REVOLUTIONARY NEW ENGLAND
1691-1776

REVOLUTIONARY NEW ENGLAND 1691–1776

BY

JAMES TRUSLOW ADAMS, A. M., LL. D.

Author of " The Founding of New England"

With Illustrations

THE ATLANTIC MONTHLY PRESS

BOSTON

PRINTED IN THE UNITED STATES OF AMERICA

Printing Statement:

Britain, America, at length be Friends,
Accept the terms which Concord, recommends!
Be ye but steady to each others Cause,
Protect, defend, and not infringe the Laws;
Ye may, together - come the World in Arms,
Bear the fierce Shock of hostile, dire alarms.
'Tis Peace, Trade, Navigation, will support
The poor with bread - in Dignity the Court.
Rush to each others Arms, be firm and true!
One Faith, one Fame, one Intrest, makes the TWO,
ET.

FRONTISPIECE FROM THE "LONDON MAGAZINE," 1774

PREFACE

In the first volume of this series, — *The Founding of New England,* — we were occupied mainly with the origins of colonial life in the section under consideration. The matters there discussed dealt to a great extent with the discoveries and early settlement, the various factors shaping the first organization and development of the colonies, and the views held both by the colonists and the English government as to the relations between the colonies and the mother country.

In the present volume the story is carried from 1691, the approximate date of the close of the narrative in the preceding, to the Declaration of Independence and the ending of the colonial status of the New England settlements. Perhaps no period of our history is richer in easily accessible original material, monographic studies or secondary historical works than that which is somewhat loosely called the Revolutionary period, from 1763 onward. Scholars of the present generation in particular have devoted themselves to a much needed reëxamination of the events of those years and a revaluation of the tendencies disclosed. As a result of their labors our views of the imperial struggle have undergone a profound alteration, and we have become far more acutely aware of the double nature of the struggle as at once a political contest between colonies and mother country, and a social revolution in the colonies themselves.

It is noteworthy, however, that, with some important exceptions, the new studies have been confined almost wholly to the more appealing and dramatic period from the Peace of Paris in 1763 to the outbreak of hostilities, and that they have largely neglected the task of tracing the origins of radical thought and the growth of grievances and of parties during the preceding half-century. The increased importance which we now attach to the domestic social revolution and the somewhat decreased influence which we attribute to the purely imperial difficulties, place us, so far as our present knowledge goes, in a somewhat anomalous position. Social revolutions are not made in a decade, particularly in a society in which, as in colonial America, the great bulk of the population consists of a property-owning, agricultural class. If, therefore, we are right in laying much stress upon the domestic, social influences in the later years of the period, as I believe we are, we must, of necessity, turn back to the earlier decades to study the causes which may have been at work during several generations to bring those influences into operation.

The attempt to trace the origin of grievances, the slow growth of revolutionary sentiment and the rise of a radical party, is the chief task of the earlier part of the present volume. In the absence as yet of such exhaustive monographs upon special phases of the first two quarters of the century as we have for the third, and in view of the scattered nature of the innumerable sources from which the social and economic history of a people must be derived, any new synthesis must at best be but partial and tentative.

The period from the Peace of Utrecht in 1713 to that of the decade from 1740 to 1750 produced no striking personalities and few events of compelling human interest. But though this may detract from the dramatic quality of the period, it by no means diminishes its historical importance. In those years of recovery from war, and of great economic expansion, we can see at work forces tending to develop democratic ideals in certain elements of the community, and foreshadowing the alignments and parties of a later time. The decade from 1740 to 1750 was marked by an intense quickening of thought and action, and so important was the change in the intellectual and social atmosphere following the extraordinary religious outburst at the opening of this short period that I have named the chapter dealing with it "The Great Divide" (Chapter IX).

The tendencies then clearly shaping the life and outlook of the people, both in their local and imperial concerns, were emphasized and focused by the events and influences of the Seven Years' War (1756–63), influences which in both their economic and psychological significance are more readily understood from our own present post-war experience.

During these earlier decades leading up to the Revolutionary period proper, we have to note, on the one hand, the efforts to advance their position by those upper classes which were endeavoring to control the life of the colonies for their own advantage, and, on the other, the demands made by the less fortunate elements for an increase of power and the betterment of their position. We observe the rapid accumulation of wealth and its increasing concentration in relatively fewer hands; the changes in business methods which operated to the disadvantage of the poorer classes; the alteration in colonial land policy, the speculation in wilderness lands, and the lessening opportunity for persons without capital to rise in the social scale. Throughout the period discontent grows, radical sentiment develops, and there is noticeable a slow slipping of political power from the higher to a lower social class, and a steady growth in self-consciousness on the part of the latter. In the sphere of imperial relations we have endeavored to indicate the prime importance of the part played by the West Indies in complicating and embittering the relations between old and New England. All of these, and the other strands in the narrative, are inextricably woven into the events of the better known decades of open discussion and rebellion following 1763. Those cannot be fully understood, however, unless we learn more than we yet know of the duller years of the preceding half-century.

It is a pleasure to record my sincere appreciation of the many courtesies received in the course of preparing this volume from Dr. Herbert Putnam and Mr. Charles Moore of the Library of Congress, and from the other members of the staff of that institution, without the ample facilities of which I could not have prepared this work. In particular I have to note the annually increasing number of transcripts from the British Documents in the Library's Manuscript Division, which are becoming every year of more vital importance to American scholars unable to examine the originals in London. The references given in my notes, although citing the English classification, are almost wholly to the Transcripts in Washington. I have also to thank Mr. Worthington C. Ford and the Massachusetts Historical Society, Mr. Albert Matthews and the Colonial Society of Massachusetts, Mr. John H. Edmonds of the Massachusetts State Archives, Mr. M. A. DeWolfe Howe of Boston, and the authorities of the State Library of New York and of the Hampton Library of Bridgehampton, New York, for many courtesies. The labor involved in the footnotes was much lightened by the assistance of my father, the late William Newton Adams.

J. T. A.

Annapolis, Maryland,
   February 27, 1923.

CONTENTS

ILLUSTRATIONS

REVOLUTIONARY NEW ENGLAND
1691-1776

REVOLUTIONARY NEW ENGLAND

1691-1776

CHAPTER I

INTRODUCTORY

Character of XVIIIth Century — Rise of New Classes — Political Effects of Revolution of 1688 — Effects of Frontier Life on the Colonists — Difficulties of the Imperial Problem.

FEW centuries have suffered so much from unappreciative interpretation as the eighteenth. It was a period, as Seeley has said, that many seem to think of only as "prosperous, but not as memorable." [1] It is true that its gigantic and almost constant struggles were mainly for the markets and raw materials of this world, and were but little influenced, as had been those of the immediately preceding generations, by the problems of the next. Nevertheless, whatever alteration there may have been in the channels through which has flowed the expanding energy of the men of European stock since the fifteenth century, there has been no diminution in that energy itself. Beneath the shifting forms in which it has been clothed at different times, — art, religion, politics, trade, humanitarianism, — we can trace the constant stream of discontent, of restlessness and of upward striving. The force abides though its expression alters, and it is hard if not impossible for those of a later time to feel in the same way as their ancestors felt the reality of the connection between the abiding force and a passing mode of its temporal expression. It is by no means unlikely that our own descendants may in time come to take as little living interest in the intricacies of the economic thought and struggles of the nineteenth century as we

[1] J. R. Seeley, *The Expansion of England*, (London, 1884), p. 17.

do in those of the religious opinions and controversies of the sixteenth and seventeenth.

If we look beneath the surface of the dull and sluggish life of the upper classes throughout most of the years from the accession of William to the outbreak of the revolution in France in order to study the movements stirring there; if we leave the pleasant but somewhat vapid company of beaux and belles, of wits and easy-going statesmen, to live with classes hardly as yet recognized by them as socially or politically existent, we shall find a new eighteenth century, by no means stagnant, and shall realize why a period popularly considered as prosperous and placid should have ended in civil war for England and the Red Terror in France. It is quite true that in the American colonies in the years from 1713 to 1763 colonial life seemed to have reached its highest level of stability,[1] but throughout that whole time one finds constant warnings, at least, of the impending storm, as in France, in the same period, one feels time and again that it needs but a match to set the world in flames.[2] In the latter country, liberty had been almost completely suppressed, whereas in the English colonies it was enjoyed to a greater degree than anywhere else in the world. This contrast, however, but makes the ultimate demand in each case the more striking, and leads us to regard more closely the spirit of an age which equally led men so dissimilarly placed to wade through blood for freedom. Events are forces momentarily made visible. Revolutions are not wrought in a decade, and one must go far back to conjure up their silent causes.

From this standpoint, the real, if less obvious, keynote of the eighteenth century is not placid dulness but, to choose a metaphor from physics, expansion and explosion. It was a period of titanic struggles, of nations for commercial supremacy, and of peoples for power and self-expression. The first is spectacular and easy to trace, the second, slow, hidden, and at times obscure. Of the ninety-four years from the accession of William to the end of the American Revolution, England was formally at war during forty-three, and actually during more.

---

[1] C. M. Andrews, *Colonial Folkways*, (Yale Press, 1919), p. 3.
[2] Felix Rocquain, *L'Esprit révolutionnaire avant la révolution*, (Paris, 1878), *passim*.

Throughout most of the eighteenth century the economic doctrine which directed trade legislation and the administration of
colonies, "the pivot round which revolves the whole early history" of European colonization,[1] was that Mercantile Theory of
which I have already written at length in an earlier volume.[2]
That theory aimed at the creation of self-sufficing empires in
which the colonies should supply the raw materials and consume
the finished products of the home countries, which, in turn,
should manufacture those products, and also carry on such trade
with the world outside as the conditions of the case required or
made profitable. I need not here repeat what I have already said
as to the utility, indeed the necessity, of such a system as a
stage in modern empire building. Whatever benefits it might
confer, however, it is obvious that in a world in which territory,
materials and markets are limited, one result that was bound to
ensue was a clash of nations in their race to secure them. The
two antagonists who clearly stood out as the chief contestants
at the opening of the eighteenth century were those who faced
each other across the narrow waters of the English Channel. In
the wars in which England was engaged from 1689 to 1697, from
1702 to 1713, from 1739 to 1748, the unofficial warfare from that
year to the reopening of the formal war of 1756–63, and in the
war of the American Revolution, the real European contestants
were always England and France, and the prize fought for was
supremacy in the world's trade. It is this long struggle, both in
its military and mercantile aspects, that forms one of the outstanding features of the period with which this volume deals,
and that exerted a determining influence upon the local history
of the colonies whose story we are to trace.[3]

The steady advance in the standard of living during the seventeenth and eighteenth centuries, and the earlier as well as the
later phases of the industrial revolution, were also of great influence in fostering discontent among the less favored classes,

[1] H. E. Egerton, *The Claims of the Study of Colonial History upon the University of Oxford*, (Oxford, 1906), p. 18.

[2] J. T. Adams, *The Founding of New England*, (Boston, 1921), chap. XII.

[3] For a broad outline of this phase of the period, *vide* Seeley, *Expansion of England*, *passim*. For a detailed study of the commercial aspects, *vide* C. M. Andrews, "Anglo-French Commercial Rivalry," *American Historical Review*, vol. XX, pp. 539 *ff.*, 761 *ff.*

and impelling them to demand a larger share in the good things of life. Feudalism, which had long continued to modify legal and social relations after it had passed as a political order, was rapidly giving way as an influence to those developing from the new economic order.[1] The breaking down of the mediæval guild organization of industry, the increasing competition of individual with individual, the boundless field opened to exploitation in the new world, and above all the opportunities and demands in America for laborers and artisans, all reacted upon the lower classes both in Europe and the colonies, and at once gave them an enlarged vision of the possibilities open to them of improving their condition, and enabled them successfully to claim a larger share in the social product. The new forms of wealth and ways of gaining it, moreover, not only increased the competition for it, but enabled new and in many cases inferior types to compete for it. Men became hardened by the keener struggle, by the passing away of personal relations between employer and employed, and by the desire for quickly acquired riches by those who had neither possessed them before nor knew their uses. "À la modestie du maître artisan du moyen age," writes a Belgian economist, "succède l'âpreté ingénieuse du fabricant moderne, à la vénération du travail, l'adoration du capital, à la religion du chef-d'oeuvre, la foi du profit." [2] The egotism of the self-made man is notorious. In the seventeenth and eighteenth centuries there were vast numbers who were acquiring the new wealth by the new means, and who were growing to believe themselves capable of everything in consequence. These types ranged from the opulent London merchant whose daughter might marry a nobleman and who believed himself a statesman, to the scarcely literate pioneer on the American frontier, rich in a clearing and a shanty, who thought himself capable of solving the imperial problem by the simple method of personal appropriation and declamation of the rights of man.

At the beginning of the period with which this volume deals,

---

[1] Even in France the nobility were entering trade. *Vide*, Henri Carré, *La noblesse de France et l'opinion publique au XVIIIᵉ siècle*, (Paris, 1920), pp. 135 ff.

[2] Léon Hennebicq, *Génèse de l'impérialisme Anglais*, (Bruxelles, 1913), p. 129.

England had just passed through that revolution of 1688 which had "brought neither glory nor political advantage to the majority of the English people." [1] There had been no change in the governing class. There had been no increase in democratic influences. The essentials of free government had not been mentioned in the Bill of Rights. There had been no increase in religious liberty, in public education, in the freedom of trade or of the press, nor in the publicity of debates in Parliament.[2] Power had indeed been transferred from the king to Parliament but not to the people. During the eighteenth century not only did not one Englishman in fifty possess a vote, but from 1701 until after the American Revolution there was not a single general election held to decide a public question.[3] Throughout the century, the real governing power lay not in the king, the House of Lords, or the people, but in an exclusive, privileged, autocratic, middle-class and class-minded group whose main interest was in trade.

The theory of the absolute sovereignty of Parliament was thoroughly established in the eighteenth century and has continued to the present day.[4] Needless to say, this theory though still held in form has been greatly altered in substance during the nineteenth century by the grant of responsible government to the dominions and by other causes.[5] As it steadily developed through the eighteenth, however, it could receive but little check from the people at home or from those in the colonies.

Another political idea upon which the revolution of 1688 seemed to have set the seal of approval and validity was that of contract. The doctrine of a covenant between the ruler and the ruled which we traced in New England in our earlier volume, and which was given philosophic form in England in the writ-

---

[1] C. M. Andrews, *Present Day Thoughts on the American Revolution*, Bulletin University of Georgia, No. 11, p. 7.

[2] Andrews, *cit. supra;* Lord Acton, *Lectures on Modern History*, (London, 1907), p. 231.

[3] F. W. Maitland, *Constitutional History of England*, (Cambridge University Press, 1919), p. 291; A. F. Pollard, *The Evolution of Parliament*, (London, 1920), pp. 170, 338 *f.*; G. B. Adams, *Constitutional History of England*, (New York, 1921), p. 396.

[4] *Cf.* A. V. Dicey, *Law of the Constitution*, (London, 1920), pp. 70 *ff.*, 425; C. H. McIlwain, *High Court of Parliament*, (Yale Press, 1910), pp. 377 *ff.*

[5] E. Jenks, *The State and the Nation*, (London, 1919), p. 265; Sir H. Jenkyns, *British Rule and Jurisdiction beyond the Seas*, (Oxford, 1902), pp. 10 *f.*

ings of Locke, Sidney and others, could not but be considered as the basic idea in the settlement of the crown upon William in spite of all the ingenious fictions employed to make the revolution appear as little revolutionary as possible. The theory leads, however, with pitiless logic, not only to democracy but through democracy to a form of government or anarchy beyond anything of which we have present knowledge,[1] and in spite of its incalculably great influence upon the beliefs and actions of the American colonists, it was never carried out by them even to its more easily attainable conclusions in practice.

These two doctrines — the sovereignty of Parliament and government based upon the consent of the governed — were the leading political ideas of the English-speaking peoples in the eighteenth century. But it was of profound importance that whereas the first took complete possession of the minds of Englishmen at home, it failed for the most part to receive the full assent of those overseas, and whereas the second was to a considerable extent put away and even discredited in England, it took firm root in America where different influences were at work.

From the very beginning of colonization on that continent there had always been evident a tendency toward expansion, and not only had settlements grown up in new spots along the coast, but pioneers were continually passing to the higher reaches of the rivers or plunging boldly through the forests. In New England, which was without mineral resources other than the rocks that encumbered her soil, and where the fur trade early ceased to be a prime factor owing to the comparatively small drainage basins of the river systems, the main reason for this constant pushing forward of the frontier was the presence of free land. The approach to history through the study of institutions marks such an advance over the old chronicles of kings that there is danger of overstressing this aspect of national development. Institutions are even more effects than they are causes of social movements. Like coral islands they are formed by the largely unconscious coöperative efforts of myriads of liv-

---

[1] F. W. Maitland, *Collected Papers*, (Cambridge University Press, 1911), vol. I, pp. 18 *ff.*

ing organisms. Although we may describe and classify such islands as they appear above the surface, we cannot understand them unless we study first the silent forces working in the unseen depths below. The most compelling of such forces in moulding the minds and institutions of the American colonists into something different from those of the first English settlers was the vast and empty continent.[1]

Nowhere else in modern societies does equality of economic opportunity and of economic status approach so near completeness as on the frontier.[2] As political power is closely allied to economic power, it follows that nowhere else is political power so diffused and the political demand of the individual merely as an individual so insistent and unanswerable. Liberty, democracy, equality on the frontier are not due to a long struggle against the results of historical development in which the necessity for clear thinking and compromise play their parts but are there inherent in the conditions.[3] The conception of an ordered society in which the claims of the individual are of necessity subordinated to those of society as a whole is replaced by the most extreme individualism. The ideals of the frontier are equality, freedom of opportunity, unrestrained liberty of exploitation, individual success, faith in the common man.

Although the tendency of frontier life is anti-social, the necessity for voluntarily forming some sort of government, and the equality due to the economic conditions, give an enormous stimulus to the belief that government derives its only sanction from the consent of the governed. Although this idea had been greatly reinforced in New England by the town and church covenants already mentioned, it was due mainly to the influence of the frontier that throughout all of the colonies by the time of the revolution this theory had come to seem "one of the axioms in political philosophy, which no one in his political senses would question."[4] Indeed, to those dwelling on the frontier, removed

[1] *Cf.* W. G. Sumner, *Earth-Hunger and other Essays*, (Yale Press, 1914), pp. 42 *ff.*

[2] The essays by F. J. Turner, now happily collected into one volume, [*The Frontier in American History*, (New York, 1920)], have greatly influenced the study of our history, and my own indebtedness to them is too great for specific references.

[3] *Cf.* Émile Boutmy, *Eléments d'une psychologie politique du peuple Américain*, (Paris, 1902), p. 129.

[4] C. E. Merriam, *A History of American Political Theories*, (New York, 1918), p. 51.

from any serious restraint upon their actions and with the unexampled physical resources of the continent open to their exploitation, liberty came to mean not a just balance of rights and
duties between individuals united in social bonds but freedom
from all curbs upon individual will and desire. The word *duty*
almost completely disappeared from the political vocabulary of
the colonial radicals, as the feeling did to a great extent from
their political life. Even the primary, and it would seem wholly
selfish, duty of self-defence became subordinated to individualism, particularism, and childish conceptions of "liberties" and
"rights." [1] Mere legal rights tended to become merged in vague
conceptions of "natural rights" and "rights of man," the watch-
words of the emotional political philosophy of the century.

Moreover, frontier life tends to develop fondness for general-
ized formulæ, and distaste for analysis and discrimination. The
frontiersman, freed from complexities, ceases to believe in them
and sees things not as they are but as he wants them to be or as
he thinks they will be. His present is the present plus a rosy future contributed by his buoyant optimism. It is this that is at
the bottom of his boasting, of his wildcat financial schemes, of
his impatience with the conservative caution of the older settlements. In fact, if we consider what are generally accepted as the
characteristics of American thought and temperament — such
as the love of vague phrases, the lack of analysis and critical
judgment, intense optimism, practical ingenuity, versatility,
religious tolerance, belief in democracy and the perfectibility of
man — we find them rooted in the environment and so far from
being derived from the religious elements among the founders
of New England as to stand, for better or worse, in direct opposition to what is most characteristic in the conscious beliefs of
New England Puritanism. [2] It was in the eighteenth century
that the American colonies grew into a nation psychologically
as well as politically, and that the American mind took on its
distinctive features. It was also in that century that throughout

[1] *Cf.* E. I. McCormac, *Colonial Opposition to Imperial Authority during the French and Indian War*, University of California Publications, vol. I, No. 8, p. 67.

[2] I say *conscious* beliefs for, as I tried to show in my earlier volume, there was implicit in the Puritan doctrine much that led to democracy, but this was in part not recog-nized and in part opposed by the Puritan leaders.

the entire length of the colonies a distinct frontier region — as contrasted with merely scattered frontier settlements — came into existence to struggle with and react upon the tide-water sections.

Frontier existence might be either shiftless or hard-working, depending upon the temperament and ambition of the individual frontiersman; but danger, isolation, freedom from restraint, and opportunity for success with little or no capital, naturally attracted the adventurous, the restless and the contentious. Democracy among the founders of Massachusetts was as much disliked socially as it was abhorred politically. Men who had occupied positions of little or no prominence in England found themselves the most important figures in the new community, and became extremely tenacious of their social and political position, refusing as far as possible to admit others within their circle. Those who after several generations, either by descent or admission, found a definite place in the higher social or business groups of the older towns would naturally not be attracted by the ruder life of the frontier, whereas those who rebelled against the position assigned to them by these provincial arbiters of place and fashion would as naturally strike out for the greater freedom of the wilderness or of a new town where they in turn might become locally important and establish new dynasties of farmers or tradesmen. More serious than the insistence of the new colonial "first families" to being recognized as socially superior to their fellow provincials were their attempts, more or less successful, to entrench themselves securely in economic, political and legal privileges. Owing to the nature of the soil and climate in New England, slavery and the creation of large landed estates had not proved economically profitable. The richer men, therefore, did not disperse throughout the colonies as they did in the South, but remained for the most part concentrated in the older seaboard and river towns. There they formed not only a wealthy class as opposed to the poorer, but a merchant and moneyed one as opposed to the small shop-keepers and artisans of the towns and the farmers of the country districts, which latter classes came to feel themselves in the financial power of the merchant as well as being looked down upon by him.

The relations between established settlements and their out-lying frontiers seem everywhere and in all periods to follow certain simple and well-defined lines. In the first place, the older settlement has accumulated capital seeking investment whereas the frontier, in spite of its natural resources, needs for their exploitation capital in the form of money or credit. The frontier, therefore, is always and everywhere in debt to the old settlement, and this relation breeds all those feelings a debtor seems by nature to entertain towards his creditor. As contrasted with one another, the older settlement is always conservative, the frontier always radical. This involves distrust on the part of the former and irritations of various sorts upon that of the latter. The East has therefore always feared and sought to check the political growth of the West (as the terms may be used in this country), whether, depending on the period, the West lay a few miles or a thousand from the coast. It has trembled for its investments in the too rapid expansion that the frontier always breeds. It has distrusted radical thought and has feared above all else that economic expansion might increase political power and transfer control to a section whose philosophy and outlook have seemed revolutionary. The main feeling of the frontier for the settlement may thus be denominated as resentment, whereas that of the settlement for the frontier is fear, the two human emotions that perhaps most militate against cool reasoning and mutual understanding.

There is a third element in this relationship. In the older settlements economic inequality results in dividing society into upper and lower classes. The lower class has more in common in many ways with the frontiersman than it has with the upper class of the settlement. Its lack of capital and of culture, a certain recklessness derived from its hard struggle for an uncertain living, its resentment against the class above it upon which it is dependent for wages as the frontiersman is for capital, all tend to unite it with the frontier and to align the two against the conservatives of the settlement capitalist class. "The West," says Professor Turner, "is a form of society rather than an area." If we may paraphrase this by saying that the frontier is a state of mind rather than a place, the lower class of the seaboard may be said to have been frontiersmen in a social, not a geographical, relation.

In the colonial period there was the further complication that America as a whole, regardless of local distinctions, formed the frontier of the older civilization of England, and bore to that country the usual relation of frontier to settlement. If, however, we fail to realize the geographical and class distinctions as they existed in America, we shall not understand the dual nature of the events of 1776. We shall fail to see that it was only after a social revolution of the men of the two "frontiers" against the capitalist class in the colonies as well as in England had forced a portion of the colonial capitalists and conservatives, in considerable measure by terroristic means, to acquiesce in a movement too strong for them, that the revolution in the colonies broadened into a war for independence against the mother country.

This volume will be largely taken up with tracing the causes that brought about that separation, but it will be well here at the outset to call attention to one of the most common and fatal fallacies in historical thinking, the fallacy of what I may call the continuous entity. People speak glibly of Greece or Rome or England as though those terms connoted at any given moment a single national thought and purpose, and as though through the ages thought and purpose were unchanging and continuous. Our daily experience with the infinitely varied and often incongruous and conflicting motives which induce men to join political parties, and the fact that national questions are always decided against the wishes of a very large part of the voting population, should guard us against this error. To personify and simplify the actions of the colonies and of England in the eighteenth century has even less foundation than it would have today with the wider franchise on both sides of the water. At no stage was it a struggle between an unanimous body of colonists and the unanimous body of the English people, but between those sections of each which had secured control of the organs of public opinion and action. As Professor MacIver has said in a notable passage addressed to sociologists but which historians should take to heart, "if one only realized the complexity of any social system, where authority direct and indirect subordinates will to will; where interests combine and clash in a multitude of ways; where every degree of ignorance and enlightenment underlies decision; where custom and convention, the mental habits of uniformity, are incessantly at warfare with the liberating enterprise and ambitions of individuality, we should avoid forever the easy simplification that finds one motive behind every social decision, one will behind every social fact." [1]

The great overseas colonial systems that developed from the discoveries in the age of the navigators were political phenomena of an entirely new type. Of them all the English Empire has become the freest, the greatest and incomparably the most interesting, as well as the most complex. From the beginning wholly novel problems, for the solution of which history offered no guiding precedents, presented difficulties which have often seemed, and at one stage proved to be, insuperable. In my earlier volume I have already discussed at some length the special sources of misunderstanding due to the purely physical element of distance, and need not here repeat what I have said of that aspect of the problem. [2]

Still another difficulty in that part of the empire which has constituted a "sphere of settlement" as contrasted with a "sphere of rule" has been the fact that Englishmen have not only demanded liberty for themselves but have been willing to grant it to others. It is, I think, indisputable that the American colonists in the eighteenth century had far more liberty than the mass of Englishmen at home, and that the average man in New England had a greater voice in the management of his own political affairs than had the average man in old England. It was certain, however, that the more liberty England allowed the colonists, the more, according to human nature, would they resent such control as she might still retain, aside from such wisdom and efficiency as she might or might not display in its exercise. Colonial representation is everywhere regarded as im-

---

[1] R. M. MacIver, *Community*, (London, 1920), p. 146.

[2] *Founding of New England*, pp. 292, 294 f., 301 f. *Cf.* Sir C. P. Lucas, *Greater Rome and Greater Britain*, (Oxford, 1912), pp. 32 ff. Although modern inventions have assisted the solution of the problem, it is still an important factor in imperial administration. *Cf. Minutes of Proceedings of the Imperial Conference*, 1911, [Cd. 5745], p. 188; *Summary of Proceedings and Documents, Conference of Prime Ministers*, 1921, [Cmd. 1474], pp. 19, 56 f.

practicable [1] and the colonial problem was largely the result not of withholding but of granting as large a share of self-govern-ment as possible. For the most part, the steady increase in the desire for greater independence has been, and is, due to the en-joyment of freedom and not to suffering endured from tyranny.

The British Empire had behind it in the eighteenth century but a hundred years or so of growth and experimentation as com-pared with the centuries during which the national state had been gradually perfected as a form of organized community. Just as a child and a man exist contemporaneously but belong to different generations of experience, so the organization of the British overseas empire and the organization of the British state belong to different cycles of political growth even though they coexist in time. Moreover, as each child has to pass through the same stages of learning and experience, so it would seem as though men in their community life had to pass through more or less the same succeeding stages in each new cycle of en-larged organization and outlook. In the national development of England at the end of the thirteenth century the county was the country for the average Englishman and his vision compre-hended only the activities of the shire.[2] For the past few cen-turies his larger outlook upon the state has been as instinctive as was his earlier more restricted one, and Englishmen at home have found it as natural to carry on and develop the state or-ganization as have Englishmen overseas to create new states of similar type. Just as it seemed an impossible task to bring men to think in terms of the nation instead of the county, so it needed a long period of stress and almost unperceived growth to make them think in terms of empire instead of England and certain individual colonies. It is a process that cannot be hurried, and even by the wisest legislation it would have been as impossible suddenly to create an imperial sentiment in the eighteenth cen-tury as a national one in the thirteenth. Moreover, in the blun-dering attempts to evolve a new form of political organization, upon a scale and under difficulties that were unequaled in

---

[1] It has been tried by Portugal and France. *Vide* A. Zimmerman, *Kolonialpolitik*, (Leipzig, 1905), pp. 23, 40 *ff*.

[2] Pollard, *Evolution of Parliament*, p. 134.

history, we must expect to find mistakes and blind gropings as we expect to find them centuries earlier in the same relative stage of national state making.

The machinery devised to administer the new organization was necessarily but clumsily contrived and operated by inexperienced and frequently selfish men. There were, speaking broadly, no rules to guide, no mistakes to warn, no long traditions of service or of sentiment to sustain. There was on the other hand, throughout the whole period with which we have to deal, an enormous and almost constant friction produced in matters great and small. Questions of impressment of seamen, of finance, of relations between debtor and creditor, of taxation, of the charter governments, of legislation, of appeals, of review of colonial legislation, of tactless officials, of Admiralty jurisdiction, of the relation of local to imperial authority, of the King's Woods, of commercial restrictions, of religion, of land policy, of Indian policy and of imperial and local defence — to mention at hazard some of those with which we shall have to deal — all tended toward disintegration. It is not the sudden lightning stroke that splits the granite of the hills but the innumerable little rifts and seams which are broadened and extended by the rains and frosts of season after season. Such were these and other causes of disaffection, disagreement and slow alienation of interest and of thought. As an offset there had as yet developed none of that consciousness of a common attitude toward life, and way of envisaging its conduct and problems shared more or less fully by those throughout the empire as contrasted with the citizens of other nations, that is today, perhaps, the strongest bond cementing the imperial structure, more subtle, but more powerful than racial, economic, political and military interests.[1] There was at best but a sentiment of loyalty to an England seen and known by few of the colonists, and to a king who was not then a symbol of imperial and racial unity but who was considered as the possessor of a power which, in fact, he neither exercised nor enjoyed.[2]

[1] *Cf.* G. M. Wrong, "The Growth of Nationalism in the British Empire," *American Historical Review*, vol. XXII, p. 51.
[2] *Cf.* Dicey, *Law of the Constitution.* p. 465 *n.*

These then are the main threads in the story which we are to follow. We shall watch that duel for empire between England and France, and trace its profound effects in many ways upon the relations between England and her colonies. We shall see how those relations were also deeply influenced and embittered by the conflict of interests between New England and the West Indies — a conflict in which those of the mother country were but indirectly involved. We shall find entangled in both of these struggles, and the later one of the Revolution, certain economic ideas still to survive by another half century the ruin that in part they caused. We shall be present at the opening of new regions to settlement and watch their influence exerted upon the political thought of the older sections and the transfer of political power from a higher to a socially lower class. We shall see how little by little the whole outlook upon life, and the political philosophy of the colonies and the mother country diverged, while one incident after another created friction and engendered passions not easily allayed when once aroused. We shall see how all these tendencies and events fatally and inevitably moved toward and ended in revolution. That revolution, however, was not a mere episode in American history or a mere mercenary quarrel between those of the same household. It was a movement wrought by the whole thought and condition of one period of the world's advance. It should be studied, therefore, not from the narrow eighteenth-century standpoint of either Englishman or colonist, but from that of a citizen of a newer and wider world, who seeks to learn the truth from the past in order that he may live wisely in the present and build enduringly for the future.

CHAPTER II

THE MACHINERY OF EMPIRE[1]

Organization of Administration — Causes of Inefficiency — Influences of Military Operations — Effect of System on the Colonists.

As one reads the literature of various nations in the past three centuries on imperial questions, one is struck by the fact that the people of the home countries seem to have passed through definite phases of belief and disbelief in the value to themselves of imperial possessions. In the seventeenth century the question was very decidedly an open one, but in the next, opinion crystallized temporarily in favor of the acquisition and retention of as large colonial domains as it was possible to acquire.[2] This belief in the value of colonies, however, was wholly a belief in their trade value. It was a period in which trade interests dominated all others[3] and we shall look as vainly for imperial pride or sense of trusteeship in England as we shall for ardent loyalty or affection in America. The policy adopted by the home country, therefore, aimed at making the colonies, which in the face of her trade rival France involved her in heavy risks and great expense, as valuable to her own commerce as possible. If this policy was fundamentally selfish and unideal it was not necessarily either tyrannical or lacking in benefit to the colonies. England took as great care for their interests as a whole as the basic eighteenth-century conception of their only possible util-

---

[1] As to the propriety of the use of the term "empire" in the 18th century, *vide* J. T. Adams, "On the Term 'British Empire,'" *American Historical Review*, vol. XXVII, pp. 485 *ff.*

[2] Among numerous English writers, *cf.* C. D'Avenant, *Discourses on the Public Revenues and on the Trade of England*, 1698, in *Collected Works*, (London, 1771), vol. I, pp. 1 *ff.*; W. Wood, *A Survey of Trade*, (London, 1719), pp. 134 *ff.* For French opinion in the 18th century, *vide* L. Deschamps, *Histoire de la question coloniale en France*, (Paris, 1891), pp. 260 *ff.*

[3] Deschamps points out how trade matters and interests crept even into pure literature in France after the end of the 17th century. *Cit. supra*, pp. 201 *ff.*

ity, and the generally low tone of political responsibility, permitted.

In her endeavor to solve the problem of their administration, she created no new organs for the purpose but merely adapted those already in existence, and it is necessary to consider briefly this machinery before proceeding to the narrative of events. Today the two links which unite all parts of the empire are the legislative one of Parliament and the executive and judicial one of the Crown.[1] This was equally true in the eighteenth century but the relative position of each in the British constitution had not then been settled, and the domestic struggle between the two helped to confuse and hamper colonial administration. This confusion was further increased by the multiplicity of agencies employed, equaled in our own day, perhaps, for resultant paralysis of action only by our own departmental machinery for the government of Alaska.[2]

First of all, there was the Board of Trade and Plantations, created in 1696 as a successor to the old Committee of the Privy Council. It had no executive power and its main functions were the gathering of data and the making of recommendations, a very considerable proportion of which were eventually carried into effect.[3] The keeping in touch with the domestic affairs of all the colonies, island as well as continental, the proceedings of their legislatures, and the economic, military and political conditions, would have been too great a task to have been performed properly even if there had not been added to it the stupendous one of supervising British trade as a whole in all parts of the world. In its capacity as a board of review it performed a function of the highest importance, the influence of which both

[1] Jenkyns, *British Rule*, pp. 10 ff.

[2] Secretary of the Interior Fall writes: "The greatest handicap now facing Alaska is that of government. . . . The administration of this vast territory, which equals in size the states of Minnesota, Wisconsin, Illinois, Iowa, Kansas, Missouri, and half of the Dakotas, is at present divided between so many different departments and bureaus, that I would hesitate to number them." He describes the resultant paralysis in terms familiar to students of 18th-century imperialism. *New York Times*, July 17, 1921, Sec. 7, p. 2.

[3] O. M. Dickerson, *American Colonial Government, 1696–1765*, (Cleveland, 1912), p. 104; M. P. Clarke, "The Board of Trade at Work," *American Historical Review*, vol. XVII, pp. 17 ff.; L. P. Kellogg, *The American Colonial Charter*, (Washington, 1904), pp. 210 ff.; C. M. Andrews, *List of Reports and Representations*, 1915, pp. 322, 324.

upon the colonies and the subsequent legal development of the United States it is hard to overrate. The review of colonial legislation, including the royal disallowance of such laws as were disapproved of by the home government, was an executive not a legislative act and was quite distinct from the royal veto on Parliamentary legislation.[1] Like all executive acts under the British constitution it was performed in the name of the king, and for that reason the Declaration of Independence took the form of an indictment of George the Third, but one gains an entirely false impression of the review if it is considered to have been the irresponsible act of an individual. The monarch had little do to with it beyond a formal approval as the king in council of the action taken by the Board of Trade and its legal advisers. The main objects of review were to prevent the continuance of laws that were opposed to those of England, to the laws of trade, or to the maintenance of the royal prerogative, and to protect British subjects, at home and in the colonies alike, from the effects of oppressive or defective acts. The number of such laws disallowed when stated alone is rather misleading and would seem to indicate considerable interference with colonial legislatures. The percentage of laws disallowed to all submitted, however, is comparatively trifling, and amounted in Massachusetts between 1692 and the Revolution to only two and eight-tenths per cent. Even of these, two-thirds were negatived in the fifteen years following the grant of the charter in 1691, which was necessarily a time of uncertainty and readjustment.[2] The colonists were always given ample opportunity to present their side of the case and most modern students of the question are agreed that as a rule the procedure was eminently fair. Action, however, was slow, cumbrous and expensive, and this combined with the Board's frankly acknowledged ignorance of colonial

[1] C. M. Andrews, "The Royal Disallowance," *American Antiquarian Society, Proceedings,* New Ser., vol. XXIV, pp. 342 *ff.*; same, *Connecticut and the British Government,* (Hartford, 1915); A. G. Dorland, *The Royal Disallowance in Massachusetts,* Bulletin Queen's University, Toronto, No. XX; E. B. Russell, *The Review of American Colonial Legislation by the King in Council,* (Columbia University, 1915); Dickerson, *American Colonial Government,* pp. 225 *ff.*; Kellogg, *American Colonial Charter,* pp. 272 *ff.*

[2] In all the continental colonies in approximately the same period, 469 laws were disallowed out of 8563 submitted, or about 5.5%. Russell, *Review of Legislation,* p. 221; Dorland, *Royal Disallowance,* p. 30.

conditions occasionally caused injustice, as it undoubtedly did resentment. In many respects, nevertheless, the system was of lasting benefit. The marked improvement, for example, shown in law making during the eighteenth century by all the colonies whose acts were subject to review, as contrasted with the badly worded and contradictory legislation of the seventeenth, was primarily due to the constant and increasing supervision of the crown lawyers. Their insistence, moreover, that laws should not conflict with those of England nor with the provisions of the charters, accustomed the colonists to the conception of a fundamental law and a constitutional test, and prepared the way for our Supreme Court with functions otherwise entirely alien to anything in the British or colonial constitutions.[1] Another function of the Council, which was also strenuously opposed by the colonial governments and made to seem a grievance, was that of hearing complaints and appeals. This right of appeal, however, was quite as inherent in a subject as was the right to hear it in the Crown.[2]

The colonists were subject to the legislation of Parliament as the citizens of our territories are to that of Congress. Indeed, as Congress has the right to pass laws in contravention of territorial constitutions, it goes even further in this respect than did Parliament, which respected the colonial charters.[3] As England's interest in the colonies was wholly commercial, Parliamentary legislation was mainly confined to laws regulating trade and manufactures, and these, as dealing with imperial rather than domestic matters, were generally accepted by the colonists, although in many cases neither observed nor enforced. Indeed, the theory of Parliamentary sovereignty was not always admitted and from the beginning of the century voices were heard both in Massachusetts and Connecticut denying that Parlia-

---

[1] The most exhaustive study is that by Russell already noted. The student may find much first-hand material in the *Calendar of State Papers, Colonial. Cf. 1696–7*, pp. 312, 587, 589; *1697–8*, pp. 87, 563; *1699*, p. 38; *1701*, pp. 26, 405, 565; *1702–3*, pp. 254, 273, 611, 858; *1704–5*, pp. 226, 296; *1706–8*, pp. 151, 171, 387, 478, 547.

[2] H. D. Hazeltine, "Appeals from colonial Courts to the King in Council," *American Historical Association Report*, 1894, p. 302.

[3] *Cf.* Carl Becker, "Law and Practice of the United States in the Acquisition and Government of Dependent Territory," *Annals American Academy of Political and Social Science*, 1900, p. 417.

ment possessed any authority whatsoever over the colonies as the colonists were not represented.[1]

A new official of whose colonial importance the eighteenth century saw the rise, was the secretary of state for the southern department. It was this individual who to a great extent initiated the policies and was in a position to carry them out. In his ample province were included not only Irish and Scotch military affairs but those of Africa and all southern Europe, as well as those of the island and continental colonies.[2] It was he who appointed the royal governors and certain other officials, and the activity and efficiency manifested in colonial administration fluctuated to a great extent with the personality of the secretary.

Among the many boards dealing with colonial matters there were the Commissioners of Customs, the Treasury, the Admiralty and the War Office. The first of these appointed the collectors of customs, the two American surveyors-general, and kept especial watch upon illegal commerce. The Treasury was charged with the control of the royal revenues and expenses in the colonies, and, although its activities have not yet received careful and detailed study, it is evident that its constant parsimony was of profound influence upon imperial concerns. The Admiralty and the War Office naturally had to do with colonial defence on land and sea, and it was to the former that the colonists looked for the important work of convoying their merchant vessels along the trade routes infested by enemies and pirates alike, which was one of the services rendered by the British navy and considered a natural right by the colonists.[3] The Admiralty also came into close touch and occasional conflict with them through the establishment of Vice-Admiralty courts for the trial of cases of illegal trade.

Although the home government thus reached into the col-

---

[1] *Cal. State Pap., Col., 1693–6*, p. 193; *1701*, p. 709.

[2] C. M. Andrews, *The Colonial Period*, (New York, 1912), p. 139; Dickerson, *American Colonial Government*, pp. 107 *ff.*; A. H. Basye, "The Secretary of State for the Colonies, 1768–1782," *American Historical Review*, vol. XXVIII, pp. 13 *ff.*

[3] The volumes of the *Cal. State Pap., Col.*, contain innumerable references to the convoy system. *Vide e.g. 1696–7*, pp. 2, 103, 133, 126, 141, 167, 177, 182, 191, 217, 220, 228, 234, 240, 245, 286, 300, 312, 316, 343, 377, 391, 394, 396 *ff.*, 436, 452, 467, 486, 531, 583, etc.

onies through customs officers and Admiralty court officials, its most important representative was, of course, the royal governor.[1] As in Connecticut and Rhode Island the colonists elected both governor and legislature, those colonies were to a great extent independent of control and it was in Massachusetts and New Hampshire that there occurred the New England examples of the struggles between the assemblies and the governors which formed such an important feature of imperial history in the eighteenth century.

As a connecting link between the central and local administrations there was the colonial agent, resident in England, whose duty was to care in every way for the interests of the colony which he represented. In the seventeenth century such agents had been appointed at crises to handle some particular negotiation, but in the eighteenth they became permanent and possessed a recognized status in the administrative system.[2]

That system, sketched above in barest outline, varied to a considerable extent in the different colonies, whose attitude toward English control, in turn, varied with their domestic politics. As a whole, however, it was doomed to failure. It is true that in the nineteenth and twentieth centuries England has built again a far mightier empire than the one she lost in the eighteenth. But it is no exaggeration to say that the world in the two periods has been totally different. Steam and electricity have reduced the problem of time and distance to a minimum. New economic doctrines have eliminated many of the dangers lurking in the fallacies of the Mercantile theory. The development of political thought has profoundly altered the relation of the individual to the state and of states to one another. New ideals of race, of nationality, of imperial unity and of the history and destiny of mankind, have played their parts in the formation of a new world-outlook.

All this, however, lay beyond the limits of our period. It was then a race between the progress of thought and the stubborn resistance of physical environment. In the eighteenth century

---

[1] The most exhaustive study of the duties of this official is that by E. B. Greene, *The Provincial Governor*, (Harvard University Press, 1898).

[2] E. P. Tanner, "Colonial Agencies in England during the 18th Century," *Political Science Quarterly*, vol. XVI, pp. 24 ff.

not a single scientific invention was made which in any way
aided the solution of the problem. Moreover, in England
thought and character were altering more slowly and in a direction different from that taken in America where the influences of
the frontier and of illimitable free land were fostering a people
who came to speak a different political language from their relatives in the mother country. One watches the drama unroll
with all the fateful certainty of doom in a Greek tragedy. The
details come to seem unimportant and almost irrelevant after
one has glimpsed the naked outline of the story. It is, however,
those details, — the faults in administration, the occasions of
misunderstanding, the conflicts of interests and ideals, — which
served to hasten the separation and brought it about within that
earlier period before there had occurred the scientific progress
and the alteration in thought which might otherwise have resulted in entirely different relations between the two great portions of the English-speaking races in the past century and a
half.

One of the contributing causes was undoubtedly the inefficiency of the English administration. That inefficiency was
due to many influences. Today there is probably no higher
standard in any body of public officials than exists in the English colonial service, but the ideal of public office held by them
was almost undreamed of in eighteenth-century Europe. Bribery and corruption were so much the order of the day as to pass
unnoticed. The income of most offices was derived from fees
and not from salaries, and the transition from legitimate fees to
bribes was almost as unconscious and indefinite as was that from
privateering to piracy. William Blathwayt, whom we met in
the earlier volume of this history as the corrupt secretary of the
Lords of Trade, was one of the most important of the permanent
officials who dealt with the colonies, although the honest Earl of
Bellomont complained of him that he had "made a milch cow
of 'em for many years together." [1] Not only did the low ideals
of public life greatly hamper the honesty and efficiency of administration in England but in the colonies an additional dif-

[1] Adams, *Founding of New England*, pp. 402 *ff.*; *Cal. State Pap., Col., 1700*, p. 372.
Bellomont's letter is printed in full in *Doct. Hist. of Maine*, vol. X, pp. 65 *ff.*

ficulty was the fact that there was little or nothing to attract an able and incorruptible man in the post of governor. As one watches such a one struggling with the nagging and obstructive tactics of colonial assemblies on the one hand, and on the other with a dilatory and frequently uncomprehending government at home, one wonders how any such were found to give up the comforts and social pleasures of life in England for a harassing existence in the colonies, where honesty received little or no financial reward and where the difficulties of the position were likely to blast, almost equally, happiness and reputation. That there were many unfit and sordid governors is only what we should expect from the period emphasized by the system, and one cannot but follow the struggles of men of a different type with the keenest interest and sympathy as one watches them striving honestly for the good of the empire and laying the foundations of that tradition of service which has done so much both for that empire and the world. Although the first really great imperial governor and the establishment of schools for the training of minor colonial officials were to wait for the nineteenth century, nevertheless, there were in the aggregate among the higher officials of the earlier period many who did try to combat the corruption and obstruction around them.[1]

In the case of minor royal officials in the colonies a still further source of corruption and inefficiency is to be found in the custom of the time which regarded the office as a sinecure, the political favorite who held it remaining in England and drawing the pay while his appointee did the work for a fraction of the income. Bellomont was not alone in his laments over the evils of this system, and many other governors complained of offices that were held "by Deputys' Deputys' Deputys, some of which are scarce capable of writing six words of sense." In one case, that of secretary and clerk of the Council in the Leeward Islands, the position was farmed out to a boy of fourteen who wrote "such nonsense and stuff" the governor was ashamed to sign it.[2]

[1] On character and training of colonial officials, cf. A. Billiard, *Politique et organisation coloniales*, (Paris, 1899), pp. 134, 143; *Minutes of Proceedings of Imperial Conference, 1911*, p. 195; Etienne Richet, *Le problème coloniale*, (Paris, 1919), pp. 65 ff.; A. Zimmerman, *Kolonialpolitik*, (Leipzig, 1905), pp. 103 ff.

[2] *Cal. State Pap., Col., 1700*, pp. 266, 401, 681; *1702*, pp. 305 f.

In addition to inefficiency in individual departments, there was hopeless confusion from the division of authority and jurisdiction among them. Not only did this make almost impossible the formulation and carrying out of any definite and consistent policy but the simplest routine matter might take months and even years in passing through its various stages from department to department. The papers in the case of the McSparran land claims in Rhode Island lay pigeon-holed for eleven years in the Privy Council Office, and it took sixteen years to settle the controversy. There are even more damning examples of official procrastination.[1]

In spite of a packet boat service introduced at the beginning of the century to expedite communication with the colonies, the long distance and the hazards of the sea made intercourse both slow and precarious. Although the government ordered that all official mail should be weighted with lead so that it might be thrown overboard and so escape capture by the enemy, more or less fell into their hands during the frequent wars. Moreover, routes were roundabout. Much New England mail went by way of the West Indies, and the handling of it by merchant sea captains was careless. To add to all other delays, when letters did finally arrive in England, they sometimes lay for weeks or even months in the custom house before being forwarded to the proper officials.[2]

In fairness to those responsible for the administrative chaos it should be remembered that during the pre-revolutionary years of the eighteenth century, England was at war, at intervals, during more than thirty of them. In fact, she was either at war, preparing for war, or recovering from its effects during almost every year of the seventy-six. At no time in the whole period, therefore, was there opportunity to develop a colonial policy or administration independent of the results and influences of sustained military operations. This dominant fact had another and perhaps more vital influence upon colonial relations than that involved in the dislocation of administrative processes.

[1] E. Channing, *History of the United States*, (New York, 1916), vol. II, p. 237; Andrews, *Colonial Period*, p. 180.

[2] *Cal. State Pap., Col., 1697–8*, p. 556; *1700*, pp. 12, 69, 266, 356, 361; *1702–3*, p. 656; *1704–5*, pp. 97, 167, 189, 268, 274; *1706–8*, pp. 111, 120, 128, 133, 178, 187, 438, 587.

The constant and enormous demand for money required in the ceaseless military operations resulted in the growth of a national debt, the rise of a moneyed class, and in the fostering above all other interests those of trade. England's military strength in the exhausting century of conflict depended largely upon her wealth, as that did, in turn, upon her commerce. We shall see toward the opening years of the American Revolution how great a factor this need for money became in the relations between the mother country and the colonies, but although less dramatic in the earlier part of the century, it was perhaps not less important. It was not merely that administration was hampered in such small ways as arose from mail being held up because postage had not been settled for; from clerks of the Privy Council being in distress because their salaries remained unpaid for two years at a time; from judges and attorneys-general being appointed for America but their salaries not allowed; from the soldiers serving there being so shamefully treated that they were inefficient and mutinous; or from defences planned by the War Office remaining unbuilt because the Treasury would not supply the funds.[1] The most important consequence of all was the failure of the home government to provide for the salaries of the royal officials in the colonies. In the case of the minor ones this brought about all the demoralizing results that flowed from the system of fees, but in the case of the governors it may almost be said to have been the lever by which the colonies raised themselves to independence.

It is now recognized that the type of government which England developed in those colonies possessing a royal governor and a popularly elected assembly was an impossible one. Of all forms of administration the most difficult to carry on is one having representative institutions but not responsible government. As has been well said it "is like a fire without a chimney."[2] There is bound to ensue a struggle between the power of the people as represented in the legislature, and the appointed executive as the

---

[1] *Cal. State Pap., Col., 1700*, pp. 14, 157, 202, 252, 355, 431, 577, 615; *1701*, pp. 16, 381; *1702*, pp. 240, 452.

[2] Charles Buller, cited by H. D. Hall, *The British Commonwealth of Nations*, (London 1920), p. 24.

representative of superior authority.[1] As an effect of this constant strife between the colonists and the representative of the home country, the latter comes to be considered almost in the light of an alien and hostile power. A recent writer on the English constitution finds the basis for it in confidence whereas, on the contrary, he finds in the system of checks and balances of our own that the keynote is distrust.[2] This is true to a great extent, and the reason for it may well lie in that struggle for control during several generations in our colonial period between the legislature as representative of the people and the executive as the representative of an authority that came to be considered as tyrannical largely because it was imposed from without in an otherwise self-governing system. Where so much liberty was granted, a demand was bound to ensue for a liberty that should be complete.

There was also a more subtle effect produced by such a system upon the thought and actions of the colonists. The attitude of a Parliamentary opposition has certain well-marked characteristics. It is captious, over-critical, and either feels or assumes a suspicion of every act of the party in power. What tempers the expression, and even the nature, of those feelings in the ordinary political opposition is the fact that it hopes or believes that some day it will come into power itself and be called upon to resolve those problems whose solution by the government it professes to find so unsatisfactory. The colonists, however, sat, so to say, permanently upon the opposition bench. No matter how violent their attacks might be upon the policy or acts of the home government, they knew that they would not themselves be called upon to assume responsibility. The problem of defence of the empire against foreign nations, and of administering all the varied and conflicting interests within it, would still rest upon England and not themselves, whatever they might say or do, and they were well aware of that fact. There was therefore nothing to temper the violence of their attacks in their endeavors to gain the maximum of advantage for themselves.

[1] H. E. Egerton, *British Colonial Policy*, (London, 1918), p. 133; A. L. Lowell, "The Government of Dependencies," in *The Foreign Policy of the United States*, (Philadelphia, 1899), p. 53.
[2] Pollard, *Evolution of Parliament*, p. 254.

The weapon which they used unsparingly in the conflict was that of the control of the purse, and its sharpest point was the salary of the governor. It was a weapon that had been placed in their hands by England herself when she gave them representative institutions and was unable to retain fiscal control by assuming all the expense of the civil and military establishment. In that struggle, whereas we have on the one hand incompetence, corruption and greed in England, on the other, we cannot absolve the colonists from sins of their own, and from policies that were too often basely petty and selfish. The imperial connection must be either "openly and frankly nothing" or "an encroachment at some point or another," [1] and it is difficult as one reads the documents in the story of the colonies' relations to England, particularly those connected with imperial defence, not to conclude that they frequently wished to have their cake and eat it too, that they often desired to retain the advantages of empire while declining in large measure its responsibilities and drawbacks.

[1] Quoted from the *Westminster Gazette* by Graham Wallas in *Our Social Heritage*, (Yale Press, 1921), p. 239.

CHAPTER III

THE DAWN OF THE CENTURY

*Culture and Ideals of the Colonists — Religious Attitude —
Morals — Law — The West India Trade — French Rivalry*

AFTER the first half century or so of colonization the American continental colonies showed most striking increases in population as contrasted with the comparatively stationary or dwindling numbers of whites in the island plantations.[1] A mainland population estimated to be about fifty-two thousand in 1650 had become two hundred and seventy-five thousand by 1700.[2] In that year there may have been six thousand persons in New Hampshire, seventy thousand in Massachusetts including Maine, six thousand in Rhode Island, and twenty-four thousand in Connecticut, or a hundred and six thousand in all. Although the New England colonies were actively engaged in the slave trade, in which Rhode Island took the lead, economic factors did not make slave-holding profitable, and the black population, bond and free, was comparatively small.[3] A few Jews, commercially important mainly in Rhode Island, some French Huguenots, and a considerable number of Scotch-Irish and Germans mostly in New Hampshire and Maine, formed almost the only elements added to the English stock.[4]

[1] F. W. Pitman gives the West Indian statistics. *Development of the British West Indies*, (Yale Press, 1917), pp. 369 *ff.*

[2] *Century of Population Growth*, (Washington, 1909), p. 4. *Cf.* also F. B. Dexter, "Estimates of Population in the American Colonies," *American Antiquarian Society Proceedings*, vol. V, pp. 22–50. All statistics in the colonial period are mere approximate estimates and should never be considered as accurate in the modern sense.

[3] W. E. DuBois, *Suppression of the African Slave Trade*, (Harvard University Press, 1916), pp. 27 *ff.*

[4] *Cf.* M. J. Kohler, "The Jews in Newport," *American Jewish Historical Society Publications*, No. 6, pp. 62 *ff.*; L. Huhner, "The Jews of New England," *ibid.*, No. 11, pp. 78 *ff.*; G. F. Daniels, *The Huguenots in the Nipmuck Country*, (Boston, 1880); E. R. Potter, *Memoir concerning the French Settlements in Rhode Island*, Rhode Island Historical Tracts, No. 5, (Providence, 1879); *Maine Historical Society, Coll.*, Ser. II, vol. III, pp. 351 *ff.*; E. L. Parker, *History of Londonderry*, N. H., (Boston, 1851); H. J. Ford, *Scotch Irish in America*, (Princeton University Press, 1915), pp. 223 *ff.*; *New Hampshire Historical Society, Proceedings*, vol. IV, pp. 143 *ff.*

During the eighteenth century the cultural life of certain classes in the older settlements became more varied and more closely in touch with intellectual movements in England than had been the case in the latter half of the seventeenth, but in the shifting frontier sections — which came to bulk larger and larger in influence as the century advanced — education and thought declined.[1] Schools and churches were not found so generally, and the hard-working life left even the children but little leisure. In an illuminating letter written from Deerfield at the time of the Indian troubles of 1703, the minister stated to Governor Dudley that the settlers feared to allow children under twelve to work in the fields for fear of the savages.[2] Another letter written about the same time from one of the southern colonies depicted the life common to the great mass of settlers throughout all of them, for it must be remembered that nine-tenths of the colonial population was engaged in tilling the soil.[3] "Men are generally carpenters, joiners, wheelwrights, coopers, butchers, tanners, shoemakers, tallow-chandlers, watermen, and what not," wrote the Reverend Mr. Urmiston in 1711, "women, soap-makers, starch-makers, dyers, etc. He or she that cannot do all these things, or hath not slaves that can, over and above all the common occupations of both sexes will have but a bad time of it, for help is not to be had at any rate, every one having enough business of his own." [4] One hesitates to analyze the "common occupations of both sexes" in the light of this list of added avocations.

This complete preoccupation with obtaining the mere means of subsistence fostered the beliefs so common in America that work of some sort is the duty of every member of the community, and that art is wholly unconnected with life, not a vital

[1] At the beginning of the century the frontier region may be said to have included all of Maine and the country lying to the north and west of a line drawn from Portsmouth to Hartford. *Acts and Resolves of the Province of Massachusetts Bay*, [hereafter cited as *Acts and Resolves*], vol. I, p. 402; *Public Records of the Colony of Connecticut*, [hereafter cited as *Conn. Col. Records*], vol. IV, p. 463. *Cf.* also, Turner, *Frontier*, pp. 43, 71, 76; and map facing p. 70 in L. H. Kimball's *Expansion of New England*, (Boston, 1909).

[2] G. Sheldon, *History of Deerfield*, (Deerfield, 1895), vol. I, p. 289.

[3] This percentage is given by Andrews, *Colonial Folkways*, p. 8.

[4] Cited in *Documentary History of American Industrial Society*, (Cleveland, 1910), vol. I, p. 271.

influence in developing personality. "If some have such Estates, that the yearly Income's enough to maintain them," wrote an unknown New England author from the country in 1719, "yet since they have the same Powers and Capacities for Business, and are under the same Supream Law with others, they seem inexcusable if they wrap up their Talent in a Napkin." "The Plow-man that raiseth Grain," he also says, "is more serviceable to Mankind, than the Painter who draws only to please the Eye. . . . The Carpenter who builds a good House to defend us from Wind and Weather, is more serviceable than the curious Carver, who employs his Art to please the Fancy." The writer does indeed add, after a panegyric on manual labor, that "when a People grow numerous, and part are sufficient to raise necessaries for the whole, then 't is allowable and laudable, that some should be imployed in innocent Arts more for ornament then Necessity : any innocent business that gets an honest penny, is better than Idleness."[1] Even then, apparently, art was to be redeemed not by its influence but by the "honest penny" to be gained in its pursuit. These were becoming the ideals of the great bulk of the colonists, who were growing away from the little cultured groups in the seaboard towns almost as much as they were from the intellectual life of England.

Even in those towns, in spite of a certain amount of reading by a few, there seems to have been little genuine culture, and the spirit developed may be said to have been that of a provincial bourgeoisie modified by the influence of the frontier. In the home country, as we have pointed out, the governing power was in middle class hands, and the days of Queen Anne were witnessing the steady growth in wealth and political strength of that commercial bourgeoisie which formed the back-bone of the non-conformist element.[2] This type in politics, notes a French historian, seizes quickly and surely upon the absurdities and faults of governments but too often lacks understanding of what is elevated and generous. It sees things from their least impor-

---

[1] *An Addition to the present melancholy Circumstances of the Province considered*, (Boston, 1719), pp. 3, 7. The author signs himself "your friend among the Oakes and Pines."

[2] W. T. Morgan, *English Political Parties and Leaders in the Reign of Queen Anne*, (Yale Press, 1920), pp. 22 *f*.

tant aspect — the higher aspect, the delicate point escape it —
"mais en revanche il a bon sens à faire peur." [1] The political history of the century on both sides of the water was repeatedly to
point to the truth of this characterization.

In the matter of reading, it is instructive to note that in one
shipment to the bookseller Usher in Boston in 1685 out of eight
hundred and seventy-four books more than seven hundred and
fifty were either school texts or religious works, whereas the
fields of history, travel and biography were represented by but
six stray volumes. [2] By the opening of the new century, however, the power and influence of the clergy were visibly declining, and with them their "sway over the book market." People
were beginning to demand a different sort of literary fare and
the taste of New England readers was becoming more liberal.
In spite of the painstaking research of recent years, however,
into what our ancestors read, and the still more painful process
of reading what they wrote, at this period, the fact seems to
remain that the cultivated individual, although not wholly
absent, was somewhat of a white robin and that there were
scarce half a dozen owners of private libraries of importance in
any of the colonies before 1730. [3] The innate tendency of the
Anglo-Saxon toward preoccupation with the practical, when
emphasized by frontier conditions or by opportunities for exploitation of abundant natural resources, overwhelms the more
intellectual side of his nature, — a process that has been quite as
characteristic of his development under colonial conditions in
Australia and New Zealand in recent years as in America in the
settlement era. [4] This is less true of the Latin, and long before
the little school known as Harvard College was founded at Cambridge in 1635, the learned institutions established by the
Spaniards in Mexico already surpassed in number and attain-
ments anything to be found within the limits of the present
United States until the nineteenth century. [5]

[1] Ch. Aubertin, *L'esprit publique au XVIIIe siècle*, (Paris, 1873), pp. 177, 189.

[2] W. C. Ford, *The Boston Book Market*, (Boston, 1917), p. 44.

[3] E. C. Cook, *Literary Influences in Colonial Newspapers*, (Columbia University
Press, 1912), p. 13. The most elaborate brief in favor of early New England culture is
Dr. T. G. Wright's *Literary Culture in early New England*, (Yale Press, 1920), which
presents the case in the most favorable light possible.

[4] *Cf.* Lord Bryce, *Modern Democracies*, (New York, 1921), vol. II, pp. 246, 279.

[5] E. G. Bourne, *Spain in America*, (New York, 1904), p. 310.

Nor for most of the first quarter of the eighteenth in New England was there any periodical press which supplied genuine discussion of public affairs. *The Boston News-Letter*, founded in 1704, and *The Boston Gazette* of 1719 contained little enough of anything, and that little was of no importance in the formation of either taste or thought.[1] The town-meetings, sessions of the assemblies, discussions in taverns, and controversial pamphlets formed the main channels for the expression of public opinion. There was practically no censorship after 1723, and as the press was open to all, the lack of good news sheets must have been due to the bovine apathy of the public and not to the heavy hand of government.[2] Indeed, the range of interests in colonial New England at the opening of the century, like that of goods and evils, was notably scant, and even to one who knows something of the pettiness of life in the remoter rural sections of today, the narrowness and more particularly the explosive individualism of early New Englanders are a bit disconcerting. One does not, of course, look for any genuine humility or a sense of humor in a Puritan. They destroy his specific characteristics as the sunshine does microbes, and that way tolerance lies. But one occasionally receives a shock.

Deerfield, for example, in 1701 was distinctly a frontier town, and was lying under the shadow of its unhappy destiny of almost total destruction by the Indians two years later. Yet we find it rocked to its foundations not by questions of defence but by that entertaining subject of dispute among the godly, the problem of social precedence in church. After deciding that age, estate, "place and qualifications" should guide those entrusted with the dangerous task of assigning sittings, it was further ruled in town-meeting that the "fore seat in the front gallery shall be equall in dignity with the 2d seat in the Body of the meeting house," the front seats in the gallery with the fourth seats in the body, and so on in a somewhat complicated scale of cross-dignities. Yet in 1730 it had to be further decided that after the

---

[1] Cook, *Literary Influences*, pp. 8 *ff*. *Cf.* extracts in Weeks and Bacon, *An historical Digest of the Provincial Press, Mass. Ser.*, (Boston, 1911), vol. I. Biographical material may be found in *The early Massachusetts Press*, by G. E. Littlefield, (Boston, 1902).

[2] C. A. Duniway, *The Development of the Freedom of the Press in Massachusetts.* (Harvard University Press, 1906), p. 103.

seating committee had done its best their findings would have to be submitted for ratification to a vote of the entire town.[1] The matter has more interest than that merely of an amusing commentary upon a certain type of the religious spirit, for it brings into clear view the parochial limits of outlook, the contentiousness, and the over-charged sense of self-importance possessed by these embattled farmers of the church-yard. Men who could quarrel bitterly over whether they were assigned for the worship of God and the confession of their own unworthiness to the second seat in the front gallery or the sixth seat in the body could be counted upon to quarrel instinctively with royal governors and imperial regulations irrespective of principles involved.

Although generalizations of such sort are dangerous, evidence indicates that in the early years of the eighteenth century the people of New England touched their lowest point intellectually and spiritually. Those years, however, also mark the turn toward a freer play of mind and a more rational envisaging of the problems of the universe. In an earlier volume I traced the tendencies in the latter half of the preceding century that were at work undermining the influence of the clergy.[2] In that period, however, the opposition to the established colonial church was based rather upon a growing indifferentism and dislike of church control in civil matters and of its persecuting zeal than upon disagreement with its teaching. But in the eighteenth century we find a rapidly growing revolt against the dogmas of Calvinism as developed in New England, which revolt exercised a most important influence not only upon religious and philosophical thought but upon political theory.

A mere reaction in any case was due upon the part of healthy minded persons from the unnatural absorption in theological matters expected in early days. Moreover, men came to feel that universal predestination and partial redemption wrecked the moral character of God. In the theory of the atonement and of the relation of the sinful soul to its Maker, as conceived in the early New England theology, a moral deity played hardly any

---

[1] Sheldon, *Deerfield*, vol. I, pp. 205, 482.
[2] *Founding of New England*, chap. XI, and pp. 451 *ff.*

part, a loving Father none whatever, and the legal and mechanical treatment of the subject has left us a mere "rubbish-heap of dead opinions." [1] The optimism which we have found to be one of the traits developed on the frontier, profoundly altered the settlers' outlook on life. In a world daily growing richer, safer and pleasanter, in which healthful labor met with a sure if moderate reward of content and prosperity, it was hard to maintain the belief that most of one's friends and neighbors were doomed to everlasting damnation. The sense of sin tended to evaporate, and the way was prepared for the later teaching by Chauncey of the benevolence of the Deity, and, a century later, for the transcendentalism of Emerson. [2] The pessimistic passivity and determinism of Calvinism, with the whole negative attitude toward life of New England Puritanism, was abandoned by many for the positive activity and optimism of a deistic conception of the universe. [3] Life they felt had been strangled by a theology which was essentially non-ethical, which paralyzed human initiative, and which was detrimental to practical religion. [4]

In spite of the "Half-Way Covenant" and lax communion, the churches slowly emptied. It was in vain that Mather drew pictures of the early treatment of the clergy by the people — "with what Reverence; with what Obedience; with what concern" they wished "to have them comfortably provided for!" "How they Rejoyced when they saw them come into their Houses as if Angels of God had appeared." [5] But even Mather himself fell somewhat under the general spell of optimism, and in a volume of garbled science and platitudinous moralizing, illumined here and there by charming passages descriptive of nature, seemed to admit the truth of God's own verdict that the world he had made was good. Dull as it is, the book thus shows an advance over the clergyman's earlier prophecy that "in the glorious times promised to the church on earth, America will be Hell." [6]

[1] G. A. Gordon, *Humanism in New England Theology*, (Boston, 1920), pp. 35, 37 *f.*

[2] G. Santayana, *Winds of Doctrine*, (New York, 1913), p. 191.

[3] I. W. Riley, *American Philosophy, — the early Schools*, (New York, 1907), p. 11.

[4] F. H. Foster, *A Genetic History of the New England Theology*, (University of Chicago Press, 1907), pp. 544 *f.*

[5] Cotton Mather, *The good old Way*, (Boston, 1706), p. 70.

[6] Cited in *The religious History of New England*, (Harvard University Press, 1917), p. 32.

Although his writings contain deistic tendencies, he had no intention of setting his feet on any new path, and in 1699 strongly opposed the formation of the Brattle Street Church which was organized mainly by men connected with Harvard, and which was an exponent of the more liberal forces then coming into play.[1] It was noted about this time that many of the boys at that college "differ much in their principles from their parents."[2] The circumstances attending the birth of the new church strengthened the liberal tendencies in the little institution of learning, and at the same time loosened the hold both upon it and upon the people of Mather himself, who in an ungoverned fit of rage had written a violently vituperative pamphlet against the innovators.[3]

Two years later Yale College was founded at Saybrook, heartily supported by Mather who hoped that the new school would form a bulwark for orthodoxy. In 1705, in a further attempt to stem the tide, some of the clergy in Massachusetts, under the lead of the Mathers, made certain proposals for the closer association of churches under a form which savored so much of Presbyterianism that many considered it to have a " prelatical, if not papistical, flavor " and the plan came to nothing.[4] A similar movement in Connecticut, however, succeeded and the Saybrook Platform, adopted at a synod in 1708, was enacted into law by the General Court.[5] Although the in-

---

[1] "The old strait Gate is now out of Date,
The street it must be broad ;
And the Bridge must be of wood, tho not half so good
As firm stone in the Road.

Relations are Rattle with Brattle & Brattle ;
Lord Brother may n't command :
But Mather and Mather had rather & rather
The good old way should stand."

From a "libel" written in Plymouth. Quoted by Samuel Sewall, *Letter Book*, vol. I, p. 255.

[2] *Cal. State Pap., Col., 1701*, p. 577.

[3] Josiah Quincy, *History of Harvard*, (Cambridge, 1840), vol. I, pp. 132 *ff.*; W. Walker, *Creeds and Platforms of Congregationalism*, (New York, 1893), pp. 472 *ff.*; *Diary of Cotton Mather*, [Mass. Hist. Soc., Coll., Ser. VII, vols. VII and VIII], vol. I, pp. 325, 330, 338.

[4] H. M. Dexter, *Congregationalism in the last three hundred Years*, (New York, 1880), pp. 491 *ff.*; Walker, *Creeds and Platforms*, pp. 483 *ff.*

[5] *Conn. Col. Records*, vol. V, p. 87.

tent of the articles adopted has never yet been settled, they provided for a closer consociation of neighboring churches and were held by some to have created full ecclesiastical courts.[1] That colony, which had originally been more tolerant than Massachusetts, had now become more reactionary and distinctly lagged behind the liberalizing movement centering more or less in Boston and Cambridge.

Perhaps of all generalizations, the most difficult and dangerous to make are those dealing with the moral conditions of peoples and periods. For many years, owing to the deliberate exclusion from printed records of entries bearing on the topic, it was peculiarly difficult to form an estimate of the standard of sexual purity developed by the Puritan code. A more honest attitude toward history and life has resulted in accumulation of evidence that enables us to judge more accurately of the Puritan results and of our own time as compared with what has been considered as America's age of religion and virtue. Owing to certain peculiar requirements by some of the churches, we are in possession of sufficient records to test this point among church members, and the entries indicate strongly that the standard of sexual morality among the unmarried youth was lower in Puritan New England than it is today for both sexes. The ruling by one of the Connecticut churches later in the century that seven-months-children should be considered legitimate and receive baptism confirms the records as to wide-spread laxity.[2] Unpleasant as this aspect of the Puritan days may be, it is by no means surprising. The Puritan does not seem to realize that activities and capabilities demand an outlet, and that if the avenues for innocent and normal recreation are denied nature will take her own revenge. In Connecticut, where the people were almost all hard-working farmers for whom Sunday was the only day of rest, it was enacted that all young persons should be subject to fine or two hours in the stocks should they meet

[1] Dexter, *Congregationalism*, pp. 488 *ff.*; Walker, *Creeds and Platforms*, pp. 495 *ff.*
[2] *Plymouth Church Records*, [*Col. Soc. Mass., Publications*, vol. XXII], pp. 251 *ff.*; C. F. Adams, "Some Phases of Sexual Morality and Church Discipline in New England," *Mass. Hist. Soc., Proceedings*, Ser. II, vol. VI, pp. 477 *ff.*; L. H. Gipson, *Jared Ingersoll*, (Yale Press, 1920), pp. 51 *ff.*; H. R. Stiles, *Bundling, its Origin, Progress and Decline in America*, (Albany, 1869); *Records of the Brewster* (Massachusetts) *Congregational Church*, 1700–1792, (privately printed, m. p., 1911).

together on Sabbath evenings either indoors or out, although church services had perforce occupied almost all of their earlier hours.[1] In Massachusetts it was illegal, on the same day, not only to go swimming but, in spite of Christ's own example, even to go for a quiet walk on the village streets or in the fields.[2]

Legislation opposed to human nature or to the desires of a large part of the people breeds hypocrisy and a contempt for law. In addition to the effort to force people to live their lives according to the most extreme views of a fanaticism which was finding response in a steadily decreasing part of the community, there were other influences also that tended to break down respect for legal authority. One of these was that all-pervasive influence upon American life and institutions to which we have to revert continually — the frontier. The frontiersman is always impatient both of restraint and of fine-drawn distinctions. In his rough and ready meting out of justice he takes little account of precedent or thought for the future. Even as late as 1782 the chief justice of New Hampshire refused to be bound by previous decisions, remarking that "every tub should stand on its own bottom." [3] One of the favorite dicta of English lawyers of the old school was that "it is better that the law should be certain than that it should be just." [4] The difference between this and the dictum of the New Hampshire judge is in part that between the complexities of a thousand years of development and the *tabula rasa* of the wilderness.

The office of chief justice was invariably held by laymen during the early period, the first lawyer being appointed to that office in Massachusetts in 1712, and in New Hampshire in 1754.[5] The feeling against lawyers is illustrated by such facts as that in Connecticut in 1698 they were legislated against in company with drunkards, keepers of disorderly houses and other people of ill-fame, and that in Rhode Island in 1730 a law

---

[1] *Conn. Col. Records*, vol. V, p. 130.

[2] *Acts and Resolves*, vol. I, p. 59.

[3] Cited by P. S. Reinsch, *English Common Law in the early American Colonies*, Bulletin, University of Wisconsin, No. 31, p. 27.

[4] James Bryce, *Influence of national Character and historical Environment on the Development of the Common Law*. Reprinted in part by Kocourek and Wigmore, *Formative Influences of Legal Development*, (Boston, 1918), p. 370.

[5] Reinsch, *English Common Law*, pp. 24, 27.

was passed prohibiting members of the profession from being elected to the House of Deputies.[1]

The unsatisfactory condition of legal theory and practice, although varying in degree in different colonies was common to them all, island and continental alike, and English merchants sometimes complained, not without reason, that they found "more security and better and more speedy justice in the most distant provinces of the Ottoman Dominions from their Bashaws" than in some of the American plantations.[2] As social conditions became more complex, layman law administered by laymen was bound to break down. There was always the uncertainty of what constituted law in the colonies. "No one can tell what is law and what is not in the plantations" complained an American at the beginning of the eighteenth century.[3] It was frequently denied that the common law of the mother country was of binding force upon the colonists or that Acts of Parliament other than those relating to trade could be extended to them, although from the time of Andros's administration increasing admiration was expressed for the common law, because the colonists felt that under it they could strengthen their position against England.

At that period, however, the interests of New Englanders were by no means confined to matters within their colonial borders or even to their relations with the English government. To the merchant in Boston and Newport as well as to the settler

---

[1] *Conn. Col. Records*, vol. IV, pp. 236 f.; *Records of the Colony of Rhode Island*, [hereafter cited as *R. I. Col. Records*], vol. IV, p. 430. The Rhode Island law was repealed at the next session. In New Hampshire a law prohibited a person from being represented by more than two attorneys as there were not enough to go around. W. H. Fry, *New Hampshire as a Royal Province*, (New York, 1908), p. 468. A Connecticut law of 1726 limited the number of lawyers permitted in the colony to eleven. *Conn. Col. Records*, vol. VII, pp. 279, 358.

[2] *Cal. State Pap., Col., 1700*, p. 512. *Cf. ibid.*, pp. 13, 509; *1699*, pp. 81, 543 f.; *1702–3*, p. 491; *1706–8*, p. 93.

[3] Quoted by S. L. Sioussat, *The English Statutes in Maryland*, (Johns Hopkins Univ. Studies, 1903), p. 30. This was written of Maryland but compare Larkin's report on Massachusetts in 1701. "As to the Laws of England, they abhor the very thought of them, and Acts of Parliament they look upon to be only obligatory wherein the Province is particularly named, though they will use either of them to serve a friend, so that none can tell what is law and what is not." *Cal. State Pap., Col., 1701*, p. 576. *Cf.* C. M. Andrews, "The Influence of colonial Conditions as illustrated in the Connecticut Intestacy Act," in *Select Essays in Anglo-American Legal History*, (Boston, 1907), pp. 450 ff.

on the frontier, trade and war with England's traditional foe were beginning to assume large importance as the century opened. The contest between the two nations themselves was fundamentally for trade and not for territory, and in so far as concerned such disputed lands as were washed by the waters of the Atlantic the commodities fought for fell into four classes — negroes from Africa, furs and naval stores from the northern American region, fish from the northern waters, and the group of tropical and semi-tropical products of which sugar was the most important. Both nations regarded their West Indian possessions as much the most valuable parts of their overseas dominions, and both the African slave trade and the temperate zone colonies were looked upon rather as "supplemental areas of supply" for the sugar plantations than of value in themselves.[1] We can readily understand how the comparative importance of New England and the English sugar islands must have appeared to the contemporary Englishman by a glance at the figures for direct trade with England in the year 1697–8.

	Imports into England	Exports from England
Island colonies	£632,653	£309,965
New England	31,254	93,475
New York	8,763	25,278 [2]

Quite distinctly, however, from the beginning of the eighteenth century, the balance between the needs of the sugar colonies and the products of each nation's supplemental areas of supply in North America began to be upset.[3] By additions to her West Indian territory and from other causes France needed a supply of temperate zone products greater than Canada could yield, whereas, on the other hand, the growth of the New England colonies resulted in a production and trade activity greater than could be satisfied by the British sugar islands. Rapid development of a trade between New England and the French islands thus became inevitable although opposed to the Mercantile doctrines held by each nation. In 1701 Gov-

[1] Cf. Andrews, "Anglo-French Commercial Rivalry," pp. 546, 553.

[2] House of Lords Mss., Historical Mss. Commission, vol. IV, New Ser., p. 446; Cal. State Pap., Col., 1702, p. 69.

[3] Pitman, West Indies, pp. 189 ff.; S. L. Mims, Colbert's West India Policy, (Yale Press, 1912), pp. 334 ff

ernor Codrington of the Leeward Islands complained to the home government that the "French begin to tred upon our heels in the sugar trade" and asked that Parliament pass an act to prevent exportation to them of provisions and lumber from Ireland and the North American colonies.[1] At the very threshhold of our period, therefore, we catch a glimpse of that divergence of interest between New England and the British West Indies, the warping effect of which upon the whole imperial structure was to prove of the highest importance.

Although by the opening of the century France had planted in her three most valuable islands a population of twenty-three thousand whites and forty-four thousand slaves, in all the vast expanse of the American continent she had as yet only about sixteen thousand settlers in Canada and a mere village at the mouth of the Mississippi.[2] Despite the fact that the numbers in the English colonies along the seaboard were perhaps twenty times as great, this disparity was by no means a fair index to the comparative strength of the two nations in the New World. The French administrative policy was one of centralized control at home with no troublesome local liberties for the colonists. Not only were the sixteen thousand Canadians under a single administration whereas the English were under a dozen, each jealous of the others and working at cross purposes, but no struggles between assemblies and governors diverted attention and resources from questions of military aggression or defence. Moreover, in many respects, the home government in France displayed an efficiency and unity of purpose distinctly greater than that of the English, and we even find the Lords of Trade complaining of the lack of good maps of America and asking the ambassador in Paris to procure some there.[3] In addition, as far as land forces were concerned, France could put much larger professional armies in the field both in Europe and America than could her antagonist.

There were two points, nevertheless, in England's favor. The

---

[1] *Cal. State Pap., Col., 1701*, pp. 417 *f*.

[2] Zimmerman, *Kolonialpolitik*, vol. IV, pp. 79, 129; Deschamps, *Question coloniale*, pp. 188, 234.

[3] *Colonial Office Papers* in Public Record Office, [hereafter cited as *C.O.*], *324 No. 10*. *Cambridge Modern History*, (New York, 1907), vol. VII, pp. 104 *f*.

A SEA SKIRMISH BETWEEN ONE ENGLISH AND THREE
FRENCH MEN-OF-WAR

From *A Relation of the severall Adventers by Sea with the dangers, difficulties, and
hardships met for several years, transcribed by John Millar*, 1717–1718, a manuscript in
the Library of Congress

first was her lack of European entanglements and aspirations, and the second was her dominance upon the sea.[1] The French dream of an empire built up in the great valleys of America, which should encircle the English and perhaps conquer them, was not an idle one. It was the power of England's fleet that enabled our ancestors to defy the forces of France in spite of their own selfish particularism and of military inefficiency both English and colonial.

In America the most important phase of the struggle is to be noted in the colony of New York, but the suffering fell for the most part upon the frontier settlements of New England. This was due to the part played by the Indian trade in the contest between the white men. The beaver was practically extinct in the territory ruled by the Iroquois who were dependent for their profits upon tribes farther to the west. The French carried on a direct trade with certain of these interior tribes through the valley of the St. Lawrence but in the case of the English the Iroquois occupied the profitable position of middlemen. Their prosperity, therefore, was bound up with the maintenance of friendly relations with the English, and it was even to their advantage to influence the "Far Indians" as much as possible in the same direction. The cheapness of the English trading goods had a secondary effect in creating a large traffic in them between the merchants of Albany and the fur traders at Montreal, which was of great value to the French and would have been interrupted by hostilities in upper New York. For that reason they directed their war-parties rather against the frontier of New England, and the New Englanders claimed with truth that both the immunity of Albany and their own sufferings were due to the illicit business which the Albany traders carried on with the enemy.[2]

The use of savage allies was countenanced and encouraged by both nations, and King William's War just before, and Queen

---

[1] Seeley, *Expansion of England*, pp. 94 *ff.*; A. T. Mahan, *The Influence of Sea Power upon History*, (Boston, 1898), pp. 209 *ff.*

[2] C. H. McIlwain, *Wraxall's Abridgment of the New York Indian Records*, (Harvard University Press, 1915), chap. II. [The usefulness of this volume is very much decreased by the absence of any index.] *Cf.* also *New York Colonial Documents*, vol. V, pp. 584, 587, 682, 687.

Anne's just after, the opening of the century partook largely of the nature of Indian warfare rather than of civilized military operations. The only organized expedition of interest in the former — the attack on Quebec by Phips in 1691 — has already been described at the end of our preceding volume.[1] For the rest of the war, the story is mainly one of wild border raids, of midnight massacres, and of barbaric cruelties inflicted on defenceless women and children in isolated farm houses and scattered hamlets. In the four-fold contest for control of the furs, lumber and fish of the West, Hudson's Bay district, Newfoundland and Acadia, it was the last only which involved New England directly.[2] Its ill-defined boundaries were held to include New Brunswick, Nova Scotia and the larger part of Maine. In the sombre and limitless forests that covered the entire region there were few settlers, and those at far separated points on the coast or the banks of rivers. It was upon these unfortunates that the French and their Indian allies fell at intervals throughout those six years, with a savage fury almost without counterpart in the history of civilized nations. It is true that in upper Canada the French settlers lived in terror of the Iroquois but the English neither goaded on the natives nor took part in the cruelties inflicted by them as did the French officers and priests. The fact that some generations later the selfish interests of a French despot led him to side with the revolting colonies against his own arch-enemy England and so to turn the scale in their favor, and the noble acts of certain individual Frenchmen,[3] have apparently obliterated all remembrance of the previous relations of our ancestors and their French neighbors for a century and a half, and France is made to appear the traditional friend as England the traditional foe of our forefathers. The fact is that France was the persistent enemy throughout practically the entire colonial period, and waged war with a ferocity and an inhumanity for which there is scarce parallel or palliation.

The anticipating or warding off of the sudden and secret attacks of the Abnakis and their French inciters and leaders

[1] Adams, *Founding of New England*, pp. 438 *ff.*

[2] *Cf.* Francis Parkman, *Count Frontenac and New France*, (Boston, 1909), pp. 352 *ff.*

[3] *Cf.* E. S. Corwin, *French Policy and the American Alliance*, (Princeton University Press, 1916), chap. I.

were made almost impossible by the character of the New England frontier. The brunt of the military burden fell upon Massachusetts though she met with scant success and her chosen leaders showed but little of skill or courage. Colonel Church, the aged veteran of King Philip's War, led a futile expedition to the eastward, and Captain Pasco Chubb, who was in charge of the fort at Pemaquid, made a cowardly surrender when called upon without firing a shot.[1] In the refusal of the colonies to afford aid to one another, in the exploits of badly officered and worse disciplined troops, and in the constant opposition to England coupled with as constant requests for help from her,[2] there is much that is anticipatory of the future but little to stir pride. The only relief afforded by the picture is to be found in the heroic deeds of individual men and women defending their homes and families, or suffering with noble fortitude the pains and perils of a savage captivity. Although Hannah Dustin's well-known exploit is the most popular of such episodes in the war, it is but typical of what many a man and woman endured and dared before the Treaty of Ryswick brought temporary peace to the harried settlers of the border in 1697.

[1] *Cal. State Pap., Col., 1696–7*, pp. 70, 142 f., 224, 313; *N. Y. Col. Docts.*, vol. IX, p. 658. For the general narrative of the war *vide* Benj. Church, *History of the eastern Expeditions*, ed. H. M. Dexter, (Boston, 1867); Parkman, *Frontenac*; S. A. Drake, *The Border Wars of New England*, (New York, 1910). *Cf.* also *Collection de manuscrits relatifs à la nouvelle France*, (Quebec, 1884).

[2] *Cal. State Pap., Col., 1696–7*, pp. 133, 141, 185, 251, 486, 494, 624.

CHAPTER IV

THE POLICY OF UNIFIED CONTROL

Imperial Defence — Need for Greater Union — Bellomont's Policies — Navigation Acts — Illicit Trade and Piracy — Rhode Island and Connecticut Violate Their Charters — Troubles in New Hampshire — Difficulties of a Colonial Governor

THE experiences of King Philip's War and the recent contest with the French had made it apparent to the home government, as well as to many of the colonists themselves, that the system by which the English in New England were divided into different jurisdictions, jealous of one another and subject to almost negligible control by the mother country, was both wasteful and unfair to the colonies themselves. In the face of a united enemy it had proved highly dangerous. When the colonists had been unable to agree as to mutual help England had undertaken to fix their respective quotas for them but without success. The main burden had fallen on Massachusetts and New York, whereas the southern and smaller northern colonies had done little or nothing, frittering away their time and energy in excuses and recriminations.[1]

The general theory of imperial defence gradually being evolved was that England should fight her European battles without colonial aid, — though the fate of the colonies might be involved, — and be solely responsible for the naval defence of the empire. On the other hand, the colonies were expected to take care of the local defence of their own frontiers as far as possible. Provided England retained control of the sea, that task would have been entirely within the strength of the colonists, could they have used their combined resources in any efficient way. This, however, both their selfishness and their jealousy

---

[1] *Cal. State Pap., Col., 1693–6*, pp. 45, 130, 137, 169, 191, 195, 237, 315, 335 *f.*, 347 *ff.*, 361, 377, 560, 581, 587, 596, 606, 635 *f.*, 646, 673, 677.

prevented them from doing, so that, with ample reserves, they were constantly asking help from England who was herself at times sorely pressed. Demands for men, money, guns, ammunition and assistance of all sorts poured in upon the Lords of Trade even from such colonies as claimed in practice a virtual independence of the mother country.[1] Dependence and independence are incompatible conditions, each of which possesses advantages. The same group of men, however, cannot fairly claim the benefits of each status simultaneously.[2] In this respect, nevertheless, the relations of the New England and other colonies to the home country were merely those commonly subsisting between any frontier and old settlement. The particularism of the colonies in their relations with one another must also be regarded merely as the characteristic attitude of communities at a certain stage of their growth. The jealousy between the American colonies, for example, was perhaps less than that which existed among the provinces of Australia in the past century and which long delayed the possibility of union on that continent.[3] Moreover, it is interesting to note, in view of what I have said about empire forming a new cycle in political development, repeating the stages of national state-making, that it does so in this matter of particularism in defence. The nationalization of such defence in England herself was obtained only after a long struggle, episodes in which were the refusal of Cornwall to acknowledge liability for the defence of the Scottish borders, and of the interior districts to bear any responsibility for the

---

[1] In addition to references already cited, *vide Cal. State Pap., Col., 1696-7*, pp. 212, 266, 568; *1702-3*, pp. 148, 188. In January 1702 the Lords of Trade had to consider requests from Massachusetts, New York, Bermuda, the Bahamas, Antigua, Nevis, Jamaica and Barbadoes. *Ibid.*, pp. 25 *f.*

[2] *Cf.* Sumner, *Earth Hunger*, pp. 121 *ff.*

[3] The following description of the Australian colonies applies equally well to the American ones of a century earlier. "Malgré les conditions communes de milieu géographique et de vie sociale, les colonies australasiennes, même dans la pleine ferveur de leur développement économique et de leur esprit d'indépendence à outrance vis-à-vis de la métropole, façonnaient leur politique selon les conceptions régionalistes les plus étroites. . . . Elles constituaient autant microcosmes politiques terriblement jaloux les uns des autres . . . tous acharnés à entraver, moyennant des barrières fiscales élevées, toute pénétration économique réciproque; et elles restaient si rebelles à l'idée de fusionner en un seul organisme que les chemins de fer étaient même construits avec un écartement différent d'une colonie à l'autre." G. Mondaini, *Colonisation Anglaise*, (Paris, 1920), vol. I, p. 327.

defence of the coasts.[1] Apparently provincial sentiment must play its part and spend its strength before a national sentiment can take its place.[2]

If, however, it was to be nearly a century, and only after the critical period following the revolution, before the particularism of the colonies was at last to give way under great pressure to the need for genuine union, both the English government and many of the colonists saw the need for combination of some sort from the days of James the Second and of Andros. Massachusetts, by means of memorials and representations through her agents in England, strongly urged the necessity of uniting the northern colonies by appointing a single governor over New Hampshire, Massachusetts and New York, with military authority in Rhode Island and Connecticut.[3] To this the proprietor of New Hampshire objected because he dreaded an increased military expense; Connecticut considered it as an invasion of her charter rights; New York feared to lose trade and prestige to Boston.[4] Union, however, was in the air, and plans for a genuine consolidation either of all or of some of the continental colonies were put forth by Penn, D'Avenant, Livingstone and others.[5]

Not only, therefore, was a different type of official chosen in the appointment of Richard Coote, first Earl of Bellomont, an able Irish peer and a Whig supporter, but a partial return was made to the theory of unified control by commissioning him governor of New Hampshire, Massachusetts and New York as well as giving him control in time of war of the militias of Rhode Island, Connecticut and New Jersey.[6] Quite in accord with the deliberate official movements of the time it was not until seven months after his appointment that he left England. Owing to military exigencies he landed first at New York and did not

[1] Pollard, *Evolution of Parliament*, p. 146 and note.
[2] *Cf.* Richard Jebb, *The Imperial Conference*, (London, 1911), vol. II, p. 180.
[3] *Cal. State Pap., Col., 1696–7*, p. 339.
[4] *Ibid.*, pp. 136, 165, 170, 189, 225, 318, 338 *f.*, 346, 352, 354, 358, 384; *N. Y. Col. Docts.*, vol. IV, pp. 259 *ff.*
[5] *N. Y. Col. Docts.*, vol. IV, pp. 296 *ff.*; D'Avenant, *Discourses on the Public Revenues*, vol. II, pp. 40 *f.*; R. Frothingham, *The Rise of the Republic*, (Boston, 1873), pp. 112 *f.*
[6] *Col. Soc. Mass., Publications*, vol. II, pp. 76 *ff.*; *N. Y. Col. Docts.*, vol. IV, pp. 266 *ff.*, 284 *ff.*; *Laws of New Hampshire, Province Period*, ed. A. S. Batchellor, [hereafter cited as *N. H. Prov. Laws*], vol. I, p. 621; *Cal. State Pap., Col., 1696–7*, pp. 399, 448 *f.*, 450, 514.

reach Boston until the middle of 1699. A hearty welcome awaited him, but the Boston of the day could have afforded but a modicum of social pleasure to the titled and witty Irishman. Of his new duties, the most pressing were to deal efficiently with the French menace, and to enforce the laws of trade against both pirate and smuggler. Although his most serious military trials were in New York and not New England, the defence of both against the French really constituted a single problem, and the conditions the Earl found are interesting for the light they throw on English administration.

Four companies of English regulars, though partially raised in the province, formed for many years the only English forces on the continent, and were garrisoned at New York and Albany when Bellomont assumed command.[1] The new Governor found that not only were the younger officers sent out of the very worst type, but that the morale of the men suffered from intolerable conditions. Living was several times as dear as in England, yet the troops were forced to submit to a reduction of thirty per cent in pay, said to be due to exchange; they were at the mercy of victualers for their food, Mr. Livingstone being accused of having "pinched an estate out of the poor soldiers' bellies"; and their uniforms were in such rags that they were forced to walk the streets of Albany indecently naked.[2] A mutiny was the natural result, and Bellomont struggled hard to remedy the conditions. Declining to pocket the thirty per cent as he might have done according to custom, he wrote to the home government in honest protest. "'Tis a great abuse," he wrote to the Lords of Trade, "and much to the King's dishonor it should be continued; it has the air of a trick and a fraud upon the poor soldiers, and I will wash my hands of it and of the Government too, unless they have full English pay."[3]

His military policy was to retain the friendship, then wavering, of the Iroquois by insisting upon fair dealing with them and

---

[1] *Cal. State Pap., Col., 1693-6*, pp. 291 *f.*, 315, 433; *1696-7*, pp. 183, 507. In addition to garrisons maintained in the West Indies, there was also a company of foot in Newfoundland. *Acts Privy Council*, vol. II, pp. 360 *ff.*

[2] *Cal. State Pap., Col., 1696-7*, pp. xviii, 533, 546, 556; *1700*, pp. xxv, 14, 202, 252, 355, 431, 572, 577, 593, 607, 874; *N. Y. Col. Docts.*, vol. IV, pp. 377, 871.

[3] *Cal. State Pap., Col., 1700*, p. 606; *N. Y. Col. Docts.*, vol. IV, pp. 712 *ff.*, 759 *ff.*

by building more forts. Those at Albany and Schenectady had been allowed to fall to ruin by the English and colonial governments until they looked less like defences than "pounds to impound cattle," and at Albany the gunners dared not even fire the guns because the platforms were dangerously rotten. In Massachusetts, where in Bellomont's opinion the Indians were "barbarously treated," he could secure only the passage of a weak act for remedying abuses and the colony could in no way be induced to strengthen its defenses. "There being now a peace," he wrote, " they have no remembrance of war." [1]

Perceiving, as many did not at that time, the enormous potential value to England of her colonies, Bellomont ardently desired to increase the efficiency and honesty of the civil administration, to foster trade, and to reorganize military defence upon an imperial basis. He rightly believed that the safety of the colonies depended upon the strength of England, which, in turn, depended upon resources derived from trade. Without concentration of material resources and administration, there could be no concentration of military and naval strength. Had the naval power of the empire, for example, been as divided and as comparatively impotent as was the military power of the colonies, there is little doubt but that the empire would have gone down before the unified power of France. Bellomont's second important duty, the enforcement of the laws of trade, was closely connected, therefore, with the primary one of defense.

The trade situation had become chaotic. The various Navigation Acts were merely the most conspicuous of hundreds of declarations defining the limits of operation of colonial industry and commerce. They had never been strictly observed and a new act was passed in 1696 intended to aid in the enforcement of the earlier ones.[2] Bellomont's task of carrying this into effect was no easy one for the laws were generally unpopular, though it is difficult to say to what extent they worked genuine hardship to legitimate business. The legislation against wool manufacture created much irritation, but as it did not prohibit house-

---

[1] *Cal. State Pap., Col., 1699*, pp. 412, 490; *1700*, pp. 252, 673; *N. Y. Col. Docts.*, vol. IV, p. 641.

[2] *7th and 8th Wm. III, c. 22*; W. Macdonald, *Select Charters*, (New York, 1906), pp. 213 *ff.*

hold spinning and weaving the restraint could not have been a serious one in a country where capital and labor were equally scarce.[1] As to the enumerated commodities required to be carried direct to England, New England produced none of them. In so far as the laws restricted the carrying trade to English owned and English manned ships, they were of enormous benefit to the colonies, for the term "English" was held to include the colonists, whose shipping was thus put on a basis of equality with that of the mother country.[2] Under this stimulus shipbuilding had become one of the most important of New England industries, competing so fiercely with English production as to bring forth bitter complaints from the carpenters at home, complaints that the government refused to heed.[3] Nevertheless, the colonists complained that it was a hardship not to be allowed to buy European goods before they had first been landed in England. The Council in Boston, Bellomont reported, "expressed great discontent at the Acts of Trade and Navigation that restrained them from an open free trade to all parts of the world; they alledg'd they were as much Englishmen as those in England and thought they had a right to all the priviledges that the people of England had." [4] One of the privileges of Englishmen in which the colonists did not share was the payment of taxes for the maintenance of the British navy. It was that navy which was bringing the whole carrying trade of the world largely into English hands — colonial as well as British — by making English shipping the safest and cheapest, because the best protected, means of transport. It should be noted that by 1714 the cost of convoys for colonial commerce, aside from other naval expense, was over £115,000 a year.[5] It bears out what I earlier said of the insistence in the colonial period upon "rights" and the disappearance of "duties" that, when the Boston merchants were claiming the rights of Englishmen

---

[1] *Cf.* however, *Cal. State Pap., Col., 1701*, pp. 658, 695; *1702-3*, p. 924.

[2] E. Channing, "The Navigation Laws," *American Antiquarian Society, Proceedings*, New Series, vol. VI, pp. 166 *f.*

[3] W. B. Weeden, *Economic and Social History of New England*, (Boston, 1890), pp. 366 *f.*; G. W. Chalmers, *Introduction to the History of the Revolt of the American Colonies*, (Boston, 1845), vol. II, p. 33.

[4] *N. Y. Col. Docts.*, vol. IV, p. 789.

[5] Chalmers, *Revolt*, vol. II, p. 4; Mahan, *Influence of Sea Power*, p. 224.

to trade where they would, they said nothing about the equivalent duty of paying for that navy which alone gave them the power to trade where they did. Theoretically the profit supposed to accrue to England from the Navigation Acts was held to constitute a contribution from the colonies equivalent to taxation, but in practice not only did the colonists constantly complain of the laws but evaded them whenever they saw fit.

New England ships by the hundreds plied up and down the American coast, to the French and English West Indies, the Dutch settlements, the Canaries, Madeira, the coast of Africa and the countries of the Old World.[1] Much of this commerce was legitimately open to them. But when they clandestinely carried enumerated commodities from other colonies to countries other than England or brought back from foreign ports goods which should have been landed first in England, they secured the extra profit always accruing in any smuggling trade. It is difficult to estimate the extent of this trade or the profits involved. As the morals of the time were not over nice, the former probably depended upon the latter.[2] Men in New Hampshire declared that that province would be ruined if the acts were enforced, and in Boston, a little later, men of such standing as Peter Faneuil were notoriously engaged in smuggling European goods.[3]

Bellomont's efforts to carry out his orders in this respect were hopeless enough, but when he included an attack on piracy in the scope of his activities, he aroused a dragon from the slime of colonial commercial life against which he was powerless. That evil had grown to enormous proportions. Privateering had come to a legal end with the Peace of Ryswick, but there was no diminution of the more lawless trade. The war had let loose a flood of desperate characters, and so low was the ethical tone of the day that Governor Fletcher, Bellomont's predecessor at New York, and leading merchants were all leagued in the nefa-

---

[1] For routes, *vide* Andrews, "Colonial Commerce," pp. 58 *ff*.

[2] Most authorities agree that the illegal trade was great. *Cf.* E. Channing, *History of the United States*, vol. II, p. 262; Andrews, "Colonial Commerce," p. 61. But also note W. J. Ashley, "American Smuggling," in *Surveys Historic and Economic*, (London, 1900), pp. 341 *ff*.

[3] *Cal. State Pap., Col., 1702*, p. 89; E. B. Greene, *Provincial America*, (New York, 1905), p. 294.

rious business, and the wealth of not a few socially prominent families is founded upon murder on the high seas.[1] The trade at New York was notorious and on a tremendous scale. Boston and the smaller ports had their share, and the waters of Rhode Island and eastern Long Island harbored numberless ships loaded with plunder and stained with blood while their commanders made their terms with the authorities for a peaceful home-coming and prominent citizens chafed at delays till they could know their gains.[2] Captains Every, Mews, Bradish, Want and many others openly sought Newport or some quiet landing spot to bring ashore their thousands, and in some cases their hundreds of thousands, of dollars to be welcomed by their partners and by the people at large. The most celebrated of these sea robbers in ballad and tradition was Captain Kidd, whose memory seems to have attracted to itself all those qualities and adventures believed to appertain to a fine and proper pirate.

He had been a privateersman in the recent war, and was engaged by Bellomont and Robert Livingstone of New York to go on a voyage to capture pirates and as far as possible break up their trade. The venture was legitimately expected to be profitable as well as serviceable, and not only Livingstone but Lord Somers, the Earl of Oxford and the Earl of Shrewsbury invested in what looked like a promising speculation.[3] The whole affair is more or less wrapped in mystery despite the efforts of those who have sought to rehabilitate Kidd's character. Pirates may have proved wary but certainly the crew proved unruly, and whether willingly or not, Kidd seems to have become engaged as a pirate himself. His capture of two rich East Indiamen created a scandal in England which threatened to have far reaching political consequences in view of the prominence of his backers.[4] Returning to New England he hovered off the coast and attempted to make terms with Bellomont, having heard rumors of what awaited him. The governor, however, inveigled him into custody and sent him to England for trial.

[1] *N. Y. Col. Docts.*, vol. IV, pp. 304, 306 ff., 323 f., 385 ff., 512 ff., 532, 551 f.
[2] *Cf. Cal. State Pap., Col., 1696* to *1701, passim.*
[3] The agreement is in *N. Y. Col. Docts.*, vol. IV, pp. 762 ff.
[4] *Cf.* Bishop Burnett, *History of his own Times*, (London, 1809), vol. III, pp. 368, 377 ff.

Kidd claimed that the vessels captured by him had been law-fully taken as they were sailing under French passes. The passes, which were genuine, were detained from him, apparently by some of the high personages involved, and the trial itself was a mere railroading of the man to his death on Execution Dock.[1] Whatever the truth of the whole mysterious affair may have been, the enterprise certainly proved a dismal failure from every standpoint.

The year 1700, however, marked a decline in the activities of such gentry, due partly to the English policing of trade routes and partly to the effect of new Parliamentary legislation applic-able to piracy in America. The proprietary and charter colo-nies had been asked to pass a law similar in effect to that in force in Jamaica but had refused. Finally, out of patience, Parliament passed one for them, and the Lords of Trade wrote to Bellomont that he need not trouble further to press for the passage of local ones, saying that "the Parliament, having in view the refractoriness of New England and other Plantations, have now past an Act for the suppression of piracy, which ex-tends to all the Plantations and foreign parts, by which those of New England may perceive that where the public good does suffer by their obstinacy, the proper remedies will be easily found here."[2] The significance of this is so clear that it seems impossible that it should have been lost upon the colonists. But without ships to patrol the coast, which the Admiralty refused to furnish; without proper men in the offices of Attorney Gen-eral and Chief Justice, who were appointed by the English government but prevented from going out by one of the usual "stops in the Treasury"; and with corrupt officials in the cus-toms houses, the Earl made slow headway against the com-

---

[1] *N. Y. Col. Docts., Col.*, vol. IV, p. 583; R. D. Paine, *The Book of Buried Treasure*, (New York, 1911), pp. 62 *ff.*; C. N. Dalton, *The Real Captain Kidd*, (New York, 1911), *passim.* Dalton gives only extracts from the trial, which, on the whole, is rather less favorable to Kidd. *Vide The Arraignment, Tryal, and Condemnation of Captain William Kidd, for Murther and Piracy . . . to which are added Captain Kidd's Two Commissions, . . .* (London, 1701). This contains the trial verbatim. There is also the important pamphlet *A full Account of the Proceedings in relation to Captain Kidd in two Letters. Written by a Person of Quality to a Kinsman of the Earl of Bellomont in Ireland,* 2d edit. (London, 1701).

[2] *Cal. State Pap., Col., 1700*, pp. 132, 164.

bined opposition of all classes to the enforcement of law.[1]
Owing on the one hand to a debauched public opinion in the
colonies, and on the other to the failure of the government to
provide him with adequate means, he had to acknowledge
himself partly beaten in this important sphere of his duty.

In Rhode Island he was not only in constant conflict over this
matter of piracy but had been instructed to enquire into other
irregularities as well. These seem to have been indulged in
partly from a spirit of independence and partly from crass ignorance. When after a long delay, the Lords of Trade received
what the Rhode Islanders sent over as a true copy of their laws,
that body complained that "the blots in some places, the blanks
in others, the want of sense in some expressions, the want of
titles to the Acts, and the disorderly placing of them" were
such that no dependence could be placed upon them. Bellomont himself reported them to be "such a parcel of fustian" as
he had never seen.[2] Although the replies of the local authorities
to the complaints of the English government as to privateers
were so disingenuous as to call forth a sharp and deserved re-
buke, many of the other complaints indicate merely a people
and officials "shamefully ignorant" for a self-governing community.[3] Indeed, Bellomont might well have said of the colony,
as the new administrator of Bermuda reported of his province
soon after, that it "is one of the distracted'st little Governments that I yet came into."[4] In this it but shared in the
general intellectual and moral decline throughout New England at this period.

As a matter of fact, neither of the colonies of Rhode Island
nor Connecticut was under obligation in accordance with her
charters to transmit her laws to England for approval. In many
respects, indeed, they were small republics, which it was never
intended they should be and which it was impossible to allow
them to remain. The refusal of one or the other to unite with

---

[1] *N. Y. Col. Docts.*, vol. IV, pp. 317 *ff.*, 354 *ff.*, 598, 700; *Cal. State Pap., Col., 1700*,
pp. 362, 392, 417, 528, 681, 758.
[2] *Cal. State Pap., Col., 1699*, p. 388 ; *1700*, p. 13; *R. I. Col. Records*, vol. III, p. 376.
[3] *Cal. State Pap., Col., 1699*, pp. 542 *ff.*; *R. I. Col. Records*, vol. III, pp. 363, 385 *ff.*;
388 *ff.*
[4] *Cal. State Pap., Col., 1702*, p. 538.

the other colonies in common defence, to recognize the authority of Vice-Admiralty courts, their denial of the subjects' right of appeal, their long delays in answering the letters of the home government, and other difficulties in administration, all raised the question of the cancellation of the charters. During Bellomont's term a bill was introduced in Parliament to resume these and the other charter governments, and, although it did not pass, it was the precursor of more serious attempts later.[1]

The colonists themselves, however bold a front they might show to the home government in pleading innocence, were quite aware that they were violating the charters. In connection with one of the perennial boundary disputes, for example, Governor Cranston of Rhode Island wrote to Governor Winthrop that many people would rejoice over the quarrel and take "the oportunity thereby to strike att our Charters" and that even though Connecticut might think herself safe, yet "you may assure yourselves that if wee split you will sinke; for wee are both upon one bottom and I am apte to conclude as many rents and leaks on your part as on ours if not some trunnel holes open."[2]

Bellomont's troubles in New Hampshire were of a different sort. He found that province to lie between Massachusetts proper and that part of her domain now known as Maine, which he thought, as it was, "odd and inconvenient." The perennial source of trouble in the Masonian claims to the title to the province still continued, Mason's claims having been transferred to one Samuel Allen of London for a small consideration, said to have been only £300, although that sanguine new proprietor reckoned the possibility of running up a rent roll of £22,000 per annum from the settlers.[3] When the new charter of 1691 had been granted to Massachusetts, Allen, probably through the corrupt influence of Blathwayt, had had New Hampshire created a royal province with himself as governor. He had ap-

[1] R. R. Hinman, *Letters from the English Kings and Queens* . . . , (Hartford, 1836), pp. 301 *ff.*; *Cal. State Pap., Col., 1696–7*, pp. 385, 459; *1699*, p. 209; *1700*, pp. 287, 560; *1701*, p. 180; *Winthrop Papers*, [*Mass. Hist. Soc., Coll.*, Ser. VI, vol. III], vol. V, pp. 63 *ff.*

[2] *Winthrop Papers*, vol. V, p. 70.

[3] *Cal. State Pap., Col., 1699*, p. 427; Fry, *New Hampshire*, p. 220; *New Hampshire Provincial Papers*, vol. II, pp. 535 *ff.*

pointed his son-in-law, John Usher of Boston, his deputy, and the history of the province had been a series of disputes and dead-locks between that choleric and tactless individual and the assembly.[1] Bellomont's own commission superseded that of Allen and by the time the governor arrived in the province in July 1699, conditions were anarchic. He managed to settle the administration so much to the satisfaction of the not easily satisfied settlers, however, that they voted him a gift of £500.[2] He fully realized the evil influence of Allen's land claims, as he had of the enormous and more or less fraudulent grants to socially prominent people in New York, where one grant alone amounted to over five hundred and sixty square miles. In spite of Allen's attempt to bribe him with £10,000 if he would accept half the province and prosecute the claim, Bellomont opposed it to the home government, pointing out the injustice to the settlers, the questionable legality of the claim, and the damage to England's interests.[3] He was particularly insistent upon the latter, showing how settlement was retarded, and pointing out the great value of the woods for naval stores.[4]

In Massachusetts, Bellomont's relations with the local government were amicable but unproductive. When his appointment had been first considered, the Lords Justices in England had wisely pointed out the necessity for not leaving the governor to depend upon the "benevolence" of the local assemblies for his salary, stating that such an arrangement for the incomes of governors would "make their authorities precarious and engage them to compliances that might be prejudicial to the King's interests." [5] Fearing the expense, however, they suggested that they be made charges upon the revenues of the colonies, but this was not done and the long conflicts began which, year by year, throughout the whole colonial system tended to transfer power from the executive to the legislature. Not long before he died, Bellomont complained bitterly but

---

[1] *N. H. Prov. Papers*, vol. II, pp. 259 ff.; *Cal. State Pap., Col., 1696-7*, pp. 161 ff., 170, 173, 339, 368 ff., 560; *1697-8*, pp. 63 ff., 72, 78 f., 94, 100 f., 565 f.
[2] *Cal. State Pap., Col., 1699*, p. 427.
[3] *N. Y. Col. Docts.*, vol. IV, pp. 334, 506, 535, 554, 673.
[4] *Ibid.*, pp. 501 ff., 587 f., 645, 668 f., 675, 678; *Cal. State Pap., Col., 1700*, pp. 195 ff., 545 ff., 563 ff.
[5] *Cal. State Pap., Col., 1693-6*, p. 541.

soberly of his position. No regular salary would be allowed him
by the assemblies, and the "gifts" bestowed upon him from
time to time made him but "their pensioner just as long as they
please." [1] The harassing matters in his various provinces proved
at length too much for the governor, who had attempted to
handle them seriously and honestly, and he died at New York
early in 1700, worn out by overwork and disappointment.

It is impossible to study carefully the mass of his voluminous
correspondence and reports, in the light of conditions as we
know them, and not feel both admiration and keen sympathy
for the man. The task set him by the English government, with
the means which they afforded, was an impossible one. At
almost every point his work involved the antagonizing of important interests. So thoroughly had piracy and illegal trading
become intrenched and debased public sentiment, that his
efforts to remedy the evil could not fail to bring down upon him
the wrath of a large part of the lower classes as well as of the
powerful merchants. In his struggles against the public opinion
of almost the whole body of colonists, his appeals for assistance
from England fell upon deaf ears, and he was granted, for the
most part, neither ships, upright judges, nor honest subordinates. Not less was he denied adequate help in his efforts to
remedy the crying abuses and the scandalous conditions in connection with military defence. In his fight against the engrossing of the public lands by exorbitant grants, he encountered
the formidable opposition of such grantees as the Van Rens-
selaers, the Schuylers, the Phillipses, the Livingstones, the
Beekmans, the Van Courtlandts and others, — an opposition
that might well have made a less courageous man hesitate.[2]

In his contests with the assemblies he was without a weapon
to secure even his living expenses, and he died with his estate
heavily depleted by his unrewarded work for an ungrateful
government at home. Had he been corrupt, the opportunities
for amassing money lay all about him. "If I could make this the
mart of piracy," he wrote from New York, "confederate with
the merchants and wink at their unlawful trade; if I would

---

[1] *Cal. State Pap., Col., 1700*, p. 416. *Cf. ibid.*, pp. 284, 362, 375, 393, 413*f.*; *1701*,
p. 181.

[2] *N. Y. Col. Docts.*, vol. IV, p. 535.

pocket all the off-reckonings, make three hundred pounds pr ann of the article of victualling the poor soldiers, muster half companies, pack an Assembly that would give me what money I pleased and let me misapply it as I pleased, and pocket a great part of the public moneys; I could make this government very valuable." [1]

The inefficiency and short-sightedness, if not the actual corruption of the home government, however, were too great, and it failed often to afford the governor even the moral support of official communications.[2] "For the Ministers sending me orders and afterwards not standing by those orders and not quickening the execution of them, is a most cruel thing," he wrote on one occasion. Again, speaking of the attempted cancellation of the excessive land grants, he wisely contended that "it were better that things of this kind were never called in question than not to be vigorously prosecuted when once they are begun." In these struggles and passionate utterances of a loyal servant of the Crown, who realized the impossibility of expecting any one man to contend with the sinister and disintegrating forces at work, and who vainly strove to awaken the English government to a sense of the issues at stake, we find the key to much of the story of administrative mismanagement and to part of the drifting away of the colonies during the balance of the colonial period. The home government failed to realize that, as Lord Derby said on another occasion many generations later, "to do nothing is in fact to take the most momentous and responsible action" and showed themselves then, as throughout many of the years remaining to them, capable only of "causing the maximum of friction with the minimum of result."

---

[1] N. Y. Col. Docts., vol. IV, p. 378.
[2] Ibid., pp. 685, 794, 825; Cal. State Pap., Col., 1700, p. 681.

CHAPTER V

ATTEMPTS AT COÖPERATION, IMPERIAL AND COLONIAL

Influence of European Situation — Dudley as Governor — Characteristic Feature of His Administration — Renewed War with French — Attitude of the Colonies — Jamaica Expedition — Ineffectiveness of Colonial Militia — Attacks on Dudley — Expeditions against Canada

THAT race for empire, of which I described the beginnings in the preceding volume, had never ceased since it first began, between the leading powers of the Old World, however the individual power of each might alter. In 1700, the contest entered upon a new and decisive phase, and the death, in that year, of the Spanish monarch Charles the Second was the cause of that of many a New England soldier and frontiersman in the decade and a half that followed. By his will he left the vast and undivided domains of his empire to a grandson of Louis the Fourteenth, the young Philip of Anjou, and in spite of former self-denying treaties Louis accepted the bequest on his behalf. At once the whole international colonial question was brought to a head. It was not merely that the closer union of the two crowns destroyed the European balance of power by the passing under the control of France of the Spanish imperial possessions, including Sicily, Naples, Milan and Flanders. The fateful and faithless acceptance of the legacy for his grandson by the French king signified even more in the union of the world's two greatest colonial empires under the greatest single military power of the day. It seemed the commercial death-blow to England and Holland, the two nations whose very life had come to depend upon their over-seas trade. On the surface it was a question of who was to rule Spain, but fundamentally it was who was to rule the commerce of the world.[1] France had grasped at the

[1] J. R. Seeley, *Growth of British Policy*, (London, 1895), vol. II, pp. 352 *ff.*; Greene, *Provincial America*, pp. 136 *ff.*; Deschamps, *Histoire de la Question coloniale*, pp. 164 *ff.*

riches of America and the Indies by placing a boy on the throne at Madrid.

At first, in spite of the desire of King William, England was slow to move. The exclusion by the French of British manufactures and the acknowledgment by Louis — on the death of the former King James the Second in 1701 — of the Pretender as King of England, brought on the crisis, however, and William himself having died, war was declared on the 15th of May 1702 in the first year of the reign of Queen Anne. England and Holland joined the coalition against France, and again the dread shadow of savage warfare fell across the New England frontier.

In the same month, another shadow, almost more dreaded by some of the irreconcilable party in Massachusetts, also crept across that colony, for on the day when war was declared, the new Governor, Joseph Dudley, was half-way across the Atlantic on his way to his new and long coveted post. Unforgiven by many for the part he had played in the loss of the Massachusetts charter and in the Andros régime, his appointment bitterly opposed by the colony's agent, Ashurst, he was about to face his old antagonists with all the power and prestige of a royal governor.[1]

In the thirteen years since his fellow colonists had placed him in Boston jail in the Revolution of 1689, he had had a checkered career as Chief of the Council at New York, Deputy Governor of the Isle of Wight, and Member of Parliament. Now that he was returning to his old home and that of his fathers, he would have been less than human had he not looked upon the circumstances of that return as affording him at once a vindication and a triumph. He showed, however, no desire to humiliate former enemies, and the colonists themselves, in spite of loose talk by some about opposing his landing by force, received him courteously if not cordially.[2] His cause, at a critical time while his appointment was pending, had been espoused by that curiously

---

[1] Adams, *Founding of New England*, chap. XVI; for his appointment, commission, and Ashurst's opposition, *vide Cal. State Pap., Col., 1701*, pp. 304, 315, 610, 670 ff.; *Winthrop Papers*, vol. VI, pp. 89, 92, 109 ff.; E. Kimball, *The Public Life of Joseph Dudley*, (New York, 1911), chap. IV; *Col. Soc. Mass. Publications*, vol. II, pp. 83 ff.

[2] *Cal. State Pap., Col., 1701*, pp. 576 ff.; S. Sewall, *Diary, Mass. Hist. Soc., Coll.*, Ser. V, vol. VI, pp. 57 f.

constituted man of God, Cotton Mather, who was himself much in need of a powerful ally just at the moment. Readers of my previous volume will recall the part that Mather had played in the witchcraft delusion, and what was there said about the people having turned against him when Calef's able defence of sanity and common sense appeared. The book had arrived in Boston in 1700, and Mather records in his diary that: "The Lord has permitted Satan to Raise an extraordinary *Storm* upon my Father, and myself. All the Rage of Satan, against the Holy Churches of the Lord, falls upon us." The "filthy Scribbles"of a "vile Fool," as the clergyman in his chaste style described the merchant's book, and the workings in the town of what he termed the "Satanic Party," had happily much undermined the Mather family influence.[1] Moreover, Elisha Cooke, an enemy of Dudley, was opposing the sending of Increase Mather to England as agent for the colony. So Mather the "patriot" assisted the ambition of Dudley the "renegade" to the temporary satisfaction of each, though the clergyman was privately calling the governor "wretch" within a week of his landing. Also, which was perhaps more tiresome to Dudley, he was giving him advice and urging him to "carry an indifferent Hand to all Parties; if in our case," as Mather wrote, "I may use so Coarse a Word as Parties." [2] A certain familiarity with the range of the minister's vituperative vocabulary is necessary for the full enjoyment of the maiden blush of that qualifying clause Suggesting the yet coarser word factions for what Mather had in mind we will delay their discussion, and merely note here that the episode of Cotton Mather championing Joseph Dudley is one worth recalling when we are tempted to consider the action of the mass of men as based upon impersonal loyalty to abstract ideas.

Dudley's commission represented a partial return to the policy of divided control, for although he was appointed governor of New Hampshire as well as Massachusetts, with command of the Rhode Island and Connecticut militia in time of war, the colony of New York was again placed under a separate gov-

[1] Mather, *Diary*, vol. I, pp. 377, 379, 383, 397.
[2] *Ibid.*, pp. 464 *f.*; Kimball, *Dudley*, p. 74.

ernor, the notorious Lord Cornbury.[1] Dudley was especially instructed to see that the members of the Council in Massachusetts were men of standing and of substance, to "use his utmost endeavor" to have a bill passed fixing salaries, to prevent illegal trade, and to urge the fortification of the northern posts.[2] All of these were contentious points, but Dudley was not a man to flinch from unpleasant duty, and he was promptly involved in a dispute with the assembly over the appointment of councilors. Under the new charter, that body possessed the unique colonial privilege of electing the members of the upper house, subject to confirmation by the governor. In 1703 Elisha Cooke, the leader of the opposition in the assembly and a consistent opponent of the new order, together with four others, were refused confirmation, an action not only well within the legal right of Dudley but, in the case of Cooke, easily justifiable as well.[3] This right, which was the only means the home government had of controlling the character of either house — in the choice of both of which the people of Massachusetts possessed more liberty than did their fellow citizens at home — was nevertheless bitterly resented by the colonists, and is an example of how the desire for freedom from restraint grew by what it fed upon. The immediate effect of the governor's action was an open breach between him and the assembly.

Other points of friction, some of which will be noted later, were by no means lacking, but on the whole the more characteristic features of Dudley's administration were the efforts made at coöperation between the colonies and England, and between the colonies themselves, under pressure of military necessity. In his first speech before the General Court, Dudley had touched upon the approaching war and the need for preparation. On land, less was to be feared from the French troops than from the savages whom it was their policy to incite to commit such atrocities as would make them realize that thereafter no peace with the English would be possible. The French knew well that the cheaper trading goods of the English would, for the most

---

[1] *Laws of New Hampshire, Prov. Period*, vol. II, pp. 4 *ff*., 13 *ff*.
[2] Kimball, *Dudley*, p. 80.
[3] *Ibid.*, p. 89; Hutchinson, *History*, vol. II, pp. 125 *f*.

part, have made the Indians prefer peace to war, although they also preferred French brandy to English rum.[1] It was a deliberate policy of arousing the worst passions in savages by a Christian nation in order to inflict damage, without loss to itself, upon a civilized foe.

Dudley, who realized the necessity for preserving peace as long as possible, held a conference with the Abnaki chiefs and entered into a treaty with them at Casco in June 1703 with all the rhetoric and passing of gifts dear to the savage.[2] French and Indian treachery were at work, however, even at the council itself, and within two months from the signing of the document, the frontier was again ablaze.[3] It was the old story of burning homes, of murdered settlers, of women and children plodding through the snow-filled forests in the train of their swiftly retreating captors to Canada. At Wells, York, Spurwink, Winter Harbor, Casco and other little settlements along the coast or rivers, the tale was the same, varying only in the heroic incidents. The enemy was everywhere and nowhere. As the slaughter continued into the winter, Massachusetts ordered five hundred pairs of snowshoes for her militia. That colony and Connecticut both offered the familiar bounty for Indian scalps, and later adopted the Reverend Mr. Stoddard's suggestion of hunting down the enemy with dogs.[4] In midwinter came the terrible and well-known attack on Deerfield, in which more than one half of the hundred and twenty-five inhabitants were killed or carried off.[5] Besides six hundred men in garrisons, Dudley had six hundred more ranging the border, and Massachusetts raised the scalp bounty to £100 for the head of every Indian over ten years old. Those under ten were to be sold as slaves, although Rhode Island refused to permit this within her borders

[1] F. Parkman, *A Half-Century of Conflict*, (Boston, 1909), vol. I, pp. 47 *f.*, 55 *f.*, 100 *ff.*; Wrong, *Conquest of New France*, p. 46.

[2] Parkman, *Half-Century of Conflict*, vol. I, pp. 36 *ff.*; Drake, *Border Wars*, pp. 150 *ff.*; Sewall, *Diary*, vol. II, p. 85; Samuel Penhallow, *History of the Wars of New England*, ed. (Cincinnati, 1859), pp. 16 *ff.*; *Acts and Resolves*, vol. VIII, pp. 286 *ff.*

[3] *Acts and Resolves*, vol. VIII, pp. 300 *ff.*

[4] *Ibid.*, pp. 38, 42, 45, 325 *f.*; *Conn. Col. Records*, vol. IV, p. 464; Sheldon, *Deerfield*, vol. I, p. 291; Turner, *Frontier*, pp. 45 *f.*

[5] Sheldon, *Deerfield*, vol. I, pp. 293–324; *Winthrop Papers*, vol. V, pp. 176 *ff.*, 245 *ff.*, 129, 131; Parkman, *Half-Century*, vol. I, pp. 55 *ff.*

for fear of stirring up the friendly natives.[1] New Hampshire had every fourth man in arms, and by summer nineteen hundred were serving under Dudley.[2] Nevertheless, the frontier towns of Maine, New Hampshire and Massachusetts continued to suffer attacks which were made almost with impunity, for hunting Indians in boundless forests was but "chasing shadows."

Unfortunately, aside from the difficult nature of the warfare, the old selfish particularism of the colonies was also at work to nullify to a great extent the efforts made by each. Dudley took a broad view of the situation as was natural from his character and experience, and secured the unwilling consent of the Massachusetts Court to extend help to the other colonies should occasion arise during its recess.[3] On his petty stage of action, however, he was experiencing the same difficulty in attempting to combine the resources of confederates that Marlborough was simultaneously struggling with in the case of the Dutch, Prussians and Hanoverians in Europe.[4]

England, fighting in all quarters of the world, naturally looked upon the military problem in its entirety and realized the necessity for the colonies to combine in their own defence. It is enlightening to turn from the haggling policy of each little colonial assembly, — island and continental alike, — and to study the instructions sent out from the Lords of Trade to the various governors throughout the entire colonial system, and the complaint of Colonel Nicholson, the able governor of Virginia in 1701, is of value both in regard to this matter and others.[5] "One of the great misfortunes," he wrote, "that the Country lives under at present, is that the Assembly cannot, or will not be made sensible of the necessity of assisting his Majesty's Province of New York with money or men, or that they are in any danger of being attacked by the French, either at sea or land; for the Country consists now most of Natives, few of

---

[1] *Cal. State Pap., Col., 1704-5*, pp. 99 *f. Acts and Resolves*, vol. VIII, pp. 38, 45 · R. I. *Col. Records*, vol. III, pp. 482 *ff.*

[2] Drake, *Border Wars*, p. 170; *Winthrop Papers*, vol. V, pp. 231, 244.

[3] Kimball, *Dudley*, p. 110.

[4] Earl Stanhope, *History of England, 1701-13*, (London, 1871), p. 42.

[5] *Cf. Cal. State Pap., Col., 1701*, pp. 29 *f.*, 50 *f.*, 77, 207, 276; *1702*, pp. 25, 41, 240, 558, 590 *f.*; *1702-3*, pp. 323, 373.

which either have read much or been abroad in the world: so that they cannot form to themselves any Idea or Notion of those things (tho' in point of Trade and of Plantation Affairs they are generally very knowing)." [1] In that true and temperate statement lies the key to much colonial history.

Although England again made the attempt to apportion the quota of the several colonies, they paid no attention to the suggestions of the home government, and, in the cases of Rhode Island and Connecticut, opposed Dudley's exercise of his legitimate authority over their militia. [2] Although the quota for Massachusetts had been set at three hundred and fifty and that for Rhode Island at forty-eight, the smaller colony refused to comply when Dudley asked for fifty men in spite of Massachusetts' having exceeded her stated proportion many times, and Connecticut gave aid but to an unfairly small amount. [3]

Aside from certain civil distractions, therefore, the military exigencies seemed to demand a more unified control of New England's resources, and at the end of 1702, Dudley suggested placing all three colonies under the administration of the strongest one during the war. [4] A couple of years later, the two smaller ones were ordered to have their agents present their "objections in point of law" against the queen appointing governors for each of them, and as this was later found to be inconsistent with the charters, it became another point against those instruments. [5]

During these years, when England was fighting for her life in many quarters of the world, she was continually receiving requests from the northern colonies for help in the shape of money, small arms, cannon, powder, troops, and ships to guard the New England coast and to convoy New England trade. [6] To many

[1] *Cal. State Pap., Col., 1701*, p. 631.

[2] *Acts Privy Council*, vol. II, pp. 402; 418; *R. I. Col. Records*, vol. III, pp. 462 f.; *Winthrop Papers*, vol. V, pp. 191, 217.

[3] *N. Y. Col. Docts.*, vol. IV, p. 706; *Cal. State Pap., Col., 1702-3*, p. 651; *1704-5*, pp. 47, 83, 211, 214, 274, 445; *Winthrop Papers*, vol. V, pp. 149 ff., 160; *Conn. Col. Records*, vol. IV, p. 444; *Acts and Resolves*, vol. VIII, pp. 303 ff.; *Maine Hist. Soc., Coll.*, vol. IX, p. 191; *R. I. Col. Records*, vol. III, pp. 515 f.

[4] *Cal. State Pap., Col., 1702*, p. 742.

[5] *Acts Privy Council*, vol. II, pp. 480 f.; C. M. Andrews, "The Influence of colonial Conditions as illustrated in the Connecticut Intestacy Act," p. 441 n.

[6] *Journal of Board of Trade, 1704-9*, pp. 45 f., 52 ff., 194, 210 f.; *Cal. State Pap., Col., 1702*, p. 25; *1702-3*, pp. 148, 165, 188; *1704-5*, pp. 101, 211 ff., 217, 312, 329, 446, 453 f.; *Acts Privy Council*, vol. II, p. 505.

of these requests she acceded. The cost of hostilities to the colonies was very heavy in proportion to their resources, but so was the enormous cost of the war as a whole to the larger ones of England, and although the mother country met the calls for help from the colonies as far as she was able, it is not surprising that she urged them to exert themselves in their own defense, and, especially, to unite in order to make their efforts more effective.[1] In considering the attacks upon the charters from time to time, it must be remembered that the need for united action as contrasted with the particularism of the several colonies was a genuine and crying one.

In waging war in four different continents simultaneously, as England was called upon to do, she needed to consider the resources of the empire as forming one fund, and an interesting experiment of these troubled years was the call by the mother country for volunteers from New England to go to the assistance of the island colony of Jamaica which was in danger of French invasion. Nothing was done by Rhode Island or Connecticut, which seemed to consider themselves as independent of the whole empire and without responsibility for anything outside their own very narrow borders. In Massachusetts and New Hampshire, however, in spite of their own pressing danger and much political opposition, Dudley succeeded in raising two companies which were duly despatched to join the naval expedition sent out from England.[2] It was one of the attempts at coöperation between the home country and her lately recalcitrant colony of Massachusetts that form perhaps the distinguishing feature of Dudley's administration, and which, if they had been more successful, might have done something to have drawn the bonds of common interests closer. The governor himself realized something of the importance of the occasion and wrote to the governor of Jamaica requesting good treatment for the soldiers, saying that "they are the first men in armes that ever went out of this province, or from the shoar of America, and if at first they meet with discouragement I am sure I shall never

[1] *Acts Privy Council*, vol. II, pp. 418, 436; *Cal. State Pap., Col.*, *1702-3*, pp. 35, 323, 827; *1704-5*, pp. 214, 217, 273, 325, 446 f., 448, 661, 677; *Winthrop Papers*, vol. V, p. 150; vol. VI, p. 129.
[2] *Cf. Col. Soc. Mass., Publications*, vol. XVIII, pp. 84 ff.

send from hence one file of Volunteers more. I therefore humbly pray on their behalf that they may be kindly dealt withal and provided so that I may have a good account of them to be made public here, and it will satisfy everybody." [1] Unfortunately the expedition was a failure from the start. The usual hindrances to efficient administration in the clumsy working of the home government — including in this case even the complication of "an irresolute and fond Lady" in high official quarters — prevented the proper and prompt outfitting of the ships. In Jamaica, disease, poor food and bad treatment rapidly thinned the ranks, and the story of the criminal lack of success in this first attempt at joint imperial action can be read in Dudley's laconic despatch a year later announcing that "the two foot companyes, Capt. Laramore and Walton, are arrived from Newfoundland . . . Laramore scap't best and brought home 30 men" — unpaid.

Apart from some courageous commanders, it was a period of disgraceful conditions in the British navy. Not only was there disorganization in the administration but in many cases the officers were brutal and wholly unfit to have command over men, and in the naval battle off Jamaica in 1702 four captains even proved themselves, what Englishmen rarely are, poltroons and cowards.[2] For many years thereafter, both the moral and physical environment of the seamen on the royal ships was unspeakably bad,[3] and for the most part the press gang was the only means of making unwilling men enter the service, and of replacing those who were continually deserting. It is typical of the constant working at cross-purposes of all departments that the governor of Jamaica had to complain to the home government that the Admiral in command there was impressing the soldiers sent to defend the island.[4] Although certain safeguards were supposed to be thrown around colonial impressment, naval officers were frequently arrogant and tactless, when not worse, and an attempt by the captain of H.M.S. Swift to

---

[1] *Cal. State Pap., Col., 1702–3*, p. 192. *Cf.* also, *ibid.*, *1702*, pp. 594, 704; *1702–3*, pp. 36, 38, 94, 159, 187, 193, 213, 421, 537, 883.

[2] *Ibid.*, *1702*, pp. x *ff.*

[3] W. L. Clowes, *The Royal Navy*, (London, 1898), vol. III, pp. 22 *f.*

[4] *Cal. State Pap., Col., 1702–3*, pp. 538 *f.*

carry off some men from Boston in the first year of Dudley's term, which led to the killing of one and the wounding of five others, was but one of many instances throughout the century.[1]

The war within the limits of New England was necessarily of the most unsatisfactory defensive sort. The strategy of preventing the raids on the frontier by attacking the French at the seat of their power at Montreal and Quebec was so obvious as to have suggested itself to almost everyone who had studied the problem. Although the colonies were not as yet ready to join in such an undertaking, Massachusetts was exceedingly anxious for the capture of Port Royal, from which place French privateers constantly sailed to prey upon New England merchantmen and fisher-boats. Dudley had already been in communication with the home government in regard to the project in 1703, and the following year sanctioned an expedition to the eastward under the veteran Colonel Church, now old and physically unwieldy but still popular. As the home authorities had not yet given their approval to the proposed attack on Port Royal, the governor forbade any attempt to capture it, and a certain want of frankness in his attitude in the whole matter was construed by his political enemies to indicate that he was involved in illegal trade with the French, of which there was always a considerable amount being carried on.[2] Although this was mere slander, the expedition, which had apparently been organized to satisfy the impatient clamor of the people, proved a futile one, and accomplished little beyond some damage to the civil population in Acadia, and to Dudley's own position.

The charge of trading with the enemy was an easy one to bring, and the tactics of colonial politicians were not overscrupulous when advantage was to be gained over a royal official. For many months after the failure of Church's expedition, Dudley was engaged in an attempt to arrange for an exchange of prisoners and to negotiate a treaty of neutrality with the French governor Vaudreuil, although the proceedings indicate that both were fencing for time and information rather than

---

[1] *Cal. State Pap., Col., 1702*, pp. 474 f.

[2] *Ibid., 1702–3*, pp. 297, 373, 410, 665; Kimball, *Dudley*, p. 112; Hutchinson, *History*, vol. II, pp. 132 ff.; Church, *History of the Eastern Expeditions*, pp. 128 ff.

that either had any thought of really making a treaty.[1] Dudley's son, William, and a certain Samuel Vetch, a son-in-law of Robert Livingstone, served as Dudley's messengers.[2] The frequent trips of Vetch, who had already been accused of illegal trading in New York, aroused the suspicions of the assembly, on the lookout for a case against Dudley, and in June 1706 they ordered the arrest of his agent together with that of three other captains and merchants. A joint committee of the House and Council decided that there was evidence that Vetch and the others had been guilty of trading under a flag of truce. It was decided to try them before the General Court, and, in spite of the fact that that body was without jurisdiction in the case, Dudley interposed no objection, although his own possible connection with the case had not then been publicly called in question. Exceedingly heavy fines were imposed upon the prisoners, but these were subsequently remitted by the Privy Council in England on account of the illegality of the trial.[3]

Although the governor's name had not been involved, his acquiescence in what he must have realized was the overstepping of its authority by the General Court may have been caused by his desire to avoid seeming to shield the accused, and in any case he knew that his political enemies were both numerous and unscrupulous. It was evident also that nothing was to come from the negotiations with Vaudreuil, so that both the political and military situations encouraged the making of an aggressive diversion against the enemy. Without waiting longer, therefore, for the help he had already asked from England, Dudley decided to make an attack upon Port Royal, and turned to Governor Winthrop of Connecticut for the assistance of that colony. Although Winthrop had urged such an expedition two years before, he now represented the disposition of the citizens of his colony as "generally very thoughtfull and cautious" and reported that they would give no assistance. Rhode Island

[1] Collection de Manuscrits relatifs à la Nouvelle France, (Quebec, 1884), pp. 425 ff.; Acts and Resolves, vol. VIII, pp. 541 ff.; N. Y. Col. Docts., vol. IX, pp. 770, 776; Hutchinson, History, vol. II, p. 141.

[2] Cal. State Pap., Col., 1701, p. 711. For sketch of Vetch's career, vide Nova Scotia Historical Society, Collections, vol. IV, pp. 11 ff.

[3] Kimball, Dudley, pp. 116 f., 184 f. All the more important references to the case are cited by Kimball in his notes.

offered some help, but practically the entire burden of raising the thousand men needed fell upon Massachusettts, which undertook the project with enthusiasm.[1]

The expedition, commanded by Colonel March, sailed in June convoyed by the province galley and the royal frigate Deptford. On a small scale the attempt was a reproduction of the attack on Cadiz in the European sphere of operations. Just as in that attack, "no discipline was kept, no spirit was displayed" as Stanhope wrote, so in the Port Royal expedition the troops were little more than a "courageous rabble," even if the application of the adjective is not questionable.[2]

The fact is that the colonial militia never formed a disciplined and effective fighting force. The officers without exception were civilians with no military training. In the private soldiers that reckless and wilful refusal to submit to any authority, which is characteristic of the frontier and which colored all colonial relations, destroyed all discipline. "I will never plead for an Haverhill man more," wrote Governor Saltonstall of Connecticut, while recruiting a few years earlier, "to tell us what we should, may or must do. . . . They go this, and that, and the other way at pleasure, and do what they list." "They were mostly Good Livers at Home," wrote another of the Port Royal expedition, "and could not bear the Thoughts on't" that they should have to garrison the place if they captured it![3] Parkman speaks of March as "a tyro set over a crowd of ploughboys, fishermen, and mechanics, officered by tradesmen, farmers, blacksmiths, village magnates, and deacons of the church."[4] In spite of a high degree of courage and skill frequently displayed by individuals in skirmishing, such material was useless for sustained military operations unless acting in concert with disciplined troops.

Owing equally to lack of ability and courage, the expedition was a shameful failure. The "army" retired to Casco Bay and sent a delegation to Boston to explain the collapse of the plans.

[1] *Winthrop Papers*, vol. V, pp. 171, 192, 367 ff.; R. I. Col. Records, vol. IV, pp. 5, 57; *Acts and Resolves*, vol. VIII, pp. 680 ff.

[2] Stanhope, *History of England*, p. 59; Drake, *Border Wars*, p. 144.

[3] Turner, *Frontier*, p. 51; *The Deplorable State of New England*, 1708, in *Mass. Hist. Soc., Coll.*, Ser. V, vol. VI, p. 128.

[4] Parkman, *Half-Century*, vol. I, p. 126.

There they were greeted by hoots and jeers of the women, the very words of whose coarse language have been preserved.[1] A commission of popular leaders was then formed to take charge of the demoralized forces, but a second attempt was as ineffectual as the first.[2]

The result was a sore disappointment to Dudley and at once gave his political opponents what they considered their opportunity. In the overcharged atmosphere of petty and local politics in the colonies, the results of factional feuds, added to the ignorance of the world at large, always brought down the wrath of some upon the unfortunate holder of public office, whether a royal appointee or an elected colonial. The treatment by Massachusetts of her agents in England, for example, was always notoriously ungrateful, whether they were sons of the soil like Increase Mather or Englishmen like Ashurst.[3] The Massachusetts Puritan possessed many fine qualities, such as strength of character and tenacity of purpose, but in one he had been conspicuously lacking from the start — generosity of spirit. No opponent could be right. No weapons could be too vile to use against those who differed from himself. Mastiffs to hunt the Indians, the gallows for heretics, lies and slander for the royal officials. It is a commentary on the spiritual atmosphere of early New England that whereas many historians have pointed to various men — Randolph, Dudley, and others — as having been the "most hated man in New England," none has ever been led to point to one as the "most loved."

As the most conspicuous official in the colony, the governor was the storm center for the feuds of faction or of party. The fact that he was a royal appointee permitted his opponents always to raise the cry of patriotism in their onslaughts upon him regardless of the real motive. The play of petty spite or personal ambition found it advantageous to clothe itself in the garb of patriotic opposition to tyranny, and helped at once to create a prejudice and to foster a tradition.

[1] *Winthrop Papers*, vol. V, p. 388.
[2] *Acts and Resolves*, vol. VIII, pp. 715 *ff.*; Kimball, *Dudley*, pp. 119 *ff.*; *Cal. State Pap., Col., 1706-8*, pp. 637, 677 *f.*; *Winthrop Papers*, vol. V, pp. 387 *ff.*, 392; Hutchinson, *History*, vol. II, pp. 150 *ff.*
[3] *Cf.* Hutchinson's comment, *History*, vol. II, p. 169.

No royal official could fail to be struck by the undoubted evils existing in the colonial administrative system. The home government properly considered that any powers not expressly granted in the charters remained in the crown, whereas the colonists, although clearly in the wrong legally, insisted that they could do anything not expressly forbidden.[1] In the case of Rhode Island and Connecticut the colonists practically repudiated the idea of any control whatever by England, and it was with difficulty that the home government could even get into communication with them. Any effort by England, however, reasonable and legitimate, to remedy this unintended and certainly thoroughly unsound development in her administrative system was immediately regarded by the colonists as illegal and tyrannical.[2] Not only did Dudley take the view natural in a royal official, but his wider training and lack of provinciality due to the offices he had held abroad led him to realize the genuine need for better administration, which could only be secured by restoring to the central government some of the powers which had been filched from it. Although some of the charges which were constantly pouring in to the home government were not true, many of them were, and there was much justification, considering the actions and attitude of the chartered colonies, for the opinion of the Board of Trade that the only remedy lay in the abrogation of the charters. A bill for that purpose had been introduced in Parliament in 1700–1701, as we have already noted, but had failed to pass owing to the pressure of other business.[3] Additional information was asked for, and Dudley, Quary, and others were constantly sending it over.[4] As a result, a second bill for resuming the charters was prepared and passed the House of Lords but failed in the Commons.[5] Nevertheless, Dudley's position as a believer in greater imperial

---

[1] Andrews, *Connecticut and the British Government*, p. 7 n.

[2] Andrews, *ibid.*, p. 2.

[3] *Journals of House of Lords*, vol. XVI, pp. 659 f., 666, 679; R. N. Toppan, *Edward Randolph*, (Boston, 1899), vol. V, pp. 272 ff.; Hinman, *Royal Letters*, pp. 301 ff., 316 ff.; *Cal. State Pap., Col., 1702*, p. 210.

[4] *Cf. Cal. State Pap., Col., 1704–5*, pp. 9, 43, 380 f., 445, 456 f., 649, 691; *Journal of Board of Trade, 1704–9*, pp. 128, 203 ff., 220, 224, 446.

[5] *House of Commons, Journal*, vol. XVIII, pp. 151, 168, 183, 262; *Winthrop Papers*, vol. V, p. 326.

control as the only means of curbing the irregularities of the charter governments and for increasing their military efficiency, and his activities with that end in view, naturally created a large party of enemies.

Two other points — the contributing toward fortifications at Pemaquid and the fixing of a definite salary, both of which the home government had instructed him to press — also caused trouble and ended in his defeat. In regard to the latter, the assembly stated that they feared " the settling of fixed salaries will be of no service to her majesty's interest, but may prove prejudicial to her majesty's good subjects." [1] The salary question, however, constituted a perennial source of trouble for every governor, and will be discussed more at length in connection with a later administration.

Opposition to Dudley also arose from various personal motives in the case of many, some of whom, such as Sewall and John Winthrop, were even allied to him by marriage. Sewall, always a time-server, wished for the appointment of Nathaniel Higginson as governor, and although pretending friendship for Dudley, worked with that end in view. Winthrop wished the post of lieutenant-governor for himself and expected to get it from the party trying to oust his father-in-law. The Mathers felt that their ambitions had been permanently thwarted when, partly through the governor's management, Leverett had been elected president of Harvard. The hatred of Elisha Cooke and the remnants of the old "revolutionary" party, particularly strong in the country towns, dated from the days of Andros, and unlike the double-faced hypocrisy of Sewall, Winthrop and the Mathers, was at least always open. [2]

Although beneath the surface constant efforts had been made to undermine the governor's position and secure his removal, the most determined one was on the occasion of the failure of the Port Royal expedition as noted above. A petition was presented in England signed by Higginson, who hoped for the post for himself, and by sundry malcontents of Massachusetts and

[1] Hutchinson, *History*, vol. II, pp. 138 *ff*.; *A Collection of the Proceedings of the Great and General Court* . . . (Boston, 1729), pp. 5 *ff*.

[2] Sewall, *Letter Book*, vol. I, p. 362; *Winthrop Papers*, vol. VI, pp. 153, 173, 194, 216, 218; *Col. Soc. Mass., Publications*, vol. XIX, pp. 150 *ff*.; Kimball, *Dudley*, pp. 175 *ff*.

G R

By His EXCELLENCY,

Joſeph Dudley Eſq.

Captain General and GOVERNOUR in Chief, in and over
His Majeſties Provinces of the *Maſſachuſetts-Bay* and
New-Hampſhire in *New-England.*

A PROCLAMATION

Againſt a Commerce & Trade with the *French* of *Canada,*
Cape Breton, &c.

WHEREAS the Articles of Commerce betwixt the Subjects of the Crown of **Great Britain,** and thoſe of **France,** upon the late Treaty of Peace, are not yet fully Adjuſted and Settled ; And His Majeſty's Commands in that Regard not yet Arrived.

I **have therefore thought fit, by and with the Advice of His Ma-jeſties Council, to put forth this Proclamation, ſtrictly to for-bid all Perſons whomſoever of holding any Correspondence, Commerce, Trade and Dealings in any manner of wiſe with** the French of Canada, Cape Breton, **or of any other Parts or Places ; Or of carrying or ſending any Proviſions, Lumber or other Sup-plies to them of what kind ſo ever, until His Majeſties Pleaſure ſhall be known therein, as they Tender their Allegiance and Duty to His Moſt Sacred Majeſty, and on Pain of His Majeſties Diſ-pleaſure, and of Suffering ſuch other Pains, Penalties and For-feitures as may be Lawfully inflicted on them.**

Given at the Council Chamber in *Boſton,* upon Tueſday the 29th Day of *March,* 1715. In the Firſt Year of the Reign of Our Soveraign Lord, GEORGE, by the Grace of GOD of *Great Britain, France* and *Ireland* KING, Defender of the Faith, &c.

By Order of the Governour,
with the Advice of the Council,   *J. DUDLEY.*

Joſeph Hiller, Cler. Conc.

GOD Save the King.

BOSTON: Printed by *B. Green,* Printer to His Excellency the GOV. & COUNCIL. 1715.

New Hampshire.[1] Almost simultaneously a scurrilous pamphlet, evidently by Cotton Mather, was also published, in which the governor and his son Paul were accused not only of trading with the enemy but of accepting bribes on many occasions in the crudest manner.[2] Both documents reached Boston in November 1707, and the angry governor at once asked the General Court for a vote clearing him of the charges, and demanded that the petition charging him with trading with the French and furnishing them and the Indians with ammunition be voted a "scandalous and wicked accusation."[3] The Council at once passed the vote but the assembly delayed until November 21. Inspite of the later withdrawal of his vote by Sewall as councilor, the case was evidently unproven, and the vote of the assembly was wrung from that body not from any friendliness for the governor but because the statements had been unfounded.[4] A yet more abusive pamphlet by the Mathers, in which general charges still wilder were made, was answered by the governor in his own defence, and the home government, after having heard both sides represented by counsel, dismissed the charges as "frivolous."[5] There is nothing in Dudley's career or character to gain for him in any marked degree the affection or even the respect of the historian, but the efforts to oust him from office seem to have been mainly disgraceful attempts to blast his reputation and secure his dismissal in order that others should attain their respective private ends.

In spite of the failure of the expeditions against Canada the plan of reducing that province was not laid aside, and in the summer of 1708 Vetch was busily engaged in urging upon the Lords of Trade a comprehensive plan along the usual double line of attack.[6] He was undoubtedly working in conjunction with Dudley who had seen the futility of trusting wholly to provincial troops and officers, and who in October secured the drawing up of a Memorial from the Massachusetts General Court

---

[1] Hutchinson, *History*, vol. II, pp. 145 f. note.

[2] "A Memorial of the present deplorable State of New England," etc., *Mass. Hist. Soc., Coll.*, Ser. V, vol. VI, pp. 37 ff., 52 f., 55.

[3] Kimball, *Dudley*, p. 185 n.

[4] Sewall, *Diary*, vol. II, pp. 202, 204; Kimball, *Dudley*, p. 187.

[5] *Deplorable State of New England; A modest Enquiry;* Kimball, *Dudley*, pp. 188 f.

[6] *Journal, Board of Trade, 1704–9*, pp. 530 f., 534 f., 547, 553 ff.

to the Queen asking for English assistance in the proposed campaign, which Vetch added to his own presentation of the case, thus once more drawing the colonies and the mother country into attempted coöperation.[1]

The English government decided the matter favorably and on March 1, 1709, Vetch, now Colonel, was handed his instructions. He was ordered to proceed at once to New York and to inform the governor there that "taking into consideration the frequent applications the colonists have made to be delivered from the French" an expedition was being prepared by England to assist them. New York was to furnish eight hundred men, New Jersey two hundred, Connecticut three hundred and fifty, and Pennsylvania one hundred and fifty, the joint force to be at Albany not later than the middle of May with three months' supplies. They were then to establish headquarters at Wood Creek and have boats ready to proceed up Lake Champlain. Massachusetts and Rhode Island were to provide twelve hundred troops "according to their usual proportions," provisions, pilots, and flat-bottomed boats for landing. England was to furnish the arms and ammunition, five regiments of regulars and the ships of war, which were to be at Boston by May 15. The governors of Massachusetts and Rhode Island were to confer at Boston, and those of Connecticut, New York and Pennsylvania at New York. The military plans involved a land attack on Montreal and a naval one upon Quebec.[2]

Vetch, with Colonel Nicholson, who had also been attached to the expedition, sailed from England March 11, but, owing to a very bad voyage, was delayed five weeks and forced to put into Boston April 28, having run short of water. There the two at once communicated their instructions to Dudley and the

---

[1] So says Hutchinson, *History*, vol. II, p. 160. Kimball's statement, (*Dudley*, p. 123) following Parkman, (*Half-Century*, vol. I, p. 134), that Vetch carried the Memorial to England for the colony would seem to be incorrect. The Memorial was passed in October, and Vetch had already been many months in England. His paper entitled "Canada surveyed, or the French Dominions upon the Continent of America briefly considered in their situation, strength, trade and number; more particularly how vastly prejudicial they are to the English interest, and proposing a method of easily removing them" was presented to the Board of Trade on July 27, and Vetch was in constant attendance all summer and fall. *Vide Journal Board of Trade, passim.*

[2] Instructions to Col. Vetch, Mar. 1, 1709, *C.O. 5 No. 9; Ibid., Brit. Mus. Add. Mss. 32694;* Sunderland to the governors, Apl. 28, 1709, *C.O. 5 No. 10; Ibid., Brit. Mus. Add. Mss. 32694; cf. N. Y. Col. Docts.,* vol. V, pp. 70 *ff.*

Council, and despatched letters to the other colonies. In spite of the death of Lord Lovelace at New York, of a "feud" between the governor and assembly in New Jersey, and of trouble with the Quakers in that colony and Pennsylvania, the preparations went forward as planned.[1] By the middle of July, the land forces, although short over three hundred and fifty men on account of the Quaker colonies, were at Wood Creek, where they had built forts, roads and boats, and where, with the Indian allies, they were impatiently awaiting news of the fleet and orders to proceed, as were the forces at Boston.[2] But no word came from England, and Vetch could only write home how uneasy were the people, and may "God hasten in the fleet."[3] Meanwhile, however, the project had long been abandoned in England. The ships which were to have sailed in March were still at home the end of July. As early as June 11, Sunderland noted that the expedition had been abandoned "for some time," although no word was sent to the waiting colonists whose expenses and losses in trade were mounting to over £100,000.[4]

At last the fleet, destined now for the Bahamas and not Canada, arrived at Boston on the 11th of October, apparently bringing the first word of the abandonment of the expedition.[5] On

[1] Journal of the Proceedings of Col. Vetch and Col. Nicholson, June 21, 1709, *C.O. 5 No. 9; R. I. Col. Records*, vol. IV, pp. 70, 73 *f.*, 81 *f.*, 108; *Conn. Col. Records*, vol. V, pp. 91 *f.*, 108; *Winthrop Papers*, vol. VI, pp. 208 *ff.*

[2] Letter from Nicholson to Sunderland, July 8, 1709, *C.O. 5 No. 9*; Vetch to Sunderland, June 28, 1709, *C.O. 5 No. 9*. *N. Y. Col. Docts.*, vol. V, p. 78.

[3] He wrote "how vastly uneasie, all Her Majesties Loyall subjects here upon the Continent are, att the not arrivall of the ffleet, which is like to disappoynt the great expectation & faire prospect they had of securing to themselves and their posteritie a lasting happiness & tranquility, as well as an advantageous trade both to themselves, and All the Brittish Empyre; the hopes of which made them so readilie & heartily comply, nay, out doe Her Majesties orders, by me signified to them att so vast an Expense, that it cost Her Majesties subjects Embarked In this Affaire one hundred thousand pound, besides the loss of their trade, which the Embargo upon All Shipping for these three months past hath occasioned. Add to this the alarming the ffrench (which could not be evited, after our advanced party went to wood Creek) hath given them occasion, to fortifie both places better then ever they were before pray God hasten In the ffleet." Vetch to Sunderland, Aug. 12, 1709, *C.O. 5 No. 9*. Cf. Dudley to Sunderland, Aug. 14, 1709, *C.O. 5 No. 9*.

[4] "Md. taken from Ld. Sunderland's book of lres & Instructions," etc., *C.O. 5 No. 9*; "Acct. of Everything in the Office to be found relative to the intended Expedition to Canada," *Brit. Mus. Add. Mss. 32694.*

[5] In letters to Dudley and others dated July 27. In the "Md taken from Ld Sunderland's book" etc., *cit. supra*, there is a note of a letter sent to Vetch with the news dated July 1, but there is no other trace of its ever having been sent.

the 14th Dudley and the governors of Connecticut and Rhode Island with members of the General Courts of each colony held a "congress" at Newport, and decided in accordance with the suggestions of the home government to utilize the forces under arms in an attack on Port Royal, but the naval officers had no orders to act jointly in any such undertaking, and after much correspondence declined to do so.[1]

Thus ended the second attempt at coöperation, and in spite of the failure of New York and the colonies to the south to do their part, the fiasco was almost wholly caused by the inefficient and clumsy working of the home government. The New England colonies had shown excellent spirit. Colonel Nicholson, although a former royal governor, had been unanimously elected commander-in-chief of the land forces, and had become extremely popular.[2] Even after this failure, and in spite of the wholly unnecessary disappointment inflicted upon the colonists by the incapable government at home, their desire to coöperate was undiminished for the one great object of ridding themselves of the French menace. Although the direct expense of the abortive expedition incurred by the New England colonies, exclusive of Connecticut, had amounted to over £46,000,[3] they made strong representations to the Queen in favor of a renewal of the attempt the following year, even if only to take Port Royal.[4] The tide of good feeling was at the flood for the time being, and

[1] Votes at the Congress of Govts, etc., Oct. 14, 1709, *C.O. 5 No. 9;* Dudley to Capt. Clifton, Oct. 12; Dudley, Nicholson, etc., to Gov. Ingoldsby, Oct. 18; Clifton to Dudley, Oct. 18; letters to captains of H. M. ships, Oct. 19; Dudley, Vetch, etc., to Sunderland, Dec. 6, 1709. All in *C.O. 5 No. 9.* The congress, which included the governor-elect of Newfoundland, seems to have sat at different places, as Dudley states Newport, and Saltonstall says Rehoboth. *Winthrop Papers,* vol. VI, p. 211.

[2] The assembly in Boston voted that they "do gratefully Acknowledge the uncommon zeal, which his Honor Nicholson hath Shewn for Her Majesty's Service, and his good Inclination to Assist and Promote the Welfare, of Her Majesty's good Subjects" etc. Resolution in House of Representatives, Mass. Oct. 27, 1709, *C.O. 5 No. 9. Cf. R. I. Col. Records,* vol. IV, p. 73.

[3] Account of Charges for the intended Expedition to Canada, in Dudley's letter of Oct. 24, 1709, *C.O. 5 No. 9.* The amounts were Massachusetts, £30,800, New Hampshire, £3,500, Rhode Island, £6,700, to date, and £5,000 more to be incurred by all before the troops could be disbanded. The £60,000 given by Kimball as the cost, was that of the two years 1709 and 1710. Kimball, *Dudley,* p. 125. *Vide* Dudley to St. John, Nov. 15, 1710, in *Gay Transcripts,* vol. X, pp. 10 *ff.* (In library of Mass. Hist. Soc.)

[4] Address to Her Majesty from members of the Governors Congress Oct. 14, 1709; Address of the principal inhabitants, etc. Oct. 24; *ibid.,* Dec. 6, 1709. All in *C. O. 5 No. 9.*

the efforts of Dudley and Vetch for the conquest of Canada had brought about a hitherto unparalleled situation. Not only had the jealous provincials elected a royal officer as their own commander-in-chief, but the governors of Rhode Island and Connecticut, the two colonies whose inveterate separatism England was endeavoring to break down, were uniting in a harmonious congress with the royal governor of Massachusetts, and urging the British government to send over troops and officers to work with them in a common cause. There is nothing to indicate that the statesmen at home had the slightest realization that an opportunity had presented itself for improving the relations between the colonies and the mother country. Throughout the century, indeed, they exhibited an utter lack of that imagination that is essential in imperial statesmanship.

As a military measure, not as a step in colonial policy, a joint attempt upon Canada recommended itself to the government, and in May of the following year, Sunderland wrote to the Board of Ordnance to provide the same stores as in the preceding one.[1] No plans, however, could be decided upon, and the home government blew hot and cold.[2] In the middle of May, Vetch wrote from Boston that the people were "mightily discouraged" the "Season being so farr advanced; without my having the Least orders, relating to the Expeditions being renewed," and Nicholson in England was no better off for information.[3] It was only in July that the fleet arrived at Boston with orders for Lord Shannon to coöperate with the colonials for an attack upon Quebec.[4]

Owing to their experience the preceding year, the colonies had made no preparations in advance of the instructions received by them, but all in New England now obeyed with alacrity. A new

---

[1] Account of all found in the office relating to the intended expedition to Canada, 1710. *Brit. Mus. Add. Mss. 32694.*

[2] In March and April the government abandoned the project of an attack on Canada in favor of one merely on Port Royal. Account of the Commissions, Instructions, etc., *C.O. 5 No. 9.* In May the larger plan was taken up again. In July Shannon was ordered to try either, depending on preparations he found made in New England. Lord Shannon's Instructions, July 1710, *C.O. 5 No. 9.* In August, word was sent to New England that it was too late for the fleet to sail. Account, etc. *cit. supra.*

[3] Vetch to Sunderland, May 15; Nicholson to Sunderland, May 12, 1710. Both in *C.O. 5 No. 9.*

[4] Lord Shannon's Instructions, July 1710. *C.O. 5 No. 9.*

congress of the governors met at Boston and preparations were pushed with all speed. The delay entailed, however, had been too great, for the season was now too far advanced to permit of operations in the St. Lawrence, and the joint expedition resulted only in the capture of Port Royal, on October 2.[1]

Although no more had been accomplished, the capture of that "nest of spoilers" filled the colonists with joy, as well it might, for in 1708 alone the French privateers from that port had taken no less than thirty-five vessels, mostly from Boston, and carried off four hundred and seventy prisoners.[2] That indeed was not a matter of great importance to Connecticut, which possessed no commerce and was wholly agricultural, so that it is not strange that, when a third expedition was talked of for the next year, that colony should plead its inability to furnish as large a quota as in the earlier efforts. Indeed all the colonies were feeling the strain of expense greatly, and strongly urged the home government to force New York and the colonies as far south as Maryland to do their share, although heartily in favor of a renewed attempt to destroy the French power in Canada once for all.[3] It may be noted that one of the curious features in the relations of the colonies to England was the constant demand made by one colony or another that the mother country should force other colonies to contribute fixed quotas although each for itself refused to acknowledge her right to do so.

Unfortunately the final effort at coöperation was bungled even worse by the authorities in England than had been the other three. The same plan of two combined attacks, the one by way of Albany, and the other by the St. Lawrence, was adopted as usual. The choice of Nicholson to have charge of the land expedition was excellent, but the fleet and forces for

---

[1] Address from Connecticut to the Queen, Aug. 7; from Massachusetts to the Queen, Aug. 22; both in *C.O. 5 No. 10.* Nicholson and Vetch to Sunderland, Sept. 16; Articles of Capitulation, Oct. 2; Address of Council of War to Queen, 1710. All in *C.O. 5 No. 9. R. I. Col. Records*, vol. IV, pp. 93 *ff.*, 198 *ff. Cf.* Nicholson's Journal, and other documents in *Nova Scotia Hist. Soc., Coll.*, vol. I, pp. 159 *ff.*

[2] Wrong, *Conquest of New France*, p. 55.

[3] Saltonstall to Sunderland, Nov. 21, 1710, *C.O. 5 No. 10*; Memorial of Mass. General Court to Queen, Nov. 11, 1710, *Gay Transcripts*, vol. X, pp. 66 *ff.*; Memorial of Jer. Dummer, Jan. 3, 1711, *C.O. 5 No. 9; ibid.*, Mar. 1, 1711, *C.O. 5 No. 10.*

the attack on Quebec were placed under command of two thoroughly tactless, overbearing, and incompetent men. The presence of Sir Hovenden Walker and General Hill, the latter the brother of the Queen's favorite, Mrs. Masham, spelled disaster from the start. Moreover the usual delays had not only kept the fleet from sailing so that it did not arrive at Boston until June 24, but even Nicholson did not reach America, with the first intimation to the colonists that an expedition was under way, until June 8, so that when Walker and Hill arrived all the matters of raising troops, providing provisions, and all other details of preparation were necessarily in confusion.[1] For six weeks, until July 30, the fleet remained at Boston while preparations which might just as well have been completed before its arrival were being made. Nicholson at New York did what he could, and as usual got on well with the colonials, but at Boston the air was filled with charges and recriminations between the English commander and the General Court. The good feeling established by Nicholson was largely destroyed, and the Journals of Colonel King and General Hill afford a vivid picture of incompetence and exasperation.[2] There was undoubtedly much profiteering, but on the whole the Massachusetts authorities seem to have done all they could to facilitate matters, including a loan of £40,000 for subsisting the troops, and the fixing of prices at which goods could be sold, as well as undertaking a search for hidden stores.[3]

It must have been a relief to both sides when the ships finally sailed on the 30th of July on their ill-fated voyage. It was three weeks before they reached the mouth of the St. Lawrence where the final catastrophe occurred. There on the night of August 22, through having steered a wrong course eight transports

---

[1] *R. I. Col. Records*, vol. IV, pp. 120 *ff.*; *Conn. Col. Records*, vol. V, p. 243.

[2] Mr. Hill's Journal, *C.O. 5 No. 9*; Journal of Richard King, May 4 to Aug. 12, 1711, *Gay Transcripts*, vol. X, pp. 81 *ff.*; Abstract of the Proceedings of the Governor, Council and Assembly of Mass. Bay, June 8 to July 2, dated Oct. 31, 1711, *C.O. 5 No. 10*; King to St. John, July 25, *Gay Transcripts*, vol. X, pp. 104 *ff.* The items attributed by J. G. Palfrey, [*History of New England*, (Boston, 1875), vol. IV, p. 282 *n.*] to King's Journal are from Hill's.

[3] Jer. Dummer, *A Letter to a Noble Lord concerning the late Expedition to Canada*, (London, 1712), pp. 11 *ff. Cf.* Dudley to St. John, Nov. 13, 1711, *Gay Transcripts*, vol. X, pp. 143 *ff.*

were cast away on the rocks with a loss of over a thousand men.[1] As a result of two councils of war it was finally decided to attempt nothing further in any direction although none of the royal ships had been damaged, and the fleet ignominiously sailed back for England.[2] Nicholson, who was at Lake Champlain with the Connecticut troops waiting the word to move on Montreal, was notified and the entire expedition was abandoned.[3] A golden opportunity not only for the capture of Canada but for the establishing of better working relations between the colonies and the mother country had passed. Partly owing to circumstances and partly to Dudley and Nicholson, there had been moments in the former's administration when the colonies had caught a glimpse of working together harmoniously among themselves and with England. Owing to the incompetence of the English administration in all departments, that glimpse had faded and given place to bitter memories of Jamaica, of the dreary summer of hope deferred in 1709, and of the ghastly night in the St. Lawrence with its toll of dead, and the shameful abandonment by the royal navy. The last attempt had left the colonists sore from their personal contacts with the English troops and officers, burdened with debt, and with their prestige fallen in the eyes of their French enemies and their own Indian friends. Port Royal was the only fruit of all their efforts. The vision of a common interest passed, and each colony relapsed into its selfish isolation, while the authority of the mother country became again a power rather to be thwarted than invoked. The possible opportunity of drawing the colonies peacefully and willingly into the wider life of empire passed over the horizon with the ships and troops of Walker and of Hill.

---

[1] Hill to Dartmouth, Sept. 9, 1711; letter of Geo. Lee, Sept. 12, 1711; Vetch to Walker, Aug. 26, 1711; all in *C.O. 5 No. 9.* King's Journal continued, Aug. 15, to Sept. 10, 1711, *Gay Transcripts*, vol. X, pp. 132 *ff. Winthrop Papers*, vol. VI, p. 246. Estimates of loss run from 800 to 1500. W. Kingsford, *History of Canada*, (London, 1888), vol. II, pp. 464 *ff.*

[2] Consultation of Sea Officers Aug. 25, 1711; Resolution of Council of War, Sept. 8, 1711; both in *C.O. 5 No. 9. Nova Scotia Hist. Soc., Coll.*, vol. IV, pp. 98 *ff.*, 105 *ff.* Although nothing was done at the time to discipline Walker, he was later struck off the flag list and deprived of his half-pay. His flag captain in the expedition was dismissed from the service. Clowes, *Royal Navy*, vol. II, p. 529 *n.*

[3] In spite of Connecticut's heavy loss, the General Court asked England to plan another expedition for 1712. *Conn. Col. Records*, vol. V, p. 294.

CHAPTER VI

THE RISING TIDE

Opening of a New Period — Effects of Peace — Change in Land Policy — Extension of Frontier — Growing Problem of the West India Trade — Rise in Living Costs — Paper Money — Effect on Political Parties — John Wise and Colonial Political Philosophy — Increasing Demands of the People for Control — Character of the Democracy

THE division of history into periods, or of a historical work into chapters, is merely a concession to a peculiarity of our mental constitution which seems unable to grasp any subject unless thus arbitrarily broken up into morsels of convenient size. But that utterly mysterious play of cosmic energy, call it by what name we may, which for hundreds of thousands of years has been peopling the earth with its myriads upon myriads of human beings, each called into being for the merest second of sentient existence, and then gone into the unknowable again, like the spray of some eternal water-fall, knows nothing of such divisions. Even the patterns formed by a few of these little lives for some brief moment, the lines of development that we trace in some small chosen period, merge not only before and after but on all sides into the illimitable and indivisible sea of existence.

In the living present it is not so difficult to become aware of the complexity of life and of its continuity. We realize that all sorts of things are going on about us all at once; that probably no two people in the country think alike on all subjects; that an infinite number of movements, tendencies, facts of all kinds, are influencing ourselves and all about us; that this year has developed unperceived out of the last and will slip with as little sudden alteration into the next. But in reading history we are apt to be deceived into thinking in terms of distinct periods, of comparatively few movements, and of few intellectual **and** political groups largely because of the necessity for division and selection in the historian's arrangement of his material.

From the standpoint of this required simplification, we may take the events described at the end of the last chapter, and the signing of the Treaty of Utrecht in 1713 as marking a period, or a change in tendencies, in the history of New England, though Dudley continued in office a couple of years longer. We need not here concern ourselves with the details of the political job by which Colonel Elizeus Burgess, who was subsequently appointed governor, was bought off for £1,000, some say by one of the parties in Massachusetts, and some by his successor Colonel Shute who assumed office in 1716.[1] The episode is of note mainly as an example of the way in which public offices of importance and trust were considered in England in that day, and openly bought and sold with little regard to the interest of the public or the state.

Chalmers, who considered that it was Shute who had bought the place, rather unfairly characterized him as unfit for it no less on account of his "religious and political prepossessions" than on account of his "natural imbecility." "Natural imbecility" is no light handicap for even a royal governor, but happily the evidence points to the new appointee being not quite so bad as the English historian has painted him, and in any case, the next period in New England history, which lasted for a generation, was to be controlled by forces of greater significance than governors of Massachusetts. As we have already pointed out, the local struggle in Boston between the assembly and the royal representative would have followed much the same course regardless of the character of the latter, though his strength or weakness, his popularity or unpopularity, might have altered slightly both the speed with which executive power was absorbed by the legislative and the amenities of that somewhat painful process. The struggle was the outcome of conditions, not personalities, and like many causes of friction between the colonies and the home government, was at work during the administration of every governor throughout the remainder of the colonial period.

[1] Chalmers, *Revolt*, vol. II, p. 11; Sewall, *Diary*, vol. III, p. 34 *n*. A. McF. Davis, *Currency and Banking in Massachusetts Bay*, (New York, 1900), vol. I, p. 112.

The signing of the Treaty of Utrecht marked the close of a generation of border warfare, of colossal expense and of unproductive effort. New England for the next three decades enjoyed, for the most part, the blessings and opportunities of peace, and the period was marked by great expansion of trade, by financial inflation, by the secularizing of thought, and by a growing self-consciousness politically. As a result of the years of war and of the terms of the treaty, England had not only added to her possessions in America the colonies of Nova Scotia and Newfoundland but had increased enormously her trade advantages and naval resources at the expense of the other contestants. Holland was no longer one of the great powers. France was exhausted. England, it is true, had rolled up an enormous national debt but her commerce had increased even during the war, and, most important of all, her naval supremacy was now assured. In her combination of an unrivaled navy and of the greatest merchant marine in the world, both based upon the possession of strong positions in all the disputed quarters of the globe, England had ceased to be merely "one of the sea powers" and had become "*the* sea power, without any second."[1] It had been, however, at vast expense. New England was complaining of the debts which she had incurred in her local border warfare and the Canadian expeditions, but England's own debt had risen to the unexampled figure of over £54,000,000 and of that sum, in the four years 1708 to 1711, nearly £2,000,000 had been solely for the naval protection for the colonies.[2] The unprecedented taxes which resulted called for a new economic policy, and it is from the beginning of Walpole's administration of the finances in 1715 that we find England adopting a more aggressive attitude toward the protection of her manufacturing interests. Nor was she in a position to add to her burdens by taking on any additional share of the cost of the civil administration in the colonies or of assisting them in any military adventure.

In New England the Treaty of Utrecht brought peace with the French, and a treaty with the eastern Indians, signed at

[1] Mahan, *Influence of Sea Power*, pp. 219 *ff.*

[2] N. A. Brisco, *The economic Policy of Robert Walpole*, (New York, 1907), p. 20; Chalmers, *Revolt*, vol. I, p. 354 *n.*

The Partners Ketch of Which George Gatison was Master when they first Came ye Turks in her which when she Came Home I was put in Master —

ONE FACTOR IN ENGLAND'S SEA SUPREMACY — A KETCH OF
THE LATE SEVENTEENTH-CENTURY

From *A Relation of the severall Adventers by Sea with the dangers, difficulties, and hardships met for several years, transcribed by John Millar*, 1717–1718, a manuscript in the Library of Congress

Portsmouth in the same year, brought the long desired cessation of hostilities with the savage allies of that civilized but unchivalrous foe.[1] The forty years of intermittent fighting had resulted in a marked retrenchment of the colonial frontier. In Maine not a single new town had been founded between 1675 and 1715, and at the end of Queen Anne's War over a hundred miles of the coast had become destitute of inhabitants.[2] There was practically no extension of settlement in New Hampshire, and although Connecticut planted a few towns to the northward, the entire period had been one of increased concentration of population in the older settlements rather than of expansion. There had, indeed, been a distinct movement out of New England, and by the early years of the new century the influence of the section had been carried by emigration to the colonies to the south by settlers in such towns as Bedford, Rye and Westchester in New York, Elizabeth, Newark, Shrewsbury, Cape May and others in New Jersey, and even as far as Dorchester in South Carolina.[3] Nor was that influence negligible, for Governor Hunter was by no means alone in his anxious irritation with the descendants of the "Saints" when he wrote, in 1715, that "I confidently affirm, that all the opposition and vexation I have met with in New York and New Jersey, have been in great measure owing to those who came to us from New England." [4]

Peace, however, was to have a profound effect upon the frontier and upon the economic and political life of the Puritan colonies. In the generation following the signing of the treaty, the settlers, who had been growing more and more cramped within their old limits, swarmed to the newer lands on the border. The movement was particularly notable in western Massachusetts whither Connecticut men of the hardier type arrived by way of the Connecticut and Housatonic valleys. Moreover, it became a period of renewed immigration from Europe, fifty-four ship loads of emigrants from Ireland reaching

---

[1] Text in Penhallow, *Indian Wars*, pp. 78 *ff*.
[2] L. K. Mathews, *Expansion of New England*, (Boston, 1909), pp. 61, 85.
[3] Mathews, *cit. supra*, pp. 66 *ff*.
[4] Chalmers, *Revolt*, vol. I, p. 317. *Cf.* Greene, *Provincial Governor*, p. 179, for similar statements by other governors.

the port of Boston between 1714 and 1720. Indeed, in 1718, such numbers of these Scotch-Irish arrived as markedly to raise the price of provisions in the colony. For the most part, they proceeded to New Hampshire, and gave a new inflexibility to the character of the settlers among its granite hills.[1]

Mere extension of the bounds of settlement was of comparatively slight importance in itself. The facts which were of extreme significance were that during the period of forced concentration from 1675 to 1713, the pressure of population upon the lands within the then limits of settlement had caused them to increase in value, and that the speculative fever accompanying the prosperity of the ensuing years of world peace caused a speculation in the new lands, and a marked change in the land policy of New England. These effects, in turn, were felt in an increase in the differentiation between frontier and old settlement, and in a growing bitterness between the members of the propertied class and those who began to feel that they were being exploited by them.

In the seventeenth century, the general policy in all the New England colonies had been not to sell the lands within their borders but to grant them to groups of settlers organizing and actually settling in new towns, under careful restrictions. Each of these town "proprietors" received a certain amount of land in fee, and all used the balance in common for pasturage and wood. At first these "commons" had but little value, and a share in them could be easily acquired for a nominal sum by new comers, to whom it was sometimes even freely granted. But as land became scarcer and more valuable within the limits of the older towns, the proprietors insisted upon their rights of ownership as against the towns-people generally. The eighteenth century was marked by clashes between these two parties and by the gradual breaking up of the commons into individual ownership by those claiming proprietors' rights.[2] This

[1] S. P. Orth, *Our Foreigners*, (Yale Press, 1920), p. 11; Ford, *The Scotch Irish in America*, p. 224; *New Hampshire Historical Society, Proceedings*, vol. IV, pp. 143 ff.; Parker, *History of Londonderry*, pp. 34 ff.; *Col. Soc. Mass., Publications*, vol. XIII, pp. 277 ff.

[2] For the early system, *vide* M. Eggleston, *The Land System of the New England Colonies* (Johns Hopkins University, 1886); A. B. Maclear, *Early New England Towns*, (Columbia University, 1908); C. M. Andrews, *River Towns of Connecticut*, (Johns Hopkins University, 1889), pp. 36 ff.; cf. *Conn. Col. Records*, vol. VI, pp. 394 ff., 449.

loss of the use of the commons for pasturage and wood, and also the decreasing amount of land available and its increasing price, which left the poorer people little prospect of establishing their children on lands of their own even when they themselves were not suffering, led many to move to the frontier, with no friendly feelings for the more fortunate classes in the old settlements from which many of the poorer felt they were being driven out by necessity.

But even in the wilderness they encountered in many cases what they considered oppression from the capitalists, for under pressure from the latter, the colonial governments had begun to alter their policy regarding lands, and were granting them to groups of speculators who had no intention of suffering the hardships of actual removal themselves but were merely counting upon reselling to such as they could induce to emigrate, retaining for themselves substantial tracts which would increase in value on account of the labor of the pioneers. Wherever we touch the life of the period, in the literature, in the colleges, the churches, or in the fields of politics and economics, we find that the old ideal of a church state has passed. A new town, for example, is no longer the swarming out of a congregation grouped about a new church but is mainly a planting by land speculators of persons forced out from the old settlements by economic necessity. It is noteworthy, speaking of this very point, that a writer in 1716 in trying to find a solution for the financial evils of the time attempts to make his appeal only to economic selfishness, urging that if "those Gentlemen that have Ingrost vast Tracts of Land, without any design ever to settle them by themselves, Servants or Slaves, should Voluntarily throw up into the Country's Hands, one half of what they have so Ingrost, in order to furnish Conveniences, for such Settlements, they might be gainers by it in the other half." [1] In some cases, frauds were perpetrated upon the settlers by persons having no title to the lands whatever.[2]

[1] "Some Considerations upon the several Sorts of Banks," etc. in A. M. Davis, *Tracts Relating to the Currency of the Massachusetts Bay*, (Boston, 1902), pp. 177 *f*.

[2] *Cf.* the publication of a proclamation by the governor of Connecticut regarding such a fraud at Tolland, Feb. 19, 1716–7, in *Records of the Governor and Council of the Colony of Connecticut, 1712–28* in Mss. in Library of Congress. *Cf.* Mathews, *Expansion of New England*, pp. 80 *ff.*, 91 *ff.*; *Conn. Col. Records*, vol. VI, pp. 355 *ff.*

Many factors combined in the years of expansion following the Peace of 1713 both to extend the genuine frontier section and to set it off to an increasing extent against the older settled areas. In the early days, the difference had been less marked and was mainly that of locality without differentiation as to wealth or occupation. By the time we have now reached, however, the distinction was becoming great. The seaboard towns had ceased to be for the most part agricultural and had become largely commercial. Wealth had accumulated, the range of opportunity had lessened, social distinctions were rigidly insisted upon, and snobbishness was much in evidence. Money was the dominant power, economically, socially, politically. The seaboard of New England was merely old England writ small, in a somewhat cleaner and more wholesome moral atmosphere. There was much more in common between the rich West India merchant in his counting house in Boston or Newport, and his correspondent in London, than there was between him and the pioneer farmer and backwoodsman, whose sentiments regarding the capitalists of the older settlements we have already noted in an earlier chapter.

Trade, based largely upon the fisheries, which were known as the "New England Silver Mine," had now become the leading interest in the coast towns. The New Englanders had regarded the return to France, on various occasions, of Nova Scotia as "execrable treachery" largely because of its importance in the fisheries, an importance which formed the main reason for rejoicing over its recapture in 1710 and its retention in the Treaty of Utrecht.[1] Although perhaps the largest quantity of this fish, which on the whole formed the main staple of New England export, was shipped to the Catholic countries of Europe in exchange for wines from the Azores and the Canaries, manufactured goods from England, and some illegal purchases on the continent, the growth of a trade with the French West Indies became so great from 1713 to 1730 as greatly to alarm the merchants and planters in the English islands and those in England dealing with them. In addition to the "refuse fish" which was sent as food for the slaves, there went horses, provisions and

[1] Andrews, "Anglo-French Commercial Rivalry," p. 547.

lumber in large quantities. In return came sugar, molasses for the New England rum manufacturers, and some specie.

If the theory of the Mercantilists was to be carried into practice without detriment to some part of the empire, the consumption and production among its several parts should have been so adjusted as to be approximately equal. Moreover, aside from this delicate trade balancing, illegal traffic was bound to come about if outside markets offered cheaper raw materials or higher prices for products than were afforded by those within the closed commercial system. In an earlier chapter, it has been pointed out how the growth of the northern British plantations combined with the stationary situation in the Sugar Colonies of the same empire upset the balance between them, and caused the New England colonies to look to the foreign West Indies and Caribbean settlements for a larger market in which both to buy and sell.[1] Although at first the main part of this trade was carried on with the Dutch at Surinam, circumstances during the war and after combined to develop a large business direct with the French islands. The semi-tropical possessions of France were greatly increased after 1700, especially by the addition of the rich island of Santo Domingo, and as all were greatly in need of provisions and the other supplies that New England afforded, prices were temptingly high for the Yankees.[2] Moreover, the French, for various reasons, were able to undersell the English in the sugar and molasses markets, and, finally, were free from the four and one-half per cent export duty levied in the English islands. All of these facts combined made the rapid growth of a trade between New England and the French Sugar Islands inevitable. The insular English correctly considered that this was detrimental to their interests in several ways, and complaints against the New Englanders by the West Indians began to be heard as early as 1701, followed by a much more earnest presentation of the islanders' case a dozen years later. As a result, in 1713, a bill was ordered prepared by an order in Council for the relief of the islands, but in accord with the leisurely method of transacting business the order was not read by the members

---

[1] *Vide supra*, chap. III.
[2] Pitman, *West Indies*, p. 203.

until 1715.[1] A year after, they took the matter into consideration, looked into the legality of the New England trade, and somewhat unexpectedly and happily finding it prohibited by the almost forgotten French treaty of the previous generation, issued a circular letter to the colonial governors ordering them to see that the trade was stopped. Although Shute, who was then governor in Massachusetts, issued his proclamation and duly communicated the instructions to the governors of Rhode Island and Connecticut, the merchants and sea captains and church elders continued to traffic quite as unconcernedly and profitably as before.

The Board of Trade was cognizant of the economic necessity of the business for the New England colonies, not merely for the sake of profits for their merchants but to enable them to acquire specie and credits with which to pay the annually recurring balance due to England herself, as the exports from that country to New England always heavily exceeded the imports. The reason for their action, therefore, was probably partly political and partly economic. They wished to damage the growing prosperity of the French and hinder their rivalry, though at the expense of the prosperity of their own continental colonies and home manufactures. But if the question came down merely to the domestic imperial one of which group of colonies, — the Sugar Islands or New England, — should be made to suffer for the sake of the other, the trade figures given below would leave little doubt as to which contemporary opinion could be expected to have favored.

English Imports and Exports, June 24, 1714 — June 24, 1717

Imports from		Exports to
£187,059	Antigua	£30,855
364,557	Barbadoes	140,697
332,266	Jamaica	147,931
34,485	Montserrat	4,921
85,078	Nevis	12,729
98,772	St. Christopher	11,182
£1,102,217	Total	£348,315
£65,016	New England	£139,269 [2]

[1] Pitman, *West Indies*, pp. 198 f., 206.
[2] *Kings Mss. 205, Pt. I*, f. 54. If we add the other provision colonies of New York and

Considering the above figures, and the fact that both in production of provisions and in fishing, the New England colonies directly competed with England, it is little wonder that general opinion in that country agreed with Wood who wrote in 1719 that "without our Southern Plantations, our Northern Colonies can be of no real Advantage to us; since what they are at present, must cease on the Decay or Loss of the Sugar Islands, from whence their Value to Great Britian chiefly arises, and for want of which they would otherwise be prejudicial Colonies to their Mother Country."[1]

The enormous debts incurred in the late wars, the steadily increasing foreign trade, and the inevitable adverse balance with England, all raised financial problems of grave import for the colonies. As we saw in the previous volume, the first step toward paper money had been taken as a result of the unfortunate expedition against Quebec in 1690 and the wild financing of the time in Massachusetts.[2] At first the intention of the various colonies was good, and the issues were limited in amount and intended to be redeemed within a short period, but as time went on they were increased by leaps and bounds, and the periods for repayment steadily lengthened. Had the amounts been limited to the ability of the colonies to redeem them and had their redemption been assured within a reasonable period, their parity with metal currency could have been maintained. This was comprehended, as such matters usually are, by only a small part of the community, and the increasing issues and decreasing chances of redemption resulted in lowering the conversion value of the notes and driving out the sound money. When the first paper was issued in Massachusetts in 1690, there was apparently about £200,000 in silver in circulation. By 1714 the paper had risen to £240,000 and silver had almost entirely disap-

Pennsylvania the figures are increased by £27,658 imports and £70,490 exports for the continental colonies. *Ibid.* The trade between England and New England was wholly carried on through Massachusetts. *Vide* Letter from Gov. and Company of Conn. to Lords of Trade, Dec. 12, 1709; Gov. Cranston to same, Dec. 5, 1708, both in *C.O. 5 No. 1292.*

[1] *Survey of Trade*, p. 49.

[2] Adams, *Founding of New England*, p. 442. There is some evidence that paper bills were in circulation as early as 1652, but their nature is uncertain. Davis, *Currency and Banking*, vol. II, pp. 61*f.*; J. B. Felt, *An historical Account of Massachusetts Currency*, Boston, 1839, p. 33.

peared.[1] Massachusetts had led the way, but the exigencies of the military operations in the years 1709–10 induced New Hampshire, Connecticut and Rhode Island to follow along the same path.

Dudley, throughout his term as governor, showed a full realization of the necessity for prompt redemption, but as the paper gradually declined, as silver disappeared, and as the prices of goods rose accordingly, the demand for "cheap money" became only the more insistent from the ignorant and the debtors who were benefiting at the expense of their creditors.[2] Continued inflation naturally resulted in a steady rise in the price of commodities, which worked great hardship upon many classes as it has been doing in the recent years of the Great War and after. Silver which had been seven shillings an ounce in 1704 rose to fourteen shillings by 1722, or in other words the buying power of the paper money depreciated fifty per cent in eighteen years.[3] A contemporary writer complained that the cost of living had doubled, and that although "this raising on one another in Trade helps some, yet it hurts more" and that the salaried classes were suffering severely.[4] The new governor, Shute, realized the source of the trouble as had Dudley, and told the Massachusetts assembly that "we shall never be upon a firm and lasting foundation 'til we recover and return to silver and gold, the only true species of money."[5] Nevertheless his stand was as unavailing as had been Dudley's in his latter years. The governors were by no means alone in their opposition, and the appeal to return to sound methods addressed jointly to the governments of Massachusetts, Connecticut and Rhode Island by Hutchinson, Belcher, and others in 1720 was but one of many

[1] A. M. Davis, *Colonial Currency Reprints*, (Prince Society, Boston, 1910), vol. I, p. 34.
[2] The most important pamphlets issued at the time are reprinted by A. M. Davis in his *Tracts relating to the Currency*, and *Colonial Currency Reprints*.
[3] *Extracts from the Itineraries of Ezra Stiles*, (Yale Press, 1916), p. 7; the same proportion held good in Connecticut, *vide* H. Bronson, "A historical Account of Connecticut Currency," *New Haven Historical Society Papers*, vol. I, p. 52; also in Rhode Island, *vide* H. Phillips, Jr., *Historical Sketches of the Paper Currency in the American Colonies*, Series, I, (Roxbury, 1865), p. 153.
[4] *The present melancholy Circumstances of the Province*, (Boston, 1719), p. 13.
[5] Davis, *Currency and Banking*, vol. I, p. 61.

protests made against the effects of the reckless ignorance of the paper money men.[1]

Throughout New England the question of the currency divided the people into bitterly hostile parties. The dispute was one with which America was to become all too familiar, for every great advance of the frontier has been marked by the same demand for "cheap money," or an expansion of the currency, and the paper money men of New England were merely the precursors of the Greenbackers, the Populists and the Free Silverites of later times. Nor were they alone even in their own day. The same currency heresies and the same paper money schemes to assist the debtor at the expense of his creditor had then but recently been tried in Barbadoes, where the irredeemable paper issued fell to a discount of forty-five per cent in eighteen months and the English Board of Trade had to exert its authority to prevent the complete financial ruin of the island.[2]

Those who best understood the nature of money and the financial laws governing the use of credit, and who suffered most immediately from the wildcat financing, were the minority who formed the educated and moneyed class in the community. On the other hand, those who demanded the "cheap money" which in their opinion would cure the very evil of which it was in fact the cause, or which they counted upon to help them pay their debts by enabling them to do so in a medium of decreased purchasing power, were the ignorant, the debtors and worse, who were in the majority. The advocates of paper money were thus usually found in the assemblies, whereas the governors, Councilors and wealthy men were on the other side. The paper money advocates therefore early became identified with the "popular party" and helped to foster the bitter feeling between the men of the two frontiers of which we spoke in an earlier chapter, and the conservative class of the old settlements. As England had necessarily to throw the weight of her authority on the side of honesty and sound money, she shared largely in the resentment felt by the men of the border and the lower classes

---

[1] Felt, *Currency*, pp. 72 *f.* *Cf.* also Connecticut's offer to join with the other New England governments to remedy the evil, Jan. 23, 1719. *Records of Governor and Council of Connecticut, 1712-28*, Mss. in Library of Congress.

[2] Pitman, *West Indies*, pp. 141 *ff.*

in the towns. It is difficult to overrate the influence of the long drawn battle over the currency upon the development of party spirit within the colonies and of that between them and the mother country.

Just at the time that this contest was adding its influence to the drawing of a party distinction between what may be considered the little colonial aristocracy of wealth and privilege, and the people generally, and while the extension of the frontier — from now on to be almost continuous — was bringing its democratic tendencies to bear upon the life of New England, other influences were also at work to develop the popular ideals of liberty and democracy. A quarter of a century earlier, Locke had published his second essay on "Civil Government" which was of the most profound influence upon American thought and was even to provide phrases for the Declaration of Independence. The simple society of America, whether represented by the mechanic or tradesman in the towns or the settler in his clearing on the frontier, agreed almost by instinct with such dicta as that "the natural liberty of man is to be free from any superior power on earth, and not to be under the will or legislative authority of man, but to have only the law of nature for his rule," or that men being "by nature all free, equal, and independent" have the right to the uncontrolled enjoyment of their "life, liberty, and estate." [1]

In the preceding century, colonial thought in New England on political matters had been hampered at every turn by being conditioned by the Biblical and theological standpoint. Democracy was implicit in the Mayflower compact and in the many church and town covenants, but for the most part it had not been so recognized by the leaders of thought and action in the Puritan colonies, who with John Winthrop had repudiated it as "the meanest and worst of all forms of government." [2] But in the beginning of the eighteenth century the works of the English political writers of the liberal school, Locke, Sidney, Cumberland and others, were beginning noticeably to influence colonial thought which was moving rapidly from the field of religion to that of politics.

[1] John Locke, *Of Civil Government*, (London, 1905), pp. 20, 54, 60.
[2] *Cf.* Adams, *Founding of New England*, pp. 143*f.*

Although it was a church dispute that brought forth the two volumes from the man who has been called "the first great American democrat" yet both the spirit and the language of the works of the Reverend John Wise are far removed from the theological wrangling of the Puritan period. When arguing against democracy, Winthrop had considered as a valid argument that it would be "a manifest breach of the 5th Commandment" and that there "was no such government in Israel." [1] Wise, on the other hand, writes that "there is no particular form of civil government described in God's word, neither does nature prompt it. The government of the Jews was changed five times." [2] Government, he declares to be "the effect of human free-compacts and not of divine institution," and that it is solely "the product of man's reason." He finds the only motive for its establishment to lie in the safety and happiness of the individual — its only end "to cultivate humanity, and promote the happiness of all, and the good of every man in all his rights, his life, liberty, estate, honor." "All power," he says, "is originally in the people." One of the natural "immunities" of man, he finds to be "an equality amongst men, which is not to be denied by the law of nature, till man has resigned himself with all his rights for the sake of a civil state." Agreeably to his doctrine of equality, he considers democracy to be the most ancient form of government, and that possibly "the fairest in the world" is "a regular monarchy settled upon a noble democracy as its basis." Speaking of the form of church government which will least expose "people to hazard, either from the fraud, or arbitrary measures of particular men," he declares that "it is as plain as daylight, there is no species of government like a democracy to attain this end. There is but two steps from an aristocracy, to a monarchy, and from thence but one to a tyranny." [3]

Belonging to the school of Locke, although he derived his ideas more directly from the German Puffendorf to whom Locke

[1] *Life and Letters of John Winthrop*, (Boston, 1869), vol. II, p. 430.

[2] *Vindication of the Government of the New England Churches*, (Boston, 1772). I quote from this later edition.

[3] *Ibid.*, pp. 18, 27, 43. *Cf.* Algernon Sidney, *Discourses concerning Government*, 2d edit. (London, 1705), pp. 11 *ff.*, 47 *ff.*, 115 *f.*

himself was indebted, the work of Wise contains many echoes
from an earlier day in New England itself. But just as Locke in
treating of the rights of the individual brought them out of the
atmosphere of abstraction in which they existed in the works of
his predecessors, and made them seem "the concrete privileges
of actual living men" and as the only legitimate end for which
government could exist,[1] so Wise by appealing to the law of
nature instead of scripture, by his disregard of the old theological distinctions between the elect and the unregenerate, and
by his insistence upon the natural equality of all men, and by
the brilliancy and force of the style in which he clothed his
thought, placed the doctrines of liberty, of equality and of the
people as the only source of power, in a far more vital relation
to contemporary thought than had his forerunners in the preceding century either in Rhode Island or Connecticut. The
founders of the most powerful colony in New England had
grounded such rights as they grudgingly admitted individuals
might possess in the civil government solely upon their being
the elect of God. But "it is impossible to reconcile the Puritan
ideal of a reign of the Saints with the ideal of a Government
founded on consent"[2] and the Puritan doctrine had to be
utterly destroyed before American democracy could take its
place. These rights of the individual, Wise derived wholly from
the social necessities of men and from their inherent equality and
liberty in a state of nature. We thus pass into a new field of discussion and enter upon political ground occupied a half century
later in the controversy with the mother country.

The seed had been sown, and the soil of colonial life was
every year becoming more suited to its growth. Quite as much
as the ideas of Sidney, Locke, Wise and of others, which were
blown about by the winds of doctrine, the conditions of existence in New England, more particularly in the rural and frontier sections, were developing a deep-rooted and instinctive
belief that political rights were not derived from government
but from something inherent in the nature of man himself. The
authorities at Yale, in 1714, might warn the students against

[1] W. A. Dunning, *A History of Political Theories*, (New York, 1919), vol. II, p. 364.
[2] Maitland, *Collected Papers*, vol. I, p. 16.

the works of the philosophers then "all in vogue" there; [1] the
aristocratic Mathers might battle with Wise, the son of an
indented servant; the privileged class in the seaboard towns
might struggle against the "leveling tendencies" of the time;
but all in vain. The boundless continental expanse of free land
offered a barrier against which such efforts broke as hopelessly
as the waves against New England's shore.

Throughout all her colonies, the men in the rural sections and
on the border, although literate to a fair degree in the more
settled portions, were for the most part ignorant of books and
of life outside their extremely restricted range of personal observation. One has only to picture the condition of any remote
rural section he may know today, and to think of it in terms of
no transportation, of only the most primitive sort of lowest
grade schools, of no libraries, books, magazines or newspapers,
to gain some idea of the life of the masses in the colonial period
outside of the very few larger towns. It was from such sections
that in the main were made up the assemblies in each of the
New England colonies. The governors, elected by the freemen
in Connecticut and Rhode Island, appointed by the crown in
New Hampshire and Massachusetts, were usually men of property and of standing. The Councils, also, as a rule, were made
up of the more conservative and well-to-do men from the larger
centers, but as the deputies in the assemblies were elected solely
by the voters of the several towns which the deputies represented and in which they had to live, it was in those bodies that
the thought of the country and frontier was most directly and
uncompromisingly evident.

The clashes were constant between these assemblies and the
governors and councils, the latter representing education,
wealth, social standing and power, whereas the deputies represented a people largely ignorant and exceedingly narrow, whose
only property was in the lands they tilled or the labor of their
hands, and who were frequently in debt to the merchants and

---

[1] E. C. Smith, "The 'New Philosophy' against which students of Yale College were
warned in 1714," *American Antiquarian Society Proceedings*, New Series, vol. XI, p. 252.
Cumberland's *De Legibus Naturae*, 1694, was early put in the Yale library, and the
second edition of 1727 soon after publication. Foster, *Genetic History of New England
Theology*, p. 48 *n.*

landowners of the older settlements. Owing to the overshadow-
ing fact that in most colonies the governor and council were of
royal appointment, the struggle against them by the assemblies
has been made to assume merely the appearance of a struggle of
the colonist against royal authority, of a contest for liberty
against English oppression. It was so in part, as it was bound to
be under that particular form of colonial machinery,[1] but for a
considerable portion of the century it was in reality quite as
much a struggle between two sections of the community based
upon the opposition of the frontier to the old settlement, of the
country to the town, of labor to capital, and of the pioneer's
dislike of all restraint.

This will come before us over and over again, even in the case
of Massachusetts, but in Connecticut we may study the situation with no complicating element of royal appointees. That
colony, as we have frequently pointed out, was almost an independent republic. She elected all her own officials, she had
practically no communication with the home government, her
laws were not subject to review, there was no representative of
the crown within her borders. If the constant bickerings of the
assemblies, those "Guardians of the Peoples' Liberty" as the
Massachusetts pamphleteers called them,[2] with governors and
councils were directed in reality only against royal usurpation,
then here there should have been profound peace. It might be
that the British lion and the colonial lamb could never be taught
to lie down together, but here there were none but lambs to
frisk in friendly frolic. Yet in 1724, to lift the veil at one corner,
on the occasion of electing a governor to fill the unexpired term
due to the death of Saltonstall, the lower house was so insistent
in its obstruction that the Council had to abdicate its function
and resign its rights "rather than run the hazard of our charter,"
and to allow the two houses to vote as one, which meant that
the more numerous deputies would outvote the smaller number
of Councilors.[3] Saltonstall himself, a few years earlier, had been

---

[1] The history of Canada from 1791 to 1837 is in the main that of the same struggle
between an assembly elected by the colonists and a governor appointed by the crown
with which we Americans are so familiar. C. P. Lucas, *Lord Durham's Report*, (Oxford,
1912), vol. I, p. 34.

[2] *English Advice to the Freeholders, etc. of the Prov. of Mass. Bay*, (Boston, 1722).

[3] *Conn. Col. Records*, vol. VI, pp. 483 f.

so hampered by the intractableness of the assembly that he declined for a time to accept his tenth nomination as governor. So used have we become to thinking of opposition to colonial governors as opposition to royal "tyranny" that it is well to ponder the words with which this popularly elected chief magistrate in the most independent of all the colonies declined to accept the burden of ruling his free people again. So firmly persuaded is he, he says, that law and order are "fit and necessary for upholding not only the honor but the usefulness and even being of government, that it 's impossible for me to do otherwise. Now if this be like to beget and increase an uneasiness among the people, if the maintaining some small degree of that respect due to government be not agreeable with our Constitution, it will be much better I should resign my charge, and never trouble others or myself any further with what in my opinion is so necessary and in theirs so grievous."[1] Against this governor, at least, his constituents were not struggling in opposition to royal authority or supposed oppression. Although the people's own elected representative, he was almost overcome, as were in part the royal governors, by the spirit of the frontier, — its lawlessness, its ignorance, its provinciality, and its self-assertiveness. Nor were disputes over salaries, the importance of which in imperial relations cannot be overestimated, confined alone to those colonies which had a royal chief executive. Saltonstall himself was engaged for some years in a contest with the Connecticut assembly over his own trifling salary of £200 which that colony claimed to be too poor to pay in full. When he accepted office again after the election of 1724, he had a dignified speech spread on the minutes of the Council in which he said of the salary, with biting sarcasm, "let us forget the debates we have had about it, and be as careful of husbanding our time in the publick affairs as we seem to be of our money in this particular instance."[2]

One of the main threads in the colonial story is thus not merely the steady encroachment of the legislatures upon the power of the executive, but of the lower houses upon the upper,

---

[1] Cited from Mss. by Palfrey, *History*, vol. IV, pp. 493 *f*.
[2] *Conn. Col. Records*, vol. VI, p. 443 and note.

that is of the people at large upon the small class privileged by wealth, education and position. It is impossible in a single volume to recount the movement in the several colonies in all its details. In Massachusetts, during the few years of Shute's administration, the assembly advanced its claims so fast and with such pertinacity as to result in the governor's return to England and practical abdication. His relations, indeed, with the General Court were almost impossible from the beginning. Though given the usual instructions from home to require the granting of a fixed salary, he was no more successful in that point than his predecessors or successors, and that particular contest presents no unusual features, except that it was marked by the characteristically bad manners of the legislature during those years. When at the end of his first six months of office, the Court granted him £300 in depreciated bills, in consideration of his assurance of watching out for their interests, both the amount and the terms of the grant were insulting, but the governor contented himself with thanking the legislators and ironically remarking that the sum would "help in defreying the Charge of my Transportation." [1]

In his efforts to reduce the evils of paper money he failed as completely as in those to secure a fixed salary. The paying of the expenses of government by issuing notes due several years later instead of collecting taxes was too alluring. In 1721, however, not only was the governor forced to consent to the issue of £50,000 redeemable only in from five to nine years, but the deputies in the same session tried to secure still greater control over the finances by distinctly limiting the uses of each sum granted. Although this was an encroachment upon the coördinate rights of the Council, and that body attempted to defeat the assembly, it was unsuccessful and the deputies won the point.

The contest was carried on after Shute's abrupt departure in 1723, when the lieutenant-governor, Dummer, was administering affairs, and the colony was engaged in the war with the eastern Indians. As the deputies refused to vote supplies even for bills already legally incurred by the Court or for the abso-

[1] *Collection of the Proceedings*, p. 27.

lutely necessary expense of the war, without the obnoxious requirement, the Council finally had to yield rather than incur the dangers which the deputies refused to consider.[1] The financial disputes were thus becoming a matter between the deputies and Councilors rather than between the people and the governor, and reached another acute stage in 1727 which well displays both the temper and ignorance, not to say dishonesty, of the lower house. The notes issued in 1723–4 were then drawing due, and provision was necessary for meeting them. The Council requested that the assembly initiate the required legislation for the purpose, whereupon the deputies impudently sent a message to the lieutenant-governor that having no business to transact they were ready to adjourn. When the necessity of redeeming the colony's credit and honor was again called to their attention, they replied that they had no responsibility for the engagements made by any former assembly. They added that if any such had been made which might seem to them detrimental, they would break them, and that as to the bills, the promise of the government to redeem them formed no element in their value which arose solely from the fact that they were accepted in circulation.[2]

In almost any legislature there might be found, perhaps, one or two members of no higher intelligence or integrity than is shown in such statements, but that such should be the considered judgment of a majority of the hundred members of the Massachusetts assembly is an extraordinary commentary upon the character of that body at this period. It more than bears out the governor's report that most of the deputies were men of "Small fortunes & meane Education."[3]

Under the terms of the charter, the power of adjourning the Court was vested in the governor, but in their general effort at encroachment the deputies attempted to draw a distinction between his power to adjourn the Court as a whole and their own claim to adjourn the assembly. They also refused to consider it within his province to designate the place of meeting, and when

---

[1] Davis, *Currency and Banking*, vol. I, pp. 65 *f*., 70 *ff*.

[2] *Ibid.*, vol. I, pp. 74 *f*.

[3] Memorial of Gov. Shute to the King, in W. S. Perry, *Historical Collections relating to the American Colonial Church*, (Hartford, 1873), vol. III, p. 122.

unable to make their points good expressed their resentment by voting him but £500 as salary, which was then worth about half that sum owing to the depreciation in the bills.[1] They also made an unsuccessful effort to encroach upon the right of the Council by attempting to make that much smaller body act "conjunctly" with the body of over one hundred deputies when the Court was acting in a judicial capacity, an attempt that recalls the similar effort at encroachment on the part of the Connecticut deputies.[2]

Yet another minor quarrel occurred between them and Shute over the election of a speaker for the assembly, which resulted in the colony's having to accept an explanatory charter in which the governor's negative voice was clearly defined, the terms of the original one of 1691 having been doubtful in this particular.[3]

One of the most serious aspects of this struggle of the lower branch of the legislature to absorb the legislative, judicial and executive powers of the government all into itself is found in connection with military affairs in the course of which the assembly endeavored to wrest control from Shute, Dummer and the Council alike. The treaty of Utrecht did not define the boundaries of Acadia but left them to be determined by commissioners of the two powers, who did not meet for forty years. The peace, however, led as we have seen to a rapid expansion of the frontier settlements, and English pioneers pressed into Maine as elsewhere. War had ceased between the two nations, and the French, therefore, could not oppose the English settlements by force, but there is ample evidence to show that they did not hesitate to urge on the savages to a cruel warfare against the peaceful pioneers.[4] Although without such urging, the natives

[1] Shute's Memorial, cit. supra, p. 123; The Report of the Lords of the Committee upon Governor Shute's Memorial, 1725, pp. 4 f.

[2] Citations from Council Records by Palfrey, History, vol. IV, p. 446.

[3] Shute's Memorial, cit. supra, p. 123; Report of the Lords, cit. supra, pp. 3 f. Cf. also Mr. Cooke's Just and Seasonable Vindication respecting some Affairs transacted in the late General Assembly, etc. (Boston 1720), pp. 9 ff.; and Representation of the Lords of Trade to the Lords Justices relative to the Encroachment upon the Royal Prerogative by the House of Representatives of Massachusetts Bay, Sept. 3, 1723, Brit. Mus. Add. Mss., 35908.

[4] J. P. Baxter, The Pioneers of New France in New England, (Albany, 1894), pp. 91, 93 ff., 265; Parkman, Half Century, vol. II, pp. 235, 237, 252; N. Y. Col. Docts., vol. IX, p. 936; Mr. Hamilton's Relation of Mons. Vaudreuil's Proceedings, Dec. 7, 1723, C.O. 5 No. 10.

would not have opposed the English by force, as apart from other reasons their trade was valuable, nevertheless, the advance of settlement brought in its train the usual difficulties and injustices between the whites and Indians, more particularly over land titles, and the natives felt, with some truth probably, that they had a grievance against the English.[1] It was the old story repeated on every advance of the whites into new territory. In 1717, Shute met the natives at a conference at Arrowsick Island, and although he handled the negotiations very badly, a new treaty of friendship was negotiated.[2]

The main instrument by which the French carried on their machinations was a Jesuit priest, Sebastien Rale, who was settled at the village of Norridgewock in Maine. Various minor conflicts had already occurred between the savages and the settlers, which promised to become serious, when in 1720 the priest sent a "railing letter" to Shute threatening the whole border, followed by one from the savages themselves in the following year.[3] War was considered unjust and unnecessary by Connecticut and by many in Massachusetts itself, although it is difficult to see how it was to be avoided unless the frontier were to be abandoned.[4] The Massachusetts assembly was anxious to march troops to the border, and the feeling between them and the governor was increased by his refusal to sanction such action, and delaying it again in the following year, 1721, in hope of avoiding a general war. In the following July, however, war was formally declared by him against the natives, and less formally, but quite as genuinely, by the assembly against the governor and Council.[5] The deputies not only insisted upon laying out the whole detailed plan for the campaign before voting any supplies, but demanded the discharge of the officers in command, which the governor as the rightful commander-in-chief of the province naturally refused. They also declined to pass a law for

[1] On Indian grievances, cf. Adams, *Founding of New England*, pp. 340 ff.; *N. Y. Col. Docts.*, vol. IX, pp. 941 ff.

[2] A verbatim report of the proceedings is in *N. H. Prov. Papers*, vol. III, pp. 693 ff. Cf. Baxter, *Pioneers, cit. supra*, pp. 68 ff.

[3] Printed by Baxter, *Pioneers*, pp. 96 ff., 111 ff.

[4] Parkman, *Half Century*, vol. II, p. 239; *Conn. Col. Records*, vol. VI, p. 335; *Talcott Papers*, (Conn. Hist. Soc. Coll., vols. IV and V) vol. I, pp. 32 ff., 42 ff.

[5] Palfrey, *History*, vol. IV, pp. 421 f.; Baxter, *Pioneers*, pp. 313 f.

mutiny and desertion, and instead sent a committee to visit the forces at the front. In accordance with a suggestion of the assembly, Shute had ordered an advance toward the Penobscot under Colonel Walton, which plan had to be changed justifiably on account of altered circumstances. The deputies immediately requested the governor to send an express to Walton "to appear forthwith before the House to give a reason wherefore the orders relating to the expedition had not been executed." The governor was naturally irritated by this exhibition of combined arrogance and ignorance, and refused the impertinent demand. The assembly next asked that the entire conduct of the war be managed solely by a committee consisting of four Councilors and seven deputies, in other words by themselves. This the Council refused by an unanimous vote. Meanwhile, the governor had sent for Walton to report, and when he arrived in Boston, the deputies requested to have him appear immediately before them. Shute replied that if there was to be a legislative inquiry it should be by the whole legislature and not one house only. Thereupon the assembly commanded Walton to appear, refusing to unite with the Council and insisting that they alone had the right to investigate the action of any person in the public service.[1] The carrying on of the government had become impossible and it was at this point that Shute left for England. The change in the chief executive, however, made no alteration in the attitude assumed by the deputies. An election had resulted in returning a house even more ignorant and narrow-minded than the last. Its members demanded from Dummer, the lieutenant-governor, that the two military commanders be dismissed from service without even receiving the back pay due them, but both Dummer and the Council refused to sanction this wholly unwarranted and unjust demand. Thereupon the house stated that they would vote no more supplies unless their orders were complied with, and Dummer, fearing to take the responsibility for what might happen on the frontier, was forced to consent. The officers were discharged, and Walton remained unpaid because he had obeyed the orders

---

[1] Palfrey, *History*, vol. IV, pp. 426 *ff.*; *Journal of the House of Representatives of Massachusetts*, 1723, p. 63.

of his commander-in-chief instead of those of the "narrow-minded rustics" who had possessed no authority over him whatever.[1]

The story of the military operations before peace was finally declared in 1725 offers only the usual incidents of border warfare against savages, and cannot be recited in detail though it would be a relief to turn from the doings of the factious and irresponsible legislators to those of the gallant Americans who did the fighting, and to tell once more the ballad tale of "Lovewell's Fight." [2] Neither Connecticut, except for some defensive measures taken for her own frontier, nor Rhode Island had accorded any aid, although both had been asked. It is interesting to note that the Massachusetts deputies, who were so pertinaciously defying constituted authority, seeking to absorb all the power of governor and Council into their own incapable hands, and refusing to vote supplies to protect their own frontiers, nevertheless had the audacity to ask England to require the two neighboring colonies to furnish quotas of men and money. Even Connecticut, jealous of the slightest suggestion of control by England in her own affairs, considered applying to her to force Rhode Island and New York similarly to assist in her defence.[3]

The struggle in which the Massachusetts deputies had been engaged had not been one for efficiency of operations nor directed against royal authority as such. The substitution of a debating body of a hundred members in place of an individual as commander-in-chief of an army engaged in active operations in the field was a farce, and the other encroachments that they attempted were quite as much against the Council as against the governor. Nevertheless, the significance of the story is great, for it clearly exhibits the working upward toward political self-consciousness of those democratic elements that were to be

---

[1] The characterization is Parkman's. *Half Century*, vol. II, p. 243.

[2] The treaty is in Penhallow, *Indian Wars*, pp. 119 ff. For Lovewell, *vide* F. Kidder, *The Expedition of Capt. John Lovewell*, (Boston, 1865). T. Symmes, *The original Account of Capt. John Lovewell's "Great Fight,"* ed. N. Bouton, (Concord, 1861).

[3] Memorial to His Majesty, June 25, 1725; Memorial of J. Dummer to Duke of Newcastle, n. d. — both in *C.O. 5 No. 10*; *Conn. Col. Records*, vol. VI, pp. 335, 425, 435, 502 f., 512; *R. I. Col. Records*, vol. IV, pp. 320, 351 ff.; *Records of Governor and Council of Connecticut, 1712–28*, Mss. in Library of Congress, pp. 200 f., 205 f., 257 f.

of profound influence both upon the imperial and domestic relations of the colonies. It was the men of the lower economic and social classes in Boston, the men of the narrow life of the back country villages, the men of the fields and frontiers, who were demanding that the governor, whether royal or not, and the merchants and socially elect who formed the Councils, should turn over to them the entire control of the government. They were men of restricted views, of little experience, and in great degree ignorant both of government and of the problems which they claimed the right to solve.

Much has been written of the New England town meeting as a school for political education, but the picture has other sides, two of which we have touched upon elsewhere. Moreover, although the importance of strong and vital local institutions can hardly be overrated, yet it may be questioned whether the extraordinary absorption in the petty matters of local jurisdiction as developed in the town meeting did not do something to destroy the wider interest of the voter and to provincialize his thought. The open discussion gave him, indeed, fluency in debate and a certain sense of responsibility for his government, but it also gave him enormous conceit. He came to believe himself capable of solving every question in all its details. He also came to envisage the whole matter of administration in both colony and empire as though it were a village matter of fence building or road mending. Thus in attempting to destroy the executive power of the governor, and the coördinate legislative power of the Council, the deputies were in reality trying to reduce the governmental machinery to the simple formula of a town meeting, of a single debating body before which every question of every sort should be brought and by which every action should be taken.

Their efforts were a phase in that continuous movement for the transfer of power to the people as a whole and of their demand for an increasingly direct influence upon affairs of which we have not yet seen the end, and of which it is too early yet, perhaps, to judge the ultimate effect. The popular movement was directed equally against privilege in any form — the speculator who claimed title to wilderness lands, the merchant in his seaboard counting house, and the local aristocrat comfortable in an assured social position — as well as officials representing royal authority from overseas. That in its progress it broke the bonds which bound the colonies to the mother country was incidental to a far wider sweep of events. That its leaders proved themselves ignorant in many cases, as in that of the currency question, or lawless, as they have done on every frontier and in every revolution, was inherent in its nature. In the following chapter we will examine another incident in the struggle against the Massachusetts governor and the frontier spirit which well illustrates the latter aspect, and it only remains here to call attention to the harmony between the doctrines of the philosophers who were gaining the ear of the younger Americans and the political action of the latter. Wise's dicta that all men are by nature free and equal, and that all power originates in the people and returns to them, were being applied, consciously or not, by the deputies in their struggles to grasp the whole power of government. There was, indeed, no talk, perhaps no thought, as yet, of throwing off the imperial connection. There was something far deeper at work — an attempt to gather all power into the hands of the common people, an attempt to destroy all privilege, political, economic and social. This was not a movement peculiar to the American colonies. The same desires and aspirations were beginning to stir in the common people of England and the common people of France. As in colonial philosophy the changes furnished "an almost chronological reduplication of the European cycles," [1] so in the colonial revolutionary movement, the colonists but felt the influence of a current which was flowing through the life of eighteenth-century Europe as well. In America it was vastly accelerated and deeply influenced by the frontier conditions which heavily weighted the scale toward democracy and radicalism, but though modified it was not unique. The civil war between England and her colonies and the separation that ensued cannot be interpreted in terms of royal governors or of Parliamentary acts. One might as well interpret an eruption of Vesuvius in terms of the action of human beings on its vine-clad slopes. The

---

[1] Riley, *American Philosophy*, p. 11.

crust of society in America was new and thin. The eruptive forces broke through there sooner than in Europe but they were the same. In the relations of the colonies to the mother country throughout the eighteenth century, various events modified the feeling of the colonists, and hastened or retarded the final event. They are therefore of interest in tracing the development of the drama, but the final outcome loses its significance if considered only as a political event and not as deeply rooted in the social revolutionary movement of modern society.

CHAPTER VII

DIVERGING INTERESTS

Beginning of the Industrial Revolution — Rise of Colonial Capitalists — English Colonial Policy — The King's Woods — Frontier Commercial Ethics — Land Titles — Connecticut Intestacy Case — The Charters — Dispute over Burnett's Salary

In an earlier day, historians were wont to treat the gradually diverging interests of Englishmen in the eighteenth century mainly as a growing conflict between England and her continental colonies. A more detached point of view, increasing knowledge of human nature, and the immense amount of work done by scholars on the documents of the period, have enabled us to realize that the story is far more involved than that, and we are no longer content with "simple ideas of complex facts."

The gradually broadening lines of cleavage between the colonies and the mother country need no particular comment here. Three other spheres of diverging interest between Englishmen in various parts of the empire, however, must be taken into consideration in order to understand the better-known story of New England's opposition to old England. Two of these — the divergence between the newly developing sections and classes in New England itself, and the conflict of material interest between those colonies and the Sugar Islands — have already been discussed and will be again even at the risk of wearisome repetition, for the period is characterized not so much by incident as by continuing causes and tendencies, all gradually growing more and more effective until they culminate in the final tragedy of civil war and revolution.

The third instance of these diverging interests is to be found in the beginning of clearly marked class conflict in the mother country herself. As contrasted with mere demands for higher wages, the so-called "Industrial Revolution" used to be thought of as beginning with the introduction of machinery, but in the light of recent research that beginning must now be pushed considerably further back. The early eighteenth century, as we have pointed out in another connection, was marked by a great growth of capital seeking investment, and by the development of the instrument of credit which multiplied many-fold the economic power of those already possessing some capital in the form of money or of goods. It was not a time of great or general economic distress, but it was one in which were becoming distinctly evident those alterations in the structure of English economic society which were so to affect the opinions and philosophy of those in power as to result in a complete reversal of the relations between the government and the laboring class of the community, and to a considerable extent of those of the mother country to the colonies. It was not, however, until 1756, in those momentous mid-years of the century, that the revolutionary change culminated in the embarking by Parliament upon a new industrial policy. Conditions, nevertheless, had been steadily developing in one industry after another from the beginning of the century which made that policy seem natural to the country's rulers, however radical it may have looked to its laborers and operatives.[1]

In many industries the necessity for having a much larger amount of capital than had been customary in the past, or than was within the possibility of an artisan's acquiring, was gradually taking from him the chance of ceasing to be a paid workman and becoming a "master" himself. In other words, technical skill without capital was becoming powerless to permit the emergence of the workman from the class of the mere wage earner. With the steadily rising scale of living as exemplified by the well-to-do, there had come in the past constant demands for increased wages from laborers and artisans, although in many cases the interests of employer and employed were recognized by both as being the same in spite of such struggles over the division of profits. But with the increasing necessity for capital, and in quantities greater than the wage earner could accumulate from the products of his labor, there began that

[1] Sidney and Beatrice Webb, *The History of Trade Unionism*, (London, 1911), p. 44.

"definite separation between the functions of the capitalist and the workman" which is "the fundamental fact in the modern organization of labor." [1]

This naturally occurred earliest in such trades as tailoring, woollen manufacturing, the worsted industry and others which lent themselves most readily to division of labor, and so to control by capital. The influence upon the whole industrial outlook of this new cleavage between the industrial capitalist and a class of operatives permanently dependent upon wages was profound. Under the simpler conditions of earlier days, the manual workers had been accustomed to look to Parliament for protection in maintaining their standard of living but the problems now arising were too complex to be solved readily by either workmen or legislature. The paramount interests of the country were by everyone considered to be those of foreign trade, and those seemed to require the greatest possible production of goods for export at the lowest possible cost — a condition which redounded to the benefit of the capitalist and to the detriment of the laborer. Subtly but rapidly the interests of the human worker were giving way to the interests of capital. The capitalists of the new type were becoming more and more influential in Parliament, but we cannot consider the policies which they initiated as wholly dictated by a conscious selfishness. Little by little, however, they were being brought to the point of view which permitted a Parliamentary committee a century later to report to the house that "the right of every man to employ the capital he inherits or has acquired, according to his own discretion, without molestation or obstruction, so long as he does not infringe on the rights or property of others, is one of those privileges which the free and happy constitution of this country has long accustomed every Briton to consider as his birthright." [2]

We cannot here digress so far as to trace the development of facts and theory which led Parliament to doctrines so completely opposed to its earlier ones regarding its mediating function with reference to the economic welfare of all classes in the state. Nor can we discuss what were those rights of others which

---

[1] Dr. J. K. Ingram, cited by Webb, *Trade Unionism*, p. 25.
[2] Cited by Webb, *Trade Unionism*, p. 56.

according to capitalist opinion in the latter part of the eighteenth
century were the only limitations upon the enjoyment of wealth
solely according to the discretion of its fortunate possessor.
They were distinctly, however, not those rights which the mass
of English workmen, without a voice in the election of the legislative body under "the free and happy constitution," were coming to feel were those of the individual to political liberty and a
decent standard of living. Nor were they those "natural rights"
to "life, liberty and the pursuit of happiness" which philosophy
and the frontier were causing to seem axiomatic to the artisans
and farmers in America. But it is of supreme importance that
they and their fellow classes in England were being led by
events to assume the undoubted existence of those "natural
rights" with all that they implied, whereas the governing class
at home, and to a considerable extent the conservative class on
the colonial seaboard, were growing to be firm believers in "natural wages" and the "rights of property" with all that *they* implied. The conflict between the wage earners and the capitalists
at home, between the classes in America, and between England
and the colonists as a whole, in this aspect of it, was thus far
deeper than a mere dispute over wages or laws regulating manufactures and trade. It was rooted in utterly differing conceptions of primary values in human life.

On the one hand, the group in control of the organs of government were coming to lay the whole stress upon rights of property regardless of the "natural rights" of the individual human
being. On the other, multitudes of such human beings were
coming to lay their whole stress upon what they considered
their "natural rights" — too often a euphemism for natural
desires — with but little respect, when they conflicted, for the
rights of capital. The rapid economic development of the century hurried both parties along the road which was eventually
to lead to conflict within England, within the colonies, and between the two. It is not a mere coincidence that the years following 1756 which saw in England that "revolutionary change in
the industrial policy of the legislature which must have utterly
bewildered the [English] operatives" [1] saw also those innova-

[1] Webb, *Trade Unionism*, p. 44.

tions in England's dealing with the colonies which hastened the coming of revolution and civil war. The slow gathering of strength by the forces which produced that final imperial catastrophe have been obscured by the overemphasis which the rapidly moving and dramatically appealing political events of the decade from 1765 to 1776 have seemed to demand. Having thus briefly noted the beginning in England of some of the conditions leading to the events of the latter years, we must return to the farms and towns and limitless forests of New England to consider further aspects of our local story.

In the earlier part of the eighteenth century conditions there, as in all the colonies, were not favorable to the growth of manufactures, which, as we have just noted, were beginning to operate as a new force in the mother country and in her colonial relations. Not only did colonial capital, as in all new countries, tend to assume a fixed form in land, but the lack of currency and of a sound system of finance, with the resulting instability of prices, militated against both investment in manufacturing plants and their profitable operation. These were still further hampered by the scarcity of skilled labor and the high wages paid to all colonial workmen due to the presence of free land and the opportunities offered to the agriculturist to rise from the wage earning to the propertied class.[1]

It is true that colonial fortunes had begun to accumulate and that in the first quarter of the century they assumed larger proportions than had been the case in the preceding one. Thomas Amory, a Boston merchant who died in 1728, at the age of forty-five, left an estate there valued at £20,000 without counting his property in Carolina and the Azores. A little later, Peter Faneuil, another merchant, had accumulated a fortune sufficient to allow of having £14,800 of Bank of England stock as well as other stocks and bonds in the home country.[2] That an active New England business man should have had so large an

---

[1] V. S. Clark, *History of Manufactures in the United States, 1607–1860*, (Washington, 1916), pp. 123, 145.

[2] Weeden, *Economic and Social History*, vol. II, pp. 571, 618. Gov. Belcher, in 1733, estimated his own fortune at from £60,000 to £70,000 colonial currency or at least £20,000 sterling. *Belcher Papers*, (Mass. Hist. Soc. Coll., Ser. VI, vols. VI and VII), vol. I, p. 315.

amount invested in English securities is a commentary on the lack of investment opportunities other than those in trade and land in America. There were, of course, the fishing industry and lumbering, including small saw-mills run by water power, and also shipbuilding, but all the conditions of colonial life combined to foster individual rather than corporate enterprise, and the safe investment of surplus capital in liquid form required its transfer to the old country.[1]

The liquid capital which from now on began to accumulate in the hands of individuals was for the most part derived from commerce and merchandising, and found its greatest profit in those branches of business. In the first quarter of the century, English goods could be sold in New England for two and one half times their prime cost, and as liberal advantage was also taken of the depreciating currency, an additional profit could be made from that source.[2] But as wealth accumulated in the counting houses of the seaport merchants, who did business, comparatively speaking, on a large scale, competition with them became more and more difficult. An industrious mechanic or farm hand might readily accumulate enough capital in a few years to become his own master in a trade or handicraft or to buy a bit of a farm in outlying sections. He remained, however, strongly individualistic as contrasted with the growing capitalism of the merchant class, which was becoming in every way closely akin to the developing capitalistic society in England. Just as the divergence of interest between the wage-earner and employer in that country was coming about from the increasing difficulty for the former of passing over into the class of the latter, so a marked divergence was developing in the colonies between the privileged merchant class, with its entrenched advantages of wealth, education and social position, and the farmers, mechanics and tradesmen who were beginning to find it more and more difficult to surmount the barriers which kept them out of the classes above them, a condition which was the more irritating from the simultaneous growth of the doctrine of equality. A careful analysis of political conditions during much of the cen-

---

[1] Clark, *Manufactures in the U. S.*, p. 145.
[2] *Ibid.*, p. 148.

tury shows that the contests were quite as frequent between these elements in colonial life as between the colonies and the mother country, examples of which we will have to note in the present chapter, as we did in the last. On the other hand the colonial merchant on account of his investments, his business relations, and particularly the credit there extended to him, was bound by the closest of ties to England. He was in constant fear of the unsound ideas and radicalism of the colonial "mob," and looked to the imperial connection to afford stability. He looked down socially upon the ignorant, bumptious and cantankerous lower orders in the colonies, and up to the great names of social life in the old country.

In that country when Walpole was called on to take charge of the disordered finances as First Lord of the Treasury in 1721, one of the fundamental features of his policy was to make England a great manufacturing and trading nation.[1] The "colonial system" of the day consisted in the main of a mass of trade legislation of great complexity "based on the idea of the mutual reciprocity of the economic interests of mother country and colony."[2] In this reciprocal system, the chief value and function of the colonies had originally been thought to lie in their supplying the mother country with the raw materials necessary for her manufactures, but in the eighteenth century a second conception came into vogue which regarded them as protected markets for those manufactures.[3] Although this altered conception was more particularly influential after the middle of the century, the legislation, as well as economic writings, which from

---

[1] Brisco, *Economic Policy of Walpole*, p. 209.

[2] Beer, *British Colonial Policy*, pp. 193 *ff*. Free trade was advocated by a few far in advance of their times but had to wait nearly a century for a favorable hearing. *Cf.* e.g. an article in *The political State of Great Britain*, vol. XLIII, pp. 20 *ff*. "We may as well think to fix the kind and gentle Breezes of the Summer, as think to confine the Course of any Trade to the Island of Great Britain. . . . It being thus impossible to fix any Sort of Trade or Manufacture to any one Province or Country, I therefore never can think it a good Politick to prohibit any Sort of Trade or Manufacture in any Part of the British Dominions; Trade must circulate, and since it must, let it for God's Sake circulate among our own Dominions as long as it possibly can; if any of our Colonies be ever able to undersell us in any Sort of Manufacture, or to incroach upon us in any Branch of Trade, Foreigners certainly may; and if we must lose any Branch of our present Trade, surely it is more for our Interest, to let it go to one of our Colonies than to let it go to Strangers." *Cf.* also, *ibid.*, vol. XLIV, pp. 536 *f.*

[3] Beer, *cit. supra*, pp. 135 *ff*.

its beginning were directed against the setting up of other than household manufacturing in the colonies, had in view the protection of the English manufacturer at the expense of any possible colonial competitor. As we have noted, the woollen industry was among the first to undergo transformation in England, and the laws prohibiting the manufacture of wool in the plantations, except as a household industry, were the first which attempted to limit the entire freedom of the colonists in this regard. From time to time other restrictive measures were asked for by special interests, but although such legislation, like our own protective tariffs, was bound to be sectional in character, the policy of the government was not a narrowly British one.[1]

In regard to the woollen industry one important fact must be kept in mind. The impression is sometimes given that the large population of the colonies was being exploited for the benefit of a small group of manufacturers at home, but this is by no means borne out by the facts. In the colonies there were no manufacturers, properly speaking, of woollen goods, and the poor man who had his wool spun in his own home was not within the scope of the law. But aside from this, not only was the industry considered the most fundamentally important one in Great Britain, accounting for nearly one-half of her exports, but the number of people said to be affected by it was about fifty per cent greater than the entire population of the American colonies. In 1739, for example, it has been estimated that one million five hundred thousand persons were dependent upon the trade in England,[2] whereas the entire population of English America was not over a million. The attempt by the government to nip in the bud any colonial competition that might endanger the industry at home, interfere with the livelihood of so enormous a proportion of England's total population, and endanger her balance of trade with foreign countries, must be considered to have

---

[1] *Cf.* the fears for the iron forges in 1729, *Talcott Papers*, vol. I, pp. 169, 220. The so-called "Hat Act," which prevented exportation from the colonies of any hats manufactured there and limited the number of apprentices, was enacted for the benefit of the English manufacturer in 1732. 5 Geo. II, cap. 22. John Adams said it was never observed in the colonies. *Works*, (Boston, 1851), vol. IV, p. 49.

[2] Brisco, *Economic Policy of Walpole*, p. 178.

been a reasonable one, little as the colonists relished any restrictions on their entire freedom of action and occupation.

In fact, the genuine desire of the government, as shown both by the legislation it enacted and by its resistance in many instances to legislation demanded, was to make of the empire a coördinating economic whole. The prohibition of certain colonial manufactures, although a cause of some friction, in all probability did not entail any serious economic loss upon the colonists and was not brought forward as a serious grievance by them until later years.[1] On the other hand, the English government by a system of drawbacks, bounties and other financial methods endeavored to increase the prosperity of the colonies in other lines. Partly in an effort to create a profitable trade for the New Englanders, and partly to make England independent of the Baltic countries, bounties were continually made use of to stimulate the production of naval stores. A certain John Bridger was sent over to instruct the people in the making of tar, resin, pitch and turpentine and although he was so far successful as to demonstrate to the suspicious New Englanders that by making tar they could earn enough money to buy two coats in the same time that it took them to make one, nevertheless, the industry never really took root.[2]

Closely connected with these attempts to establish what should have been a profitable colonial trade, was that source of perennial trouble: the question of lumber and the King's Woods. The magnificent forests of New England had been looked upon from the earliest days of settlement as affording the finest masts to be obtained anywhere for the royal navy, and in the beginning of the eighteenth century the so-called "mast fleet" sailed once a year with its precious cargo for the fitting out of the ships of war upon which the safety of the whole colonial system depended.

[1] Ashley, *Surveys, historic and economic*, pp. 320 *ff. Cf.* however, the citations from Eversfield given by Sioussat, *English Statutes*, pp. 58 *f.* note. It was stated in 1734 that owing to higher labor costs, linen cost 20% and woollen cloth 50% more to manufacture in the colonies than at home. Representation of the Commissioners for Trade and Plantations to Parliament, Jan. 23, 1733-4, *C.O. 5 No. 5.*

[2] Dickerson, *American Colonial Government*, p. 307; Eleanor Lord, *Industrial Experiments in the British Colonies of North America*, (Johns Hopkins Studies, 1898), pp. 1 *ff.*, 68 *ff.*; Council of Trade to the King, March 28, 1717, and July 6, 1715, *C.O. 5 No. 4.*

The preservation of the larger trees suitable for masts had indeed been a matter of solicitude upon the part both of the local colonial government and that of England for many years before the new charter granted to Massachusetts in 1691. By the last clause of that document there were reserved to the Crown all trees of a diameter of not less than twenty-four inches a foot from the ground and not growing upon lands already granted to private individuals. Commissioners, including Bridger, were sent over from time to time to report upon the possibilities, and Surveyors of the Woods were appointed to mark suitable trees with the "broad arrow" of the king, and to protect the rights of the English government.[1]

Lumbering, however, was one of the most profitable of colonial industries, more particularly in New Hampshire and Maine at this period, and the unpopular surveyors met with constant opposition both from the larger operators engaged in the trade and from the lawless elements in the lumber regions. The exports of lumber had been greatly increased by the growth of the West Indian trade, and this to some extent linked the interests of the frontiersman and the seaboard merchant together in this particular, and completely frustrated the efforts of the English government. During Shute's administration, Elisha Cooke, the leader of the "popular party," who was carrying on large speculative operations in wilderness lands and timber for his own account, was one of the most active opposers of the royal officers, and even advanced the theory that the Crown had no claim to any of the woods in Maine on account of the purchase of that province by Massachusetts from the heirs of Gorges in 1677, though this untenable and far-fetched view had few other supporters, if any.[2] This convenient doctrine, however, added to the creation of new towns by Massachusetts for the purpose of evading the law, may have helped to give a color of legality to the illegal depredations of the loggers, although such a veneer of righteousness was perhaps but little needed or heeded. The larger interests in lumber, as well as most of the successive

---

[1] Lord, *Industrial Experiments*, pp. 9 ff., 53 ff., 93 f.
[2] Adams, *Founding of New England*, p. 386; Lord, *Industrial Experiments*, pp. 113 ff.; *Maine Hist. Soc. Coll.*, vol. IX, pp. 383 f., 388 ff., 395.

lieutenant-governors of New Hampshire, were actively engaged in breaking the law for their own pecuniary advantage, and the whole population took sides with the loggers. It was thus impossible to secure convictions against the depredators — even in cases of violence — as judge and jury alike were on the side of the law-breakers. In the rush for private gain, magnificent trees suitable for masts were ruthlessly sacrificed, and sawn into planks or even split into shingles. By 1728 it was reported that scarce any trees were left standing within six or seven miles of the waterside between Boston and the Kennebec, and by the same date, the mast industry had been forced as far eastward as the present Portland, and far up the valley of the Connecticut. [1]

It is rather odd that we should find the lawlessness of the frontier in our later period of the "Far West" natural, interesting and picturesque, but consider it unpatriotic to suggest that any New Englanders of this earlier frontier period who found themselves in opposition to authority were anything but sober church-going citizens defending their liberties. The frontier always and everywhere breeds squatter doctrines and individualism. The speculator in a new land and the settler in the wilderness ever tend to disregard vested interests, distant authority, and any restraint placed upon their individual exploitation of the natural resources about them. When the people of New Hampshire burned the trees felled for the use of the English government, cut those marked with the board arrow, defied the royal surveyors, and boldly said that "the King has no woods here, and they will cut what and where they please" [2] they were not patriots defying royal tyranny. They were merely thoroughly characteristic frontiersmen defying all restraint. Let us interpret the events on the New England frontier of 1728 by those on the Minnesota frontier of 1852. Defending the lumbermen of that section, who were then engaged, like their colonial progenitors, in stealing government timber, that territory's delegate in Congress, speaking of the conservation laws,

---

[1] Lord, *Industrial Experiments*, p. 119; Weeden, *Economic and Social History*, vol. II, p. 578.
[2] Cited by Palfrey, *History*, vol. IV, p. 401.

said that "especially is he pursued with unrelenting severity, who has dared to break the silence of the primeval forest by the blows of the American axe. . . . After enduring all the privations and subjecting himself to all the perils incident to his vocation — when he has toiled for months to add by his *honest labor* to the comfort of his fellow men and to the aggregate wealth of the nation, he finds himself suddenly in the clutches of the law for trespassing on the public domain. The proceeds of his long winter's work are reft from him, and exposed to public sale for the benefit of his paternal government." [1]

In the colonial period the labeling of much of the disliked authority as "royal" obscures the real nature of the conflict of interest and of the bitterness engendered. The formula that explains many of the earlier issues is not patriotism against tyranny but merely the perfectly natural and universal opposition of squatter and frontier ideals to those of older settlements. Congressman Sibley, denouncing conservation in 1852 and defending the timber stealers of Minnesota as "honest" workers harassed by the government, was merely voicing the beliefs and ideals of the frontier against those of the East. As the quarrel in his day was all in the American family, its nature is clearly seen. Had the government against which he declaimed in favor of individualism, lawlessness and disregard of the future, been the English one of a century earlier, the rhetoric of the controversy would have been poured out against the "royal tyrant" instead of the "paternal government." The situation, as in many other cases, was a more universal one, the cleavage of thought deeper. In the constantly recurring troubles over the King's Woods, which marks so many years of the eighteenth century and which did so much to embitter the New Englanders of many sections against the English government, and in the later conflicts between the lumbermen and the federal government, the fundamentally sectional way of envisaging rights and property comes out clearly. There was a divergence not merely of interest but of economic philosophy, and the fact is of immense significance for both periods that such actions as England and, later, the American "East," regarded as stealing and law-

[1] Cited by Turner, *Frontier*, pp. 272 f. The italics are mine.

breaking, the colonies, and later the "West," should come to regard as "honest labor."

In connection with this matter of conservation of the royal timber, as in so many others, the radical element was naturally found for the most part in the country and frontier districts, reinforced by capitalists who took advantage of the situation for themselves. Opposition to authority was thus voiced mainly in the assembly, and in 1720 we find that body asserting the absurd claim, against the governor and Council, that the timber described as belonging to the Crown in the charter and subsequent laws did so only when standing, but that as soon as it was cut it belonged to the colony. It is little wonder that the Lords of Trade pronounced this fantastic doctrine of the lower house to be a "scandalous evasion." [1] It is amusingly enlightening to find the Massachusetts government five years later petitioning the king to require Rhode Island and Connecticut to furnish their quotas of men in the war against the French and Indians on the plea, among others, that if Massachusetts were forced to abandon Maine, his Majesty would lose his most valuable forests for masts! [2] When they wanted lumber, the king had no trees, but when they wanted help, then the woods were a royal asset. When England assigned them a quota to be met, it was an invasion of their rights as Englishmen, but when they required assistance, then England was to insist upon the other colonies furnishing it. The shock to our ancestor worship is somewhat lessened when we find the same selfish and naïvely illogical attitude on every frontier from Casco Bay to the Golden Gate, and from the island of Jamaica to the continent of Australia.

There is perhaps no more frequent cause of controversy along the fringe of civilization than land titles, and such was the case both in New Hampshire and in the more newly settled portions of Connecticut. In the former where the English government came in for a share of the resentment, as it did not in the prac-

---

[1] Representation of the Board of Trade to the Lords Justices, Sept. 3, 1723, *Brit. Mus. Add. Mss. 35908.*

[2] Memorial from Massachusetts to the King, June 25, 1725, *C.O. 5 No. 10.* Cf. Geo. Chalmers, *Opinions of eminent Lawyers on various Points of English Jurisprudence . . .* (London, 1814), pp. 110 ff., 115 ff., 136 ff.

tically republican government of Connecticut, the trouble arose mainly from the survival of disputes over the claims of Mason to the title of the province.[1] At the time of Dudley's administration New Hampshire contained only six towns, two of which were small, and the entire province was poverty stricken. Although only about one-third of it was included in the settled towns, the inhabitants were willing to allow those into whose hands the Mason claim had passed to assume ownership of the whole province outside the township limits.[2] Nevertheless, Samuel Allen who claimed title under transfer from the Mason heirs, attempted to assert a right to the commons within the towns as well.[3] Dudley, who was popular in New Hampshire if nowhere else, had evolved a statesman-like plan to settle the dispute forever, but it was never put into execution.[4] Following the Peace of Utrecht, the frontier in the little northern colony, as elsewhere throughout New England, began to be extended, and in 1719, during the period of the Scotch-Irish immigration, Lieutenant-governor Wentworth could give the new settlers only a qualified permission to settle beyond the limits of the already established towns. The founding of Londonderry was followed by grants to four other settlements which formed a new fringe of frontier around the older ones, but the grants could be made only in "as far as in us lies" on account of the uncertain claims of the assignee of the old province title.

The constant litigation and the uncertainty surrounding the inhabitants' titles to the lands they were improving could not fail to arouse a feeling of resentment, a contempt for law, and a rebellious attitude toward "vested interests." What with the recognized illegal trading in commerce, the lawless treatment of the woods, and the conflicts over land titles, it is little wonder that legal precedents should carry slight weight in New Hampshire, as has already been noted, and that the "rights of man" to "life, liberty and the pursuit of happiness" should not only become popular but develop an extremely inclusive meaning in that sparsely settled and outlying portion of the British empire.

[1] Adams, *Founding of New England*, loc. cit; Fry, *New Hampshire*, pp. 209 *ff.*
[2] *N. H. Prov. Papers*, vol. III, p. 275 *n.*
[3] Fry, *New Hampshire*, pp. 226 *ff.*
[4] Kimball, *Dudley*, pp. 141 *ff.*

Even in Connecticut, that "land of steady habits," disputes over real estate titles, in 1722, led to riotous demonstrations against court judgments, and a sufficient lapse in the habits to permit of an attack upon the Hartford jail and the delivery of some fifty popular prisoners.[1]

As we pointed out in the preceding volume, New England had originally been settled by emigrants to whom one of the greatest inducements had been the possibility of acquiring free land in fee simple.[2] It had become a country preëminently of small landholders, tenaciously devoted to their title deeds, and naturally regarding any attack upon them as overturning the very foundations of their liberties, as in truth they did. Massachusetts had had its experience with such an attack in the unwise and unjust, even if technically legal, course which Andros had pursued during his brief rule, and in rural communities memory is as long as mind is narrow. We have just noted how the question of titles was a running sore generation after generation in New Hampshire. Even Connecticut men, far removed as they seemed to be from control by England, were not to be free from the same fear engendered by a cloud on their own titles, for suddenly an exceedingly black one appeared over the Atlantic horizon and aroused consternation and terror.

As in most new countries, land was the most widely held form of property. In the majority of cases, it was, aside from a few utensils and a little household furniture, all of which a settler died possessed, and the custom had early originated of dividing the real estate of an intestate equally among the children, save that in accordance with the New Englanders' love for Moses, the eldest son received a double share. This method of division had been rendered necessary by the fact that owing to both climate and soil neither staple crops nor slave labor proved profitable in New England. Owing also to the scarcity of white labor and the high wages demanded, it was difficult for a man to farm profitably more land than he and his unmarried sons could cultivate themselves. So long as land remained cheap or

---

[1] *Conn. Col. Records*, vol. VI, pp. 322, 341 and note, 346, 387 *f*. There were also riots in 1733 in the land disputes with New York. *Talcott Papers*, vol. I, p. 277.

[2] Adams, *Founding of New England*, p. 419.

was granted by new towns, that amount could readily be acquired in fee. There was therefore practically no tenant farming, and the only way to secure an income from land was to farm it one's self. In England, the land left to the eldest son could be burdened with payments of income to the younger children. Not so, however, in New England, and this economic factor developing from physical conditions, not only overthrew one of the most deeply rooted features of the social system to which the settlers had been accustomed in the old world, but was a great element in nourishing the sense of equality and dislike of privilege in the new.

Quite apart from this conflict of colonial custom with English law, the fact had been clearly established during the Andros régime that in Massachusetts, at least, owing to technical faults in the grants to individuals by towns, scarcely a man held his farm or house lot by a valid title.[1] The sudden realization of this not only caused Connecticut to take speedy action to validate the town and individual grants, but evidently caused a searching of heart in all the colonies with reference to the customary mode of inheritance as well. In Massachusetts in 1692 during the second session of the Massachusetts legislature after the grant of the new charter, an act was passed by which the colonial custom of distributing the estates of intestates was enacted into law,[2] and this action was confirmed by the home government. A law for the same purpose, with exactly the same wording in the preamble, was enacted the following year in New Hampshire, and was among those sent home for approval in 1703.[3] After the usual leisurely examination, however, it was disallowed in 1706 for the reasons that it altered the "descent of Inheritances of persons residing in England," that it divided the estates of insolvents equally among all creditors without regard to the nature of their several securities, and — so little were colonial conditions often understood by those in authority — that it was considered "inconvenient to divide plantacions."[4] New Hampshire, however, in general paid curiously little atten-

[1] Adams, *Founding of New England*, p. 417.
[2] *Acts and Resolves*, vol. I, pp. 43 *ff.*
[3] *Laws of New Hampshire*, Prov. Period, vol. I, pp. 566 *f.*; vol. II, p. 295.
[4] *Ibid.*, vol. I, p. 646.

tion to the royal disallowance, and not only was it unobserved in this case but the identical law was reenacted in 1718 when a number of disallowed acts appeared in the official compilation of laws in force — a remarkable example of "colonial insubordination," as their editor says, "which had the merit of success." [1]

In 1699 a similar law was passed by Connecticut,[2] and as that colony's legislation did not require English approval, it escaped unnoticed at the time, to be questioned, however, a few years later in the famous Winthrop case. In 1717 Wait Still Winthrop, a citizen of Connecticut and a descendant of the first governor of Massachusetts, died intestate, and his son John was appointed administrator. As the latter claimed all of the real estate both of his father and uncle under the common law of England, his only sister brought suit for the share due her according to the colonial law, and in 1726, after several years of litigation she and her husband were appointed administrators in place of the unfraternal John. That worthy, after ignoring the highest colonial court, defying the governor, and escaping from the sheriff, fled to England. This would probably have been a relief to both his family and colony, had it not been that his purpose was to present a brief in appeal to the English Privy Council.[3] After hearing both sides, that body recommended that the law be declared void as contrary to that of England, and a decree of the King in Council to that effect was entered in February 1728.[4] The charters of such colonies as possessed them required that no legislation be passed repugnant to the laws of the mother country, so that the Connecticut act might also be considered a breach of the charter.

The colony's agent had been informed of the pending case by the Council, and requested to attend to defend the colony. As a consequence he had written hastily to the Connecticut government for funds as "every hearing will cost me forty Guineas,"

---

[1] *Laws of New Hampshire*, Prov. Period, vol. II, pp. 241, 295.

[2] *Conn. Col. Records*, vol. IV, pp. 306 ff.

[3] The best treatment of the case is by C. M. Andrews, "The Influence of colonial Conditions," etc., *cit. supra*. A clear short account is given in a note in the *Talcott Papers*, vol. I, pp. 94 ff. The brief and the action of the Council is in *Winthrop Papers*, vol. VI, pp. 440 ff. The brief for the respondent seems to be no longer in existence. *Ibid.*, p. 494 n.

[4] *Winthrop Papers*, vol. VI, pp. 496 ff.; *Conn. Col. Records*, vol. VII, pp. 571 ff.

but the colony was unable to prepare its defence in time for the proceedings, which seem to have been somewhat suspiciously expeditious.[1] The decision at once threw Connecticut into the greatest confusion. Two years later, Governor Talcott wrote that there were hundreds of intestate estates then awaiting settlement in the hope of a repeal of the English government's unjust and inconsiderate action.[2] Even worse than that, the title of practically every person in the colony had been rendered uncertain and probably void if the English law of primogeniture were to be considered as having been the law of the colony from the beginning. As many persons had voluntarily died intestate in the belief that their property would be divided among their children equally, their desire would not only be thwarted but all of the real estate holdings in the colony thrown into an inextricable tangle. Like the earlier decision of Andros, it is impossible to conceive of one more certain to arouse the fear and anger of an entire people, and to align them in opposition to those making it.

The colony at once took steps to present its case with a better prepared defence, minimizing as far as possible the argument that the law was contrary to that of England.[3] The whole question of what constituted a conflict between colonial laws and those of the mother country was brought into the forefront of the discussion, however, and the still more fundamental one of what legislative powers the colonists might have under the charter, and the nature of that instrument. Another point raised by the unexpected controversy was the authority possessed over the colony by the king and Parliament respectively. In fact, grasping John in his little family feud with his sister had exploded a gas bomb the deadly fumes of which were gradually spreading into every nook and cranny of the colony's life.

The Connecticut government debated at considerable length whether it were better to apply to the king in Council for a confirmation of their law, or to ask leave to bring in a bill in Parliament for the same purpose.[4] Fear of increasing that body's

---

[1] *Talcott Papers*, vol. I, p. 90.

[2] *Ibid.*, p. 203.

[3] Andrews, "Influence of colonial Conditions," etc., p. 450.

[4] Andrews, *cit. supra*, p. 457; *Talcott Papers*, vol. I, pp. 174 *ff.*, vol. II, pp. 418 *ff.*

colonial control, and of its possibly making embarrassing enquiries into the colony's ecclesiastical and other laws when once
started on the scent, seems to have caused the decision to have
been in favor of an application to the king. This, however, in
turn, raised the question in England whether he could grant
their wish by virtue of his prerogative, and it shows the distance
that the English constitution had traversed since the days of the
Stuarts that the Attorney General in his opinion on the point
advised that it might "be more for his Majesty's service to take
the assistance of Parliament, as that method will be the least
liable to objection."

The final decision of the Board of Trade, after hearing both
sides and the colony's agents, was influenced by several considerations.[1] The original verdict had been against the colony
because, as in many cases, the Board had been without correct
knowledge of local conditions.[2] With the new information now
at hand, they recommended that the request of the colony to
validate existing titles be granted, but stated that they would
not favor giving permission to alter the law for the future so as
not to agree with that of England unless the colonists would
accept an Explanatory Charter which would make the people of
Connecticut "at least as dependent upon the Crown and their
Native Country as are the people of Massachusetts Bay." [3]
No steps were taken, however, to pass an act in Parliament or
to force the explanatory charter upon the colony. Although
almost certain conflict was thus avoided, nevertheless the question of titles was left an open one until the dismissal of an appeal
similar to Winthrop's in 1745 settled it in favor of the colony.[4]
Meanwhile, the colonists had reverted to their former custom
as to inheritance and enforced their own law, but the effect of
those seventeen years of uncertainty as to the title held by
every owner of real estate cannot be overestimated.

To the fear for their property had been added that for their

[1] For the Agents' petition and the Council's action, *vide Talcott Papers*, vol. I.
pp. 187 *ff.*, 200 *ff.*

[2] Lechmere and his wife, (Ann Winthrop) seem to have been very badly defended by
their counsel. *Vide Talcott Papers*, vol. II, pp. 78 *f.*, 330, 434.

[3] Andrews, *cit. supra*, p. 460.

[4] *Cf. The Law Papers*, (Conn. Hist. Soc., 1907), vol. I, pp. 23 *ff.*, 68 *f.*; "Papers in the
Case of Phillips vs. Savage," *Mass. Hist. Soc., Proceedings*, vol. V, pp. 64 *ff.*

charter, for the dispute came at a time when the question of the
resumption of the charters of all proprietary colonies had again
come prominently before the English government. We have
already noted some of the reasons, many of which were valid,
that from time to time led the home authorities to consider the
only path to a more uniform and efficient colonial administration to lie through resumption of the charters and the bringing
of the colonies into more direct relations with the home government. In the first quarter century or so of our period, the mere
titles of papers containing charges against the proprietary
colonies fill twenty-one pages of an entry book, and although
much of the information upon which the government had to
rely was one-sided, nevertheless many of the charges were both
serious and true.[1] Moreover, control of colonial affairs from
1700 onward had been steadily passing from the King in Council into the hands of Parliament, and that body was constantly
growing more familiar with the thought of colonial administration by itself. The bill for the resumption of the charters in 1700
had been followed by the introduction of another in 1706, which
likewise, however, had failed of passage.[2] Nine years later
a similar one had been introduced and finally dropped in committee, although it caused great uneasiness in the colonies.[3]

The frequent difficulties in administration, however, kept the
matter before Parliament, and in 1721 the Lords of Trade reported that they believed the resumption of the charters of all
the proprietary colonies "either by purchase, agreement, or
otherwise" was essential to good government, as was also, in
their opinion, a complete change in the clumsy and confused
methods of handling colonial affairs in England itself.[4]

[1] Andrews, "Influence of Colonial Conditions," p. 444; Andrews, *Connecticut and
the British Government*, pp. 4 f.

[2] *Commons Journal*, vol. XV, pp. 151, 168, 183.

[3] *Ibid.*, vol. XVIII, p. 262; *Winthrop Papers*, vol. VI, p. 314.

[4] "The present method of dispatching business, relating to the plantations, is liable
to much delay and confusion; inasmuch as there are at present no less than three different ways of proceeding herein; that is to say, by immediate application to Your
Majesty by one of Your Secretaries of State; by petition to Your Majesty in Council;
and by representation to Your Majesty from this Board; from whence it happens,
that no one office is thoroughly informed of all matters relating to the plantations;
and sometimes Orders are obtained by surprize, disadvantageous to Your Majesty's
Service; whereas, if the business of the plantations were wholly confined to one office,
these inconveniences would be thereby avoided." Rept. of Lords of Trade, Sept. 8,
1721, *King's Mss. 205, Pt. I.*

The danger brought forth a very able defence of the charters by the colonial agent, Jeremiah Dummer, in which he attempted to show the "undoubted right" of the colonies to them, to answer the charges against the colonists, and to prove that, in any case, it would not be to the advantage of the government to resume the grants.[1]

The question, however, again came prominently before Parliament a couple of years later when Governor Shute after his return from Massachusetts laid a Memorial before the king reciting the various encroachments on the prerogative and the acts of the assembly which we noted in the preceding chapter.[2] The charges were certainly serious enough, as we have seen, and the Lords of Trade were not wholly unjustified in reporting that the inhabitants of Massachusetts "far from making suitable Returns to His Majesty for the Extraordinary Privileges they enjoy by their Charter, are daily endeavouring to wrest the small remains of Power out of the hands of the Crown, and to become independent of their Mother Kingdom." They ended their report with the ominous comment that the colony evidently could not be restrained within due bounds "without the Interposition of the British Legislature, wherein in Our humble opinion no time should be lost." [3]

Dummer was genuinely alarmed and wrote to Connecticut that he feared "this Winter may prove fatal to Your Charter," for Shute, he admitted, had proved all his charges from the Massachusetts assembly's own printed votes. Some of the Lords declared publicly that the colonists were "dancing to the Old Tune of '41" and had done such things as by any other government would be adjudged treason and rebellion. The agent feared that if Parliament — which being, as he said, "a great Body of men, does not consider things distinctly, besure not minutely, but takes everything in the Lump" — should proceed against Massachusetts, they would do so against the other

[1] Jeremiah Dummer, *A Defence of the New England Charters*, (London, 1721).

[2] The Memorial, and the Report of the Lords have already been cited *supra*. The Massachusetts assembly appointed Jeremiah Dummer agent to defend the colony. *Journal of Massachusetts House of Representatives*, 1723, pp. 10, 12.

[3] Representation of the Lords of Trade to the Lords Justices, Sept. 3, 1723, *Brit. Mus. Add. Mss. 35908*. One paragraph of the representation is printed by Hutchinson, *History*, vol II, p. 320 *n*.

colonies also. He pointed out, however, that there was division in the ministry, and how "My Lords Cadogan & Carterett draw one way & My Ld. Townsend & His Brother Walpole another." [1] It was this division, apparently, that again saved the day for the colonies. Connecticut and Rhode Island, it is true, were asked whether they would surrender their charters voluntarily, but they naturally refused, Governor Saltonstall's reply being a masterly diplomatic document. [2]

At the time of the Winthrop case, however, the situation had again become critical. Winthrop had not contented himself with merely attempting to have the law of inheritance declared void, but as part of the struggle had brought twenty-nine several complaints against the Connecticut government and had asked that a *Scire Facias* be brought against the charter in order that it be vacated. [3] Such an attack from such a source was serious enough in itself, but the long record of complaints against the colony, and the matter of the inheritance law, rendered it more so, and a controversy then raging in Massachusetts made the situation yet more dangerous. [4]

In March 1728, William Burnet, a son of the famous bishop, had been commissioned governor of Massachusetts, and at once proceeded to his new post. His short period of rule, lasting little more than a year until his death in September, 1729, was one long contest with the assembly over the salary question in an effort to force that body to comply with the royal instructions, and it was their defiance of the home authorities that Connecticut feared would react upon her own case.

Burnet was a man of engaging personality, of considerable ability, and of a strong sense of honor. He had been specially instructed to require that the Council and assembly fix a definite annual salary upon the governor "for the time being" under

[1] Dummer to Woodbridge, Sept. 10, 1723, *Col. Soc. Mass., Publications*, vol. VI, pp. 197 *ff*.

[2] It is given in full by Kellogg, *American Colonial Charter*, pp. 326 *ff*. Gov. Cranston's answer for Rhode Island is given in part in the same volume, pp. 322 *ff*. and in full by G. S. Kimball, *The Correspondence of the Colonial Governors of Rhode Island*, (Boston, 1902), vol. I, pp. 1 *ff*.

[3] The petition and the colony's answer are in the *Conn. Records, Miscellaneous Papers, Force Transcripts*, (Mss.) in the Library of Congress.

[4] For Gov. Talcott's fears of the effect of the Massachusetts quarrel on Connecticut's affairs, *vide Talcott Papers*, vol. I, pp. 176 *ff*.

threat of action by Parliament.[1] In the ensuing contest, the assembly undoubtedly occupied safer ground than the Council in denying the binding force of a mere royal instruction and in standing by a literal interpretation of the charter. The fact was, as a later governor had the sense to observe, that although his instructions were not binding upon the assembly, they were upon himself.[2] It is an example of that lack of imagination upon the part of the English authorities, to which I have already alluded, that they seemed wholly to fail to realize that the only possible result of pursuing a stubborn policy which they could not enforce by law and would not by arms would be to lower their own prestige, to create unnecessary bitterness and to hamper their governor. The colonists were not likely to be caught napping where their cherished liberties were concerned. Had they been, however, nothing could have been better calculated to keep them awake than the setting off of this alarm clock of a fixed salary dispute once a year with entire regularity and no other result.

Burnet at once communicated his instructions to the members of the General Court, but the assembly, although it voted the unusually large sum of £1,700, did so in the old way and made no permanent settlement of salary. The governor's instructions required him to refuse the grant on these terms, and the contest began. The two houses then sent an address in which they stated that it was their "undoubted right as Englishmen" and a privilege vested in them by their charter to raise the money needed for the carrying on of government, and that the ends proposed in such a grant of power would "be best answered without establishing a fixed salary." [3] In his reply, Burnet touched upon the main point and said that it was well known that heretofore the governor's salary had sometimes been kept back until he had consented to bills and that he had thus been coerced into doing so. Comparing the colonial legislature to Parliament, as the colonists were fond of doing, he also pointed out that the latter body always voted the king's civil list for life, and that as

---

[1] *Collection of Proceedings*, etc., p. 41.
[2] G. A. Wood, *William Shirley*, (New York, 1920), vol. I, p. 114.
[3] *Collection of Proceedings*, etc., pp. 39 f., 42 f., 45.

the governor was the king's representative in the constitutional scheme of a colony, the Court had Parliamentary precedent for the action requested. To this the assembly replied that although they could not say what motives might have animated the members in previous sessions, nevertheless, even if the salary of a governor had been withheld in order to secure desired legislation, such action might not have been unreasonable "nor without precedent from the Parliaments of England; when some of the greatest Patriots and most wise and learned States-men, have been Actors in them." The Council, however, refused to concur in so flat an avowal of a coercive policy.[1]

The two houses then began a controversy between themselves, the Council resolving that a fixed salary might be granted for a certain time to the present governor without danger to the province, to which the assembly would in no way agree.[2] A communication from the home government threatening action against the charter had no effect, and the House remained immovable. Requests for adjournment were met with refusals by the governor until the salary question should be disposed of. Instead, he removed the Court to Salem in October, alleging the undue influence of the people of Boston, who had voted at a public meeting against fixing a permanent salary. He also said, with a wit that the irate assemblymen probably did not relish, that as there might be something in a name, he had hesitated whether to adjourn them to Salem or to Concord. The deputies protested loudly against their being called together at any place except Boston, but the Council, with the better right, upheld the strict legality of the governor's action.[3]

The assembly next sent a Memorial to the king, giving their views of the case, in which they stated that the Council concurred with them on some points on which it distinctly had not done so. They also voted £100 Sterling to their agent Wilks in London "to enable him to serve the Interests of this Province."

---

[1] *Collection of Proceedings*, etc., pp. 47 *ff.*

[2] *Ibid.*, p. 63. Hutchinson says that a majority of the Council and about one-third of the deputies were in favor of granting a salary for two or three years. *History*, vol. II, p. 314.

[3] *Collection of Proceedings*, etc., pp. 65 *ff.*, 90 *ff.*; Hutchinson, *History*, vol. II, pp. 315, 317.

In this the Council non-concurred unanimously and said that, as they had never seen the Memorial, they could not decide whether it were for the interest of the colony or no.[1] Finally the governor prorogued the Court to meet again at Salem in April, later adjourning it to Cambridge.[2]

The new assembly was in no more tractable a mood than the former one, and not only at once voted not to consider the settling of a salary upon the governor at that session but voted £300 to the agents, Wilks and Belcher. A newly elected Council again non-concurred in the latter vote and advised the House that they looked upon it as a "very extraordinary Practice" to ask them to concur in appropriating money to forward an address to the Crown that they had not been allowed to see until several months after it had been presented to the King in Council. Furthermore, they took exception to several passages in the Memorial itself, more particularly the one in which the assembly had stated that the Council had concurred with them in agreeing not to fix a salary upon the governor, whereas neither the facts nor the records bore this out. In reply, the assembly ignored the constitutional position and duties of both governor and Council and took the untenable position that they had the right to dispose of the public money as they saw fit and that the assembly "act for, and may be said to be the People." In blocking legislation for a permanent salary, the deputies were within their rights, but in the position they now assumed they showed themselves either ignorant of the extent of their powers or wilfully ignored their constitutional limits. No progress could be made and when the Court adjourned on April 18th, the only satisfaction the governor could secure was to refuse to sign the bill for the members' salaries on the ground that "one branch of the legislature might as well go without their wages as another."[3]

Burnet under his instructions could not yield, and the assembly would not. It made one final effort to break the deadlock, incidentally showing how little they understood the gov-

[1] *Collection of Proceedings*, etc., pp. 96 ff.
[2] Hutchinson, *History*, vol. II, p. 325.
[3] *Collection of Proceedings*, etc., pp. 102 f., 104, 111; Hutchinson, *History*, vol. II, p. 321.

ernor's character, by an insulting attempt to bribe him with a grant of £6,000. To this Burnet coldly replied that if the assembly would not comply with the king's request, they might "at least forbear their endeavor to seduce one of his servants from his declared duty." [1] Within a week the sorely tried official was dead, from a fever following an accident, and the assembly had won its victory. Much has been made by some historians of a grant made to his widow and children, but the fact is that although money was granted not a shilling was paid to them until four years after his death, when £3,000 in depreciated bills was at last paid "on account" after repeated and urgent solicitation by the next governor. [2] One wonders what liberties the assembly may have thought would be endangered by paying to the unfortunate woman money long past due to her dead husband. However, as we have pointed out before, generosity of spirit was not developed by the New England brand of Puritanism.

In the struggle lasting more than a year, both sides had clearly stated their positions, and they were irreconcilable. The conservative class in the community as represented in the Council had endeavored to mediate, and were closer in their sympathies to the views of the home government than they were to the radical elements in the colony. On the one hand, they unduly minimized the dangers, perhaps, in a royal governor uncontrolled by the power of the purse, and on the other, they could not watch without foreboding the passing of power into the hands of more or less ignorant and irresponsible persons from outside their own circles of education, financial standing and responsibility. There may have been many who preferred settled peace, quiet and a royal governor to the more than doubtful outlook of government by practically a single chamber, and that made up largely of agitators and radicals. Nevertheless, the latter had won. The struggle with Burnet marked the crisis between the home government and the assembly on

---

[1] Cited by Palfrey, *History*, vol. IV, p. 526.

[2] *Belcher Papers*, vol. I, pp. 399, 405, 407. Many of the documents concerning Belcher's relations with the assembly, during his term of office may be found in *The Political State of Great Britain*, vol. XLIII, pp. 335 *ff.*, vol. XLIV, pp. 176 *ff.*, 199 *ff.*, vol. XLVI, pp. 28 *f.*

the salary question, and although England fatuously kept bringing it up, she never seriously disputed it again. Both the radicals
and the conservatives saw that she did not back up her representative with the power either of the law or the sword. Once more
"tumult had procured concession." A weapon with the keenest
of edges had been surrendered to the people, and the prestige
of authority had been lowered. The struggle between Burnet
and the assembly represents more than a transfer of power from
England to her colony. It marks also another step in the transfer of power from the Council to the assembly, from the conservative to the radical elements in the colony itself. The divergence of interest between the colony and the mother country
presaged civil war. It was the divergence of interest between
the men of wealth, education and social standing, and those
of the shop, of the farms, and of the frontier that presaged
revolution.

CHAPTER VIII

EXPANDING ENERGIES

Broadening and Secularizing of the Colonial Mind — Expansion and Business Methods — Crisis in West Indian Relations — The Molasses Act — Finance — The Land Bank and Attempted Revolt — Panic of the Conservatives — The Cartagena Expedition

"DEEPER than men's opinions," writes Lord Morley, "are the sentiments and circumstances by which opinion is determined." [1] Few men base their political actions upon abstract ideas however much they believe themselves to be doing so. Back of the idea for which they may think themselves to be struggling lies a whole complex of capacities, experiences and influences which urge them along certain lines. Our adoption of a political philosophy is not the result so much of thought, however we may flatter ourselves, as it is of the circumstances and influences to which we have long been subject.

The generation of colonists in the period at which our story has now arrived, that from 1730 to 1760, was particularly rich in experience. It was a time of changing social customs, of expanding commerce, of wars, of religious questionings, and of the setting free of thought. What impresses us most in studying it, is the increasing variety and interest in the content of colonial life. New standards are introduced. Wealth replaces real or hypocritical "godliness" in determining a man's position in the community. Individuals are no longer stretched upon the Procustean bed of New England Puritanism to ascertain their fitness. It is a time of rapidly expanding energies, and those mainly in secular lines.

During the years of Shute's administration in Massachusetts, the freedom of the press in New England had finally been vindicated, first against the demands of the irate governor, and then

[1] *Notes on Politics and History*, (New York, 1914), p. 54.

against those of the assembly.[1] In 1719, the fifteen years of journalistic dullness provided through the medium of *The Boston News-Letter* were somewhat disturbed by the entry of a competitor, *The Boston Gazette*, and two years later much more effectually by the appearance of *The New England Courant*. In its columns a small group of men, — popularly known as the Hell-Fire Club, — including James the elder brother of Benjamin Franklin, proceeded to attack many of the cherished shibboleths of New England conservatism. Although they incurred the wrath of the assembly and the clergy, — Mather called them "profane Sons of Corah," — they did represent a popular reaction against clerical domination.[2]

That such a publication should be allowed and successful for even a few years speaks much for the change that was coming over the thought of the people. Moreover, in the *Courant's* pages America had its first taste of literature as provided by journalism, and the essays reprinted from the *Spectator* and those written in imitation of them formed quite a new literary fare for the public, a fare that was continued to it in *The New England Weekly Journal* founded in 1727. From 1730 onward, the change in taste from theological to secular that was heralded in the preceding decade in the *Courant* and the *Journal* is noteworthy whenever we can look over the shoulders of the people and see what they were reading. The appallingly theological character of the early New England libraries had changed but little until the beginning of the century. Even in 1723, Harvard possessed no copy of Addison, Steele, Dryden, Pope or Swift and had but recently acquired a Milton and a Shakespeare.[3] Two decades later, the Redwood Library in Newport was ordering £500 worth of books from London of which forty were on medicine, twenty-four on law, one hundred and nine on natural history, science and art, thirty-seven on politics, and a hundred and thirty-five "good general reading." [4]

---

[1] Duniway, *Freedom of the Press*, pp. 91 *ff.*

[2] *Ibid.*, p. 98; Cook, *Literary Influences*, p. 27.

[3] Cook, *Literary Influences*, p. 23. Efforts have been made to prove a more catholic taste but without very convincing results. *Vide* Wright, *Literary Culture in early New England, cit. supra.*

[4] W. B. Weeden, "Ideal Newport in the 18th Century," in *American Antiquarian Society Proceedings*, New Series, vol. XVIII, pp. 111 *f.*

In this broadening and secularizing of the public interest the colleges played their part, albeit somewhat unwillingly. Harvard early became deistic in tendency and we have already found the authorities at Yale feeling it necessary to warn their students against the dangers of the "new philosophy." One of those so warned was young Samuel Johnson, a Connecticut lad who later visited the English Johnson, as well as Pope, and received honorary degrees from both Cambridge and Oxford. Brought up in the gloomy Calvinism of New England orthodoxy, he early went over to the Church of England and became one of its most important colonial supporters. The rationalism of the colleges was slowly eating into Calvinism, but of even more influence probably than the books the young men were reading was the atmosphere in which they were living, and which led them to accept those ideas which were in harmony with it. In the new world, with its rapidly increasing prosperity and comparative absence of restraint, it was inevitable that men should feel free and optimistic. In many ways Johnson was a typical resultant of the forces at work. In his *Introduction to the Study of Philosophy*, published in 1731, he made the chief end of God to be the happiness of mankind, instead of making it man's chief end to glorify the Deity.[1] "The great end that above all things concerns us," he wrote again, "is that we be truly happy in the whole of our nature and duration."[2] Continually he preached and wrote against both determinism and the "horror, despair, and gloomy apprehension" of predestination.[3]

The same causes that were at work in this prosperous young country to undermine the belief in a dependence upon a temporal monarch were also at work to undermine the belief in a similar relation of absolute dependence upon the unconditioned will of the Calvinistic deity. The optimism of the frontier, and the dislike of restraint were finding more and more frequent expression in political, religious and philosophical thinking. The new ideas were taking root because they had found a con-

[1] W. Riley, in *Cambridge History of American Literature*, vol. I, p. 82.

[2] Cited by Riley, *American Philosophy*, p. 69.

[3] Riley, *American Philosophy*, pp. 72 ff.; *Cambridge History of American Literature*, vol. I, pp. 82 ff.

genial soil in the unlimited free land to be subdued on the empty continent. Among the uncultivated classes of the farms and forests they were growing unconsciously from the effects of the environment. Among the cultured class the same ideas were receiving philosophical treatment and literary expression. Although the idealism of the English philosopher Berkeley never took deep root in colonial America, it is noteworthy that when he came to Rhode Island in 1729 and spent a few years near Newport, there were enough men there to join with him in founding the Literary and Philosophical Society, which became a powerful factor in the intellectual life of the colony. Of considerable influence also were the eight hundred and eighty volumes of philosophy and literature which he gave to Yale College, and which were the source, according to a contemporary rhymester, to which

> "Yalensia owes the power of knowing more
> Than all her Sisters on the western shore." [1]

As Calvinism was thus slowly yielding to the optimism of the frontier and the deism of the colleges, both influences were also bringing about a more tolerant attitude on the part of many toward religious beliefs. "I have no opinion," wrote Governor Belcher in 1731, "of those stingy, narrow notions of Christianity which reigned too much in the first beginnings of this country." Speaking of beliefs that he did not share, Benjamin Colman wrote that nevertheless he would not say a word against them and that the souls of those who held them "look enlarged to me; and mine does the more to myself, for not daring to judge them." [2] Although this spirit was as yet far from general, its frequent expression marks a change in the community. Legal toleration in Massachusetts and Connecticut was hindered by the vested interests of the established Congregational or Presbyterian churches, and the actions of the governments and

---

[1] Riley, *American Philosophy*, p. 211. The list included the *Spectator*, Wycherley, Otway, Swift, Prior, Don Quixote, the *Tatler*, Jonson, Shakespeare, Steele, Rowe, Dryden, Gay, Pope, Milton, Cowley, Addison, Waller and Clarendon. D. C. Gilman, "Bishop Berkeley's Gift to Yale College," *New Haven Historical Society, Papers*, vol. I, pp. 162 ff.

[2] *Belcher Papers*, vol. I, p. 82; Tyler, *American Literature*, vol. I, pp. 147, 175.

of narrow-minded rustics were particularly directed against the adherents of the Church of England, who from time to time complained bitterly of having to pay taxes for the support of the established clergy, and even of physical violence toward themselves.[1] Although these conditions had been gradually ameliorated, notably by an Act passed in Connecticut in 1717, and the "Five Mile Act" of Massachusetts in the same year,[2] nevertheless, the Anglican Church continued until the Revolution to be an object of suspicion owing to the belief that the constantly expressed desire of its members for the appointment of resident bishops by the English ecclesiastical authorities threatened the religious liberties of the other colonists.[3]

The interests of Americans, however, were becoming commercial rather than religious, and their efforts were in the main directed toward exploiting the wilderness in the shortest possible time and the most profitable manner or toward the building up of their fortunes by foreign trade. The one thing they wished above all else was to be left wholly unmolested while they pursued these desirable ends. Their sense of dependence upon either a British monarch or a Calvinistic deity was fast disappearing. Their sense of sin was evaporating. But their sense of the exceptionally profitable situation in which Providence had placed them with reference to European ports, the West Indies, and the riches of illimitable land and forests, was becoming exceedingly acute.

Aside from the utilization of the land for agricultural purposes, still mostly in the form of small farms tilled by the owner and his family, its exploitation assumed two forms — specula-

---

[1] *Vide Soc. Prop. Gospel Mss., Series B, vol. I, Pt. II,* letter from Gov. Dudley, Dec. 19, 1712; documents relative to church at Braintree, 1713, *ibid.*; petition from Baptists at Reheboth, Jan. 8, 1714, *ibid.*; Council Minutes, Boston, May 7, 1713, *Fulham Mss. No. 113;* F. L. Hawks and W. S. Perry, *Documentary History of the Protestant Episcopal Church in the U. S. A.,* (New York, 1863-4), vol. Conn., pp. 39 *ff.*

[2] *Conn. Col. Records,* vol. VI, pp. 106 *ff.; Acts and Resolves,* vol. II, pp. 459 *ff. Cf.* M. L. Greene, *Development of religious Liberty in Connecticut,* (Boston, 1905), pp. 199 *ff.*

[3] For the efforts of the colonial Anglicans to have a bishop appointed during the first half of the century, *vide* A. L. Cross, *The Anglican Episcopate and the American Colonies,* (New York, 1902), pp. 92 *ff. Cf.* Bishop of London's Queries concerning the exercise of ecclesiastical Jurisdiction in the Colonies, 1725; and the Order in Council for preparing a draft for exercising ecclesiastical Jurisdiction in the Plantations, 1725, *Brit. Mus. Add. Mss., 35908.*

tion in wilderness lands for prospective settlement, and the development of its timber resources. The first was mainly the concern of colonial and English capitalists, and the second of colonial capitalists and the rough loggers and lumber-jacks whose interests coincided with those of the larger operators as opposed to those of the English government.

Even in the more settled portions of New England the richer men were beginning to accumulate larger estates, as for example the four-thousand-acre farm of Governor Belcher at Pomfret in Connecticut, which he estimated to be worth from £12,000 to £14,000 New England currency. Land in such sections was also beginning to be held in greater amounts by absentee landlords or speculators in England, moderate examples of which were a four-thousand-acre tract in Oxford, Massachusetts, held by Sir Robert Clark, and another two-thousand-acre piece held by a daughter of Sir William Ashurst. But English owners seem rather to have been interested in the wilderness lands, such as the thirteen thousand acres owned by Baron Edgcumbe in Maine and the very large holdings of the Duke of Chandos.[1] In the early days in New England, when the soil was all held by the colonial governments, and granted only to actual settlers, there was comparatively little agrarian discontent, but as capitalists gradually engrossed large tracts, the pioneers, through whose manual labor such holdings acquired the only value they possessed, began to feel that they were being exploited for the benefit of the wealthy owner in Boston, Newport or England. The advance of the frontier, frequently preceded by that of the speculative land jobber, was a marked characteristic of the generation before the revolutionary period, and was without doubt a cause of deep-seated resentment against the classes in control of capital and of the local government.

It is quite possible, indeed, that this may have created quite as much ill feeling as the contests over the royal timber, although the latter as involving the home government was the more spectacular. We have already spoken of the beginning of the troubles over the King's Woods, which had formed one of the chief points in Governor Shute's indictment of Massachu-

<hr>

[1] *Belcher Papers*, vol. I, pp. 173, 194 *f.*, 314, 382, 495.

setts. In 1728 the English government took up the question seriously and appointed David Dunbar surveyor-general with instructions to proceed to New England. It was also proposed to set aside two hundred thousand acres in Nova Scotia for mast trees, and to settle a colony of Irish and Germans in the tract between the Kennebec and the St. Croix, forming a new colony which was to bear the name of Georgia.[1] Owing to the fact that the mast industry had been pushed eastward as far as the first named river, and that the clearing of the forests, the advance of the frontier settlements, and of the ship-building industry, were all tending the same way, the country in which the home government was now interesting itself was also becoming of special interest to Massachusetts.

In our previous volume, we have written at length of the aggressive policy of expansion and annexation pursued by that colony almost from the beginning.[2] That policy had received severe checks both from the home government and the local patriotism of the other colonies, but was now being renewed in the more subtle form of peaceful penetration in New Hampshire and the country to the eastward.[3] Elisha Cooke, whom we have already noted both as a popular leader in the assembly and a speculator in wilderness lands, had been instrumental in having Massachusetts make surveys for a line of townships from the Connecticut River to the Merrimac, and up that latter stream on both sides as far as the present Concord, as well as for another line of prospective settlements in Maine.[4]

Jonathan Belcher, who had been commissioned governor of Massachusetts and New Hampshire in 1730, and who was to play a prominent part in the disputes over the eastern country, was a native of the larger colony and a retired merchant. Although he had the usual contests over the granting of a fixed salary — his instructions on that point being even more stringent than Burnet's — the assembly, though not the Council,

[1] *Acts Privy Council*, vol. III, pp. 152, 183 *ff.*; Report of Lords of Trade, May 14, 1729, *C.O. 5 No. 4.*

[2] Adams, *Founding of New England*, pp. 182 *ff.*, 216 *f.*, 227, 243 *ff.*, 328, 335 *f.*, 386 *f.*

[3] *Cf.* Wood, *William Shirley*, vol. I, pp. 50 *ff.* Dr. Wood's book was published while my own was in the press. I am glad to find that our opinions agree as to the expansion policy of Massachusetts.

[4] *Ibid.*, p. 53; Fry, *New Hampshire*, pp. 252 *ff.*

proved obdurate, and the English government finally yielded.[1] Although the assembly's attitude was strongly condemned by many of the prominent men in the colony as well as such leaders as Governor Talcott of Connecticut; nevertheless, owing to the supineness of the English government, the point had already been won by the radicals and the main interest of Belcher's administration lies in the field of economics rather than of politics.[2]

Fond of popularity and of office, his policy was to maintain the show of a prerogative man sufficiently to retain his post, and at the same time as a colonial and Massachusetts man to advance the interest of the politically potent element in that colony at the expense of the Crown and of New Hampshire. His policy and the innumerable intrigues of his administration based themselves upon the questions involved in the eastern lands, for the main desire of the colonists, toward which this native royal governor was more than complacent, was "to develop the natural resources of their country and to utilize them freely through commerce."[3] In that formula is to be found the key not only to the intricacies of Belcher's administration but to the major part of the history of the period. In the former, the chief field of activity was the eastern country already referred to. Dunbar, with whom Belcher was continually at war, and whom he described in his choice language as "the bull frog from the Hibernian fens,"[4] was there uprooting settlers and loggers, and questioning the rather uncertain titles of the pioneers and larger speculative interests. The most prominent capitalists involved were Elisha Cooke and Samuel Waldo, both of Boston. Cooke posed always as the champion of the people's rights and as their constant defender against the royal prerogative, so he could not well approach the home government as a suppliant. Waldo, however, was the New England agent for the contractor for masts for the navy, and it was he, therefore, who undertook a voyage to England to press the inter-

---

[1] Hutchinson, *History*, vol. II, pp. 33 *ff.*; Additional Instructions for Gov. Belcher, Feb. 21, 1732-3, *C.O. 5 No. 10*; *Belcher Papers*, vol. I, pp. 15, 56, 91, 114*f.*, 308, 311.

[2] *Talcott Papers*, vol. I, p. 214.

[3] Wood, *William Shirley*, vol. I, p. 49.

[4] *Belcher Papers*, vol. I, p. 145; *cf.* Hutchinson. *History* vol. II, p. 340.

ests of the eastern speculators. In this he was successful, for, after hearing all parties to the dispute, the Privy Council decided that although Massachusetts had the right of administration in the Sagadahoc section, it did not possess that of granting lands there to individuals without the royal consent, and before the section had come under its control by the new charter, many such grants had already been made.[1]

The prior settlements on these lands had been known as "towns" although they had not been incorporated as such, and when the English Council recognized the claims of Waldo and others as valid, it gave them a position of semi-independence with reference to Massachusetts. Waldo at once engaged in plans of large scope to settle and exploit the area awarded him, including supplying the navy with masts. His interests were thus becoming identified with those of the Crown, and the struggle for the control of the natural resources of the rich eastern territory was growing more complicated. Waldo soon came into conflict with Belcher, and joined Cooke, Dunbar, and the other enemies of the executive, whose eventual downfall was foreshadowed from that time.

But Massachusetts had no intention of letting the profitable exploitation of the eastern country pass from her grasp, and when Waldo sent workmen into the newly settled town of Berwick to cut masts, the colony supplied the alleged owners of the land on which the trees stood with money to fight the case, which was appealed to the Privy Council.[2] The decision was in favor of Waldo, but he was unable to enforce it because neither the governor nor the courts in America would take the necessary steps in spite of peremptory orders from the English Council.

The natural result was greatly to increase the boldness of the provincials of all classes in their encroachments upon the woods. What is known as the Exeter Riot occurred soon after, in 1734, when Dunbar's men in the performance of their duty for the Crown were viciously assaulted after Dunbar himself

---

[1] The whole story is clearly worked out by Wood, *William Shirley*, vol. I, pp. 54 ff.; *cf.* Aspinwall Papers, *Mass. Hist. Soc., Coll.*, Ser. IV, vol. IX, pp. 195 ff.

[2] Wood, *William Shirley*, vol. I, pp. 59 f.

Samuel Waldo of *Boſton*, Merchant, intending with all poſſible Expedition to ſettle Two Towns of Forty Families each, on a Tract of Land, to which his Title is indiſputable, lying on the Weſtern ſide of a Navigable River known by the name of St. *George's River*, in the Eaſtern Parts of this Province; hereby notifies all Perſons who may be deſirous to take up Lots and Settle there, that from Monday the 17th. to the 24th. Inſtant, he will be ready at his Houſe in *Boſton*, to treat with them, and give each Family that ſhall agree with him to ſettle the ſame, a Grant of One Hundred Acres of Land.

Samuel Waldo.

Boston 3d. March, 1734.

The better to accommodate the Settlement a double Saw Mill will immediately be erected on ſaid Land: and the ſaid *Waldo* will be on the ſame from the 10th to the laſt of *April* next, to direct in the laying out the Lotts, and the moſt commodious Settlement thereof.

SAMUEL WALDO'S ADVERTISEMENT OF EASTERN LANDS, 1734

had been openly insulted by some of the loggers. For many years this contest for the timber resources of the eastern country continued to be carried on in lawless fashion along the frontier, and England's legitimate rights and the vested interests of certain colonial capitalists as well were swept away by those engaged in exploiting the resources at hand regardless of both.

At the time when the country east of New Hampshire was thus becoming a center of intrigue and economic conflict, a long standing boundary dispute between that colony and Massachusetts was also nearing a crisis. In anticipation of the appointment of royal commissioners to determine the contest, the larger colony laid out over thirty townships, mostly in the disputed area.[1] Throughout the protracted proceedings, the intricate details of which cannot be given in a work of this scope, Belcher intrigued for the advantage of Massachusetts, although he was also governor of New Hampshire, and the final decision of the King in Council was in favor of that latter colony.[2] In these efforts at westward, northward and eastward expansion of the old Bay Colony many elements thus played their parts. Fundamentally, it was an attempt to secure possession of the natural resources of the section, and by establishing the political control of Massachusetts as against the Crown and New Hampshire to ensure the exploitation of such resources by her own favored citizens. Intertwined in the threads of these contests were those of intriguing politicians for and against Governor Belcher, and of private capitalists seeking their own advantage, as well as of frontiersmen and loggers seeking theirs on a smaller scale. To a lesser extent the same movement of expansion, due to the growth of population and the desire to exploit the wilderness, was in progress in Connecticut. Between 1700 and 1741, the number of towns in that colony had doubled, and in 1737 alone seven were laid out on the Housatonic River.[3]

[1] Fry, *New Hampshire*, pp. 254 *f.* For the dispute between the local and English authorities, *vide ibid.*, pp. 255 *ff.*; Hutchinson, *History*, vol. II, pp. 343 *ff.*; Jeremy Belknap, *History of New Hampshire*, (Dover, 1812), vol. II, pp. 98 *ff.*; *N. H. State Papers*, vol. XIX, pp. 179 *ff.*; B. H. Hall, *History of Eastern Vermont*, (New York, 1858), pp. 58 *ff.*

[2] He was the last governor to be in charge of both provinces. In 1740, Benning Wentworth was made governor of New Hampshire as a separate administration.

[3] Greene, *Religious Liberty in Connecticut*, p. 206 *n.*; *Conn. Col. Records*, vol. VIII, pp. 134 *ff.*; Mathews, *Expansion of New England*, p. 93.

Although six out of seven of these Connecticut towns fulfilled the conditions of settlement, many of the Massachusetts ones did not, in spite of the effort to bring settlers from Europe, and the speculative character of much of the movement is shown by the number of forfeited claims.[1]

While the expanding energies and accumulating economic resources of the colonies were thus being employed in a rapid exploitation of the surrounding wilderness, and were strongly influencing local politics and relations with the home country, the same results were being attained by an equally rapid development of over-seas commerce. We have already noted the necessity, according to the then current view of the value of colonies, of a certain balance being maintained between the products of the temperate and tropical zone sections of the empire. We have also noted how this balance became less and less perfect from the beginning of the century and more particularly from the Peace of Utrecht in 1713. Various factors were in continuous operation to emphasize this growing maladjustment in the colonial system from that time to the end of the period. In the trade between New England and the island colonies, the main exports of the former were provisions, timber in various shapes and horses. These last, according to the governor of Virginia, were useful for turning the machinery in the sugar mills and carrying the customs officers out of the way when smugglers wished to land their goods.[2] In return for these commodities, the northern plantations imported rum, sugar and molasses, the latter the basis of the important distilling business of Rhode Island and Massachusetts producing a liquid known among New England's less ardent contemporary admirers as "Kill-Devil."[3] As we have just seen, New England was undergoing a marked expansion, and a market had to be found for the steadily increasing amount of food stuffs produced and of timber

---

[1] For terms of settlement *vide Conn. Col. Records, cit. supra*; Hall, *Eastern Vermont, cit. supra*; *cf.* Mathews, *Expansion of New England*, pp. 84, 93; Sheldon, *Deerfield*, vol. I, pp. 513 *ff.*

[2] Gov. Gooch to Board of Trade, Sept. 8, 1731, *C.O. 5 No. 4.*

[3] Representation from the Commissioners for Trade and Plantation to House of Lords, Jan. 14, 1745-6, *C.O. 5 No. 5. Cf.* Pitman, *West Indies*, pp. 189 *ff.*, 205; *A Comparison between the British Sugar Colonies and New England as they relate to the Interest of Great Britain*, (London, 1732), p. 16.

cut. The natural markets for both these products were tropical sugar colonies.

While this expanding process was taking place in New England, however, a retrograde movement was under way in the British islands to the south. In Barbadoes it had been reported that there was no uncultivated land by 1724, and eleven years later the Board of Trade represented to the House of Lords that the soil there, as well as in some of the other islands, was almost worn out.[1] Jamaica alone offered virgin soil and an opportunity for increased production at reasonable cost. In that island, however, the buying up of vast tracts by comparatively few rich planters retarded the production of which the island was capable.[2] The soil in the French islands was much richer and had been less worked than that in the English ones, so that it was stated at various times that the labor of one negro in the former produced as much as that of from three to four in, for example, Barbadoes.[3] Moreover, owing to the French distaste for molasses and rum, the French planters had little outlet in their own commercial system for these important by-products of the plantations.[4] Lower freight rates, duties and interest charges, premiums on the importation of slaves, and other factors all tended to reduce the prices at which the French sold their products, a differential in their favor estimated at from twenty-five to fifty per cent.[5] In addition to all these economic elements, it seems probable from contemporary testimony that

[1] Representation from Lords of Trade to House of Lords, Jan. 14, 1734–5, *C.O. 324 No. 12*; Pitman, *West Indies*, p. 70. Similar conditions prevailed in the Leeward Islands, Pitman, p. 99. Some contended that this was the fault of the planters who had already made more than the value of them. *Some Considerations humbly offer'd upon the Bill now depending in the House of Lords relating to the Trade between the Northern Colonies and the Sugar Islands*, (London, 1732), p. 4.

[2] Pitman, *West Indies*, pp. 108 *ff.*

[3] *Ibid.*, pp. 70 *f.*

[4] Andrews, "Anglo-French Commercial Rivalry," p. 556.

[5] Representations of the General Assembly of Barbadoes to the Commissioners for Trade and Plantations, Aug. 27, 1731; Letter of Gov. Gooch, *cit. supra*; Representation of the President, Council and Assembly of St. Christophers to the Commissioners for Trade and Plantations, Sept. 24, 1731; The Case of the British Northern Colonies, n. d. — all in *C.O. 5 No. 4. Some Observations on a direct Exportation of Sugar from the British Islands with Answers to Mr. Toriano's Objections to it*, (London, 1735), pp. 4 *f.*; John Ashley, *Memoirs and Considerations concerning the Trade and Resources of the British Colonies in America*, (London, 1740), p. 64; *The present State of the British and French Trade to Africa and America*, (London, 1745), pp. 8 *ff.*

the French were showing an energy superior possibly to that of the English in their colonizing projects throughout the earlier part of the century, a fact to which we have already had occasion to allude. After noting certain changes in the administrative methods of France, a contemporary English writer adds that "she has changed (at least in this Part of the World) her very Genius too, or rather dropped what was vicious in it; and all her Undertakings here seem to have been contriv'd with as much Thought and Deliberation, as it is obvious they are carried on with a Patience and Steadiness unknown to her in former Times."[1] Moreover, as another writer pointed out, the French "work cheaper, and live harder everywhere, than Englishmen will or can do any where."[2] Finally, her temperate zone colony in Canada was even more hopelessly inadequate in relation to her sugar colonies than were the English sugar colonies in relation to the northern continental ones.

Here then were a set of conditions under which New England trade was as certain to be carried on with the French islands as water is to run downhill, regardless of legal prohibitions. Such trade, however, added another disadvantage to those under which the English in the islands were suffering, and in 1730 and the following year, the island planters petitioned the Privy Council to prohibit it. Not receiving the immediate assistance they had hoped for, they next carried the matter into Parliament, which body, as we have already several times had occasion to note, was assuming a more important rôle in the management of the colonies and was with more and more frequency appealed to by the colonists themselves when they wished to secure prompt and efficient action.[3]

Owing to various factors, including the presence in England and even in Parliament itself of a considerable number of rich absentee planters, the lobby representing the island interest was an exceedingly strong one. Nevertheless, the northern colonies received ample hearing.[4] A few years later, a member

---

[1] A Detection of the State and Situation of the present Sugar Planters of Barbadoes and the Leeward Islands, (London, 1732), p. 99.

[2] An Enquiry into the Methods that are said to be now proposed in England to retrieve the Sugar Trade, (London, 1733), p. 15.

[3] Andrews, "Anglo-French Commercial Rivalry," pp. 766 f.

[4] Commons Journal, vol. XXI, pp. 778, 788 f., 792 ff., 801, 804 f., 811, 841.

of Parliament speaking of the lengthy debates on the subject
said that both the northern and southern [island] colonies had
an equal right to the care of the legislature but that "our Northern Colonies tell us, 'If we pass the Bill, we destroy their
Trade,' and our Southern Colonies say, 'If we do not pass the
Bill, they are undone.'" [1] England's own immediate interests
were but little affected and the question for the home government was mainly one of broad policy. All economic legislation
is bound to injure some one no matter how much it may benefit
others, and, as the member of Parliament pointed out, in this
case either action or inaction seemed equally detrimental to one
set of colonies or the other. The legislature had to choose between them in the light of the sometimes false and always exaggerated statements put forth by both the contesting parties.
But the case was decided on broader grounds. "The contest is
not so much between Colony and Colony, as between the French
and us," said one writer,[2] and the following year in the debate
in the Commons one of the members put the point equally
clearly. "Some of the Counsel at the Bar," said Winnington,
"have endeavoured to turn the affair before us into such shape,
as if the Question to be determined were, whether the Northern
Colonies, or the Sugar Colonies ought most to be encouraged
by this House. This, Sir, is not at all the Question before us;
the Affair in hand is the Dispute between the English and the
French Commerce." [3] From this point of view the question
was merged in the far larger one of the struggle between French
and English, the influence of which must be reckoned with
throughout the century. To consider the dispute as merely one
between old and New England is to lose its significance.

The fall in the price of sugar in 1733 to the lowest figure yet
reached, and the persistent demands of the planters resulted
finally in the passage through Parliament of the famous Molasses Act of that year.[4] The conflict of interests and the pos-

---

[1] John Bennet, *The National Merchant*, (London, 1736), p. 17.

[2] *The Importance of the Sugar Colonies to Great-Britain Stated and some Objections
against the Sugar Colony Bill Answer'd*, (London, 1731), p. 10.

[3] *History and Proceedings of the House of Commons from the Restoration to the present
Time*, (London, 1742), vol. VII, p. 209.

[4] Pitman, *West Indies*, pp. 92, 134; *An Act for the better securing and encouraging
the Trade of His Majesty's Sugar Colonies in America*, VI Geo. II, C. xiii. It was

sible results of any action, even upon the French competition itself, were of great complexity. The bill as it finally passed represented the effect of dealing with the problem in confusion of mind and weakness of purpose. It conceded in principle the right of the northern colonies to trade with the foreign West Indies, but laid duties so high as, if enforced, would have been prohibitive of the importation from them of rum, sugar and molasses. However, without adequate customs service to see that the duties were collected, they were naturally evaded, and the penalties proved but "Scarecrows and Pasteboard Soldiers." [1]

Although the conditions from which the New England trade had evolved were too strong to be withstood by mere legislative prohibitions, and the trade therefore went on as before, nevertheless, it cannot be said that the bill left matters as they had been. Had the law been enforced, not only would it have deprived the New England merchants of a most lucrative business, have decreased shipping, ruined the production of "Kill-Devil," adversely affected the fishing industry, but would also have cut off New England from one of the main channels of trade by which it secured specie with which to pay its constant adverse balance of trade with England, and so have reduced English exports and forcibly encouraged colonial manufactures. The law, therefore, aimed a deadly blow at what the colonists held dearest, their right to "develop the natural resources of their country and to utilize them freely through commerce." It constituted a perpetual grievance against England. Moreover, as it made a large section of the colonial population smugglers and law breakers by necessity, it lowered the moral tone of the community and decreased the respect for law. Finally, the fact that Parliamentary legislation of such far-reaching import proved to be so easily nullified in practice, taught the colonists a lesson that could not be lost upon them. As in the matter of a fixed salary for the governors, the English

passed as a "money bill." *Vide A Letter to a noble Peer relating to the Bill in Favour of the Sugar Planters*, (London, 1733), pp. 9 ff. Cf. *Commons Journal*, vol. XXII, pp. 55, 99, 139, 153.

[1] Thos. Salmon, *Modern History of the present State of all Nations*, (London, 1738), vol. XXXI, p. 523.

government irritated the colonists and then showed itself apparently impotent in the face of their defiance. It is a fatal policy with animals, children or growing nations.

At the time that the West Indian planters were presenting their grievances against the New Englanders, the merchants in old England had also been complaining to Parliament of the laws in many of the colonies which discriminated seriously against them in their collection of debts lawfully due to them while favoring the colonial creditors. In fact, in some cases colonies had passed laws which were so manifestly unfair as to warrant the English merchants' characterization of them as "bare-faced fraud." [1] As a result of the representations made, Parliament passed an act in 1732 which is noteworthy in that it distinctly regulated the internal affairs of the colonies and could not be construed as merely related to them externally as regulating imperial commerce. The act provided for the method by which the evidence of a resident in Great Britain could be introduced in a colonial court, and also made lands and slaves liable for debt as though they were personal property. Nor was it by any means the first example of the regulation of internal colonial affairs by Parliamentary statute. In 1710, the act establishing the post-office in the colonies had not only regulated the rates for service but had made it a revenue-producing measure for imperial purposes, although this seems to have escaped the attention of the colonists at the time.[2] Still earlier, in 1704, Queen Anne by proclamation had fixed the rates at which certain foreign coins should circulate within the colonies, and this had been confirmed by Parliamentary statute two years later.

The currency problem in the main, however, soon became that of a depreciated paper one, and was one of the most subtle of the forces at work to create ill-feeling between the colonies and England, and between classes in the colonies. The decade from 1730 to 1740 was marked not only by extravagant additions to the amounts put into circulation by the several New England governments, but also by the efforts of groups of private individuals to add to the chaos by forming their own

[1] Russell, *Review of colonial Legislation*, p. 150.
[2] Palfrey, *History*, vol. IV, pp. 327 *ff.*

"banks," that is by arranging to issue money. In 1732, a company was started in Connecticut under the name of The New London Society United for Trade and Commerce, which had a short and stormy career and which was the prototype of the more important Land Bank in Massachusetts eight years later.[1] In 1733, Rhode Island passed an act for emitting £104,000 and alarmed the merchants of Boston by the prospect of another enormous depreciation.[2] In an effort to avert this, ten of the more prominent merchants made an agreement not to receive any of the Rhode Island bills, and in an attempt to provide a sounder medium in their stead themselves issued £110,000 in notes redeemable at definite dates within ten years in silver at a fixed ratio.[3] A year later, some merchants in New Hampshire attempted a similar issue, the details of which are somewhat obscure.[4]

In 1739, with the greatest amount of paper as yet in circulation, and with exchange on London standing at 525, the demand for "more money" took the form of a resolution in the Massachusetts assembly stating that as there was a great scarcity of bills, and as trade must "be brought under a great declension unless some further expedient can be found" therefore the assembly asked that schemes might be proposed for providing an additional medium of trade.[5] As one of the results of this request, an exceedingly crude plan was advanced for the formation of a "bank," or issue of paper money, to be secured by land. A bid for the support of the working class in Boston was made by a clause which permitted notes to be issued for loans on the personal security of "Artificers and Traders," with sureties, for not over £100 each.[6] The notes were to be re-

---

[1] Davis, *Currency and Banking*, vol. II, pp. 102 *ff.*; *Conn. Col. Records*, vol. VI, pp. 420, 449; *Talcott Papers*, vol. I, pp. 268 *ff.*

[2] *R. I. Col. Records*, vol. IV, p. 487; Potter and Rider, *Some Account of the Bills of Credit or Paper Money of Rhode Island*, Rhode Island Historical Tracts, No. 8, (Providence, 1880), p. 137. The amount is frequently mentioned as £100,000.

[3] Davis, *Currency and Banking*, vol. II, pp. 123 *f.*; Hutchinson, *History*, vol. II, pp. 341 *f.*

[4] *Ibid.*, pp. 125 *ff.*

[5] Cited by Davis, *Currency and Banking*, vol. II, pp. 130 *f.*

[6] Articles of the bank are given in *Col. Soc. Mass., Publications*, vol. IV, pp. 135 *ff.* The Silver Bank Articles are in *ibid.*, pp. 143 *ff.* For the general account I follow Davis, *Currency and Banking*, vol. II, pp. 130 *ff.* and Hutchinson, *History*, vol. II, pp. 352 *ff.*

deemable only after twenty years, and might then be paid off in commodities of wholly uncertain value. The total issue was put at £150,000.

As in the case of the danger from Rhode Island, the merchants at once took action to counter the scheme and proposed one of their own, which became known as the "Silver Bank," whereas the other was known as the "Land Bank." They undertook to issue notes based on silver, similar to those they had issued in 1733 and which were now at a premium of thirty-three per cent; to receive no notes of other governments not redeemable in gold or silver except at a discount fixed by the company; and not to receive the notes of the Land Bank at all. The governor and Council were naturally in favor of the Silver Bank and sound currency, whereas the assembly favored the inflationist Land Bank scheme, and a political contest at once ensued. The line drawn was distinctly a class one, and the entire colony was for the most part divided into Debtors and Creditors, who for some years had formed the two political parties in Rhode Island. Of the eight hundred "subscribers" to the Land Bank — which as there was no capital stock meant prospective borrowers only — there was practically none of any substance or standing.[1] Besides these persons "the needy part of the province in general favored the scheme" and of the assembly elected in 1740 over one-half were its subscribers or abettors.[2]

Petitions were presented for and against it, but the assembly refused, on the one hand, to consider the matter in a committee of both houses, and, on the other, declined to prevent the Land Bank from issuing its notes.[3] Thereupon the governor, with the advice of the Council, issued a proclamation cautioning all persons against either issuing or receiving the bills as tending to defraud men, to disturb the peace, and to injure trade.[4] This was followed by an address to the people signed by one hundred and thirty prominent merchants, including such men as Peter

---

[1] The list is in *Col. Soc. Mass., Publications*, vol. IV, pp. 169 *ff.*

[2] Hutchinson, *History*, vol. II, p. 353; *Belcher Papers*, vol. II, p. 348.

[3] A. M. Davis, "Calendar of Papers relating to the Land Bank," *Col. Soc. Mass., Publications*, vol. IV, pp. 4 *ff.*

[4] It is given in *American Antiquarian Society Proceedings*, New Series, vol. XI, pp. 462 *f.* Cf. *Belcher Papers*, vol. II, p. 349.

Faneuil, Edward Hutchinson, James Bowdoin, Andrew Oliver, Edmund Quincy, Samuel Sewall and Thomas Hancock, warning the public against the scheme.[1] No headway, however, could be made against the ignorance of some, the dishonesty of others, and the ambition of those demagogic members of the assembly who catered to both. It seemed as though the experience of Barbadoes, a generation earlier, when the debtors of the island secured control of the assembly and almost ruined the moneyed class by making a similar currency legal tender, was in a fair way to be repeated in Massachusetts.[2]

For some time the advocates of paper money, drawn mainly from the debtor and ignorant class, had proclaimed themselves the "popular party" as opposed to that of sound money, which was naturally made up of the wealthy, the educated, and the royal officials. Feeling between them now rose to a high pitch. Finding the assembly obdurate in their pursuance of a course which seemed to portend ruin for the moneyed class, many of the leading citizens joined with the London merchants in a petition for help to the Privy Council in England. That body approved Belcher's proclamation and directed him to give all possible discouragement to the scheme of the Land Bank until an act of Parliament could be passed regulating the whole question of paper money in the colonies.[3]

Meanwhile, the governor issued another proclamation again warning people against passing the Land Bank notes, and threatening to remove certain classes of public officials if found guilty of doing so.[4] Many of the militia officers and justices of the peace, among whom was Samuel Adams, father of his better-known son, resigned office, but in spite of that were forcibly removed.[5] In addition to such action, which was without warrant in law, military officers were forced to enquire as to whether their subordinates had passed the bills, and registers of deeds were ordered to make returns of all Land Bank mortgages. The

---

[1] *Belcher Papers*, vol. II, p. 463.
[2] Pitman, *West Indies*, pp. 141 *ff.*
[3] *Acts Privy Council*, vol. III, pp. 683 *ff.*; *Belcher Papers*, vol. II, p. 360.
[4] *Col. Soc. Mass., Publications*, vol. IV, p. 7.
[5] *Ibid.*, pp. 7 *ff.*; Davis, *Currency and Banking*, vol. II, pp. 147 *ff.*

Massachusetts Council even went so far as to vote that no person could plead before it as an attorney who should pass, receive, or give encouragement to the bills, which cut such persons off from all practice in the probate of wills.[1]

Nevertheless, the notes continued to be put into circulation, resignations from office were frequent, and the assembly was as obdurate as ever. There was no law preventing the issuing of circulating notes by private individuals or associations and no way of legally reaching them. The Bubble Act of 1720 in England, passed after the South Sea scandal, distinctly did not apply to the colonies. Parliament, however, as a result of the representations made to it of the alarming conditions in Massachusetts, now proceeded to pass a new act by which it declared that the Bubble Act had applied to America from its first passage and was in force there, and further that the Land Bank came within its scope. Not only is it very difficult to find any legal justification for the last, but the making the application of the statute to the colonies retroactive by twenty years was a thoroughly iniquitous piece of legislation. Persons who had engaged in entirely lawful acts, however unwise, now found themselves threatened with exceedingly heavy penalties.[2] The affairs of the company were thrown into utter confusion, and all persons who had participated in them were at the mercy of anyone who chose to use the bills as a basis for the demand for enforcing the penalties of the act.

Meanwhile, the activities of the governor, council and merchants in opposition to the bank, and the fact that the notes had not circulated as the believers in the scheme felt that they should have done, had created very bitter feeling. Upon receipt of the news of Parliamentary action, if not, indeed, before, this resulted in what might have been serious armed rebellion against the local government. According to one affidavit five thousand "Land Bankers" were preparing to march on Boston to know why the notes did not circulate, and threats were made to burn the property of those who would not receive the bills. According to other affidavits, a thousand men were said to be

---

[1] Davis, *Currency and Banking*, vol. II, p. 151.
[2] *Ibid.*, pp. 152, 160 *ff.*

ready to rise in Boston, while twenty thousand were preparing to march in from the country, and to throw the merchants' stocks of corn into the Bay.[1] The evidence indicates strongly that a secret rising on a serious scale was in reality planned to take place but was prevented by prompt action by the governor.

It was just at this time that the long intrigues against Belcher attained their object and that the executive was removed. Had this not occurred it may be questioned whether either the people or the assembly would have acquiesced peaceably in the suppression of the bank. The winding up of its affairs was the most serious problem that at once confronted the new governor, William Shirley, and a process that took a generation and involved much injustice and caused much bitterness. We cannot here go into the details of the long and complicated story, and our main interest is with the effect of the episode upon opinion in the colony.[2]

In so far as concerned the relations with England, John Adams, writing in 1774, stated as his belief that "the act to destroy the Land Bank scheme raised a greater ferment in this province [Massachusetts] than the Stamp Act did," and was appeased only by the passing of local acts in contravention of it. Franklin, also, believed that the opposition of the home government to colonial paper money was one of the most active forces in producing and keeping alive the discontent of the colonists.[3] It is probable that this was the case. Conflict over currency problems is inherently a class conflict, with ignorance and resentment on the one hand and panic and fear on the other. The history of such conflicts invariably shows a deep emotional aspect. In this case the illegal or unjust acts of both the home government and the sound money party in the colony could not fail to embitter yet further the losing side. In the episode we can clearly see the strands entering into the story of the later revo-

[1] *Col. Soc. Mass., Publications,* vol. IV, pp. 18 *ff.*; Davis, *cit. supra,* vol. II, pp. 153 *ff.*
[2] Davis, *cit. supra,* vol. II, pp. 190 *ff.*; A. M. Davis, "Legislation and Litigation connected with the Land Bank of 1740," *American Antiquarian Society Proceedings,* New Series, vol. XI, pp. 86 *ff.*; Davis, "The General Court and Quarrels between Individuals arising from the Land Bank," *ibid.,* pp. 351 *ff.*; *Correspondence of William Shirley,* ed. C. H. Lincoln, (New York, 1912), vol. I, pp. 89 *ff.* Hutchinson, *History, cit. supra.*
[3] Adams, *Works,* vol. IV, p. 49; Franklin, *Works,* ed. Bigelow, (New York, 1887), vol. III, p. 418.

lutionary years — resentment against the authority of Parliament, resentment against the royal officials in the colony and, finally, resentment against the moneyed and merchant class in Boston.

In the colonies, the growth of distinct parties is invariably shown in the currency disputes, which intensified the cleavage between classes and geographical sections. In every case it was the more ignorant and the less able or less favored class which arrayed itself against that which had achieved or inherited success due to native ability or the entrenchment of privilege. Geographically, it was, in the main, the country against the towns, although the alliance of the farmers and frontiersmen with the mechanics and laborers in the larger centers tended to a certain extent to blur the divisions. We have noted in the Land Bank scheme how the bait of a hundred-pound loan was held out to the landless mechanic and artisan of the towns. These two elements composed the "country" or "popular" party, in distinction to the "Court party" composed for the most part of the town merchants, their lawyer allies, and others particularly favored by wealth, education or social position.

As a rule the latter were able to retain control until near the years of the Revolution. Even in so-called democratic Rhode Island it was not until the election of 1755 — when Stephen Hopkins was elected governor by a very narrow majority — that the people succeeded in returning a candidate not backed by the "mercantile oligarchy" of Newport and their rich and aristocratic allies, the planters of South County, who owned unusually large estates for New England and formed a unique class in the northern colonies.[1] It must be recalled that only a small part of the New England population was enfranchised, owing to various restrictions, and that, both for this and other reasons, the merchant aristocracy was much more powerful than its comparative numbers would indicate. In the Land Bank struggle of 1740 they were indeed outnumbered in the legislature. Although the supporters of that scheme were for the greater part composed of the poorer people of the towns and

---

[1] Kimball, *Correspondence of Colonial Governors*, vol. I, p. xxxix; E. Channing, *The Narragansett Planters*, (Johns Hopkins Studies, 1886), pp. 16 *ff.*

rural districts, they had secured so firm a hold on the situation as to force the "Court party" to resort to unconstitutional methods to which the "Country party" retorted by threats of violence and revolution.

The fact, however, that only about one-fourth or one-fifth of the adult males in the colonies possessed the franchise was ordinarily sufficient to ensure control by the simple but efficient political "machines" of the merchant class and their allies.[1] Even in Connecticut, where from 1702 a personal property qualification was accepted in lieu of the otherwise almost universal one of a freehold estate, the enfranchised citizens seem to have formed no larger proportion of the total population than in the others. As late as 1761 in a closely contested town election in New Haven only two hundred and thirty-four votes were cast, yet there were over one hundred holders of public office.[2] In other words, the office holders formed one-half of the entire electorate. Throughout New England a large part of the rural population did not possess the colonial franchise and neither did the great bulk of the people in the towns. Practically not a single workman, laborer, fisherman, sailor, mechanic or small tradesman had a vote, except in purely local affairs, and even for them the franchise was by no means as wide as it is frequently stated to have been. It was only as the Revolution approached that these unenfranchised elements, forming the overwhelming majority of the people, wrested political control of the colonial governments from the class of propertied freemen, and then largely by illegal, violent, and terroristic methods.[3]

From the beginning, it had been in accordance with New England theory to consider that the incorporation of townships carried with it the right to representation by two deputies in the General Court. As a matter of fact, owing to the expense involved and frequent lack of interest in political matters, they had not availed themselves in many cases of the privilege, even

[1] For proportions of voters, *vide* A. E. McKinley, *The Suffrage Franchise in the Thirteen English Colonies in America*, (Philadelphia, 1905), pp. 355 *f.*, 419, 453, 458, 471, 487.

[2] Gipson, *Jared Ingersoll*, pp. 23, 25.

[3] *Ibid.*, p. 20.

the older towns as a rule sending only one deputy instead of two.[1] The great extension of the frontier, however, and the subdivision of some of the earlier towns, had nearly trebled the possible number of deputies in the assembly by 1742. As practically all of these represented small towns and rural districts, it was evident that the balance between the assembly and Council was becoming completely upset in favor of the lower house. Had all of the one hundred and sixty towns of that year sent their two deputies each, the number in the assembly would have been three hundred and twenty as against the unchanged number of only twenty-eight Councilors.

Owing to the fact that this had not been done and that on the whole the conservatives had been able, without great trouble, to maintain their ascendency whenever they chose to act with their full weight, the possibilities of the situation seem to have passed unnoticed until the administration of Governor Shirley in Massachusetts. When the Land Bank agitation caused the merchants temporarily to lose control in 1740, and the full extent of the growth of radicalism and the strength of the radical elements became apparent, the conservatives appear seriously to have considered the changed political balance of the province. It would seem unquestionably to have been the result of the lesson the merchants had then been taught that caused the report to be made by Shirley on the evils of this continued increase in the potential numbers of the lower house, which, as he said, "seems to promise no good effect for his Majesty's service."[2]

The Lords of Trade at once took action, and instructions were issued to the governor which practically made the right of representation of new towns or subdivisions of old ones, dependent upon their assent. This policy was maintained until the Revolution, and in many cases towns were incorporated without the right of representation.[3] Although the policy went counter to

[1] H. A. Cushing, *History of the Transition from Provincial to Commonwealth Government in Massachusetts*, (New York, 1896), p. 21 and note.

[2] Cited by Cushing, *Transition from Provincial to Commonwealth Government in Massachusetts*, p. 21.

[3] Cushing, *cit. supra*, pp. 21 *ff.*; *Acts Privy Council*, vol. III, pp. 680 *ff.*; *Acts and Resolves*, vol. III, pp. 69 *ff.*, 745; vol. IV, pp. 5, 93 *f.*, 452 *f.*, 627 *f.*, 870. *Cf.* Chalmers, *Opinions of eminent Lawyers*, pp. 267 *ff.*; John Lind, *An Answer to the Declaration of the American Congress*, (London, 1776), pp. 23 *ff.*

the principles of the colonists, it does not seem to have been extolled generally as a grievance until the more heated politics of a later time. It is interesting, however, as showing the fear of the rural and rapidly growing frontier sections already felt by the conservative classes, and also how naturally those classes in the colonies allied themselves with the English government against the radical elements in the colonies themselves. The Land Bank episode had evidently made the merchant-aristocrats see clearly the possibilities of a class struggle for power, which the incipient revolutionary movement of the Land Bankers had revealed to them in no uncertain light. By defeating the wishes of the radicals they had drawn down upon themselves bitter feelings of resentment. By appealing successfully to the home government for assistance in the maintenance both of sound money theories and their own political ascendency, they had involved that government in the animosity felt for themselves.

Despite all these increasing points of friction, however, there was as yet no serious thought of separation from the mother country. In most of the cases, indeed, it was merely a question of struggles between American radicals and conservatives, the former fighting for their "rights" indiscriminately against the restraints imposed by the wealthy elements in the colonies and by the English government alike. In the Land Bank affair, the armed resistance, such as it was, was directed rather against the former than the latter. The radicals, however, including the farmers, the workmen in the towns, and the frontiersmen of various types, were becoming more and more aware of a conflict of interest between themselves and privilege, whether of the colonial merchant, of the English Parliament or the imperial Crown. A decrease of privilege was bound to be demanded sooner or later as the radicals became both stronger and more conscious of their strength. Partly from ignorance and partly from its abounding physical vitality and optimism, the frontier always exaggerates its own power. When the demand for an increase in privilege on the part of the English government precipitated the inevitable struggle, the radicals notoriously overrated their own military strength, and had it not been that the

European political situation led the French monarch to strike at England by aiding the revolting colonies, they would finally have failed. Had it not been for their mistake in overestimating their ability to defy England, it is possible that even the radicals would have hesitated to drive public opinion along the line of revolt. Such overestimation, as we have just said, is common to all peoples of new countries, but in addition England seemed fated to lead the colonists of each generation to believe that she was weaker than she was. Politically, she always allowed herself to be defied. Militarily, whenever she joined the colonists in a combined operation, she showed herself at her lowest point of efficiency and competence.

Young men who had taken part in the disastrous expedition against Canada in the English fleet under Sir Hovenden Walker in 1711 were still in the prime of life when the home government again decided to ask the coöperation of the American colonies in a military and naval undertaking. Forced by popular clamor, England had declared war — the "war of Jenkins's ear" — against Spain on October 19, 1739. It was decided to make the West Indies a theater of operations, and in January of the following year the colonial governors were requested by the English government to raise as many troops as possible to join in a combined naval and military expedition.[1]

On April 2d additional instructions were forwarded to each of the governors stating that although the government was sending only three thousand arms, more would be provided in the West Indies and that the total number of troops, therefore, should not be limited to that number. The field and staff officers, as well as one lieutenant and one sergeant in each company were to be appointed by the home authorities.[2] For the other officers, blank commissions were to be furnished to the governors to be filled in by them with the names of Americans.

---

[1] Newcastle to colonial governors, Jan. 5, 1739–40, *Brit. Mus. Add. Mss. 32693*. The instructions are printed in *Talcott Papers*, vol. II, pp. 191 *f.*; and Kimball, *Correspondence of Colonial Governors*, vol. I, pp. 127 *ff.*

[2] Instructions to Gov. Belcher, Apl. 2, 1740. *C.O. 5 No. 10*. Similar instructions were sent to Connecticut. *Talcott Papers*, vol. II, pp. 229 *ff.* Additional instructions followed a few days later. Secret Instructions to Gov. Belcher, Apl. 2, 1740, *Brit. Mus. Add. Mss., 32693*. Cf. *Talcott Papers*, vol. II, pp. 235 *ff.*; Kimball, *Correspondence of Colonial Governors*, vol. I, pp. 143 *ff.*

Proclamations were issued in the several colonies, and the people responded with considerably more alacrity than had been anticipated. Not only were the three thousand volunteers raised with ease, but many more offered themselves. Colonel Blakeney who had been sent out from England to take charge of the recruiting reported that all showed remarkable spirit in their desire to engage in the war against the hated Spaniard. He also noted that "from the highest to the lowest, the Inhabitants of these Provinces seem to set a great Value upon themselves, and think a Regard is due to them, especially in the Assistance they are able to give the Mother Country on such Occasions."[1] The pride and self-confidence of the colonists was evidently increasing.

In Massachusetts, Belcher was distinctly unenthusiastic toward the enterprise, and his confidential letters show that if not hostile to it he certainly was not active in forwarding it.[2] The friends of Shirley, who had already for many years been a resident of Boston, had long been intriguing to have him made governor and saw in the expedition an opportunity for him to show his zeal and to shine in comparison with the luke-warm Belcher.[3] We cannot here go into the details of the curious contest that ensued. The governor suddenly realized the situation, and became, on the surface, an enthusiastic partisan of the expedition.[4] Largely through Shirley's efforts, ten companies, numbering a thousand men in all, were raised instead of the four expected. The enlistments in the other New England colonies were also far beyond expectations. Suddenly, however, Belcher again changed his attitude, possibly because he feared that the brilliant showing might be credited to his rival instead of to himself.

An excuse presented itself in that owing to the fact that the English government had sent too few commissions signed in blank, and also too small a supply of the military stores

---

[1] Col. W. Blakeney to Newcastle, Aug. 21, 1740, *C.O. 5 No. 41*. *Cf.* also same to same, June 25, July 8, July 31, Sept. 11, *ibid*.

[2] *Belcher Papers*, vol. II, pp. 283, 305, 309.

[3] Wood, *William Shirley*, vol. I, pp. 85 *ff*.; *Shirley Correspondence*, vol. I, pp. 17 *ff*.; letter of Chauncey Townshend to Newcastle, Mar. 28, 1740, *Brit. Mus. Add. Mss. 32693*.

[4] *Belcher Papers*, vol. II, pp. 311 *ff*., 315 *f*., 321.

promised, the commissions and supplies were sufficient for only four companies. Although this shortage was due to an under-estimation of the willingness of the colonists to raise more than the three thousand troops suggested, it had a most depressing effect upon their spirit throughout all the colonies.[1] Belcher seized upon the pretext and disbanded six of the ten companies raised, although one of them was reorganized and finally sailed with the other four for the Indies.[2]

We cannot concern ourselves with the detailed story of the military operations, and are interested only in their effects on the minds of the colonists. There can be few expeditions, if any, in the annals of either the British army or navy which can show such a record of incompetence, mismanagement, lack of co-operation between the two branches, and such a staggering total of wholly unnecessary casualties.

The mismanagement in America had already made a painful impression upon the colonials, but on the arrival of the thirty-five hundred American troops at Jamaica it was found that no arrangements whatever had been made by England for either paying or feeding them, although the English troops were well cared for, and the Americans suffered much distress.[3] The sub-sequent losses, both from military casualties and from disease, were largely due to the incompetence of the English com-manders and were extraordinarily heavy. A careful analysis of the returns of the regiments from August 1740 to August 1741 indicate that approximately thirty-seven or thirty-eight hundred Americans were in the expedition at one time and another, and that by the latter date only about eleven hundred were still surviving.[4] It was stated by one of the English officers that owing to sickness after the disastrous battle of St. Lazarre

---

[1] Blakeney to Newcastle, Aug. 21, 1740, *C.O. 5 No. 41; Correspondence of Rhode Island Governors*, vol. I, pp. 172 *ff.*; *Shirley Correspondence*, vol. I, p. 25.

[2] State of Gov. Belcher's Proceedings in dismissing the Massachusetts Levies. John Sharpe. Dec. 3, 1740. *Brit. Mus. Add. Mss. 32695;* Copy of Vote of House of Representatives relating to the six companies, Sept. 5, 1740; Copy of the Declaration to the six companies, Sept. 6, 1740; Shirley to Lt. Gov. Clarke, Sept. 8, 1740; Belcher to Blakeney, Sept. 1, 1740; Blakeney to Newcastle, Sept. 20, 1740; all in *C.O. 5 No. 41.* W. K. Watkins, "Massachusetts in the Expedition under Admiral Vernon in 1740," *Soc. of Col. Wars (Mass.) Year Book* (1899), pp. 65 *ff.*

[3] Blakeney to Newcastle, Dec. 14, 1740; same to same Oct. 23. Both in *C.O. 5 No. 41.*

[4] The returns are in *C.O. 5 No. 41.* It is impossible to make them tally exactly.

WILLIAM SHIRLEY, GOVERNOR OF MASSACHUSETTS
From a portrait by T. Hudson

the combined force of English and Americans "between Tuesday morning and Friday night . . . had dwindled from 6645 to 3200." [1] In November, General Wentworth reported that the troops had been moved to Jamaica only with immense difficulty, "the greatest part of the sailors on board the transports being dead." [2] Entirely contrary to the terms of their enlistment, many of the American troops were impressed by the naval officers and forced on board the vessels, in a number of cases being carried off to Europe. Nor was this done ignorantly, for Blakeney, who was a man of honor, protested to the Admiral and showed him the royal orders.[3]

Although there were, of course, many naval officers who were both able and honorable, the conditions in the service at that period were indescribably cruel, immoral and brutal — one might almost say brutish — and there were undoubtedly good grounds for the protests contained in the memorial from the field officers of Colonel Gooch's American regiment which was sent to General Wentworth complaining of the treatment of the troops on board the transports.[4] On the other hand, Wentworth was continually complaining of the quality of the colonial soldiers, which complaints have unfortunately been echoed by the historian of the British army.[5] Many of the troops, particularly from the southern colonies, were of the riff-raff of the population, and were undoubtedly a poor lot, particularly the Irish Papists against whom complaints were most bitter. This by no means applies to all of the troops, however, as is evidenced in part by the fact, overlooked by Wentworth in his reports and by their modern detractor, that after the fatal battle of St.

[1] "Expedition to Cartagena in 1741" in Capt. Knowles's letter of Sept. 10, 1741, *C.O. 5 No. 41*; on the attack, *cf.* Newcastle to Lord Chancellor, June 19, 1741, *Brit. Mus. Add. Mss., 35407.*

[2] Wentworth to Newcastle, Nov. 29, 1741, *C.O. 5 No. 42.*

[3] Wentworth to Newcastle, June 20, 1741; same to same, Nov. 2, 1741; same to same, Dec. 20, 1741; Wentworth to Vernon, July 14, 1742; all in *C.O. 5 No. 42.*

[4] Feb. 3, 1741–2, *C.O. 5 No. 42.* The reader may get a vivid picture of conditions on the Cartagena expedition from Smollett's *Roderick Random.* The novelist was on the expedition and I find his account is borne out by the official papers, in regard to general conditions.

[5] J. W. Fortescue. *History of the British Army,* (London, 1899), vol. II, pp. 72, 78. The author's well-known idiosyncracies in the matter of colonials needs no comment, but in this case he has made statements so absurdly exaggerated as to refute themselves were there not plenty of official evidence to do so.

Lazarre, it was the Americans who were chosen for the peculiarly difficult and dangerous work of covering the retreat of the English forces from the wholly untenable position in which the English officers had placed them.[1] Moreover, while blackguarding the Americans in his English despatches, Wentworth was making every effort to secure additional enlistments from America.[2] It appears that the complete and disastrous failure of the expedition from every standpoint, made any scapegoat convenient to divert, however slightly, the attention of the home authorities from the quarrels and incompetence of the leaders.

The effort that the colonists had made at coöperation with the mother country, an effort so great and made so willingly as greatly to surprise the English authorities, had thus resulted not merely in heavy losses, but in increased misunderstanding and bitterness between the British and the provincials, and in exhibiting to the latter at close range the weakness and incapacity of both branches of the English service in their most exaggerated form. In the rapid expansion of the colonists' energies, it was not likely that the "great value" which Blakeney had found that they set on themselves was likely to diminish — a value which the English recruiting officer reported that they considered "especially in the assistance they are able to give the Mother Country."[3] The unfortunate exhibition which that country had just afforded them could not fail to make them set their own value still higher, and to mislead them to a certain extent when the point at issue was to be not assistance but resistance to the home land in less than another generation of continued colonial growth and expansion.

[1] A Journal of the Expedition that sailed from Spithead to the West Indies, Oct. 1740, *C.O. 5 No. 41.*
[2] Wentworth to Newcastle, Aug. 14, 1741; same to same, Nov. 29, 1741, both in *C.O. 5 No. 42*; *Law Papers, (Conn. Hist. Soc. Coll.)*, vol. I, pp. 15 *ff.*
[3] *Cit. supra.*

CHAPTER IX

THE GREAT DIVIDE

New Forces, 1740 to 1750 — Jonathan Edwards — The Great Awakening — Capture of Louisbourg — Its Return to France — Redemption of Paper Money — Changes in Social and Intellectual Life

THE forces which we noted in the last chapter as in operation were destined to bring about most striking results during the decade from 1740 to 1750. The events of the first half of the period are among the most spectacular in the history of New England in the spheres of thought, emotion and action, and make visible for us the strength of that movement of liberation and expansion which we have been tracing. Its bursting forth in all three spheres was almost volcanic in intensity, and although the results at the time seemed to be disappointing they were in reality both profound and lasting. Old landmarks were swept away, the sense of individual freedom was greatly increased, and the belief of the colonists in their own undisciplined strength — one of the most subtle elements in the weakening of the imperial connection — was enormously emphasized.

For half a century, many factors had combined to undermine the old New England theology and theocracy. The political power if not the social prestige of the clergy had been steadily declining, and the tenets of Calvinism had been yielding to Deism and Arminianism. In regard to the beliefs of the latter, those modern readers who are weary of the eternal wrangling of priests and sectaries over matters of which they do and can know nothing positively may find relief in the simple analysis by Bishop Morely, a century earlier, who when asked what it was that the Arminians held replied "the best bishoprics in England." To penetrate a little deeper, however, their doctrines of free-will as necessary for responsibility; the self-limitation of the divine sovereignty in dealing with free agents; the universality of redemption, and the denial of the responsibility of Adam's descendants for his guilt, were all radically opposed to the Calvinism of the New England churches, as were also both the doctrines and the temper of the Deists. The spread of both heresies had been alarming the ministers of orthodoxy for some years before the period covered by the present chapter, when there arose as their defender one of the most notable figures in the history of New England thought. Few even of New England clergymen have risen to a higher pitch of spiritual pride than Jonathan Edwards when he pictured a Last Judgment in which the ministers were to sit as co-judges with Christ upon the unfortunate members of their congregations.[1] The distance which separates intellectual New England of the eighteenth century from that of the seventeenth, however, is indicated by the fact that Edwards's life was completely divorced from politics, and that although the ablest theologian of his day he remained aloof from the concerns of the civil state.

Opposing with all the strength of a mind unequaled in his place and generation what he conceived to be the errors of his opponents, he became a dominating force, positively and negatively, in New England thought for a century and a half.[2] Although lacking philosophic thoroughness and developing a theology that was divorced from both philosophy and human nature, he in part swung New England back to the horrors of its Calvinism and preached a gorilla God of such fiendish deviltry as surpassed the bloodiest heathen Moloch. The description that Lecky gives of one of his volumes as "one of the most revolting books that have ever proceeded from the pen of man"[3] might be applied to several, and judged by human moral

---

[1] "How dreadful will it be to you to hear him [your clergyman] declaring how inexcusable you are upon these accounts! How will you be cut to the heart, when you shall see him approving the sentence of condemnation, which the Judge shall pronounce against you, and judging and sentencing you with Christ, as an assessor in judgment; for the saints shall judge the world; and when you shall see him rejoicing in the execution of justice upon you for all your unprofitableness under his ministry!" Edwards, *Works*, (New York, 1856), vol. IV, p. 297.

[2] F. J. E. Woodbridge, "Jonathan Edwards," *Philosophical Review*, vol. XIII, p. 394.

[3] W. E. H. Lecky, *History of the Rise and Influence of the Spirit of Rationalism in Europe*, (London, 1913), vol. I, p. 368 *n*.

standards I know of no more blasphemous descriptions of the
Supreme Being than those contained in the series of imprecatory
sermons preached by Edwards at Northampton. These, it is
true, form but a part of his work in other sections of which are
to be found many passages of much sweetness and charm, but
they are those by which he is best known today and by which he
most directly and deeply affected the popular religious life of his
time. The picture of God which he gives in them must be considered the one to which his beliefs led him and which he
deliberately tried to impress upon his generation.[1] To those who
were beginning to assert the freedom of man's will, and to dis-
believe in predestination, the damnation of infants and infinite
punishment for finite sins, Edwards preached determinism, collected the most infamous passages from the Jewish scriptures
to show God's wrath against children,[2] and painted a hell that
has no equal in all the horrors of theological literature. He
blasted the morality of the universe and damned the character
of God. The latter he described as holding the souls of men
"over the pit of hell much as one holds a spider or some loath-
some insect over the fire." It is useless to cry in supplication to
such a Deity, he continues, for "though he will know that you
cannot bear the weight of omnipotence treading upon you, yet
he will not regard that, but he will crush you under his feet
without mercy; he will crush out your blood, and make it fly,
and it will be sprinkled on his garments so as to stain all his
raiment. He will not only hate you, but he will have you in the
utmost contempt."[3]

Edwards pictured those saved by grace as looking out from
heaven upon the tortures of those whom God has damned forever, and feeling their own happiness exalted by the sight. "It
will not only make them more sensible of the greatness and free-
ness of the grace of God in their happiness . . . it will give
them a more lively relish of it; it will make them prize it more.
When they see others, who were of the same nature, and born

[1] As his biographer points out, these sermons were written out in full, showing them
to be his deliberate utterance. A. V. G. Allen, *Jonathan Edwards*, (Boston, 1889),
p. 116.
[2] *Works*, vol. II, pp. 379 ff.
[3] *Ibid.*, vol. IV, pp. 318, 320.

under the same circumstances, plunged in such misery, and they so distinguished, O it will make them so sensible how happy they are." Although these others "were by nature, and perhaps by practice, no more sinful and ill deserving than" themselves, it will give them a lively sense of the goodness of God to behold their torments. "How joyfully will they sing to God and the Lamb when they behold this!" [1]

In spite of his efforts to avoid the conclusion, Edwards had himself to postulate this god as the author of the sin which he punished.[2] Yet he calls this creature "infinitely lovely" and of "infinite excellency and beauty" — though his garments are spattered with the blood of human beings created by himself, whom he hates with an eternal and infinitely malignant hatred for sins of which he is himself the author. Such had the teachings of Christ become in the frenzied fantasies of New England's ablest theologian, who proclaimed them as the eternal truth and had the blasphemous audacity to describe himself as sitting with that same Christ in final judgment on the members of his congregation, condemning those whose lives and thoughts did not agree with his to that hell which he pictured to their tortured imaginations as they writhed below his pulpit on Sabbath mornings. It is little wonder that, as Dr. Gordon says, no one with a "respectable intellect" holds the New England theology today, and that Edwards's system is "morally incredible" and beneath the "moral consciousness of the average respectable person in any civilized community." [3] Edwards himself possessed not a "respectable intellect" but the greatest that had yet appeared in New England, and, in view of that, the picture which he drew of the Deity for his own and succeeding generations constitutes perhaps a greater sin against the supreme power of the universe than any venial ones of the body or social customs for which he condemned the young people of

---

[1] *Works*, vol. IV, pp. 276, 283. *Cf.* in this same volume the sermons entitled "The Justice of God in the Damnation of Sinners," "The Eternity of Hell Torments," "Sinners in the Hands of an angry God," and "The End of the Wicked contemplated by the Righteous."

[2] *Ibid.*, p. 231, vol. II, pp. 155 *ff.*, 476; Allen, *Jonathan Edwards*, pp. 87 *ff.*; Foster, *Genetic History of New England Theology*, p. 79.

[3] Gordon, *Humanism in New England Theology*, pp. 15, 66.

his congregation. There are mistakes and temptations more fatal and more subtle than those of the flesh.

The theology of the New England school had become almost completely divorced from the needs of human nature. It was intellectualism run mad. Its premise that man's heart was totally and completely evil without a trace of good in it was false, and finally failed to carry conviction. Its insistence upon the immutable decree of God condemning the greater part of mankind to eternal torment, irrespective of merit, as compared with those whom he chose to reserve to an eternity of bliss, not only blunted the moral sense but logically made fruitless any efforts of the individual to live a moral life. Great as was the theological structure reared by the orthodox New England ministers they failed to grasp the fundamental fact that "the essence of religion is a striving toward being, and not towards knowing," and that its philosophical or theological formulæ are its most evanescent aspects.[1]

As interests widened, these formulæ became comparatively of less appeal merely as mental exercises. They had ceased to possess an emotional content for a large part of the people, and left wholly untouched their genuine religious needs based upon a sense of "sin," of things as they are as compared with what they might be, and of the desire for a release from such a state. While life had been flowing on, changing unceasingly, the church had remained stationary, slowly petrifying. Failing either to guide or follow the spiritual needs of the people, it was largely abandoned by them, and the oft-raised cry of "empty churches" was heard on every side. Religion had been too deeply stamped upon the New England consciousness for it not to remain one of the leading factors in the life of the people, as to thought, custom and prejudices, but not only was the old orthodoxy displaced from its undisputed position, but religion itself was now become but one of the elements, and not the leading one, in New England life.

Both in old England and new, the reaction ensuing upon the Puritan revolution had been a "starving time" in the emo-

---

[1] J. H. Leuba, *Studies in the Psychology of Religious Phenomena*, (Worcester, 1896), pp. 313 *ff*.

tional life. Should anyone apply the key to open the cover over
these long suppressed emotions it might be anticipated that a
great outburst would follow which might take almost any direction. It is this outburst, lasting from 1734, but more particularly from 1741, to 1744 which in New England is known as
the "Great Awakening."

The first to turn the key was Edwards, whose illogical calls
to his hearers to repent and reform, when that repentance was
powerless to save them from the horrors of a hell already inevitably decreed as their portion, were clothed in a literary style
of such extraordinary power as still to be felt when read in print
two centuries later and in an age not easily moved by such
appeals.[1] The awakening effect upon his little congregation in
Northampton was immediate though not lasting, and it was
only with the itinerant preaching of Whitefield in 1741 that the
movement attained its full momentum. The example of the
latter was followed by a small host of other itinerants of every
shade of conscientious zeal and ignorance, who considered themselves as inspired and whose frenzied appeals to their hearers
released the spring which held back the emotional flood so long
pent up. "Les inspirés sont les ennemis nés de tous les clergés"
as a recent writer has said [2] and many of these itinerant evan-
gelists "exhausted ecclesiastical billingsgate" to describe those
ministers who disapproved of their revivalistic methods.[3] In
many cases, as in that of Edwards, the established ministers
believed in the efficacy of the new means, and everywhere congregations and even families became divided into "New Lights"
and "Old Lights" according as they approved or disapproved of
the methods of the "Exhorters."[4] The excesses committed dis-
pleased many and made them question the reality of the spiritual benefit of the movement. "There is a Creature here,"

[1] As to this illogical position of Edwards *vide* Allen, *Jonathan Edwards*, pp. 109 *ff*.;
E. G. L. Van Becelaere, *La philosophie en Amérique depuis les origines jusqu'à nos
jours*, (New York, 1904), p. 40.
    [2] C. Guignebert, *Le Christianisme antique*, (Paris, 1921), p. 164.
    [3] C. L. Becker, *Beginnings of the American People*, (Boston, 1915), p. 188.
    [4] The best general account is still that by Joseph Tracy, *The Great Awakening*,
(Boston, 1842). *Cf.* Jonathan Edwards, "Narrative of surprising Conversions," and
his "Thoughts on the Revival of Religion in New England," in *Works*, vol. III, pp.
231 *ff*., 274 *ff*.

says one opponent, "whom perhaps you have never heard of before. It is called an Exhorter. It is of both Sexes, but generally of the Male, and young. Its distinguishing Qualities are Ignorance, Impudence, Zeal." [1] "Numbers of people continued the greatest Part of the Night in the utmost Disorder," writes another observer; "they were groaning, crying out, fainting, falling down, praying; exhorting, singing, laughing, congratulating each other, which they did by shaking Hands and Embraces (the latter was commonly practised by different Sexes) and by the fifth Night, there were almost three Hundred thus affected." At another meeting the people "would break forth into as great Laughter as could be, to think, as they exprest it, that they should go Hand in Hand to Heaven. Then they would speak it over again, and shout out into a great Laughter, laughing and singing, jumping up and down, and clapping their Hands together; and some would be so filled with Joy, as they pretended, that they could not stand or walk: And all this, when at the same Time, there were threescore Persons lying, some on the Floor, some across the Seats, while others were held up and supported in great Distress." [2]

As might be expected from what is now known of the relation of the religious process of conversion with the bodily changes succeeding the age of puberty in both boys and girls, the greater number of persons everywhere affected were young people.[3] Also, as in all revivals, the forces of suggestion and hypnotism were clearly present. Describing one service a minister says, "Some had Fits, some fainted; and it was observable, that God made use of the Concern in some to create a Concern in others; and some that did not appear much concerned when the public Exercise was ended; yet seeing others distressed, fell into deep Distress under a Conviction of Sin and the Sense of the Divine Wrath due to them." [4]

[1] *The State of Religion in New England*, (Glasgow, 1742), p. 8.
[2] Chas. Chauncey, *Seasonable Thoughts on the State of Religion in New England*, (Boston, 1743), p. 240.
[3] Edwin D. Starbuck, *The Psychology of Religion*, (London, 1901), pp. 28 *ff.*; William James, *The Varieties of religious Experience*, (New York, 1902), pp. 198 *ff.*; Thomas Prince, *The Christian History*, (Boston, 1744-5), vol. I, pp. 191, 196, vol. II, pp. 20, 108, 140, 167 *f.*, 347.
[4] *Christian History, cit. supra*, vol. II, p. 106; Starbuck, *cit. supra*, pp. 171 *f.*

The Reverend Mr. Chauncey of Boston was a leading opposer of the movement from the first, and others looked askance at it as the excesses grew, but the exhorters and those of the clergy who went over to the "New Lights" were "vainly fond of their own imaginations, and invincibly set upon propagating them." [1] Many of the itinerants claimed the right to examine and judge the settled ministers, and when not satisfied pronounced them unconverted. For a while it seemed impossible for any one to speak against the new doctrines and preaching. Those who opposed Whitfield "were stigmatized as Enemies of God and true Religion" and were "openly represented both from the Pulpit and the Press, as in danger of committing the Sin against the Holy Ghost if not actually guilty." "Very few ministers have dared to open their Mouths in favour of Reason, Virtue, Order or anything that is thought to be against this Work," wrote another observer. [2]

Allowing for all the effects of hysteria and the influences of contagion, nevertheless, people were hungering for what they called "vital religion." When John Adams, some years later, voiced his discontent with the "whole cart-loads of trumpery that we find religion encumbered with in these days" and stated his belief that "the design of Christianity was not to make good riddle-solvers or good mystery-mongers, but good men" he was also voicing the weariness of countless numbers who were asking for bread and were being offered the desiccated husks of a theology growing more and more heedless of the needs of the human heart.

Moreover, short as may have been the apparent effects of the "conversions" and however disappointing the subsequent moral lapses of the majority, nevertheless, a people could not pass through an intellectual and emotional crisis of such violence and universality without its leaving deep traces upon their minds and outlook. For one thing, the unity of the individual sects, their parochialism, and the dictatorial powers of the clergy were broken up for good. "The Communion of Churches is in a great

---

[1] C. Chauncey, *Enthusiasm described and caution'd against*, (Boston, 1742), pp. 6 *f.*
[2] *A Letter from a Gentleman in Boston to Mr. George Wishart*, (Edinburgh, 1742), reprinted by Clarendon Historical Society, 1883, pp. 6 *f.*; *State of Religion in New England*, p. 8.

degree lost," wrote Samuel Niles in 1745, "the beautiful Harmony of Ministers as Fellow-helpers in their Work, turned too much into party Views." [1] Provincial religious solidarity, even in New England, became a thing of the past. The movement was not limited to any one group of colonies, and, although religious in its nature, was non-sectarian.[2] It was a schism which split all sects, a schism between those of each who were content with the old preaching and the old theology, and those who demanded a different and more vital religion. It was an uprising everywhere against the old form of parish despotism and an insistence upon the right of the individual soul to receive such spiritual help and guidance as suited it best. It was essentially democratic and individualistic, a demand, as against the state, the state-aided churches and even the lay majorities, for the right of the individual to choose his own way. Although attempts have been made to estimate the number of lasting conversions, such a method of gauging the result of the movement is not only impracticable but is on the wrong line. Its most important effect was the impetus it gave to social, religious and political tendencies. The fact that it cut across the boundaries of colonies and sects, and for the first time united great numbers in all of them in a common and emotional experience was in itself of fundamental and far-reaching import. Those throughout the colonies who separated from the old churches were bound together by a common opposition to the privileges conferred by a union of church and state. The movement thus created a new solidarity among large classes in the several colonies who had had no common bond before and gave a powerful impetus to the opposition against privilege in any form — an opposition already woven of so many different strands — and to the democratic tendencies of large groups. Beneath all the froth and excitement which remind one of a colossal negro camp meeting, we can trace the movement as one of discontent, as an uprising against an established order, as a demand for the right of the individual to expand along his own lines, to express

[1] *Tristitiæ Ecclesiarum*, (Boston, 1745), p. 4.

[2] There is no satisfactory account of the movement in the middle and southern colonies. The study by C. H. Maxson, *The Great Awakening in the Middle Colonies*, (University of Chicago Press, 1920), is helpful but inadequate.

his own unique emotional life, and to choose his own spiritual food and guides. As such it was successful. That the religious emotionalism should not have continued at its extreme pitch was only natural, and we should not be deceived by the fact that "conversions" both in the Old and New Light churches stopped suddenly after 1744. The energies set free for individual expression sought other channels, but the colonies were never the same afterward. The educational, social and political effects were even more profound than the religious ones. The new schools, colleges and churches which were the outcome of the schism remained as standing protests against entrenched privilege and were seed-beds for the growth of individualistic and democratic ideas which came to fruition in the political rather than the religious events of the next half century.

In New England, the movement came to a sudden end as far as the phase of religious excitement was concerned in 1744, but it is noteworthy that the following year was marked by an outburst of energy in another field which resulted in the most spectacular military achievement in the history of the colonies. Although the maritime war against Spain, which we noted briefly in the last chapter, had seemed, as an English historian of British foreign policy has said, "to lose itself in a morass" [1] England had found herself drawn into the larger operations of the war of the Austrian Succession, and as a result war was formally declared against France in the spring of 1744. A contest between the two colonizing powers of the North American seaboard was bound to involve the colonies of each, and Governor Shirley of Massachusetts believing such an outcome inevitable had been doing his utmost to strengthen the defences of New England in the few years since he had assumed office.[2] An intercolonial conference at Albany, participated in by representatives from Massachusetts, New York, Connecticut and the Iroquois resulted in securing both a pledge of friendship from the natives, and, as a consequence of a threat by the latter, a promise of neutrality from the eastern Indians in Maine and Nova Scotia.[3]

[1] H. E. Egerton, *British Foreign Policy in Europe*, (London, 1918), p. 62.
[2] Wood, *William Shirley*, vol. I, pp. 116 *ff.*
[3] *Ibid.*, pp. 197 *ff.*; *Law Papers*, vol. I, pp. 172 *f.*; McIlwain, *Wraxall's Abridgment of the Indian Records*, pp. 233 *ff.*

The inefficient French governor at Louisbourg, however, thought he saw a chance to strike a blow at the English and promptly attacked and captured the little New England fishing station at Canso, and then proceeded to an attempt against Annapolis. In spite of reinforcements previously sent by Shirley, the latter place would have proved an easy prey to the superior force of the French had not their leader shown himself wholly incapable.[1] As it was, the attack was abandoned and the main effect of the two operations was to exasperate the New Englanders.[2] This was effected through the influence upon the rival fisheries of the two nations, of the capture of Canso and of the over-running of part of Nova Scotia. In our previous volume, we pointed out how the long duel for empire between England and France, lasting a century and a half, had begun in an obscure fight between unknown fishermen off the coast of New England in 1611, and from that time onward the allegiance owned by the cod was possibly the most important international question in northern America.[3] It was that fish, shying at a French hook to gulp, perhaps, an English one, the multitudes of small fur-bearing animals scurrying to elude pursuit, and the silent trees of the northern forests, and not any dream of future imperial power and peoples, that ever and again brought the terror and slaughter of war to the New England border.

Shirley from the first had shown himself intelligently alive to the economic aspects of the struggle, particularly the enormous importance of the fisheries.[4] To protect these and to serve as a naval base both for warships and privateers, the French had fortified Louisbourg at such enormous expense that it is said the king and his council had asked whether its streets were "pav'd with Gold, or its Walls compos'd of Lewisdores." [5] The desirability of reducing this "Dunkirk of America," as the

---

[1] Parkman, *Half Century of Conflict*, vol. II, pp. 60 *ff.*; Wood, *William Shirley*, vol. I, pp. 212 *ff.*; *Shirley Correspondence*, vol. I, pp. 134 *ff.*

[2] *Lettre d'un Habitant de Louisbourg*, 1745, University of Toronto Studies, Historical Series II, vol. I, p. 15.

[3] Adams, *Founding of New England*, p. 54; Andrews, "Anglo-French Commercial Rivalry," pp. 546 *ff.*

[4] *Shirley Correspondence*, vol. I, pp. 137, 162 *f.*, 243, 284 *f.*, vol. II, pp. 1 *f.* Cf. *The Importance and Advantage of Cape Breton, truly stated and impartially considered* (London, 1746), pp. 71 *ff.*

[5] Admiral Warren to Newcastle, Nov. 23, 1745, *C.O. 5 No. 44.*

colonists termed it, was so obvious as to have been recommended by one person and another in positions of responsibility for several years before its governor made his irritating attack upon Canso and Annapolis.[1] At that time, however, information was given to Shirley of the weakness of its garrison, which was in reality in a shameful condition due to the inefficiency, neglect and venality of the French authorities. So outrageous had the condition become in 1744 that a mutiny of the troops was suppressed only with difficulty.[2] Food was scarce, and in spite of the strong defences of the place, there was considerable prospect of success could it be attacked in the proper force.

Shirley rightly regarded the fortress as the key to the entire French position in North America, and realized in addition the part it might play as a strategic point in the whole imperial system of trade.[3] As an imperial official, his outlook was wider than that of the local New England merchants, fishermen, loggers and farmers whom he would have to count upon, in large measure, for the execution of the enterprise. As in all self-governing communities every motive would have to be played upon to gain their approval. Quite as essential was the securing of naval assistance from England, without which success would be impossible. In spite of his representations to Newcastle, and the urging by the colony's agent, Kilby — who was acting, however, on his own initiative — no assurance of British help had been received when Shirley startled the General Court in Boston by a proposal to undertake the capture of the fortress.

The colony, owing to the course it had pursued for a generation in the matter of paper money, was practically bankrupt, and Shirley made his proposal on the very day when the Court was passing a bill for raising £7,500 for government expenses by means of a lottery — a coincidence the jocular significance of which was but too apparent.[4] After two days debate, the as-

[1] On the vexed and not very important question as to who first proposed its capture, vide J. S. McLennan, *Louisbourg from its Foundation to its Fall*, (London, 1918), p. 130; Parkman, *Half Century*, vol. II, pp. 64 f.; Wood, *William Shirley*, vol. I, pp. 225 f., 229.

[2] McLennan, *Louisbourg*, pp. 47 f., 95, 107, 109, 123 f. Cf. *Memoirs of the Principal Transactions of the last War*, (London, 1757), for a general account of the siege.

[3] *Correspondence*, vol. I, pp. 161 ff.

[4] Wood, *William Shirley*, vol. I, pp. 243 f.; *Acts and Resolves*, vol. III, pp. 195 ff. 219.

sembly, possessed of no courageous rashness, naturally rejected
the proposal as too hazardous unless England and the other
colonies would assist.

William Vaughan and a few others, however, who were enthusiastic for the scheme, immediately secured petitions signed by
several hundred citizens of Marblehead and Boston, and the
matter was again brought before the Court. Although not yet
in a position to promise either, Shirley expressed his belief that
England would both send assistance and reimburse the colony
for part of the expense. Several days were spent in secret deliberation, when finally the decision was taken to risk everything
upon the attempt.[1] Meantime, although not yet known in
Massachusetts, instructions had been issued by the English
government permitting Shirley to consent to the emission of
more paper money owing to the exigencies of the war, and that
government had also assumed the pay of the colonial troops.[2]

Shirley had early won the support of the prominent merchants, impelled by the hope of gain in the fisheries and in
trade, and every other possible motive was now brought into
play — religious bigotry, fear of invasion, glory and the chance
of plunder — in an effort to win the enthusiastic support of the
people at large.[3] The governors of the neighboring colonies were
appealed to for assistance, and all plans were pushed rapidly.[4]
In the absence of instructions, Commodore Warren, who was
cruising with the West India squadron, was obliged to refuse
the coöperation which Shirley requested, but fortunately Newcastle was showing more interest and energy than was known
or than might have been expected, and orders reached Warren
to join the expedition in time for him to reach Canso not long
after the forces sent to that rendezvous from Boston, preceded
a few days by the contingent from New Hampshire. The total
levies included about thirty-three hundred men from Massachusetts — of whom Parkman says over a third came from

[1] Parkman, (Half Century of Conflict, vol. II, p. 69) follows Hutchinson, (History, vol. II, p. 368) in stating that the plan was carried by only one vote, but this seems to have been an error. Vide Wood, William Shirley, vol. I, p. 255 n.
[2] Shirley Correspondence, vol. I, pp. 141 f., 144 f.
[3] McLennan, Louisbourg, pp. 133 f.
[4] Shirley Correspondence, vol. I, pp. 171 ff.; Law Papers, vol. I, pp. 252 ff.; Wood, William Shirley, vol. I, pp. 268 ff.

Maine — five hundred from Connecticut, and three hundred from New Hampshire. Rhode Island eventually raised half of the latter number but too late to take part in the siege.[1] William Pepperrell, a rich merchant of Kittery, was chosen commander of the expedition.[2]

Shirley had displayed a most commendable amount of energy and tact in dealing with the legislature and people of his own colony, with the touchy governor of New Hampshire, with the other colonies, the home government and all the other factors in a complex situation, but although his tastes were military his genius was not, and the expedition, including his own general orders, contained more elements of farce than of military science. The energy and courage which he put into the preparations were happily not balked of final success, mainly because of the assistance of the English fleet, the utter incapacity of the French and the dogged persistence and youthful dash of the undisciplined colonial troops. The original plan to take the fortress by surprise was, of course, impracticable, and the French had ample warning of the impending attack.[3] The fleet had already taken up its station for some days off Louisbourg when the troops arrived on the 30th of April, were disembarked with considerable skill, and the siege begun. Planned by a lawyer, the land forces composed of fishermen, farmers and mechanics, led by a merchant who was ignorant of the rudiments of war, it was nevertheless crowned by complete success.

The easiest, as well as perhaps the most decisive, event of the siege was the capture of the Grand Battery, situated opposite the entrance to the harbor. This was abandoned by the French in a panic without striking a blow, and was promptly occupied by the English.[4] The unexpected sight of smokeless chimneys

---

[1] Parkman, *Half Century of Conflict*, vol. II, pp. 81 *f.*; *Shirley Correspondence*, vol. I, p. 196.

[2] This seems to be the accepted spelling. Usher Parsons, *Life of Sir Wm. Pepperrell*, (Boston, 1856), p. 2.

[3] *Lettre d'un Habitant, cit. supra*, pp. 11, 23 *f.*

[4] There are ample documents in print covering the events of the siege. Among them may be mentioned, "Journal of Sir Wm. Pepperrell," *American Antiquarian Society, Proceedings*, New Series, vol. XX, pp. 130 *ff.*; *Pepperrell Papers, Mass. Hist. Soc., Coll.*, Series VI, vol. X; *Shirley Correspondence, passim*. The most important may be found cited by Wood, *William Shirley*, vol. I, pp. 281 *ff.* Parkman's account, as usual, is excellent. *Half Century of Conflict*, vol. II, pp. 90 *ff.*

WILLIAM PEPPERRELL
From a portrait by T. Smybert

within the barracks had led Vaughan to suspect the truth, and he bribed a Cape Cod Indian with a flask of brandy to reconnoitre. The savage found all safe and empty. Whereupon, somewhat neglectful of the part played by the humble flask, the leader grandiloquently reported to Pepperrell the capture of the battery "by the grace of God and the courage of thirteen men."[1] The enemy's cannon were now turned against the besieged, and in addition the New England troops, with enormous difficulty, hauled others from the shore across what had been considered an impassable swamp, harnessed two or three hundred to a gun. Their ardor and energy were astonishing but their lack of discipline and their scornful rejection of expert advice would have cost them dear had not the French given up every advantage by criminal blundering and inaction. As one of the British said of the colonial troops "if they had pickaxe and spade they would dig a way to Hell itself." We may add that it was certainly not the fault of their ministers if they did not know the way there, and that they certainly would have captured it if it had been defended with as little ability and courage as was displayed by the French. It was also said at the time that the siege resembled "a Cambridge commencement," which in those days was anything but a serious occasion, and those who took part in what was half a siege and half an uproarious holiday used later to laugh at the whole affair and marvel at their almost miraculous preservation.[2]

In spite of an unsuccessful attempt to take the island battery, in spite of disease — at one time half the troops were unfit for service — of accidents due to unskilled gunnery, and of innumerable other difficulties of one sort and another, the besiegers were at last gladdened by an offer of surrender by the French on the very day when they had planned a final assault, which it was probably fortunate for the attacking party never took place. On the 17th of June, the garrison surrendered and marched out of the fortress with the honors of war.

Although the land forces had borne the main burden of the

---

[1] Jeremy Belknap, *History of New Hampshire*, vol. II, p. 168.
[2] *Ibid.*, p. 170. Belknap had talked with many of the survivors.

attack, their success would have been impossible without the coöperation of the fleet. This was serviceable in more ways than merely by its capture of a French sixty-four gun ship which was taken while on her way to relieve the fortress in May, and which yielded a new supply of powder and ammunition sorely needed by the besiegers. Happily, although minor occasions of friction were by no means lacking, the colonial army and the royal navy worked together in a harmony that was in complete contrast to the relations subsisting between the two branches of the service in the recent expedition to the West Indies.[1] This was due in part to the character and interests of the naval commander Warren who understood the Americans and had married a New York woman, and in part to the tact and patience of Pepperrell. Although the somewhat dilatory movements of the latter, combined with his ignorance of military matters must have seriously irritated Warren, as did also the utter lack of discipline among the colonial troops, nevertheless he seems to have appreciated the good points of the provincials, as did Shirley.

The joint expedition undertaken by the colonies and the mother country had thus been a complete success, which was heartily acclaimed on both sides of the ocean. Good news was sorely needed in England for the battle of Fontenoy had recently been lost and the Pretender had just landed in Scotland, so that old England's enthusiasm over the Canadian victory was quite as spontaneous as New England's. A perverse fate, however, seemed always to hang over any efforts at close coöperation and to cause them to end in increased bitterness no matter how promising their beginnings. Warren, who had been made governor of the empire's new acquisition, had been released within a year at his own request and replaced by Admiral Knowles who hated all colonials from the bottom of his soul, and exhibited toward them on every occasion that manner of supercilious superiority which is the most irritating trait abroad in such Englishmen as happen to possess it. In addition he had that spirit of the martinet which the navy occasionally breeds. At

---

[1] Shirley had anticipated possible trouble and cautioned Pepperrell. *Correspondence*, vol. I, pp. 205, 236 *f.*, 250. The Massachusetts legislature was very touchy on the subject. *Cf.* McLennan, *Louisbourg*, pp. 171 *f.*; "Roger Wolcott's Journal of the Siege of Louisbourg, 1745," *Conn. Hist. Soc., Coll.*, vol. I, p. 156.

every point at which he came into contact with colonists, in the West Indies, at Louisbourg, at Boston, friction immediately resulted. In one respect, if known at the time, his action must have caused the deepest dissatisfaction, and we may here anticipate a little in order to dispose of the matter to which it related.

The capture of the French stronghold had been almost the only feat of arms in the entire war in which the English nation could take any pride, and its possession was the only counter with which the ministry could bargain at the peace of Aix-la-Chapelle. Not only was the capture a source of legitimate and enormous self-satisfaction to the New Englanders but the retention of the fortress was considered by them as absolutely essential to their safety and trade. Warren, who like Shirley, took an imperial rather than a local view agreed with him as to the strategic value of the French base in spite of the staggering expense which he foresaw it would entail.[1] Knowles, on the other hand, had been at his new post but a month when he began writing home violently denying that the place had any value, complaining of the colonials, and strongly advising against any effort to maintain the fortress.[2] He not only lamented over the possible "vast expense of this bewitching idol" but so absurdly overdrew the picture in his hostility to everything American that he was led into such futile nonsense as to say that even if the English were to be "in quiet Possession of the Town of Quebec tomorrow it would be impossible to keep it, had we no other Enemy but the Weather," oblivious apparently of the fact that the French had already maintained themselves there for a century and a half.[3] Poor little spiteful, self-important Knowles was evidently not of the stuff that pioneers and empire builders are made of. How much influence his childish petulance and gloom may have had upon Newcastle and the ministry it is hard to say. The final return of Louisbourg to the French in the treaty of 1748, however, was a cause of such deep and lasting resentment on the part of the colonists, who felt that their interests had been wholly overlooked and that they

---

[1] Warren to Newcastle, Nov. 23, 1745, *C.O. 5 No. 44.*
[2] Knowles to Newcastle, July 8 and 9, 1746, *C.O. 5 No. 44.*
[3] Same to same, January 20, 1746–7, *C.O. 5 No. 44.*

were being deprived of the just reward of their great efforts, that it is worth while to trace somewhat in detail the progress of the negotiations.

In the latter part of 1746 suggestions were made to Newcastle from Lisbon that if peace were to be effected between England and Spain, the way would be paved for the retention of Cape Breton.[1] The private secretary of the King of Portugal indeed suggested that in that case facilities might be afforded for the English to attack the French part of St. Domingo and retain Louisbourg.[2] Six months later Sandwich wrote from the Hague that he was convinced England could conclude peace upon her own terms but that it would "require address and management to get over the Article of Cape Breton, by which the people of Amsterdam jealous of us in a commercial light will endeavour to rob us of our popularity in this country" and strongly advised an effort to get a private pledge from the Pensionary that he would support England in that point if she would not continue the war.[3] In August, Newcastle wrote that an answer had been discussed in reply to a French note, and that the other ministers had wished to say that the "King would not refuse to consent to an *Arrangement* about Louisburgh, provided all other points were settled to His Majesty's satisfaction" and that the king had approved but that he had got the monarch to consent to altering it. The minister added "for God's sake moderate the Prince of Orange or all is undone."[4] On the same day, Chesterfield wrote that the king expected the cession of Cape Breton but that if Sandwich should be unable to obtain it for him, he was to insist upon the demolition of the fortress.[5]

That diplomat reported a few weeks later that the Dutch had

---

[1] M. de Tabuerniga to Newcastle, Sept. 5 (N.S.) 1746, *Brit. Mus. Add. Mss. 32806.*

[2] Keene to Newcastle, Oct. 26, 1746, *Brit. Mus. Add. Mss. 32806.* It was intimated that Spain would secretly sign a separate treaty without consulting France, and meanwhile would amuse the French by publicly insisting on England's restoring Cape Breton. Sandwich to Chesterfield, Feb. 10, 1747, *Brit. Mus. Add. Mss. 32807.*

[3] Sandwich to Newcastle, May 3, 1747, *Brit. Mus. Add. Mss. 32808. Cf.* Same to same, Mar. 10, 1747, *Brit. Mus. Add. Mss. 32807,* marked "very private." "Can we ever finish upon worse terms than the surrender of Cape Breton and a neutrality for the Low Countries? Yet if we finish at present in conjunction with the Dutch I fear those two articles must be part of our Treaty."

[4] Newcastle to Sandwich, Aug. 4, 1747, *Brit. Mus. Add. Mss. 32808.*

[5] Chesterfield to Sandwich, Aug. 7, 1747, *Brit. Mus. Add. Mss. 32808.*

then been brought to support all the English demands including that for Louisbourg, and that they would insist "with us for the absolute cession of that possession on the part of France, as long as we Ourselves think it consistent with common Prudence to persist. . . . If we gain the point of the Demolition, after having been beat out of the other, I think we shall be able to defend Ourselves upon the Supposition of our having made it useless to the Enemy," otherwise that Parliament would take a very unfavorable view of their action.[1] Three weeks later, he reported that France was willing to cede Cape Breton but in that case would insist on keeping her conquests in the Low Countries "which it would be impossible for us to recover in less than a War of Six Years longer."[2]

The English people themselves were intensely anxious to retain the new colonial conquest. "The generality of our Nation," Sandwich had written earlier, saw the value of it, and were "ready to continue the war for the defence of it, or to express their rage and resentment in the strongest terms if it is given up. All opposition in Parliament seems to be attentive to that point, their writings as well as the language of their leaders from the first to the last sufficiently shew that it is there they intend to form their attack because it is upon that question that they are sure of having the people on their side."[3] Everywhere, however, the military results of the war had been unsatisfactory for England — even in India she had been outgeneraled by the French — and the time when she might have made peace and retained Louisbourg had gone by, if, indeed, she might have done so at any time. The new campaign was going badly. Money was almost impossible to obtain, and the government securities were lower even than they had been during the Rebellion.[4] In January 1748, Newcastle had to write to Sandwich that the ministry desired to conclude peace practically without reservations.[5] In April, unable to reconcile the discord among the allies and to check the progress of French

[1] Sandwich to Bedford, Aug. 29, 1747, *Brit. Mus. Add. Mss. 32808.*
[2] Sandwich to Chesterfield, Sept. 11 (N.S.) 1747, *Brit. Mus. Add. Mss. 32808.*
[3] Sandwich to Newcastle, Mar. 13, 1746-7, *Brit. Mus. Add. Mss. 32807.*
[4] Lord Mahon, *History of England,* (London, 1853), vol. III, p. 513.
[5] Newcastle to Sandwich, Jan. 19, 1747-8, *Brit. Mus. Add. Mss. 32811.*

arms, the ministers had to admit that they would be forced
to sign a separate peace with France on her own terms.[1] In order
to regain lost possessions in Flanders and India, it became
necessary to yield the new acquisition in America. So low,
indeed, had England fallen for the moment that two hostages
— the Earl of Sussex and Lord Cathcart — had to be sent to
France as pledges for the return of Cape Breton.

In New England, however, these conditions were ignored, and
the easy conquest of the strongest position in all America had
enormously increased that "great value" which we found in the
last chapter the colonists were beginning to set on themselves.
They had assisted in the only successful conquest of the war,
and now that conquest was taken from them. In the commercial controversy with the West Indies the decision had been
given against them in such a way as would have ruined their
trade had the terms been enforced. Now their trade was again
sacrificed, they felt, in favor of imperial interests on the continent of Europe and in far off India. Such conflicts of interest
were bound to occur in any far-flung empire. Decisions in favor
of one section would necessarily at times be to the disadvantage
of others. The imperial bond was of enormous value to the
colonies even from the point of view of trade, but the general
view of the relation was that England afforded military protection in exchange for certain trade advantages yielded to her
by the colonists. But the events of the two decades prior to
1750 were causing New England to overrate her own military
power, on the one hand, and to feel increasing resentment on the
other over the restrictions imposed upon her commerce. The
final outcome of the joint colonial and royal effort at Louisbourg
was thus even more disastrous upon sentiment toward the home
country than had been any of the earlier experiments in
coöperation.

Before this result was known, however, the colonists showed
themselves eager to follow up the success at Louisbourg by the
conquest of all Canada.[2] Shirley, as usual, was a leader in the

---

[1] Mahon, *History of England*, vol. III, p. 514.
[2] Wood, *William Shirley*, vol. I, pp. 295 *ff.*; V. H. Paltsits, "A Scheme for the Conquest of Canada in 1746, *American Antiquarian Society, Proceedings*, New Series,
vol. XVII, pp. 69 *ff.*

plans made for the joint action of the colonies as far south as Pennsylvania. The English ministry took up the project with considerable interest in spite of the Duke of Bedford's later misgivings lest too great conquests and the possession of a large force of men might give the colonists an undesirable sense of independence toward the mother country.[1] Preparations for an expedition of so large a scope, involving the united action of England and more than half a dozen of the colonies, naturally moved slowly, but Newcastle promised English assistance, and the colonies raised and equipped some eight thousand men. The plan of attack was the old standard one of joint operations by way of the St. Lawrence and Lake Champlain.[2] Matters, however, were still in the stage of discussion, when the French assumed the offensive and despatched a large fleet from Brest for the recapture of Louisbourg, or, if that should not prove feasible, for an attack upon Boston. The armada was said by some to contain as many as ninety-seven vessels carrying fifteen thousand troops, and the West India squadron was believed to be on its way to join it.[3] The French effort proved a colossal failure. Disease, storms, lack of supplies, the death of the commander and the suicide of the next in command — all served to render the imposing menace a complete fiasco.

The French in Canada, meanwhile, were by no means inactive, and the slow movements of the Newcastle government and the lack of willing coöperation among the American colonies gave them opportunity to harass the northern frontier as of old.[4] Finally, after Massachusetts and some of the other colonies had already incurred heavy expense for two successive years, word came from England that after all no help could be expected thence and that the expedition had been definitely abandoned.[5]

---

[1] *Shirley Correspondence*, vol. I, pp. 329 *ff.*, 342 *ff.*; Wood, *William Shirley*, vol. I, p. 318.

[2] *Vide* Plan of an intended Expedition against Canada, Admiralty Office, Apr. 7, 1746; Newcastle to the Governors of New Hampshire and other colonies, Apr. 9, 1746; both in *C.O. 5 No. 42*.

[3] Wood, *William Shirley*, vol. I, pp. 347 *f.*; Parkman, *Half Century of Conflict*, vol. I, pp. 145 *ff.*

[4] *A short Narrative of the Mischiefs done by the French and Indian enemy . . . drawn up by the Reverent Mr. Doolittle*, (Boston, 1750), reprint *Magazine of History*, Extra number No. 7, (New York, 1909), pp. 203 *ff.*

[5] Newcastle to Shirley, May 30, 1747, *C.O. 5 No. 42*.

Once more, as in the earlier Canadian expeditions planned for 1709, 1710, and 1711, the New Englanders had relied upon promised military assistance from the home country only to find, at vast expense, that they were leaning on a broken reed. Under the circumstances, it was impossible that a certain amount of contempt and distrust should not fail to be mingled with a great deal of natural irritation.

The cost of the military preparations, particularly the expedition against Louisbourg, had been enormous, and at the peace of Aix-la-Chapelle, the colonists found their enemy reinstated and themselves practically bankrupt. The peace as Carlyle says was a "mere end of war because your powder is run out, mere truce till you gather breath and gunpowder again," but the New Englanders did not yet know that. Meanwhile, the bulk of the expense had fallen upon Massachusetts, and the amount which she had expended was stated to be over £183,000 Sterling, represented by approximately £2,000,000 in her depreciated paper money. William Bollan, a son-in-law of Shirley and one of the agents for the colony in England, solicited the home government for reimbursement to the colony of the sum spent. Finally after many delays and much difficulty, the ministry was induced to accede to the request and a bill passed Parliament for the purpose. Meanwhile, Thomas Hutchinson, the speaker of the Massachusetts assembly and the ablest financier of the province, had recognized that the receipt of so vast a sum in silver would afford the colony an unexpected way out of the morass of paper currency could the provincial authorities be induced to use the payment for the redemption of the outstanding notes. The plan received Shirley's somewhat sceptical approval but was merely met with a smile when laid before the House.[1] It was twice rejected by the assembly, and although Hutchinson exercised much pertinacity, tact and sound judgment, it is probable that his efforts might have been fruitless had it not been for the pressure brought to bear by the English government. The London merchants and some "New England Gentlemen" petitioned that no money should be paid to the colonies unless they would agree to call in all their paper cur-

---

[1] Hutchinson, *History*, vol. II, p. 392.

THOMAS HUTCHINSON, GOVERNOR OF MASSACHUSETTS
From a portrait by J. S. Copley

rency.[1] This had so much influence with the Lords of the Treasury that the Connecticut agent in London wrote to the governor that as a "means of removing all Cloggs" to the payment he recommended that the colony take measures to redeem their paper. Governor Law wrote to Shirley of the situation and stated that he believed there was no use for the colonies to go to further expense in trying to secure reimbursement unless they would call in the paper currency, and it is evident that the final decision to do so was brought about very largely by the interposition of the English authorities.[2] The opposition among the debtor class was strong at first, and in spite of the favorable effect upon trade, the action of Parliament, two years later, in passing an act preventing any New England colony from making paper money legal tender in private transactions was distinctly unpopular and a source of great irritation in the colonies. The paper money of Connecticut was also redeemed by 1756, at about one-ninth of its face value, both colonies thus resorting to repudiation on a heavy scale.[3] But New England theology always advocated justification by faith and not by works.

The period was distinctly one of lax commercial morality on both sides of the water, emphasized in New England by the facts of the frontier and of restrictive legislation which made the bribery of customs officials or the making out of false invoices and clearance papers a mere matter of daily routine. Moreover it was a period of decreasing self-restraint. To those who think of the Boston of the mid-eighteenth century as a dour Puritan town, the following little extract from the diary of Captain Francis Goelet may prove enlightening. "Having an invitation from the gentlemen to dine at Mr. Sheppard's, went accordingly

---

[1] *Law Papers*, vol. III, pp. 268, 284. These papers shed much new light on this whole transaction. Other references are *ibid.*, pp. 219 *f.*, 223, 226, 230, 232, 249, 257, 265, 268, 270 *f.*, 276, 286 *ff.*, 294 *ff.*, 297, 310, 337.

[2] Other references that should be consulted are Hutchinson, *History*, vol. II, pp. 391 *ff.*; Davis, *Currency and Banking*, vol. I, pp. 203 *ff.*; Wood, *William Shirley*, vol. I, pp. 398 *ff.*; An Account stated which if pursued proves the ruin and destruction of the Massachusetts, 1747, and An Account stated proving the method to secure and safeguard New England, 1747, both in *Brit. Mus. Add. Mss. 33029*; *Acts and Resolves*, vol. III, pp. 430, 454 *f.*, 457 *f.*, 493; *Trumbull Papers*, pp. 45, 48, 60, 66, 69, 72, 84; Kimball, *Correspondence of colonial Governors*, vol. II, pp. 80 *ff.*, 116 *f.*; *Conn. Col. Records*, vol. IX, pp. 410 *f.*, 447, 453, 474, 512; vol. X, p. 157.

[3] Bronson, "Historical Account of Connecticut Currency," pp. 75 *ff.*

where was a company of about forty gentlemen. After having dined in a very elegant manner upon turtle, etc., drank about the [sic] toasts, and sang a number of songs, and were exceeding merry until three o'clock in the morning, from whence went upon the rake. Going past the Commons in our way home, surprised a company of country young men and women with a violin at a tavern dancing and making merry. Upon our entering the house, the young women fled. We took possession of the room, having the fiddler and the young man with us with the keg of sugared dram. We were very merry. From thence went to Mr. Jacob Wendell's where we were obliged to drink punch and wine, and about five in the morning made our exit and to bed." [1] Of the two thousand and odd men selected from the besieging force at Louisbourg to do subsequent garrison duty, over a thousand were officially reported drunk daily.[2] It was in many ways a brutal age. Governor Shirley and the Council, consisting of the pick of the cultivated and wealthy men of Boston, at the beginning of the new war in 1744, passed a resolution that all Indians living beyond a certain arbitrary line to the eastward should be considered enemies, and offered a bounty of £50 for the scalps of any of their women or of their children under twelve years of age.[3]

Throughout the whole period there is evidence of a growing spirit of lawlessness, to which we earlier called attention, and of an increasing tendency for the unenfranchised lower classes to give expression to their disapproval of men and measures or to their momentary gusts of passion by mob action. This was by no means always directed against royal officials. A serious case, however, in which the latter were involved occurred in Boston in 1747, while preparations were under way for the expedition against Canada.

In no responsible quarters, perhaps, was the inhumanitarianism of the age erected into a more callous system than in the

[1] *New England Historical and Genealogical Register*, 1870, p. 43. I have modernized the spelling and to some extent the punctuation, the original having the somewhat disheveled appearance which would seem to be justified by the circumstances.

[2] Knowles to Newcastle, July 9, 1746, *C.O. 5 No. 44.* Although this is Knowles's testimony it is borne out largely from other sources.

[3] *Acts and Resolves*, vol. III, p. 218.

royal navy.[1] The treatment that the men received, even more than the small pay, made resort to the press gang system inevitable in order to replace the vacancies caused by the constant desertions. In this abominable work the naval authorities enjoyed a curious immunity. Army officers complained frequently, as we have noted at the time of the siege of Jamaica, that soldiers needed for defense were impressed by naval officers regardless of the exigencies of the sister service. In 1741 the Custom House in England complained that although smuggling was rife, the navy was impressing customs officers, but they could get no redress.[2] Representations may be found, through the Parliamentary journals, which were fruitlessly made by English merchants of ships held up for lack of men owing to the impressment of their crews, but all to no avail. In the colonies this vicious system was peculiarly obnoxious, and was the cause of constant friction between English naval officers and the people, as we have already noted. Loud complaints had been made in 1741 of the acts of the commander of the royal ship Astraea in impressing men at Boston in an especially brutal and irritating fashion,[3] but six years later an attempt by officers of Commodore Knowles's ships, then in Boston harbor, resulted in a serious riot. Only a couple of years before in another case, two Boston men had been killed, and a boy concerned in the affray was even yet in jail charged with murder and awaiting orders on his case from England.[4] When, therefore, Knowles attempted a wholesale impressment of the men on the vessels lying at anchor, the whole town was immediately in a blaze. So serious did the disturbance at once become that Shirley took refuge in Castle William, and Knowles threatened to bombard the town unless his officers, who had been seized, were released. Shirley, however, dissuaded him from this final imprudence.

There were particular reasons why the practice of impressment was becoming peculiarly irritating to Boston besides those

---

[1] Cf., e.g. the treatment of prisoners of war, Francis Abell, *Prisoners of War in Britain, 1756 to 1815,* (Oxford, 1914), *passim. Cf.* J. R. Hutchinson, *The Press Gang Afloat and Ashore,* (London, 1913).

[2] *Calendar of Treasury Books and Papers, 1739–41,* p. 473.

[3] *Mass. Archives,* 64: 163–176; 64: 198–201.

[4] *Shirley Correspondence,* vol. I, pp. 415, 421 *f.*

already mentioned. With its increasing importance, that place was becoming more frequently a port of call for the royal ships and consequently seamen were more likely to be impressed there than at the rival ports of New York and Newport, in consequence of which sailors were drifting to the latter two towns and giving the merchants there an advantage over their Boston competitors. In addition, only recently Parliament had passed an act by which the Sugar Islands were exempted from the practice, and this had added to the continually sore feeling over the discrimination shown in favor of the islands by the Molasses Act.[1] So general was the resentment felt, and so slight was the control of those in authority, that for three days Boston was in the hands of the mob, the militia having failed to respond to the governor's call. At length, however, order was restored, the naval officers released, as were most of the impressed men also, and Knowles sailed to sea.[2]

In a long report on the affair to the Lords of Trade, Shirley had an interesting comment to make upon the significance of that much vaunted New England institution, the town-meeting. "What I think may be esteem'd the principal cause of the Mobbish turn in this Town," he wrote after a fair presentation of the colonists' case, "is its constitution; by which the Management of it is devolv'd upon the populace assembled in their Town Meetings; one of which may be called together at any time upon the Petition of ten of the meanest Inhabitants, who by their Constant attendance there generally are the majority and outvote the Gentlemen, Merchants, Substantial Traders and all the better part of the Inhabitants, to whom it is Irksome to attend at such meetings, except upon very extraordinary occasions." [3] The beginnings of American municipal misrule could not be more clearly shown than in this comment — the "constant attendance" of the lower class politicians, and the "irksomeness" of that same attendance upon the "Gentlemen," with the inevitable consequences. Although in the beginning of New England,

[1] *Shirley Correspondence*, vol. I, p. 417.

[2] *Vide* Vote of Council and House of Representatives, Nov. 19, 1747; Resolves of House of Representatives, same date; Shirley's Proclamation, Nov. 21; Votes of Town of Boston, Nov. 20; all in *C.O. 5 No. 42*.

[3] *Shirley Correspondence*, vol. I, p. 418.

the right to vote in town meetings had been restricted to the "freemen" only,[1] in the course of time the town franchise became so widened as to include practically all the male inhabitants of legal age, of whom perhaps only one-fifth to one-fourth possessed the colonial franchise, and were without representation in the General Court. This situation gave the demagogue and the ambitious politician of the unenfranchised orders a peculiar advantage and a peculiar grievance. On the one hand it provided him with a public and an arena for his budding talents and ambitions, and, on the other, it excluded him from participation in the larger political life of his little provincial world. A man conscious of his political influence with the people, and who had felt the intoxication of the applause of the mob and yet found himself blocked from further advance, would naturally drift into an attitude of opposition to the existing political order. The conflict inherent in the system of an appointed governor and an elected assembly is now generally recognized. It is possible, however, that second only to that, in the production of political friction, was this situation in regard to the local and colonial franchise, although it has received no study as yet. Nothing could be better calculated to breed up a class of demagogues and radical agitators opposed to a government than one in which — if I may be permitted a "bull" — they were allowed to speak but denied a voice. The effect of such a system would naturally appear when political interests should become dominant and a class of professional politicians arise.

In the mid-years of the century, commercial and political interests did rapidly supersede those of religion in the minds of the mass of even New England people. A change crept over the news sheets, which became both more political and more vigorous. In the earlier years a man who felt himself a leader, who aspired by his voice to sway the destinies of his little commonwealth, had naturally sought the pulpit rather than political office, but in connection with Jonathan Edwards we have

[1] *Massachusetts Records*, vol. II, p. 197, act of 1647. The general impression is that the town meeting was a much more democratic affair than it really was. Both the town franchise and the control of the personnel of the Boards of Selectmen was vested in church members only, until the charter forced on Massachusetts by the Crown in 1691. The above act with its far-reaching implications, is worth much more careful study than seems to have been accorded to it.

already noted the change that had come in this respect. So greatly, indeed, had the situation altered by 1750 that Jonathan Mayhew, the patriot preacher of Boston, when he delivered a political sermon in that year felt called upon to defend himself against the possible charge that it was "out of character for a Christian minister to meddle with such a subject." [1] The increasing population, the more diversified life, the increasing importance and popularity of political questions, and the growing self-consciousness of the colonists, were attracting men to play the popular rôle. No one can doubt the provincial patriotism of Mayhew, but in the sermon just noted he said "there are men who strike at liberty under the term licentiousness; there are others who aim at popularity under the disguise of patriotism. . . . There is at present amongst us, perhaps, more danger of the latter than the former." [2] It was easy for the rising politician to identify the interests of his own career with those of his province. Entirely apart from causes of discontent in the relations with England, ample as we have shown those to have been, the growth of distinct parties within the colonies themselves yielded opportunities to party politicians. There must be differences of opinion among people in order to bring forth parties, but it then becomes the interest, conscious or not, of the politicians to intensify and perpetuate those differences or to develop others. One of the chief of these for political effect had been the question of paper money, both for the breadth of its appeal and the passions which it aroused. Implicit in it was the greater alignment of the people into classes. Although contemporary observers in the colonies at this period denied that there was any disloyalty in the sense that the colonies were contemplating throwing off the imperial connection,[3] nevertheless, recent events, as we have attempted to show, were beginning to give New Englanders a confidence in their own power and a self-consciousness which was beginning to draw distinctions

[1] Preface to sermon on Unlimited Submission. In J. W. Thornton's *Pulpit of the American Revolution*, (Boston, 1860), p. 47.

[2] *A Discourse concerning Unlimited Submission and Non-resistance to the Higher Powers, with some Reflections on the Resistance made to King Charles I*, (Boston, 1750), p. 55.

[3] *Shirley Correspondence*, vol. I, p. 244; Otis Little, *The State of Trade in the Northern Colonies*, (London, 1748), p. 10.

between themselves as Englishmen and as New Englanders. "With the Bravery, Spirit, Fortitude and Magnanimity of Englishmen, or rather of New-England men," wrote a violent opponent of specie resumption in 1749, "let us take a survey of our Circumstances." [1] Many questions naturally merged the opposition to the privileged class in the colonies with the opposition to England. Speaking of that country's action as to the return of Louisbourg to the French, and of the use of the silver payment for redeeming the paper money, the above writer continues "can we say the Publick, or any Individual (the Governor and a few more excepted) have received any Recompence? On the contrary, has not our Loyalty and publick Spirit been made a Stale of, to lessen the Weight of the People by shifting their Property, the Foundation and Cause of Power into the Pockets of those, who have thereby been enabled to raise Prerogative to an enormous Height?" [2] After declaiming against what he considered the declining influence of the people at large, he warns his readers that they must struggle to guard the exercise of "their moral Right to Freedom and Happiness, that can only be done by maintaining the august and awful Influence and Power of the People." [3]

I repeat that there was as yet no clear intention to separate from the mother country, but there were developing both a party opposed to the privileged classes in the colonies, and a political philosophy which was to make easy the transition from revolution to independence. We have already noted the incipient armed revolt by the Land Bankers in Massachusetts, and the chill which that incident gave to the merchant oligarchy in Boston. In 1755 the similar ruling powers in Rhode Island were successfully opposed politically for the first time in an election for governor, when Stephen Hopkins defeated the merchants' candidate by a narrow majority. [4] Throughout New England the unenfranchised debtor class and radicals were becoming

[1] *Letter to the Freeholders and qualified Voters relating to the ensuing Election*, (Boston, 1749), p. 2.
[2] *Ibid.*, p. 3.
[3] *Ibid.*, p. 12.
[4] W. E. Foster, *Stephen Hopkins*, Rhode Island Historical Tracts No. 10, vol. II, pp. 3*ff.*, 16.

more and more vocal and threatening the comfortable established order for the merchants.

Moreover, their philosophy was being provided for them in
ample quantity and appealing form. "If those who bear the
title of civil rulers," preached Mayhew in 1750, "do not perform
the duty of civil rulers, but act directly counter to the sole end
and design of their office; if they injure and oppress their
subjects, instead of defending their rights and doing them good,
they have not the least pretence to be honored, obeyed, and
rewarded." "When once magistrates act contrary to their office,
and the end of their institution — when they rob and ruin the
public, instead of being the guardians of its peace and welfare —
they immediately cease to be the ordinance and ministers of
God, and no more deserve that glorious character than common
pirates and highwaymen." [1]

About the same, William Livingstone in New York was writing in regard to the Anglican doctrine of passive obedience and
non-resistance that "to propagate such fustian in America
argues a disposition prone to senility." [2] Not only was the doctrine of the divine right of kings rapidly passing but the doctrine of divine right itself was giving way to the newer one of
"natural right," just as the Calvinistic theology was giving place
to a rationalistic attitude toward religion. The same half
decade that heard the words of Mayhew and Livingstone in
favor of the natural right of resistance to an unjust ruler, also
saw the founding at Harvard of the Dudleian lectureship for
the study of the principles of natural religion. Although first
printed many years later, Charles Chauncey's volume on the
Benevolence of the Deity was probably written in these same
years. In that extraordinary burst of optimistic utterance he
not only pictures a God delighting in the happiness of his crea-
tures, and a universe operated by laws and secondary causes —
not the irresponsible and despotic "special providences" of the
old theology — but he lays down in the strongest terms his own
belief both in the freedom of the will and the necessity for such

---

[1] *Cit. supra.*
[2] Cited by Riley, *American Philosophy*, p. 27.

freedom to justify the moral character of God and man.[1] "This power in us men," he says, "whether it be called self-determination, or by any other name, is the only basis of moral obligation. Unless this be first supposed, to talk of moral agency is a contradiction to common sense."[2]

New England was still loyal, it is true, but the New England of 1750 was not that of 1740. At the beginning of the decade, its men seem still far off in a misty past, remote from our ways of thought. At its end, we recognize them as one with ourselves, standing clearly revealed in the light of our own common day, modern as we are modern. Somehow in those ten years of extraordinary emotion and action, they had crossed the great divide. They were not disloyal, but, what was more fatal for the old ties, they were growing more and more aware of deep-seated conflicts of interest in the empire, they were feeling wronged, they were coming to have an overweening sense of their own strength, and, locally, the power was slipping year by year into the hands of those who were opposed to the irksomeness of privilege and restraint in any guise whatever.

[1] *The Benevolence of the Deity, fairly and impartially considered* (Boston, 1784), pp. 27, 60, 78.
[2] *Ibid.*, p. 128.

CHAPTER X

THE WRONG TURNING

England's New Colonial Policy — Western Expansion and Rise of Speculative Business — Colonial Indian Policy — Conflicts of Economic Interests — Need for a Revision of Imperial Relations — Plans for Colonial Union — Effect of Their Failure

FROM the early mid-years of the century England was considering making many of those changes in her colonial administration which, in the main, she did make after the Seven Years' War. That struggle, though it emphasized in her opinion the necessity for such changes, so far from suggesting them merely delayed them. On the other hand, though the colonists might have resisted these innovations at any time, the effects of the war economically, intellectually and politically made such resistance inevitable. In the years immediately following 1750 there was no thought that in another decade England would have come into possession of Canada and all the Mississippi Valley, yet her intentions were forming to centralize the control of Indian policy, of land policy, to pass on a greater share of the expense of colonial administration to the colonists in some form of taxation, to unify the administration to a greater extent and, commercially, to cause the colonies to adhere more closely to the strict ideals of the Mercantile System for her own benefit.[1] The policy entered upon by English statesmen after 1763, therefore, was not one which had been forced upon them by the mere exigencies of a post-bellum situation. It was a return to a policy interrupted by the war, and which represented the altered attitude of the English upper classes at this period, to which allusion has already been made, and which was manifested in many ways.[2]

[1] McCormac, *Colonial Opposition to Imperial Authority*, pp. 2 f.; Victor Coffin, *The Province of Quebec and the early American Revolution*, (Madison, Wisconsin, 1896), p. 411; G. B. Hertz, *The old Colonial System*, (Manchester, 1905), p. ix.

[2] *Vide supra*, chap. VI.

In 1748 Newcastle gave up the office of Secretary of State for the Southern Department and was succeeded by the Duke of Bedford whose "total negligence and inability for office was far from being known to mankind in general" until that year.[1] It may have been that in his office "all was jollity, boyishness and vanity" as Pelham wrote, but Lord Halifax at the Board of Trade was paying far more attention to colonial business than it had received for a long time past, and in the period between his accession and the outbreak of the Seven Years' War most of the questions that loomed so large between 1763 and 1776 came up for serious discussion.

In the same year that Halifax went to the Board, Thomas Sherlock succeeded Gibson as Bishop of London, and during his incumbency pressed for the appointment of bishops in the colonies. His motives seem to have been in part, at least, political, and by uniting the colonies under ecclesiastical jurisdiction he hoped apparently more and more to intertwine them with the English church-state system.[2] This of course was bitterly opposed to the general sentiment of the New England colonists, and although Sherlock received no encouragement from the English government his efforts could not fail to increase the colonial feeling of distrust and opposition. The Privy Council, indeed, disliked Sherlock's agitation on account of its possible effect in England as well as in the colonies, but it was well known in New England that prominent leaders of the Anglican church there, such as Timothy Cutler of Massachusetts, Samuel Johnson of Connecticut, and Andrew McSparran of Rhode Island, were all urging a local episcopate.[3] As the Church of England clergy were in favor of closer control by the mother country this provided another element in the cleavage between local Whigs and Tories, a cleavage that to a considerable extent was also one between town and country, for the feeling against the English church was strongest away from the larger centers. Cutler clearly points to this when he

[1] Cited by Egerton, *British Colonial Policy*, p. 145.

[2] Cross, *Anglican Episcopate*, pp. 113 ff.

[3] Cutler to Bishop of London, Apr. 24, 1751, *Fulham Mss. Mass.*; Johnson to same, Sept. 17, 1750, Mar. 26, 1751, Sept. 25, 1751, *ibid., Conn;* McSparran to same, Mar. 26, 1751, *ibid., New York and Rhode Id*; Roger Price to same, Apr. 19, 1751, *ibid., Mass.*

speaks of the gradual wearing away of prejudice in the towns where the church had long been established and of the "monstrous ideas" which prevailed regarding it in the more distant areas.[1]

Just at this same period the whole question of the policy to be pursued with regard to the vast territory of the "western country" began to obtrude itself upon the colonial and the home authorities alike, and both in the colonies and in England opposing parties were formed based upon conflicting economic interests. We have already seen that there were two schools of thought in the mother country as to the value of colonies, the one believing it to lie in their supplying home manufactures with raw materials, and the other considering it to be rather in providing markets for manufactured products. The former party cared nothing for an increase in colonial population and everything for an increase in colonial produce, whereas the latter laid the whole stress upon an increase in the number of consumers. The first, therefore, wished to have the trans-Alleghany country remain an untenanted wilderness yielding the furs derived from the Indian trade, and the second to have it become populated as rapidly as possible with farming communities buying English goods.[2]

There was a somewhat similar conflict of opinion among the colonists. We have already noted the steady increase in speculation in land on the part of the colonial capitalists to the enriching of themselves at the expense of the poorer elements in the communities. Of New England a contemporary writer states that "a wretched Insensibility . . . has prevailed in imaginary Riches, of vast Tracts of waste Lands, from being really so in their Improvement; and to this Day" the holders "remain obstinate, having obtained them for a Trifle, they hold the Terms of Settlement so very high, that the Industrious, who would improve them, dare not undertake it."[3] Even when settlers did buy lands from these speculators, and by their labor

---

[1] Cutler to Bishop of London, Apr. 24, 1751, *Fulham Mss. Mass.*
[2] C. W. Alvord, *The Mississippi Valley in British Politics*, (Cleveland, 1917), vol. I, pp. 106 *ff.*
[3] *A Letter to a Member of Parliament on the Importance of the American Colonies* . . . (London, 1757), p. 17.

increased the value of the holdings, the grasping non-resident owners endeavored to avoid paying taxes on the lands which they frequently had secured for a song by those methods best known to such as secure favors from legislatures.[1] It may be suggested to those who look back to a reign of the Saints or forward to one by the Socialists, that there is nothing in recorded history from the Sea Kings of Crete to our present war-profiteers to indicate any essential alteration in human nature, and that the colonial capitalists and New England deacons were quite as ready to feather their own nests and to exploit their fellow colonists as were the capitalists and merchants of old England or of today.

To these capitalists and their little allies who had small shares in their enterprises, who hoped to reap great riches from the development of the lands within the borders of the old colonies, the suggestion of opening up new territories to settlement in the West threatened all their prospects, and they became naturally allied to the party in England which wished to preserve the wilderness for the sake of furs. On the other hand, money was accumulating and there were others who saw their opportunity in promoting western speculative land enterprises. In 1747 the first step forward was taken on any considerable scale, when prominent Virginians in combination with important English financiers petitioned the Crown for a grant of five hundred thousand acres along the upper Ohio River.[2] The following year, the Board of Trade reported favorably on the scheme, the Ohio Company was chartered, and the race for the West began. The British government, which up to this time had had no Western policy, was now forced to consider one, and by its action had committed itself at first to opening the West to settlement under imperial control.

There was, however, another element in the situation. Several of the colonies, including Massachusetts, Connecticut and Virginia, claimed wide extension of their boundaries westward to the "South Sea" under their original grants. If these were allowed in the wild scramble now clearly foreseen for

[1] Cf. *Acts and Resolves*, vol. IV, p. 626; *Boston Evening Post*, Oct. 11, 1756; *Letter to a Member of Parliament, cit. supra*, pp. 17 *f*.
[2] Alvord, *Mississippi Valley*, vol. I, p. 87.

western expansion, such colonies would, in time, evidently far
outstrip in political influence those limited to definite seaboard
areas, a prospect naturally distasteful to the jealous inhabitants
of the latter. A decision as to Western policy, now first considered and which was to be postponed by the war, was by no
means a simple matter regarded from either the imperial or
colonial standpoints. Meanwhile the exploitation of the land
was apparently to be pressed as rapidly as possible by speculators, large and small.

A group in Connecticut organized the Susquehannah Company to purchase from the Indians a tract of two hundred
square miles in what was claimed to be the western portions
of Connecticut on the Susquehanna River in the present state
of Pennsylvania.[1] The stockholders numbering at first about
one hundred were increased to five hundred, and later to eight
hundred and more "wholesome persons," the stock being sold
at $4 a share or $2 a half share, quite in the method of modern
oil or mining promotions.[2] A very questionable purchase was
made from the Indians through a person of bad reputation, one
Colonel John Lydius,[3] but in 1755 the General Court of Connecticut was prevailed upon to sanction the scheme, in spite of
the protests of Pennsylvania, and to say that the Indians
"finding" the land "not necessary for their own use have, for
very valuable considerations" sold it to the company.[4] The
governor, Roger Wolcott, when called upon, gave a written
opinion in favor of the enterprise of which three of his sons
were prominent promoters.[5] The Indians' view of the deal,
however, was publicly expressed at a meeting with the Commissioner, William Johnson, at Albany in 1755, at which Colonel

---

[1] *Pennsylvania Archives*, 2d. Ser., vol. XVIII, pp. 4 *ff.*; O. J. Harvey, *History of Wilkes-Barré*, (Wilkesbarre, 1909), vol. I, pp. 248 *f.*

[2] *Pennsylvania Archives*, cit. *supra*, pp. 22 *ff.*; *Conn. Col. Records*, vol. X, p. 378; C. W. Alvord, *The Illinois Country*, (Springfield, 1920), pp. 286 *f.*

[3] *Pennsylvania Archives*, cit. *supra*, p. 23; C. H. McIlwain, *Wraxall's Abridgment of Indian Affairs*, (Harvard University Press, 1915), p. cvii, *n.*; Harvey, *History of Wilkes-Barré*, vol. I, pp. 268 *ff.*, 277, 286 *ff.* The deed was made out to 753 grantees, (text *ibid.*, pp. 271 *ff.*) and Harvey regards the transaction in a much more favorable light than most investigators.

[4] *Conn. Col. Records*, vol. X, p. 378; *Fitch Papers*, vol. II, p. 96.

[5] *Wolcott Papers*, (*Conn. Hist. Soc., Coll.*) (Hartford, 1916), p. 428; *Conn. Col. Records*, vol. X, p. 378.

Lydius and over eleven hundred Indians were present. "You have promised us," said one of the Oneida sachems to Johnson, "that you would keep this fire place clean from all filth and that no snake should come into this Council Room. That man sitting there (pointing to Col. Lydius) is a Devil and has stole our Lands, he takes Indians slyly by the Blanket one at a time, and when they are drunk, puts money in their Bosoms, and perswades them to sign deeds for our lands upon the Susquehanna which we will not ratify nor suffer to be settled by any means."[1]

Although the company voted the same year to apply to the Crown for confirmation of the purchase and a royal grant, the plans were interrupted by the war, as were so many others. Not only, however, were scheming capitalists forcing the problem of a land policy upon the imperial government, but that of an Indian one as well. England had been content before 1748 to leave the native question to be settled in the main by the individual colonies. It was becoming increasingly evident that they were incompetent to handle it.

The friendship of the Six Nations was a matter of vital importance to the English, both in itself and in relation to the struggle with the French, yet Massachusetts, Pennsylvania and New York pursued their own separate, selfish and conflicting courses with these people regardless of any settled policy or of the interests of the whole.[2] For example, when Governor Morris of Pennsylvania complained to Governor Fitch of Connecticut with regard to the dangers inherent in the actions of the Susquehanna Company, Fitch replied that he was "very sensible that to take any steps to disaffect the Indians in our Alliance or to raise Contests between the Governments at this Critical Conjuncture must be prejudicial to the safety and Peace of these Governments," but that he was unacquainted with the scheme, and did not know who the persons might be who were interested in it, though he had "been informed some live in this Government"! Considering that it was perhaps the largest

---

[1] *Wraxall's Abridgment*, p. cvii; Harvey admits that the sachems were treated with individually and not at any general meeting. *History of Wilkes-Barré*, vol. I, p. 269.

[2] *N. Y. Col. Docts.*, vol. VI, p. 741.

enterprise ever undertaken in the little colony, that his immediate predecessor, Governor Talcott, and a large number of the
Assembly, as well as over eight hundred other citizens including
his own son, were embarked in it, it is simply incredible that he
should have really been as ignorant as he claimed.[1] He promised
however, to lay the matter before the "Assembly for their
consideration." The only result of this was that a few months
later, although the enterprise was a private business venture,
the assembly went out of its way to give it a public endorsement.[2]

None of the assemblies could be induced to adopt any general,
just or far-sighted policy. The treatment of the natives by
traders and land-grabbers, many of the latter being among the
most prominent families in the colonies, was disgraceful and
utterly without conscience or honor. Indian children were
stolen by the whites and kept as servants. Liquor was the
constant means employed to facilitate fraudulent transactions.
The savage was cheated in every way, and, as the law stood,
before he could secure redress, if at all, he had to fee a lawyer,
take out a writ, file a declaration, wait twelve months — frequently from two to five hundred miles from his home, without
support — and then neither his evidence nor that of any other
Indian would be admitted at the trial. As Governor Colden of
New York said in his report on conditions, it was "but too
obvious what the consequences of this treatment must be."[3]
Always there was the question of the land to which we are led
again and again in the colonies both for its influence upon
Indian relations and upon those resulting between rich and poor
among the whites. The home government had left Indian
affairs largely to the colony of New York, but in the ablest
contemporary record of conditions we read that "an unaccount-
able thirst for large Tracts of Land without the design of culti-
vation, hath prevailed over the inhabitants of this and the

[1] *Fitch Papers*, vol. I, pp. 71 *f*. He was personally opposed to the policy of expansion,
and an effort has recently been made to put his conduct in a more favorable light.
Vide Edith A. Bailey, *Influences toward Radicalism in Connecticut, 1754–1775*, Smith
College Studies in History, vol. V, pp. 233 *f*.
[2] *Conn. Col. Records*, vol. X, p. 378.
[3] *N. Y. Col. Docts.*, vol. VI, pp. 546, 741.

neighboring Provinces with a singular rage. Patents have been lavishly granted (to give it no worse term) upon the pretence of fair Indian purchases, some of which the Indians have alleged were never made but forged. Others bought of Indians who were no Proprietors, some by making two or three Indians Drunk and giving them a trivial consideration. They say that the Surveyors have frequently run Patents vastly beyond even the pretended conditions or limits of sale." [1]

In 1726 the natives "by a solemn deed" had placed their lands under the jurisdiction of the Crown to be protected as hunting lands for themselves and their posterity. Confronted by the growing troubles due to the Ohio Company grant, the activities of the Connecticut speculators and equally disturbing schemes in Pennsylvania, the Lords of Trade advised the Crown in 1755 to make no more grants and to use every effort to defend the rights of the savages — a policy naturally extremely distasteful to the powerful and aggressive land schemers in the colonies.[2] But owing to the complete failure of colonial Indian administration, due largely to sinister financial influences, it was evident that the English government would have to take the problem in hand in order to render justice to the savage and to protect the settlers against the French.

Without adopting the economic interpretation of history to the exclusion of all others, which I think is unhistorical and ignores a true psychology of man, yet we do find the economic motive at the bottom of most of the relations subsisting between the colonies and the mother country. In fact to a considerable extent the "policies" of each were not considered as continuous policies at all, but as the sum total at one time of the resultants of the various stresses and strains between different economic groups working in opposition to one another as their interests dictated. Perhaps the most continuous factor was that which decreed that whenever the financial interests of the most powerful English groups conflicted with those of colonial groups the latter had usually to give way. As the interests of New England were more frequently opposed to those of the home merchants

[1] Wraxall's Report, N. Y. Col Docts., vol. VII, p. 17.
[2] Report of Lords of Trade on Mr. Penn's Proposal, Dec. 11, 1755, C.O. 5 No. 7.

and manufacturers than was the case in the southern or West Indian colonies, the New Englanders felt more frequently that they were singled out as the object of attack. A good example of the complexity of each individual question that arose was that of iron manufacture which came up for final decision in 1750. As we ourselves have found in the matter of the tariff, it is not easy to define a raw material, for the finished product of one process may be the starting point for another. In England the manufacturers of bar iron considered it as a finished product, whereas those who carried the manufacturing process further regarded it as raw material. Although, as we have already seen, manufacturing had not as yet developed to any great extent in the colonies, the middle of the century saw the beginning of a number of new lines, notably that of iron. By 1750 there were four slitting mills in Massachusetts, eight iron and steel mills in Connecticut, and one bar iron plant in New Hampshire, though none as yet in Rhode Island.[1] No one in England questioned the doctrine that colonial manufactures should not be allowed to compete with those at home, but here was a more difficult problem. As a result of the contending forces, in which the interests of New England were almost wholly ignored, Parliament passed an act allowing bar iron to be imported into England but at the port of London only, (where it had formerly been imported from Sweden), and prohibiting the colonists under a penalty of a £200 fine from carrying the process of manufacture any further. Although the budding industry would probably not have amounted to much for many years, the definite notice thus served on the colonists that their interests would continue to be sacrificed to those of industrial groups in England could not fail to arouse antagonism at a time when their sense of growing importance was acute, and capital was accumulating in sufficient quantity to be actively seeking new outlets.[2]

[1] G. R. Minot, *Continuation of the History of Massachusetts Bay*, (Boston, 1798), vol. I, p. 171; *Wolcott Papers*, pp. 74 *f.*; *R. I. Col. Records*, vol. V, pp. 313 *ff.*; *N. H. Prov. Papers*, vol. VI, p. 8; Weeden, *Social and Economic History of New England*, vol. II, p. 684; Kimball, *Correspondence of colonial Governors*, vol. II, pp. 129 *f.*

[2] Hutchinson says that at this time plans were made to bring over immigrants "to introduce useful manufactures." *History*, vol. III, p. 11. *Cf.* Weeden, *cit. supra*, vol. II, p. 686.

The conflict of economic interests, however, was not confined to groups in the continental colonies and the mother country. As we have already shown, the problem of economic adjustment was a triangular one in which the West Indies played a part which seemed perforce to be always inimical to New England.[1] The absentee owners of plantations who lived in England had always been numerous, and were sufficiently so about 1740 to found what was known as the "Planters Club" in London.[2] These rich absentees had always formed an influential Parliamentary group by combining with the English merchants trading to the islands, and had procured the passage of the "Molasses Act" of 1733, which by the heavy duties imposed on importations into New England on the products of the French West Indies had been designed to kill that lucrative trade. That trade, however, had always continued although for the most part as acknowledged smuggling, the duties collected amounting to only about £800 annually.[3] It may be noted here in connection with this illicit trade that although the noted case involving Writs of Assistance did not come up until the next decade such writs were being issued to customs officers in Massachusetts in 1755, and had been in use for a number of years and issued to at least five different officers before James Otis made his famous attack upon their legality in 1761.[4]

In view of the approaching expiration of the Molasses Act, the West India interests began about 1750 to bring all possible pressure upon the Board of Trade and Parliament to secure a new act which would totally prohibit all imports of French sugars and molasses into New England.[5] At the very beginning of the new controversy, however, the colonial agent in London

---

[1] In the economics of the day Africa with its slave trade played a leading part, but although the interests of the Indies and of old and New England were all heavily involved there was less natural conflict.

[2] L. M. Penson, "The London West India Interest in the 18th Century," *English Historical Review*, (July 1921), p. 377.

[3] Beer, *British Colonial Policy*, p. 34.

[4] Josiah Quincy, Jr., *Reports of Cases argued and adjudged in the Superior Court of the Province of Massachusetts Bay, between 1761 and 1772*, (Boston, 1865), (Appendix on Writs of Assistance, by Judge Horace Gray, Jr.), pp. 402 ff.

[5] *Wolcott Papers*, pp. 1, 35 ff., 48 ff., 97, 110 ff., 170, 197; Kimball, *Correspondence of colonial Governors*, vol. II, p. 146; *Acts Privy Council*, vol. IV, pp. 517 f.; Pitman, *West Indies*, pp. 298 ff.

was able to write, somewhat colloquially, to the governor of Connecticut that the Board of Trade had "given the West India Gentlemen the go by," and the agitation though continued for some years finally profited them nothing.[1] Two points, however, emerged from the lengthy discussions which clearly foreshadowed future events of the greatest importance, and which are usually relegated to the period following the war. One was that due to the pressure from certain English economic groups British colonial policy was swinging to a preference for temperate rather than tropical zone colonization, that is for colonies that should absorb manufactures rather than for those which merely provided raw products — a policy which was to result in 1763 in the retention of Canada and the return to France of Guadaloupe. The other point was the suggestion frequently thrown out that the duties under the Molasses Act be lowered to such an extent as to be collectible and to constitute a revenue instead of a prohibition; in other words, that the colonies should be taxed for their own support.[2]

The question of a direct Parliamentary tax upon the colonists as distinct from the indirect contributions made by them under the various laws regulating trade, was by no means a new one. An elaborate plea for such a contribution in the form of a stamp tax had been made by Sir William Keith in 1728.[3] Walpole, however, would have nothing to do with it, and when asked for an opinion said that he "had old England set against him and did they think that he would have New England likewise?"[4] Various plans were suggested from time to time, and

---

[1] *Wolcott Papers*, p. 35.

[2] E.g. Malachy Postlethwaite suggested that the duty be made 1d. a gallon and that thus "a considerable sum of money might be raised for the advantage and security of our North American colonies." "Measures of this kind might lay a good foundation for such future American funds as to prevent those colonies from being longer burdensome to their mother-country for their security." *Great Britain's Commercial Interest explained and improved*, (London, 2d. edit., 1759). Cf. also *State of the British and French Colonies in North America . . . in two Letters to a Friend*, (London, 1755), pp. 63, 147.

[3] A short Discourse on the present State of the Colonies in America with Respect to the Interest of Great Britain, 1728, *C.O. 5 No. 4*. For Keith's colonial doctrines, cf. also his Proposals for the better Government of the Plantations, 1728, *King's Mss. 205, Pt. I.* Cf. Beer, *British Colonial Policy*, pp. 31 ff.; Kate Hotblack, *Chatham's Colonial Policy*, (London, 1917), pp. 168 ff.

[4] Philip Yorke, Earl of Hardwicke, *Walpoliana*, (London, 1781), p. 7. Hardwicke says that it was soon after the Excise scheme and that the reply was made to the Earl of Chesterfield.

in 1753 Henry Pelham seriously considered one of these but finally discarded it saying that "we have talked it over and it will not do."[1] From this time on, however, colonial taxation was a matter of frequent discussion in pamphlets and press, and it is not unlikely, even aside from the enormous debt piled up by the war, that some such scheme would eventually have been tried. The British taxpayer was becoming exceedingly restive, and not wholly without reason. Even before the declaration of the Seven Years' War, the national debt amounted to approximately £72,500,000, and landowners were paying six and a half shillings in the pound, or about thirty per cent of income without including tithes and poor rates.[2] As comparatively few troops were maintained in those colonies which later became the United States, we are apt to forget that the military establishment in America as a whole entailed considerable expense upon the British taxpayer, aside from the naval expenses for convoys. In fact, neither conquered territory nor standing armies were new elements in the imperial system when the Peace of Paris was to bring its new problems. Even as early as 1728 England had maintained regular troops at Annapolis Royal, Placentia and Canso, as well as in New York, South Carolina, the Leeward Islands, Bermuda, Jamaica and Providence, at a cost of about £39,000, and the stations, number of troops and cost had all increased from time to time until by 1754 the last amounted to about £75,000 annually.[3]

Taxation, of course, was intimately bound up with military expenditure, and this, in turn, as far as the colonies were concerned, with their extreme military inefficiency, the latter being due to their inter-provincial jealousies and quarrels, and to chronic disputes between governors and assemblies. Again, expense and military efficiency were bound in with the whole question of Indian policy. No one could foretell just when war

---

[1] Hardwicke says that he himself and Newcastle dissuaded him from it. *Walpoliana*, Supplement XX. This Supplement is exceedingly rare. There is a Ms. copy in the Library of Congress. My reference is to fol. 2 of this Ms.

[2] Stephen Dowell, *History of Taxation and Taxes in England*, (London, 1884), vol. II, p. 130; R. M. Garnier, *History of the Landed Interest*, (1893), vol. III, p. 163. Laborers paid about 3*d*. in the £.

[3] *British Army in America*, vol. I, *passim*. [Two volumes of original Mss. English government records in the Library of Congress.] *Cf.* Beer, *Old Colonial System*, pp. 11 *ff*.

might break out once more between England and France, but it was well recognized that the Treaty of 1748 was but a truce, which fact had to be accepted by British statesmen. War, whether imminent or not, had to be reckoned with as a certainty sooner or later, and everything indicates, I think, that England had reached the point where she would have attempted to reorganize her colonial administrative system in any case.

War in America had never really stopped, and the uncertainty as to the Acadian boundary, the unscrupulous machinations of the French priests in stirring up the Indians, the English colonists' policies as to land and the natives, the steps taken by the French to check the Ohio Company's advances in the Ohio Valley, all formed but the prelude to operations upon a larger scale.[1] In August 1753, the Earl of Holderness sent a circular letter to the colonial governors warning them of hostilities planned by the French, and advising them to be on their guard.[2] They were ordered to keep in communication with one another, but as England did not wish to be the aggressor in the approaching struggle, they were not to act outside the certain limits of English dominion — though those were in reality most uncertain.[3] There were ample reasons in the complications of the situation in Europe why England should not have wished to begin the war at this time, and indeed as late as January 1755, Newcastle was still hoping, not entirely without reason, that war might be avoided altogether for the present.[4] Nevertheless, whether war were to come at once or not, the English government had evidently decided that it could no longer leave the colonies "as a Rope of Sand, loose and inconnected," as Governor Glenn of South Carolina phrased it in urging a colonial union for defence.[5] Indian af-

---

[1] S. G. Drake, *A Particular History of the Five Years French and Indian Wars*, (Boston, 1870), pp. 107 *ff.*; Francis Parkman, *Montcalm and Wolfe*, (Boston, 1912), vol. I, pp. 39 *ff.*, 96 *ff.*, 133 *ff.*; Richard Waddington, *Louis XV et les renversements des alliances*, (Paris, 1896), pp. 16 *ff.*

[2] Holderness succeeded Bedford as Secretary of State in 1751 and served until March, 1761.

[3] Shirley, *Correspondence*, vol. II, pp. 12 *f.*

[4] Sir Julian S. Corbett, *England in the Seven Years' War*, (London, 1918), vol. I, pp. 15 *ff.*, 37 *f.*

[5] Glenn to Lt.-Gov. Dinwiddie, Mar. 14, 1754, *C.O. 5 No. 14*. Gov. Clinton had advised a union in 1750. *Wolcott Papers*, p. 23.

fairs, owing to the extreme dissatisfaction of the natives with their treatment, were in a critical condition, and in September 1753, the Lords of Trade wrote to the governor of New York that a joint meeting should be held with the natives and the governors of Virginia, Pennsylvania, Maryland, New York, New Jersey, Massachusetts and New Hampshire, and that all the provinces if possible should be comprised "in one general Treaty to be made in His Majesty's name it appearing to us that the practice of each Province making a separate Treaty for itself in its own name is very improper and may be attended with great inconveniency to His Majesty's service." [1] Thus an important step was taken toward an imperial rather than a separatist Indian policy. Moreover, closer association of the colonies for military purposes was seen to be essential and in June of the following year the Secretary of State requested the Lords of Trade to prepare a plan of union for the colonies. This had been strongly urged by a number of the ablest colonial governors, among them Shirley, who wrote that Massachusetts was in favor of taking such a step. [2] In fact, a few weeks later the Lords of Trade wrote that "it seems to be the opinion and is the language of almost every Colony that a general Union of strength and interest is become absolutely necessary," [3] and they decided that such a plan should if possible be put into effect. As they distinctly stated that its preparation would take too much time to permit it of being available for the present crisis, it is evident that they were intending to inaugurate an entirely new and permanent policy for the colonies, and not merely one to meet a temporary emergency. [4] The colonists' own abortive attempt to form a union at Albany usually receives but scant treatment in our histories. It was, however, one of the most important crises in the relations of the colonies to the mother country. The failure, whether the fault of England or the colonists, rendered the revolution inevitable, for it was clearly impossible that the former system should continue much longer. Had the colonies been located on scattered islands,

[1] *N. Y. Col. Docts.*, vol. VI, pp. 801 *f.*
[2] *Ibid.*, p. 844; Shirley, *Correspondence*, vol. II, p. 22.
[3] *N. Y. Col. Docts.*, vol. VI, p. 846.
[4] *Ibid.*, p. 903.

they might have continued to be treated as disconnected units. This had practically been their position in the early days when they had been far remote from one another, separated by almost impassable forests or by long water routes. But as they grew they came to form practically one continuous settlement all along the coast. To the westward likewise there came to be a continuous frontier against the French and Indians. The jealousies of the colonies could not alter the fact that in many cases the action of one affected all. The Indian question had become one. The military problem had become one. The financial problem, in so far as it was related to the other two, had become one. The old separatist policies of dealing with the savages, with the French, and of contributing separate quotas of men and money in wholly indeterminate and always unjust proportions, had completely broken down. The colonists might insist upon remaining Virginians or Rhode Islanders. Their problems and their dangers had become American. Concerted action had become absolutely necessary, and there were but two ways in which it could be attained. Either the colonies could have formed a union — as in Australia, South Africa and Canada — and the home government could thus have had a single and powerful unit to work with and through, or else the unifying of Indian, military and fiscal policies had to be undertaken by the home government itself. The attempt to carry through the first failed. The attempt to accomplish the second was bound to result in revolt.

The effort to devise some workable form of colonial union was undertaken simultaneously on both sides of the water toward the middle of 1754. The congress of delegates from the colonies who met at Albany in June had been summoned to do so by the British government, but only for the purpose of arranging a joint policy with the Indians, the more far-reaching scheme of a permanent union of the colonies not being taken up in England until the very month in which the congress met. The Lords of Trade then expressed the opinion that no time could have been better in which to have tried to inaugurate it than at the congress.[1] Many of the leading men in the colonies,

[1] *N. Y. Col. Docts.*, vol. VI, p. 846.

however, aside from the royal governors, had realized for some time the necessity for union, and it was so arranged that the matter did come up for discussion at the congress in spite of there being no orders from England to include it in the agenda. Benjamin Franklin in particular, commenting upon a plan proposed by Archibald Kennedy of New York in 1751, had strongly advocated some sort of colonial union and had said that "it would be a very strange thing if Six Nations of ignorant savages" could form such a union, and ten or a dozen English colonies could not have an equal understanding of their interests.[1] Unfortunately Franklin over-rated the understanding of his fellow colonists, for they did in fact prove to be less politically minded than the savages.

On the 19th of June twenty-five delegates met at Albany representing the four New England colonies and New York, Pennsylvania and Maryland, although only those from Massachusetts were empowered to commit their colony to a permanent "union and confederation."[2] The congress constituted an assembly, as Hutchinson said, "the most deserving of respect of any which had been convened in America" considering the number of colonies represented, the character of the delegates and the purpose of the meeting.[3] Although the matter of the Indian treaty naturally became the subject of first and longest discussion, the question of union was also pretty thoroughly canvassed.[4] An unanimous agreement was reached that such a union was absolutely essential for the preservation of the colonies and that it could be established only by Act of Parliament.[5] A plan previously prepared by Franklin was then

[1] Kennedy's plan is in his *The Importance of gaining and preserving the Friendship of the Indians to the British Interest considered*, (New York, 1751). Franklin's letter is in his *Works*, ed. Bigelow, vol. II, pp. 217 ff.

[2] Hutchinson says "some of the delegates had very full powers, while others were limited, and held to make report to their constituents." *History*, vol. III, p. 22. *Cf. Conn. Col. Records*, vol. X, p. 268 n.; *R. I. Col. Records*, vol. V, pp. 384 f.

[3] The list of delegates is in *N. Y. Col. Docts.*, vol. VI, p. 853. Thomas Hutchinson's name is omitted there although he was one of the Massachusetts delegates.

[4] The proceedings given in *N. Y. Col. Docts.*, vol. VI, pp. 853 ff. For accounts given by participants, *vide* Hutchinson, *History*, vol. III, pp. 21 ff.; Stephen Hopkins, *A true Representation of the Plan formed at Albany* . . . (Providence, 1755), reprinted in Rider's *Rhode Island Tracts, No. 9*, (Providence, 1880).

[5] Franklin, *Works, cit. supra*, vol. II, pp. 351 f.

discussed and adopted with slight modifications.[1] It is not
necessary to examine it in detail. The main features were an
executive appointed and supported by the Crown, and a legislature of forty-eight members elected by the several colonial
assemblies. The legislature was to regulate Indian policy; purchase the Indian lands in the name of the Crown; raise and pay
the military and domestic naval forces; and levy taxes and make
laws, the last subject to veto by the executive and approval by
the Crown. Apparently the delegates, with the exception of
those from Connecticut who strongly disapproved of it, unanimously agreed to present the plan to their assemblies for
approval, only after which it was to be transmitted to Parliament.[2] Without exception every assembly refused to concur in
it, even that of Massachusetts treating it with decided cool-
ness. [3] As Franklin said, all cried out for the absolute necessity
of union, but when called upon to decide upon some definite
form "their weak Noddles are perfectly distracted." No special
meetings of the legislatures were called, and the plan therefore
was not submitted until August in Rhode Island, October in
Connecticut and November in Massachusetts.[4] Connecticut
not only refused to join the union but undertook to oppose it in
England should the other colonies try to effect it.[5]

[1] Franklin, *Works, cit. supra*, vol. II, pp. 345 *ff.*; *N. Y. Col. Docts.*, vol. VI, pp. 889 *ff.*

[2] Hutchinson, *History*, vol. III, p. 23; *N. Y. Col. Docts.*, vol. VI, p. 891; Hopkins,
True Representation, pp. 42 *f.*; Beer, *British Colonial Policy*, p. 22; Trumbull, *History*,
vol. II, p. 355; *R. I. Col. Records*, vol. V, p. 394. The instructions to the Connecticut
delegates were exceedingly narrow-minded even in the matter of joint defence. Among
other things they were enjoined to use every argument "that may occur to them
. . . that they think may tend to render the duty of this government under the present
situation of affairs no greater than of necessity," and that they "make no presents to any
Indians, unless the other governments by doing so make it necessary, and that they
oppose everything of this nature so far as they see convenient." *Conn. Col. Records*,
vol. X, p. 268 *n*. Their expressed disapproval of the congress is noted in *Fitch Papers*,
vol. I, p. 40.

[3] It is doubtful if Massachusetts had really been very enthusiastic in spite of having
given power to her delegates. Shirley was very keen about it, however. Shirley, *Correspondence*, vol. II, pp. 43 *f.* In reply to his urging, the Court merely answered
"Your Excellency must be sensible that an Union of the several Governments for their
mutual Defence, and for the Annoyance of the Enemy, has long been desired by this
Province, and Proposals made for this Purpose; we are still in the same Sentiments,
and shall use our Endeavours to effect it." *Boston Evening Post*, May 20, 1754.

[4] *R. I. Col. Records*, vol. V, pp. 393 *f.*; *Conn. Col. Records*, vol. X, pp. 292 *f.*; *Boston
Evening Post*, Nov. 11, and 18, 1754.

[5] *Conn. Col. Records*, vol. X, pp. 292 *ff.*; *Mass. Hist. Soc., Coll.*, Ser. I, vol. VII, pp.
203 *ff.*, 210 *ff.*; *Fitch Papers*, vol. I, pp. 34 *ff.*

That colony in writing to the home government took a strong line against centralizing the control of Indian affairs, and it is most distinctly shown in the report adopted by the assembly, and in the representation made to the Lords of Trade that the influence of the stockholders of the Susquehannah Company had much to do with the official attitude of the colony. For example, in both of those documents we find it stated that "if His Majesty should be graciously pleased to encourage his subjects to settle and plant a government or colony on such lands, in their country, as the Indians will readily sell, to be formed and conducted as the New England colonies have been, nothing would tend more to secure those Indians to His Majesty's interests."[1] Considering what has been noted above as to the Indians' supreme desire to prevent any encroachments on the Susquehanna lands, which they wished above all to retain as hunting grounds, and as to the manner in which their "willing" consent had been obtained, no further comment is required as to the official attitude of the colony in blocking the plan for union, and as to the advice it gave the home officials. It may, however, come somewhat as a shock to those who take a sad pleasure in comparing the sordidness of modern statesmanship with the assumed simplicity and sturdy uprightness of our colonial forefathers to find that the influence of finance upon politics is not a discovery of the present age.

Although the plan was never formally presented to the English government, they did see a copy of it and were not favorably impressed.[2] Meanwhile they had formed their own plan, although this was never formally offered to the colonists

---

[1] *Fitch Papers*, vol. I, pp. 41 *f.*, 53.

[2] Franklin stated in 1789 that "the Crown disapproved it, as having placed too much Weight in the Democratic Part of the Constitution; and every Assembly as having allowed too much to Prerogative." Beer says this is a "gross misrepresentation." *British Colonial Policy*, p. 23 *n.* Franklin was always a special pleader and cared more about making his point than he did about keeping punctiliously near the truth, and this statement was made 35 years after the event. However, there may have been more truth this time than Beer allows, for Gov. Morris writing in 1755 said, "the plan formed at Albany, was upon such Republican Principles, that I do not wonder it was not relished at home." Cited by W. T. Root, *The Relations of Pennsylvania with the British Government*, (University of Pennsylvania, 1912), p. 301 *n.*

and was allowed to drop.[1] This contemplated merely a combination for military purposes, and it may be, as is usually stated, that Parliament would not have consented to the one adopted at Albany. Had the colonists, however, been sufficiently far-sighted to have united voluntarily in some such combination, it is difficult to see just what England could have done. The whole history of the period must be considered in the light of its dominant factor which was the constant armed rivalry of England and France. The home country could not have undertaken to fight its colonies and the French nation at the same time, and it might well have been that a colonial union, however distasteful in some of its features, which would have added greatly to her military strength in America, and simplified Indian, military and fiscal problems, might not have been considered by her as a cause for civil war if presented to her as a *fait accompli* in the then state of European politics. But the facts were that there was not at that time a single American statesman, with the possible exception of Franklin, and that the great majority of the provincial politicians forming the assemblies were too selfish, ignorant and narrow to realize that the time had come when a unified control of policy and action had become necessary, and that if they could not overcome their own separatism, and educate the people to wider views, a conflict would become inevitable with the mother country. It is as certain as any "might have been" in history that if the colonies could have agreed upon a just and sane Indian policy, could have united effectively for military action, could have decided upon some method of taxing themselves for joint American military expense, and thus presented a possible form of administration and a united front to England, that country would not have embarked upon her policy of the next decade, a policy as unwelcome and vexatious to herself as it was to the colonies.

The breaking down of provincialism, however, is a slow process. Nations have to traverse stages of development as do

[1] *N. Y. Col. Docts.*, vol. VI, pp. 901 *ff. Cf.* Draught of a Plan, in *Brit. Mus., Add. Mss. 32736*, (this has marginal notes not in the printed version), and the Lord Chancellor's Letter regarding Plan, Aug. 25, 1754, and Remarks upon the Plan, both in same *Mss.*

individuals, and, as we have already pointed out, there seems to be a definite mental evolution in colonial societies, and none can escape that of provincial jealousy. Circumstances had moved too rapidly for the colonists and produced a crisis in which union was necessary before they were capable of compassing it.[1] Although both in the colonies and in England union continued to be discussed unofficially, the moment had gone not to return.[2]

The failure of the colonies either to unite in their own defense or in the determination of an Indian policy — for that part of the Albany deliberations had been as little successful as had the other — of necessity threw the whole burden of decision upon England. As the voluntary quota system of providing money — which had been as unfair to the more public-spirited colonies as it had been unsatisfactory to England — had proved a failure, and as the colonies apparently could devise no other, the question of providing funds for colonial defense was also brought to the front again. In July 1755, the Lords of Trade sent a circular letter to the colonial governors asking for information upon which to base a complete policy for the colonies. "Having under consideration," they wrote, "the state of His Majesty's Colonies in North America, more especially with respect to the defenceless state of their frontiers and the irregular management of Indian affairs; and it appearing to their Lordships to be absolutely necessary, as well for the safety and welfare of the

---

[1] We may be allowed to illustrate our point by again referring to the Australian colonies before federation. "The governments . . . oft-times assumed in their intercolonial relations the attitude of rival and competing corporations; they approached intercolonial questions from the standpoint of provincial hucksters anxious to drive a good bargain at the expense of a sister colony, rather than of citizens of a common country." They were so "jealous at the same time of any interference from without, that they refused to sacrifice the smallest portion of their autonomy even in response to the demands of their common interests and welfare." "The attitude of each colony at any moment depended largely upon the state of domestic politics . . . provincial politics were as restless and unstable as the sea; scarcely a season passed but the executive of one or the other of the colonies was in the midst of a political crisis." C. D. Allin, *The early Federation Movement in Australia*, (Toronto, 1907), pp. 412, 414. This is an exact description of the American colonies at the same stage of their growth.

[2] Shirley had a plan, Franklin, *Works*, vol. II, pp. 376 *ff.*, as had also Hutchinson, *Mass. Archives*, VI: 171. There were two plans evolved in Connecticut, *Fitch Papers*, vol. I, pp. 20 *ff. Cf.* also *State of the British and French Colonies, cit. supra*, p. 58; *Proposals for uniting the English Colonies on the Continent of America* . . . (London, 1757); Postlethwaite, *England's Commercial Interest*, vol. I, p. 424; John Mitchell, *The Contest in America*, (London, 1762), p. 41.

colonies, as to ease the Mother Country of the great and heavy expense, with which it has been of late years burthened on account of services relative to these points, that some general system should be laid down, and some certain, general and permanent provision made for the defence of the frontiers and for the management of Indian affairs," the governors were instructed to furnish information as to the situation among the natives, the number of troops and forts needed against the French, and the best way of providing the necessary funds "with the least burthen and inconvenience to His Majesties subjects." [1]

Whatever new burdens might result from the war, the extent of which was not even as yet foreseen by English statesmen, a new policy was evidently forming, which could only have been fended off by the colonists by their having the ability to formulate a comprehensive one of their own. But this they had just shown themselves incapable of doing. The normal development for colonies planted upon various parts of a continental area, is for them first to attain an exaggerated sense of their separate existence and a premature feeling of self-importance and strength. As their growth and expansion gradually force them into closer relations with one another, inter-colonial jealousies arise and what may be termed the bickering stage ensues. The only remedy for the ills of this stage is colonial union of some sort and the attainment of what has come to be known as the dominion status. It is possible that this forms not simply a stage in imperial evolution but a peaceful step toward nationhood as well. In the case of the American colonies, events pushed them ahead too rapidly for their political development. The premature break with the mother country by violent means instead of peaceful secession, and the troubles of the young nation for many years after independence was won, may in great measure be traced to the failure of the colonies to rise to a sense of their common danger, common interests and common responsibilities at the commencement of the greatest struggle in which they had yet been engaged.

[1] Lords of Trade to Shirley, July 16, 1755, *C.O. 5 No. 15.*

CHAPTER XI

THE FATE OF A CONTINENT

Influences of War — Causes of Seven Years' War — Situation in New England — Attitude of Colonies in the Struggle — Evil Effects of the System of Defense — Braddock — Outline of the Campaigns — Canada Conquered

IT was a matter of profound importance to the New Englanders, both intellectually and politically, that just at the time when they had reached the critical stage described in the last two chapters they were called upon to pass through that ordeal by battle which is always of deep influence upon the life and thought of a people. A prolonged war in which the economic and human resources of a society are taxed to their utmost markedly affects the relations of its members to one another, and involves for many a reëxamination of the theories upon which such relations are based. The experiences of all classes — though the result is frequently not felt until some years later — greatly stimulates their intellectual life. War lets loose disruptive forces which even when they do not threaten the destruction of the social fabric profoundly alter its structure. The popular political philosophy of any age is unconsciously an attempt to rationalize the already accepted economic and political ideas. In the period following war, therefore, the intellectual stimulus given by it prompts men to observe the altered social conditions and status created, and in endeavoring to provide a rational basis for the new outlook to orient an altered philosophy. All these factors, the influences of which are but too apparent to us today, may be seen shaping the events of the whole period from the outbreak of the Seven Years' War to the armed arbitrament of the dispute between England and her colonies.

It is interesting to note the intellectual ferment incidental to war at work in the youthful mind of one of the leading figures in the events which were to follow, and happily there is preserved a letter of the young John Adams, then a lad under twenty, to an intimate friend in the opening years of the struggle. "Be not surprised," he says, "that I am turned politician. This whole town is immersed in politics. The interests of nations, and all the *dira* of war, make the subject of every conversation. I sit and hear, and, after having been led through a maze of sage observations, I sometimes retire, and by laying things together form some reflections pleasing to myself," just as the youth of the world has been doing in these latter years. It may be noted that Adams was not writing from Boston but from the frontier town of Worcester. After speaking of the rise and fall of empires, and of the arrival of the Pilgrims on the shores of his own colony, he continues, "perhaps this apparently trivial incident may transfer the great seat of empire into America. It looks likely to me : for if we can remove the turbulent Gallicks, our people, according to the exactest computations, will in another century become more numerous than England itself. Should this be the case . . . the united force of all Europe will not be able to subdue us. The only way to keep us from setting up for ourselves is to disunite us." [1]

The war which was thus beginning to influence the thoughts of American youngsters, although fought upon the continents of Europe, Asia, Africa, and America, and upon the high seas, had its immediate origin in disputed boundaries beyond the fringe of English settlement in the wilds of Acadia and on the western slopes of the Alleghanies.[2] The bounds of the former had been left undecided by the treaty of Aix-la-Chapelle in 1748, whereas the question of French and English claims beyond the Alleghanies rested entirely upon indeterminate problems of prior discoveries, charters, and settlement.[3] Negotiations between the two powers, in which Governor Shirley — on leave

---

[1] John Adams, *Works*, vol. I, pp. 23 *f*. Letter dated Oct. 12, 1755.

[2] In spite of all the European elements in the struggle Waddington says that "il faut chercher l'origine de la querelle qui ensanglanta l'Europe . . . dans les démêlés insignifiants de frontières dont les vastes solitudes de l'Amérique du Nord furent le théâtre." *Renversement des Alliances*, p. 1.

[3] Cf. *Founding of New England*, pp. 41 *f*. Horace Walpole summed up the situation in characteristic fashion. *Vide, Memoirs of the Reign of King George II*, (London, 1846), vol. I, pp. 394 *ff*.

from Massachusetts for that purpose for nearly three years —
had taken his part, dragged their tedious and unavailing course
from 1750 until July 1755.[1] It is not enough, however, to attribute the final rupture to the insufficiency and weakness of diplomats, the incapacity of ministers, and the egoism and vanity of
monarchs. The situation, apart from any delimitation of frontiers drawn upon inexact maps in Paris, was bound to result in
armed conflict. On the one side, there were the rapidly growing
English colonies all along the seaboard from New England to
Georgia, filled with a population of abounding energy, tempted
by the lure of Indian trade, of rich lands for the settler, and of
unlimited tracts for the speculator. On the other side, there
was the long, scattered line of French garrisons and small posts
stretched from the mouth of the St. Lawrence to the Great
Lakes, and thence down the Mississippi to the Gulf of Mexico,
with perhaps sixty thousand colonists in Canada, a thousand at
Detroit, and a mere handful at New Orleans.[2]

This domain, embracing the two greatest river valleys on the
continent and all the tributary streams flowing from the French
side of the mountain barrier anywhere from the height of land in
Maine to the foothills of Georgia, was a magnificent empire. But
it was for the most part an empire on paper. It was merely a
staked claim. The energy of the English had been intensive.
They had settled and ploughed and sown. They had established
farms and plantations, and then as population had increased,
new groups had gone a little west, and settled and ploughed
and sown again. The march had been as steady and unoppos-
able as a slow moving force of nature. There seems to have
been curiously little of the English spirit of adventure among the
colonists luring them to the unknown. There was always a scattered line of pioneersmen ahead of the settled frontier, always
the sound of the axe and the crash of the falling tree, but these
men did not go into the wilderness to explore it but to destroy it
for the sake of gain. On the other hand, the French were every-

[1] Waddington, *Renversement des Alliances*, pp. 52 *ff.*
[2] Waddington, *cit. supra*, pp. 2 *f.* ; Zimmerman places 80,000 for the continent as the
highest possible figure, *Europäische Kolonien*, vol. IV, p. 155; Deschamps allows 54,000
for Canada in 1759, *Question coloniale*, p. 234; Paul Leroy-Beaulieu says 82,000 in 1759,
Colonisation chez les peuples modernes, (Paris, 1902), vol. I, p. 154.

where — for a moment. Witty and courtly gentlemen, broken-down adventurers, priests and ignorant *coureurs des bois* alike explored the endless forests, the prairies, the illimitable rivers. But it was impossible that in the long run sixty or seventy thousand explorers, traders and settlers could hold a line three thousand miles long against over a million English who were beginning to feel cramped within their borders east of the mountains and who were casting covetous eyes at the riches beyond. "Le monde n'appartient pas aux curieux qui le parcourent et l'explorent: c'est aux patients seuls et aux travailleurs qu'il finit par rester," says the French historian of colonization.[1] The monarchs in Europe were as impotent to stem the advancing tide of English settlement and exploitation as King Canute to halt the advancing tide of ocean. The mountain barrier which had been of prime importance in holding back and concentrating the English settlements in the early period, had done its work.[2] The forces which had been made powerful by that concentration had now become so great that they were ready to burst through the barrier in a dozen places regardless of what polished diplomats might say around a table at Versailles. While the negotiations became more and more hopeless, lost in a maze of verbiage and conflicting testimony, as a river loses itself in the sands of a desert, events in the American forests were moving to their appointed end.

In Acadia the French inhabitants, from the time of the treaty of Utrecht, by which France had ceded that province to England, had never accepted the situation. As the great conflict approached, although the two nations were at peace, both Acadians and Indians were continually stirred to animosity against the English by French officials acting under orders from the French king, and by French priests, more particularly one blood-thirsty brute in a cassock, named Le Loutre. English settlers were murdered by the savages and the whole northeastern frontier was kept in a continual state of alarm. Finally, in 1755, came the well-known order to deport the French Acadians who were as little loyal at the end of forty years as they

[1] Leroy-Beaulieu, *Colonisation chez les peuples modernes*, vol. I, p. 154.
[2] Cf. *Founding of New England*, pp. 3 *f.*

had been at the beginning, and whose presence was a menace which could no longer be tolerated unless England were willing to abandon territory which was indubitably hers. Few events have elicited more sympathy, most of which is unjustified. The Acadians were an extremely simple, ignorant, priest-ridden peasantry, scarce one of whom could write his own name.[1] Their religion had been respected, and they had been treated with an unusual amount of consideration by the conquerors, although persistent in their refusal to take a complete oath of allegiance or to bear arms in defence of the government. The real responsibility for their deportation lies upon the French king and his agents, who continually goaded them on to disloyalty.[2]

On the borders of New York and Pennsylvania, we have already noted the restlessness of the Six Nations, among whom the work of French emissaries was but too well seconded by the resentment caused by the Indian policies of the colonies and by the operations of the Connecticut, New York and Pennsylvania land-grabbers. Farther to the south a French effort to counter the advance of the Ohio Company pioneers had been made by Céloron de Bienville, who traveled through the country, negotiating with the Indians and setting up lead plates, taking possession of the country in the name of his king. Next came the seizure of one of the company's trading posts on the Alleghany by French forces, who told Washington that it "was their absolute design to take possession of the Ohio, and, by God, they would do it."[3] The following year occurred the first armed conflict in force when Washington and his troops were defeated at the Great Meadows, and still, after some fifty months, the interminable negotiations continued at Paris. The plenipotentiaries found the question complex and the city charming.

But the situation in America was becoming far more serious than the extreme disparity in numbers between the two con-

[1] In the oath subscribed to in 1720, 227 out of 245 had to sign by a mark. *Selections from the Public Documents of the Province of Nova Scotia*, (Halifax, 1869), opp. p. 84.

[2] Parkman, *Montcalm and Wolfe*, vol. I, pp. 94 *ff*. Almost all the documents in the case may be found in the *Nova Scotia Documents, cit. supra.*

[3] Parkman, *Montcalm and Wolfe*, vol. I, p. 139.

testants would indicate. In Louisbourg, France possessed the strongest fortress on the continent; Crown Point and Ticonderoga controlled the northern route into New York, as Frontenac, Oswego and Niagara commanded those from the west; from Fort Duquesne the whole frontier of Pennsylvania, Maryland and Virginia could be harried; and, lastly, in their Indian allies, whom they never hesitated to let loose on defenceless women and children, the French had a weapon as effective as it was inhuman. Not only were the French far better fitted than the English to bind the savages to themselves by becoming assimilated to the native life, but the objects and nature of their dominion tended to conserve the alliance. The Indians could continue to hunt in the forests to the very threshold of a French garrison post, whereas the magnificent woods which sheltered their game fell before the advancing English farmer like the walls of Jericho at the sound of Joshua's trumpet, and left the savages stripped of all they held dear, even to the very means of subsistence. Finally, although there was almost grotesque venality and financial rottenness among the officials at Montreal,[1] the English were rendered nearly impotent by their parsimony — "parsimony to prodigality" as Livingstone called it — by their bickerings with the royal governors, by their jealousy of each other and, in some cases, by racial antagonism.

Although New England was more homogeneous in population and showed more public spirit than the other colonies, even there prospects were not bright for any effective defence against the coming storm. New Hampshire, pleading poverty, refused to vote more than a few troops for a few months for the protection of her own borders, and it was impossible to make any use of them for that reason. Massachusetts, Shirley wrote, had done something but hesitated to do more until she saw what Connecticut and the other colonies would do.[2] Connecticut, as we have seen, instructed her delegates to Albany to use every "argument that may occur to them" to make Connecticut's contribution as small as possible. Farther south, New York was

[1] Parkman, *Montcalm and Wolfe*, vol. II, pp. 25 *ff.*; William Wood, *The Fight for Canada*, (Boston, 1906), pp. 47 *ff.*
[2] McCormac, *Colonial Opposition to Imperial Authority*, pp. 16, 25.

in the midst of a quarrel with its governor, and rendered only tardy and almost useless aid for the defence of the Virginian border. The assembly of Pennsylvania, in chronic warfare with the proprietors, was sufficiently oblivious to the pressing danger to say that "they would rather the French should conquer them than give up their privileges." Maryland, owing to a similar quarrel, would vote no money, and even when war had broken out, a militia law was opposed on the ground that it "would abridge the Liberty to which as Englishmen they have an inviolable right." In Virginia, the assembly took advantage of a trifling dispute with the governor to refuse any grants even to defend her own harassed settlers on her own frontier.[1] It was the old story, repeated in every emergency, of the complete inability of the colonies to unite for common defence or even adequately to provide for their own. No reliance could be placed upon voluntary joint action or upon quotas of men or money to be determined by the colonies themselves, in spite of their very considerable resources.[2] It is, after all, little wonder if the English people, sorely burdened with taxation, and viewing the unsatisfactory situation in America, should consider, however impractically, the advantages of a more centralized control and of a system of taxation which would reimburse them for the expense of the assistance asked for by the colonies, or which, unasked, was necessary for their defence.

Many years later, Franklin in his examination before the House of Commons, tried to show that the war had been waged solely for English and not for colonial interests. He claimed that it was wholly for the Indian trade and that that trade was entirely a British concern; that no disputed territory was claimed by any colony or had been granted to any colonist; and that the colonies were "in perfect peace with both French and Indians" before Braddock's defeat.[3] This was going beyond even Franklin's characteristic special pleading, for his statements were both untrue and unfair. Not only were many colonists interested in one capacity and another in the Indian

---

[1] McCormac, *cit. supra*, pp. 28 *ff.*, 63 *f.*, 67, 74 *ff.*
[2] Beer, *British Colonial Policy*, pp. 70 *ff.*
[3] Franklin, *Works*, vol. III. pp. 438 *f.*

trade;[1] not only did some of the colonies claim the disputed areas; not only had land in them been granted to colonists — such as the Washingtons and other American stockholders in the Ohio Company; not only had there been armed conflicts before Braddock sailed from England; but the colonists themselves had asked England's aid in a struggle they acknowledged to be largely for their own benefit and which they admitted they could not carry on without her assistance.

Although our interest lies in New England, we may glance at the conditions in the most public spirited of the colonies to the south before considering New England more particularly. Even when the territory which Virginia claimed in the West was actually invaded by the French, the assembly could not be induced to grant sufficient money for the most inadequate defence. Washington frequently complained of the inferior quality of the "loose, idle persons" who were all that would serve as militia, and of the scandalously small and uncertain pay for officers and men, stating that he would rather have no remuneration at all or "dig for a maintenance . . . than serve upon such ignoble terms."[2] The assemblymen, with that consideration for votes which is the most cowardly characteristic of popular legislative bodies, decreed that all citizens qualified to vote for candidates for assembly should be exempt from military service.[3] Not only did the Virginians ask aid from England when they could just as well have defended themselves, but in the very message to the king in which they thanked him for having sent imperial troops from New York and South Carolina to their defence, added that they hoped he would pay for them himself.[4] In the other southern colonies the situation was even more hopeless. Unpleasant as it may be to rehearse these facts, they are essential to an understanding of England's position.

[1] At the beginning of the war the bulk of the fur trade was in the hands of the French, but the Americans were competing to some extent. Alvord and Carter, *The Critical Period, Illinois Hist. Coll.*, vol. X, p. 323. Sir William Johnson wrote that "what the Trade was in the time of the French, no two persons can agree about." *Ibid.*, p. 336. By the end of the war, he wrote, "thousands subsist by it, who must be ruined without it, and fail of making their remittances to Europe." *Ibid.*, p. 307.

[2] McCormac, *Colonial Opposition to Imperial Authority*, p. 78.

[3] *Ibid.*, p. 80.

[4] *Ibid.*, pp. 79 *f.*; W. Knox, *The Controversy between Great Britain and the Colonies reviewed*, (London, 1769), pp. 129 *f.*

As I have already pointed out, they are also characteristic of colonial development at a certain stage, and not merely of the American colonies. When at the end of 1755, the Massachusetts assembly answered Shirley's plea for additional funds after the unsuccessful campaign of that year by saying that "securing his majesty's territories is a design which his majesty only is equal to project and execute and the nation to support; and that it cannot reasonably be expected that these *infant plantations* should engage as principals in the affair" [1] they were anticipating an endless line of similar complaints and evasions from other colonies at similar stages. For example, a patriotic Australian historian, who considers Australia's position at the present time to be that of an independent nation, states that those colonies before confederation "with vehement argument" "bargained . and haggled over every pound they were asked to pay for the defence, not of the Empire, but of the local interests of Australia. With eloquence they demanded that the British Government should undertake a brilliant colonial policy, and with eloquence they explained that 'struggling dependencies' must, of course, be exempt from the brilliant expenses." [2]

In New England, although the smaller colonies asked aid from the mother country, the stand taken by the most powerful one, Massachusetts, is so clearly set forth that we may confine ourselves to that. We may note, however, in passing, that Connecticut, though she had instructed her delegates to the Albany Congress to commit the colony to as little as possible, asked arms from the English government a few months later, and in 1756, when the situation was more alarming asked that England should find, arm, and subsist a regiment to be kept in the colony but upon the pay of Great Britain — certainly a noteworthy request from a colony which had claimed practical independence whenever it pleased her.[3]

In January 1754, the Massachusetts assembly sent a message to Governor Shirley stating that the French were making such encroachments "as threaten great danger, and perhaps in time,

[1] Hutchinson, *History*, vol. III, p. 38.
[2] A. G. Wood, in *Australia, Economic and Political Studies*, (Melbourne, 1920), p. 384.
[3] *Conn. Hist. Soc., Coll.*, vol. I, pp. 269, 283.

even the entire destruction of this province (without the interposition of his majesty) notwithstanding any provision we can
make to prevent it." [1] In April they sent up a second message
stating that the French were pursuing a long-laid plan to subject
the entire continent to the Crown of France; that even in time
of peace they were "continually exciting the Indians settled
among them to come upon our Frontiers, to kill and captivate
Our People and to carry their Scalps and Prisoners to Canada";
that this prevented the Massachusetts settlers "from extending
our Settlements in Our Own Country"; and that these disadvantages could not be removed without England's help. They
prayed the governor "to represent to His Majesty the exposed,
hazardous State of these His Governments" and to ask him to
take steps to destroy all French forts or settlements anywhere
within boundaries claimed by England, and particularly to
remove at once the French population from Nova Scotia. They
also asked, with easily understood reference to their neighbors,
that "Affairs which relate to the Indians of the Six Nations and
their Allies under some general Direction as His Majesty shall
think proper may be constantly regarded, and that the Interests of particular Governments or Persons may not be suffered
to interfere with such Direction; that the several Governments
may be obliged to bear their proportion of the Charge of defending His Majesty's Territories . . . and that in case of any great
and heavy Charge His Majesty would be graciously pleased to
Relieve Us." They admitted that the numbers of the French
bore but a small proportion to themselves, but pointed out that
the colonies suffered under various disadvantages, among which
was their "consulting temporary Expedients" in face of the
systematic French plan and that they were "in Danger of continuing to do so untill it be too late." [2] Some months later, in
September, came the attack on Stockbridge, and Israel Williams wrote to the governor from Hartford that "I conclude by
this time you are fully inform'd of the hostile attacks of the
Indians, and the mischief done by them in our own Frontiers,

[1] Knox, *Controversy between Great Britain and the Colonies*, p. 115.
[2] Shirley, *Correspondence*, vol. II, pp. 47 *ff*. The entire message was printed in the
Boston Evening Post of May 20, 1754.

and the neighboring Governments in one of which they have made terrible waste burning and destroying all before 'em. It is now open war with us, and a dark distressing scene opening."[1]

These facts, and others which might be cited, not only completely disprove the assertions made later by Franklin and others that the war was waged wholly for England's own interests and in no wise for those of the colonists, but go far toward explaining the attitude of many in the mother country on the subjects of taxation and greater control, as well as the indignation excited by the colonists' later claims of having had nothing to gain in the war for themselves. Meanwhile, the colonies were affording point to the statements as to their disunion by engaging in boundary disputes, punctuated by bloody rioting, between Massachusetts and New York, and New York and New Jersey, which called forth caustic rebukes from the Lords of Trade about internal peace being thus "disturbed by trivial Disputes of this kind, at a time when the Colonies are so loudly called upon to exert with the greatest unanimity their utmost Strength in their own defence."[2]

For the sake both of the Americans and of her own imperial interests, England was determined to grant aid to the colonies in their widening struggle with France, and, as early as December 1754, despatched General Braddock as commander-in-chief with two regiments to the succor of Virginia, with orders to organize expeditions to take Fort Duquesne on the Ohio, Niagara on Lake Ontario, Fort Frederick on Lake Champlain, and the French posts at Chignecto.[3] Money as well as men was needed, however, and the unsolved problem of providing it continued henceforth to perplex England and the colonies alike. The inadequacy had long been recognized of the old system by which each colonial assembly voted funds when and to what extent they pleased, taking into consideration the relations which might happen to subsist at the moment between themselves and the proprietors or royal governors rather than the

---

[1] Shirley, *Correspondence*, vol. II, pp. 84, 86 *ff.*

[2] Beer, *British Colonial Policy*, p. 50. Such disputes recurred in 1757 in the very midst of the war. *N. Y. Col. Docts.*, vol. VII, p. 273.

[3] The secret instructions are summarized by Waddington, *Renversements des Alliances*, p. 373. *Cf.* Corbett, *Seven Years' War*, vol. I, pp. 24 *ff.*

exigencies of the military requirements, and always fearful lest in a temporary lapse of generosity they might do a little more than their share compared with their less public-spirited neighbors. The English government pressed the colonists to agree upon some plan by which they might provide a general fund for the common defence, but to no avail. Many Englishmen at home as well as many in America felt that the only remedy was Parliamentary taxation, but to this, naturally and properly, the colonies would by no means consent. In fact, the main lines of the whole later controversy, a controversy merely deferred by the war, had been clearly laid down by 1754. Among the objections urged by Connecticut to the Albany plan of union had been one against the levying of taxes by the proposed central colonial government which it considered to be "a very extraordinary thing, and against the rights and privileges of Englishmen."[1] Franklin, in three private letters to Shirley in regard to a plan of union proposed by the latter, had clearly stated that "it is supposed an undoubted right of Englishmen not to be taxed but by their own consent, given through their own representatives" and "that the colonies have no representation in Parliament" and for Parliament to tax them would be "treating them as a conquered people, and not as true British subjects."[2] He developed, furthermore, that distinction between external and internal taxation (called by him at this time "secondary" and "immediate"), which was to play a considerable part at one stage of the later discussions.[3] When the war was well under way, both Massachusetts and Connecticut made great exertions and contributed heavily to the common cause, but throughout the course of the entire contest there was not an operation that was not hampered, made uncertain of success, and unnecessarily costly by the jealousy, recalcitrancy, and bickering spirit of one or all of the colonial assemblies.

Though so deeply affecting the life of New England, all the chief military events of the struggle were enacted outside of her borders, and we can give but a general outline of its purely mili-

---

[1] *Fitch Papers*, vol. I, p. 39.
[2] *Works*, vol. II, p. 379.
[3] *Ibid.*, pp. 381 *f.*

tary history. On October 26, 1754, a circular letter was sent by the English government to the colonial governors stating that two regiments were to be sent to the defence of the colonies, and asking that three thousand men be enlisted in America and a general fund provided, until "a plan of general union of His Majesty's Northern Colonies, for their common defence, can be perfected." Shirley and Sir William Pepperrell were each appointed colonel of a regiment, and England sent over two thousand stand of arms for their use.[1] The two regiments of regulars were sent from England with considerable promptitude and Braddock was in Virginia by the end of February. Two months later a council of war was held at Alexandria, at which Shirley and a number of the other governors were present, and at which the first business which required consideration was the unanimous failure of the several assemblies to provide any money for the general fund.[2] In spite of this unpromising beginning, it was decided that Braddock should move against Fort Duquesne, and another expedition under command of Colonel William Johnson, the Indian agent, against Crown Point, and a third, under command of Shirley, against Niagara.

The choice of Braddock was an unfortunate one, although his bravery was beyond question. Horace Walpole described him as "desperate in his fortune, brutal in his behaviour, obstinate in his sentiments, intrepid and capable."[3] Aside from the lack of certain qualifications in the general, however, the obstinate assemblies and dishonest colonial contractors seemed bent upon delaying and ruining the expedition beyond hope of success. Its well-known and fatal ending, in ambush upon the banks of the Monongahela, needs no retelling. The news struck the colonists throughout the entire seaboard with consternation and terror, its effect upon the wavering friendship of the Indians, which the colonists' policies had already gone far to alienate, being particularly dreaded. For the latter reason it was

---

[1] Shirley, *Correspondence*, vol. II, pp. 98 *ff.*; Sir T. Robinson to Shirley, Feb. 10, 1755, *C.O. 5 No. 211.*

[2] Minutes of the Council at Alexandria, Apl. 14, 1755. *C.O. 5 No. 15.* It was the opinion of the assembled governors that no such fund could ever be raised except by act of Parliament.

[3] *Memoirs of George II*, vol. II, p. 29.

forbidden that the facts should be printed in any newspaper in the colonies.[1]

Upon the death of Braddock, Shirley was appointed commander-in-chief of all the forces in America, and as Hutchinson says had reached his zenith though "his friends saw the risk he was running and wished he had contented himself with his civil station."[2] Meanwhile, he had been active in promoting the military operations of his own colony. An expedition of five hundred men to the eastward in Maine had proved as futile as it was costly, but another undertaken jointly with the English against the French forts in Nova Scotia was successful. In the latter, Massachusetts shared to the extent of furnishing two thousand men, all the expenses being borne by the Crown.[3]

Thinking that the attention of the French in Canada would be distracted by the operations in Nova Scotia, Shirley broached a scheme to the Massachusetts assembly in February 1755, to send an expedition to fortify the heights on Lake Champlain commanding the French post at Crown Point, which later developed into the plan to attack the French position directly.[4] This was part of the triple movement approved at the council of war at Alexandria, and when Braddock was defeated, among the papers which fell into the hands of the French was one which gave them information of Shirley's proposed attack. Reinforcements were at once sent from Montreal, under the able Baron Dieskau who had recently arrived from France with additional regular troops.[5] Haste was an essential of success for the English, but with seven colonies involved in negotiating with one another about the expedition matters moved slowly.[6] Connecticut adopted a generous attitude, and not only raised a thousand men but promised more if necessary and allowed New York to

---

[1] "Our Governor has given the Printers here orders not to print anything about Gl. Braddock's Defeat and It would be wrong it should be printed anywhere in the Continent for sometime, lest the News [sic] reach our Indians & Army above which may be of bad Consequence." General letter from the Post Officers at New York, July 28, 1755, *Mass. Archives*, 54: 515.

[2] Shirley, *Correspondence*, vol. II, pp. 241 *ff*.; Hutchinson, *History*, vol. II, p. 38.

[3] Hutchinson, *History*, vol. III, pp. 27 *ff*.

[4] Shirley, *Correspondence*, vol. II, pp. 127 *ff*.

[5] Parkman, *Montcalm and Wolfe*, vol. I, p. 300.

[6] New Hampshire, Massachusetts, Rhode Island, Connecticut, New York, New Jersey, and Pennsylvania.

enlist within her borders.[1] Massachusetts also made great efforts, and in September claimed she had nearly eight thousand men in the field in one quarter and another.[2] There were innumerable delays, however, due to intercolonial jealousy over quotas of men and stores, the appointment of officers, and other matters, and by the end of August at a council of war at the Great Carrying Place it was estimated that only thirty-two hundred effectives were in the army, whereas six thousand French were mistakenly thought to be concentrating at Crown Point.[3] "The expedition goes on very much as a snail runs," wrote a colonial colonel from the American camp, and added, "it seems we may possibly see Crown Point this time twelve months." "As to rum," he reflected sadly, "it won't hold out nine weeks. Things appear most melancholy to me." [4] Reinforcements were called for but, although eventually sent, they arrived too late to be of service.[5] Dieskau had no intention of waiting for the enemy's pleasure, and on September 8th made a surprise attack with slightly superior numbers upon Johnson's advancing forces. The fight lasted throughout the day, and the savage allies of both opponents added to its horrors. Although unexpectedly ambushed owing to bad scouting, the colonials fought well, or, as Dieskau said, like good boys in the morning, like men at noon, and devils in the afternoon. The French commander was wounded and captured, but although the result wore the guise of victory for the Americans, the expedition was a failure. In spite of Shirley's urging, Johnson declined to utilize his advantage by a forward movement, claiming lack of supplies, discipline and men.[6] The Mohawks, who had lost heavily, refused to remain, the colonials sickened by hundreds and deserted in bodies. It was decided to disband the army leaving merely small garrisons at one or two points.[7] Enormous expense

[1] *Fitch Papers*, vol. I, p. 98; Fitch to Robinson, Aug. 8, 1755, *C.O. 5 No. 16.*

[2] Shirley, *Correspondence*, vol. II, p. 285.

[3] Council of War, Aug. 22, 1755, *C.O. 5 No. 16.* The true number of French was but little more than half of this.

[4] Cited by Parkman, *Montcalm and Wolfe*, vol. I, p. 304.

[5] There was the usual quibbling. Massachusetts claimed she had 4,300 men in the expedition but this was denied by New Hampshire which put the Massachusetts figure at only 1,500. Wentworth to Robinson, Sept. 3, 1755, *C.O. 5 No. 16.*

[6] Shirley, *Correspondence*, vol. II, pp. 270 *ff.*, 280 *ff.*

[7] Councils of war at Lake George, Oct. 20 and Nov. 18, 1755, *C.O. 5 No. 17.*

had been incurred and nothing had been gained, except by Johnson who was made a baronet and granted £5,000. The English government, however, expressed lively appreciation of the colonists' efforts, ordered ten thousand stand of arms and ammunition to be sent to them, and stated that Parliament would be asked to grant them financial aid.[1]

Meanwhile, Shirley had proceeded along the Mohawk River with a force of only about fifteen hundred effective men for the planned attack upon Niagara. Small as the force was, it included a regiment from New Jersey which Johnson had counted upon being added to his force, and this diversion which he attributed to Shirley, as well as some interference by the latter with Johnson's properly exclusive relations with the Indians as Commissioner, resulted in permanently poisoning the relations between the two most important colonial leaders. The French had advance information of Shirley's plans, as they had had of Johnson's, and owing to this, to the failure of supplies and boats upon which Shirley had counted, and to the defeat of Braddock, the expedition against Niagara was even more of a failure than had been that upon the lakes. Leaving a garrison at Oswego, Shirley returned to New York and Boston to project plans for the coming year.

Massachusetts and Connecticut in particular had made very considerable efforts. Between them, they claimed to have had twelve thousand troops in the field, of which one-third were from the smaller colony, which also sustained nearly one-half of the expense.[2] In other respects, however, the situation was extremely discouraging. No leader in the colonies was the equal of the Marquis de Montcalm whom the French government soon sent over to replace the captured Dieskau. The commissary department of each colony had broken down. Any prompt and efficient military action had been shown to be impossible when carried out by seven distinct and jealous gov-

---

[1] Robinson to the New England governors, Nov. 11, and to Shirley, Nov. 11, 1755, *C.O. 5 No. 211*; Shirley, *Correspondence*, vol. II, p. 401.

[2] *Fitch Papers*, vol. I, p. 161. Connecticut paid in full for her 4,000 troops. The Crown supported 2,600 out of the 8,000 from Massachusetts. Representation of the case of His Majesty's Province of Massachusetts Bay, Sept. 26, 1755, *Brit. Mus., Add. Mss. 33029.*

ernments, each with its internal difficulties politically. Moreover, although war had not yet been formally declared between
the two powers, it was seen that it would be waged on a grand
scale, and for this colonial troops were by no means fitted.
Washington's complaints of the quality of the riff-raff which
formed most of his force has already been noted, and was
repeated by nearly every general officer. In many cases the
junior officers were no better than the men, and Johnson complained that as they were elected by the soldiers, discipline was
out of the question, and they were but so many "heads of a
mob." Physically the soldiers could not stand inaction, and a
long encampment, in those unsanitary days, was said to be
"the Bane of New England Men." They grew curiously home-
sick, always an American trait, after a few weeks, and heavy
desertions were constant throughout the war.[1] In a report on
the character of colonial troops, Johnson gave it as his opinion
that "they are so constituted" when acting by themselves,
"that neither by their Form or Discipline to be fitt for the various Duties and Services of a Campaign of any continuance, nor
for the difficulties, Fatigues, and Events of a Siege." On the
other hand, he considered them as entirely suited for a short
expedition of two or three weeks, and that when acting as aux-
iliaries to regular troops for work in the wilderness they were the
"best of any Forces in the World." In spite of the self-satisfaction common to all young and provincial peoples, the trouble
was too obvious not to be realized even by the colonial assemblies themselves, and that of Massachusetts wrote confidentially
to their agent in England that their men, not only in garrisons
but when kept long in any branch of the service, "soon grow
troublesome and uneasy by reflecting upon their Folly in bringing themselves into a State of Subjection, when they might have
continued free and independent."[2] Free and independent, it
may be noted, only so long as someone else protected them
against the national enemy, whenever they chose to regard as

[1] Parkman, *Montcalm and Wolfe*, vol. I, p. 325; Council of war at Lake George,
Oct. 20, 1755, *C.O. 5 No. 17*; *Journal of Capt. John Knox*, (Champlain Society, 1916),
vol. III, pp. 26, 61, 70; McLennan, *Louisbourg*, p. 241.
[2] A Representation of the Case of His Majesty's Province of Massachusetts Bay,
cit. supra.

"folly" their suffering the toils and inconveniences of doing it for themselves. There is a stage in the evolution of colonies as in the growth of boys when a high degree of understanding sympathy is required not to regard their opinion of themselves with marked irritation. Washington was to realize the truth of all this but too well twenty years after, as his correspondence testifies.

The situation in all its aspects was thus distinctly more menacing at the end of the first year's campaigning than it had been at the beginning, nor did the following year bring better fortune, although the position of the colonies was regularized by the formal declaration of war between England and France. Early in the year England kept her promise of financial help by reimbursing the six northern colonies to the extent of £115,000 out of an estimated total expense on their parts of £170,000.[1] This gift at once encouraged the New England colonies to accede to the elaborate plans for the new campaign as laid down by Shirley, though they insisted that the troops raised should be used against Ticonderoga and Crown Point only, leaving the governor to arrange otherwise for the other two expeditions planned against the western posts and up the Chaudière toward Quebec. The number of Shirley's political enemies, however, had been increasing, and not content with merely pointing out his shortcomings as a military leader, had not hesitated to charge him with being a traitor to his country. The matter was taken up at home by the ministers and even by the king himself. It was said that the governor had raised a force of ten thousand men in Pennsylvania with some traitorous design. "I don't suspect Shirley of Treachery," wrote Fox, "but I have no doubt of his having great Schemes and that he trusts the Execution to Traitors and that he ought not to stay in North America," adding that "His Royal Highness is for a rougher method."[2] Both the king and Newcastle were for having him sent to England as a prisoner.[3] The whole "strange dark

---

[1] Lords of Trade to Treasury, Feb. 12, 1756, *C.O. 324 No. 15*; same to Secretary of State, Jan. 16, 1756, *ibid.*; *Fitch Papers*, vol. I, pp. 198, 222; Shirley, *Correspondence*, vol. II, p. 535.

[2] Fox to Newcastle, Mar. 27, 1756, *Brit. Mus., Add. Mss. 32864.*

[3] Hardwicke to Newcastle, Mar. 28, 1756, *Brit. Mus., Add. Mss. 32864.*

affair," however, ended merely in his recall from America with promise of other employment, which, nevertheless, was long in forthcoming.[1] The charges, which are incredible and unsustained, were apparently concocted by his enemies for the purpose of securing his removal. He continued in the colonies for some months and exerted himself to the utmost for the English cause, in support of which he had lost two sons in the preceding year. His temporary successor in command was to be General Webb, who in turn was to hand over the command to General Loudon or General Abercromby. Shirley was given no instructions as to their plans, and unless the whole year was to be wasted could only go on with such preparations as seemed wise to himself. Webb and Abercromby did not arrive until the end of June, and the Earl of Loudon not until a month later. The latter, who possessed the title of a nobleman but not the nature of a gentleman, took an immediate dislike to Shirley, and for the rest of the season seems to have had more interest in his personal campaign against the deposed governor than in that against the French.[2]

The earl was soon in Albany, and having decided against any attack on the western posts, determined to confine his efforts to a move against Ticonderoga. He found himself at once enmeshed in the difficulties of joint campaigning with colonials. Each of the New England colonies had made it a practice to operate through a war committee charged with the purchase of all supplies. A second committee in each case would be sent with the soldiers to arrange for the transportation of troops and

---

[1] Fox to Shirley, Mar. 13, 1756. *C.O. 5 No. 212*; Shirley, *Correspondence*, vol. II, p. 425. He was ordered to return at once on a frigate provided for that purpose. In Fox's first letter it was stated that his recall was "not owing to any Dissatisfaction with your Services; But on the contrary. It is the King's Intention as a Mark of His Royal Favor to appoint you to be Governor of Jamaica." The government had no intention of doing so, nor had the king. Hardwicke had pointed out that he feared the affair "will be followed with great Confusion in the Colonies," and it is likely that the matter was arranged as it was so as not to arouse feeling in America, where, on the whole, Shirley was popular.

[2] The quarrel may be followed in Shirley, *Correspondence*, vol. II, pp. 522, 529, 538 *f.*, 547, 551, 558; G. S. Kimball, *Correspondence of William Pitt*, (New York, 1906), vol. I, pp. 172 *ff.*; Papers relating to provisions for the Army, 1756, *Brit. Mus.*, *Add. Mss.* 35909; Documents relating to delay in Provisions, 1756, *C.O. 5 No. 46*; Maj-Gen. Shirley's Answer to Earl of Loudon's Representations, Sept. 1758, *War Office, 1 No. 1*; *The Conduct of Major-General Shirley . . . briefly stated*, (London, 1758).

material. Each colony wished to keep all control over its own supplies, and thus, as Parkman points out, "four independent committees were engaged in the work of transportation at the same time, over the same roads, for the same object." No wonder Loudon wrote to the colonial commander Winslow that "I wish to God you could persuade your people to go all one way."[1] Another and even more serious difficulty arose. In a composite service the question of official precedence is always a matter of serious concern. Intercolonial jealousy was particularly sensitive on this point.[2] Sometimes the difficulty would be overcome by all the New England colonies granting a commission to the same officer, who thus had four masters.[3] More often no common ground could be agreed upon and the conduct of the war suffered lamentably in consequence. Rhode Island, for example, gave instructions that no troops from that colony should serve under any but Rhode Island officers save the commander-in-chief only.[4]

When colonials and regulars of any nation act together it always engenders a special bitterness, for to the invariable jealousy between the regular and volunteer officer is added the supercilious feeling of superiority of the national, and the sensitiveness to slight of the colonial.[5] After the Boer War, for example, not to mention later and more invidious instances, the methods adopted by the British regular to rid himself of the company of the colonials called forth protests from Canada, New Zealand and the Cape.[6] At the very beginning of Braddock's expedition the question had given trouble, the home government having ruled that no regular officer of any rank whatsoever should take orders from any colonial officer, so that a colonial major-general found himself subordinate to an Eng-

---

[1] Parkman, *Montcalm and Wolfe*, vol. I, pp. 397 *f.*, 400.

[2] *Fitch Papers*, vol. I, pp. 101, 104 *f.*

[3] *Ibid.*, pp. 106, 108.

[4] *R. I. Col. Records*, vol. VI, pp. 118, 124 *f.*

[5] The same difficulties were experienced with the French forces in Canada. Wood, *Fight for Canada*, p. 66; Parkman, *Montcalm and Wolfe*, vol. I, p. 389.

[6] P. A. Silburn, *The Colonies and Imperial Defence*, (London, 1909), p. 153. Six years after the war not five per cent of the colonials who had held commissions remained in the service, and it is said that these "met the same cold reception meted out to the Colonial cousin in the past."

lish captain.[1] Many of the colonial officers were exceedingly inefficient, it is true, but so also were many of the British, particularly when acting under the new conditions in America. It was a matter on which, from several points of view, there was much to be said on both sides, but however it was settled it was bound to cause ill feeling. For some weeks the dispute went on at Albany as to whether the large body of colonials assembled at Fort Edward would agree to act with the regulars under Loudon if their officers were made subordinate to the English. The colonials finally agreed to the English viewpoint but with the request that they be allowed to act in different expeditions from the English as far as possible.[2]

Meantime, while Loudon and the colonials were parleying over precedence, while at Fort Edward five hundred men were sick out of twenty-five hundred, and while the garrison at Oswego was vainly waiting for supplies, Montcalm was watching his opportunity and preparing an unsuspected and sudden blow. A few days after the unwilling compromise had been effected by which the colonials and English finally agreed to act together if necessary, the staggering news was received that Oswego had fallen. Sixteen hundred English had surrendered to the French, amid the usual scenes of drunkenness and butchery which marked all actions with Indian allies. The always pessimistic Loudon was panic struck. He immediately gave up all idea of an advance against Ticonderoga, and hurriedly sent to all the colonies north and south, for reinforcements.[3] In view of the complete failure of the summer's campaigning, the lateness of the season, and the colonists' lack of confidence in the capacity of the British generals, the assemblies showed no disposition to answer the calls.[4] In Europe, affairs had gone as badly as in the colonies, and

[1] H. Fox to Capt. Demeré, Aug. 25, 1754, C.O. 5 No. 211. A similar order was issued May 12, 1756, Parkman, Montcalm and Wolfe, vol. I, p. 413. Cf. Beer, British Colonial Policy, pp. 173 ff.

[2] Council of Field Officers, July 22, 1756, C.O. 5 No. 46; Loudon to Winslow, July 31; Same to same Aug. 9; Winslow to Loudon Aug. 10; Provincial Field Officers to Loudon Aug. 12, 1756; all in C.O. 5 No. 47. Shirley, Correspondence, vol. II, pp. 497, 499, 501 ff., 512, 517.

[3] Loudon to Winslow, Aug. 20, 1756; same to governors of the southern colonies, Aug. 20; same to governors of New England colonies, Aug. 20; all in C.O. 5 No. 47.

[4] Mass. Assembly to Shirley, Sept. 8, 1756; Loudon to Fox, Oct. 3; Fitch to Loudon, Sept. 20; Mass. Committee of War to Loudon, Sept. 21; all in C.O. 5 No. 47.

even before the fall of Oswego, Newcastle was as panicky as his
American chief. "We have reasons to fear constant Miscar-
riages," he wrote in June: "Our Armies run away in America
and Our Fleets in the Mediterranean . . . we have hardly One
Ship more to add to Our Squadron Abroad, or One Battalion to
Our Forces employed in the Mediterranean, and in North
America." [1] Gloom settled upon the colonies, conscious of their
own weakness and with no confidence in British help, a gloom
not lightened by renewed quarrels with Loudon over the necessary but irritating question of quartering the troops for the
winter. [2] The Massachusetts legislature denied that the Parliamentary quartering act extended to the colonies as they were
not expressly included, but admitted, in words that were to give
trouble later, that the authority of Parliament over the colonies
was always acknowledged. "There is not a member of the General Court," they stated, "and we know of no Inhabitant within
the Bounds of the Government that ever questioned this
Authority." [3]

By October, however, it was evident that Newcastle would be
forced to resign, and before the close of the disastrous year, Pitt
had risen to power. In the King's speech at the opening of
Parliament in December "the succour and preservation of
America" was given a leading place, and in stirring words Pitt
aroused the fighting spirit of the English. [4] Although new energy
was put into the struggle, the next year was to be no less disastrous for the colonists than the preceding. The chief movement
was to be directed against Louisbourg, and it was planned that
Loudon was to move his troops from New York to coöperate
with a fleet under Admiral Holburne, which was to meet him at
Halifax. By April, party politics had forced Pitt's resignation,
and incompetence and contrary winds had held the fleet in
England until May. [5] The plan had been Loudon's, and in spite
of the fleet's delay he was anxious to reach the rendezvous.

[1] Newcastle to Col. Joseph Yorke, [marked "very private"] June 11, 1756, *Brit. Mus., Add. Mss. 32865.*
[2] *Acts and Resolves*, vol. IV, pp. 47 *f.*, 112 *ff.*
[3] *Ibid.*, vol. IV, p. 117.
[4] Corbett, *Seven Years' War*, vol. I, pp. 150 *ff.*
[5] Holderness to Loudon, Apl. 8, 1757, *C.O. 5 No. 212.*

Late in June he moved his troops to Halifax, and a month later was met by Holburne's ships, but although he then had over twenty-five thousand troops under his command, the delay had been fatal.[1] The French had assembled a still more powerful fleet at Louisbourg, and the expedition was ruined. Nothing was attempted, and in September a gale of unprecedented fury completely destroyed the English fleet as a fighting machine.

As usual, the French were quick to seize the opportunity which the blundering English afforded. For the sake of his ill-starred expedition, Loudon had drawn off all the best troops from the frontier of New York. As soon as he realized the situation Montcalm decided to strike, and advanced down the lakes with a mixed army of French regulars, militia and Indians. By the fifth of August he was in front of Fort William Henry at the lower end of Lake George, where a brave Scotch officer, Lieutenant-Colonel Monro was in command with twenty-two hundred men. Although much outnumbered, Monro decided to defend the place to the last, trusting in aid from General Webb who was fourteen miles away with sixteen hundred men.[2] That general, however, who had never shown any ability, refused to move to the help of the garrison, and contented himself with calling on the colonial assemblies for reinforcements that could not possibly have arrived in time. Monro and his men made a heroic defence, but by the night of the eighth practically all the cannon were disabled, the walls had been breached, and small-pox was raging among the soldiers.[3] The following day surrender was made on honorable terms, among which was the promise that the garrison, with the women and children, should be escorted by a French detachment to Fort Edward to avoid massacre by the Indians.[4] The French officers, however, scarcely made an effort to save the conquered English. The sick were murdered in their tents, the retreating column assaulted and plundered. All discipline was lost, and many of the Eng-

---

[1] Troops under Loudon, July 24, 1757, *War Office Papers, 1 No. 1.*

[2] Parkman, *Montcalm and Wolfe,* vol. I, pp. 510 *f.* There were about 800 more between Webb and Albany.

[3] *Ibid.,* p. 519; Col. Frye's Journal, Sept. 4, 1757, *C.O. 5 No. 18; R. I. Col. Records,* vol. VI, pp. 82 *ff.,* 167 *f.; N. Y. Col. Docts.,* vol. X, pp. 597 *ff.*

[4] Account No. 2 of the Military Operations in America, 1756–7, *C.O. 5 No. 18; N. Y. Col. Docts.,* vol. X, pp. 617 *f.*

lish were killed as they fled through the woods. For days, the survivors, half starved, were arriving at Fort Edward.[1] Montcalm personally seems to have done what he could, but he evidently had entirely lost control of the situation, and the conduct of his officers is beyond extenuation. The New England colonies hastened to send up reserves but too late to be of help, and they soon returned to their homes for the winter. Rangers under the colonial leader, Rogers, continued skirmishing through the snow-filled forests and over the frozen waterways, but picturesque and daring as were many of their exploits, they were of no effect on the situation as a whole.

Of far greater influence than the abortive operations in America upon the final outcome of the war was Pitt's return to power early in the summer after three months' retirement.[2] Although his first thought was for America, it was too late for him to undertake new plans there for the year's campaign, and that of 1758 was the first for which he was responsible. At the close of December, however, a step was taken which did as much as any one thing to assure the success of Pitt's new policy for the colonies, when it was ruled that colonial commissioned officers should rank after regular officers of the same grade only.[3] Pitt's plans were matured by the same date, and early in February all the colonial governors were requested to have the colonies raise, arm and clothe a number of troops equal at least to that of the preceding year, England undertaking all responsibility for food and supplies.[4] Loudon was recalled and Abercromby appointed in his place. Although this was an unfortunate appointment it seems to have been necessary and Pitt did his best by making the young Lord Howe second in command, — "the best officer," as Wolfe wrote, "in the British Army." Young Howe at once and deservedly endeared himself to the Americans.

The forces under Abercromby were to advance up Lakes

[1] Frye, Journal, cit. supra; Affidavit of Surgeon Miles Whitworth Oct. 17, 1757; affidavits of Capt. Wm. Arbuthnot, Oct. 17, 1757, both in C.O. 5 No. 18; Parkman, Montcalm and Wolfe, vol. I, pp. 524 ff.; N. Y. Col. Docts., vol. X, pp. 631 ff., 645 ff.

[2] June 29, 1757.

[3] Warrant for settling Rank of Provincial Officers, Dec. 30, 1757, C.O. 5 No. 212.

[4] Kimball, Pitt Correspondence, vol. I, pp. 3 ff.

George and Champlain, capture Ticonderoga and Crown Point, and proceed to unite with a naval force under Boscawen in the capture of Quebec, the fleet first taking Louisbourg on its way. The land forces designed to operate with Boscawen in his own operations were placed under Colonel Jeffery Amherst with Wolfe as second. These two campaigns and the operations planned for the south, called for fifty thousand troops, of which Pitt hoped to raise one-half in the colonies.[1] Pitt's policies, particularly that with regard to the rank of provincial officers, produced a veritable revolution in colonial sentiment, and the New England colonies at once voted about fourteen thousand troops.[2] The details of transport and supplies were most efficiently cared for by Pitt himself, but the vagaries of ocean winds and the blind chance of a stray bullet ruined the plans so carefully laid. The fleet, which left England on February 19th alternately encountered terrific gales and complete calms, and was nearly three months in making the crossing to Halifax.[3] Though the forces under Boscawen and Amherst worked together in perfect harmony to final success in their first objective, Louisbourg did not fall into the hands of the English for the second time until July 27th.[4] There were wild rejoicings both in England and America, but it is interesting to note, as a straw in the wind, that although six hundred colonial rangers had taken part in the siege, there were voices raised in Boston against celebrating a victory won by the British and not by the provincials.[5]

While Boscawen and Amherst were discussing whether it were too late to proceed to Quebec to attempt the second part of the plan, news came which forced them to abandon all hope of the immediate conquest of Canada. On the 4th of July, Abercromby with his six thousand regulars and nine thousand colonials had proceeded up Lake George in an imposing flotilla of a thousand bateaux and whale boats provided by the foresight of Pitt. Two days later while the troops were passing through the

---

[1] Beer, *British Colonial Policy*, pp. 59 *f.*

[2] *Ibid.*, p. 60 *n*; Kimball, *Pitt Correspondence*, vol. I, pp. 203 *f.*

[3] Corbett, *Seven Years' War*, vol. I, pp. 314 *f.*

[4] For details of the siege *vide* McLennan, *Louisbourg*, pp. 236 *ff.*; Parkman, *Montcalm and Wolfe*, vol. II, pp. 59 *ff.*; Knox, *Journal*, vol. III, pp. 1 *ff.*

[5] Parkman, *cit. supra*, p. 80.

dense woods in the narrow strip of land between the two lakes, Lord Howe was instantly killed by a bullet from an unseen foe, and in the words of Major Mante, "the soul of General Abercrombie's army seemed to expire." [1] The general, however, decided to push on and arrived before Ticonderoga he ordered a general assault from the worst possible position, and sacrificed victory and the army to his own stupidity. Both regulars and colonials behaved with admirable courage, but the English were forced to withdraw with nearly two thousand casualties. [2] Reckless before attack, Abercromby proved a coward after it, and gave hurried orders to send the heavy artillery all the way to New York without delay, and from this time was dubbed "Mrs. Nabbycrombie" by the colonials. They were furious both at the unnecessary sacrifice and the equally unnecessary abandonment of the enterprise. "I have told facts," wrote one, "you may put the epithets upon them." Feeling against the English could not fail to run high among the nine thousand colonists in Abercromby's army and their fellow citizens at home who saw their friends sacrificed and the heavy expense of the operations rendered useless by the incompetence of the British leader. This seemed the more obvious when contrasted with a brilliant success, won against that leader's advice, by Colonel Bradstreet and three thousand colonials who some weeks later captured Fort Frontenac on Lake Ontario, and thus inflicted a blow on the French position second only to the capture of Louisbourg. It may be noted again that the friction and criticism born of the coöperation of regular and colonial troops seems destined almost invariably to develop self-consciousness and a sense of solidarity among the colonials. Nearly a century and a half after Canada had become English her troops fought with the British against the Boers in South Africa, with the usual result that "a popularly exaggerated idea of the achievements of the Canadian contingents, friction in Africa with imperial officers and loss of confidence in the War Office and the staff . . . quickened the

---

[1] Cited by Parkman, *Montcalm and Wolfe*, vol. II, p. 102.

[2] *N. Y. Col. Docts.*, vol. X, pp. 721 *ff.*; *R. I. Col. Records*, vol. VI, pp. 217 *f.*; Kimball, *Pitt Correspondence*, vol. I, pp. 297 *ff.*; Parkman, *Montcalm and Wolfe*, vol. II, pp. 103 *ff.*

consciousness of Canada as a distinct national entity." [1] The effect of such coöperation on the part of the American colonists and the British from 1756 to 1763 must be considered as reflected in the course of events that followed the close of the war.

By 1758 the tide of success had turned, though it had not yet become obvious to the English. The Canadian farms had scarcely been tilled; peculation in the government was ruining everything; only a quarter of the money intended to secure the allegiance of the Indians was reaching them; the Canadians were dispirited; it was estimated that the English had about sixty thousand men against their ten or eleven thousand. Early in the spring Montcalm wrote that Canada would assuredly fall that campaign or the next, barring a naval diversion, unforeseen good luck, or more gross blunders by the English.[2] Although the French still held Ticonderoga and Crown Point in the center, their left had been forced back by the capture of Louisbourg, and their right by the English victories at Fort Duquesne and Frontenac.[3] Whereas England was greatly increasing her effort in America, France was adopting a local European policy, and Montcalm was instructed to withdraw wherever necessary, so as merely to defend the indispensable footing in Canada with the least resources possible.[4] "Eh, monsieur," said Berryer to Bougainville, when the latter asked aid for Canada, "quand le feu est à la maison, on ne s'occupe pas des écuries." [5] The way was clearly being opened for the completion of Pitt's plan of 1758 now renewed for the coming campaign. The more capable Amherst was sent to replace Abercromby for the advance from the center, and Wolfe was given command of the land forces to operate with Admiral Saunders in the attack upon Quebec.

Owing to the weakness of the French position, there was nothing for the French forces to do but to withdraw before Amherst's advancing army of eleven thousand men, about

---

[1] O. D. Skelton, *Life and Letters of Sir Wilfrid Laurier*, (New York, 1922), vol. II, p. 286.

[2] *N. Y. Col. Docts.*, vol. X, pp. 960 *ff.*

[3] Capt. C. R. Bradshaw, "Campaign of 1759," *Journal of United Service Institution of India*, vol. XXXVIII, p. 284.

[4] *Ibid.*, Despatch cited, p. 285.

[5] Cited by Deschamps, *Histoire de la question coloniale*, p. 234.

equally made up of regulars and provincials. In July, Ticonderoga and Crown Point were abandoned without a shot save by a small rearguard left to delay the English advance.[1] Almost simultaneously came word of the capture of Fort Niagara in the west. Amherst, however, failed to advance toward a junction with Wolfe at Quebec, and busied himself with consolidating his position and making unnecessarily elaborate preparations. A painstaking officer, he was without imagination, and seemed incapable of distinguishing between the essential and the unimportant. It was nearly always the fate of the colonials to have to serve under the least competent of British commanding officers, officers of a type which, as an English historian has rather kindly phrased it, "the British army seems to evolve in the fat years of peace."[2] The provincials, indeed, were well prepared to sympathize with George the Second who, when told that Wolfe was mad, replied that in that case he wished he "would bite some of my other generals."

The story of that officer's brilliant exploit in the capture of Quebec, with the splendid coöperation of the navy, need not be repeated here, colonial forces participating only to a very minor extent.[3] In fact, nearly twice as many New England men shared in a distant naval expedition in 1762 as in the capture of the Canadian stronghold which they had so long and so ardently desired, for over eleven hundred Connecticut and Rhode Island troops took part in the attack upon Havana following Pitt's extension of operations to the West Indies. That expedition proved nearly as disastrous to the colonials as had the terrible Cartagena one of twenty years before, and of the nine hundred and seventeen men from the larger colony over three hundred and seventy-four were lost.[4]

[1] Knox, *Journals*, vol. III, pp. 20 ff.

[2] Williams, *William Pitt*, vol. I, p. 336.

[3] Perhaps no other military event has been so completely documented as has this siege. *Cf.* A. Doughty and G. W. Parmelee, *The Siege of Quebec and the Battle of the Plains of Abraham*, (Quebec, 1901), 6 vols. The story of the fall is given in vol. III.

[4] A. B. Gardiner, "The Havana Expedition of 1762," *R. I. Hist. Soc., Publications*, New Ser., vol. VI, pp. 186 ff.; W. K. Watkins, "The Capture of Havana in 1762," *Soc. Col. Wars, Year Book* [Mass.] (1899), pp. 157 f.; E. E. Hale, ed. *An authentic Journal of the Siege of the Havana*, (London, 1762), reprint, Cambridge, n. d. Dr. Hale's statement that 5,000 New England men took part is an error. *Cf.* also, *Soc. Col. Wars*, [New York], *Publications*, vol. XIV, pp. 56 f.; *R. I. Col. Records*, vol. VI, pp. 339 f., 363.

Although the French minister Choiseul foresaw the end and was anxious for peace, the triumphant English were in no mood to stop with the capture of Quebec.[1] Indeed, there was still a small but effective French force in Canada, and Montreal was as yet in the enemy's hands. In 1760, Amherst resolved to retrieve his delay of the previous summer, and planned a triple movement on the city, from Quebec on the east, up the New York lakes from the south, and down the St. Lawrence from the west by way of Lake Ontario. It was a critical combination to attempt, but was crowned with success and resulted not only in the capture of Montreal but in preventing any force escaping westward to continue to harass the frontiers. On the 8th of September Vaudreuil signed the capitulation, and as Parkman wrote "half the continent changed hands at the scratch of a pen."[2] The stream of American history was thenceforth to flow in new channels, though many months were to pass and momentous decisions were to be taken before that fact was made known and certain by the scratch of another pen at the treaty of Paris in 1763.

[1] Richard Waddington, *La guerre de sept ans*, (Paris, n. d.), vol. III, pp. 543 *ff.*

[2] This is not true in a literal sense, for the "Illinois Country" was not included in the capitulation, though it was in the treaty of Paris.

CHAPTER XII

WAR AND BUSINESS

Financial Effects of the War — Growing Disparity of Wealth and Its Effect — Rise of " Big Business" — Its Influence on the Legislatures and People — The Land Question — Increasing Discontent — Smuggling — Writs of Assistance —Popular Leaders — Politics — Increasing Friction with England

In the closing three years of the war, from the capture of Montreal in 1760 to the peace of Paris in 1763, the colonials, to a great extent, lost interest in its operations, the theater of which, so far as America was concerned, was shifted from the continent to the West Indies. The continental conquests, indeed, had to be held by armed forces, but the colonies considered the acquisition as a *fait accompli,* and failed to meet their requisitions in as large proportion as they had done in the years immediately preceding. This was as true of the continental operations as it was of the Havana expedition noted at the close of the last chapter. The one thing that the colonists always and ardently desired was to be let alone, to be allowed to make money in their own way, to exploit all the resources of a new land and of overseas commerce, unhampered by French or Indian enemy or English imperial officials or policy. Throughout the struggle, in so far as its larger aspects were concerned, they cheerfully threw the entire responsibility upon England, and continued to trade with the enemy upon a larger scale than ever, caring only for the defeat of France upon their own frontiers. That accomplished by the help of the mother country, their war was over.

Although this attitude was partly due to the extreme narrowness of their provincial outlook, and partly to innate human selfishness, it is also true that some of the colonies had made great sacrifices and were less able than formerly to meet the demands of the military situation. The policy adopted by

England at the beginning of the struggle of repaying the colonists a considerable part of their outlay had been erected into a
considered system by Pitt, and in the last five years of the war,
Parliament had reimbursed the continental colonies to the
extent of nearly £900,000 Sterling, equivalent to about two-
fifths of their expenses.[1] A very considerable portion of this
went to the colonies of Massachusetts, Connecticut and New
York, which had furnished about seven-tenths of all the colonial
troops, although they contained only about one-third of the
white population.[2] New Hampshire had done comparatively
little, although in 1765 she claimed an unliquidated war debt of
£18,000.[3] Rhode Island's debt amounted to £5,000 less, but her
loss in shipping had been heavy. Her people had chosen to play
their part in the profitable rôle of privateers, and the loss of
ninety to a hundred vessels must be considered in the light of
the enormous profits they were making.[4] For example, one
prize in 1757 netted £78,000, and another a few months later
£93,000, these two alone thus bringing into the colony profits
amounting to the entire war cost in Massachusetts in her
year of heaviest military expense.[5] This was approximately
£179,000 in 1758, or, not allowing for the sum returned her by
England, about ten times her normal expense for government.[6]
Her total expenses during the entire war were estimated at
£818,000, those of Rhode Island at £81,000, and those of Connecticut at £260,000.[7] By the end of 1758 the land tax in Boston
had risen to about sixty-seven per cent of the income, and that
in the rural districts to about twenty per cent.[8] After the end of

[1] Beer, *British Colonial Policy*, pp. 54*f.*, 57*f.*
[2] *Ibid.*, p. 68.
[3] State of the Debts incurred by the British Colonies in North America . . . Jan. 29,
1766, *C.O. 324 No. 17.*
[4] Foster, *Stephen Hopkins*, vol. II, p. 24.
[5] G. S. Kimball, *Providence in Colonial Times*, (Boston, 1912), p. 269.
[6] *Mass. Archives*, 78:113. The expense of the government was £18,000 in 1760, and
that for Connecticut £3,500 in 1762. Annual expense of Establishments in Colonies
in Time of Peace, *C.O. 324 No. 17*, dated Jan. 29, 1766. In 1759 England paid Massachusetts £59,575, or more than one quarter of the amount given to the colonies. *Mass.
Misc. Mss.*, *1755-66*, Library of Congress.
[7] State of the Debts, *cit. supra*. Another estimate places the cost to Massachusetts at
£1,039,390. *A brief State of the Services and Expences of the Province of the Massachusetts
Bay in the Common Cause*, (London, 1765), p. 20.
[8] Kimball, *Pitt Correspondence*, vol. I, p. 362.

hostilities Massachusetts was raising by taxation £37,500 annually for the sinking of her debt, so that taxes must have been
triple the normal rate, although it was expected that the debt
might be cleared in about four years.[1] The colonists were accustomed to very light taxation, the entire cost of the colonial
government in Connecticut, for example, being only £4,000 a
year, or about fifteen cents per capita for its population of one
hundred and thirty thousand.[2] The great bulk of the people
were poor, the poorest being found in the lower classes in the
towns and among the frontiersmen. The strength of New England lay in her farming class of the more settled sections, but
even in their case, wealth consisted almost wholly in land. Not
only were the people poor but in many sections extremely
ignorant.[3] Many contemporary observers agree moreover in
commenting upon their dishonesty, pointing particularly though
perhaps undeservedly to the Rhode Islanders, though one
southerner admitted that "for rural scenes and pretty frank
girls" Newport was the pleasantest place he had found in his
travels.[4] Even in such a Massachusetts town as Worcester in
1755, John Adams reported that all the conversation he could
find was "dry disputes upon politics and rural obscene wit." [5]
Nor in many cases did even politics serve to lift the rural mind
out of the petty affairs of the village. Even at the beginning
of the Seven Years' War, either on account of poverty or lack of
interest, eighteen towns out of sixty-eight in Connecticut, and
fifty-eight out of one hundred and fifty-three in Massachusetts
failed to send representatives to their General Courts.[6]

As a matter of fact, a great gulf had widened between the
rich town merchant or other capitalist and the ordinary colo-

[1] [Francis Bernard] *Select Letters on Trade and Government of America*, (London,
1774), p. 31. In 1761 Barbadoes and Jamaica incurred debts of £30,000 and £50,000
respectively which they paid off in one year by taxation with the help of £10,000 received from England. Letter of Lords of Trade to Parliament, Feb. 25, 1766. *C. O.
324 No. 17.*

[2] *Fitch Papers*, vol. I, p. 211. Of this amount £490 was for education.

[3] *Cf.* Robert Rogers, *A concise Account of North America*, (London, 1765), pp. 45, 51,
55, 59.

[4] *Hamilton's Itinerarium*, ed. A. B. Hart, (St. Louis, 1907), p. 103. *Cf.* p.178, and A.
Burnaby, *Travels through the Middle Settlements in North America in the years 1759 and
1760*, (London, 1798), p. 97, as well as the accounts of other contemporary travelers.

[5] *Works*, vol. I, p. 28.

[6] *State of the British and French Colonies*, pp. 132 f.

nist. The more or less cultured men and women of the socially elect who had servants and fine houses, whose portraits hung on their walls, and both sexes of whom went clothed in "the rich, deep, glaring splendor" of their silks and satins, velvets and brocades, had little in common with the barefoot farmer and his equally barefoot wife, or with the artisan of the towns. As we are apt to think of New England as thrifty, simple and homespun in contrast with the "cavalier" luxury of the south, it may be illuminating to quote what a North Carolina planter wrote home as to the life of the young girls of fifteen or so in his own social class as he found it at Boston at this time. "You would not be pleased," he wrote, "to see the indolent way in which" they "generally live. They do not get up even in this fine Season till 8 or 9 o'clock. Breakfast is over at ten, a little reading or work until 12, dress for dinner until 2, afternoon making or receiving Visits or going about the Shops. Tea, Supper, and Chat closes the Day and their Eyes about 11." [1] This was indeed a far cry from the earlier children of Deerfield who had not been allowed to work in the fields, temporarily, under twelve for fear of the Indians, or even from the children of the farmers and artisans of 1763.

Wealth was increasing, but with even more rapidity it was concentrating. In Boston, in 1758, Charles Apthorp died leaving over £50,000, and there were others equally or even more wealthy.[2] Fortunes were fast being built up to enormous figures for that day by the privateering merchants of Rhode Island, while in New Hampshire Benning Wentworth, who had been bankrupt in 1740, had acquired a hundred thousand acres of land and a fortune in money twenty years later, and was living in princely style in a palatial mansion of fifty-two rooms.[3] This growing disparity of wealth between the few and the many, increased the feeling between the poor and the rich which we have already noted as steadily developing throughout the century. Demagogues were not lacking to add fuel to the as yet smouldering fires. "Because God has made some poor," wrote

[1] *Letters of James Murray, Loyalist*, (Boston, 1901), p. 110.
[2] Elias Nason, *Sir Henry Frankland*, (Albany, 1865,) p. 45 n.
[3] L. S. Mayo, *John Wentworth*, (Harvard University Press, 1921), p. 21; Gipson, *Jared Ingersoll*, p. 92.

one regarding the Excise tax in Boston, "must Men therefore make them poorer still, to enrich themselves? . . . As the main End and design of Government is to protect and defend the poor and weak against the Power of the rich and potent Part of the Community it would thence follow, on your Principles, that the poor must pay all, or near all . . . unless you choose to consider them as Criminals, and as such make them pay for their own Execution." [1] In connection with the currency question in Rhode Island, another wrote of those "Plagues of Society, who remain as a Scourge for our Sins, call themselves honest Merchants, Men of Honor and Integrity, substantial and sober Farmers . . . But for my Part I will suffer on the Rack before I will own that they have any more Religion, Virtue, or Honor than a Highwayman." Even the title of this broadside is suggestive, for it is headed "A Letter to the Common People." [2]

Feeling between the "court" and "country" parties was only in part directed against England and English policies. The attack was directed against privilege in any form. This cannot be over-emphasized, for it is apt to be lost to sight in the more dramatic moments when the contest assumed the form of a struggle between colony and mother country. "There is an overweening fondness," wrote John Adams in 1817, "for representing this country as a scene of liberty, equality, fraternity, union, harmony and benevolence. But let not your sons or mine deceive themselves. This country, like all others, has been a theatre of parties and feuds for near two hundred years." [3] In spite of this clear warning by one of the great actors in the drama, the sons did, for some generations, choose to deceive themselves, and it is only in recent years that the real nature of the American revolution is beginning to emerge from beneath the falsifications of encrusted legend.

Much of the colonial wealth was being accumulated by doubtful methods — the use of official position, the privateering that was akin to piracy, smuggling and bribery, the engrossing of public lands, price fixing and war profiteering. We of this day

[1] *Boston Evening Post*, Oct. 21, 1764.
[2] T. R. Cooper, "A Letter to the Common People of the Colony of Rhode Island, (Providence, 1763), *Broadside Collection, Connecticut*, in Library of Congress.
[3] *Works*, vol. X, pp. 241 *f.*

need no historical examples to teach us the effects of the opportunities of war upon the economic conscience of rich and poor
alike. These were emphasized in the New England of the period
by the laws of trade, complacent customs officials and the
natural resources of the neighboring frontier. Even these were
not sufficient for those who were so rapidly amassing fortunes,
and an inter-colonial group of financiers of the time formed
themselves into an interesting price fixing combination that
was a forerunner of the "big business" of today. Organized by
Rhode Island merchants, an agreement was entered into by all
the manufacturers of spermaceti candles in New England, and
later embraced those of Philadelphia. Under the name of the
United Company of Spermaceti Candlers a dozen or more of the
largest houses, including the Jews, made an agreement which
was distinctly in restraint of trade, as we would say today. It
included fixed prices at which the dealers in the raw material
should be allowed to sell their product to the "trust," and at
which the finished candles could be marketed; the rates of commission to be paid in the trade; the allotment of the entire
supply of raw material in America among the signers of the
agreement; measures for preventing any other houses from becoming competitors, and for forcing the raw material dealers
to sell at the prices fixed by the combination.[1] The plan, which
was inaugurated in 1762, is of great interest as showing how
colonial boundaries were being eliminated in the minds of the
moneyed group as contrasted with the as yet extremely provincial outlook and provincial "patriotism" of the smaller people
of town and country. The combination cornered the entire
North American supply, and by mere threat of its power seems
to have controlled the trade successfully, and to have prevented
competition, for some years at least. The whalers who found
themselves forced to sell part of the product of their toils at a
fixed price along the entire seaboard, and the smaller manufacturers who found themselves shut out from any chance to compete, must have regarded the powerful combination with no
kindly eyes. It was another sign that the freedom of the new

[1] *Commerce of Rhode Island*, [*Mass. Hist. Soc., Coll.*, Ser. VII, vols. IX and X]
(Boston, 1914), vol. I, pp. 88 *ff.*, 97 *ff.*

land was passing and that the average man was coming to be more at the mercy of a small class who lived a life and controlled opportunities from which the common people were more and more excluded. Even the itinerant country peddler found himself being hampered and forced out of business by the merchant groups by methods with which we are entirely familiar today.[1] This process, which as yet can be best studied in Pennsylvania, may well have accounted for the passage of an act by Connecticut in 1765, by which the cost of the license granted "to any pedlar, hawker or petty-chapman" was increased from £5 to £20, which latter would seem to have been an almost prohibitive amount for such small scale business in that period of acute trade depression.[2]

As yet manufacturing occupied but a minor place in the economic life of New England. This was due, as has already been pointed out, far more to the presence of free land than to the few restrictive laws, laxly enforced, enacted in England. During the war, a writer noted that in spite of the great increase in population labor was as dear as forty years before "for no man will be a servant whilst he can be a master," and he thought that it would require "several ages" for labor to become cheap on account of the land still obtainable.[3] As far as a mere living went, there was much truth, if some exaggeration, in Franklin's remark that "the boundless woods of America" were sure to "afford freedom and subsistence to any man who can bait a hook or pull a trigger."[4] The three economic mainstays of New England life were the land, fisheries and foreign commerce. The first was utilized by the "small people" for farming, and by the capitalists for speculation and lumber, and the increasingly devious ways followed by the "big business" of the day may be well illustrated by the latter trade.

By 1760 the chief logging centers were in New Hampshire and Maine, of which the most important were along the Piscataqua, with the small but growing town of Portsmouth at its mouth.[5]

[1] A. M. Schlesinger, *The Colonial Merchants and the American Revolution*, (New York, 1918), p. 28.
[2] *Conn. Col. Records*, vol. XII, p. 356; *Fitch Papers*, vol. II, p. 346.
[3] *State of the British and French Colonies*, p. 141.
[4] *Works*, ed. Bigelow, vol. III, p. 485.
[5] It had 700 houses in 1765. Rogers, *Concise Account*, p. 46.

It was here that Benning Wentworth maintained his regal
state, and controlled absolutely the destinies of the colony
through his own great wealth, his political influence as governor,
and the filling of almost every important office with his relatives
and family connections. Although two hundred vessels sailed
annually for the West Indies and Europe,[1] the main interest of
the colony was in timber, and it was asserted that the governor
had paid the surveyor-general £2,000 to relinquish his office,
worth but £200 a year, in order that he himself might be appointed to the post.[2] His own interest was rather in land, however, as we will note later, and it was his brother, Mark Hunking
Wentworth, who was unquestionably the "lumber king" of the
colonies. He was one of the richest men in New England, and
lived in a house but little less magnificent than that of the governor. Owing to the enormous inroads on the forests, which had
denuded the country but built up the power of the Wentworths,
it was becoming more difficult and costly to get the logs to
market from this portion of the great New England pine belt.
That belt, however, extended southwest from Nova Scotia to
beyond the Connecticut River.

The colony of Connecticut produced no staple for export, and
although it did some business with the West Indies in "large,
genteel fat horses"[3] and supplies, its export business, never
large, was diminishing and tended more and more to pass
through the ports of the neighboring colonies. A contemporary
English traveler compared the province to "a cask of good
liquor, tapped at both ends, at one of which Boston draws, and
New York at the other, till little is left in it but lees and
settlings."[4] Although this situation may not have consciously
affected the small farmers and breeders to any great extent, it
was growing obvious to the enterprising men who conducted business upon a larger scale, and whom we have found undertaking
the speculations in western lands. The latter attractive prospect
had been temporarily blighted, as we have seen, but another

[1] Rogers, *Concise Account*, p. 46.
[2] Gipson, *Jared Ingersoll*, p. 94.
[3] As exported by Benedict Arnold. Cited from *Conn. Gazette*, Feb. 14, 1766, by
Gipson, *Jared Ingersoll*, p. 233.
[4] Quoted by Rogers, *Concise Account*, p. 54.

opportunity for exploitation seemed to present itself in bringing to market down the Connecticut River masts and other timber from that part of the pine belt crossing its upper waters. As this would interfere with the immensely profitable business of the Wentworths, and might even mean the decline of Portsmouth and the rise of New London in its place, it was realized that their hostility would be incurred at once, and that Benning Wentworth, as surveyor-general, could be counted upon to use his office to block the scheme.[1]

Of all the colonies, Connecticut had been the most independent and the most averse to suffering the exercise of any imperial control. Throughout all of them, one of the most hated instruments of imperial organization was the Court of Vice-Admiralty, for reasons which we have already noted. This was particularly true in Connecticut, which was within the jurisdiction of the court located at New York, and which at this very time had been annoyed for some years by an unfortunate affair with the treasure of a Spanish ship,—a case which had been dragging along in the Admiralty Court to the no small danger of the Connecticut charter.[2] The last thing that anyone would have thought possible would be that this independent little republic would petition the Crown to establish one of the hated imperial courts within her borders.

An Admiralty Judge, however, in addition to his jurisdiction over maritime cases, possessed extensive powers with regard to trespasses against the King's Woods. If Connecticut could secure a judge naturally interested or amenable to influence, in favor of Connecticut rather than New Hampshire, it might go far to neutralize Wentworth's powers as surveyor-general, and the "interests" might then proceed with their lumbering in the upper river valley. The proportion of citizens who consciously could expect to benefit by the logging deal must have been very small, whereas antagonism to English control, to Admiralty Courts and to interference with squatter predilections for stealing government timber, was bred in the bone of the colonists. It is highly significant, therefore, of the growing influence of the

[1] *Cf.* Gipson, *Jared Ingersoll,* pp. 94 *f.*
[2] *Fitch Papers,* vols. I and II, *loc. cit.; Wolcott Papers, loc. cit.;* Gipson, *Jared Ingersoll,* pp. 61 *ff.*

capitalist groups in the popular legislatures that the assembly should be found voting that the governor be asked to apply to England for the appointment of an Admiralty Judge "within and for this Colony." [1] The affair dragged, however, although Jared Ingersoll as agent pushed it in England, and in the end the influence of the Wentworths proved too strong and the scheme failed. [2] But the episode is another indication of the tightening grasp of the wealthy group of aggressive speculators and business men upon the resources of the colonies, of their placing their own financial interests above provincial patriotism, and of their growing class opposition to the interests and deepest feelings of the poorer colonists.

In the matter of opening new land to settlement, although the main interest of the two classes was in less direct opposition, we can also trace growing friction between them, and the tendency toward the concentration of wealth and increase of power in the smaller groups. The colonists were unskilful and unthrifty farmers. Aside from other causes of pressure, there were always many who wished to move on from the lands which they had worn out to other and richer ones on the fringes of settlement. The desire to make provision for their large families, the dislocation and restlessness due to the war, and the pioneer spirit all combined to foster an unusually strong movement outward as soon as the danger of the French and Indians was removed. It is estimated that between 1760 and 1774 thirty thousand persons emigrated from Connecticut alone, and in the same period one hundred new towns were planted in New Hampshire. [3] In the latter colony, Benning Wentworth, in the course of his administration as governor, had made grants of about two hundred tracts to various groups, reserving for himself in each case five hundred acres, or some hundred thousand in all, which were to be increased in value by the labors of the settlers without cost or effort on his part. For every grant he had also exacted a fee in proportion to the ability of the grantee, and the lands had gone to the highest bidders to the increasing exasperation of the

[1] *Conn. Col. Records*, vol. XI, p. 358.
[2] Gipson, *Jared Ingersoll*, pp. 79 ff.
[3] Bailey, *Radicalism in Connecticut*, p. 229; Mathews, *Expansion of New England*, p. 113.

poorer settlers.[1] The year 1761 must have been a most profitable one, for in a few months the chief magistrate's "coffers chinked to the tune of well-nigh eighty new townships." [2] In his anxiety to benefit from the great rush then setting in for western New Hampshire and the lands now included in the state of Vermont, the governor was paying but slight attention to colonial boundaries, and of the new towns sixty-eight were within territory claimed by New York. That colony had also made allotments there, and from these various conflicting claims over what became known as "the New Hampshire Grants" bitter disputes eventually arose resulting in riots, bloodshed and border feuds.[3] The speculators, however, cared little for such difficulties, and Massachusetts also undertook to make grants of doubtful validity for ten towns in Maine, hoping to overcome the defective title by enlisting the influence of Governor Bernard in having the grants validated by England by granting him the island of Mount Desert.[4] Nearly four thousand persons were prepared to emigrate as soon as the towns should be opened.[5]

In Connecticut, the same period of wild speculation witnessed a renewal of the efforts of the groups of Delaware and Susquehanna proprietors, and in 1760 the former sent out settlers to take possession of their more than doubtful claims, calling forth a protest from Pennsylvania.[6] Some months later, the Susquehannah Company voted to unite with the Delaware proprietors in sending a joint agent to England to petition for a charter, but two years later decided to proceed immediately with settling the lands without further formalities.[7] This at once brought protests from the Indians. In spite of an attempt by the insistent proprietors to bribe Sir William Johnson to use his influence with the natives to alienate their lands, he declined

---

[1] Mayo, *John Wentworth*, p. 21.

[2] *Ibid.*, p. 22.

[3] *N. Y. Col. Docts.*, vol. VII, pp. 608 *ff.*; *New York Historical Society, Collections*, (1869), pp. 281 *ff*

[4] Jasper Mauduit, *Mass. Hist. Soc., Coll.*, vol. LXXIV, p. 69; *Barrington-Bernard Correspondence*, (Harvard University Press, 1912), pp. 51, 57, 66.

[5] *Ibid.*, p. 71.

[6] *Fitch Papers*, vol. II, pp. 124 *ff.*

[7] *Penn. Archives*, Ser. II, vol. XVIII, pp. 37, 41, 43; Harvey, *History of Wilkes-Barré*, vol. I, pp. 384 *ff.*

and advised his wards to send representatives to Hartford to protest, which they did in May 1763.[1] Governor Fitch, who was opposed to the expansionist policy of the Susquehanna group, told the Indians that the colony had nothing to do with the matter and that, having received orders from England to prevent the settlement, he had communicated them to the company. In August, in spite of warnings from England and from the Indians, some of the proprietors met some Mohawk sachems at Albany and negotiated a new deed. There was in fact no valid claim save from some such instrument, for even some of those interested in the company did not hesitate to laugh at the colony's insisting upon the old charter limit of the "South Sea," and derided the conception of "a Government 60 miles wide and 3000 miles long." Indeed, the colony itself in the previous century had admitted that New York constituted its western boundary.[2] On representations made to England by Pennsylvania, new and more stringent orders were at once sent out that the Connecticut settlers were "forthwith to desist from the" undertaking.[3] They came too late. Goaded by their wrongs, real and fancied, the Indians had readily listened to the chief Pontiac, and a general uprising, starting at Detroit, had again brought on a savage war. As an incident in the general conflict, the little settlement of the Susquehannah Company at Wyoming was attacked and destroyed on October 15th. After this sacrifice to their avarice the promoters of the company did desist for a time from their undertaking.

Their activities, however, had fanned discord in many directions. Not only was a renewal of them destined later almost to plunge the two colonies of Connecticut and Pennsylvania into civil war, but parties had been formed within the smaller colony bitterly opposed to one another. A number of the Council and possibly one-half of the members of the assembly were involved in the scheme, which drew in more and more of the radical element of the people. It is noteworthy that the party lines formed

---

[1] Harvey, *cit. supra*, pp. 411, 416; *Jared Ingersoll Papers, New Haven Colony Historical Society Papers*, vol. IX, pp. 284 *f*.

[2] *Jared Ingersoll Papers*, p. 287; Gipson, *Jared Ingersoll*, p. 317.

[3] Harvey, *cit. supra*, p. 432; *Fitch Papers*, vol. II, pp. 240 *ff*.; Letter from Egremont to Gov. Fitch, Jan. 27, 1763, *C.O. 5 No. 1280.*

at this time, as well as the geographical division of the colony
politically, was maintained in the later disputes in the years of
the revolution, and that those who were in favor of the scheme
— which was opposed by the English government — were those
most opposed to the mother country later.[1] Moreover, when the
final orders came from England, over seven hundred people were
waiting to move to the company's alleged property, and these
naturally threw all the blame on the English government.[2]

Aside from the conflicting claims and various sources of discontent resulting from the expansion and land speculation of the
closing years of the war, there was another profound effect,
which cannot, perhaps, be overestimated in judging the temper
of the people. The new lands were, for the most part, extremely
cheap compared with those in the already settled areas. For
example, in 1762, Massachusetts sold at auction nine townships
in its western section at from thirty-three to seventy cents an
acre.[3] The effect of this competition upon land values was felt
throughout the colonies. In the same year, Dr. Stiles wrote that
"many are selling their lands in order to remove" and that land
at Voluntown had declined from £30 Old Tenor to £15 an acre,
and that at East Haddam they had declined twenty-five per
cent, and at Stafford fifty per cent. The next year he noted that
lands around Stonington, Groton and other places on the
Sound had declined one-half in value, and that the people were
in debt for all their stock and half their lands.[4] In 1765 the
governor of Rhode Island wrote that the fall in the value of real
estate in that colony had been fully as great.[5] When we recall
that almost the entire wealth of the great majority of the colonists consisted of their farms, we can realize the widespread alarm
and discontent that would necessarily result from a sudden drop
of from one quarter to one half of their value within a year or so.
In addition, toward the end of the war there came also a decline
in general business and the price of farm products, emphasized
in part of New England by severe droughts in 1761 and 1762.[6]

[1] Bailey, *Radicalism in Connecticut*, pp. 237 *ff.*
[2] Ezra Stiles, *Itineraries*, p. 189.
[3] Mathews, *Expansion of New England*, p. 110 *n.*
[4] Stiles, *Itineraries*, pp. 50 *f.*, 81, 188.
[5] *R. I. Col. Records*, vol. VI, p. 473.
[6] Kimball, *Correspondence of colonial Governors*, vol. II, p. 336.

For one reason and another, therefore, a great proportion of the people found themselves owing to the merchants debts which they could not meet, their incomes diminished, their property declining in value at a prodigious rate, and themselves facing bankruptcy and eviction. In contrast, they could watch the small class of capitalists, speculators and war profiteers accumulating money on an unprecedented scale.

Those who from despair or from the mere hope of bettering themselves left their old homes for the new lands, also found cause for discontent. In innumerable towns there was the question of the validity of title, but in addition there was everywhere the conflict of interest between those who went to settle, and those who stayed at home as absentee proprietors and enjoyed the increase in value of their lands at the expense of the toils of the pioneers. Dr. Stiles, who bought and sold shares in towns as a modern speculator deals in stocks, owned an interest of thirteen thousand acres in the Susquehannah Purchase, shares in Charlestown on the Saratoga River, in South Kingstown, Concord, Danvis, Lempster, Killington, Harwinton, Cornwall, North Haven, Sherburne and elsewhere throughout the northern colonies, wherever lands were being opened up.[1] Like all such speculators he endeavored as far as possible when selling his shares not to alienate the "privileges of the town" with them, so as to retain control over the town affairs including taxation. Of the grantees of Maidstone, Vermont, for example, not one ever went to live in the town, all remaining in Connecticut whence they managed the town affairs without giving the actual pioneers any voice at all. In many other cases the majority of the proprietors were non-resident even when some were among the settlers. The pioneers thus found themselves doing all the hard work of development while the rich proprietors sat at ease in the old settlements, refusing to bear their just share, if any, of taxation for needed improvements, and merely watched their lands rise in value.[2] The effect was naturally greatly to embitter the feeling of the settlers along the entire frontier against the old settlements. In the closing years of the war, therefore, the

---

[1] Stiles, *Itineraries*, pp. 99, 184.
[2] *Ibid.*, p. 87; Mathews, *Expansion of New England*, pp. 134 *f.*

agricultural population, which meant the vast majority of all New Englanders of that time, was not only deeply anxious about its position, but a large part had distinct economic and political grievances against the small colonial money lending and investing class of the established centers.

The great bulk of colonial debt, however — placed by some as high as nine-tenths of the total — was that owed by the merchants to their English correspondents, and we must consider the position of the former which was also deeply affected by the war.[1] It is practically certain that almost no New England merchant carried on his business without indulging in smuggling on a considerable scale, though it is impossible to ascertain just what proportion the volume of illegal trading may have borne to the total, and it is also necessary in fairness to distinguish between different varieties of technical law-breaking.[2] Manufactured goods and brandy were smuggled in from European ports in contravention of the laws of trade, but the importation of wines and fruit both in small packages and bulk constituted a more important branch of smuggling. Although business with the French West Indies, which the English authorities had considered illegal under the treaty of 1686, was declared lawful by the Attorney-General in 1755, the trade was nevertheless burdened with such heavy duties under the Molasses Act of 1733 as to be impracticable if the specified duties were paid. This entire business, which formed a great part of New England commerce, was almost wholly carried on by smuggling, openly connived at by the authorities. In addition, upon declaration of war with France in 1756, all trade with the enemy became illegal and also of great military importance. England's fleets might prove more than the equal of those of France, but the constant supplying of the enemy with food and supplies by the colonists went far to neutralize the advantage of that sea power upon which both their own safety and that of England depended. Of the guilt of the colonies in this regard there is no doubt. The trade was constant and heavy. To some extent it may be palli-

---

[1] *Acts Privy Council*, vol. IV, p. 388.

[2] Ashley, *Surveys, Historic and Economic*, p. 337; Schlesinger, *Colonial Merchants*, p. 41.

ated by the fact that New England's prosperity and consequent ability to carry on the war depended to a considerable extent upon this very business,[1] but as the war continued it was carried on to an extent and in a manner that evidenced entire disregard of its effects upon the struggle.

The English authorities, civil and military, had found themselves powerless to interfere with what was prolonging the contest and blocking the way to victory. It is true that various acts were passed from time to time by the colonial assemblies which were aimed at controlling the trade in food-stuffs and with the enemy, but the trade was too profitable and New Englanders had become too much accustomed to illicit traffic to be hindered by purely legal or moral considerations.[2] Colonel Byrd of Virginia had not been far from the truth when he had written some years earlier that "the Saints of New England . . . have a great dexterity at palliating a perjury so well as to leave no taste of it in the mouth, nor can any people like them slip through a penal statute." [3] The terms of the Molasses Act were so drastic that evasion seemed justifiable if not, indeed, absolutely necessary. Had England simply failed to enforce the act, its ignoring by the colonists would have had little more'moral effect than our failure today to observe many old and forgotten laws upon our own statute books. But the law was not a dead letter. Though England derived no advantage from it, the customs officers did, and its evasion by otherwise reputable merchants involved constant bribery and corruption of the officials, the effect of which could not fail to react upon character. A customs officer might agree to accept a bribe of a dollar a hogshead in lieu of duty; collectors might grant false clearance papers; forged ships' documents might be bought and sold; even a governor might sell "flags of truce" to cover the illicit traffic; but whatever the methods employed by the merchants to defeat the laws or to avoid paying duties — and they were infinitely various — the fact is that the merchants and their captains and

---

[1] Hubert Hall, "Chatham's Colonial Policy," *American Historical Review*, vol. V, p. 666.

[2] *Conn. Col. Records*, vol. XI, pp. 22, 105; *R. I. Col. Records*, vol. VI, p. 11; *Acts and Resolves*, vol. IV, p. 70.

[3] Cited by Schlesinger, *Colonial Merchants*, p. 40.

agents carried on a very large part of their daily business by bribery or perjury.[1]

Even many of the Judges of the Admiralty took part in the orgy of corruption, which perhaps bears upon the curious action of the Rhode Island assembly in applying to the Crown for the appointment of a special court for that colony, an action oddly parallel to that of Connecticut.[2] Rhode Island was not only as jealous of any encroachments by the English government as was its neighbor, but was above all other colonies the seat of illegal trade. That a colony, a large part of whose population was engaged in smuggling, should ask for a court ostensibly to prevent it has its humorous side, and the solution would seem to be that, in view of the growing complacency and approachableness of judges, it was hoped that by securing the appointment of the right person things might be arranged a little more easily than being under the jurisdiction of the judge at Boston, Massachusetts having complained not a little of late that her trade was being ruined by the unfair competition of the notoriously illicit traffic of Newport and Providence. This is borne out by the fact that the assembly in its application named the person whom it wished to have appointed. An amenable judge of high rank is always of more value to large interests than to petty offenders, and it is suggestive to find at the same period the two most independent of the charter colonies asking for the establishment within their limits of the most hated organs of imperial control. The reasons are obvious, and exhibit in both cases the encroachment of the selfish interests of the rich upon the independent ideals of the generality of the colonists. The combination of courts, legislatures and the "interests" is no new phenomenon in American life, and is one of those we must take into account in considering the American Revolution as distinct from the imperial civil war.

With regard to a very considerable part of the smuggling trade, it is questionable how much of the wholesale corruption indulged in by the merchants may have been due to the nature

---

[1] Schlesinger, *Colonial Merchants*, p. 40; Pitman, *West Indies*, pp. 298, 306, 308, 312, 321, 328 f.

[2] *R. I. Col. Records*, vol. VI, p. 107; Kimball, *Pitt Correspondence*, vol. I, p. 178; Kimball, *Correspondence of colonial Governors*, vol. II, pp. 275 f.

of the laws and how much to the mere desire for greater gain.[1] There were some at least who preferred to conduct their business lawfully and who strenuously objected to the competition of the smugglers, though the latter included many of the most distinguished mercantile houses. In 1756, a Boston merchant wrote to his Rhode Island correspondent to caution him against venturing too much smuggled tea "in one bottom" as it was "an unsettled point" whether even a false customs certificate would screen it if it could not be proved to be legally imported, and "in short the Gentlemen here in Fair Trade are determined to prevent the Importation of Hollands goods at all adventures, and 't is probable may employ people to be on the lookout."[2] It is evident, therefore, that in some lines, at least, business could be carried on at a profit honestly and that the "Fair Traders" ranged themselves on the side of government in trying to prevent the unfair competition of what had come to be known as "the smuggling interest." In fact, there is not a little evidence that even in West India produce the northern consumer was not supplied at a cheaper rate by the smuggler than by the honest merchant, and that the former was merely "making exhorbitant gains and usurping control of the market to the prejudice of the fair trader."[3]

As the war progressed and the price of goods and provisions rose, the temptation became greater. The routes and methods of forwarding cargoes became as varied and devious as were the dealings with the officials,[4] and the wrath of the military and naval authorities increased proportionately as they saw their efforts thwarted and neutralized by the acts of the colonial merchants. In the latter part of 1759 General Crump wrote to Pitt that in the previous eight months not a single vessel had been able to reach the French West Indies from Europe, and that the islands were sustained wholly by the illegal American trade. Admiral Cotes called this trade "iniquitous," and Commodore

---

[1] When we find New England merchants enquiring about the possibility of smuggling into England herself, it is evident that it was wholly for illegal gain and not on account of any hampering restrictions. Cf. *Rhode Island Commerce*, vol. I, p. 110.

[2] *Rhode Island Commerce*, vol. I, p. 66; cf. *Jasper Mauduit*, p. 137.

[3] Pitman, *West Indies*, pp. 308 *ff*.

[4] *Cf.* Beer, *British Colonial Policy*, pp. 88 *ff.*; Pitman, *West Indies*, pp. 297 *ff.*

Moore described those who were engaged in it as "traitors to their country." [1] It has been asserted that commercial supremacy in the West Indies was the central point of Pitt's policy.[2] It is certain at any rate that the fruits of the war he had waged so brilliantly could not be gathered unless the French possessions in the islands were conquered, and what prevented them from falling into his hands was the support they received from the colonists — to a great extent, the New Englanders. It is little wonder that the situation should arouse the wrath of the great statesman. Its only cure seemed to be the enforcement of the act of 1733, and in 1760 he sent a circular letter to the colonial governors stating that the enemy was "principally, if not alone, enabled to sustain, and protract, this long and expensive war" by means of "this dangerous and ignominious trade," and calling upon them to take every lawful step to bring the offenders to "exemplary and condign punishment." [3]

The replies of the New England governors are interesting. Although the trade was notorious, and although at the very time, a few months previously, when Wolfe was battling for Quebec, Boston merchants were ferreting out a new way of trading with the enemy through New Orleans,[4] a committee of the Massachusetts Council reported on Pitt's despatch that "they cannot find that there has been any illegal trade, or any Trade at all, carried on by His Majesty's subjects of this Province either to the French Islands, or to the Rivers Mobile and Mississippi, or to any of the French Settlements on the Continent of America, since the Commencement of the present War." [5] Governor Fitch of Connecticut wrote that he had been unable to find any evidence of trade with the enemy among his people.[6] Governor Hopkins of Rhode Island also stated that

[1] Beer, *cit. supra*, p. 104.

[2] Hotblack, *Chatham's Colonial Policy*, p. 54.

[3] Kimball, *Pitt Correspondence*, vol. II, pp. 320 *f.*

[4] N. M. Miller Surrey, *The Commerce of Louisiana during the French Régime*, 1699–1763, (Columbia University, 1916), pp. 458 *ff.*; Hertz, *Old Colonial System*, p. 77.

[5] Report of a Committee of the Massachusetts Council, Boston, Nov. 7, 1760, *C.O. 5 No. 19.*

[6] Fitch to Pitt, Apl. 25, 1761, *C.O. 5 No. 20.* This portion of the letter is given in *Fitch Papers*, vol. II, p. 112 but omitted by Kimball, *Pitt Correspondence*, vol. II, p. 420. *Cf.* his earlier reply, *ibid.*, p. 359.

no provisions or warlike stores had gone to the French by the permission or connivance of the government, but, in refreshing contrast to the replies from the supposedly more godly colonies to the north and west, he admitted that there had been trade and made a strong and frank plea for its necessity.[1]

Although the efforts made by the authorities to hinder this trade during the earlier years of the war had not been successful, they had been more so in Massachusetts than elsewhere. Governor Bernard did indeed write in 1764 that "if conniving at foreign sugar and molasses, and Portugal wines and fruit, is to be reckoned Corruption, there was never, I believe, an uncorrupt Custom House officer in America till within twelve months; and, therefore Incorruption in the best of them must be considered, not as a positive, but comparative term."[2] In the previous chapter we noticed the introduction of Writs of Assistance in 1755, and it was by means of these instruments that a few of the officers had been able to accomplish what little they had in hindering the illicit trade. These writs, which had been introduced in England by a statute of Charles II, later extended to the colonies, gave the holder the right of general search and seizure, neither particular goods nor place being specified. Although contrary to the spirit of the English constitution, they were legal in the mother country and there seems little ground on which to debate their equal technical legality in America.[3] The difficulty with a warrant for specific search, in a community almost wholly in league with the smugglers, was the advance notice necessarily given to the offender before the officer could arrive with his warrant. In view of the general situation outlined, the writ of assistance, introduced in Massachusetts largely as a war measure, seemed to be the only weapon that promised any chance at all of stopping the traffic with the enemy. Although Paxton and the few other officers who held them had not been able to accomplish much more than the harassing and irritating of the merchants engaged in the contraband trade, the latter began to regard with jealous eyes the complete absence

---

[1] Kimball, *Pitt Correspondence*, vol. II, pp. 373 ff.
[2] Gray, Writs of Assistance, Quincy, *Reports*, p. 424 n.
[3] Gray, *cit. supra*, p. 540.

from annoyance of their competitors in Rhode Island and Connecticut. Coincident with the receipt of Pitt's despatch, which seemed to promise more drastic efforts to break up the smuggling trade, there is evident a concerted attempt on the part of the Boston merchants to destroy the machinery of administration by which alone that result could be attained.[1] Even in Rhode Island, the merchants seem not to have gained all they had hoped from the appointment of their own judge, and in both colonies suits were brought at common law for the recovery of sums forfeited under decisions of the Admiralty Court.[2]

In one of the Boston cases, that of *Erving vs. Cradock*, the merchant Erving sued the collector Cradock for damages after he had been allowed to compound for the smuggling which he admitted, by the payment of £500 fine. In spite of his acknowledged guilt, the provincial court awarded Erving nearly £600 damages. Appeal was taken to the Superior Court, and although the judges charged the jury to find for the defendant, they likewise brought in a verdict of about £550 for Erving. The tendency of the other cases was equally to nullify the administration of the laws by the customs officers and the Admiralty Court. In fact, as Governor Bernard wrote to the Board of Trade, the suits had been brought with a view "of discouraging a Court immediately subject to the King and independent of the Province and which determined property without a jury; and on a necessity of putting a stop to the practices of the Custom house officers, for that the people would no longer bear having their trade kept under restrictions, which their neighbours (meaning Rhode Island) were entirely free from." "One Gentleman," he added, "has been so candid as to own to me, that it was their intention to work them up to such a pitch as should make it necessary for the Ministry to interpose and procure them justice (as they call it) in repealing or qualifying the Molasses Act." [3] As part of this concerted move to secure a

---

[1] Professor C. M. Andrews thinks it likely that the "Merchants Club" of Boston was back of the movement. "The Boston Merchants and the Non-Importation Movement," *Col. Soc. Mass., Publications*, vol. XIX, p. 161 n.

[2] Beer, *British Colonial Policy*, p. 120; Pitman, *West Indies*, p. 323; *R. I. Col. Records*, vol. VI, pp. 371 f.

[3] Cited by Pitman, *West Indies*, p. 325 n.

modification of the act or to nullify the means of its enforcement, the merchants decided to attack the validity of the writs of assistance.

It must be recalled that Massachusetts had her own duties and imposts which she levied to raise part of her colonial income, and her own customs officers. From 1748 to 1756 she had authorized her commissioner to appoint his own deputies who were empowered "to search in all suspected places" for smuggled wines and spirits and to seize such as had not paid the Massachusetts duty.[1] It was only in the latter year that the law provided for specific warrants.[2] It may be coincidence, but this was done at the first session of the legislature after Paxton, the English Surveyor of the Port, had applied for his first writ of assistance and received it from the court.[3] Although the system of general search warrants was open to serious objection, the colonists evidently had not objected to it when used by themselves, and only began to do so when it was employed by the imperial government. In other words, it was a question, at first, not of personal liberty but of interference with profits. As the writs in the hands of the customs officers ran for only six months after the death of a monarch, the demise of George II in October 1760 necessitated an application to the court for their reissue, just at the time that the Boston merchants were combating the whole trade system in view of increased English activity and the Rhode Island smuggling competition. They at once seized upon the opportunity, and sixty-three of them presented a petition to the court to be heard against the grant of the writs.[4] A few months earlier the new governor, Francis Bernard, had arrived at Boston and found the parties there so equally divided as to make it, as he wrote, "madness for me to have put myself at the head of either of them."[5] He was at once, however, drawn unwillingly into a position of considerable delicacy and difficulty. It was said that Shirley had

---

[1] *Acts and Resolves*, vol. III, pp. 406, 471, 522, 581, 622, 701, 762, 845. Beer in citing these references overlooked the first, thus making the acts date from 1749 instead of 1748. *British Colonial Policy*, p. 122 *n.*

[2] *Acts and Resolves*, vol. III, p. 1006.

[3] Gray, Writs of Assistance, Quincy, *Reports*, pp. 402 *ff*.

[4] The petition is given in full by Gray, Writs of Assistance, Quincy, *Reports*, pp. 412 *f*.

[5] *Barrington-Bernard Correspondence*, p. 53.

promised the office of judge to James Otis, Senior, when a vacancy should occur. In September, Stephen Sewall, the chief justice, died, and Otis wished Bernard to advance one of the other members of the bench to that office and to be made himself a judge. This Bernard refused to do, appointing the Lieutenant-Governor, Hutchinson, to the vacant post.[1]

Although much was made of the appointment in the way of party capital, there is no reason for thinking that the paternal disappointment influenced the action of the younger Otis, who was now chosen one of the counsel to represent the case of the merchants. The hearing was held in February 1761, the legality of the writs being defended by Jeremy Gridley, the Attorney-General. His technical position was sound and there was little to be said from the strictly legal standpoint for the opposite side. Oxenbridge Thacher, for the merchants, followed, but the speech of the day apparently was that by the younger James Otis, "a plump, round-faced, smooth-skinned, short-necked, eagle-eyed politician," as a contemporary described him.[2] Able, but violent and eccentric, self-centered and frequently intolerable in manner, tainted with the insanity that was later to end his career, the young lawyer burst into the technical legal discussion like "a flame of fire." We have no verbatim report of his speech, and there is but little to be gained historically by continuing to substitute the increasingly fervid accounts that John Adams penned as he grew older.[3] Although in the days of his old age and failing memory he was to indulge in such panegyrics as placed young Otis above Cicero and Demosthenes, there is nothing in his diary at the time or the contemporary notes which he made of the speech to indicate any such extraordinary quality in it or interest regarding it.[4]

[1] Hutchinson, *History*, vol. III, pp. 86 ff.; John Adams, *Works*, vol. X, pp. 183, 281. There is nothing to support Adams's contention that Hutchinson was appointed for the special purpose of securing a decision in favor of the writs. *Cf.* Gray, Writs of Assistance, Quincy, *Reports*, p. 411. Adams's various references to the whole matter of the writs and the speech of Otis are unreliable.

[2] Cited by J. K. Hosmer, *Life of Thomas Hutchinson*, (Boston, 1896), p. 58.

[3] *Works*, vols. II, pp. 521 ff.; X, 183, 233, 247 f.

[4] *Ibid.*, vol. II, pp. 124, 522 ff.; vol. X, 233. It would seem time in view of Adams's innumerable inaccuracies, and on all sound principles of historical criticism, to discard all of his later accounts of the speech and to consider only the notes he made at the time. This, of course, would apply to Minot's and all other derivatory accounts. We do not, in fact, know the turn of a single phrase that Otis uttered.

Whatever it may have been that Otis said, his utterance was undoubtedly a passionate one, appealing to the instinct for liberty rather than to legal precedents or technicalities. It made enough impression upon the judges as to cause them, partly, probably, in view of the state of public opinion, to withhold their decision until they should be further advised from England. When that advice was given in favor of the legality of the writs, as indeed it could hardly fail to be, the instruments continued to be issued for many years, and it is from this time and in this connection that the more general decline in Hutchinson's popularity began. The underlying principle at stake was whether a legislative act which invaded what citizens declared to be fundamental rights of the individual should be enforced by the courts. Hutchinson considered honestly that they should be until altered by the legislature. On the other hand, Otis seems to have argued that there are certain rights so sacred that the courts should refuse to enforce laws infringing them, thus arguing for one of the fundamental principles underlying all the constitutions of the American states and nation.[1] Both men were unquestionably honest in their opinions and Hutchinson's stand was unassailable from a legal standpoint. He himself was a wealthy man, his family were engaged in foreign trade, and he could have nothing to gain by adding to its hampering restrictions. His strict legalistic interpretation of the case, however, was opposed not merely to the interests of the smuggling merchants but to what was to be the winning side in the struggle of public opinion in regard to the relations of the individual to the state. Whereas his own popularity began to decline, Otis at once became the idol of the populace in Boston, and at the next election was made one of the four representatives of that town in the general assembly. In shifting the discussion from legal technicalities and questions of trade to the fundamental liberties of the subject, he both widened the basis of the dispute and inflamed the emotions of the people. It is from this time onward that in the storms of controversy we detect more clearly and ominously the rising ground swell of passion.

[1] This ground is taken in the contemporary notes of his speech by John Adams. *Works*, vol. II, p. 522. *Cf.* Address of Chief Justice Rugg, *Col. Soc. Mass., Publications*, vol. XIX, p. 430.

It was a propitious time for the appearance of a popular leader. Almost every group and class in New England had some grievance, some of which we have touched upon in this chapter. The war had brought about a profound economic disturbance. It had also had a very distinct psychological effect. It was a most dangerous time for the English administration to adopt any change in policy that, rightly or wrongly, might be construed by the people as an interference with their rights or as adding to their burdens. The poor were resentful; the rich, flushed with gain, were greedy and in no mood to brook interference with their operations. Bernard, in his first speech to the assembly, had taken occasion to remind them of the "blessings they derive from their subjection to Great Britain, without which they could not now have been a free people; for no other nation upon earth could have delivered them from the power they had to contend with." It is significant that in their reply the Council altered the word "subjection" to "relation," and that the assembly went further, saying that although they were indeed "sensible of the blessings derived to the British colonies from their subjection to Great Britain" nevertheless "the whole world must be sensible of the blessings derived to Great Britain from the loyalty of the colonies." They then went on to speak of Massachusetts "in particular; which, for more than a century past, has been wading in blood, and laden with the expenses of repelling the common enemy; without which efforts, Great Britain, at this day, might have had no colonies to defend."[1]

About this time, in the neighboring provinces of New York and New Jersey arose the question of the independence of the judiciary, and although New England was not at the moment directly involved, the disputes had a decided influence in alarming public opinion. The question was not one to be settled easily in fairness both to England and to the colonists. In the mother country, the independence of the bench had been secured as a result of the constitutional struggles of the seventeenth century, by appointing judges during good behavior and attaching permanent salaries to the office. In the colonies, the salaries

[1] Hutchinson, *History*, vol. III, pp. 83 *f.*

were granted annually by the assemblies, and with considerable frequency were reduced or withheld whenever the court rendered a decision which was unpopular. In connection with the matter of the writs of assistance for example, when it was found that the court favored the legality of their issuance, the salaries of all the judges had been reduced and the extra amount usually given to the chief justice had been withheld entirely.[1] This common practice was evidently an unwarranted exercise of the power of the purse, and the only safeguard possessed by the imperial government was that in the colonies the judges held office at the pleasure of the Crown instead of during good behavior. But of late years it had become the practice in New York, with the consent of the home government, to appoint them according to the latter tenure. During the war, however, the judges thus appointed had shown a distinct partiality for offenders engaged in illegal trade, they being closely connected by blood and marriage with the leading families and larger merchants. This situation, incidentally, gives us another sidelight on the alliance of the courts and business during the pre-revolutionary years.

When it became necessary to renew judicial commissions on the accession of George III, the governor refused to reappoint the judges except at the pleasure of the Crown unless they were granted permanent salaries and so removed from the temptations incident to their livings being dependent upon the popularity of their verdicts.[2] The assembly insisting upon its own control over judicial decisions, refused to allow any salaries but those granted annually, which meant, as Governor Colden said,

[1] Minot, *History of Massachusetts*, vol. II, p. 109. In 1763 Gov. Bernard of Massachusetts wrote that the judges' salaries "which depend upon the Assembly and fees together do not amount to £140 Sterling each, half of which is expended in travelling charges. The Attorney-General used to have a Salary, but of late that has been refused by the Assembly, upon a pretence of their having the right to join in his appointment, but they sometimes pay him for public business tho' in a scanty manner." The governor properly considered this a disgraceful condition, adding that the salaries of the judges really amounted to only about £80 a year clear, and that for this they were "dependent upon the Assembly, where frequent attempts are made and sometimes successfully, to lower even this poor pittance. To do this, the very Judgments of the Court, where they have been unpopular, have been used as means to lower the Salaries of the Judges." Answer of Bernard to Queries of Commissioners of Trade, Sept. 5, 1763, *Kings Mss.* 205, Pt. I.

[2] Beer, *British Colonial Policy*, pp. 188 *ff.*; *Acts Privy Council*, vol. IV, pp. 498 *ff.*

"undue influence, not only in cases where the King's rights may be disputed, but likewise in private suits, where a leading man in the assembly may be a Party." This situation, in New England as well as in New York, would have been bad enough had the assemblies been made up entirely of fair-minded and honest men, but, if we are to accept John Adams's unflattering picture of them, their control over the courts, jointly with the capitalists, could hardly have been reassuring to simple but honest citizens. Describing the unfit keepers of the filthy country inns of the day, he speaks of the latter as "full of people drinking drams, flip, toddy, carousing, swearing; but especially plotting with the landlord, to get him, at the next town meeting, an election either for selectman or representative," and that thus the "offices, which belong by nature and the spirit of all government to probity and honesty" are bestowed "on the meanest, and weakest, and worst of human characters." [1] We have already noted that our simple and homespun ancestors had discovered the relations between "big business" and politics. The alliance with the saloon is evidently not a modern discovery either. Evil as the control of the assemblies over the courts was, there would have been undoubted danger had the colonists possessed no control over judges who might be wholly in the interest of England. As the late Mr. Beer well points out, in this, as in so many other concerns of the imperial administration at this time, an *impasse* had been arrived at and the only way out was blocked by mutual lack of confidence. [2]

It was becoming apparent, indeed, in many directions that if England should, on the one hand, undertake to carry out that policy of more unified and firmer control which she had been contemplating when the war broke out, or, on the other, should popular leaders arise who could so stir the emotions and guide the minds of all the discontented elements among the people as to concentrate those discontents against any one subject, no man could tell what might ensue. The topics and incidents which we have noted formed merely some of the elements in a most complex situation, a situation presenting problems that

[1] *Works*, vol. II, p. 126.
[2] *British Colonial Policy*, p. 192.

may well have been insoluble, and which certainly demanded for their solution statesmanship of the highest order. Meanwhile, the war, already over for some time in America, was at last drawing to its close and diplomats were preparing to flock to Paris to wrestle with the terms of peace.

CHAPTER XIII

THE PRICE OF PEACE

Controversy over the Terms of Peace — The Value of Colonies — The West Indies — The Problem of the West — Proclamation of 1763 — Indian Affairs — Influence of War on Imperial Ideals — Ferment in the Colonies — English Social Outlook — Increased Expenses of Imperial Administration — Method Adopted to Meet Them — New Trade Measures — Effect on Colonists — Economic Crisis — Position of the Merchants

In treating of the war we have necessarily confined ourselves to that portion of it which was of direct interest to New England, and could not describe the events in the other theaters of action in what was a world-wide struggle for empire. Similarly, owing to the limited scope of this work, we must ignore the complicated relations of the nations to one another and the political conditions in England which gave rise to what the majority of Englishmen considered a shameful peace. John Wilkes, with characteristic irreligious wit, had said of the preliminary terms made at Fontainebleau that it was "certainly the peace of God for it passeth all understanding," [1] and the definitive Treaty of Paris pleased him and many other Englishmen but little better. Nevertheless, it was forced through the House of Commons by means of bribery and corruption in a degree scandalous even in the eighteenth century. Pitt, no longer minister, and so ill that he could hardly appear, spoke for over three hours against the betrayal, but Fox's bribes had done their work too well and, although a turbulent crowd outside the doors roared their disapproval, the House passed the proposals by an enormous majority. [2]

---

[1] Cited by H. Blackley, *Life of John Wilkes*, (London, 1917), p. 65.

[2] Pitt had resigned in 1761. For the negotiations concerning the peace *vide* Corbett, *Seven Years' War*, vol. II, pp. 327 *ff.*; Williams, *William Pitt*, vol. II, pp. 126 *ff.*; A. von Ruville, *William Pitt*, (London, 1907), vol. III, pp. 82 *ff.*; Kate Hotblack, "The Peace of Paris," *Royal Historical Society Transactions*, Ser. II, vol. II, pp. 235 *ff.*

By the treaty England added to her possessions in America the French province of Canada and the Spanish dominions in Florida, and acquired an undisputed title to the western lands as far as the Mississippi, with the exception of New Orleans. In the West Indies, however, she returned to France the rich conquests of Guadaloupe and Martinique, retaining only a few small islands totaling less than half a million acres, most of which were unsuited to sugar planting. These terms bring us to consider again both the question of what constituted the value of colonies in the eyes of statesmen of the period, and the century long conflict between the interests of the West Indians and the New Englanders. The crisis in imperial affairs brought out a voluminous pamphlet literature which leaves little doubt that although the old Mercantile doctrine was still largely in the ascendant, the conception of colonies was slowly altering. In the main the discussion centered around the comparative value to England of Canada and the West as against Guadaloupe; that is, of colonies which afforded possible markets for English manufactures against those which served as sources of supply for raw material.[1] The West Indian planters, who, as we have seen, formed a most influential mercantile and Parliamentary group,[2] were strongly opposed to any extension of sugar growing colonies as tending to reduce their monopoly of the industry and control of prices — a monopoly, however, which was strongly resented by the English consumers.[3] Nevertheless, as England's interests were becoming increasingly manufacturing rather than agricultural, and as the temperate zone colonies afforded a broader market for manufactured articles than the tropical, the planters found allies in the struggle among the manufacturers, and to some extent the landowners at home.[4]

Moreover, those who advocated the retention of Canada not only pointed out the advantages of a northern market for

---

[1] The best summary of the discussion is by Beer, *British Colonial Policy*, pp. 132 *ff*. *Cf.* also W. L. Grant, "Canada *vs.* Guadaloupe," *American Historical Review*, vol. XVII, pp. 735 *ff*. In a reëxamination of all the more important pamphlets, I find no essential point not well brought out by Beer.

[2] Fifty-six were said to be members of Parliament at this time. *Fitch Papers*, vol. II, p. 278.

[3] Pitman, *West Indies*, pp. 335 *f.*, 344 *ff.*

[4] The latter because of their interest in wool. Beer, *cit. supra*, p. 139.

manufactures but the necessity of protecting the continental colonies from any further hostilities from the French.[1] The fear, however, was expressed by many that the very removal of this menace might induce the colonies to throw off their allegiance and to revolt. "A neighbor that keeps us in some Awe," wrote one, "is not always the worst of neighbors," and he noted that "there is a Balance of Power in America as well as in Europe."[2] Another thought that although this was indeed a genuine danger, it could be averted by keeping the colonists disunited and preventing them from forming any general union which "might breed a new monarchy."[3] One of the ablest writers on American matters during the war had already foreseen that if France did not conquer she would nevertheless in time attempt to make the colonies independent of her rival and to secure their trade.[4] It was to this war of revenge on her part, rather than to the removal of her menace from their frontiers, that the colonies did eventually come to owe their independence.

Those groups who were in favor of the older view of colonies as sources of supply insisted upon the superior value of the tropical possessions, and claimed that the trade of all other colonial parts of the empire was based upon that of the islands. To think of extending the dominions in North America or Africa, without a similar extension in the West Indies, wrote one, "would be almost as rational as to think of fattening a Beast, after you had sewed up his Mouth."[5] "It is our sugar islands," wrote another, "that raise the value of North America, and pour in such wealth upon the mother-country; the more we have of these islands, America becomes from that cause the more important and valuable: in America we have more than enough, in the sugar islands a great deal too little, the nearer they can be proportioned to one another, the better for both."[6] This disproportion and the need of wider markets for the grow-

[1] *The comparative Importance of our Acquisitions from France* . . . (London, 1762), p. 36; *A Letter addressed to two great Men,* (London, 1760), pp. 34 f.

[2] *Remarks on the Letter addressed to two great Men,* (London, 1760), pp. 50 f.

[3] *Thoughts on Trade in general* . . . (London, 1763), p. 38.

[4] Mitchell, *Contest in America,* p. 208.

[5] *An Examination of the Commercial Principles of the late Negotiations,* (London, 1762), pp. 24 f.

[6] *Reasons for keeping Guadaloupe at a Peace,* (London, 1761), p. 6.

ing northern colonies, on which we have already touched several times, was recognized in the dispute, but it was claimed by many that the New England trade with the newly acquired islands would continue whether they remained English or should be given back to the French.[1]

Although by the final decision to retain Canada and the West, the colonists were relieved from the French pressure on their borders, nevertheless, the balance between themselves and the tropical colonies, already upset, was now hopelessly and permanently disturbed. Not only were the English islands incapable of taking off any larger share of the rapidly expanding commerce of the now enormously increased continental dominions, but as the French had lost their only temperate zone possessions, they also were more than ever dependent upon the business which the New England merchants were anxious to transact with them. The prohibitive Molasses Act thus became more of an economic anomaly than it had been before.

The selfishness of the English West Indians, however, could still be counted upon to insist upon some manipulation of duties that would relieve them from any competition disturbing to their serenity. Moreover, those in England who felt that, in the increasingly keen commercial rivalry foreseen with France, the New England trade would give their French competitors an advantage, would demand restrictive measures, while those who had long felt the effects of competition of New England shipping and mercantile activity would favor laws to curb them. It was evident, therefore, that the failure, on the one hand, to retain the larger West Indian conquests, and the enormous addition, on the other, to the temperate zone territory, foreshadowed a renewal of the three-cornered struggle between English, West Indian and New England commercial interests, and that in this respect the peace but precipitated a new crisis.

In truth, the treaty was a veritable Pandora's box, and a host of troublesome problems were not slow in emerging. By the transfer of Canada and the West, England had both come into possession of an immense new territory and been burdened with

[1] *A full and free Inquiry into the Merits of the Peace*, (London, 1765), pp. 63 f.; *Thoughts on Trade in general, cit. supra*, p. 18.

the whole problem of the Indians and their trade. The system of control by the several colonies having broken down, the English government in 1761 had taken it over and made it an imperial function by the appointment of two commissioners, one for the north and one for the south. There was no lack of evidence that in addition to the disgraceful character of the colonial traders, the main cause of unrest among the savages had been their justified fear of the seizure or illegal purchases of their lands by the colonial speculators, a fear that led to the continuance of native hostilities in Pontiac's War after the main struggle was over. In connection with New England, we have already seen the part played by the Susquehannah Company of Connecticut, but when the terms of peace were known, many other companies sprang into life with the object of rapidly exploiting the lands beyond the old frontier.[1] The British government was not averse to settlement of the new territory, but in view of the hostility of the savages during the war and the subsequent rising, the more pressing problem appeared to be that of native pacification. The land and Indian problems were so closely related as to demand a policy dealing with both simultaneously.

The statesman in England who knew most about the colonies at the time was Lord Shelburne, who was favorably inclined toward them and of democratic tendencies, and the policy adopted and embodied in the Proclamation of 1763 may in the main be considered as emanating from him.[2] That policy, in brief, consisted in the establishment of three new colonies — Quebec, East and West Florida — none of which in any way conflicted with the older ones. As soon as possible they were to be placed under governments similar to those in the royal colonies, with popularly elected assemblies, Shelburne's own wish having been to have the governors so elected also.[3] Two points in the Proclamation, however, provoked the hostility of certain elements in the older colonies. These were the provisions more directly concerning the land and Indians in the western coun-

---

[1] Alvord, *Mississippi Valley*, vol. I, pp. 94 *ff.*
[2] *Ibid.*, pp. 140 *ff.*, 177 *f.*
[3] *Ibid.*, p. 177.

try. On the one hand, the Proclamation placed traders under certain restrictions, and, on the other, forbade colonial governors to make any grants of land within a reserved area and required the removal of any settlers already there, or on other lands not properly acquired.[1] The plain intention in creating a reservation was to reassure the natives, by running a boundary line — along the ridge of the Alleghanies — to the westward of which they would feel that their land would be safe from encroachment until such time as they might willingly and peacefully sell it to the British government. Although it was later said that it had been the intention to confine the colonists to the coast, this was not the case, and the plan was merely a temporary expedient.[2] Washington used that very term in describing it, and Grenville said that the "design of it was totally accomplished so soon as the country was purchased from the natives." [3]

However, the plan met with immediate opposition. Both the traders, whom nearly all contemporary authorities described as base and abandoned, and the land speculators, much preferred the old method of "a Bull feast at Albany and a little Rum" to any regulations, hoping that the Indians might "consume like a March snow and no Enquiry be made concerning lands pattented." [4] In view of the disastrous results of leaving the Indian question to be handled by the separate colonies, and the immensity of the new problems, the English policy in its inception cannot be considered unreasonable, and it is indeed impossible to suggest a better one. But aside from the traders and speculators there were now great numbers in the colonies anx-

---

[1] The reserved area lay, roughly, between Hudson's Bay territory, the Alleghanies, the Floridas and the Mississippi. The Proclamation has many times been reprinted. *Vide, Annual Register for Year 1763*, (London), pp. 208 *ff.*; Sir Henry Cavendish, *Debates of the House of Commons in 1774 on the Quebec Act*, ed. J. Wright, (London, 1839) pp. 297 *ff.*; W. P. M. Kennedy, *Documents of the Canadian Constitution*, (Toronto, 1918), vol. I, pp. 18 *ff.*

[2] C. W. Alvord, "The Genesis of the Proclamation of 1763," *Michigan Pioneer and Historical Collections*, vol. XXXVI, pp. 41 *f.*; *Mississippi Valley*, vol. I, pp. 199 *f.*; Coffin, *Province of Quebec and the early American Revolution*, pp. 401 *ff.*; Max Farrand, "The Indian Boundary Line," *American Historical Review*, vol. X, pp. 782 *ff.*; Board of Trade to Halifax, Oct. 4, 1763, *C.O. 324 No. 21*; same to the King, May 18, 1764, *C. O. 324 No. 17.*

[3] Cited by G. H. Alden, *New Governments West of the Alleghanies*, Bull. Univ. of Wisconsin, vol. II, p. 43.

[4] Alvord and Carter, *Critical Period*, p. 505.

ious to swarm to new lands, and as the years went by and no
steps were taken to settle the Western question, owing partly
to rapid changes in the government at home, the effect on
colonial sentiment was little less than disastrous. A prohibition
which had been intended to be temporary seemed to have
become permanent, and the colonists believed that a deliberate
effort was being made to establish a monopoly and to keep them
out of the great heart of the continent.[1] With new restrictions
on their trade at sea, and with expansion to the western lands
which they had helped to win denied to them, they were being
squeezed by the British government like nuts in a cracker.
That the government was guiltless of any intentional tyranny
does not lessen its responsibility for the results.

The necessity for taking over the administration of Indian
affairs and for protecting the natives from the land-grabbing
colonists had been due to the failure of the colonial governments
to unite upon any reasonable policy among themselves and to
control their own citizens. The failure of the colonial requisition system in military matters was similarly the cause of the
decision of the English government to rely on it no longer and
to protect the new domain with regular troops from home, a
policy of far-reaching consequences. During the rising under
Pontiac, when the English commanding officer had asked for
aid from the colonies, New Hampshire, Massachusetts and
Rhode Island had refused, and Connecticut had sent but a
small body of troops after much delay.[2] In view of such facts,
men like Washington, the Lees, Fitzhughs and others interested in western land petitioned the English government to
establish garrisons at specified places.[3] Franklin thought that a
system of imperial garrisons might be by no means unwise even
if the colonies were taxed for them as it would save them the
trouble and expense of a militia.[4] It was estimated in England
that ten thousand men would be required for the purpose at an
expense of about £300,000 a year.

[1] Coffin, *Province of Quebec and the early American Revolution*, p. 432.

[2] Beer, *British Colonial Policy*, pp. 263 f. Little aid was derived from any of the
colonies and there was no coöperation.

[3] Alvord and Clark, *Critical Period*, pp. 22 f., 26 f.

[4] *Works*, ed. Bigelow, vol. III, p. 299.

We have pointed out many times how certain tendencies in our colonial history were by no means peculiar to the time and place but common to the history of other colonies at the same stage of development. The same parallelism may be found in imperial relations, and England has now been a colonial power long enough and has been engaged in a sufficient number of great wars to enable us to predict that after each of them there will develop an effort to reorganize the colonial system, an easily understandable characteristic of *post-bellum* psychology. It was immediately after the South African war that on his return from its battle fields Chamberlain launched his campaign for "a new government for the British Empire," and those who are following attentively the results of the last Great War on English imperial relations are aware of the efforts being made to "draw the bonds of empire closer" and to use colonial resources to help pay the war debt.[1] Whatever may be the justice of such efforts, the result is always to arouse a spirit of opposition in the more independent colonials and to drive many who had formerly been content with the looser bonds into the extreme radical group.[2] It was but two or three years, for example, after Chamberlain proclaimed the need for a new organization of the imperial structure that Sir John Colomb had to admit that "the voices that call for real British unity are drowned by the shoutings for constitutional rights reverberating throughout the Empire from one self-governing State to another."[3] In Canada at the present time, the reaction to the efforts of the British imperialists is indicated by the fact that such men as Mr. John S. Ewart, formerly content to remain associated with the empire through the link of the Crown, have felt forced to declare for independence and a republican form of government.[4]

The Seven Years' War was no exception. For several years before its close Governor Bernard of Massachusetts, although in many ways favorable to the colonies, had been writing home

---

[1] *Cf. e.g.*, John S. Ewart, *The Kingdom Papers*, (Toronto, n.d.), vol. II, pp. 272 *ff.*, 347 *ff.* Also his *Independence Papers*, (Ottawa, 1921), *passim*.

[2] *Kingdom Papers*, vol. II, paper No. 21; *Independence Papers*, pp. 108 *ff.*

[3] Cited by Sir Howard d'Egville, *Imperial Defence and closer Union*, (London, 1913), p. 161.

[4] *Cf.* citations above and Mr. Ewart's current writings at the present time.

advising a remodeling of the colonial governments upon "a true English-constitutional bottom," and unfortunately giving honest but quite false impressions as to how such a remodeling would be regarded in America.[1] In England Shelburne was wisely attempting to increase the efficiency of the machinery there for dealing with colonial matters.[2] The new imperial control of Indian affairs, lands, and the prospect of a standing army were, on the scale proposed, all innovations although foreshadowed before the war. Rumors were reaching the colonists of drastic alterations and they were becoming uneasy.[3] Wholly false stories of the amount that England intended to raise by taxation were spread about, and the old question of the establishment of an Anglican episcopate came up again to alarm those in New England who were not of that church.

Bishops had always been held in abhorrence in that section, and many years later John Adams wrote that the controversy "spread an universal alarm against the authority of Parliament" and was one of the important factors in developing revolutionary feeling.[4] It is very possible that this was the case, for in spite of the decline in religious interest, of the considerable body of Episcopalians, and of the spread of Deism, New England was still strongly Puritan in feeling and attached to Independency in the church. It is this core of Puritanism, with its sternness, its belief in its own infallibility and its narrowness and bigotry as well as its finer qualities, which has always been a dominating influence in New England, and without consideration of which its history cannot be understood.

Although a considerable portion of the people were literate, they were not educated, and aside from desire had little opportunity for reading. The ideas they got were derived from the Sunday sermon and from conversation. Among the poorer classes in the towns, and particularly in the country districts, political philosophy was in the main a mere instinctive desire to be let alone to attend to their daily business with no hampering

[1] *Barrington-Bernard Correspondence,* pp. 44, 93, 99.
[2] Lord Fitzmaurice, *Life of Earl of Shelburne,* (London, 1875), vol. I, pp. 241 ff.
[3] *Cf. e.g.,* enquiries as to what England was intending in *Rhode Island Commerce,* vol. I, pp. 101, 107.
[4] *Works,* vol. X, pp. 185, 288 f.

regulations or taxes. Of the implications in a world of competing empires at sea, or of competing races and civilizations in the American hinterland, they knew little and cared less. With no background and little outlook, hitherto almost wholly unhampered in the exploitation of their opportunities, it is no wonder that tyranny was thought to lie in any attempted restriction. Moreover, there is no fallacy relating to colonies more dangerous perhaps, then and today, than the one lurking in the writings of such brilliant historians as Seeley and Freeman, who regard the "Expansion of England" or "Greater Britain" as meaning a mere transplanting of Englishmen overseas. Quite apart from any racial mixture, the native born becomes in time something different, though he may himself require a shock before he realizes the change. In the case of an individual, however loyal both before and after, such a shock is often provided by a visit "home." In the case of a community it may come with the sudden realization of a difference in point of view upon a question of vital importance. In the ten years following the Seven Years' War, the statesmen of England in their efforts to "tighten the bonds of empire" were to bring home to a considerable part of the Americans the fact that such a change had occurred. In the resulting confusion of thought and action, the discontented elements in the community, discontented because in debt, because of the growing inequality of wealth, because of political disabilities, because of a dozen real or assumed grievances, were to see their opportunity.

Such a movement as set in, however, required leaders. Heretofore we have dealt mainly with tendencies, which we tried to show would lead inevitably to some great change. A particular crop, nevertheless, does not grow merely because the soil is ready for it. The seed must be sown and cared for. The relations between England and the colonies, and between the classes in the colonies, would in time have suffered a profound alteration in any case, but the particular manner of that change and the time of its coming were largely the work, both conscious and unconscious, of individuals on either side of the water. If the colonists generally had but little knowledge of books, this was not so of their leaders who now come to the front. Although the literary center of New England had shifted at this period from Boston to New Haven, the libraries both public and private in the Massachusetts capital, in Newport and Providence afforded ample materials for the student of government.[1] It was a time, as Otis wrote, when "the cards were shuffling fast thro' all Europe," and there were not only uneasy turnings of the common people in England, but in France the revolutionary movement was gaining rapid momentum.[2] But although the works of Montesquieu, Voltaire and Rousseau were to be had in Boston, and the first was not seldom quoted in argument, the writers to whom the revolutionary leaders appealed were rather the English ones already occasionally mentioned, and above all, Locke.[3] It is easy, however, to overestimate the importance of literary sources. At bottom the colonial revolutionary movement was directed toward the complete enfranchisement of the individual, toward the liberation of his energies, and as far as possible the release from all hindrances to the full expression of his personality.[4] The masses of those who took part in it needed, it is true, leaders to make it effective, and those leaders strove to give it literary expression and a reasoned base. As time passes, books remain, whereas the gossip of the village tavern and the unspoken emotions in the heart of the mass are lost forever. But although it follows that the tendency is always to over-emphasize the intellectual aspect of any great movement of the past, it is a mistake to consider that man's political actions necessarily or even mainly spring from reasoned premises. In spite of those among the wealthy and cultured who chose the popular side, had the question been decided by them as a class, the war of the revolution would not have taken place. It was

---

[1] M. C. Tyler, *Literary History of the American Revolution*, (New York, 1897), vol. I, p. 11; Foster, *Stephen Hopkins*, vol. I, pp. 126 ff.

[2] James Otis, *Rights of the British Colonies asserted and proved*, (Boston, 1764), p. 40; Rocquain, *Esprit révolutionnaire*, pp. 252 f.

[3] Rousseau's *Nouvelle Héloise* as well as works by Scarron, Rabelais, Racine and others were offered in Boston frequently enough to indicate at least a moderate public interest in French *belles-lettres*. *Boston Post Boy*, Mar. 15, 1762, Sept. 15 and 29, Oct. 31, 1763. The same journal advertised several of Voltaire's works Sept. 12, Oct. 17, and 24, 1763. Rousseau's *Treatise on the Social Compact or the Principles of political Law* made its first appearance, so far as I have found, in *Boston Gazette*, Dec. 17, 1764.

[4] For an interesting comparison of the French and American movements and their sources, *vide* Henri Michel, *L'Idée de l'Etat*, (Paris, 1898), pp. 31 f., 60 f., 88.

those elements in the colonies who were already chafing at the infringements of privilege upon that social, economic and political freedom which to a considerable extent had been theirs in the simplicities of a new world society, who responded to the leadership of such a man as Sam Adams, and who in the end gave the radicals control of the situation and decreed the birth of a new nation.[1]

It is a striking contrast to turn from the ferment of this new society and the extreme individualism engendered by it, to the ordered unity of the social hierarchy of eighteenth century England, with its "air of distinguished satisfaction and dignified self-control." The great land-owning families were still supreme, and as has been well said "English institutions suited them admirably; a monarchy so reasonable nobody could mind; Parliament was a convenient instrument for their wishes, and the English Church the very thing to keep religion in its place."[2] The little free school of New England, poor as it was in the country districts, and the farmers and frontiersmen, making their political wills obstreperously known in town meetings or tavern gatherings, had little in common with that system of education in England which was merely the nursery of a race of rulers, and with a rural population that slept under the absolute sway of the justice of the peace.[3] For the most part, in spite of the exceptional and generous action of not a few individuals, the English ruling class had come honestly to consider that England's greatness depended upon their own undisputed leadership and her commercial supremacy upon their exploitation of the working class, which for two centuries had been steadily falling more and more under the control of capitalistic power and enterprise. It is true that there were mutterings in England of a coming storm and even serious riotings here and there. For example, the miners, in 1765 — who worked below ground for from sixteen to seventeen hours a day for fourteen pence, and whom the owners wished to tie to the same collieries

---

[1] *Cf.* the interesting letter from Lord Acton to Lady Blennerhasset in *Selections from the Correspondence of the first Lord Acton*, (London, 1917), vol. I, pp. 277 *ff.*

[2] J. L. and B. Hammond, *The Village Labourer*, (London, 1911), pp. 342 *ff.*

[3] *Ibid.*, p. 24; Ramsay Muir, *Short History of the British Commonwealth*, (London, 1920), vol. I, pp. 782 *ff.*, 792.

for life — publicly remonstrated that this arrangement "they conjecture will take away the antient character of this Kingdom as being a free nation," but they were overawed by troops rapidly sent by the government, in spite of some protest by public opinion.[1] Several times between 1763 and 1776 troops had also to be employed against the weavers of Spittlefields rising against the abuses in their trade, though public opinion again made itself felt to a certain extent. It was helpless, however, against the conditions of Parliamentary representation of which we have already spoken. In 1761, men who had made fortunes in both the East and West Indies were bidding enormous sums for seats in the House of Commons. Not only were seats advertised for sale in the newspapers, but £5,000 was left by will for the purchase of one, and another was reckoned among the assets of a bankrupt.[2] Even Pitt, who was in favor of reform is reported to have said that representation is "not of person but of property; and in this light there is scarcely a blade of grass which is not represented." [3]

Although opinion was coming to demand reform as well as to censure the increasing use of troops against labor, the temper of the nation was nevertheless becoming more imperialistic in regard to colonial possessions. From the middle of the century the enormous growth of the cotton industry changed the whole tone of thought at Manchester and the development of that trade and the extension of markets became its touchstone of public policy.[4] Between such a system as is indicated above and that of the little merchant oligarchies of the American seaboard towns understanding might be difficult but negotiation was certainly possible. Between the miners and weavers and other sections of the English public which were attempting to make their weight felt against the system and those in America

[1] J. L. and B. Hammond, *The Skilled Labourer*, (London, 1919), p. 16.
[2] Von Ruville, *William Pitt*, vol. III, p. 239; G. S. Veitch, *The Genesis of Parliamentary Reform*, (London, 1913), p. 3.
[3] Veitch, *cit. supra*, p. 37. I am inclined to think that the real author of this remark was not Pitt but Lord Camden who said in the Stamp Act debate in 1766, "there is not a blade of grass growing in the most obscure corner of this kingdom, which is not, which was not ever, represented since this constitution began; there is not a blade of grass which, when taxed, was not taxed by the consent of the proprietor." *Parlt. Hist.*, vol. XVI, p. 179.
[4] G. B. Hertz, *The Manchester Politician*, (London, 1912), p. 14.

who were also fighting against privilege whether at home or overseas, there was much in common but there was no contact. But between the ruling class in England and the common people in America there was an impassable gulf, and should the former attempt to bridge it for their own interest there was likely to be but one result.

Unfortunately there was much that seemed to make the attempt both necessary and justified. Although under the influence of the new regulations and taxes, many of the colonists denied that they had had anything to gain by the war, several of the colonies, including Massachusetts, Connecticut and Virginia, had petitioned for England's help, and there was undoubtedly much truth in Grenville's statement that "the immediate Defence of our Colonies from imminent Danger was the sole occasion" of the conflict.[1] It had cost England over £82,000,000, of which £60,000,000 had been added to the national debt.[2] The expense of the new military establishment for the protection of the old frontier and the new acquisitions, which although resented by some had also been requested by others among the leading men in the colonies, would run to about £300,000 a year. The landed interest in England was already heavily taxed, and in view of the growing unrest it did not seem wise to add to the heavy burdens already being borne by the laboring class. The thought of shifting a small part of the load to the colonists, for whose benefit it had in part been incurred, was a natural one, however unwise. As the system of voluntary grants had always worked badly, even when the colonists' own safety was immediately at stake, and had broken down completely in the recent native uprising, and as they had shown themselves both incapable and unwilling in devising any other, Parliamentary action seemed to be the only sure method of deriving a dependable income from American sources.

Pending the passage of some such new fiscal legislation, the

[1] *The Regulations lately made concerning the Colonies*, (London, 1765), p. 4. Lionel Curtis accepts the attribution of this pamphlet to Thomas Whately, *Commonwealth of Nations*, (London, 1916), Pt. I, p. 311. Whately himself claimed authorship. *Vide Bowdoin-Temple Papers*, [*Mass. Hist. Soc., Coll.*, Ser. VI, vol. IX.], p. 77. Beer thought that it was written under Grenville's guidance if not by him. *British Colonial Policy*, p. 221.

[2] Dowell, *History of Taxation*, vol. II, p. 131.

only immediate prospect of revenue appeared to lie in the duties already supposed to be collected under various acts. These had been so laxly enforced hitherto that it had cost £7,600 a year to collect £1,900.[1] The way had been pointed out by Pitt's stricter enforcement of the acts as a war measure in 1760. Aside from income, however, and although the new acquisitions in India as well as in America were beginning to influence the conception of empire in the direction of the more modern meaning of that term, the old ideal of a self-sufficing Mercantile Empire was still strong.[2] The newer and purely fiscal question of income for imperial purposes was complicated, therefore, by the older one of the regulation of trade according to the Mercantile doctrine.[3] A most dangerous element was added to the situation by the influence of the West India interest which was insisting upon the reënactment for its own benefit of the Molasses Act which was about to expire.

As one of the first steps toward stricter enforcement, Parliament had passed an act by which naval commanders in American waters might serve as customs officers, with the usual percentage of profits arising from seizures.[4] The terms of this act were sent by the government to the colonial governors in July 1763 with orders to see that all trade laws should be strictly enforced for the benefit both of the "Publick Revenue" and of the "Fair Trader." [5] The effect was instant. Of the various sorts

---

[1] *Regulations lately made*, p. 57; *Fitch Papers*, vol. II, p. 255; Order in Council, Oct. 5, 1763, *C.O. 5 No. 65*; *Acts Privy Council*, vol. IV, p. 569.

[2] As it is yet in a modified form, for although some of the cruder elements in the old Mercantile doctrine have been eliminated, the doctrine of a self-sufficing empire within which trade should be carefully regulated among its members for the good of the whole is much in evidence yet. *Cf.* A. P. Newton, *The old Empire and the New*, (London, 1917), p. 91. There has even been talk in the last few years of reviving the Navigation Acts directed against Germany's mercantile fleet as the earliest act was against Holland. *Cf.* C. E. Fayle, "The Navigation Acts," *Edinburgh Review*, (July, 1918), pp. 22 ff.

[3] In the instructions to the governors and in the order in Council we read that the reason for the stricter enforcement is "that through neglect, connivance and fraud, not only the Revenue is much impair'd but the Commerce of the Colonies is diverted from it's natural Course, & the salutary provisions of many wise Laws are in great measure defeated." *Fitch Papers*, vol. II, p. 255; Order in Council, Oct. 5, 1763, *C.O. 5 No. 65*.

[4] 3 Geo. III, c. 22.

[5] *Fitch Papers*, vol. II, pp. 247 ff. This was followed by further orders in October. *Ibid.*, pp. 255 ff.; *R. I. Col. Records*, vol. VI, p. 375.

of illicit trade carried on, all of which were technically considered smuggling, some had become so well established as to
be looked upon as legitimate, more particularly the West Indian
business. Of the latter, Lieutenant-Governor Hutchinson wrote
in Boston two days after receiving the unexpected orders, that
"such indulgence has been shown of late to that branch of
illicit trade that nobody has considered it as such; vessels arriving and making their entries for some small acknowledgment as
openly as from our own Islands without paying the duty." [1]
The opposition to the enforcement of the other trade laws had
largely died down in Massachusetts, and since the flurry in 1760
Writs of Assistance had continued to be issued without opposition. The fact seems to have been that the trade laws as a whole
were not oppressive and that the better class merchants preferred to comply with them, the smugglers being regarded as
actually smugglers and as a pest to the honest merchant. But
the West India, and to some extent the wine, trades were on a
different footing, the former being absolutely essential to the
economic life of New England. The fear that the Writs of
Assistance would be used to put an end to that business was
apparently the main if not the sole cause of opposition to them,
and the mercantile rather than political character of that opposition, in spite of Otis's speech, is indicated by the peaceful
acceptance of the writs after it had become evident that the
West India trade was not to be molested. Indeed the only complaint of the Massachusetts merchants was that in other lines
they were paying the duties, whereas their competitors in Rhode
Island and Connecticut continued to smuggle with impunity,
and were thus getting an unfair advantage. [2]

But the news that the Molasses Act also was to be enforced
created a panic, and as Bernard wrote "caused a greater alarm
in this country than the taking of Fort William Henry did in
1757." "The Merchants," he added, "say, 'There is an end of
the trade in this Province; that it is sacrificed to the West
Indian Planters; that it is time for every prudent man to get
out of debt with Great Britain as fast as he can, and betake

---

[1] Quoted by Gray, Writs of Assistance, Quincy, *Reports*, p. 430 *n.*
[2] Answer of Gov. Bernard to Board of Trade, Sept. 5, 1763, *Kings Mss. 205, Pt. I.*

himself to husbandry.'" [1] "They are a strange People," he wrote in another letter, and "are either for [taking the Government by storm and] enforcing such a remission of the laws of trade as they think fit; or else in a fit of Despondency they give up themselves and their trade to ruin. They never think of a middle way; to remonstrate, with decency, upon the real hardships they lay under, and to crave redress, which I cannot think would be hard to obtain." [2]

If this was the case at first they soon recovered and undertook to present their grievances. In January 1764 the assembly in Rhode Island prepared a remonstrance to the Board of Trade showing that the West Indian business was the foundation of the colony's commerce, without which it could not possibly pay for its importations from England, or, indeed, subsist. It was pointed out that of the fourteen thousand hogsheads of molasses imported annually for the distilleries, not more than twenty-five hundred could be procured in the English islands. This remonstrance was to be forwarded to England provided that two other colonies would join in it. [3] Meanwhile, in Boston, some months before, a group of one hundred and sixty-four merchants had organized "The Society for encouraging Trade and Commerce within the Province of Massachusetts Bay," an action probably taken in view of the disturbed business conditions following the war and the agitation expected in connection with the possible reënactment of the expiring Molasses Act. [4] A committee was appointed to prepare a presentation of the case against the prohibitive duty of 6d. a gallon on foreign molasses and showing the essential character of the West Indian trade. Although this was written and forwarded to the agent in London it failed to reach him, and even their letter arrived only five days after the new Sugar Act had become law. [5]

[1] *Select Letters*, p. 9.

[2] Cited by Gray, Writs of Assistance, Quincy, *Reports*, p. 431 *n*. The words in brackets were erased in the original.

[3] *R. I. Col. Records*, vol. VI, pp. 378 *ff*.

[4] Some of them had for years been members of the less formal Merchants' Club, which Professor Andrews thinks may have been behind the agitation against the writs of assistance. C. M. Andrews, "The Boston Merchants and the Non-Importation Movement," *Col. Soc. Mass., Publications*, vol. XIX, pp. 161 *ff*.

[5] Andrews, "Boston Merchants," p. 167. The text of the paper, called "The State of the Trade" is given by Mr. Andrews, in *Col. Soc. Mass., Publications*, vol. XIX, pp. 382 *ff*.

Whether or not the terms of that law were economically workable, the English government by stupidly ordering the enforcement of the old and prohibitive act, and by unnecessarily threatening to destroy the whole foundation of New England commerce, had created the worst possible atmosphere for the consideration of their new measure. Unfortunately George Grenville, who had become head of the cabinet in April 1763, possessed a most distressing gift "of blundering into dangerous crises" in spite of honesty, industry and courage.[1] Moreover, he was a firm believer in the laws of trade, and today would be an ardent supporter of "closer union" and imperial preference. The provisions of the new act indicate a confused attempt to reconcile the conflicting and incompatible interests of the New Englanders with those of the West Indian planters, and the need of revenue incident to the new imperialism with the desire to regulate trade according to the canons of the old. It contained a number of minor changes, some of them in favor of the colonies, in duties or trade regulations, but these were of little importance. The two provisions which vitally affected the New England merchants were those which placed the duty on molasses at 3*d*. as compared with 6*d*. under the old Molasses Act, and that relating to seizures.[2] The prohibitive and unfair nature of the higher rate had long been recognized in England, and no attempt had been seriously made by the English government to enforce it, but as we have seen, a small *douceur* was paid to the customs officials. How much this may have been, and what relation it bore to the value of the molasses if any, we do not know. It was recognized, however, that the trade could bear only a very moderate duty if a revenue was to be obtained. The Boston merchants claimed that any duty at all would be prohibitive, but this was false, and they did pay eventually 1½*d*. when that became the rate.[3] Many in the colonies agreed that

[1] Frederic Harrison, *Chatham*, (New York, 1905), p. 148.

[2] 4 Geo. III, c. 15.

[3] *Cf. Proposals for uniting the Colonies*, p. 24; *R. I. Col. Records*, vol. VI, p. 381; *Col. Soc. Mass., Publications*, vol. XIX, p. 382; Hutchinson, *History*, vol. III, pp. 108 *ff.*; *Ingersoll Papers*, p. 296; *Jasper Mauduit*, pp. 130, 135, 139, 158, 172; *Bowdoin-Temple Papers*, pp. 24, 30; Gray, Writs of Assistance, Quincy, *Reports*, p. 435; Beer, *British Colonial Policy*, p. 279. It may be noted that after the formation of the federal government in 1789, New England agreed to a duty of 2½ cents per gallon. Channing, *Hist. of U. S.*, vol. IV, p. 64.

2*d.* would be a reasonable figure, and Grenville himself would have placed it at that, but the West India lobby was too strong, and the figure was finally placed just high enough to make it economically impossible of enforcement and to result in new and justified opposition in New England.

The other clause in the act which the colonists reasonably thought might prove extremely oppressive in practice was that which provided that cases arising under it might be tried by any Vice-Admiralty court in America, and consequently that a merchant might find himself haled all the way to Halifax to defend himself. Not only that, but as he could claim no damages if the judge decided that there had been reasonable grounds for suspicion, he was practically without protection. The whole system of Vice-Admiralty jurisdiction ran deeply counter to the sentiment of the colonists, and various incidents led them to expect the worst from the new regulations.[1] The fact that no colonial jury would ever convict in a smuggling case, and that some at least of the Vice-Admiralty judges had been bought by merchants may have been considered as offering justification for the new system in the eyes of English officials.[2] Nevertheless, the alarm and resentment caused must be considered as wholly warranted, and regarded from the standpoint of policy, it must be admitted that the whole customs system, as Jared Ingersoll said, partook too much of "burning a Barn to roast an Egg," a procedure naturally annoying to the owner of the barn.[3]

Although the maintenance of the old trade system played a part in the new efforts at enforcement, the main motive, as shown by the preamble to the Sugar Act, was the raising of a revenue "for defraying the expenses of defending, protecting and securing" the colonies, and it was well understood that the duties collected would amount to but a small part of the sum required from America even though the colonies were not to be asked for more than a fraction of the total. Parliament therefore agreed — "in a thin house, late at night, and just at the

---

[1] *Annual Register,* (London, 1765), pp. 18 *ff.*

[2] *E.g.* during the war, Philadelphia merchants had given a retainer to the judge in the Bahamas to return any Pennsylvania vessels seized there. Beer, *British Colonial Policy,* p. 127.

[3] *Ingersoll Papers,* p. 297.

THE PRICE OF PEACE

rising, without any debate " [1] — that stamp duties should be levied in America for the same purpose. It was proposed to start investigations with the idea of bringing in a bill the following year, the delay being allowed not only for discussion at home but to permit the colonists to present any alternative suggestions for raising the necessary money, that they might have to offer.

Serious as were these various acts of the government, exaggerated rumors of what was intended added to the alarm of the colonists. It was said that the troops were to be sent over "under pretence for our Defence; but rather designed as a rod and check over us," and that more taxes would follow.[2] Such a man as Governor Hopkins of Rhode Island did not scruple to inflame his assembly with the utterly false statement that the British ministry had formed a plan to "raise as much money in America as hath been expended for its defence" which "must complete our ruin." [3] Moreover, although it had not been the intention of the ministry that any of the money raised by colonial taxation should be shipped to England but that, on the contrary, it should remain in America and be expended there, the phrasing of the act was ambiguous and misleading, and the colonists were justified in fearing that their normal adverse balance with the mother country would thus be disastrously increased.[4] Hopkins estimated that the duty on molasses alone would amount to £14,375 Sterling "to be paid yearly by this little colony ; a larger sum than was ever in it at any one time," adding that "this money is to be sent away, and never to return ; yet the payment is to be repeated every year." [5] Of the proposed Stamp Tax another wrote that "all the Sterling money circulating in the Provinces would not be sufficient for that and paying the late duties imposed." [6] Added point was lent to this

[1] John Almon, *A Collection of interesting, authentic Papers relating to the Disputes between Great Britain and America,* (London, 1777), p. 5. [Hereafter cited as *Prior Documents.*]

[2] *Ingersoll Papers,* p 291

[3] *R. I. Col. Records,* vol. VI, p. 414.

[4] The Minute of the Treasury Board directing that the money be kept in America was dated July 9, 1765. Text in *Prior Documents,* p. 38. *Cf.* [Chas. Lloyd] *Conduct of the late Administration,* (London, 2d edit. 1767), pp. 37 *f.*

[5] *R. I. Col. Records,* vol. VI, p. 421 ; *Annual Register,* (London, 1765), pp. 22 *f.*

[6] *Bowdoin-Temple Papers,* p. 47.

misconception by the act also passed by the Parliament of 1764 prohibiting the issue of paper money in any of the colonies, thus extending the prohibition already applying to New England to the rest of the continent.[1]

Moreover, the bubble of fictitious war-time prosperity had now been pricked. The usual effects of the feverish activity and soaring prices incidental to war had been emphasized in America by the temporary presence there of great bodies of troops, and the extremely heavy payments from England for their maintenance which upset the normal current of exchange. As usual in such periods, it had been thought the good times would last forever, and people had carried on speculation wildly in all lines. Disillusionment and bitterness are the inevitable after-fruits of all such periods. Grievances felt at the moment are considered to be the causes of the troubles which in reality are due to others far more deeply seated and of more general operation. It must be borne in mind, however, that the background of the events from 1763 onward for several years was one of commercial depression, of deep anxiety and of bitter financial resentment in the colonies. In the last chapter we spoke of the financial distress among the entire farming population, and of the enormous fall in the value of farm lands. Trade was soon affected also, and to the great fall in the price of land was added the inability of the farmer to market his crops. "I have lately travailed through the interior parts of this and New York Province," wrote Ingersoll from Connecticut, "and everywhere found the farmer complaining that he could not sell his wheat." [2] Of the two hundred and sixty-five law suits in the New Haven County Court in 1761 most of them were for debts, and a little later we find new laws covering insolvency appearing on the Connecticut statute books.[3] A broadside issued in that colony in 1764 speaks of the "Obstructions in Trade, the general Inability of People to make due Payments." [4] Rhode Island was also suffering, and in New Hampshire a writer in a weekly paper noted that "merchants and farmers are breaking and all things

---

[1] 4 Geo. III, c. 34. *Cf. Acts Privy Council*, vol. IV, pp. 623 *ff.*, 641 *ff.*
[2] *Ingersoll Papers*, p. 297.
[3] Gipson, *Jared Ingersoll*, p. 252; *Conn. Col. Records*, vol. XII, pp. 127, 228, 357.
[4] *Broadside Collection*, folder "Connecticut," Library of Congress.

going into confusion." [1] This crisis in New England was marked in Boston by the failure of several of the greatest merchants. "Trade has met with a most prodigious shock and the greatest losses to some people thro' Mr. Wheelwright's failure ever known in this part of the world," wrote John Hancock of one of these.[2] The depression in varying degrees also extended throughout the other colonies to the southward which were not affected by the English legislation.[3]

Although a reaction following the war was general and inevitable, the unwise and unjust attempt to enforce the old Molasses Act just on the eve of its alteration, and the passage of the acts of 1764, undoubtedly helped to precipitate the crisis in the commercial colonies in the north. The acts did not directly affect the farming part of the population nor the people of the great staple colonies, and there is no little evidence to show that even the merchants were alarmed over the economic and not the political consequences of English action, and that they were not opposed to either the laws of trade as a whole or to the payment of duties and taxes so long as they could still carry on their business at a profit. Had the English ministers not aroused a wholly needless spirit of opposition by their attempted enforcement of the impossible Molasses Act in 1763, and had they placed a duty of from 1d. to 2d. only on that article in 1764, the new laws would probably have been observed without evasion and with little friction. Even after the agitation of those two years many colonials who knew the colonies well, such as Ingersoll and Franklin, did not anticipate the serious troubles arising from the Stamp Act of 1765. That being the case, how much more likely would their judgment have been justified had the British government not stirred up the unnecessary agitation preceding that act. The English ministers, however, by their action in 1763 and by placing the duty too high the following year to please the West Indians, had forced the colonial merchant class into dangerous opposition. The members of that

---

[1] Cited by Schlesinger, *Colonial Merchants*, p. 59.

[2] A. E. Brown, *John Hancock, his Book*, (Boston, 1898), p. 61. The letter is dated Jan. 21, 1765.

[3] *Cf.* Schlesinger, *Colonial Merchants*, pp. 62 *ff.*; Andrews, "Boston Merchants," pp. 181 *ff.*

class would naturally use every argument and influence possible to consolidate public opinion against the acts, and in doing so would be aided by the radical elements in the community always willing to fish in troubled waters, and only too ready to seize so promising an opportunity of striking against the exercise of external control.

How far the movement initiated by the Boston merchants in August 1764 to boycott certain lines of English goods may have had for its object the influencing of opinion in England, and how much that of consolidating sentiment in the colonies against that country, we do not know. Hutchinson says that it did have the latter effect and helped to unite the people in opposition to Parliament.[1] A few weeks later, a writer in the *Providence Gazette*, recognizing that the real enemy in the all-important matter of the molasses duty was the West Indies rather than England, proposed to suspend business entirely between the continent and the English islands to teach the planters a lesson.[2] However, except in changing permanently the former extravagant custom of expense at funerals, the economy and non-importation movement did not gain much headway at this time, although the general interest it excited may be inferred from the unanimous resolve of "the young Gentlemen of Yale College" in agreeing to abstain from "any foreign spirituous liquors." It was thought that this would "not only greatly diminish the Expences of Education" but prove excellent for the health.[3]

A far more useful weapon was the proposed stamp tax which by promising to interfere with the profits of both lawyers and newspaper owners brought both those classes into immediate alignment with the merchants. Moreover, by its common effect upon the peoples of all the colonies alike, it created a far more general grievance than those inherent in either the molasses duty or the Admiralty court. The colonies had always acquiesced in England's regulation of their foreign trade and laying of duties, so that in that respect also the new acts did

---

[1] *History*, vol. III, p. 117.
[2] Cited by Schlesinger, *Colonial Merchants*, p. 63.
[3] *Boston Gazette*, Dec. 3, 1764.

not afford the opportunity of raising such constitutional questions as freely offered themselves in connection with the radical departure from any precedent in practice involved in such taxes as were proposed in the Stamp Act.

In the course of this narrative, we have had occasion to note the many causes of friction that from time to time occurred in the relations between the colonies and the mother country, some of which were continuing and others of which remained merely as rankling memories or were forgotten entirely. In connection with no one of them was colonial opposition ever unanimous, and each tended also to emphasize the conflict of parties among the colonists themselves. At the time when England was now embarking upon her new imperial policy, the state of public opinion was extremely complex, and as was natural was confused by the conflicting interests and views of the various groups among the colonists. We have seen, for example, how although Vice-Admiralty courts were abhorred by the merchants as a rule, the erection of one in Connecticut had been urged by the special group interested in lumber speculation. That same colony was rent by the disputes between the Western land speculators, who were involving the colony in all the risks incident to their expansionist policy, and those who, having no interest in the lands, had no intention of suffering the possible penalties. The former declaimed against the new policy of England in temporarily closing the West to settlement, whereas that prohibition was a relief to those who had opposed them tooth and nail. Again, the generality of those in eastern New England who owing to their remote situation had no immediate interest in the defence of the frontier or speculative lands to defend, objected strenuously to the establishment of garrisons of regular troops, which, on the other hand, was either asked for or willingly acquiesced in by such unquestioned patriots as Washington and Franklin, who did have such interests. These cases, which could be many times multiplied did space permit of a thorough analysis of the situation, typify the many cross-currents in popular sentiment and the complicated results of any policies adopted by the home government.

The most powerful single group possessing at once solidarity,

self-consciousness and a certain amount of intercolonial communication if not organization was that of the merchants. It
was their interests which had been most directly affected by the
English legislation of 1763 and 1764, and the first efforts to stir
up opposition therefore came from them. Their problem was to
organize public opinion by showing to the other groups and
classes how their particular interests were also involved. It was
not difficult for them to show by some exaggeration how the
duty — *any* duty, they said — on molasses would involve the
ruin of the rum distilleries, the fisheries and the slave trade,
the former two being among New England's most important
industries. Five thousand seamen, they claimed, would be
immediately turned out of employment. All the allied workmen, the shoemakers, the tanners, coopers and even the
farmers would suffer.[1] However wide they might be shown to
be, the economic effects of the legislation still would not
affect all the colonies or even the entire population of New
England equally and immediately. Broader grounds of discontent were necessary and were not wanting, and the agitation by
the merchants received enormous impetus from the radicals,
although ordinarily the two groups had little enough in common. The hard times, the growing disaffection between classes
in the colonies, and the broad underlying influence of the ideals
of individualism and unrestraint fostered by the frontier, made
a fertile combination for the propagandist and agitator.

If the conditions were thus ready, so also was the man, and
the forces of revolt found an incomparable leader in Samuel
Adams. A Puritan of the Puritans, uncompromising, unswerv-
ing, wedded heart and soul to the revolutionary cause, utterly
impractical in the ordinary business of life but a remarkable
manager of men and organizer of movements, a failure in the
broader aspects of statesmanship but an unsurpassed politician
in the special circumstances of time and place, he now first
comes forward to a position of prominence. There was little
in common between him and the merchants, but for the time
being both gained enormously by the help of the other. The
gulf between them was indeed great. Not only was Adams a

---

[1] "The State of the Trade," *cit. supra*, pp. 385 *ff*.

SAMUEL ADAMS
From a portrait by J. S. Copley

profound believer in democracy and a radical, whereas the merchant class was aristocratic and conservative, but among the latter there were few at that time, or for many years later, who willingly considered the necessity for separation from the mother country, their sole desire being for reform. Many, indeed, throughout the colonies amused themselves with figuring the probable population in the future at the extremely rapid increase which was maintained, and felt that in time the great disparity between England and her then far more populous colonies would probably mean a peaceful separation, but few anticipated or desired independence in their own day. It is impossible to say just how early Adams conceived the plan of working for an immediate rupture, but it was at a time long before such an idea became generally popular, and I believe it to have been very early in his own career.[1] At any rate, from 1758 onward he made it his constant rule to seek the acquaintance and means of influencing every brilliant man he could, attempting to warn him "against the hostile designs of Great Britain."[2] These followers, though of such diverse character as Otis and Hancock, he managed for the most part with consummate skill, as he did also that body the management of which has given him much of his reputation, the Boston Town-meeting.

The radicals and conservatives were thus acting together in opposition to the first steps taken by the English ministers to carry out their new imperial policy. But as the years passed and thought became clarified, and the issues more sharply defined, the unnatural alliance could not be maintained, and conservative and radical, Tory and Whig, were to become Loyalist and Patriot, the struggle between whom was to equal in intensity of animosity and bitterness that between the rebels and the mother country herself.

[1] *Cf.* J. K. Hosmer, *Samuel Adams; the Man of the Town-meeting*, J. H. U. S., vol. II p. 39; W. V. Wells, *Life and Public Services of Samuel Adams*, (Boston, 1865), vol. I, p. 207; Hutchinson, *History*, vol. III, p. 134.

[2] John Adams, *Works*, vol. X, p. 364.

CHAPTER XIV

THE INSOLUBLE PROBLEM

The Question of Taxation — Stamp Act — The Reaction of the Colonists — Imperialism — Mob Violence — Increase in Radicalism — Breakdown of Established Governments — Stamp Act Congress — Failure of Stamp Act

In the year 1764 Boston had a population of about sixteen thousand persons, and it is a popular superstition that its town-meeting was a thoroughly democratic forum where, if ever in this troubled world, the voice of the people might make itself heard. The fact was, however, that the average number of voters in the decade from that year to the revolution was only about five hundred and fifty-five, or three and one-half per cent of the population.[1] Not only so, but of these sturdy citizens who turned out thinking they were freely voting for their own rulers, nearly all were unconsciously puppets in the hands of political leaders. That extremely useful machine tool, the caucus, had been deftly used for many years, although the discovery that such was the case seems to have come somewhat as a shock to the young John Adams. "This day learned," he wrote in his diary in February 1763, "that the Caucus Club meets, at certain times, in the garret of Tom Dawes. . . . There they smoke tobacco till you cannot see from one end of the garret to the other. There they drink flip, I suppose, and there they choose . . . selectmen, assessors, collectors, wardens, firewards and representatives are regularly chosen before they are chosen in the town. Uncle Fairfield, Story, Ruddock, [Sam] Adams, Cooper, and a *rudis indigestaque moles* of others are members. They send committees to wait on the merchants' club, and to propose and join in the choice of men and measures. Captain Cunningham says they have solicited him to go to these caucuses; they have assured him of benefit in his busi-

[1] McKinley, *Suffrage Franchise*, p. 356.

ness." [1] At this stage, therefore, it is evident that the "people" whose voice was heard consisted of the members of the Caucus and Merchants' Clubs harmoniously and unobtrusively working together in the sphere of practical politics, each for the "benefit of his business."

Evidently among the measures which they were thus wont to agree upon was the action taken by the town-meeting in May 1764, when a committee of five was appointed to draw up instructions for the representatives of the town in the General Court relative to the Sugar Act. These instructions were written by Samuel Adams and although they dealt mainly with the blow directed at the colony's trade by the new act, they also advanced to broader ground.[2] "If our Trade may be taxed why not our Lands? Why not the Produce of our Lands and everything we possess or make use of?" wrote Adams. "If Taxes are laid upon us in any shape without our having legal Representation where they are laid, are we not reduced from the character of free Subjects to the miserable State of tributary Slaves?" The representatives were also instructed to require the agent in England to remonstrate for the continued exercise of the colony's supposed charter rights, and to request the other colonies to join in common action.

As a result of these representations, a committee of the Massachusetts Assembly, acting without the Council, prepared a letter which, together with a pamphlet written by Otis, was forwarded to the agent, Mauduit.[3] Although Otis suggested that the power of Parliament was not unlimited, and was circumscribed by the constitution, its sovereignty over the colonies for the general regulation of trade, at least, was as yet unquestioned in the writings and public papers of this period, and in the autumn session of the General Court the assembly in their answer to Governor Bernard's speech agreed that it was their duty to acknowledge obedience to the Sugar Act until they could secure its repeal.[4] Likewise Otis in his pamphlet asserted

[1] *Works*, vol. II, p. 144.

[2] *Writings of Samuel Adams*, ed. H. A. Cushing, (New York, 1904), vol. I, pp. 1 *ff*.

[3] *Rights of the British Colonies*, *cit. supra*; Hutchinson, *History*, vol. III, p. 108. The letter to Mauduit is in *Brit. Mus. Add. Mss. 35910.*

[4] [Alden Bradford] *Speeches of the Governors of Massachusetts from 1765 to 1775* . . . (Boston, 1818), p. 18. [Hereafter cited as *Mass. State Papers.*]

that "let the Parliament lay what burdens they please on us, we must, it is our duty to submit and patiently bear them, till they be pleased to relieve us."[1] The grievance of taxation without representation appeared prominently in most of the utterances, but the assumption had not yet been made that colonial representation in the English Parliament was an impossibility. The grievance, therefore, might be construed to consist quite as much in the lack of representation as in the taxation, a blunder that was to be quickly retrieved when it was found that the political weapon thus formed was much like a boomerang. Although in the course of discussion the Stamp Act was mentioned, the main stress was laid upon the trade burden of the Sugar Act and upon the Admiralty Courts even as late as a petition to Parliament at the end of the year.[2] In order to find a reason against those burdens, the general supervision of Parliament being acknowledged, the difference between internal and external taxation was brushed aside for the moment and the customs duty represented as a tax. There was, indeed, much confusion of thought evidenced, and the stands taken by various writers, and by the same writers on different points, were incompatible. Nevertheless, the merchants in enlisting the efforts of the more radical leaders of the people to aid them in ridding themselves of the burdens on trade had set them to finding a rational basis for objection, and, confused as these earlier writings were, they suggested doctrines which would lead straight to revolution should England force the colonists to continue this dangerous rationalizing process. It may be pointed out that the issue as yet was largely a sectional one, in which the West Indies were pitted against New England, and the interests of the southern continental colonies hardly involved at all. The next move by England, however, was destined at once to give a tremendous impetus to the discussion of constitutional questions, to afford the radicals an

---

[1] *Rights of the British Colonies*, p. 40. Stephen Hopkins while reserving a certain sphere for the local legislatures admitted the right of Parliament to legislate on matters of general concern to the empire. *Grievances of the American Colonies*, (London, 1766), pp. 19 f. This was a reprint, with some alterations, of the same pamphlet published the year before at Providence, R. I., under the title of *The Rights of the Colonies examined.*

[2] *Bowdoin-Temple Papers*, pp. 32 ff.

opportunity, and to merge the minds of all the colonists in a single wave of political emotion.

Of that one-third of the total cost of the peace-time military establishment in America which alone it was the desire of the English government to raise eventually by American taxes, only a small part was expected from the duties under the Sugar Act. Grenville had asked the colonies for their advice as to how the balance might be found in the way most agreeable to themselves, his own suggestion being a stamp tax such as we used after the Civil and Spanish wars. Such a tax was then in use in England without being unpopular, and Massachusetts herself had utilized the same method of raising money during the recent struggle.[1] Nor was the thought of its use for colonial taxation by any means new, writers and amateur statesmen having recommended it for many years, and with some frequency during the war.[2] In fact, during its continuance acts for levying such a tax both in New York and Massachusetts had been prepared in England although not introduced into Parliament.[3] Most American historians today concede that, from the standpoint of strict legality, that body did possess the constitutional right to levy such a tax upon the colonists, an opinion that was certainly almost universally held in England at the time.[4] "Except the gentlemen interested in the West Indies and a few members that happen to be particularly connected with some of the colonies and a few of the heads of the minority who are sure to thwart and oppose the Ministry in every measure," Ingersoll, the Connecticut agent, could find hardly anyone, in Parliament or out, who was opposed to the measure.[5] The question in Grenville's mind, therefore, was one of expediency. England's debt had grown to £140,000,000; the French though beaten were longing for revenge and had their spies in the American colonies reporting on the possibilities of

---

[1] *Acts and Resolves*, vol. III, pp. 793 ff., 834; vol. IV, pp. 86, 140; *New England Hist. and Gen. Register*, vol. XIV, pp. 267 ff.; *Mass. Hist. Soc. Proceedings*, vol. XLII, p. 176; *Mass. Archives*, 103: 292; 102: 437.

[2] *Cf.* e.g. *Proposals for uniting the Colonies*, p. 23.

[3] Gipson, *Jared Ingersoll*, pp. 116 f.

[4] *Cf.* Mellen Chamberlain, *John Adams*, (Boston, 1899), pp. 137 ff.

[5] *Ingersoll Papers*, p. 317.

the situation; [1] both on account of foreign and savage foes, an army was necessary in America; the colonial systems of defence and Indian policy had broken down; permanent garrisons were necessary, but the colonists would not serve.

The ministers admitted that the colonists did not have direct representation in Parliament, but said that even if they were given such direct representation they could not certainly expect to return a majority of the House of Commons and so control the whole empire. "What then?" they said to the colonial agents, "shall no steps be taken and must we and America be two distinct kingdoms and that now immediately, or must America be defended entirely by us, and be themselves quite excused or be left to do just what they shall please to do? Some perhaps will do something and others nothing. Perhaps from the nature of our situations it will happen and must be expected that one day we shall be two distinct kingdoms, but we trust even you wont think yourselves ripe for that event as yet. . . . We own on our part we dont choose to predict, nor yet to hasten the time of this supposed period, and think it would be to our mutual disadvantage for us to attempt a separation." [2]

To all this, the agents, as one of them wrote home, could answer merely that "we must own there is a weight in your arguments and a force in your reasonings — but after all we must say we are rather silenced than convinced. We feel in our bosoms that it will be forever inconvenient, 't will be forever dangerous to America that they should be taxed by the authority of a British Parliament by reason of our great distance from you." [3] This stand and that taken later by the colonists at home were unquestionably and absolutely right, but the harassed finance minister was faced by the very practical problem of paying the expense of government. If England should give up the tax, wrote Ingersoll, "Mr. Grenville asked us if we could agree upon the several proportions each colony should

---

[1] F. Kapp, *Life of John Kalb*, (New York, 1884), pp. 43 *ff.*; Cornélis de Witt, *Thomas Jefferson, étude historique*, (Paris, 1862), pp. 407 *ff.*

[2] *Ingersoll Papers*, pp. 321 *f.*

[3] *Ibid.*, p. 321.

raise. We told him no." [1] The horns of the dilemma, therefore, seemed obvious if dangerous. In the absence of colonial union the only alternative to imperial administration and taxation that the colonists could offer was the old disjointed voluntary requisition system of jealously conflicting jurisdictions and interests which, as we have seen throughout this volume and as the colonists admitted themselves, had always broken down. Many colonists claimed, with truth, that a considerable part of the gains in the West and Canada were imperial rather than colonial, yet England's aid had been invoked in the war, and even now Washington and others were asking for permanent garrisons of English troops. What then? Who was to pay for the war? Who was to pay for the garrisons? The colonies had already paid much, but so had England. On the other hand the fear by the colonial agents of taxation by Parliament was entirely justified. Here then was a new impasse. Nor need we attribute stupidity to Grenville, or a wish to tyrannize, for this very question of the apportionment of expense for imperial defence remains today unsettled in the British empire and is, perhaps, an insoluble one.

The first solution a British ministry tried proved a colossal blunder, but the colonists had themselves no practicable solution to offer. In answer to the request of the ministry for suggestions in the preceding year, they had sent in petitions, it is true, but in these merely denied the right of Parliament to tax them at all. Connecticut had indeed suggested that instead of internal taxes additional revenue might be raised from duties on slaves and the fur trade — the incidence of the one, it may be noted, falling as far to the north, for the most part, as the other did to the south of the canny little colony.[2] Although all these and other protests and petitions went before the Privy Council, by an initial mistake in statesmanship they were not allowed before Parliament on account of an old rule which was supposed to forbid receiving petitions against money bills.[3] When the

---

[1] *Fitch Papers*, vol. II, p. 325.

[2] *R. I. Col. Records*, vol. VI, pp. 414 *ff.*; Bradford, *Mass. State Papers*, pp. 22 *ff.*; *Conn. Col. Records*, vol. XII, p. 670.

[3] *Acts Privy Council*, vol. IV, p. 692; *Parlt. Hist.*, vol. XVI, pp. 35 *n. ff.*, 40; Hutchinson, *History*, vol. III, p. 115.

stamp bill itself came up in the Commons it aroused no interest, only two or three members troubling to speak on it, and it passed both houses in March 1765 with less opposition, as the *Boston Gazette* said, than there would have been "to a common Turnpike Bill." [1] The only speech in the debate which was reported was that by Colonel Isaac Barré, a short and fiery harangue of some thirty lines which has come down to us in as many versions, and is probably known in one or another of them to every schoolboy in the country. Terming the colonists "sons of liberty" he vehemently attacked the ministers' policy. "Children planted by your care! No! your oppression planted them in America. . . . They nourished by your indulgence! They grew by your neglect," he declaimed in the now hackneyed words. [2] The speech, sent home by Ingersoll and others, was printed throughout the colonies, and the fervid rhetoric had its effect. [3] It is noteworthy, as presaging the unexpected union of New England and West India interests as a result of the act, that during the debate the only member of Parliament to deny the right to tax the colonies was Alderman Beckford, whose fortune was invested in Jamaica, and of whom Walpole had written in 1759 that "a tax on sugar touched his vitals." [4]

The momentous act thus placed upon the statute book required the use of revenue stamps upon packages of playing cards and dice, upon a long list of legal papers, liquor licenses, pamphlets, newspapers, almanacs and other written or printed documents, and provided that infractions of the law must be tried in the Admiralty Courts. [5] In spite of the protests received from the colonies, the ministers did not expect that the act would meet with serious opposition in America, and this feeling

---

[1] *Parlt. Hist.*, vol. XVI, p. 37; *Boston Gazette*, June 3, 1765.

[2] *Parlt. Hist.*, vol. XVI, pp. 38 *ff.*; Frothingham, *Rise of the Republic*, pp. 175 *n.*

[3] Gipson, *Jared Ingersoll*, p. 140 *n.*; *Ingersoll Papers*, pp. 310 *f.*

[4] H. Walpole, *Memoirs of Geo. II*, vol. III, p. 177.

[5] 5 Geo. III, c. 12. The essential portions of it may be found in almost any source book, *e.g.* MacDonald, *Select Charters*, pp. 282 *ff.*; same, *Documentary Source Book*, pp. 122 *ff.*; West, *Source Book*, pp. 373 *ff.*; *American History Leaflets*, No. 21. The last states that the act is not included in the printed editions of the Acts of Parliament. Although not in the *Revised Statutes*, it may be found in both Ruffhead and Pickering, *Statutes at Large.* One of the most alarming clauses in the act was that which provided that the tax should be paid in Sterling money and not in kind, the former always being very scarce in the colonies. *Cf.* Andrews, "British Merchants," pp. 181 *f.*

seems to have been shared by many of the most prominent colonials themselves, even among those opposed to the act. Richard Henry Lee in Virginia applied for the position of Stamp Distributor; Benjamin Franklin advised Jared Ingersoll to accept the position for his colony when it was tendered to him; and Ingersoll himself for several months was pestered with applications from colonists who wished to become his deputies.[1]

At first, indeed, there was no excitement although much foreboding and a general determination to prevent the execution of the act if possible.[2] It was not to go into operation until the first of November, and apparently nothing serious was expected to occur in the meantime. At the meeting of the Massachusetts legislature in June, held soon after the passage of the act was known, the House agreed to ask representatives from the assemblies of the other colonies to meet their own delegates at a congress to be held in New York on the first Tuesday in October to consider the situation, and to agree upon some general application to the king and Parliament for relief.[3] It was said that the more radical element in the House had scarcely a working majority but that the conservatives joined with them in order to secure control of the movement. In this they were so far successful that although James Otis was chosen one of the delegates, the other two were described by Governor Bernard as "fast friends of government." Nevertheless, the conservatives were very soon to lose their hold on the situation, and the year was to be marked by a breakdown of authority, and the rise of mob rule quite as much as by discussion of constitutional principles and remedies. Newspapers and pamphlets, however, teemed with the ideas put forth by men of all shades of opinion in the effort to find rational grounds for sustaining or opposing the action of the government and for a constitutional theory of colonial relations.

On the first page of this volume I spoke of the constant stream of human discontent, restlessness, and upward striving as clothing itself in ever-varying forms of thought and outward expres-

[1] Gipson, *Jared Ingersoll*, p. 145 n.; *Ingersoll Papers*, pp. 323 ff.
[2] Hutchinson, *History*, vol. III, p. 119.
[3] Frothingham, *Rise of the Republic*, p. 178 n.; *Mass. State Papers*, p. 35.

sion and yet one at bottom. As we follow the innumerable generations of man from the dawn of history in Sumer and Accad onward through the brilliant civilizations of Crete and Greece and Rome, so varied in externals and accidentals yet in the fundamental strata of human emotion and instinct so uniform, we seem aware of forces continuously at work far below the surface of conscious life. As the spade of the archeologist reveals nation after nation which has risen, flowered and fallen, leaving hardly more impression than the swarming of midges in a sunbeam, one comes to question whether, in truth, this long story of men has been as much influenced by ideas as we would like to believe and whether the play of thought may not be result rather than cause, a sort of brilliant phosphorescence overhanging the subconscious and mysterious operation of non-rational forces in the historic process. There certainly seems, at any rate, no basis on which to dispute the statement recently made that "most of our so-called reasoning consists in finding arguments for going on believing as we already do."[1]

As we have seen, all the influences of the American environment had combined to develop a certain outlook on life and a certain attitude toward England without much conscious reasoning. Suddenly these were questioned, and the colonists at once set about finding reasons to justify them in continuing to believe as they had. They began by arguing on constitutional grounds. Finding the logic of the situation against them they retreated from one position to another until in the final years they were forced to take their stand solely on "natural rights" and the "law of God"; in other words, on purely dogmatic assertions that what they chose to believe had a sanction above any argument. Such ideas had been wafted about the colonies for many years, as we noted when speaking of John Wise as early as 1717, and they had found a congenial soil, but at this stage of the controversy the colonists evidently hoped to convince by reason rather than over-ride by dogma.[2]

[1] J. H. Robinson, *The Mind in the Making*, (New York, 1921), p. 41.

[2] Otis, indeed, found the foundation of government "in the unchangeable will of God" and proclaimed "*salus populi suprema lex esto*" to be the "law of nature, and part of the grand charter given to the human race," but the laying of the main stress on such unprovable generalities belonged for the most part to the later period. *Cf. Rights of the British Colonies*, pp. 9 *f.*

Although the provisions of the Stamp Act renewed the question of trial without jury, the discussion centered mainly about the question of taxation. In their dislike of the innovation of direct taxation by Parliament the colonists were probably more nearly unanimous than on any other question that came up during the decade now beginning, even such men as Governor Bernard and Thomas Hutchinson deploring the inexpediency of the measure as deeply as any of the radicals. Nevertheless, as we have noted, the general power of Parliament to legislate for the colonies was as yet freely admitted. The hawser that bound them to England was frayed by friction and rotted by neglect. It would stand little strain, but for the present its real condition was not recognized. Throughout a long period Parliament had too frequently and too consistently legislated for the colonies for them suddenly to question the legality of its general power. The Post Office Act, the acts relating to the wages of American seamen, to the manufacture of iron and hats, to the King's woods, to colonial debts, to paper currency, the innumerable acts of trade, as well as many others, formed too imposing a series of precedents. For a century and a quarter Parliament had been thus legislating without serious or sustained constitutional protest from the colonies. A protest, therefore, to be constitutional and not revolutionary would have to be based, however speciously, upon the supposition that in the Sugar and Stamp Acts Parliament had done something which it had not done hitherto. That something was considered to be the imposition of taxes or duties upon the colonists for the purpose of revenue rather than for the mere regulation of imperial trade. Even this was not without precedent, as witness the Post Office Act, but the case was far less clear as a matter of precedent than that of the general power of legislation. Two arguments, therefore, were at once brought forward. One, in order to explain why the colonists declined to submit to the Stamp Act whereas they had always — theoretically — submitted to the levying of duties under the acts of trade, drew a distinction between internal and external taxation. The other, in order to provide a basis for disputing the 3d. duty on molasses, denied the legality of any taxation without representation.[1]

Otis in his first pamphlet had fully admitted the right of Parliament to pass laws restraining trade, but added that he would rather "see this carried with a high hand, to the utmost rigor, than have a tax of one shilling taken from me without my consent. . . . If a shilling in the pound may be taken from me against my will, why may not twenty shillings; and if so, why not my liberty or my life?"[2] This proved rather too much, for the same line of argument would apply to many of the other unquestioned Acts of Parliament as well. Indeed, Otis himself retreated from this position the following year and wrote that "it is certain that the Parliament of Great Britain hath a just, clear, equitable and constitutional right, power and authority, to bind the colonies by all acts wherein they are named. Every lawyer, nay every Tyro knows this." He admitted that Parliament had the constitutional power to "impose taxes on the colonies, internal and external, on lands as well as on trade," basing his opposition to the exercise of the right merely on justice and expediency.[3] In the chief pamphlets produced in Rhode Island and Connecticut, however, the same distinction was made between internal and external taxation, it being claimed that the right to levy the former had been granted to the colonies by their charters.[4] Although this distinction between taxes laid at the water front and internally found some supporters in England, it was evidently impossible to maintain it logically. "What a pother," said one of the Irish members of Parliament, as to "whether the money is to be taken out of their coat pocket

---

[1] Cf. Daniel Dulany, *Considerations on the Propriety of imposing Taxes on the British Colonies*, (Annapolis, 1765), p. 28.

[2] *Rights of the British Colonies*, p. 54.

[3] *A Vindication of the British Colonies against the Aspersions of the Halifax Gentleman*, (Boston, 1765), pp. 4f., 15. Also his *Brief Remarks on the Defence of the Halifax Libel on the British-American Colonies*, (Boston, 1765), pp. 23 ff.

[4] S. Hopkins, *Grievances of the American Colonies*, p. 31; *Reasons why the British Colonies in America should not be charged with internal Taxes*, Conn. Col. Records, vol. XII, pp. 658 f. The English point of view may be found in [W. Knox] *The Claims of the Colonies . . . examined*, (London, 1765). For the more flippant and irritating treatment of the question by Englishmen, *vide* [Soame Jenyns] *The Objections to the Taxation of the American Colonies . . . considered*, (London, 1765), pp. 9, 11, 16.

or out of their waistcoat pocket!"[1] Psychologically there is a difference but constitutionally there is none, and the colonists had to abandon the contention. It is interesting, however, as showing their groping efforts to rationalize a position that, instinctively and justifiably, they had already assumed. When questioned before the House of Commons in the following year, Franklin was asked whether the colonists if they denied external taxation might not deny internal also. "They never have hitherto," he answered, "many arguments have been lately used to shew them that there is no difference . . . at present they do not reason so, but in time they may possibly be convinced."[2] Forced to admit that there was no difference, they could only undertake a still wider examination of parliamentary sovereignty.

Of the other argument, no taxation without representation, Martin Howard, a prominent lawyer in Newport who had been one of the Rhode Island commissioners to Albany in 1754, wrote that "it is this dry maxim, taken in a literal sense, and ill understood, that, like the song of *Lillibullero*, has made all the mischief in the colonies."[3]

After a century and a half there is no need to analyze anew this popular rallying cry, which like most such does not admit of a logical justification. We have already described the condition of Parliamentary representation in the England of the period. The constitutional theory did not call for the right to vote by every person taxed but only for "virtual representation," that is the representation of every class in the commonwealth by its chosen representatives in Parliament. Although the colonial representative system showed no such glaring inconsistencies as had in time grown up in England, the cry of "no taxation without representation," unless understood in the same sense of merely virtual representation, had almost as little justification in America as in the mother country. In all the colonies the franchise was rigidly restricted to but a fraction of

---

[1] Cited by S. G. Fisher, *The Struggle for American Independence*, (Philadelphia, 1908), vol. I, p. 88.

[2] *Parlt. Hist.*, vol. XVI, p. 158.

[3] *A Letter from a Gentleman at Halifax to his Friend in Rhode Island*, (Newport, 1765), p. 11.

the population, there being fewer voters proportionately in New England than in the middle and southern colonies. In Massachusetts and Connecticut only about one person in fifty took part in elections, although a larger proportion was entitled to do so. In Rhode Island the enfranchised "freemen" formed only about nine per cent of the population. In New York over one-half of the males over twenty-one years of age were without political privilege of any sort. In Pennsylvania the conditions were notorious, and throughout the whole century, until the unenfranchised elements secured control by revolutionary means in 1776, the three eastern counties had manipulated the franchise of the entire colony for their own benefit.[1] This colonial situation was wholly ignored in the new rallying cry, and many who shouted loudest would have been the last willingly to have put their slogan into practice in America. Nevertheless, it did voice a legitimate aspiration, and its reiteration in the quarrel with England taught the unenfranchised elements in the colonies a lesson and helped to arouse the genuinely revolutionary movement which caused many who were opposed to the English measures to prefer the inconveniences and even the serious injustices of English control to the uncertainties of "mob rule."

Franklin and others had long toyed with the thought of colonial representatives sitting as members of Parliament at Westminster, but the realization of the difference in interest between England and the colonies, and the fact that, however numerous, the colonial representatives could always be outvoted, prevented such a plan from gaining colonial acceptance although often brought forward.[2] The claim advanced in Eng-

---

[1] McKinley, *Suffrage Franchise*, pp. 356, 378, 420, 487; C. L. Becker, *History of political Parties in the Province of New York*, 1760-76, Bull. Univ. of Wisconsin, No. 286, p. 11; C. H. Lincoln, *The revolutionary Movement in Pennsylvania*, (Univ. of Penn. Publications, 1901), p. 52.

[2] It is needless to cite the numerous pamphlets in which the subject was discussed. An English writer strongly in favor of the scheme wrote that "every man will call that an Utopian scheme which he either cannot comprehend, or is averse to put in practice." *Reflexions on Representation in Parliament* . . . (London, 1766), p. 15. The contemporary journals had many articles on the subject, *e.g.* The *Boston Gazette*, Jan. 28, June 17, July 29, 1765. There is a good résumé of various schemes which have been proposed for colonial representation in an imperial parliament, by A. L. Burt, *Imperial Architects*, (Oxford, 1913), pp. 14-65.

land that the colonists were already virtually represented in
Parliament as much as those Englishmen at home who did not
themselves vote, failed to take into account the point that
owing to the fact that the interests of the colonists were in
many cases different from those of any group or class at home
this was not a parallel case, and of course the suggestion entirely
failed to carry conviction in America. Nor was the theory either
safe or just. British imperialism as yet was admitted to be
merely commercial exploitation, and as Lord Cromer has said
"the principle that lies at the root of all sound administration . . . is that administration and commercial exploitation
should not be entrusted to the same hands." [1]

The real question lay far deeper than constitutional quibblings
over taxation. It was the fundamental one of the moral validity
of imperialism, of whether a group of men in one part of the
world has the right to rule others in another part against their
will, however wisely and however well. Like the question of the
right of a majority it admits of no easy or universal answer.
Both English statesmen and colonial leaders were feeling their
way toward the solution of a problem that is perhaps insoluble,
the reconciliation of freedom and empire. There was at the time
no guide, for as a contemporary writer said "there is no similar
case in all the records of history to serve as a precedent or clew,
to direct their steps; and all they can do is to grope their way." [2]
What lent dignity to the cause of the colonists and a touch of
sordidness to that of England in the period under review, was
the nature of imperialism as understood at the time. There is
always, perhaps, a sordid background to any imperialism, but
the magnificent work done by English administrators in many
quarters of the world in the past century has not only lent a new
glamor to the conception but has done much to validate it. It
may be that in time the British Empire may really become
what it is now popular to call it, a genuine Commonwealth of
Free Nations, but in the years before the American revolution
and for many years after, all that lay in the future. To Pitt as
much as to Grenville, empire meant commercial supremacy and

[1] *Ancient and modern Imperialism*, (London, 1910), p. 69.
[2] *The Justice and Necessity of taxing the Americans demonstrated*, (London, 1766), p. 6.

commercial exploitation for England. "Colonies," it was said in a pamphlet written or inspired by the latter, "are only Settlements made in distant Parts of the world, for the Improvement of Trade ; but if they were allowed to transfer the Benefits of their Commerce to any other Country than that from which they came, they would destroy the very Purpose of their Establishment."[1] It must, I think, be admitted that England then wanted the American colonies solely for a profit. She wanted to rule Americans and keep them "in proper dependence" for what there was in it commercially. On the other hand, although the economic grievance was the most obvious one on the side of the colonists, and they were as anxious for profits as were their British cousins, there is something rather finer in struggling to be free to make one's own way than in struggling to keep some one else in subjection to help make it for us. The effort to judge justly of the difficulties of the problem from the English standpoint; of the economic and political atmosphere of the time; of the influence of the American environment; and of the vast quantity of dross intermixed with such pure gold as there was in American doctrine, should not disguise the fundamental situation in the eighteenth century.

In New England in 1765, two questions began to emerge from the discussion of that year. If it was denied that Parliament had the right to levy internal taxes in America and if there was no constitutional difference between that and enacting trade laws with duties, would not colonial protest have to be against Parliamentary action in a far larger sphere ? And if taxation, or possibly any legislative action by Parliament, was invalid in America because the colonists were not directly represented, as was claimed, then would not the unenfranchised colonials demand the right to the colonial franchise ? Although the privileged classes in the colonies — by no means desirous of a genuinely revolutionary overturn — were playing with fire to an extent they did not at first realize, the events of the summer were to give them ominous warning.

While the more cultivated and thoughtful colonists were writing pamphlets discussing constitutional points, and the

---

[1] *The Regulations lately made*, p. 89.

minorities privileged to share in the political administration were passing resolutions in the assemblies, leaders among the lower classes — some sincere and some merely agitators seeking personal influence — began to organize the unenfranchised elements into secret societies under the name of "Sons of Liberty," adopting the phrase from Barré's speech.[1] It was this organization, extending throughout many of the colonies, and composed for the most part of the least educated, least responsible and most unruly elements among the people, that carried out most of the mob violence and outrages of the next ten years; though in the beginning, at least, the responsibility must be shared by some of the more important radicals who took part in the movement. The two groups whose interests were particularly affected by the Stamp Tax, however, were the lawyers and printers. From about 1758 lawyers had suddenly risen into prominence and had taken the lead in public matters,[2] and news-sheets by this time had become far more effective weapons in forming public opinion than they had been earlier in the century. Both of these influential sources of leadership were almost solidly aligned against the measure.

In spite of the apparent calm which deceived some of the best observers, public feeling was in a highly dangerous state. Only a spark was needed to start a conflagration. It was furnished not by New England but by Virginia. The wealthy and aristocratic members of the Virginia Legislature, indeed, were far more interested at the moment in trying to hush up a financial scandal than in the Stamp Act, and were taking no measures against it. But under the leadership of Patrick Henry, the democratic elements in the assembly, in revolt against the hitherto unchallenged influence of the "first families," voted the famous Virginia Resolves. It is uncertain how many were actually passed, but six were published in the newspapers throughout the colonies, and as they were assumed to be authentic, had as much effect as though they had been.[3] The

[1] J. H. Trumbull, "Sons of Liberty in 1755," *New Englander*, (Apl. 1876), pp. 299 *ff.*; H. B. Dawson, *The Sons of Liberty in New York*, (New York, 1859); C. L. Becker, "Growth of revolutionary Parties and Methods in New York Province," *American Historical Review*, vol. VII, p. 61; same, *Political Parties in New York*, pp. 49 *f.*

[2] Hutchinson, *History*, vol. III, p. 104 *n.*

[3] *Virginia Magazine of History and Biography*, vol. X, pp. 8 *ff.*

last two affirmed that the inhabitants of Virginia could not be bound by any laws imposing any taxation except such as were made by the colonial assembly, and that anyone who should maintain the contrary should be considered as an enemy to the colony. All contemporary observers agree as to the tremendous and almost instant effect of the publishing of the resolves in the papers. They threw "Boston into a flame," and in Connecticut "the peoples Spirits took fire and burst forth into a blaze." [1] The excitement was fanned by the printers who from now on "stuffed their papers weekly . . . with the most inflammatory pieces they could procure and excluded everything that tended to cool the minds of the people." [2] A veritable frenzy took possession of the colonists, comparable only to that of the Great Awakening, its contagious nature being evidenced by the fact that even the negro slaves shared in it.[3] Peter Oliver in his biased but occasionally amusing account of the "Origin and Progress of the American Rebellion," says that one evening a Bostonian told his slave to go on an errand. The slave refused, saying with tears in his eyes, "me 'fraid, Massah, Tamp Act he catch me." [4] It was a psychological quite as much as a political manifestation, and, indeed, the whole revolutionary period offers a fascinating field for psychological study.

The springs of the mob action of that summer throughout New England are to be found in mass meetings, speeches and violent propaganda, without a preliminary course of which mob outbreaks seldom occur.[5] Unconsciously probably, the press and some of the more prominent radicals, as well as more ignorant local leaders of the Sons of Liberty, were employing all the methods which the most scientific student of crowd psychology today could suggest to bring about the very outbreak that followed.[6] Although the Inter-Colonial Congress had been called to consider the question of the tax in October, the people were meanwhile wrought upon by being told that they were to be

[1] *Ingersoll Papers*, pp. 157, 367; Précis of Gov. Bernard's Correspondence, 1765, *C O. 5 No. 43.*
[2] Cited by Gipson, *Jared Ingersoll*, p. 165 n.
[3] Jonathan Mayhew, *The Snare broken*, (Boston, 1766), p. 17.
[4] *Egerton, Mss. 2671 f. 89.*
[5] E. D. Martin, *The Behaviour of Crowds*, (New York, 1920), p. 38.
[6] *Cf. ibid.*, chap. V; W. McDougall, *The Group Mind*, (New York, 1920), p. 62.

made "slaves"; that there was not enough money in the colonies to pay the tax; that England was to make the colonies pay the entire cost of the war; that troops were to be sent to overawe them; and that in spite of their sacrifices all the gains had gone to Great Britain. No language was too violent to apply to the Tories. Otis, whose manners, however, were notoriously bad, spoke of a group in Newport as a "little, dirty, drinking, drabbing, contaminated knot of thieves, beggars and transports . . . collected from the four winds of the earth, and made up of Turks, Jews and other Infidels with a few renegado Christians and Catholics." [1]

But even the unpopularity of the recent acts, and the laws of mob psychology do not wholly account for the general outbreak. The case bears somewhat of an analogy to the great uprising in England in 1381, although on a much smaller scale. That earlier movement, which used to be considered inexplicable merely as a response to the passage of even an intensely unpopular tax, we now see to have been due to the accumulation of a great variety of local grievances frequently bearing no relation to each other, but which could all be focused in a fight against established authority. As the historian of that episode writes, "things had been working up for trouble during many years — only a good cry, a common grievance which united all malcontents, was needed to bring matters to a head." [2] In 1381 it was the Poll Tax which did so, in 1765 the Stamp Tax. We need not rehearse the multifold discontents rife in the colonies at this time, which we have already noted. Some of the grievances were against England, some against the privileged classes in the colonies, some, though not so recognized, against mere economic law. There was scarcely a group in New England, however, that did not have a grievance of some sort. The crowd always looks for the source of its troubles in some enemy, some conspiracy against its interests, and when the crowd spirit has taken hold of a people it is easy for the leaders to merge all resentments into some common channel directed against individuals. Anyone who does not go with the crowd at once be-

---

[1] *Brief Remarks on the Defence of the Halifax Libel*, p. 5.
[2] C. Oman, *The Great Revolt of 1381*, (Oxford, 1906), p. 2.

comes an enemy of the people, a traitor to the commonweal. In 1765 the storm fell first upon the collectors appointed under the new law. It mattered nothing that the conservative elements had already taken measures to oppose the tax by constitutional means. From this year onward, there was clearly added to the question whether the rights of the colonies were to be maintained, a second query, by whom and by what methods, and this was the more pregnant of the two. In other words, to the question of home rule was added that of who was to rule at home.[1]

In Boston the leader of the mob in its acts of violence seems to have been one Mackintosh, a shoe-maker, but one or two merchants and the publisher of the radical organ, the *Boston Gazette*, were deep in the counsels of the Sons of Liberty. On the 8th of August the list of stamp distributors was made public, and an inflammatory article appeared in the *Gazette*. A few days later a stuffed figure intended to represent Andrew Oliver, the Massachusetts appointee, brother-in-law of Chief-Justice Hutchinson, was found hanging to a tree. That evening a mob of some thousands proceeded to a new building of Oliver's, which they thought was intended for a stamp office, and tore it down. From thence they went to his own house, beat down the doors, and destroyed a considerable part of his furniture. Some of the leaders of the mob were known, and the governor issued a proclamation offering a reward for the discovery of the offenders, but the executive power was so weak that Oliver, fearing for his family, resigned his office. A couple of days later, the authorities having taken no action, the mob surrounded Hutchinson's house, a false report having been spread that he favored the tax. This was wholly untrue, but the unpopularity he had incurred in some of his too many offices, his ultra-conservative views, his wealth and high social position, all made him a shining mark for the activities of a mob. Although he was in his house at the time, a neighbor called to the rioters that he was not, and after some difficulty they were got to disperse, having merely broken the windows and greatly alarmed the family. On Sunday the 25th, however, the Reverend Jonathan Mayhew preached a

[1] Becker, *Political Parties in New York*, p. 22.

provocative sermon on the text "I would they were even cut off which trouble you." The next evening the mob was called together again, supplied with liquor, and after having destroyed the records of the Vice-Admiralty court, and plundered the house of the comptroller of the customs, once more proceeded to that of the Chief-Justice. This time the family barely escaped with their lives, and the mob spent the night in pillaging and almost completely demolishing the mansion, which was one of the finest in Boston. Without counting the loss of Hutchinson's invaluable collection of public and private papers, the damage amounted to the large sum for those days of £2,500.[1] Although many magistrates and field officers stood by, no one dared to interfere, and the town was in terror the whole night. The next morning a great number of the citizens, including participants in the outrage, met in Faneuil Hall and expressed their not altogether sincere detestation of the acts of the mob, but the government was powerless. Although Mackintosh was arrested by the sheriff, a number of merchants assured that official that unless the prisoner were released no guard would turn out to defend the town, and the sheriff had to yield to their intimidation. A few other known leaders in the riot were put in prison but were rescued by the people, and the government never dared to undertake further proceedings, although the governor's cadets did disperse the mob when it again attempted to gather for plunder. Bernard truly wrote home that the authority of government had broken down. The conservative element, however, was beginning to take the alarm, and "the people of any property," the governor wrote in September, were "being very much cooled by their apprehensions of confusion and distress."[2] The assembly for long insisted that the action of a mob could not be considered that of the town, but the fact that the movement had been set on foot by the radical leaders, that the prisoners were rescued and that neither juries nor officials would do their duty, places the responsibility beyond question. Had the town in reality condemned the action of the mob, as they

[1] Hutchinson, *History*, vol. III, pp. 120 ff.; *Boston Gazette*, Sept. 2, 1765; Précis of Gov. Bernard's Correspondence, 1765, *C.O. 5 No. 43.*

[2] F. Bernard, *Select Letters*, p. 27; Letter of Gov. Bernard, Sept. 7, 1765, *Brit. Mus Add. Mss., 35911.*

pretended to do, it would have been possible to have brought the offenders to justice after the first excitement. That, on the contrary, they were shielded even by the violent methods of a jail delivery, and that no action could ever be taken against them, shows that either they were in complete accord with public opinion or that the law-abiding citizens who pretended to condemn their acts were a cowardly lot.

In Connecticut the stamp distributor was Jared Ingersoll, the colonial agent in England. He had been opposed to the tax, and it was only after he had done all he could to prevent its passage that he had accepted the office for the good of the colony upon Franklin's suggestion. It was thought by many good Americans that if the Act were to be enforced it would be better to have colonials as officials rather than rapacious office-seekers from over-seas, and Ingersoll was amazed on his return to Connecticut to find himself the object of bitter hostility. The first attack upon him in the press was made by Napthali Daggett, professor of Divinity at Yale College, who owed him a grudge of ten years' standing in connection with a purely collegiate question. In fact, the alignment of parties in that colony offers a marked continuity regardless of the questions at issue. As Dr. Benjamin Gale, who lived in the center of the eastern radical section, wrote at this time of the Sons of Liberty, they were the offspring of "several factions which have subsisted in this Colony, originating with the New London Society — thence metamorphosed into the Faction for paper Emissions on Loan, thence into the New Light, into the Susquehannah and Delaware Factions — into Orthodoxy — now Stamp Duty opponents."[1]

Although Ingersoll was not without his defenders, the articles in the press became more and more vituperative. In August came the news of the Boston riots and the forcing of Oliver's resignation. On the 21st Ingersoll was hanged in effigy at Norwich, and the following day at New London, where even the children were made to say "there hangs a traitor, an enemy to his country."[2] The hangings in effigy were repeated in other

---

[1] Gipson, *Jared Ingersoll*, pp. 157 ff., 327.
[2] *Ibid.*, pp. 168 f.

towns and the excitement increased, fanned as usual by the incendiary press and harangues by mob orators. At Lebanon, where Jonathan Trumbull lived, effigies of Ingersoll and the devil were tried together, condemned and executed. At Lyme another mock trial was held, Ingersoll being accused in extraordinarily violent language of having conspired with the devil to murder his brethren and his mother, "Americana." He was condemned to be whipped and hung on a gallows fifty feet high, which sentence was executed upon the effigy.[1] All of this crude propaganda, carried out apparently by the Sons of Liberty, was calculated to arouse the worst passions of ignorant people. Soon a mob gathered about Ingersoll's house in New Haven, threatening to tear it down unless he resigned his office. Ingersoll, who had given a bond of £3,000 for the performance of his duties, could not do so until the colonial government had taken some action. Governor Fitch, who had irritated the people by delaying to call the legislature together, now issued a call to meet at Hartford on September 19th. Although Ingersoll had again several times been threatened, he had stood his ground, and the more law-abiding citizens in New Haven had themselves become alarmed by the actions of the men in the eastern section of the colony, where it was said armed bands were gathering to march on the town. The collector left, however, in company with the governor to attend the session at Hartford. Near Meriden they were met by a crowd of Sons of Liberty who declared their intention of marching on New Haven. When ordered to disperse by the governor, they announced that they represented the people who "did not intend to take directions from anybody," and that large bands from the east were moving toward the town with eight days' rations. In an attempt to head these off Ingersoll wrote that he would resign if the people wished it and would meet them at Hartford.[2] On his way, however, he was intercepted by some of the easterners, captured and finally, in peril of his life, forced to resign his office. Meanwhile, the General Assembly heard of the plight he was in at Wethersfield but felt themselves powerless to oppose the mob,

[1] Gipson, *Jared Ingersoll*, pp. 170 f.
[2] *Ibid.*, pp. 178 f.

which numbered about a thousand men. The object of the rioters accomplished, however, no further violence was offered, and they escorted Ingersoll to Hartford, he riding in advance on a white nag, which put him in mind, as he said, of the passage in Revelation describing "Death on a pale horse and Hell following him."[1] Arrived at the capitol, they marched around the State House, where the legislature was sitting, and finally made off to the east again.

The governor, who had made enemies of the eastern men in his stand against colonial expansion in the Susquehanna matter, and who was in general a conservative, urged the assembly unsuccessfully to prosecute the rioters. This action and his taking, at the last moment allowed him under law, the oath to enforce the Stamp Act, ended his political career. In the election about one-half the members of the assembly were also replaced by new and more radical men. Freedom of action on the part of elected officials or of speech by private citizens was now largely disallowed by self-appointed guardians of the people. At a meeting at New London resolutions were passed stating that "every officer neglecting the exercise of his office may justly expect the resentment of the People, and those who proceed may depend upon their protection." Ingersoll, some of whose letters to England had been published in a purposely garbled form to inflame feeling against him, was forbidden by the Sons of Liberty at Pomfret to write anything whatever regarding governmental questions under penalty of realizing "all the Horrors of falling a defenceless Prey into the Hands of a free and enraged Populace."[2]

Although all the Connecticut officials were elected by the people themselves, the real government from now on passed into the hands of the Sons of Liberty and was carried on by them in extra-legal and revolutionary meetings. Like the conservatives at Boston, Roger Sherman, who had supported the movement at first, soon became alarmed at "the practice of great numbers of People assembling and assuming a kind of legislative authority," and wrote that it would "tend to weaken

---

[1] Gipson, *Jared Ingersoll*, p. 186.
[2] *Ibid.*, pp. 204, 206.

the authority of government and . . . to such disorders as will not be easily suppressed or reformed." [1] The radical sentiment at this time was almost wholly confined to the eastern part of the colony, and the assumption of power by the committees of the Sons of Liberty, who were in correspondence with similar committees in other colonies, who met and passed resolutions and who overawed the authorities, was nothing less than a revolution by the lower unenfranchised minority of one section. The people of the colony as a whole were undoubtedly strongly opposed to the Stamp Tax, but as the officials comprising the entire machinery of government, from the governor and legislature down, were elected annually, there would seem to have been no reason why unconstitutional methods should have been resorted to except for the desire of the extreme radical minority to secure control to themselves by threats of force — a movement quite independent of the quarrel with England. As the "Libertines" and "Sons of License," as the Liberty Boys were called by their enemies, were thus overawing the colonial government, the conservatives became alarmed at their rapidly increasing numbers. A few months after the events here touched upon, they were said to number ten thousand in this little colony alone, well armed and ready to act, under the command of Colonel Israel Putnam. [2] We must pass over any discussion of other lawless acts of that summer, all tending to show the breakdown of constituted authority even in conservative Connecticut, and pass to consider the case of Rhode Island where we find the same symptoms of mob rule.

It seems unquestionable that in that colony smuggling was carried on to a very considerable degree, not merely the semi-respectable smuggling of molasses, but what was even then considered as smuggling without excuse by the honest merchants of other colonies, and which we have already found to have resulted in complaints by the merchants of Boston and elsewhere of the illicit interference with fair trade by the Rhode Islanders. It was natural, therefore, that there should at all times be a large lawless element in the colony, and that feeling

[1] Cited by Gipson, *Jared Ingersoll*, p. 207.
[2] *Montresor Journals, New York Historical Society, Coll.*, (1881), p. 355.

against the English revenue officers should be particularly bitter. In June 1764, an attempt by a customs officer to seize a cargo of sugar clandestinely landed up a creek had resulted in conflict between a mob and the officers of the little English armed vessels, the *St. John* and the *Squirrel*. Although this was a case of ordinary smuggling and the mob had even seized the battery at Newport and opened fire on the ships, the colonial government did nothing to uphold authority.[1]

The question of impressment which was always making trouble in the colonies, as indeed, in England itself, was particularly acute in Rhode Island where the main business was shipping, and the people were in a state of constant, and frequently just, irritation against the English officers. Just a year after the affair of the *St. John*, in June 1765, a particularly "hot press" was instituted by Captain Antrobus of *H.M.S. Maidstone*, against which the governor protested vehemently.[2] An account in a letter from Newport brings clearly before us the evils of the system. For four or five weeks, it says, the officers "have visited every Vessel entering the Harbour, our Wood Boats, and the very smallest Coasters not excepted. . . . We already feel the Effects; Seamen's Wages advanced nearly one Dollar and a half per Month; our Wood Wharve almost clear of Wood, the coasters from the neighboring Governments shunning our Port, to escape the hottest Press ever known in this Town; and if a speedy Stop does not take Place, the lamentable Condition of the poorer part of the Inhabitants the approaching Winter will be truly affecting, as in May, June, July and August the Town is mostly supplied with Wood."[3] Finally a mob of some five hundred, said to have been mostly boys and negroes, gathered, and captured one of the *Maidstone's* boats and having hauled it to the center of the town, burnt it. Although the leaders were known, no action was taken against them by the colonial authorities.

The excitement over the Stamp Act at this time was bound to have its effect where the atmosphere was already so highly

[1] *R. I. Col. Records*, vol. VI, pp. 427 ff.; *Acts Privy Council*, vol. IV, pp. 690 ff.
[2] *R. I. Col. Records*, vol. VI, pp. 444 ff.
[3] *Boston Gazette*, June 17, 1765.

charged, and in August a large number of people in Newport formed a procession carrying effigies — with halters around their necks — of Augustus Johnston, the stamp distributor, and of Dr. Thomas Moffat and Martin Howard. The latter two had no official positions but had made themselves obnoxious to the radicals by their writings on the question of the tax and of colonial relations to England. The effigies were hung on a gallows, and the following day a mob proceeded to the houses of the three men. Howard's was attacked first, plundered of everything it contained and almost completely destroyed. Moffat's fared little better, but at Johnston's, although the furniture was destroyed, the mob growing weary, perhaps, spared the building itself. Several days before, Johnston had been forced to resign his office and made to say that he would not execute it against "the will of our Sovereign Lord the People." [1] Howard and Moffat, whose only crime had been in stating their views, took refuge on an English vessel in the harbor and escaped to England. Although the damage claimed amounted to over £2,700, the governor wrote to the English government that it was merely "some little injury" to the property, and although a pretense was made of placing the ring-leader in custody, no further action was taken against the well-known individuals who had led the riot.[2] The issue in the cases of Moffat and Howard had nothing to do with England and was purely one concerning the right of colonial free speech and the ability of the colonial government to protect its citizens. The question, as in Boston, New Haven and elsewhere, was whether citizens expressing unpopular opinions were to be liable to have their houses burned over their heads, their property plundered and their lives endangered, without protection and without recourse. It was no wonder that conservatives began to fear the "people" and sound patriots like Sherman to dread the overturn of all authority in the mere effort to get rid of a tax.

While the forces of disorder had thus been gathering strength throughout New England during the summer, and the power

[1] S. G. Arnold, *History of Rhode Island*, (New York, 1860), vol. II, p. 258.
[2] *R. I. Col. Records*, vol. VI, pp. 483, 514, 590; *Cal. Home Office Papers, Geo. III*, vol. I, pp. 609 *ff.*

of authority rapidly slipping from the hands of the authorities, preparations for the more lawful method of protest had been going forward in the appointing and instructing of delegates to the congress called for October.[1] On the 7th of that month, twenty-seven delegates, representing the nine colonies of Massachusetts, Rhode Island, Connecticut, New York, New Jersey, Pennsylvania, Delaware, Maryland and South Carolina met at New York.[2] The representatives from the other colonies were abler men, for the most part, than those sent from New England, and although Ruggles of Boston was elected to the innocuous office of president, none of the chairmanships of committees went to the New Englanders. Of the New England group Otis was the most striking, but owing to his erratic behavior, his lack of manners and his frequently coarse language, he was better fitted to shine as the leader of the Boston populace than in the higher atmosphere of an inter-colonial conference. Nowhere had the excitement been more intense than in the cosmopolitan commercial town on the Hudson, and it was in no calm environment that the delegates met for their deliberations. Articles in the *New York Gazette* had recently appeared advocating complete independence of England, showing a sentiment that was not as yet felt, or at least avowed, in most of the colonies.[3] Influenced by the rising tide of disorder and the talk of the extreme radicals, it is not surprising that the Court Party in England did not look upon the gathering of delegates with friendly eyes, and considered the congress "a dangerous federal union."[4]

It did, in fact, mark an important step in the formation of a new nation. By the imposition of a direct internal tax, levied upon all the colonies, the mother country at one stroke had done

---

[1] The term *congress* was by no means new in the colonies, but as there has been some discussion as to the first suggestion of its use as applied to this gathering of colonial delegates, it may be of interest to note that in the Library of Congress copy of Otis's *Rights of the British Colonies*, which was owned by Sam Adams, the word *congress* used in another connection, is underlined [p. 14] apparently by Adams.

[2] H. Niles, *Principles and Acts of the Revolution*, (Baltimore, 1822), p. 451.

[3] Dawson, *Sons of Liberty*, pp. 77 f. Some months later the *Boston Gazette* warned English statesmen who were talking of the desire of the colonists for independence to see to it that "this string be no more sawed, lest it be cut asunder in good earnest." Jan. 27, 1766.

[4] Albermarle, *Memoirs of the Marquis of Rockingham*, (London, 1852), vol. I, p. 829.

more to foster a spirit of union born of hostility than the French had done in a century and a half. It is true, and it is a fact that should always be borne in mind, that at no time, with the possible exception of this, were more than one-half to two-thirds of the Americans in favor of extreme measures against the home country. As John Adams pointed out, even the last Whig and Tory contest in Boston in 1775 was decided only by five to two.[1] Nevertheless, England had now brought about union of sentiment to an extent that nothing short of an act weighing upon all the colonies alike could have done.

The gathering at New York represented a different order of political event from the burnings in effigy and mob outrages. An assemblage made up of representatives from nine governments, and approved by the people of four other colonies,[2] and including in its membership such men as Otis of Massachusetts, Philip Livingstone of New York, John Dickinson of Pennsylvania, Thomas McKean and Caesar Rodney of Delaware, and John Rutledge and Christopher Gadsden of South Carolina, was a portent which should not have failed to impress any imperial government neither wholly ignorant nor wholly reckless.

As a result of their fortnight's deliberations, the congress put forth four state papers — a declaration of "the rights and grievances of the colonists," and three separate petitions to the king, to the House of Lords and to the Commons.[3] In the declaration, the colonists held that they were entitled to all the rights of Englishmen, and that among them were those of not being taxed without being represented and of trial by jury. They denied that they were represented in Parliament or that they ever could be. The late Acts, they claimed, subverted their rights and liberties, and, moreover, were sure to be commercially detrimental to England. With an indirect reference to the rejection of their petitions by Parliament they reaffirmed their

---

[1] *Works*, vol. X, pp. 61, 63.

[2] Owing to local circumstances Virginia, New Hampshire, North Carolina and Georgia had not been able to send delegates, but the assemblies had written approving the action of the congress. Niles, *Principles and Acts*, p. 451.

[3] The texts are in Niles's *Principles and Acts*, pp. 457 *ff.*; Hutchinson, *History*, vol. III, pp. 479 *ff.*; R. I. Col. Records, vol. VI, pp. 465 *ff.* and elsewhere.

right to be heard by the king or either house. In the memorial to the Commons they admitted the right of Parliament to make regulations for trade but claimed a distinction between that and taxation. It will be noted that these able and admirably drawn papers mark a distinct advance in the controversy, due to Gadsden. No reference is made to the charters, so dear to the heart of the New Englanders, but the claim to rights was based solely upon being Englishmen. It was only when that position too was shown to be untenable that the colonists later generally came to base them solely upon their rights as men. After having recommended union to the colonies and the appointment of special agents to present their grievances in England, the congress adjourned on the 24th. The president, Timothy Ruggles, refused to endorse its action and was censured by the Massachusetts assembly.

Five days later, before Otis's return, that assembly adopted a series of resolves, drawn by Sam Adams, which marked another forward step, although both charters and Acts of Parliament were named as foundations for the rights of the colonists. Adams, however, somewhat in advance of colonial thought in general, asserted that the essential rights of the British constitution "are founded in the law of God and nature, and are the common rights of mankind" wherefore "the inhabitants of this Province are unalienably entitled to those essential rights in common with all men : and that no law of society can, consistent with the law of God and nature, divest them of those rights." [1] Adams at this time owned without reserve in private conversation that his aim was independence, according to Hutchinson, who thought that the "Great advance" made at that session of the legislature was due to his influence.[2] It was these resolves, apparently, to which Peter Oliver alluded when he wrote that they did not meet with universal approval and that one Bostonian, referring to the assemblymen who had passed them, said that "if the D—l don't take them Fellows, we had as good have no D—l at all." [3]

---

[1] Samuel Adams, *Writings*, vol. I, pp. 23 *ff.*; Hutchinson, *History*, vol. III, pp. 476 *ff.*
[2] *History*, vol. III, p. 134.
[3] Origin and Progress of the American Rebellion, *Egerton Mss. 2671*, f. 94.

The Stamp Act was to go in force on November 1st, and on that day in Boston, although the authorities had taken steps to "prevent any Pageantry" for fear of a tumult, the church bells were tolled, the flags on all ships half-masted and effigies of Grenville and Huske were hung on the Liberty Tree, to be carted through the town later and cut to pieces. Similar scenes were enacted throughout New England.[1] Although the Act was in force and no will could be probated, no deed drawn, no ship cleared from the harbors, in fact almost no business transacted legally without stamps, there were neither stamps nor distributors, the former not having been allowed to enter the colonies, and the latter having all resigned.[2] The stamps for Massachusetts were in the castle in the harbor, those for Connecticut at the fort in New York. It was evident that nothing but armed force could put the act in execution. The movements of economy and non-importation had been broadened and both were legitimate weapons in the hands of the colonists, but now a new question arose. Should they adopt a similar method with the stamps and merely avoid using them by suspending all business dealings requiring them, or defy the law and carry on business without them?

In Massachusetts, Governor Bernard, who was by no means the man for the crisis and much of whose conduct from now on was most injudicious, had prorogued the legislature after an unfortunate speech to which the assembly had replied with considerable ill-feeling.[3] A writer in the *Gazette*, who assumed the *nom de plume* of Humphrey Ploughjogger and a country idiom, wrote that "I can't sleep a nights, one wink hardly of late, I hear so much talk about the stamp act and the governor's speech, that it seems as if 't would make me crazy."[4] For five or six weeks no business requiring stamps was transacted in the colony, and the inconvenience and loss were very great. Several vessels arriving from England brought news of the

---

[1] *Boston Gazette*, Nov. 4, 1765; Nov. 11, 1765; Hutchinson, *History*, vol. III, pp. 174 f.; Bernard to Pownall, Nov. 1, 1765, *C.O. 5 No. 43*. Huske was believed to have suggested the act to Grenville.

[2] There had been less disturbance in New Hampshire, but the distributor there had also been obliged to resign in September.

[3] Texts in Hutchinson, *History*, vol. III, pp. 467 ff

[4] *Boston Gazette*, Oct. 14, 1765.

probable repeal of the Act, but this merely made the colonists more earnest in their opposition.

Although Oliver had resigned his office as distributor, he was forced by the Sons of Liberty, with much indignity, to appear at the Liberty Tree, on December 17th, and in the presence of two thousand people to declare on oath that he would never take any measures to enforce the act.[1] The shoemaker, Mackintosh, the leader of the earlier rioters, stood at his right hand; no grand jury would consider the proceedings unlawful, and apparently they were instigated by the popular leaders. One of the remarkable features of the day was that the militia having refused to muster at the governor's order, Mackintosh, who claimed to have one hundred and fifty trained men, took charge of the town and paraded the streets arm in arm with Colonel Brattle, a member of Council, although known as the leader of the mob in various riots, including the destruction of the lieutenant-governor's house.[2] The following day at town-meeting the citizens prepared a memorial to the governor stating that no stamps could be procured, and praying that the courts might reopen and all business go on as before, and that the citizens might be heard by counsel. The timid Council, of which Hutchinson was president, advised the governor that the decision be left to the judges of each court to determine for themselves, which was voted "not satisfactory" by the town. The customs officers soon gave way, granting clearances without stamps, and the judges of some of the inferior courts consented to do without them. Hutchinson, who was chief justice, could not bring himself to take the illegal step, and resigned his office.[3] As soon as the assembly met again, they sent a message to Bernard stating peremptorily that the courts "must open immediately." The Council non-concurred in the action of the assembly, and Hutchinson as president incurred further unpopularity. The judges, however, opened court of their own volition before the news arrived of the repeal of the Act.

Similar struggles, although varying in details, went on in the

---

[1] Hutchinson, *History*, vol. III, pp. 139 *ff.*; *Boston Gazette*, Dec. 23, 1765.
[2] Bernard to Pownall, Nov. 5, 1765, *C.O. 5 No. 43.*
[3] Hutchinson, *History*, vol. III, pp. 141 *ff.*; *Mass. State Papers*, pp. 67 *f.*

other colonies. In Connecticut, although the customs houses soon opened, the conservatives in the main won a victory over the Sons of Liberty as to the courts, not from any desire to enforce the Act but in order to keep the opposition within legal limits. A great struggle between the two groups, equally opposed to the Act but differing as to methods, occurred in the town-meeting at New Haven in February. The conservatives, among other arguments, pointed out that the illegal opening of the courts would be inconsistent with the petitions presented by the congress; that the titles to real estate would be clouded; and that debtors resisting execution would "squirm in every possible method" and plead the illegality of papers without stamps.[1] Although the radicals outvoted the conservatives two hundred and twenty-six to forty-eight, the courts refused to open.

The general opposition and intense feeling against the Act naturally gave a great impetus to the economy and non-importation policies adopted the year before in opposition to the Sugar Act. "I don't believe," wrote "Ploughjogger" in the *Boston Gazette*, that "our young folks would leve to dance together at husking frolics and to kiss one another a bit the less, if they wore woolen shirts and shifts of their own making, than they do now in their fine ones. I do say, I won't buy one shilling worth of anything that comes from old England till the stamp act is appeal'd" [sic].[2] However this may have been, the young Tory blades had to do without their kisses and frolics in Providence, where the girls solemnly agreed to permit no addresses from any youth who favored the tax. There was less time for frolicking, however, for the maids and matrons throughout all New England, in order to increase the supply of home-spun, took to spinning from sunrise to dark, and the whirr of wheels must almost have drowned the constant talk and resolves of the men. Following the lead of the merchants of New York and Philadelphia, two hundred and fifty in Boston, in December, signed a formal agreement to import no articles, with some necessary exceptions, from England until the Stamp

---

[1] Gipson, *Jared Ingersoll*, pp. 214 f.
[2] *Boston Gazette*, Oct. 14, 1765.

Act was repealed. Although the idea had not originated in New England, and Boston was the last of the great ports to act, many of the smaller ones soon fell into line.[1]

Not only had the English government succeeded in uniting the North American colonies for the first time by their fatal experiment, but they had also brought the conflicting interests of the New Englanders and the West Indians into an unexpected harmony, for the island planters liked being taxed no more than did their continental neighbors. At Antigua a mob seized and burned the tax stamps, as did also the people of Nevis and St. Christophers, instigated, it is said, by the crews of some New England vessels.[2] The Barbadians, however, although they claimed their "spirit had flamed as high as did the North Americans" showed a caution that refused to be moved even by threats of starvation sent them from the continent. To urgent appeals that they defend their natural rights they replied with some humor that the continental colonists had not reflected on the Barbadians' relation to the British navy, and "what a wretched Figure Arguments, depending upon the Rights of Nature only, would have made in such a well-cleaned and little Spot as this, where we have no Woods, no Back-Settlements, to retreat to, in Case those Arguments should not be able to stand their Ground against such a Force of Rhetoric as might be brought to combat them in the open Field."[3] Nevertheless, instead of the long opposition to all their interests which the New Englanders had always encountered in Parliament from the powerful West India group, that group, now touched themselves in their most tender spot, could be counted upon to join in the effort for repeal, an effort which engaged not only all the strength of the colonists throughout the new world, but almost all the economic interests of the empire. The colossal blunder was soon, in part, to be retrieved, but its effects could not be

---

[1] Schlesinger, *Colonial Merchants*, pp. 78 ff.; Andrews, "Boston Merchants," pp. 198 ff.

[2] V. L. Oliver, *History of the Island of Antigua*, (London, 1894), vol. I, p. cxx; *Hist. Mss. Comm. 11th Rept. App.*, Pt. V, p. 332; Tucket to Gov. Thomas, Dec. 21, 1765, *C.O. 5 No. 218*; R. H. Schomburgk, *History of Barbadoes*, (London, 1848), p. 331; Conway to Gov. Thomas, Mar. 13, 1766, "H. S. Conway, Letters to America 1765-6," Mss. in Library of Congress.

[3] *Letter to a North American on Occasion of the Address to the Committee of Correspondence in Barbadoes*, (Barbadoes, 1766), p. 27.

undone. It was an ominous sign that amidst the growing social and political unrest, the iron-willed Sam Adams, already aiming at independence, should write to Gadsden that he considered the Stamp Act a blessing in disguise, in that it had united the colonies, and that he felt "a Disposition to hint many things more." [1]

[1] *Works*, vol. I, pp. 108 *ff.*

CHAPTER XV

DARKENING SKIES

Repeal of the Stamp Act — Declaratory Act — Constitutional Principles in the Empire — Attitude of Colonial Radicals — Townshend Acts — Violent Resistance in Boston — Massachusetts Provincial Congress — Religious Agitation — Non-Importation Movement — Approach of Revolution

WHILE the events described in the last chapter had been transpiring in America, the conflicting political forces and factions in England had caused the overthrow of the ministry and the formation of a new one under the lead of the young Marquis of Rockingham.[1] The chief minister had good intentions and was a friend to the aspirations of the colonists, but he lacked experience, was of mediocre ability and more at home on the turf than in politics.[2] The dignified Conway was made Secretary of State to deal with the colonies, but although he also was favorably inclined toward them, he was of so irresolute a character that it was said if there were two doors to a room he was tortured as to which to take. Townshend dubbed the new government a "lutestring ministry fit only for the summer," and the shrewd Lord Chesterfield wrote that it was "a heterogeneous jumble of youth and caducity," and anticipated that it would soon center "in Mr. Pitt and Co." [3] The brief and not unjust description will have to suffice, for it would take us too far afield to attempt to describe the sinuosities of contemporary English politics, dependent as they were upon personalities and factions.

It was this well-intentioned, but for the most part youthful and inexperienced, group of ministers that was called upon to

---

[1] Albermarle, *Rockingham Memoirs*, vol. I, pp. 218 *ff.*
[2] Alvord, *Mississippi Valley*, vol. I, p. 233.
[3] Albermarle, *Rockingham Memoirs*, vol. I, p. 224; *Correspondence of William Pitt*, (London, 1838), vol. II, p. 316 *n.*

deal with the upheaval in America due to the acts of their predecessors. As the protests of America had been economic as well as political, so the question in England, by this time, had become one of threatening trade disaster quite as much as of theoretical sovereignty, and the ministers found powerful allies among the merchants and manufacturers in the effort to retrace the steps of colonial policy. The amount owing to their English correspondents by importers in the continental colonies was said to range all the way from £4,000,000 to £6,000,000, although the total value of all estates in America was also computed to be not much over the latter figure.[1] The non-importation movement and the plea of the Americans that if the Stamp Act remained in force they would be unable to meet their obligations, vastly alarmed the English exporters, not only on account of the loss of current business but still more on account of the enormous outstanding balance due. The cancellation of orders, however, was beginning to result in a serious stagnation of trade, and the numbers of discharged workmen to run into thousands. In January 1766 petitions were flooding Parliament from mercantile houses of London, Bristol, Manchester, Lancaster and twenty or more other trading centers, representing the necessity of a complete and immediate repeal of the Act.[2] A few weeks later an examination of prominent merchants before a Parliamentary committee brought out the facts of the situation in detail, the question even being raised of the possible effect on English trade should the colonies declare their independence.[3]

Severely as the effects of the Act were felt in America, it bore proportionately even more hardly on the West Indian planters.[4] The merchants trading to the islands, therefore, did not long delay in adding their influence to that of the Americans, and at a joint meeting held at the King's Arms Tavern in London they

---

[1] [John Mitchell] *The present State of Great Britain . . . impartially considered,* (London, 1767), pp. 282 f.; *Rhode Island Commerce,* vol. I, p. 140; Beer, *British Colonial Policy,* p. 299 n. The balance due to eight London merchants alone was £956,579. Examination of Merchants before Committee on American Papers, Feb. 11, 1766, *Brit. Mus. Add. Mss. 33030.*

[2] *Parlt. Hist.,* vol. XVI, pp. 135 f.

[3] Examination of Merchants, *cit. supra.*

[4] *Bowdoin-Temple Papers,* p. 50.

not only agreed to urge the repeal of the Stamp Act but also the reduction of the molasses duty to 1*d.* a gallon and certain other commercial changes in favor of the continent.[1] For the first time the islanders realized that their interests were common with those of the Americans, and not only did the relations become cordial, but the English merchants later wrote to Hancock that the West Indians had rendered great assistance in securing the repeal of the Stamp Act, and hoped that the union then begun would continue.[2]

Benjamin Franklin, who happened to be in England, also played his part, and underwent a long examination before the House of Commons. Although some of his answers were distinctly disingenuous and a few rather wide of the truth, his shrewd common sense played amusing havoc with his questioners.[3] He bluntly stated that the colonists would never submit to the Stamp Tax until compelled by force of arms; that it would drain them of all specie with which to make remittances to England; and that there were no English manufactures that they could not make for themselves. He denied that they had ever questioned the authority of Parliament other than as to internal taxation, and thought that they would pay little attention to a formal declaration by Parliament of its right to tax provided that it was not carried into practice.

[1] "At a Meeting of the Committees of the West Indian and North American Merchants at the King's Arms Tavern 10th Mar. 1766,

"Agreed unanimously that such Points as are adjusted at this meeting shall have the general concurrence & assistance of the whole Trade on both sides to carry them into Execution.

"Agreed that the Duty on the foreign Molasses imported into North America be reduced to one penny Sterling per Gallon and that every possible method be adopted to enforce the full and just collection of that Duty.

"Agreed that the Importation of foreign Rum to North America be prohibited. . . .

"Agreed that the consumption of foreign Sugars be permitted in North America on payment of a Duty of 5 shillings pr hundred weight.

"Agreed that all Sugars imported into Great Britain from North America be deemed foreign, and Warehoused. . . .

"Duty on Wines to be altered." Agreement of West India and North American Merchants, *Brit. Mus. Add. Mss. 8133* C. Also *ibid., 33030.*

[2] Letter of 30 merchants to John Hancock, June 13, printed in *Boston Gazette*, Sept. 8, 1766.

[3] The examination is given in full in *Parlt. Hist.*, vol. XVI, pp. 137 *ff.*; Franklin, *Works*, ed. Bigelow, vol. III, pp. 407 *ff.*; and elsewhere. His statement that the colonies had not been attacked at all in the late war until after Braddock's defeat was not true, and the statement that they had raised 25,000 men was extremely misleading to say the least. *Parlt. Hist.*, vol. XVI, pp. 139, 153 *f.*

Glorious News.

Conftitutional LIBERTY Revives!

NEW-HAVEN, Monday-Morning, May 19, 1766.

Mr. *Jonathan Lowder* brought the following moft agreeable
Intelligence from *Bofton*.

BOSTON, Friday 11 o'Clock, 16th May, 1766.
THIS Inftant arrived here the Brig Harrifon, belonging to John Hancock, Efq; Captain Shubael
Coffin, in 6 Weeks and 2 Days from LONDON, with important News as follows.

From the London Gazette.

Weftminfter, March 18th, 1766.

THIS day His Majefty came to the Houfe of Peers, and being in his royal robes feated
on the Throne with the ufual folemnity, Sir Francis Molineux, Gentleman Ufher of the
Black Rod, was fent with a Meffage from His Majefty to the Houfe of Commons,
commanding their attendance in the Houfe of Peers. The Commons being come thither accordingly, His Majefty was pleafed to give his Royal Affent to An ACT to REPEAL an Act made
in the laft Seffion of Parliament, intitled an Act for granting and applying certain Stamp-Duties
and other Duties in the Britifh Colonies and Plantations in America, towards further defraying the
Expences of defending, protecting and fecuring the fame, and for amending fuch parts of the feveral Acts of Parliament relating to the trade and revenues of the faid Colonies and Plantations,
as direct the Manner of determining and recovering the penalties and forfeitures therein mentioned.
Alfo ten publick bills, and feventeen private ones.
Yefterday there was a meeting of the principal Merchants concerned in the American trade, at
the King's Arms tavern in Cornhill, to confider of an Addrefs to his Majefty on the beneficial Repeal of the late Stamp-Act.
Yefterday morning about eleven o'clock a great number of North-American Merchants went in
their coaches from the King's Arms tavern in Cornhill to the Houfe of Peers, to pay their duty to
his Majefty, and to exprefs their fatisfaction at his figning the Bill for Repealing the Stamp-Act,
there were upwards of fifty coaches in the proceffion..
Laft night the faid gentlemen difpatched an exprefs for Falmouth with fifteen copies of the act,
for repealing the Stamp-Act to be forwarded immediately for New-York.
Orders were given for feveral Merchantmen in the river to proceed to fea immediately on their re-
fpective voyages to North-America, fome of whom have been cleared fince the firft of November laft.
Yefterday meffengers were difpatched to Birmingham, Sheffild, Manchefter, and all the great
manufacturing towns in England, with an account of the final decifion of an auguft affembly relating to the Stamp-Act.

✸✸✸ BOSTON. ✸✸✸

When the King went to the Houfe of Peers to give the Royal Affent, there was fuch a vaft Con-
courfe of People, huzzaing, clapping Hands, &c. that it was feveral Hours before His Majefty
reached the Houfe.
Immediately on His Majefty's Signing the Royal Affent to the Repeal of the Stamp-Act, the
Merchants trading to America, difpatched a Veffel which had been waiting, to put into the firft
Port on the Continent with the Account.
There were the greateft Rejoicings poffible in the City of London, by all Ranks of People, on
the TOTAL Repeal of the Stamp-Act. The Ships in the River difplayed all their Colours, Il-
luminations and Bonfires in many Parts. In fhort, the Rejoicings were as great as ever was known
on any Occafion.
It is faid the Acts of Trade relating to America would be taken under Confideration, and all
Grievances removed. The Friends to America are very powerful, and difpofed to affift us to the
utmoft of their Ability.
It is impoffible to exprefs the Joy the Town is now in, on receiving the above great, glorious
and important News. The Bells in all the Churches were immediately fet a Ringing, and we
hear the Day for a general Rejoicing will be the Beginning of next Week.

Extract of a Letter from New-London, *to* New-Haven, *dated May* 17, 1766.
"I give Joy on the total Repeal of the Stamp-Act. We have the news at New-London Saturday Night 9 o'clock, at 10 the Guns in the Fort are firing on the Joyful occafion ; Drums beating,
&c. I am now with the Gentlemen of the Town on the Occafion."
N. B. *Like Rejoicings now* (Monday Morning) *in New-Haven.*

NEW-HAVEN : Printed by *B. Mecom*, for the Entertainment of the People
in general, and his good Cuftomers in particular.

Mr. Lowder *having rode very hard to bring the above Glorious Tidings, it is not doubted the Sons of*
Liberty will be generous in helping to defray his Expences. 'Tis defired that fuch Donations be left at Mr.
Beers's Tavern.

BROADSIDE CONCERNING THE REPEAL OF THE
STAMP ACT, 1766

In the great debate in the two Houses the arguments dwelt on the two points of legal right and practical expediency.[1] "King, Court, Favorite, Torys, Scotch and the late Administration" were all against the repeal, and the violence of the mobs and radicals, more particularly in the northern colonies, did much to prejudice the cause and make repeal more difficult.[2] Although a great majority favored it on the ground of expediency, only a small minority, including Pitt, disbelieved in the right of taxation, and, indeed, they stood on far more doubtful constitutional ground than did those who maintained it. The repeal finally was carried by a vote of two hundred and seventy-five to one hundred and sixty-one in the Commons and a majority of thirty-four in the Lords.[3] To satisfy the two houses a Declaratory Act was also passed asserting the right of king and Parliament to bind the colonies "in all cases whatsoever" and declaring all the acts of the colonial assemblies to the contrary "utterly null and void."[4] Little attention was paid to this outside Parliament, however, and the repeal was hailed with delight on both sides of the water. In England it was said to have caused more universal rejoicing than any other event, perhaps, that could be remembered, and in Boston Mayhew wrote that he had "never known so quick and general a transition from the depth of sorrow to the height of joy as on this occasion."[5] On the night when the news was received in that town the church bells started ringing at one o'clock and by two in the morning the streets were full of people playing musical instruments, beating drums and firing guns. Somewhat more ominously, the jail was emptied of debtors.[6] The papers had been following the debate closely and Pitt's speech was printed

---

[1] *Parlt. Hist.*, vol. XVI, pp. 161 *ff*. *Cf*. "Debates on the Declaratory Act and the Repeal of the Stamp Act," *American Historical Review*, vol. XVII, pp. 565 *ff*.; H. H. Hodge, "The Repeal of the Stamp Act," *Political Science Quarterly*, vol. XIX, pp. 252 *ff*. J. West's Notes to Newcastle on debate on repeal of the Stamp Act, *Brit. Mus. Add. Mss. 32974* give a vivid sense of the progress of the debate. There is much other material in this same series of Newcastle Papers.

[2] Onslow to Newcastle, Feb. 23, 1766, *Brit. Mus. Add. Mss. 32974;* "Stamp Act Papers," *Maryland Historical Magazine*, vol. VI, p. 290.

[3] 6 Geo. III, c. 11.

[4] 6 Geo. III, c. 12.

[5] *Annual Register*, 1778, p. 46; Mayhew, *The Snare broken*, p. 12.

[6] *Boston Gazette*, May 26, 1766.

in full ending with the famous "I rejoice that the Americans have resisted" in large capital letters.[1] A more serious note was sounded by two communications from the English merchants, the later one signed by fifty-five firms, congratulating the Americans on their success in the repeal but begging them to abstain in future from lawless violence in opposition to Parliamentary Acts, as such greatly hindered desired reforms.[2] Indeed, even such a mild Bostonian pastime as burning the king's favorite in effigy on the Common could scarcely be considered conciliatory.[3]

Although the repeal of the Stamp Act overshadowed all else in the minds of the colonists, it was but a part of the scheme of remedial legislation carried out by Parliament, which followed somewhat closely that laid out by the joint committee of the North American and West Indian merchants. The tariff on molasses was reduced to 1d., the figure that the colonists had agreed was economically fair, and certain other changes were made in duties, all favorable to the Americans. On the other hand, all colonial exports to European ports north of Cape Finisterre had now to be entered at an English port, and as the molasses duty was applied to imports from the English islands as well as foreign, it obviously became a duty for revenue. The grievances which remained, however, and they were not unimportant, were felt only by the merchants and fishermen, and not by the people at large.[4] John Adams probably reflected the general feeling truly when he wrote in his diary six months later that the repeal had "hushed into silence almost every popular clamor," [5] and for the time being the radical agitators were left without a cause. Nevertheless, the sudden piercing of the sun through the storm clouds of the political sky was but a false presage of clearing, and we can now recognize that the atmosphere was much too heavily charged to be permanently clarified

[1] *Boston Gazette*, May 12, 1766.
[2] The two letters were dated Feb. 28 and Mar. 18, 1766, Library of Congress Mss. *Mass. Papers*. The second was printed in the *Boston Gazette* of June 16, 1766. The first is given in *Mass. Hist. Soc., Proceedings*, Ser. II, vol. XI, pp. 446 ff.
[3] *Boston Gazette*, Feb. 24, 1766. Grenville also had been burned in chains in effigy at Portsmouth a few weeks earlier. *Ibid.*, Jan. 13.
[4] Schlesinger, *Colonial Merchants*, pp. 84 ff.
[5] *Works*, vol. II, p. 203.

without a far greater convulsion than had yet occurred. A majority in England may well have been in favor of repealing a particular tax because of its inexpediency; here and there a leader of thought might sympathize with the instinctive wish of Americans to be masters in their own house; politicians in the struggle between the king and the Whig oligarchy might make use of the colonial situation to harass their political opponents; but the fight over the repeal had clearly brought out the inherent difference in view between rulers and ruled in an empire in which the latter were arriving at the point where they were not only self-conscious but conscious of their strength. In regard to taxation, Pitt might admit that the Americans were in open rebellion and rejoice in their resistance, but even he was in favor of asserting uncompromisingly the sovereign power of Parliament to "bind their trade, confine their manufactures, and exercise every power whatsoever except that of taking money out of their pockets without their consent" — a position equally inimical to common sense, to reason and to colonial sentiment.

The Stamp Act in its passage and repeal had been like some great tidal wave that had swept across the Atlantic engulfing all the colonies in a common fate and then receding. It had deposited soil in which new ideas were to grow and had also left much débris in its wake. Among minor matters was the question of compensation for those who had suffered in the riots occurring in many of the colonies.[1] A bill passed Parliament *recommending* that the colonial governments reimburse the sufferers, the "King's Friends" under the lead of Bute having vainly striven to substitute *require* for the gentler word.[2] Although in the circular letter sent to the governors the matter was merely recommended, Bernard in Massachusetts referred

---

[1] The circular letter to the colonial governors conveying the Act of Parliament referring to this matter, [a copy of that which was sent to the New England colonies is given in *R. I. Col. Records*, vol. VI, pp. 497 *f.*] had an additional paragraph added for such colonies as had made no opposition to the Stamp Act. These were Jamaica, Barbadoes, Grenada, Bahamas, the two Floridas, Bermuda, Pennsylvania, Nova Scotia, and Quebec. Circular letter, June 12, 1766, *C.O. 5 No. 66.*

[2] Grafton says the vote went against the ministers. Sir W. R. Anson, *Autobiography of the Duke of Grafton*, (London, 1898), p. 69; "Letters of Denys DeBerdt," *Col. Soc. Mass., Publications*, vol. XIII, pp. 322 *ff.*

Contemporary Cartoon Satirizing the History of the Stamp Act

to it as a requisition and stirred up unnecessary feeling.[1] The conservative patriot elements and many of the common people heartily condemned the mob actions of the ultra radicals, and were in favor of making compensation, but the amounts were large, — the Boston town-meeting admitted the damage there alone mounted to over £4,000, — and there seems to have been a general feeling that the localities in which the people had called the tune should pay the piper.[2] At first, however, the Boston representatives in the General Court were strong enough to prevent the main cost being saddled on that town, where of right it belonged, although not strong enough to have it assumed by the colony as a whole.[3] Finally, the General Court referred the matter back to their constituents, and as a result a provincial bill was passed indemnifying Hutchinson and the others for the bulk of their losses but, at the suggestion of one of the lawyer representatives from the western section, some of whose clients were in jail in connection with the riots, a clause was added granting pardon to all who had participated in the outrages.[4] This clear usurpation of the royal prerogative, entirely beyond the power of the colonial legislature, created a painful impression in England in view of the conciliatory policy adopted there, and gave the enemies of the colonies fresh ammunition with which to carry on their war.[5] The whole episode illustrates admirably how a colonial policy in England dependent upon local political exigencies, carried out through a tactless governor in a colony where the political situation was again complicated by local animosities, could constantly embroil the mother country and colonies, and embitter the relations between them.

The possibilities of friction and misunderstanding were, indeed, becoming unlimited. The average man bases his

[1] *Fitch Papers*, vol. II, p. 399; Hutchinson, *History*, vol. III, p. 159. He had used the word in the preceding November. Bernard to Lords of Trade, Nov. 30, 1765, *Brit. Mus. Add. Mss. 35912.*

[2] *Boston Town Records, Report of Record Commissioners*, vol. XVI, p. 192; Almon, *Prior Documents*, pp. 113 ff.; J. Adams, *Works*, vol. II, pp. 202, 204.

[3] Almon, *Prior Documents*, pp. 106 ff.

[4] Hutchinson, *History*, vol. III, p. 158; *Mass. State Papers*, pp. 82 ff.; *Journals Mass. House of Representatives*, 1766, pp. 124 f., 134 f., 142 ff., 153 ff., 159, 191 f., 202 ff., 209 ff.

[5] *Trumbull Papers* [*Mass. Hist. Soc., Coll.*, Ser. V, vol. IX] pp. 225 f., 237. The act was properly disallowed in England, but meanwhile the money had been paid. Hutchinson, *History*, vol. III, p. 160.

opinions upon a modicum of reasoning and a huge mass of assumptions, which latter he unconsciously derives from his environment and which he as little thinks of calling in question as the laws of nature. When the mass of assumption is much the same for two individuals or groups, they can argue their differences, but when it is not they are, without realizing it, speaking different languages and there is little chance of a sympathetic understanding. A century and a half of contrasted environments and diverging lines of development had largely brought about such a condition for Englishmen on the two sides of the water. Colonies were at best an anomaly in the British Constitution, and owing to their different mental backgrounds the Englishmen at home were pulling in an entirely different direction from those overseas in the effort to stretch that Constitution to cover new needs. It is not strange that it was rent in their hands, for a wholly new situation had in truth arisen which was unprovided for. Men, however, are always loath to admit that such can be the case. Rather do they ever pour the new wine into old bottles, clothe the new ideas in faded words, and twist worn-out creeds to breaking. They seem to crave the "protective coloration" of familiar phrases. Like the early navigators who feared to fall over the rim of the unpassed horizon, they fear to set out upon an uncharted sea of life. Perhaps with our little knowledge and vast capacity for going wrong it is as well that we do thus linger at old landmarks and advance but tremblingly to meet the onslaught of the unfamiliar.

The controversy had set the colonists to work to formulate a constitutional theory that should at once be plausible in England and satisfactory in America. Here and there the knot was keenly cut and independence openly proclaimed as a hope or a threat, but as yet these voices found faint echo from the people. What the average man dimly craved was to be left alone to handle his own affairs in his own way. He was quite willing to proclaim a lip allegiance to the king, and vaguely realized that as the acts of his colonial legislature could not be valid beyond the limits of his own colony, a general superintending power must be left somewhere in the English government.[1] Whenever

---

[1] Hutchinson, *History*, vol. III, p. 172.

this was exercised so as to be burdensome, however, he felt it to be a grievance. In spite of the Declaratory Act, the obvious fact as it seemed to him was that England had selfishly tried to tax him, and, under pressure, had renounced the effort. He had won this right to exemption from internal taxation on the ground that he was not represented, but the crowd dislikes subtle distinctions and the difference, useful at first for argument, between external and internal taxation could not be maintained. In popular discussion, therefore, the area claimed for the freedom of a self-determining individualism slowly crept from the land out over the sea.[1] Moreover, it began to include all the colonists' activities at home. If, as seemed to have been admitted in practice, Parliament did not have the right to tax the farmer or mechanic because he was unrepresented, why did it have the right to interfere with their business in any way? "Whose natural right is infringed by the erection of a North American wind-mill, or the occupation of a water-mill on a man's own land?", wrote an anonymous citizen in the *Boston Gazette*. "A colonist cannot make a button, a horse-shoe nor a hob-nail, but some sooty iron-monger or respectable button-maker of Britain shall bawl and squawl that his honor's worship is most egregiously maltreated, injured, cheated and robb'd by the rascally North American republicans. . . . Do your honors really believe that North-America was created for the sole emolument of your very respectable dinnerizing corporations? Is this country the property of the merchant tailors and woolen drapers? Have they or any other high born British mechanic, an indefeazible right to the agonies, toils, and bloody sweat of the inhabitants of this land and the profits and produce of all their labors?"[2] This was increasingly the language of the street corner and the tavern, which is ever nearer akin to action than the more dignified phrasing of state papers. But for a while there was a lull in the storm. Merchants in the several colonies complained of minor hardships in the transaction of business, and in particular of a stupid misconstruing of his instructions by the governor of Newfoundland which seriously hampered the

---

[1] *Barrington-Bernard Correspondence*, p. 135.
[2] *Boston Gazette*, Apl. 29, 1765.

fisheries. Nevertheless, political feeling though still over-heated was simmering down in the two charter colonies where there was no royal governor, and in New Hampshire Wentworth was getting on well with the people. In Boston, Bernard, partly from his own tactlessness and lack of political insight and partly from the over-wrought liberty nerve of the assembly, was constantly embroiled with that body. It made little difference whether it was his own foolish exercise of the veto power over the election of popular councilors, or the hypercritical censoriousness of the assemblymen over his incurring unexpected expense for the care of royal troops passing through the port.[1] Bernard, though he had fared well in his earlier post in New Jersey, and might have done valuable work under certain conditions, was wholly unfitted to deal with the crisis in Boston and should have been recalled. The situation was not unrealized in England, and Shelburne's secretary, in a report to his chief, wrote that the governor valued "himself more upon a good argument than a wise measure," and that having been foiled in his effort to "chop logic with the General Assembly" he had "retired to his closet to vent his chagrin in womanish complaints."[2] But if the governor had no tact, he had ten children, and friends at home, and had to be taken care of until another source of income more congenial for himself and less dangerous for the empire could be found for him.

While public opinion was thus fermenting in America, another ministerial upheaval had occurred in England, and Chesterfield's prediction that affairs would soon be in the hands of "Mr. Pitt and Co." had come to pass. The American crisis was not the only one. The laboring class was suffering severely and there were serious riots and social and political discontent. The French, as usual, had made a rapid recovery from defeat, and a French-Spanish Bourbon alliance was assuming threatening shape. When Pitt undertook the task of dealing with the critical situation in July 1766, it was no longer as the "Great Commoner" but as the Earl of Chatham with a seat in the Lords.

---

[1] Cf. *Mass. State Papers*, pp. 56 *ff.*; Hutchinson, *History*, vol. III, pp. 149 *ff.*, 169 *ff.*; *Prior Documents*, pp. 126 *ff.*
[2] Fitzmaurice, *Life of Shelburne*, vol. II, pp. 53 *f.*

For the moment, his acceptance of the title had ruined his popularity and the French minister, Choiseul, enormously pleased, compared him to Samson shorn of his hair. In forming his ministry, Chatham had hoped by drawing men from various parties to abolish faction and unite all in forwarding his policy. Shelburne became Secretary of State for the Southern Department, which included the colonies, and the brilliant but unstable Charles Townshend Chancellor of the Exchequer in spite of Chatham's foreboding. It is impossible to say what might have been accomplished had the new earl been able himself to remain at the head of affairs. Scarcely had the new ministry got in the saddle when the illness that was to wreck his health and the hopes of the country began to show itself, and during the fatal months till his resignation in the autumn of 1768 he was inaccessible in his house in the country, and the ill-assorted members of his weak ministry, like planets released from the force of gravitation, pursued diverging or conflicting courses, while the blazing meteor, Townshend, scattered destruction broadcast until his sudden death in September 1767.

The financial situation was alarming. Not only was the new war debt colossal, but a series of bad harvests had so raised the price of corn that the Connecticut agent wrote from London that "the distress of the poor for want of bread is very terrible and affecting." [1] The American expenses were heavy, and the repeal of the Stamp Act had left the question of an American revenue still in the air. The opposition to colonial taxation felt by Chatham, Shelburne and by Conway who was also in the ministry, was well known. The House of Commons was startled, therefore, when in answer to a question of Grenville on the army estimates, Townshend suddenly announced that although he considered the difference between internal and external taxation of the colonies to be ridiculous, he would pledge himself to find an adequate revenue by a mode of taxation to which the colonies could not logically object. So complete was the disruption of even the loose cabinet system of the day that Shelburne, in alarm, at once wrote to Chatham that he could not imagine what Townshend meant to do, though his own administrative

[1] *Trumbull Papers*, p. 250.

province included the very colonies that the Chancellor was planning to tax.[1] The House was wild with delight, and for the next few months both the Chancellor and the Commons may fairly be said to have "run amuck" in their handling of the American problem. Shelburne's wise and conciliatory plans were tossed aside. Chatham's policy of an exhaustive investigation into the grievances was ignored. Instead, in May, to punish New York for its opposition to the enforcement of the Mutiny Act which had been extended to America, the legislature of that colony was forbidden to meet until the Act had been complied with. Another Act created a Board of Customs Commissioners to have charge of the entire customs service in America.[2] This, an English observer thought, would prove "a very wise and beneficial Measure" provided that on their arrival in the colonies the commissioners should "escape hanging."[3] The following month, the English land tax having been reduced twenty-five per cent, the famous Townshend Acts were passed levying an import duty in the colonies on glass, lead, tea, painters' colors and paper.[4] Still more ominously, the act recited that the revenue was to go not only to the military establishment but to "defraying the charge of the administration of justice, and the support of civil government in such provinces where it shall be found necessary." It was "a fatal and irretrievable blunder."[5] The colonists were told they were fools to think that duties for revenue were not taxes, and then new duties were laid upon them. In view of what had gone before, there could be but one answer to this criminal folly.

The colonies, moreover, were still in the midst of the post-war depression of business, much emphasized by the extreme scarcity of metal currency with which to pay both customs dues and the adverse balance with England. This was a condition common to all the colonies and the Newport merchant, Aaron Lopez, received word even from his correspondent in Jamaica that

[1] Fitzmaurice, *Life of Shelburne*, vol. II, p. 38.
[2] 7 Geo. III, c. 41.
[3] Letter from Edward Sedgwick to Edward Weston, *G. W. Digby Mss., Hist. Mss. Comm. Rept.*, p. 406.
[4] 7 Geo. III, c. 46.
[5] D. A. Winstanley, *Lord Chatham and the Whig Opposition*, (Cambridge University Press, 1912), pp. 144*f*.

THE HONORABLE CHARLES TOWNSHEND, CHANCELLOR OF THE
EXCHEQUER
From a portrait by Sir Joshua Reynolds

"there is not money enough in this parish for the Planters to bribe the Marshalls."[1] The Act passed by Parliament in 1764 prohibiting the issue of paper money as legal tender had greatly hampered colonial trade and, in spite of petitions for relief in the form of some remedial legislation, no action had been taken.[2] The extremely long credits carried — usually a year between New England importers and the English merchants, and running sometimes to seven years in the West Indies[3] — added to a very considerable over-expansion of speculative business, increased the American difficulties. The embarrassments and failures noted in the previous chapter continued, and in 1766 the locally important firm of Trumbull, Fitch and Trumbull went down with a heavy crash in Connecticut. Farms were mortgaged; tradesmen could not collect their accounts; merchants could not tell whether they were solvent or not. These facts not only should have been but were known in England, and it is against this dark background of discontent and deep anxiety that we must watch the unbalanced Chancellor of the Exchequer play his light-hearted antics, gathering pennies and disrupting an empire.

Steps were immediately taken to reform the customs service, and the new commissioners were located at Boston. The number of officials all along the coast were greatly increased and much activity was displayed. The character of the smuggling trade had changed to a considerable extent owing to the new laws. The reduction of the molasses duty to 1*d.* had made it much less profitable to attempt to run contraband cargoes of that article, and until the precarious condition of the East India Company in 1769 caused that company to advance the

---

[1] *Rhode Island Commerce*, vol. I, p. 276.

[2] Shelburne passed on a number of such petitions to the Board of Trade in 1767 in which the colonists stated that it was "impossible for them to make remittances to their creditors in England, to extend their trade, or even to pay their internal debts." Shelburne to Lords of Trade, Feb. 13, 1767, *C.O. 5 No. 223. Cf.* Andrews, "Boston Merchants," pp. 184 *ff.*

[3] "From the nature of that trade [North American] it is tedious the credit is 12 months on an average — this complaint has been ever since I can remember." Examination of Merchants, *Brit. Mus. Add. Mss. 33030, cit. supra.* "Some few of the Northern Colonies are the most tedious. Their interest is larger — some pay within the twelve month. I should not think myself ill paid if paid within 18 months with six months interest." *Ibid.,* Cf. *Rhode Island Commerce,* vol. I, p. 174.

price of tea in England, the new fiscal arrangement made its importation cheaper from that country than from Holland. The duties on various manufactured goods tended to increase their production in the colonies rather than their import from foreign countries, and, indeed, in that respect, the Townshend Acts were regarded even by some patriotic Americans as a blessing in disguise.[1] The main smuggling traffic, therefore, became centered in the importing of wines from Madeira and the Azores to avoid the rather high duty of the act of 1764, although the rate was not mentioned among the more serious grievances and the duty in general had been paid.[2]

About the middle of February 1768, Captain Daniel Malcolm, a Boston merchant, expecting his schooner loaded with Fayal wines to enter the port, asked the customs officer "what indulgence he might expect in regard to the duties" and was told, none. When the schooner arrived it was anchored five miles down the harbor, and during the night over six thousand gallons of wine were removed and carted to town protected by armed men. Although the whole affair was conducted with a good deal of noise and was notorious, nevertheless when the vessel docked the master swore that she had come from Surinam in ballast only, and the customs officers did not dare to interfere.[3] In spite of this, a few weeks later, the effigies of two of them were hung on Liberty Tree, and when they were cut down a mob terrified the town with considerable tumult. On the first of March, partly at the instigation of Malcolm, a meeting of ninety-eight merchants was held and it was decided to enter into a non-importation agreement for a year, and letters were sent to the other ports as far south as Charlestown asking for coöperation.

Meanwhile the British ministry had hurled more inflammable material upon the smouldering fire of colonial resentment. On February 11th the Massachusetts assembly had voted a circular letter to be sent to all the other colonies. This document, drawn

---

[1] Cf. *Trumbull Papers*, p. 352; Gipson, *Jared Ingersoll*, pp. 262 f.

[2] Schlesinger, *Colonial Merchants*, p. 98; Hutchinson, *History*, vol. III, p. 189.

[3] *Letters to the Ministry from Gov. Bernard, Gen. Gage and Commodore Hood*, (Boston, 1769), p. 18; Hutchinson, *History*, vol. III, p. 188. There were 60 pipes of wine, a pipe containing about 106 imperial gallons.

by Samuel Adams and couched in guarded phrases, pointed out
the danger of having the salaries of the civil officers of the colonial governments, including the judiciary, paid by England;
the impossibility of the colonies ever being represented in Parliament; the injustice of such duties as were levied for revenue
only, and asked for common counsel and united action.[1] The
assembly had already despatched letters of formal protest to the
home government some weeks earlier.[2] When a copy of the
circular letter was received in England it seems to have excited
the utmost resentment, and Lord Hillsborough, who had been
appointed to the new office of Secretary of State for America,
sent instructions to all the governors, in which he denounced the
letter as "dangerous and factious," tending to the subversion of
the Constitution, a "flagitious attempt to disturb the public
peace," and called upon them to have their assemblies treat it
with "the contempt it deserves."[3] That a man capable of pen-
ning such a document, which reads even to its absurd anti-
climax like the scolding of an angry child, should have been
chosen to handle the American problem in such a crisis enables
one to realize the utter hopelessness of the English political situation. Rarely has a great nation ever been so cursed with
imbecility in high places as England was in those crucial years in
her history of empire. The ill-advised letter naturally gave a
great impetus to solidarity of feeling among the colonies and
assisted the merchants in their endeavors.

Locally, in Massachusetts, an episode occurred about the
time the letter was received which, while it reflects little credit
upon the chief figure, added much to the anti-English sentiment
among the people. Among the men whom Samuel Adams had
attached to himself none was more prominent than the young
John Hancock, who had inherited one of the largest of New
England fortunes from a merchant uncle, although not his ability for business. In fact, he succeeded in almost completely dis-
sipating in time this splendid colonial fortune of £50,000 ster-

---

[1] Adams, *Writings*, vol. I, pp. 184 *ff.*; *Prior Documents*, pp. 191 *ff.*; *Journal Mass.
House of Representatives*, 1768, pp. 164 *ff.*
[2] *Prior Documents*, pp. 177 *ff.* Answers from many of the other colonies are given,
ibid., pp. 214 *ff.*
[3] *R. I. Col. Records*, vol. VI, p. 541.

ling and a reversion of £20,000 additional.[1] Exceedingly vain, of very mediocre talents, fond of applause and easily influenced, he readily fell under the spell of the determined Adams, who realized to the full the value of such a popular young gentleman with bulging money bags. In spite of some early vacillation, however, Hancock remained true to the cause he had chosen and rendered considerable service. He at once became the idol of the radicals, but as the years went by he somewhat lost the esteem of the public — due in part, perhaps, to his lack of ability, somewhat absurd personal characteristics, and that side of his nature which is shown in the scandal of his inexplicable handling of Harvard's financial affairs.

Early in June, one of Hancock's vessels arrived, loaded partially with wine from Madeira. Only a small part was declared at the custom house, and when an officer went on board he was forcibly confined in the cabin while the rest of the wine was taken ashore.[2] A few days later the ship was seized by the customs officials, who, fearing a rescue, took her down the bay and anchored her under the stern of the ship of war Romney which had recently arrived. A mob soon gathered, assaulted one of the officers, burned a small boat belonging to the service, broke the windows in the houses of the comptroller and collector, and held the town in terror. "The Sons of Liberty have declared open war," wrote a Bostonian to a correspondent in Newport, and his letter gives us a glimpse of how such rioting affected the ordinary hum-drum, home-keeping citizen. "Jenney was much agitated a Friday night," he added, "as the mob continued some time in King Street, with their usual Exclamations, and what is to come next God knows."[3] The commissioners, whether justly or not, fearing for their lives took refuge on the Romney, which had been sent for their protection, and later retired to

[1] Hutchinson, *History*, vol. III, p. 298.
[2] The accounts vary slightly. *Cf.* Hutchinson, *History*, vol. III, pp. 189 *f.*; A. E. Brown, *John Hancock, his Book*, (Boston, 1898), p. 156; *Letters of Gov. Hutchinson and Lt.-Gov. Oliver*, 2d. edit. (London, 1774), p. 2; *Letters to the Ministry*, p. 20; *Acts Privy Council*, vol. V, pp. 254 *ff.*
[3] *Rhode Island Commerce*, vol. I, p. 240.

Castle William.[1] On the 15th they wrote to Admiral Hood at Halifax asking for additional protection.[2]

The day before, in consequence of anonymous placards put up by the Sons of Liberty, an enormous mass-meeting had been held which passed resolutions calling on the governor to order the Romney to leave the harbor, and which went far beyond any position previously taken in denying not only that the colonists should submit to any taxes not laid by themselves but to any laws at all passed by any legislative body in which they were not represented.[3] John Adams, to whom Hancock entrusted his defence, also took the same ground in his pleading in court.[4] Although the people had been irritated by the impressment of some seamen by the captain of the Romney, it is noteworthy that the new crisis had come from the attempt of the customs officers to enforce a law four years old and which to a considerable extent had been obeyed. The immediate action of the Sons of Liberty, behind whom were such men as John and Samuel Adams, shows to what an extent the blundering course of the ministers in creating general irritation had again given the radicals the lead. The extremists on both sides of the water were developing a dangerous situation. In their address to the governor, the Sons of Liberty had not only denied the right of Parliament to make any laws for the empire but had threatened armed resistance, and in England, a few months earlier, Hillsborough was asserting to the Connecticut agent that "if you refuse obedience to our laws, the whole fleet and army of England shall enforce it." [5]

In June, while the excitement over the affair of Hancock's sloop was still at its height, the English government managed to arouse feeling to a yet higher pitch. Bernard received a letter from Hillsborough instructing him to require the new assembly to rescind the action of the former one in having sent the circular

---

[1] Admiral Hood's order to Capt. Corner, May 2, 1768, *Admiralty, Secretary, In Letters, No. 483*.

[2] Commissioners to Admiral Hood, June 15, 1768; Hood to Admiralty Office, June 23, 1768; Gen. Gage to Hood, June 24, 1768. All in *Admiralty, Secretary, In Letters, No. 483*.

[3] Text of address, Hutchinson, *History*, vol. III, pp. 488 *f*.

[4] John Adams, *Works*, vol. II, p. 215 *n*.

[5] *Trumbull Papers*, p. 297.

letter to the other colonies and to dissolve the Court immediately if it did not comply. So far, the two parties in the house had been of about equal strength, Hutchinson having missed election to the Council by only three votes.[1] The effect of the unwarranted action of the minister, however, was immediately felt, and the House voted a refusal to rescind by a majority of seventy-five, and petitioned the king for the removal of the governor.[2] The Court was immediately prorogued, and the following day was dissolved by Bernard.

The commissioners had not been alone in asking for military protection. As early as March, the governor had intimated to the secretary of war that troops were necessary though he dared not ask for them for fear of the Sons of Liberty.[3] The commissioners, now shut up in the Castle, were receiving anonymous letters threatening their lives and also an attack upon the Castle. The inspector-general, who had been away from Boston, was beset upon his return by a crowd of fifty men which rapidly grew into a large mob, and he was roughly handled with considerable indignity. Without military force or even a municipal police to uphold authority or to protect his family, the governor now lost courage entirely and pleaded both with General Gage at New York, and the home government, to send troops "not to quell a Riot or a Tumult, but to rescue the Government out of the hands of a trained mob." [4] It is useless to attempt to gloss over the situation. With a tumultuous public meeting threatening armed resistance, with the assembly on the side of the mob, with members of the grand jury taking part in the riots and refusing to find indictments, without either arm of the local government civil or military daring or willing to act, it must be admitted that legal government as established had indeed largely broken down. There was much truth in the governor's phrase, "a trained mob." Just as we have seen Sam

[1] Hutchinson, *History*, vol. III, pp. 178, 194.

[2] *Journal Mass. House of Representatives*, 1768, pp. 68 *ff.*, Appendix, *ibid.*, pp. 94–14 [sic, mispaged]; *Prior Documents*, pp. 203 *ff.*

[3] *Barrington-Bernard Correspondence*, pp. 148 *f.*, 151.

[4] Bernard to Capt. Corner, July 4, 1768; Commissioners to Admiral Hood, July 4; Anonymous letter to the Commissioners, July 7; Admiral Hood to Sec'y of Admiralty, Aug. 5; all in *Admiralty, Secretary, In Letters, No. 483*. Cf. also *Barrington-Bernard Correspondence*, pp. 167 *f.*

Adams and others manipulating the town-meeting and elections through the caucus, we can readily feel back of the apparently irresponsible proceedings of the street, deft fingers manipulating the wires, although the conservative patriots disclaimed and probably disliked such extreme methods. We have endeavored to trace throughout this volume, the gradual growth of radical sentiment in New England. There was, however, a vast body of conservative sentiment, and the two parties were probably about evenly balanced, with most of the wealth, culture and social power on the side of the conservatives. If government was breaking down, it was because the English ministry, thoroughly disorganized as it was itself, was antagonizing both parties by forcing unwise policies through unfit officials. The fantastic folly of Townshend and the splenetic dullness of Hillsborough were worth an arsenal to Sam Adams and his group.

Only a complete change of colonial policy could have delayed the inevitable separation of mother country and over-grown colonies until it might have been effected peacefully, perhaps, well in the nineteenth century. The ministry preferred force. In September an officer arrived at Boston to prepare quarters for a regiment ordered from Halifax and two more that were to sail from Ireland.[1] As the thoroughly conservative Governor Wentworth of New Hampshire wrote to Rockingham, if it was thus intended to enforce the revenue acts they would not pay half the expense, and if it was intended to secure the dependence of the colonies it would "exceedingly operate the other way." [2] A little later, in the House of Commons, Pownall, an ex-colonial governor of the better sort, said that this "is not government, it is war. . . . The sword indeed is not drawn but the hand is upon it. The word for action is not indeed yet given but mischief is on tip-toe." [3]

In Massachusetts, the rumor that troops were coming created the utmost excitement. On September 5th an article in the *Gazette*, after arraigning the various acts of the English officials, asked whether these had not in truth dissolved the tie between

---

[1] Hutchinson, *History*, vol. III, p. 202.
[2] Albermarle, *Rockingham Memoirs*, vol. II, p. 89.
[3] *Parlt. Hist.*, vol. XVI, p. 497.

the mother country and colonies, and asserted that the colonists would never be slaves but would rather put their lives in their hands and "cry to the Judge of all the earth."[1] The legislature having been dissolved by Bernard as a punitive measure in accordance with Hillsborough's orders, there was no legal body representing the province. It was decided therefore at a town-meeting to call a convention of delegates from all the towns in the colony, and a circular letter for that purpose was sent out by the Select Men of Boston.[2] It was worded moderately and called attention to the taxation of the colonists without their being represented, to their inability to have their "decent, humble and truly loyal" petitions reach the king, and to the alarming situation threatened by the sending of troops. Although the town-meeting which had voted for the convention had also requested that all citizens provide themselves with fire-arms in view "of an approaching war with France," and it was common talk that the troops would not be permitted to land, the proceedings of the convention when it met were of moderate tendency. A petition was presented to the governor reciting the grievances and requesting that he would cause an assembly to be convened. This petition Bernard refused to receive, holding that the convention (to which ninety towns had elected delegates), was illegal, and he threatened the members with legal penalties if they did not disperse immediately. A second address was likewise refused, and the convention adjourned after publishing an account of their proceedings.[3] On September 28th, the day before they broke up, the first of the troops, about a thousand men, arrived and were landed without molestation, the Irish regiments arriving about six weeks later. Much time was consumed and feeling aroused in a dispute over the question of quartering but, in spite of Gage having come on from New York to arrange matters, the colonists won their point and the soldiers were billeted at the expense of the Crown in houses rented for the purpose.[4]

---

[1] Cited by R. Frothingham, *Life and Times of Joseph Warren*, (Boston, 1865), p. 78.
[2] Text in Hutchinson, *History*, vol. III, pp. 492 *f.*
[3] Hutchinson, *History*, vol. III, pp. 209 *ff.* Seventy delegates from 66 towns were actually present at the meetings.
[4] Minutes of Council at Boston, Oct. 17, 1768; Answer of Justices of Peace to Gov.

For some months feeling had also been aroused in quite another quarter by the agitation again of the question of establishing an Anglican episcopate in the colonies, and a violent controversy was carried on in the newspapers, reaching its height in this and the following year.[1] The agitation was purely of colonial origin and there is nothing to indicate that any change was being seriously considered in England.[2] The Massachusetts assembly, writing to their agent, DeBerdt, in January, had expressed the greatest alarm at the prospect, and throughout the year the papers teemed with articles playing on the religious fears and prejudices of the people.[3] It was a matter of discussion in every hamlet, and in June "the principal gentlemen" of Norwich, who had a dinner to celebrate the election of Wilkes to Parliament, gave as one of the forty-five toasts, "No Bishops in America to eat up the Tithe Pigs"![4] One questions a little how much the fear was genuine among the leaders and how much it may have been used to add to the general resentment against England, and to enlist the aid of the clergy in the political cause. Sam Adams had a number of articles signed "A Puritan" in the *Gazette* playing on the passion against Catholicism. In one of them he expressed surprise that "so little attention is given to the danger we are in, of the utter loss of those religious rights, the enjoyment of which our good forefathers had more especially in their intention, when they explored and settled this new world. . . . To say the truth, I have from long observation been apprehensive, that what we have above everything else to fear, is POPERY."[5] This was good propaganda for firing New England passions, but it may be doubted whether it represented the reasoned judgment of

Bernard, Oct. 24; Letter from Gage to Hillsborough, Oct. 31, all in *Brit. Mus. Add. Mss. 35912.* The last includes the address from the Council to Gage. *Cf. Letters to the Ministry,* pp. 56 ff.

[1] Cross, *Anglican Episcopate,* pp. 195 ff.

[2] *Cf.* Letter of Pownall to Cooper, May 25, 1769, *Kings Mss. 202.*

[3] S. Adams, *Writings,* vol. I, p. 149. For articles in the Boston papers, *vide Boston Chronicle,* Jan. 11–18, Jan. 25–Feb. 1, Feb. 1–8; *Boston Gazette,* May 9, May 16, May 23, June 6, 1768.

[4] *Boston Gazette,* June 27, 1768.

[5] *Writings,* vol. I, p. 201. *Cf.* Jonathan Boucher, *View of the Causes and Consequences of the American Revolution,* (London, 1799), pp. 148 ff. for the same issue and its political effect in the south.

the astute revolutionary leader. In August, an article appeared
criticizing the clergy for holding aloof from politics and urging
them into the arena, an evidence of how times had changed.
The radicals realized the great influence the pulpit could wield
and were using every means to stir up the ministers to exert it.
"If any should ask what I would have the Clergy do," said a
writer, "I have only to answer, A word to the wise is enough." [1]

Discontent was so rife that it would seem as though very little
fanning of the flames was necessary. In Connecticut, for example, the old Mohegan land claim case was still pursuing its
leisurely way in England, although the trouble had been started
a generation before by a group of the colonists themselves.[2] It
involved, however, the validity of title to a considerable extent
of territory in the eastern part of the colony — where radical
sentiment was always strongest — with resultant irritation on
the part of landowners. Hillsborough, too, in his ignorance of
the powers of the charter government, was threatening a revision of colonial laws, and a possible remodeling of the charter
entirely.[3] Just across the border, in New York, there was much
agrarian inquietude, and recently riotous mobs of several hundred had been ranging the eastern parts of the lands of Mr. Van
Rensselaer, threatening his life, and even attacking the sheriff
when supported by a hundred and fifty men under him.[4] Such
episodes were indicative of the unstable state of colonial society
and the general uneasiness of the lower classes. But the English
government was managing to force the imperial issue to the
front so that it overshadowed the others. Each resistance to the
acts of the ministers, however, revealed a little more of the
underlying discontent and the emergence of the spirit of violence. The day was coming when the whirlwind would be
reaped.

Although the merchants in their agreement had touched only
on economic grounds and had claimed that non-importation was
necessary in view of the financial situation, the obvious attempt
again to nullify Parliamentary action with this weapon brought

---

[1] *Boston Gazette*, Aug. 15, 1768
[2] *Trumbull Papers, loc. cit.*
[3] *Ibid.*, pp. 254 *ff.*
[4] *Boston Gazette*, July 14, 1766.

forth angry protests in Parliament, which also severely condemned the convention of the Massachusetts towns.[1] In January 1769, resolutions censuring in the severest terms both the acts of the colonial mobs and the circular letter sent to the other colonies by Massachusetts in February were passed. The two Houses also sent an address to the Crown asking for full information concerning all acts of treason committed in Massachusetts during the year so that the leaders might be brought to England for trial under an old statute of Henry VIII.[2] In the Commons, Pownall and others labored valiantly to defeat the measures. "It was indecent to bring us resolves ready cut and dried, only for the drudgery of passing them : it was indecent to do it in the confused manner we did it : it was indecent to do it without evidence" said one member, but the number of the King's Friends was overwhelming and "at length, at four o'clock, the whole House in confusion, laughing, &c. the Resolutions and Address were agreed to."[3] The iniquitous raking up of an obsolete statute that men might be transported three thousand miles to be tried by prejudiced strangers, without being able to present proper evidence or witnesses, and to the possible ruin of their lives and fortunes, met with strong but futile resistance. Hillsborough said that it was only designed to "hang it over the Americans' heads to keep them in order," which shows the utter ignorance of the English statesmen in regard to the men they were dealing with, and is a commentary on their intelligence.[4]

During 1769, the non-importation movement gathered strength, both New England towns and those of the colonies to the south coming in one after another throughout the year, but Rhode Island did so reluctantly, and New Hampshire did not join until after the "Boston Massacre" the year after.[5] Although some merchants signed the agreements with enthusiasm, many did so only from a sense of duty or from being terrorized.

---

[1] *Trumbull Papers*, pp. 300, 307 ff.; *Parlt. Hist.*, vol. XVI, pp. 477 ff.

[2] *Parlt. Hist.*, vol. XVI, pp. 476, 490, 492, 511.

[3] *Ibid.*, p. 487.

[4] "Letters of DeBerdt," *Col. Soc. Mass., Publications*, vol. XIII, pp. 379, 382; Hutchinson, *History*, vol. III, pp. 222 f.

[5] Andrews, "Boston Merchants," pp. 212 ff.; Schlesinger, *Colonial Merchants*, pp. 131, 149 ff.

The method of coercion was much the same in all the colonies. Merchants, tradesmen, retailers, and others who held out were boycotted, excommunicated politically, subjected to indignity and violence, were tarred and feathered, hung in effigy, ducked in ponds, or had their goods burned.[1] Indeed, the movement was by no means the voluntary action of a united people. Word was received from England in June that the Townshend Acts were to be repealed in part, and this intelligence served to divide the merchants yet more.[2] In Boston, a new agreement was signed, which was to remain in force until the revenue acts of 1764 and 1766 should be repealed as well. Fourteen firms refused to sign, but on threats that their names would be published as "enemies to their country" six were coerced.

Among others, John Mein, a printer and stationer and founder of the *Boston Chronicle*, had refused from the beginning to join the movement, and from time to time published in his paper the names of those among the signers who were violating the agreement and clandestinely importing goods at a considerable profit, among them John Hancock. The anonymous letters published in the *Gazette* in defence of the accused were more scurrilous than convincing.[3] Mein's business was ruined, he himself was attacked by a mob, and finally had to escape to England. There was probably much truth in his accusations, and in any case they were fruitful in sowing discord and suspicion, and materially weakened the movement in New York and Philadelphia.[4] The original agreement was to expire

---

[1] Andrews, *cit. supra*, pp. 221 *f.*

[2] Circular letter of Hillsborough, May 13, 1769. *N. J. Archives*, Ser. I, vol. X, p. 110. Hillsborough sent the letter in a garbled and much less conciliatory form than had been agreed upon by the ministers. Anson, *Grafton Memoirs*, pp. 230 *ff.*

[3] The articles by Mein were also published separately. *Vide A State of the Importations from Great Britain into the Port of Boston from the beginning of Jan. 1769 to Aug. 17, 1769*, (Boston, 1769). Mein pictures Hancock as "Johnny Dupe, Esq. alias the Milch-Cow of the 'Well Disposed' . . . a good natured young man with long ears — a silly conceited grin on his countenance — a fool's cap on his head — a bandage tied over his eyes — richly dressed and surrounded with a crowd of people, some of whom are stroaking his ears, others tickling his nose with straws, while the rest are employed in riffling his pockets," pp. 127 *ff.* This is mild compared with the language of the "Well Disposed" toward Mein. *Cf.* also Mein's *A State of Importations . . . beginning Jan. 1, 1770*, Boston, 1770; *Boston Chronicle*, Aug. 17-24, 1769; *Boston Gazette*, Aug. 28, 1769.

[4] Andrews, "Boston Merchants," pp. 227 *ff.*; Schlesinger, *Colonial Merchants*, pp. 164 *ff.*

WILLIAM JACKSON,

an IMPORTER; at the

BRAZEN HEAD,

North Side of the TOWN-HOUSE,

and *Oppofite the Town-Pump, in*

Corn-hill, B O S T O N.

It is defired that the SONS and DAUGHTERS of *LIBERTY,* would not buy any one thing of him, for in fo doing they will bring Difgrace upon *themfelves,* and their *Pofterity,* for *ever* and *ever,* AMEN.

EDICT AGAINST WILLIAM JACKSON, IMPORTER, 1770

January 1, but a new one had been made extending the time until the Townshend Acts should be repealed. Infractions were becoming so frequent, however, by the end of the year, that in January a meeting was held at which it was decided to break down all opposition by force, and as a result several merchants had to flee from Boston for their lives.[1] "Those daring Sons of Liberty are now at the tip-top of their Power," wrote a Milton woman, "and even to speak disrespectfully of the Well-Disposed is a Crime equal to high Treason."[2] The movement, which was soon to break down, was indeed passing rapidly from the hands of the conservative merchants into the control of the radicals whose aim was wholly political, and who stood to lose nothing by a continued cessation of trade. Beginning as a merchants' device to obtain redress of trade grievances, it ended as a weapon for the radicals for the enforcement of political claims.[3] The effect of the movement commercially upon England was slight, owing to a fortuitous combination of circumstances. Better crops and the Russo-Turkish War had so greatly increased demand for goods as largely to off-set the decreased exports to America, and the situation had wholly altered from the time of the Stamp Act agitation.[4] Politically, the effect was probably detrimental.

In New England, the conservative classes had taken the alarm, for the established governments were evidently becoming helpless or passing into the control of the more radical and violent elements among the people. A change was coming over the political life of the section. Not only were the conservatives everywhere being driven from public life, and radicals, backed by the Sons of Liberty, elected to assemblies and councils, but the town-meetings were beyond control. At these, it was said, "the lowest mechanics discuss upon the most important points of government, with the utmost freedom, which being guided by a few hot and designing men become a considerable source of

---

[1] Andrews, *cit. supra*, pp. 232 *ff.*; Hutchinson, *History*, vol. III, pp. 253 *ff.*

[2] *Letters of James Murray*, p. 122.

[3] Andrews, *cit. supra*, p. 259.

[4] *Trumbull Papers*, pp. 318, 337, 347, 384, 386; Pownall to Cooper, Sept. 25, 1769, *Kings Mss. 202*; Value of all goods exported from England, 1767–1769, *Wm. Sam'l Johnson Papers*, Library of Congress; Schlesinger, *Colonial Merchants*, pp. 236 *ff.*; S. Adams, *Writings*, vol. II, p. 165.

The true Sons of Liberty

And Supporters of the Non-Importation
Agreement,

ARE determined to rëfent any the leaft
Infult or Menace offer'd to any one or
more of the feveral Committees appointed by the Body at. Faneuil-Hall, and
chaftife any one or more of them as they
deferve ; and will alfo fupport the Printers
in any Thing the Committees fhall defire
them to print.

ᴕAS a Warning to any one that fhall
affront as aforefaid, upon fure Information given, one of thefe Advertife-
ments will be pofted up at the Door
or Dwelling-Houfe of the Offender.

Notice Posted by the Sons of Liberty, 1770

sedition. Men of character avoid these meetings and the strongest have generally the best of the argument, and they could not oppose any popular measure without being exposed to insult and resentment."[1] Throughout the year 1769 acts of violence steadily increased. In Boston, for example, an officer of the *Rose* frigate who had attempted to impress men without authority, was killed by being harpooned through the throat by some sailors in resisting him.[2] A man who had informed the customs officers of smuggled goods, was captured by a mob of a thousand people and tarred and feathered.[3] James Otis, who had written to the *Gazette* complaining of the language of the commissioners regarding Americans, meeting one of them a few days later, had a personal encounter and was severely injured. Sam Adams at once utilized this incident by claiming in an anonymous article in the *Gazette*, that this was a "preconcerted plan to assassinate Mr. Otis," though there was not the slightest evidence for such an accusation.[4] A few days after the attack on Mein, another informer was caught. "On the 29th in the evening we had what the Friends to liberty call an assemblage of the people," wrote an observer, "at any other time it would be called a very great Mob. Several thousands of the lower class of the people and some it is said of the middle sort, being collected together, and keeping the Town in a Tumult, from dusk to 8 or 9 o'clock."[5] The informer caught, he was stripped naked, tarred and feathered, and carted through all the principal streets of the town with much disorder, which, as another chronicler states, "occasioned much terror &c. in some fearfull People among the Inhabitants."[6]

In Rhode Island, the armed sloop Liberty of the revenue service which put into Newport after capturing two vessels with contraband, was seized by a mob, scuttled and burned, and the two captured ships rescued and sent on their cruises with-

---

[1] Cited by Gipson, *Jared Ingersoll*, p. 270.

[2] Hutchinson, *History*, vol. III, pp. 231 *f.*; Commodore Hood to Sec'y of Admiralty, May 5, 1769, *Admiralty, Secretary, In Letters, No. 483*; J. Adams, *Works*, vol. II, pp. 526 *ff.*

[3] *Letters and Diary of John Rowe*, ed. A. R. Cunningham, (Boston, 1903), p. 202.

[4] Adams, *Writings*, vol. I, pp. 380 *ff.*; Palfrey, *History*, vol. V, pp. 412 *ff.*

[5] Letter to Commodore Hood, Oct. 31, 1769, *Admiralty, Secretary, In Letters, No. 483*.

[6] *John Rowe Diary*, p. 194.

out any arrests or action on the part of the local government except a proclamation by the governor.[1] In 1766, when Benedict Arnold had taken on himself in New Haven to tie up an informer naked to the whipping post and give him forty lashes, he had been condemned by the sentiment of the town-meeting, which passed a resolution that "the growing disorder and violence and breaches of law in this town are become . . . dangerous to civil society," and that they were "justly alarmed." [2] Three years later, however, so great had been the development of radical feeling that an informer was tarred and feathered without any notice being taken, and the following week another was publicly made to acknowledge that informing was a "heinous crime" and was threatened with dire penalties.[3] In New York city there had been serious riots that greatly alarmed the propertied classes. In New Jersey rioting on a large scale had taken place in Essex and Monmouth counties, the rioters preventing the sitting of the courts, claiming that the lawyers had oppressed the people with exhorbitant fees, although the governor thought, and apparently rightly, that the true cause was the reluctance of some and the inability of others to pay their debts.[4]

In the public papers of the day we trace all the moves in the struggle of imperial relations. It is in the private letters and diaries that we sense the social upheaval, and hear the rumble of approaching revolution. James Murray, writing from Milton, Massachusetts, in 1770 and speaking of the arrival of his young nephew and niece from England, says, that "they are very fine children and I am much pleased now that they are come as I was feared about their coming, on account of the factious spirit now at great height here, indeed it cannot rise much higher without the poor people, many of whom are almost starving for want of employment, going to plunder the rich and then cutting their throats. The children I intend to keep here . . . their goods will be easily disposed of if they can be got clear of the clutches of the Sons of Liberty. How that can

---

[1] *R. I. Col. Records*, vol. VI, pp. 593 *ff.*
[2] Gipson, *Jared Ingersoll*, p. 234.
[3] *Ibid.*, p. 278.
[4] *N. J. Archives*, Ser. I, vol. X, pp. 172 *ff.*, 177.

be effected, Jacky Clark is now going to town to consult and contrive. . . . There are seventy houses in town empty and like to continue so and the number even to increase." [1]

It was not merely occasional outbursts such as have been noticed and the number of which could be increased, but the general atmosphere of the day, and the sense that the old order was breaking up that more and more alarmed the conservatives. "A little rioting," as Professor Becker says, "was well enough, so long as it was directed to the one end of bringing the English government to terms. But when the destruction of property began to be relished for its own sake by those who had no property, and the cry of liberty came loudest from those who were without political privilege" it became a different matter.[2] The conservatives were beginning to feel that with the passing of royal authority the foundations of colonial society and their own privileged position might also be undermined. If the rising tide did engulf society, it might wreck it wholly, and many men who bitterly resented the folly of the British government could not fail seriously to weigh in their minds the still greater danger of encouraging possible anarchy at home. Nor was the danger unreal. There were in fact days so dark after the struggle was over and the new republic founded that patriots who had fought through to that end despaired of their work. In 1770, men of property, who had a stake in the colonies and whose whole lives depended upon the maintenance of an ordered society, might well ponder their course and view not only the acts of the English government but the new symptoms manifesting themselves in their own communities with foreboding and alarm.

---

[1] *Letters of James Murray*, p. 132.
[2] *Political Parties in New York*, p. 31.

CHAPTER XVI

THE ISSUE DEFINED

Repeal of Townshend Acts — Duty on Tea Retained — Increasing Prosperity and Position of the Merchants — Adams Continues his Agitation — Troops Sent to Boston — Clash with the Citizens — Discussion of Imperial Relations — The Gaspee Affair — Hutchinson Letters — Talk of Independence — Destruction of the Tea — Boston Port Bill — Quebec Act — Radicals Oppose Conciliation

AT the time at which we have now arrived, the history of New England is epitomized in that of Massachusetts. Each of the other colonies, it is true, had its special problems. In New Hampshire the questions of the King's Woods and land titles were giving trouble, as was that of the rival jurisdictions of New York and New Hampshire in what is now Vermont. In Connecticut the old Susquehannah matter was renewed, reopening the fight between the factions in favor of expansion or restriction. There, too, the problem of the Writs of Assistance was appearing somewhat belatedly. In Rhode Island paper money and smuggling were creating disturbances and aligning parties. In all of the colonies the division was becoming more sharply defined between conservatives and radicals, each issue as it arose serving to intensify and embitter their opposition, but the effects of all these issues, as well as of the constitutional one between Americans and the mother country, were brought to a focus in Massachusetts and are best treated with reference to that province in a volume of too small compass to contain the local history of each colony in detail.

On the last day of July 1769, Governor Bernard, having been recalled, much too late for the good of the service, sailed for England. The publication in Boston of certain confidential letters written by the governor to the home authorities, in which he outlined what he considered as desirable changes in the form of the colonial government, had greatly inflamed feeling against him, and caused a petition for his recall.[1] His departure was made the occasion of a somewhat ungenerous demonstration, flags being displayed everywhere, the bells rung, and cannon fired incessantly until sunset.[2] Lacking sound political judgment, the governor in his representations and suggestions had undoubtedly done much harm to the cause of mutual understanding between the ministers and the local government, and by order of the town of Boston a reply called *An Appeal to the World* was prepared and published — written as usual by the indefatigable Sam Adams.[3]

Thomas Hutchinson, the lieutenant-governor, by virtue of his office, became acting chief executive on Bernard's recall, and a few months later received his commission as governor, a promotion much against his inclination.[4] Of distinguished colonial ancestry, he was as passionately fond of the land of his birth as was Sam Adams himself. He possessed a legitimate desire to serve in public office, and for over thirty years had been not only appointed but elected to one position after another of public trust. Indeed, until the troubled pre-revolutionary days, no one had stood higher in the esteem of his fellow-citizens.[5] To him, Massachusetts owed in part her sound currency system and he had rendered distinguished services on the bench. His history of Massachusetts contains the best historical work done in America in the colonial period, and displays a rare impartiality considering that he was himself one of the chief actors in the storm center of a time of extraordinary virulence of abuse. Always a conservative he very naturally hesitated to deliver over supreme power to the untried hands of the multitude.

[1] Hutchinson, *History*, vol. III, pp. 226 ff.

[2] *Boston Gazette*, Aug. 7, 1769, cited by Frothingham, *Joseph Warren*, p. 105 n.

[3] *An Appeal to the World, or a Vindication of the Town of Boston*, (Boston, 1770). It is reprinted in S. Adams, *Writings*, vol. I, pp. 396 ff.

[4] Commission dated Nov. 28, 1770. *Col. Soc. Mass., Publications*, vol. II, pp. 164 ff. *Cf.* Hutchinson, *History*, vol. III, pp. 288 ff.

[5] He had been a Selectman of Boston, Town Representative in the General Court, Colonial Agent in England, Speaker of the Assembly, Member of Council, Judge of Common Pleas, of Probate, Delegate to the Albany Congress, Lieutenant-Governor, and a member of boundary and other commissions.

With a mind deeply imbued with legal principle — "I will live and die by the law," he had once said when governor — he had no sympathy with the increasing irregularity in government or with mob rule. Intensely loyal to the idea of imperial unity, he regarded the growing bitterness between colony and mother country and possible independence as calamities. Full of honors, possessed of an ample private fortune, and in his seventieth year, there is no reason to doubt his own statement that he entered upon his new duties with regret. He had disapproved intensely of the Stamp Act, of the retention of the duty on tea, and of many other steps taken by England, but when confronted by the lawlessness inherent in any revolutionary movement, and by the problem of having to choose between conflicting loyalties to colony and empire, he chose to identify himself with the larger political unit, and in what seemed to him the interest of stable government to increase the power of the central authority. As a consequence, the radicals covered his name with unmeasured obloquy and for nearly a century his memory suffered the fate of those of the men who, however honestly, chose the losing side.[1] As Sam Adams typifies the rising democracy, so Hutchinson represents the gentlemanly, cultivated colonial aristocracy. His age, his position, his whole tradition, tended, however, to bring him into fatal collision with the new movement and with the ideas beginning to animate the assembly. It is not necessary to enumerate the successive conflicts that occurred between them, conflicts that served, however, to embitter the radicals against that power overseas which the royal governor represented and whose orders he had to put into execution as far as possible.[2]

The revival in business, following the severe post-war depression did much to bring about a temporary period of political calm. Prosperity in varying degrees returned to all the colonies — indeed, too rapidly in some, leading to over-extension of

[1] It is pleasant to feel that some measure of justice has at last been done to a man who during the greater part of his life rendered conspicuous and valuable service to America. In 1917, the Colonial Society of Massachusetts presented a doorway, in his memory, to the First Church in Boston. *Vide Col. Soc. Mass., Publications*, vol. XIX, pp. 413 *ff.*

[2] *Cf.* Hutchinson, *History*, vol. III, pp. 307 *ff.*, 336 *ff.*

credit. The colonial war debts were fast paid off and taxes lightened. In Massachusetts the entire debt was cleared and commerce had never been more flourishing.[1] The lessened imports due to the non-importation agreement, and unexpectedly heavy demands in Europe for American produce even caused a reversal of the usual current of exchange, and specie flowed westward instead of eastward to settle trade balances, thus eliminating for a time the troublesome question of the currency.[2]

The repeal of the Townshend Acts, which had been promised the preceding year, was finally moved by Lord North, the new prime minister, March 5, 1770, with the exception of the duty on tea which was to be retained merely as a matter of principle, like the Declaratory Act.[3] Efforts were made by friends of America as well as opponents of the ministry to secure the repeal of that also but without success, North holding that "the properest time to exert our right of taxation is when the right is refused," and that if the authority of England were not maintained then it would be relinquished forever.[4] Although in the cabinet the preceding year, the suggested repeal of the duty on tea with the others had been lost by only one vote, the strength of the ministerial party was shown by a vote in the Commons of two hundred and four against one hundred and forty-two defeating an amendment to include that duty in the general repeal.[5]

As far as the merchant class had been concerned, their quarrel with England, although couched in the language of political controversy, had been in reality a quarrel over trade restrictions, intensified by trade depression, and when business improved and most of the restrictions were taken off, the merchants retained no desire to press constitutional points. Indeed, with the removal of the heavier restrictions and the return of prosperity, the desire to raise constitutional questions as to

---

[1] Hutchinson, *History*, vol. III, pp. 349 *ff*. *Cf.* Schlesinger, *Colonial Merchants*, pp. 240 *ff*. On the other hand, Reynell & Coates, a prominent Philadelphia firm, wrote to a correspondent in 1773 that "it must be allow'd the Times are very dull indeed & have been so for some years." *Reynell Papers, Mss.*

[2] Schlesinger, *cit. supra*, p. 242.

[3] *Parlt. Hist.*, vol. XVI, pp. 853 *ff*.

[4] *Ibid.*, p. 854.

[5] *Ibid.*, p. 874; Anson, *Grafton Memoirs*, p. 234.

taxation evaporated to such an extent that even so determined a patriot as John Adams could smile over whether he were drinking the smuggled or "dutied" herb. "Dined at Mr. Hancock's," he wrote in his diary in 1771, "spent the whole afternoon, and drank green tea, from Holland, I hope, but don't know." [1]

Smuggling increased and there were the usual complaints about officious customs officials, but for the most part the merchants objected to certain duties, and evaded them, only as reducing profits and not as infringing their political rights.[2] Duties which were so low as to make the risk of smuggling high in comparison were paid without contention. After the repeal of the Townshend duties, the only two articles which made that risk worth taking for New England importers were wine and tea.[3] The tea duty, like others, was wholly acquiesced in, but when the advance in the price in England caused Holland tea to show a far larger profit, the latter was smuggled in enormous quantities, concealed in rice barrels, wine casks and other receptacles.[4]

Now that after depression and panic and non-importation, the golden flood was once more rolling in, the merchants were quite content to let sleeping dogs lie — and the British lion. Moreover, they realized that the masses were beginning to take too seriously the question of the rights of the individual which they themselves had stressed for their own purposes in the recent controversy, and to apply them in a way that the men of property had never intended. They feared, in a word, that a movement initiated by them for a limited object was getting beyond control, and they did not at all like the evident tenden-

[1] *Works*, vol. II, p. 255.
[2] For complaints *vide Observations of the Merchants at Boston . . . upon several Acts of Parliament*, (London, 1770), pp. 19 ff.
[3] Hutchinson, *History*, vol. III, p. 350.
[4] Hutchinson estimated that it paid to smuggle even though one chest in three were seized. He thought, however, that not more than one in a hundred was discovered. Hutchinson to Hillsborough, Aug. 25, 1771, [marked "private"] *C.O. 5 No. 246*. He believed that practically all the tea imported into Massachusetts came from Holland. Same to same, Sept. 10, 1771 [also "private"] *C.O. 5 No. 246*. Vice-Admiral Gambier considered the illicit trade amazing all along the coast. Letter to Sec'y of Admiralty, Jan. 21, 1771. *Cf.* same to same Nov. 6, 1770, and Letter on illicit Trade in Tea, — —, 1770, all in *Admiralty, Secretary, In Letters, No. 483*.

cies toward social as well as political revolution which their own propaganda had helped to foster.[1] But everywhere radical leaders, standing socially between the aristocratic merchant class and the common people, were not willing to let the matter rest so lightly.

In New England, Sam Adams was, of course, the arch-agitator, and was tireless in his efforts to stir the people to a sense of grievance. Declaring that they were not dependent upon "merchants or any particular class of men" and that "they *will not* be slaves," he continued his propaganda in the press dwelling upon every possible point to inflame passion. How far the movement had deviated from its original character of a protest by the mercantile element against trade grievances is indicated in a letter from William Lee to his brother in Virginia. "By no means trust anything to the merchants," he writes, "for, in general, gain is their God; but force them to co-operate with the wishes of the people." [2] In New England, Adams was no longer seeking redress of grievances but complete independence, and was already covertly suggesting armed resistance.[3] He was quite willing to make use of mob violence when it served the cause he had at heart, and at the very beginning of the period treated of in this chapter there occurred an incident that afforded him incomparable material for playing upon the emotions of the populace, if, indeed, that incident cannot be largely traced to the effects of the inflammatory writings of himself and others.

As we saw in the last chapter, the several acts of violence in Boston had resulted in the temporary stationing of troops there for the protection of imperial interests and the maintenance of domestic order. There was, indeed, no reason why Boston should not have been made a permanent garrison town. Troops were frequently quartered at New York, and at this time regular garrisons were maintained in at least twenty-six other places in the New World portion of the empire.[4] The specific object for

---

[1] *Cf.* H. B. Dawson, *Westchester County during the American Revolution*, (New York, 1886), p. 6.

[2] *Letters of Wm. Lee*, ed. W. C. Ford, (Brooklyn, 1891), vol. I, p. 90.

[3] *Writings*, vol. II, pp. 65, 68, 259, 294 *ff*.

[4] *Viz.* Quebec, Montreal, St. Augustine, Pensacola, Mobile, "South Carolina," Annapolis Royal, Halifax, Placentia, St. Johns Island, St. John's in Newfoundland,

which the troops had been sent, however, aroused intense opposition on the part of many. Nevertheless, we must not forget
in studying the history of this period from the standpoint of the
winning side, that there were continuously two sides and two
parties, and that whereas the radicals were infuriated by the
presence of the troops, a very considerable element of peaceable
law-abiding Bostonians looked upon them as affording protection against the frequent threatenings of the mobs. "I have
been running from mobs ever since Sixty-five" wrote the witty
and sprightly Peggy Hutchinson.[1] "Had it not been for the
two regiments," wrote James Murray, "the mobbing would
have been greater and more general than in the year 1765."[2]
What with intimidation of unpopular Tories, ranging from
threatening anonymous letters to tarring and feathering, the
growing frequency of lawless crowd action ranging from win-
dow-breaking to the burning and sacking of houses, it must be
confessed that Boston was not a place conducive to quiet nerves
for that part of the population — and it is always a large part —
which asks only to be let alone to attend to the daily task of
making a living.

There is plenty of evidence that the radicals set about foment-
ing trouble between the soldiers and the people in order to bring
about a forced withdrawal, and they must share to a very great
extent the guilt for the blood soon to be shed. "Endeavors had
been systematically pursued for many months," wrote John
Adams toward the beginning of 1770, "by certain busy characters, to excite quarrels, rencounters, and combats . . . between the inhabitants of the lower class and the soldiers, and
at all risks to enkindle an immortal hatred between them."[3]
On February 22, 1770, one of the minor customs officers, who
had at times been an informer, was driven into his house by a
mob, who were forcing their way in after him when he fired into

Louisbourg, Bermuda, Providence, Grenada, St. Vincent, Dominique, Tobago, Crown
Point, Oswego, Niagara, Detroit, Pittsburg, Ticonderoga, Oswegatchie and Michil-
limackinac. The cost of this American establishment in 1770 was £231,838. *Army
in America*, [*Mss.*] vol. I, Library of Congress, Mss. Div.

[1] P. O. Hutchinson, *Diary and Letters of Thomas Hutchinson*, (Boston, 1884), vol. I,
p. 108.

[2] *Letters of James Murray*, p. 162.

[3] *Works*, vol. II, pp. 229 f.; *Letters of James Murray*, p. 163.

the crowd killing an eleven-year-old German boy named Seider.[1] Although the officer had not provoked the attack, and at most could have been considered guilty only of homicide in self-defence, a jury, against the order of the court, found him guilty of murder. The radicals also seized upon the opportunity of inflaming the emotions of the masses, and the boy was given a most impressive funeral as a "martyr" to the cause of liberty, although if he can be considered a martyr at all it was to the lawlessness of the mob and the recklessness of the agitators.

Just at this time the Boston journals were filled with more than the usual amount of inflammatory and demagogic material, and to such an extent had the moulders of public opinion excited the public mind that prominent Tories felt it necessary to sleep with loaded guns by their beds.[2] Instances, true or false, of soldiers having insulted civilians were published and the question canvassed as to whether the troops would dare to fire on the people. On the 2d of March, as a result of provocation by some workmen at a ropewalk, a serious affray occurred between the military and the laborers. On the evening of the 5th, the very day on which the repeal of the Townshend Acts was moved in Parliament, occurred the fatal affray ever since known, quite unfittingly, as the "Boston Massacre." During the early hours, groups both of citizens and soldiers wandered about the streets as if anticipating something out of the ordinary. About eight o'clock a bell was rung as the usual signal of fire. At once a crowd assembled near King Street and insulted the sentry posted at the Custom House. A sergeant and six men were hastily ordered out to protect the sentry, Captain Preston immediately following to prevent rash action. The mob, however, increased and assaulted the soldiers with sticks and stones, daring them to fire. Nevertheless, they did not do so until one who had been knocked down with a club struggled to his feet and at once shot his musket into the crowd, followed by all but one of the others. Preston had given no order. The crowd was shouting tauntingly "Fire, fire" and "Why don't you fire?" It is impossible to say whether in the confusion the soldiers mistook the

[1] Hutchinson, *History*, vol. III, pp. 269 *f*., 287.
[2] Frothingham, *Joseph Warren*, p. 120.

cry of some one in the crowd for an order or whether they fired in the mere excitement of self-defence. There is also a question as to whether shots may have been fired from the near-by Custom House. Three men were killed outright and two mortally wounded.[1] Regrettable as the incident was, it was without intention on the part of the authorities. The mob, led by a half-breed negro, had been the aggressor. The wisdom of the English government in posting troops in the town may well have been at fault, but the local authorities had unquestionably been unable or unwilling to maintain order and to protect the citizens in their lives and property. A very recent governor of Massachusetts has informed us that it is the primary duty of a government to preserve order, and there is no doubt that to most men mob action as a contemporary event is quite a different matter from mob action as an historical incident. Whatever the larger aspects of the case, the immediate blame for the occurrence must be laid at the door of those radicals who in the newspapers and speeches had been doing their utmost to kindle resentment and ill-feeling against the soldiers and to bring on just such a clash as occurred. Captain Preston and his little squad at once surrendered themselves to the civil authorities, and some months later, after a very fair trial which reflects credit on the town, and in which they were defended by John Adams and Josiah Quincy, Junior, all of the prisoners were found not guilty with the exception of two who were convicted of homicide and given a comparatively slight penalty.[2]

As in the case of the killing of the boy Seider, the episode derives its importance mainly from the use the radicals made of the incident as propaganda. There have been in our history innumerable street affrays in which men have been killed by soldiers or guards of constituted authority, not a few of which

[1] Among the sources the reader may consult Hutchinson, *History*, vol. III, pp. 271 *ff*.; *Letters of James Murray*, p. 163; *Mass. Hist. Soc., Proceedings*, vol. VI, pp. 480 *ff*.; *Col. Soc. Mass., Publications*, vol. VII, pp. 2 *ff*.; *Maryland Historical Magazine*, vol. IV, pp. 284 *ff*.; *American Historical Review*, vol. VIII, p. 317; *A short Narrative of the horrid Massacre* . . . (London, 1773); *The Trial of the British Soldiers* . . . (Boston, 1824). Many of the documents are collected by Frederic Kidder in *History of the Boston Massacre*, (Albany, 1870). *Cf.* also P. W. Chandler, *American Criminal Trials*, (Boston, 1841), pp. 303 *ff*.; Channing, *History of U. S.*, vol. III, p. 119 *n*.

[2] Adams and Quincy accepted the unpleasant task only from a stern sense of duty and deserve all praise for having done so.

have occurred in this year of grace 1922, but in the case of the "massacre" the facts were distorted, the entire blame at once laid upon the troops, and every effort made to inflame the most violent passions of the people, even in the official report prepared by order of the town. "The number killed and wounded," wrote Daniel Chaumier to a southern correspondent, "you will have learnt by the papers, being almost the only truth in them." [1] Although Preston and his men were entitled to be considered innocent until proved otherwise at their trial, the Boston town-meeting at once formally voted them to be "murderers." [2] In spite of the fact that English correspondents were assured that the trial would be fair, the radicals never accepted the verdict, and dinned the words "massacre" and "murder" into their hearers and readers on every occasion.[3] Some of the clergy joined the hue and cry. The Reverend John Lathrop, for example, preached on those who had wantonly murdered their fellow-citizens, and called for the death of the soldiers, thus continuing one line of Massachusetts ecclesiastical tradition.[4] For many years the anniversary was used as an occasion to rekindle passion. Five years later Dr. Warren in one of the commemoration orations was still talking in a similar strain. "Take heed, ye orphan babes," he cried, "lest, while your streaming eyes are fixed upon the ghastly corpse, your feet slide on the stones bespattered with your fathers' brains." [5] On the first anniversary of the day when the taunting rioters had been "inhumanly murdered," as the *Boston Gazette* phrased it, an exhibition was held in the windows of the house of Paul Revere. After the church bells had been tolled, the curtains at the windows were raised and at one of these there "was the appearance

---

[1] *Maryland Historical Magazine*, vol. IV, p. 285. *Cf. Boston Gazette*, March 12, 1770. Chaumier adds in his letter "by no means a friend to military power, yet I have always held it a Maxim that in a civilized Government the lives of an hundred such mobbing Spirits as we are in daily and nightly fear of here, are not to be set in competition with the life of one single honest and peaceable subject."

[2] *Boston Town Records, Record Comm. Rept.*, vol. XVI, p. 13.

[3] *Bowdoin-Temple Papers*, p. 218; S. Adams, *Writings*, vol. II, pp. 77 ff., 102 ff., 135 ff.

[4] *Innocent Blood crying to God from the Streets of Boston. A Sermon occasioned by the horrid Murder . . .* (Boston, 1771), p. 6.

[5] *Orations delivered at the Request of the Inhabitants of Boston to commemorate the Evening of the 5th of March, 1770*, (Boston, 1785), p. 65.

of the Ghost of the unfortunate young Seider, with one of his Fingers in the Wound, endeavoring to stop the Blood from issuing: Near him his Friends weeping: And at a small distance a monumental Obelisk with his Bust in front: — On the front of the Pedestal were the names of those killed on the Fifth of March: Underneath the following Lines,

> Seider's pale Ghost fresh bleeding stands,
> And Vengeance for his Death demands.

In the next Window were represented the Soldiers drawn up, firing at the People assembled before them — the Dead on the Ground — and the Wounded falling, with the Blood running in streams from their Wounds." [1]

Immediately after the clash in the streets the demand for the removal of the troops from Boston to the Castle in the harbor became irresistible. After considerable negotiation between representatives from the town-meeting, the commanding officer, the Council and Hutchinson, in which Sam Adams took a leading part, the order was finally given, and in the course of a few days the town was at last freed from the presence of the soldiers, who were soon to be ironically dubbed in England "Sam Adams's Regiments." [2]

Prosperity and the absence of any general and deeply-felt grievance in the colonies as a whole, however, gradually did their work, in spite of the efforts of the radicals to keep things stirred up and of occasional outbursts of violence. John Adams decided that having "learned wisdom from experience" he would retire from public life and mind his own business and his own farm.[3] Hancock also preferred to drop political wrangling over constitutional points, and for more than a year would have nothing to do with Sam Adams.[4] The influence of the latter, indeed, markedly declined.[5] In 1771, the parties in the assembly

---

[1] *Boston Gazette*, March 9, 1771, cited by F. Hudson, *Journalism in the United States*, (New York, 1873), p. 106.

[2] Hutchinson's account is in his *History*, vol. III, pp. 273 *ff*. *Cf.* R. Frothingham, "Sam Adams Regiments in the Town of Boston," *Atlantic Monthly*, vol. VIII, pp. 179 *ff.*, vol. IX, pp. 595 *ff*.

[3] *Works*, vol. II, p. 260.

[4] Hutchinson, *History*, vol. III, p. 346; Wells, *Life of Samuel Adams*, vol. I, pp. 396 *ff.*, 437 *ff.*, 469, 475.

[5] *Cf.* election returns for 1772. Wells, *Life of Samuel Adams*, vol. I, p. 471.

were about equally divided,[1] with the influence of the wealthier
and cultivated classes thrown on the side of peace and harmony.
We have already noted that the reasons for this were the fear of
the lower sort of radicals and the repeal of most of the obnoxious
duties.

But although the settlement of the important trade grievances satisfied the colonial merchants and removed the basis for
any wide-spread agitation which would include all classes, there
was, in reality, no change in the policy of the English government, which was merely repeating its tactics of the Stamp Act
repeal. Nor were English statesmen making any serious effort
to grapple with the problem of imperial organization. In
America, on the other hand, there had been an enormous
quickening of political speculative thought. Governor Hutchinson was of the English school and was writing despatches advising minor tinkering with the laboring machinery of administration — such as making the Council a body of royal appointees
instead of one elected by the assembly.[2] Articles were beginning
to appear in the colonial press, however, that in many ways display a broader view of England's real problem than may be
found for another hundred years, and which have a strangely
twentieth-century tone. We almost hear the voice of General
Smuts or others of the same school, in an article in the *Boston
Gazette* in 1772. "The true plan of government which reason
and the experience of nations points out for the British empire"
wrote "American Solon," "is to let the several parliaments in
Britain and America be (as they naturally are) free and independent of each other. . . . And as the King is the center of
union . . . the various parts of the great body politic will be
united in him; He will be the spring and soul of the union, to
guide and regulate the grand political machine."[3] A writer
in the *New Hampshire Gazette* suggests the same thought. One
king should be at the head of all, he writes, and each local legis-

---

[1] J. Adams, *Works*, vol. II, p. 263.

[2] Hutchinson to Hillsborough, Jan. 22, 1771 ["private"] *C.O. 5 No. 246*.

[3] Issue of Jan. 27, 1772. The writer points out that in another century America will
number 60,000,000 people and that it will be impossible for England to hold them
except by some such voluntary tie. *Cf.* General Smuts, *The British Commonwealth of
Nations*, (London, 1917), p. 7.

lature separate from every other. "The Government thus united in one Sovereign, though divided into distant Parliaments, will be actuated by one Soul. It will have all the advantages of a powerful Republic, and a grand extensive Monarchy. . . . If the supreme Legislature is considered as only in the Majesty of the King as the common Head of all his Parliaments, and exercising his authority with their [several] consent[s], while no one of them encroaches upon the rights of the rest, harmony will reign through the whole Empire; every part will enjoy freedom and happiness; it may be extended farther and farther to the utmost ends of the earth and yet continue firmly compacted until all the kingdoms of the World shall be dissolved."[1] However far the empire may continue to progress in that direction, those who were then propounding such doctrines, crudely enough it is true, were nearly a century and a half ahead of their successors in the empire of today, and they had a far more statesmanlike grasp of the fundamentals of the problem, as well as a greater imperial ideal, than had the statesmen in England who were guiding the destinies of the parent state.[2] The period of mere obstructionist tactics on the part of the colonists was drawing to a close and that of constructive political thought was beginning.

But calm discussion and genuine efforts at conciliation were by no means to the taste of the more radical leaders. "This country must do something more than either reason or write" said a writer in the Gazette "or it will soon be the most ignominious of the earth."[3] Nevertheless, though the radicals piped, the sounder elements in the community, busy and prosperous, refused to dance. Even the announcement that the governor's salary was henceforth to be paid by England and that he would no longer be dependent upon the assembly, although arousing much opposition, passed with less disturbance than might have

[1] Reprinted in Boston Gazette, Feb. 17, 1772. Such doctrines occasionally found echo in England. Cf. the interesting writings of the strong anti-imperialist John Cartwright, e.g. A Letter to Edmund Burke, (London, 1775) and American Independence the Interest and Glory of Great Britain, (London, 1775).

[2] There was evidently considerable interest in England on the part of the reading public in colonial problems. Thomas Pownall's Administration of the British Colonies had reached its 6th edition by 1777.

[3] Boston Gazette, July 6, 1772, cited by Frothingham, Joseph Warren, p. 183.

been anticipated.[1] The removal of the judges from popular influence created more resentment but it was not until 1774, by which time much new water had run under the mill, that they were formally impeached by the assembly.[2] These new grievances, however, were real, and it is evidence of the sincere desire of a very substantial part of the community to sink political agitation that not more was made of them than there was. Adams was turning definitely away from the merchants and the well-to-do in his efforts at agitation. The North-End Caucus Club was much increased in membership and took in a large number of mechanics, and it is noteworthy that in order to flatter that class, although there were always some prominent Whigs at the meetings, a mechanic was invariably chosen to preside.[3]

We have already noted the character of the town-meetings, and it was at these that radical opinion was most loudly voiced. For several years the instructions that were regularly given to the town's representatives in the assembly had been becoming more and more rabidly anti-English and abusive.[4] At the meeting of October 28, 1772, it was voted that the payment of the judges' salaries from England tended "to compleat the system of slavery, which originated in the House of Commons," and a committee was appointed to make a statement of the rights of the colonists "as Men, as Christians and as Subjects."[5] This report, adopted at the meeting of November 20th made a strong appeal for the sympathy of the common man. There should "be one rule of Justice for rich and poor" it quoted from Locke, "for the favorite in Court, and the Countryman at the Plough." It gave warning to the farmers that if the House of Commons were not curbed "our lands will go next or be subject to rack rents from haughty and relentless landlords who will ride at ease, while we are trodden in the dirt." Following upon this dema-

---

[1] Hutchinson, *History*, vol. III, pp. 357 *ff.*; S. Adams, *Writings*, vol. II, pp. 171 *ff.* 246 *ff.*
[2] S. Adams, *Writings*, vol. II, pp. 349 *ff.*; Hutchinson, *History*, vol. III, pp. 361 *ff.*, 386.
[3] Frothingham, *Joseph Warren*, p. 170.
[4] *Boston Town Records, Record Comm. Rept.*, vol. XVI, pp. 31, 132 *ff.*
[5] *Ibid.*, pp. 89, 94 *ff.*; S. Adams, *Writings*, vol. II, pp. 350 *ff.*

gogic appeal, a circular letter was sent to the other Massachusetts towns asking for concerted action.[1]

The people, however, seemed sluggish. The heavy ground
swell left by the political storms of the past few years appeared
to be subsiding. Suddenly a lightning flash in Rhode Island pre-
luded a new storm and the elements along the entire seaboard
were again in commotion. The revenue officers had had but
little success in interfering with the enormous smuggling trade
of that little colony so conveniently fitted with handy creeks
and coves, and Admiral Montague had ordered Lieutenant
Dudingston of the schooner *Gaspee* to send his prizes to Boston
as it was impossible to secure their condemnation at Newport.
On June 9, 1772, the *Gaspee* ran aground on a sand spit about
seven miles below Providence, and at midnight was attacked by
a crowd of perhaps a hundred men and boys, who captured the
helpless vessel, burned her and disappeared again in their small
boats.[2] Dudingston, who had made himself particularly obnoxious to the Rhode Islanders, was the only one wounded.

The matter was at once taken up in England and even Dartmouth, mild-mannered and friendly to the colonies, was stirred
to wrath. The offence was declared to be high treason, and a
special commission was appointed consisting of the governor of
Rhode Island, the chief justices of Massachusetts, New York
and New Jersey, and the judge of Admiralty at Boston. The
most stringent instructions were sent to apprehend the culprits
and to send them to England for trial.[3] It was this last that
stirred the continent. The Virginia assembly at once appointed
a standing committee of correspondence, and the other colonies
were invited to do the same, thus making continental in scope
the plan already adopted locally by Adams. In Rhode Island,
however, so completely were the culprits shielded by public
opinion that the commission was unable to obtain any evidence,

---

[1] *Boston Town Records, cit. supra*, pp. 196 *ff.*; S. Adams, *Writings*, vol. II, pp. 369 *ff.*
[2] Most of the documents are given by W. R. Staples in *The Documentary History of the Destruction of the Gaspee*, (Providence, 1845). Practically the same material was reprinted by J. R. Bartlett in *The History of the Destruction of his Britannic Majesty's Schooner Gaspee*, (Providence, 1861), which was reprinted again in *R. I. Col. Records*, vol. VII, pp. 55 *ff.* Channing used some new English material in his account. *History of U. S.*, vol. III, pp. 124 *ff.*, 151.
[3] The draft of instructions is in *C.O. 5 No. 1284*.

and the outcry died down with the complete collapse of the English case.

In Massachusetts, Hutchinson allowed himself to be drawn into a discussion of the constitutional relations between England and the colonies, which merely resulted in creating bad feeling and in eliciting from the assembly the statement that if, as the governor said, there could be no line drawn between the supreme authority of Parliament and the total independence of the colonies, then the colonies must be totally independent. Such a suggestion, however, was a matter of so great importance to all the colonies, they added, that "we should be unwilling to propose it without their consent in congress." [1] A few months later an episode occurred that destroyed all possible influence for good of the governor and has tarnished the reputations of several of the patriot party, or at least has raised very delicate questions in ethics regarding them. In London, Franklin had come into possession, by means even as yet unknown, of a stolen collection of personal letters from Hutchinson, Lieutenant-Governor Oliver, and the revenue official, Paxton, to Thomas Whately, a former member of Parliament. Hutchinson's imperial views and leanings were well understood in the colony, and there was nothing in his letters that was new. Those of the other two were somewhat more inimical to the interests of the province, and the political effect of the letters if published, particularly in garbled extracts, might be very great. Franklin, after giving a pledge that they should not be published, sent them to the speaker of the Massachusetts assembly. They were read to that body, which at once passed resolutions so strongly condemnatory as to mislead the public as to the real nature of the letters, and an address was sent to the agent in England to be presented praying for the removal of both the governor and his lieutenant. [2] Shortly afterward despite all pledges of honor, and after much preliminary and

---

[1] S. Adams, *Writings*, vol. II, pp. 424 *ff.*; *Journal of Mass. House of Representatives*, 1773, [Jan. 3] pp. 138 *ff.* The documents in the controversy are all given by Hosmer in his *Life of Hutchinson*, pp. 363 *ff.*

[2] *Journals of Mass. House of Representatives*, June 1773, pp. 58 *ff.*; Hutchinson, *History*, vol. III, pp. 400 *f.*, 411 *f.*; *Letters of Gov. Hutchinson and Lt.-Gov. Oliver* . . (London, 1774) [2d. edit.]

misleading propaganda, the letters were published. The publication raised a storm on both sides of the water. In America, the radical element was furious over their contents, and in England Franklin was arraigned like a thief before the Privy Council, and, it must be confessed, did not come out of the affair very brilliantly.[1] He was immediately deprived of his office of postmaster-general, resigned as agent for Massachusetts, and before long returned to America having lost all his influence in the mother country.

In Massachusetts, radical sentiment was gaining ground and it was in the atmosphere of bitter party feeling and mutual recriminations between Whig and Tory that a new false step by England followed by an act of violence by the Boston radicals was to light a train of powder which was to smoulder its slow length of two years to the explosion of open revolt. Although but a very small element in the colonies wished for independence, the less responsible radicals in favor of it were becoming bolder and were openly advocating the extreme course. In a pamphlet dealing with the Gaspee case, John Allen denied that England had any more right to interfere with smuggling in Rhode Island than she had "to send an armed schooner into Brest and demand the property of France." "Some would be glad to know," he continued, "what right the King of England has to rule over America." [2] The same idea of England as a foreign country is frequently found. In connection with the judges' salaries a writer in the *Gazette* asks, as though it were a parallel case, "What would the English say if the king of France should come at the head of a hundred thousand men to impose laws upon England." [3] In the same issue an article advocated forming an independent commonwealth on the pattern of Holland.[4] "How shall the colonies force their oppressors to proper terms?" asks another writer some months later. "This ques-

---

[1] As to how he got possession of the letters *vide Mass. Hist. Soc., Proceedings*, vol. XVI, pp. 46 ff.; *Massachusetts Gazette*, Apl. 18/25, 1774; Hutchinson, *Diary and Letters*, vol. I, pp. 82 ff. Franklin's examination is given in Almon's *Collection of scarce and interesting Tracts*, (London, 1788), vol. IV, pp. 222 ff., in *Letters of Gov. Hutchinson, cit. supra*, pp. 77 ff. and elsewhere.

[2] [John Allen] *An Oration on the Beauties of Liberty* . . . (Boston, 1773), pp. xviii, xxiii.

[3] Nov. 2, 1772, cited by Frothingham, *Joseph Warren*, p. 192.

[4] *Ibid.*, p. 198.

tion has often been answered by our politicians," he continues, by the advice to "form an independent State . . . I can't find that any other is likely to answer the great purpose of preserving our liberties : I hope, therefore, it may be well digested and forwarded, to be in due time put into execution." [1] In a song composed for the anniversary of the "Massacre" a poet wrote that

> A Ray of bright Glory now Beams from afar,
>   Blest dawn of an Empire to rise;
> The American Empire now sparkles a Star,
>   Which shall shortly flame wide thro' the Skies.[2]

The more cautious preferred to let events take their course, trusting to the more rapid increase of population in America as compared with England to bring them all they wished, and were anxious to avoid "prematurely bringing on the contest." [3] Others feared the disasters which they thought inevitable were "American independence as practicable as some wild Bostonians think." [4] That the question should be thus openly discussed in the press marks a distinct advance in the radical position.

The agitation, whether actively fomented by the French or not, was being very closely watched by them, and they had agents in every colony engaged in spreading pro-French if not anti-English propaganda.[5] The influence of French fashions and literature was increasing, notably that of Montesquieu whose false views of the English Constitution were largely to mould American opinion. We now find him quoted with considerable frequency, and even a full-page advertisement proposing to publish an American edition of his works "which ought to be in

---

[1] *Boston Gazette*, Oct. 11, 1773, cited by Frothingham, *cit. supra*, p. 245.

[2] *Massachusetts Gazette*, Feb. 28 /Mar. 7, 1774.

[3] Letters of Samuel Cushing, *Mass. Hist. Soc., Coll.*, Ser. IV, vol. IV, p. 363.

[4] *Massachusetts Gazette*, May 2 /9, 1774.

[5] A London despatch printed in Boston said "A Gentleman of Note lately returned from North America hath said that to his certain knowledge the Court of France has two or more Gentlemen of Observation in almost every Province on that Continent who have the English language, with a friendly, engaging deportment, and are very industrious in removing from the Minds of the Colonists the old Bugbear Ideas . . . that the Pope and the Devil are inseparably connected with French Faith, French Alliance and French Commerce." *Massachusetts Gazette*, Oct. 25 /Nov. 1, 1773.

TRADESMEN'S
PROTEST

AGAINST THE

PROCEEDINGS

OF THE

MERCHANTS

Relative to the New IMPORTATION of TEA.

Addreſſed to the TRADESMEN and INHABITANTS of the Town and Province in general, but to the TRADESMEN of BOSTON in particular.

☞ *AVOID THE TRAP.* *Remember the iniquitous Non-Importation Scheme.* ☜

BOSTON, Nov. 3, 1773.

WHEREAS we have repeatedly been impoſed upon by the Merchants of the Town of Boſton, and thereby incurred heavy Taxes upon us, and we ſtand unjuſtly charged with the blame : And as it is now propoſed by ſaid Merchants to prevent the Importation of Tea from the India Company, whereby that Article may be ſold for leſs than half the Price they can afford it ; who now call for our Attendance for that Purpoſe at Liberty-Tree, You are hereby adviſed and warned by no means to be taken in by the *deceitful Bait* of thoſe who falſely ſtile themſelves Friends of Liberty:

THE

PROTEST.

We the TRADESMEN of the Town of BOSTON therefore PROTEST againſt ſaid Meeting in the following Manner, Viz.

I. THAT the preſent propoſed Meeting is illegal and underhanded ; and as it is our humble Opinion that it is ſubverſive of that CONSTITUTIONAL LIBERTY we are contending for, and that ſuch Proceedings will tend to create Diſorder and Tumult in the Town, it is earneſtly wiſhed every well-diſpoſed Member of the Community would uſe his Endeavors to prevent them in future:

II. THAT the Method of notifying ſaid Meeting is mean and deſpicable, and ſmells of *Darkneſs* and *Deceit*, as the Notification for warning the ſame was not ſigned, and was poſted in the Night.

III. WE are reſolved, by Divine Aſſiſtance, to walk *uprightly*, and to eat, drink, and wear whatever we can *honeſtly* procure by our Labour ; and to Buy and Sell when and where we pleaſe ; herein hoping for the Protection of good Government : Then let the *Bellowing* PATRIOT throw out his thundering Bulls, they will only ſerve to ſooth our Sleep.

THE TRUE SONS OF LIBERTY.

Printed by E. RUSSELL, next the Cornfield, Union-ſtreet.

every Man's hands." [1] A Connecticut pessimist writing in the *Courant* and lamenting the evils of the day, places at the head of a list of things unhappily in fashion in that staid colony French Doctors, French Monkeys and French Frocks. [2] The total influence was probably small, and the evidence is interesting mainly as showing that the colonists were no longer looking solely toward England as their standard and model.

Just at this stage the English statesmen made a colossal blunder, due not to a desire to tyrannize but to sheer political and commercial stupidity. For some years the government had derived a considerable income from the East India Company, which it could ill afford to lose. The affairs of that company, however, by 1773 had reached desperate straits. The extraordinary famine three years previously had devastated the great dependency, in Bengal alone over one-third of the population having died, and in 1771 more than that proportion of cultivable land being deserted. [3] Partly due to this cause, and partly to the war with Hyder Ali and to mismanagement, not only were the company's dividends cut in half but it faced bankruptcy, and the government the loss of an important item of revenue. [4] The smuggling of Holland teas into America had also largely reduced the company's exports, and there were seventeen million pounds of the herb in its warehouses in England. In an effort to solve the commercial difficulties of the company and its own fiscal ones, Parliament hit upon the plan of relieving the company of certain duties previously paid and of permitting it to export its tea direct to America instead of selling it through merchants. [5] It was decided to retain the 3*d.* duty paid in America, out of deference it was said to the wishes of the king,

---

[1] *Massachusetts Gazette*, Oct. 19, 1772. *Cf. Ibid.*, Sept. 3, Oct. 1, Nov. 12, 1770, Feb. 18, July 15, Aug. 5, 1771, Mar. 23, 1772, June 13, Oct. 17, 1774; *Boston Chronicle*, Apl. 25, 1768; *Boston Gazette*, June 15, 1767, Feb. 11, Aug. 19, Sept. 23, Dec. 23, 1771, Nov. 9, 1772, for traces of French influence.

[2] *Connecticut Courant*, June 8, 1767. *Cf.* Issue May 11, 1767.

[3] Sir W. W. Hunter, *Annals of rural Bengal*, (London, 1897), pp. 19, 63; A. Loveday, *The History and Economics of Indian Famines*, (London, 1914), pp. 29 *ff.*

[4] Robert Grant, *A Sketch of the History of the East India Company*, (London, 1813), pp. 308 *ff.*, 330 *f.*, 342; Ramsay Muir, *The Making of British India*, (London, 1915), p. 102.

[5] 13 Geo. III, c. XLIV. *Cf.* Max Farrand, "The Taxation of Tea," *American Historical Review*, vol. III, pp. 266 *ff.*

but even so the company was enabled to reduce the price twenty-five per cent in America and thus undersell the Dutch product.

As we have already seen, the Boston merchants had been paying the duty for over two years and there was nothing in the new Act that in any way opened any new question in regard to the principle of taxation. What was new was the monopoly granted to an English corporation, for the American merchants who imported from England could not pay middlemen's profits and compete with the company, and those who had been smuggling from Holland were also undersold. News of the Act reached America in September 1773, and there is ample evidence to show that along the entire seaboard the opposition at first was directed solely against the monopoly and not against the retention of the old tax.[1] The radicals, however, were quick to see that the merchants, who had broken with them for the reasons we have given, would again be driven into opposition to England by this new step. All their own propaganda for several years had dealt with constitutional questions, and therefore in order to broaden the base of the new agitation they disguised and befuddled the issue by raising again the old cry of no taxation. On this rallying cry, the merchants once more joined with the radicals, forgetting for the moment their fears of revolution in the more immediate one of possible trade ruin.

It was everywhere decided that the tea should not be allowed to land, and when the first ships bringing the East India Company's own consignments arrived at their destined ports, with the exception of Boston, the captains and the consignees were induced by argument to accede to the wishes of the combined radicals and merchants. At Boston, however, the consignees, two of whom were sons of Governor Hutchinson, refused to resign. Most of the merchants joined in the popular demand through the town-meeting, but neither the requests of that body nor an attack upon the house of one of the consignees by a mob

---

[1] Schlesinger, *Colonial Merchants*, pp. 265 *ff.*; Extracts from letters from Boston and Philadelphia, 1773, *C.O. 5 No. 133*; [Samuel Seabury] *The Congress canvassed . . .* n.p., 1774, p. 7; W. B. Reed, *Life and Correspondence of Joseph Reed*, (Philadelphia, 1847), vol. I, p. 53; [John Drinker] *Observations on the late popular Measures*, (Philadelphia, 1774), pp. 12 *f.*

brought any yielding. Sam Adams, who saw the great opportunity offered to the waning cause of the radicals, now arranged for a joint meeting of the committees of correspondence of Boston and several nearby towns. That body, meeting on November 22, five days before the arrival of the first tea ship, voted to prevent the landing of the tea and to arouse the other towns to "immediate and effectual action." [1] As soon as the ship Dartmouth arrived with the first consignment, a joint meeting of the inhabitants, unenfranchised as well as voters, of Boston, Dorchester, Roxbury, Brookline and Cambridge was held. In this extra-legal and irresponsible body the merchants and conservatives were thrust aside, and it was voted not only that the tea should not be landed but that the duty should not be paid, and that the same principles should apply to any private shipments for account of merchants. This same body, made up to a considerable extent of unenfranchised residents and radical voters, now replaced to a great extent the legal town-meeting in the direction of affairs.

It was contrary to law for a ship to receive clearance papers unless its cargo consigned to the port had been entered and paid the duty, and technically Hutchinson would have had to exceed his authority had he permitted the tea to be returned without first being landed. This, however, the mass meeting refused to allow. Moreover at the end of twenty days the ships would be liable to seizure for non-payment of duties. On December 16, the last day allotted to the Dartmouth, nearly eight thousand people, a large part of whom had flocked in from the surrounding country, attended a meeting to learn the result of a final conference with the governor. Meanwhile the radicals had made their preparations. When early in the evening word came that the governor in accordance with his sworn duty would refuse to issue a pass for the ship until the customs officers had cleared her, Sam Adams solemnly announced that "this meeting can do no more to save the country." These anticipated words were immediately answered from outdoors by a war-whoop, and a company of men disguised as Indians went directly to the ship,

---

[1] The best brief account of these events is that given by Schlesinger, *Colonial Merchants*, pp. 283 *ff.* Hutchinson's version is in his *History*, vol. III, pp. 422 *ff.*

B O S T O N, December 2, 1773.

WHEREAS it has been reported that a Permit will be given by the Custom-House for Landing the Tea now on Board a Vessel laying in this Harbour, commanded by Capt. HALL : THIS is to Remind the Publick, That it was solemnly voted by the Body of the People of this and the neighbouring Towns assembled at the Old-South Meeting-House on Tuesday the 30th Day of *November*, that the said Tea never-should be landed in this Province, or pay one Farthing of Duty : And as the aiding or assisting in procuring or granting any such Permit for landing the said Tea or any other Tea so circumstanced, or in offering any Permit when obtained to the Master or Commander of the said Ship, or any other Ship in the same Situation, must betray an inhuman Thirst for Blood, and will also in a great Measure accelerate Confusion and Civil War : This is to assure such public Enemies of this Country, that they will be considered and treated as Wretches unworthy to live, and will be made the first Victims of our just Resentment.

The P E O P L E.

N. B. Captain *Bruce* is arrived laden with the same detestable Commodity ; and 'tis peremptorily demanded of him, and all concerned, that they comply with the same Requisitions.

WARNING AGAINST LANDING TEA, POSTED IN 1773

and with perfect order dumped £10,000 worth of tea overboard.[1] The obstinacy of the consignees, and the clinging to the strict letter of his powers by the elderly and unyielding governor in the face of an unforeseen and perilous situation had given the radicals their opportunity. There was absolutely no new principle at stake. The tea might have been landed under protest. Violence might have been reserved for a second attempt by the British government if the protest went unheeded. But the lawless act promoted by Adams could not fail to bring matters to a crisis and precipitate a struggle between mother country and colony, which was exactly what the conservatives wished to avoid and what Adams wished to bring on.

Although the patriot leaders cannot be held responsible for all the minor outrages that were frequent in Boston and elsewhere, these must be taken into account in trying to understand the attitude of many who were opposed to the course of the British government but who dreaded yet more the growing power of the roughs and extreme radicals. Tarring and feathering was the order of the day. It was even suggested in the *Gazette* for any merchant who should raise the price of coffee.[2] The tea consignees, who had been forced to flee the town, were warned in public placards that as "Traitors to their Country, Butchers who . . . are doing everything to Murder and destroy all that shall stand in the way of their private Interest" they would be violently dealt with if they dared to return to their homes.[3] A few days later Malcolm, a customs officer, was seized, tarred and feathered.[4] Buckets full of the scourings of privies were thrown through the windows of those unpopular with the toughs and roughs or smeared over their front doors.[5] Mobs had become one of the main topics of conversation, wrote John Adams, and

[1] 340 chests valued at £9,659. Memorial of East India Co. to Earl of Dartmouth, Feb. 16, 1774, *C.O. 5 No. 247.* The amount is usually stated to have been £15,000, but this included the tea from two other ships likewise thrown overboard later. A third was cast away on Cape Cod. The contemporary account from the radical standpoint is in the *Boston Gazette,* of Dec. 20, 1773.

[2] *Boston Gazette,* Dec. 20, 1773.

[3] *Ibid.,* Jan. 17, 1774. It is signed "Chairman of the Committee for Tarring and Feathering."

[4] *Ibid.,* Jan. 31, 1774; John Mein, *Sagittarius's Letters and Political Speculation,* (Boston, 1775), p. 15.

[5] Letters of John Andrews, *Mass. Hist. Soc., Proceedings,* vol. VIII, pp. 339, 370. [Hereafter cited as *Andrews Letters.*]

The BOSTONIAN'S Paying the EXCISE-MAN, or TARRING & FEATHERING

PAYING THE EXCISE-MAN, A CONTEMPORARY CARTOON, 1774

"render the populace, the rabble, the scum of the earth, insolent and disorderly, impudent and abusive." After describing an attack by one on the house of a man in Scarborough, which afforded him a case on his legal circuit, he says, "the terror, the distress, the distraction and horror of this family cannot be described by words" and he adds that, although he had often defended violence, "these tarrings and featherings, this breaking open houses by rude and insolent rabble in resentment for private wrongs, or in pursuance of private prejudices and passions" should be stopped.[1]

In the major outrage of the tea episode it is questionable whether Sam Adams had not over-reached himself, for with some exceptions the act was generally condemned throughout the colonies, except by extremists. Such men as Franklin and John Dickinson in the patriot party heartily disapproved of it, and the Tory Harrison Gray of Boston called it "a diabolical action."[2] Although owing to Adams's committees of correspondence, about forty of the nearby towns were induced to pass resolutions in favor of the action, such endorsements were by no means unanimous even in eastern New England. The Bristol town-meeting resolved that dangers were to be feared from other quarters as well as from England and that the "anarchy and confusion which may prevail will as naturally establish tyranny and arbitrary power. . . . Many on the side of liberty when they see it degenerating into anarchy, fearing their persons are not safe, nor their property secure, will be likely to verge to the opposite extreme." At York John Adams, who himself approved, reported that he found more persons "who call the destruction of the tea mischief and wickedness than anywhere else." Several Massachusetts towns took adverse action and Newport was coerced into ratification only after many months.[3] On the ground of mere opposition to unjust taxation there was indeed no answer to the reasoning of such men as Dr. Cooper

---

[1] *Letters of John Adams addressed to his Wife*, (Boston, 1841), vol. I, pp. 8, 13.

[2] *Col. Soc. Mass., Publications*, vol. V, p. 57; C. J. Stillé, *Life and Times of John Dickinson*, (Philadelphia, 1891), p. 100; [Harrison Gray] [*The two Congresses cut up* . . . (Boston, 1774), p. 4.

[3] Schlesinger, *Colonial Merchants*, pp. 299 ff.; J. Adams, *Works*, vol. II, pp. 323, 340 n. The resolutions of the towns may be found in the issues of the *Boston Gazette* from Dec. 6, 1773 to Apl. 4, 1774.

who wrote that, as the duties were regularly paid on wine and molasses, the colonists in order to act consistently should either refuse to pay those or agree to pay the one on tea, for they were all imposed on exactly the same principles and had the same effect.[1] As an irresponsible piece of reckless bravado designed to precipitate a crisis, the Tea Party was a success; but thoughtful men could not fail to condemn an act of violence that had no logical justification, and the results of which could not be foreseen. Sam Adams once prided himself on not looking ahead, but that is not a statesmanlike quality nor a safe one. He had made a blunder but, luckily for himself and fatally for the empire, he was to be saved by the English ministers making a still worse one.

If the action of the radicals in their wanton destruction of property met with condemnation from many of the soundest elements in the colonies, it may be imagined how it would strike the English government. On the 7th of March, 1774, Lord North asked Parliament for the means of suppressing the disorders in America, and a week later introduced a bill closing the port of Boston to commerce until it had made restitution to the East India Company for the destruction of its property — a method of punishment and reimbursement not without precedent in English history and law.[2] Although the ministry themselves seem to have been divided as to their course, the passage of the bill met with but little opposition.[3] Lord Camdem told the Massachusetts agent that "if an angel had come from Heaven it would not have availed" though the minority was somewhat larger than he expected.[4] So unnecessarily irritating and provocative had been the action of the radicals that such staunch friends of the colonies as Colonel Barré and Thomas Pownall voted for the measure, the latter even being in favor of bringing Sam Adams and a few other ring-leaders to England and trying them for treason, as the ministry considered doing.[5] In fact the

[1] [Myles Cooper] *A friendly Address to all reasonable Americans,* (n.p., 1774), p. 8.
[2] *Parlt. Hist.,* vol. XVII, pp. 1159 *ff.*; 14 Geo. III, c. 19.
[3] Fitzmaurice, *Life of Shelburne,* vol. II, pp. 303 *f.*; W. B. Donne, *Correspondence of Geo. III,* (London, 1867), vol. I, pp. 175 *ff.*
[4] *Bowdoin-Temple Papers,* p. 369.
[5] *Parlt. Hist.,* vol. XVII, p. 1169; Hutchinson, *Diary and Letters,* vol. I, pp. 183, 219 *f.*

cabinet decided to issue a warrant for Hancock, Cushing, Adams and Warren, and the attorney and solicitor-general were directed to prepare the papers. The Crown officers, however, objected. "Don't you see," the attorney-general said to Pownall, as he came out from the meeting with the ministers, "that they want to throw the whole responsibility of the business upon the solicitor-general and me; and who would be such damned fools as to risk themselves for such —— fellows as these? If it was George Grenville, who was so damned obstinate that he would go to hell with you before he would desert you, there might be some sense in it." He walked off and the project was temporarily dropped.[1] The law officers supported the government, however, as to its legal right to remove the custom house from Boston and to cause that town to cease to be a legal port of entry.[2]

The Port Bill was to go into effect on June 1st, but during the few months after it had been introduced in March several other acts were also passed dealing with the American situation, which we may note before turning to affairs on that continent. Three of these grew directly out of the troubles at Boston. A new Quartering Act provided that where there were no barracks in the exact places where troops were ordered the local authorities must make arrangements for their lodging.[3] Another, dealing with the administration of justice, provided that persons who in the opinion of the governor or his lieutenant could not have an unbiased trial in the colony might be sent to England with all the witnesses.[4] Still another provided for the "better regulating the government" of the colony by modifying the charter so that thereafter councilors should be appointed by the Crown instead of elected by the assembly; jurors should be appointed by the sheriffs instead of elected by the freeholders, and town-meetings, save an annual one for the election of officers, should

[1] *Mss. of Capt. Knox, Var. Coll., Hist. Mss. Repts.* vol. VI, pp. 269 *f.*
[2] Questions referred to Attorney and Solicitor General by Earl of Dartmouth, and their report, Feb. 10, 1774, *C.O. 5 No. 247.*
[3] 14 Geo. III, c. 54. This was to avoid the plea of Boston that when troops were sent there they could be kept only at Castle William in the harbor, which defeated the purpose for which they were sent.
[4] *Ibid.,* c. 39; *Parlt. Hist.,* vol. XVII, pp. 1199 *ff.*, 1274 *ff.*, 1289 *ff.*, 1316 *ff.*, 1350 *ff.*

not be held without the written consent of the governor.[1] Although both of the bills just noted met with more opposition
than the one closing the port, protests being recorded against
each of them by dissenting minorities in the Lords, both passed
without difficulty.[2]

A fourth bill which was also passed about the same time had
ostensibly no reference to the older colonies, although its effect
on sentiment in them was perhaps as diastrous as that of any
enacted during those years. This was the Quebec Act.[3] Largely
on account of rapid changes in the ministries and partly from
lack of revenue due to the repeal of the Stamp Act, the whole
question of Canada and the western country, which had been
treated in what was expected to be temporary fashion in the
Proclamation of 1763, had been allowed to drift. Although
there had been some settlement from the older colonies across
the mountains, there was much truth in North's statement that
the Illinois country — which was added by the bill to the
province of Quebec — was as yet but "the habitation of bears
and beavers."[4] In Quebec proper the enormous disparity between the English population of about six hundred and the
seventy thousand or more French, prevented the establishment
of such a representative form of popular government as had
carelessly been promised in the earlier proclamation. It seemed
unfair to have the English ruled by the French or to have the
small body of English rule a hundred times their own number of
the other nation. Trial by jury under such conditions also presented obvious difficulties. Furthermore, by the terms of the
capitulations when Canada was conquered, the French had been
promised the exercise of their religion. In an effort to give more
definite form to the government of the province, to remove
existing difficulties and to fulfill pledges, it was enacted that
the government should be by an appointed governor and council; that the colonists could not be given the privilege of self-

---

[1] 14 Geo. III, c. 45; *Parlt. Hist.*, vol. XVII, pp. 1192 *ff.*, 1277 *ff.*, 1300 *ff.*, 1321 *ff.*
[2] *Parlt. Hist.*, vol. XVII, pp. 1321 *ff.*, 1351 *ff.*
[3] 14 Geo. III, c. 83; *Parlt. Hist.*, vol. XVII, pp. 1357 *ff.*; Cavendish, *Debates of the House of Commons in 1774 on the Quebec Act, passim*; Kennedy, *Documents of the Canadian Constitution*, pp. 86 *ff.*
[4] Cavendish, *Debates, cit. supra*, p. 10.

taxation; that the Catholics should enjoy the exercise of their religion; that trials should be without jury; and, for efficiency in the administration of the great stretch of wilderness west of the old colonies and north of the Ohio River, that that section should be added to Quebec. The two American scholars who have made the most thorough study of this phase of the British legislation are of opinion that it was in no way aimed at the liberties of the older colonies.[1] A careful study of the debates indicates to my mind that the innocence of the English ministers can scarcely be considered quite so complete. At least, the opposition to the passage of the bill both in the Lords and Commons was bitter and its effect on American sentiment was pointed out in no ambiguous terms. There can be no doubt that that effect was disastrous in the extreme.

The more one studies public opinion in England and in the colonies in relation to each other at this period, the more one is struck with the utter lack of comprehension of each side with regard to the other.[2] In a very real sense the American revolution in one of its aspects was a civil war — not the obvious one between the mother country and colonies but one between conflicting parties in each. Nevertheless, even those trans-Atlantic groups which seemed to be pursuing common ends were in reality far apart in their views. Even the meanings attached to such terms as "representation" and "the English Constitution" differed on the two sides of the water, and added to the confusion of thought. If this was true of the imperialists of the upper classes of the old and new worlds, it was even more strikingly evident among the common people. The stronghold of radical sentiment in America was in the lower economic and social strata, and it was the common people in England that were most favorable to the aspirations of the colonists, as was to be the case in the great struggle of the following century.[3] Travelers from one country to the other, however, were quick to observe differences. In 1775, Josiah Quincy wrote home from

[1] Coffin, *Province of Quebec and the early American Revolution*, pp. 404 *ff.*; Alvord, *Mississippi Valley*, *loc. cit.*, especially vol. II, pp. 216 *ff.*

[2] *Cf.* C. H. Van Tyne, *The Causes of the War of Independence*, (Boston, 1922), chap. XII.

[3] *Correspondence of Wm. Pitt*, vol. IV, pp. 341, 401.

England that he was more and more "confirmed every day that
the commonalty in this country are no more like the commonalty in America than if they were two utterly distinct and
unconnected people." [1]

This ignorance of each other's characters had a fatal effect on
their political relations. The Americans thought that England
would not resort to arms to enforce her claims, and Englishmen
at home were convinced that the Americans were merely putting up a bold front and would never offer armed resistance on
any large scale. Of this there is ample evidence, even on the
parts of those who had the best opportunity of knowing sentiment on both sides. Quincy who was in England spying out
the land, wrote home that he was told that England would
never carry on a civil war against America. Richard Henry
Lee, whose brother was sheriff of London, was absolutely sure
at the opening of the congress of 1774 that the same ship that
carried the news of strong measures to England would bring
back redress. On the other hand, General Gage, who had an
American wife, told George the Third that the Americans "will
be Lyons whilst we are lambs but if we take the resolute part
they will undoubtedly prove very meek." Shelburne wrote to
Pitt at the time of the passage of the Port Bill, that the opinion
was general that America would not and could not resist. [2]

Apart from this ignorance of one another due to the obstacle
of distance, there were good reasons why each should so mistake the other. For a hundred and fifty years, England had not
made serious efforts to coerce the colonies. Although she appeared more bent at this time upon enforcing her policies, the
experience of five generations seemed to show that the old
colonial methods of opposition would win after all without a
serious clash. On the other hand, Englishmen and the Loyalists
in America found it difficult to believe that, when faced with
actual conflict against the whole power of Great Britain, the
colonists would dare carry matters to extremity. It appeared to

[1] Josiah Quincy, *Memoir of Josiah Quincy, Jr.*, (Boston, 1875), p. 259. *Cf. American Husbandry*, by an American, (London, 1775), vol. I, pp. 66 *f.*

[2] Quincy, *Memoir*, p. 224; *Letters of Members of the Continental Congress*, ed. E. C. Burnett, (Washington, 1921), vol. I, p. 3; Donne, *Correspondence of Geo. III*, vol. I, p. 164; Fitzmaurice, *Life of Shelburne*, vol. II, p. 299.

them a hazard beyond reason, and they were right. The colonies could not have won single-handed against England, and could not have won at all without the character and genius of Washington. But at this time the final coming in of France for her own purposes could not be counted upon, and the character of Washington, which indeed developed with the war, was little known. The judgment of the conservatives was thus more nearly correct than that of the radicals, though, due in part to forces operating outside of America, events decided in favor of the latter. This misconception that each side had of the other was an undoubted factor of prime importance in shaping the contest, so that a situation was created which left the way open to no appeal but that of the sword. It had been more than once suggested since the disagreements began that a commission should be sent to America to enquire into conditions on the spot, but this common-sense method seems never to have received serious support.[1] Even Hutchinson appears to have misjudged the situation and, when relieved of his office and called to England at his own request, he is said to have approved of the Port Bill and to have misled the king as to its probable effects.[2]

The news of the passage of the Act shutting the port was received in Boston on May 10th, and three days later both the committee of correspondence and the town sent letters to the committees of correspondence of the other colonies stating that Boston was "suffering the stroke of vengeance in the common cause of America" and asking for assistance.[3] On the same day, General Gage, fated to be the last royal governor of Massachusetts, arrived superseding Hutchinson.[4] He was also com-

[1] Cf. Donne, Correspondence of Geo. III, vol. I, p. 219.

[2] Ibid., pp. 194 f. There is some doubt as to the authenticity of the interview as reported.

[3] S. Adams, Writings, vol. III, pp. 107 ff.

[4] He had received the usual set of instructions "given to Governors in the Exercise of the ordinary and more permanent Powers and Authorities incident to that Command," but as the circumstances of the time called for additional instructions these were given in a letter from Dartmouth dated Apl. 9, 1774. In carrying the Port Bill into effect he was authorized to use the troops should "the Madness of the People" or the "Timidity, or want of Strength of the Peace Officers" demand it. He was also instructed to collect all possible evidence against the ring-leaders in the opposition so as to permit of proceedings being brought against them, the king considering the punishment of these offenders "very necessary and essential." I am indebted to the courtesy of Albert Matthews, Esq., and the Colonial Society of Massachusetts for copies of the Instructions and Lord Dartmouth's letter.

mander-in-chief of the forces in America and was soon followed by four regiments. In the letter to the other colonies the Boston committee had attempted to make it appear that England was really striking at all of them in her over-harsh measure against the one town for its treatment of the tea, and they asked for a general suspension of trade with Great Britain. This suggestion, however, that the whole of America should embroil itself anew with the mother country in order to help the Boston radicals extricate themselves from the results of their rash act, did not meet with the hearty and unanimous response that Adams hoped. The merchants generally and the whole conservative class had by no means approved of the destruction of the tea, and were again drawing back from the violence of the radicals. "The heads of the mobility grow dangerous to the gentry" wrote Gouverneur Morris to Penn from New York, "and how to keep them down is the question." They are counting their chickens, he adds, not only before they are hatched but before one-half the eggs are laid, and are already disputing whether the future government of America shall be "founded upon aristocratic or democratic principles." "I see, and I see it with fear and trembling" he continues, "that if the disputes with Great Britain continue, we shall be under the worst of all possible dominions, we shall be under the domination of a riotous mob." [1] In Philadelphia every effort was made to have the patriot John Dickinson speak at a meeting in favor of giving help to the Bostonians, but no entreaties, not even "the generous circulation of the convivial glass" as a "conversational aperient" would entice him into approving the position of the Boston radicals who, he believed, had wantonly destroyed all hopes of reconciliation. [2] Not only did many throughout all the colonies believe that Boston should pay for the property destroyed and so secure relief, but so did many in that town itself. A subscription was started there among the merchants and George Erving offered £2,000 if the total could be raised. [3] The proposition was ably debated at a meeting of the tradesmen,

[1] Force, *American Archives*, Ser. IV, vol. I, pp. 347 *ff*.
[2] Stillé, *John Dickinson*, p. 106.
[3] *Andrews Letters*, p. 329.

but it became evident that the common people were opposed to it and a few days later at a town-meeting the subject was not even broached.[1] Meanwhile Boston was beginning to suffer severely, for Gage exceeded even the rigor of the Act and would not allow provisions to be ferried across at Charlestown, so that every article of any sort had to be hauled from Salem or Marblehead at heavy expense by wagoners who, when they struck a particularly bad spot in the long road, "whipped their horses and damned Lord North alternately." [2] Mainly through the instrumentality of the committees of correspondence in the other colonies, large supplies of provisions were sent to assist the large numbers of Boston's unemployed, shipments being received from even so far as South Carolina, but welcome as were this generous aid and the wide-spread expressions of sympathy, it was not the response to which the radical leaders had trusted.[3] The split between the radicals and conservatives was rapidly widening. An agreement not to purchase any goods imported from England until the Act was repealed, styled a "solemn league and covenant" met with instant response in the country districts of Massachusetts but not in the other colonies, and the merchants remained cold. More and more the revolutionary impulse was coming from below. "Those worthy members of society, the tradesmen," wrote Thomas Young from Boston, "we depend on, under God, to form the revolution of the other ranks of citizens, in Philadelphia and New York. They are certainly carrying all before them here. The yeomanry of our country towns are another effectual support." [4]

The case against the Port Bill was ably presented in a pamphlet by Josiah Quincy, Junior,[5] and the general opinion of the colonists everywhere was adverse to the measures adopted by the ministry, but there was deep division as to methods to be pursued by the colonists owing, to a great extent, to the increas-

[1] I. Q. Leake, *Memoir of Gen. John Lamb*, (Albany, 1850), p. 90. *Cf.* Force, *American Archives, cit. supra*, pp. 289, 295.

[2] *Andrews Letters, cit. supra*, p. 336.

[3] Correspondence regarding the relief of the sufferers, *Mass. Hist. Soc., Coll.*, Ser. IV, vol. IV, pp. 1 *ff.*

[4] Leake, *Memoirs of Gen. John Lamb*, p. 89.

[5] *Observations on the Act of Parliament commonly called the Boston Port-Bill . . .* (Boston, 1774). This is reprinted in the *Memoir*, pp. 293 *ff.*

ing fear of the radicals. John Andrews of Boston, who spoke of the bills passed by Parliament as those "infernal acts" and who, he says, was as "well dispos'd in the cause of Freedom as any of our opponents," lamented "the cursed zeal that now prevails." "Animosities run higher than ever" he wrote, and "unless some expediency is adopted to get the port open by paying for the tea (which seems to be the only one) am afraid we shall experience the worst of evils, a civil war."[1] Similarly a certain John Gooch wrote that although the Port Act proved "equally Pernistious to both Parties," all was "tumult and confusion" and that the mob which had taken the reins of government was "a most miserable Charioteer."[2]

On the 17th of May the town of Providence had suggested that a general congress be called to consider the rights of the colonies and the formation of a union.[3] New York, in reply to the letter from the Boston committee, after merely condoling with that town also suggested a congress to consider the situation.[4] This was the suggestion of most of the other colonies, and as the weeks wore on, it became evident that no earlier concert of action could be hoped for by the radicals, and that, much against the wishes of Sam Adams, the contest for control would have to be transferred to such a general meeting of delegates, which it was finally agreed should be held in Philadelphia in September. Meanwhile the established government in Massachusetts was rapidly breaking down. The royal appointees to the Council, known as "mandamus Councilors" were hunted from the country districts and those who did not resign were forced to take refuge in Boston under the protection of Gage. A representative to the Provincial Congress complaining of the lack of public order cited over thirty cases of serious mob violence throughout the colony, directed for the most part against prominent persons.[5] "Nothing but mobs and riots all this

---

[1] *Andrews Letters, cit. supra*, p. 329.
[2] *The Cumberland Letters*, ed. C. Black, (London, 1912), pp. 58, 61.
[3] Force, *American Archives*, Ser. IV, vol. I, pp. 333 f.
[4] Dawson, *Westchester County*, pp. 51 ff.
[5] Force, *American Archives*, Ser. IV, vol. I, pp. 1260 ff. Even in Boston, with the English troops, people were not wholly safe from the mobs. *Copley-Pelham Letters*, Mass. Hist. Soc., (Boston, 1914), p. 218.

summer" wrote Peter Oliver in his diary, and in September a crowd of four thousand surrounded his house at Cambridge and forced his resignation.[1] Jurors, when appointed, refused to serve and in county after county throughout August, by one method and another, the courts were prevented from sitting. In Boston the judges had been impeached by the assembly.[2] At Worcester a mob of five thousand forced the judges, lawyers and sheriff to pass bareheaded between files of citizens and swear not less than thirty times that they would not hold court under the new Parliamentary Acts.[3] "All legislative, as well as executive power was gone," wrote Hutchinson, "and the danger of revolt was daily increasing." Gage sent word to Dartmouth that "civil government is near its end; the courts of justice expiring one after another."

In fact, however, civil government was not so much near its end as it was passing from the hands of the hitherto constituted authorities into those of the revolutionists. When Gage, hopeless of being able to effect anything by a meeting of the General Court in view of the situation as to the Councilors, canceled the writs for the autumn election, the towns professed to consider the action illegal, and elected representatives to a provincial congress. This body met in October and, although without any legal justification, undertook the administration of the affairs of the colony, backed by the opinion of the majority. There were thus two governments, the one established by the charter modified by Parliament, possessing but the shadow of power at Boston, and the wholly revolutionary one sitting at Concord, which latter steadily gathered to itself all the administrative functions.[4] Those who were loyal to the imperial ideal and dreaded a violent overturn, regarded its proceedings with no small anxiety. "Our provincial congress had adjourned themselves for three weeks," wrote the merchant John Andrews. "Had much rather they were dissolv'd — as they are principally

---

[1] Hutchinson, *Diary and Letters*, vol. I, p. 151. *Cf.* Cushing, *Transition from Provincial to Commonwealth Government in Massachusetts*, pp. 58 *ff.*; Force, *American Archives*, Ser. IV, vol. I, pp. 745, 763 *f.*

[2] J. Adams, *Works*, vol. II, pp. 329 *ff.*; *Annual Register*, (1774), pp. 224 *ff.*; *Boston Gazette*, Mar. 7, 1774; *Journal Mass. House of Representatives* (1774), pp. 194 *ff.*

[3] Cushing, *cit. supra*, pp. 85 *ff.*

[4] *Ibid.*, pp. 61 *ff.*, 114 *ff.*

composed of spirited, obstinate countrymen who have very little patience to boast of. Am therefore much afraid they will adopt measures that may impede the adjustment of our differences — as the more prudent among 'em bear but a small proportion." [1]

Conciliation, however, was the last thing the radicals wished. Their whole energies were bent upon forcing action by the congress sitting at Philadelphia, where, in turn, the conservatives hoped to guide matters to a peaceful solution. The question ostensibly before that body was that of imperial relations between England and her colonies, but lurking back of that in the minds of radicals and conservatives alike was a second, and to many a more important one — if the imperial government as heretofore established does not rule, who will? Sam Adams, stern Puritan and staunch democrat, with his abiding faith in the common man, would answer, "the people whose voice is the voice of God." The conservatives would say, "the mob, who even now have been tarring and feathering, threatening men's lives, burning their houses, destroying their goods, capable of nothing but bloodshed and anarchy if they secure complete control." The anxiety and suspense were intense. The majority of colonists condemned the acts of the English ministers, but if few could be found to defend the policy of England, many loved her. The glory of her past was theirs, and though few had stepped upon her shores, the island kingdom still was "home" in common speech. In spite of the maddening results of folly in high places, the thought of severing the ancient ties was infinitely painful to the majority of those whose knowledge and sympathy were not limited by the bounds of farm or town. Moreover, the same eyes that honestly dimmed at the thought of fratricidal war, also peered anxiously into a future where all known landmarks seemed to be lost and where the shrouded outlines of a strange new order, in which the power to rule came from below instead of from above, made a mockery of their inherited instincts and life-long preconceptions. The old order was indeed crumbling, and looking, not backward through history, but forward to an unknown future, there was no assurance that a new and fairer one would arise from its ruins.

[1] *Andrews Letters*, p. 380.

On the other hand, in city shop and country farm, in fishing hamlet on the coast and rude clearings on forested hills, the passionate opposition to any interference with economic and political freedom was rapidly gaining momentum among those who had been used to make their own way and order their own lives. There was, indeed, "a great tide flowing in the hearts of men," sweeping them and their destinies onward to the waters of an unknown sea. Above the growing roar of rushing waters, the leaders of thought might shout their rationalizing formulæ of constitutional debate, but in the heart of the individual revolutionist there was but the passionate desire to live his life, to express his personality, to utilize his powers, unhampered by any rule imposed from above, of government, of class, or of economic privilege. Here and there a man of wealth and social standing, hoping to guide the current into safe channels or with a faith akin to Adams's own in the future of democracy, joined with the extremer radicals. The tumult and the bitterness grew. Meanwhile, General Gage, now governor in name only, fortified Boston Neck, and, having modified his belief that four regiments would quiet America, was anxiously writing home for heavy reinforcements to secure a position becoming daily more precarious.

CHAPTER XVII

THE DEFEAT OF THE CONSERVATIVES

Continental Congress — Suffolk Resolves — Conservatives Defeated in Congress — Opposing Parties — Trouble on the Frontier — First Acts of War — Lexington and Concord — The Restraining Act — English Opinion — Ticonderoga — Bunker Hill — Canadian Expedition

On the 10th of August, 1774, the four representatives of Massachusetts to the Continental Congress set out from Boston for Philadelphia. They were John Adams, Samuel Adams, Thomas Cushing and Robert Treat Paine. "Am told they made a very respectable parade," wrote John Andrews, "in sight of five of the Regiments encamped on the common, being in a coach and four, preceded by two white servants well mounted and armed, with four blacks behind in livery, two on horseback and two footmen. Am in hopes their joint deliberations will effect something for our relief; more particularly to concert such measures as may be adopted by the Mother Country, so as to settle a friendship between us that may be lasting and permanent." [1] From all the other colonies except Georgia delegates were similarly setting forth on the same fateful errand. From New Hampshire went Major John Sullivan and Colonel Nathaniel Folsom, from Rhode Island Stephen Hopkins and Samuel Ward, and from Connecticut Eliphalet Dyer, Silas Deane and Roger Sherman. It would be impossible to say whether the meeting of the delegates was more favored or feared by the people at large. Both radicals and conservatives hoped that they might win control, and on the other hand feared to lose. Extremists like Sam Adams did their best to commit the colonies to a course from which there could be no turning back

[1] *Andrews Letters, cit. supra*, p. 339. For the incidents of the journey *vide* J. Adams, *Works*, vol. II, pp. 340 ff.

before the Congress met, but without success. It is probable that the great majority of the colonists felt much as did Andrews. They wished their grievances redressed and their liberties maintained, but by some method that would not involve a break with England, and all the terrors and uncertainties of civil war. This majority was flanked on either side by smaller parties, one of which wanted to precipitate a crisis and risk all for independence regardless of any English concessions, and the other of which feared the social revolution so greatly as to prefer, in the worst of cases, failure to obtain redress rather than the risk of revolution incident to war.

The Continental Congress was the most representative gathering of Americans that had yet assembled, there being a larger number of conspicuously able men from the southern colonies than from New England. It is noteworthy that there were only eleven merchants and that over two-thirds of the members were lawyers.[1] From the first it was evident that there would be a serious struggle between the conservatives and radicals for control. Although the choice of Carpenters Hall instead of the State House as a meeting place, out of deference to the mechanics, and the election of Charles Thomson, a Son of Liberty, as secretary, were minor victories for the radicals, the balance was fairly even for the first three weeks.[2] The decision, however, that the delegations from each colony should cast but one vote gave an appearance of unanimity that was far from actual, resolutions entered as unanimous being favored by not more than two-thirds of the members.[3] Galloway, one of the Pennsylvania delegates, a conservative and a man of large wealth, says that the "men of loyal principles" acted openly and on the defensive whereas the radicals "were secret and hypocritical," concealing their real designs by every possible means. This seems to have been true to a considerable extent, for even with the aid of Virginians and South Carolinians, — who, Rodney of Delaware said, were far more radical than the Bostonians, — John Adams feared the failure of their plans.

[1] Schlesinger, *Colonial Merchants*, p. 409; Burnett, *Letters of Members*, vol. I, p. 1.
[2] *Cf.* Burnett, *cit. supra*, vol. I, pp. 54 f.
[3] *Journals of the Continental Congress*, ed. W. C. Ford, (Washington, 1904), vol. I, p. 25; Schlesinger, *Colonial Merchants*, p. 412; Burnett, *cit. supra*, vol. I, pp. 7, 12, 15.

"We have had innumerable prejudices to remove," he wrote. "We have been obliged to keep ourselves out of sight, and to feel pulses, and to sound the depths; to insinuate our sentiments, designs, desires, by means of other persons, sometimes of one province, sometimes of another."[1] In this sort of political manoeuvering, his colleague Sam Adams was a past master. In Galloway's opinion he managed at once the "faction" in Congress and those in Massachusetts, arranging for the despatch from Boston of inflammatory messages at opportune times.[2] Whether this was so or not, a message did arrive from that town, the very day after Congress convened, falsely stating that Boston had been bombarded, colonists had been killed and that the whole country had risen to arms as far as Connecticut. The effect of this false news, John Adams noted, "was very great."[3]

At a meeting of delegates from the towns in Suffolk County, Massachusetts, on September 9th, a series of resolves had been adopted which were brought before Congress on the 17th with a request for endorsement. The preamble was most violent in its language, speaking of the vengeance of Great Britain "which of old persecuted, scourged, and exiled our fugitive parents" and which now pursued their "guiltless children with unrelenting severity." The streets of Boston were said to be "thronged with military executioners" and the people were called upon to "disarm the parricide which points the dagger to" their bosoms. It was claimed that no obedience was due to the recent Acts of Parliament, that the government as then established was illegal, that all taxes should be paid to the revolutionary organization, that troops should be raised and that all commercial intercourse with Great Britain and the West Indies should be suspended.[4] Could the Congress be induced to endorse these whirling words, it would go far not only to shutting the door to any possible reconciliation but toward bolting and barring it. Nevertheless, after warm debate, the passage of two resolutions was secured endorsing the Suffolk Resolves.[5]

[1] Burnett, cit. supra, vol. I, pp. 27, 55, 60.
[2] Ibid., p. 55.
[3] Ibid., pp. 13, 19 f., 36.
[4] Congress Journals, cit. supra, pp. 32 ff.
[5] Ibid., vol. I, pp. 39 f. Two of the dissenting members asked to have their dissent entered on the minutes, but this was refused and it was given out that the resolution had been adopted nem. con.

In spite of this action, and partly to test the real intentions of Congress, the conservatives presented a plan drawn by Galloway for a new form of union with Great Britain, which it was thought by many would entirely solve the questions at issue and save the empire. It received warm support from Duane and Jay of New York, and from Edward Rutledge of South Carolina, the last calling it "almost a perfect plan." The Rhode Island delegation was divided. Although the plan was entered upon the minutes by a vote of six colonies to five, the radicals rallied so strongly that it was never again considered, and they even succeeded in having all traces of the suggestion and vote expunged from the record. No better proof than this is needed of the fear of the radicals lest some reconciliation be effected, even had we not John Adams's statement that Galloway's suggestion had been the "most alarming" difficulty that was encountered by the Congress.[1] It was now evident that the conservatives had been beaten, that those who had favored a congress in the hope that some plan for reconciling the differences with the mother country might be found, had lost, and that the fate of the colonies was in the hands of the extremist group.

On the 14th of October, Congress adopted a series of resolutions stating that, based upon the law of nature, the English Constitution and the colonial charters, the colonists were entitled to certain rights of life, liberty and property, and that these had been violated by the recent legislation in Parliament. Although the right of that body to regulate external commerce was admitted, this in reality was nullified by the denial of the Parliamentary right of taxation in any form and by the denial of the possibility of the colonists ever being represented in England. The maintenance of imperial troops in America and other grievances, including the Quebec Act, were alluded to, and the threat of armed revolt was clearly made. In order to obtain redress "we have for the present" the paper read, "only resolved to pursue the following peaceable measures." These were addresses to the king and the English people, and a colonial

[1] *Congress Journals*, vol. I, pp. 43 *ff.*; Burnett, *cit. supra*, vol. I, pp. 51 *ff.*, 80. (For convenience I cite from Burnett's collection of documents even in cases in which, in other connections, I have cited the original works.)

agreement of non-importation, non-consumption and non-exportation until England should yield.[1]

It was this agreement, or "Association" as it was named, that constituted the most important action of Congress. That extralegal body could claim no power of legislation whatever. The delegates had been elected by various methods, in some cases by the assemblies, in others by the radical committees of correspondence, but in no case by a general election of the people. Conservatives and radicals could unite in an attempt to reconcile the differences with England by means of joint deliberation and negotiation, but as soon as the Congress undertook to enforce its will upon the people it ceased to be merely a mediating organ and became a revolutionary government. This was accomplished by the Association. Not only did the signers agree that after certain dates they would wholly abstain from importing and buying certain goods and from exporting any commodities to England or the West Indies, but these conditions were to be forced upon all colonists alike. Committees were to be chosen in "every county, city and town" who should see that the Association was complied with, and if anyone dared to act contrary to its terms he was to be publicly branded as an enemy to American liberty, and cut off from society. No social or commercial intercourse could be had with him. In view of the violence prevailing, the threat was by no means an idle one. Moreover, goods imported by anyone, whether a signer or not, were to be seized by the committees and either stored or sold, in which latter case the owner was to be reimbursed only for the cost, the profits to be given for the relief of the poor in Boston.

The publication of this document at once brought out a storm of protest from the moderates. In pamphlets and the press they heartily condemned the actions of Congress. It had made "our breach with the parent state a thousand times more irreparable than it was before," wrote one. "In God's name are not the people of Boston able to relieve their own poor?" he continued. Do the Bostonians "expect a literal completion of the promise that the Saints shall inherit the earth? In my conscience I believe they do" and the irate author endorsed the

[1] *Congress Journals*, vol. I, pp. 63 *ff.*

recently expressed opinion that the Bostonians think that "God had made Boston for himself and all the rest of the world for Boston."[1] What right, he continued, had Congress to order the seizure of people's goods, to legislate for them, and to place the fate of every man in the hands of irresponsible and illegal committees? Although he admitted he might be laughed at for the notion, yet he felt there was grave danger Congress might develop a republic out of the situation. "Could anything be more unjust, tyrannical, arbitrary and oppressive?" wrote Harrison Gray of the right of seizure vested in the committees. "Can the edicts of the most despotic princes under heaven exceed it?"[2] The terms of the Association, said a writer in the *Massachusetts Gazette*, "would shock the soul of a savage" . . . they constitute "such a system of lawless tyranny as a Turk would startle at."[3] It was felt that the moderates in the congress had been outwitted. "You had all the leading cards in every sute in your own hand," said a Boston writer, "and yet . . . you suffered sharpers to get the odd trick."[4]

Nor was opposition confined wholly to writing. The long series of resolves refusing to sustain Congress that were passed by towns and counties in New York are well known.[5] In Connecticut protests were made at town-meetings or by large parts of the populations of Ridgefield, Newtown, Danbury, New Milford, and Reading.[6] At Marshfield in Massachusetts there was an effort made to organize a Loyalist Association that should have its committees and work in opposition to the revolutionary organization.[7] It is always more difficult, however, to organize a conservative defence than a radical attack. The machinery of the radicals was already in working order and had been made continental in scope by the congress. The tarrings and featherings and other mob violences had also intimidated the conservatives except where they were notoriously in the majority. In the

[1] [Samuel Seabury] *The Congress canvassed*, pp. 5, 15, 17 f.
[2] *The two Congresses cut up*, p. 9.
[3] Cited by Schlesinger, *Colonial Merchants*, p. 437.
[4] *Massachusetts Gazette*, Feb. 6, 1775, cited by Schlesinger, *Colonial Merchants*, p. 438.
[5] Force, *American Archives*, Ser. IV, vol. I, pp. 1203, 1211, 1230; vol. II, pp. 151, 273, 282, 304, 313.
[6] *Ibid.*, vol. I, pp. 1202, 1210, 1235, 1215 f., 1258 f.
[7] *Ibid.*, vol. I, pp. 1178, 1198, 1249.

middle colonies they were so in many localities, but in New England, although they were present in very considerable numbers, they were so scattered as to make effective action against the aggressive and lawless radicals as difficult as it was dangerous. The assemblies of both Connecticut and Rhode Island, the Provincial Congress in Massachusetts and the Provincial Committee of the extra-legal convention of towns in New Hampshire, soon endorsed the acts of Congress, and the committee system called for to enforce the Association was put into operation in all four colonies.

The line was now far more clearly drawn between the conservatives and radicals, or as we may call them now, Loyalists and Patriots, than at any previous time, for the opposition to England had assumed a form that was difficult to distinguish from open rebellion. Great numbers, who condemned the Acts of Parliament as heartily as did the patriots, could not bring themselves to raise the standard of open revolt without having exhausted every effort at peaceful remonstrance. New England was seething, and the situation was daily becoming more warlike. On October 19, 1774, an order-in-council had been issued in England prohibiting the exportation of arms and ammunition to the colonies.[1] This order and the confidential letter conveying it from Dartmouth was divulged by the governor of Rhode Island, and in that colony the cannon and other stores at Fort George were immediately ordered to be taken to Providence, and additional troops raised.[2] Word of England's action was forwarded to Boston and thence to Portsmouth. The popularity and ability of Wentworth had thus far prevented any serious outbreak in New Hampshire, but events had moved too rapidly for him, and the first attack upon royal troops took place in that colony, on December 13th. Pursuant to plans made by the local committee, Fort William and Mary was assaulted and, in spite of determined resistance by the small garrison, was captured and a hundred barrels of powder seized.[3]

A number of local questions that we have already noted as

---

[1] *Acts Privy Council*, vol. V, p. 401. The order was for six months, and was renewed from time to time until 1783.

[2] *R. I. Col. Records*, vol. VII, pp. 262 ff.

[3] *N. H. Prov. Papers*, vol. VII, pp. 420 f.; Mayo, *John Wentworth*, pp. 140 ff.

dividing parties in the colonies were also reaching the point of violent action, and although in reality they were wholly colonial in nature they were drawn into the stream of the major contest with England, and the animosities aroused and the party cries raised were merged in those of the larger question. For example, in Connecticut, the dispute between parties within that colony and between that colony and Pennsylvania over the Susquehannah settlement had become acute. Those who favored asserting Connecticut's untenable claims and committing the colony to the Western adventure were for the most part in the radical patriot party. As late as the fall of 1772 they had been unable to induce the assembly to assert a colonial claim to the lands, and had adopted the policy of keeping quiet, and crowding their settlers in as fast as possible.[1] Finally, as it was said, "by selling rights to some and giving to others they . . . so increased their numbers that the General Assembly could not procure a vote to exclude the members of the Susquehannah Company from sitting and voting" in their own case.[2] However the matter may have been managed, the assembly did reverse its position and voted that the western lands belonged to Connecticut and erected them into a township annexed to the Connecticut county of Litchfield.[3] It is noteworthy that the three delegates to the Continental Congress were Susquehannah stockholders and members of the committee appointed to press the new claim against Pennsylvania. The party split in the colony over the English and Susquehannah questions was the same, and undoubtedly many of the speculators were using anti-English feeling to push their scheme.[4]

A similar case occurred in the New Hampshire Grants. The conflicting claims of New Hampshire and New York, with the resultant uncertainty as to land titles, had not prevented a large number of people from settling in the region about the Green Mountains. In the northern part particularly, the population

---

[1] Harvey, *History of Wilkes-Barré*, vol. II, p. 754.

[2] *Connecticut Courant*, Feb. 22, 1774, cited by Harvey, *cit. supra*, p. 792.

[3] *Conn. Col. Records*, vol. XIV, pp. 161 *f.*, 217 *f.*

[4] The Susquehannah question appeared several times in the congress and occasioned no little ill-feeling. *Vide* Burnett, *Letters of Members*, vol. I, pp. 397 *f.*; also *loc. cit.* in index under caption "Wyoming."

was characterized by all the qualities of frontier squatters, and lynch law replaced that of the courts. The original settlers had received titles from New Hampshire, and the claims of jurisdiction by New York were bitterly resented. In an effort to arrange the question at Albany, Ethan Allen had met a number of New York land speculators, lawyers and the King's Attorney, but to no effect. It is said that when the latter advised the settlers to make the best terms possible, for might often prevailed over right, Allen replied merely that "the Gods of the Valleys are not the Gods of the hills," and suggested that the Attorney meet him at Bennington for further explanation.[1] As early as 1771, Allen had organized a regiment of which he was colonel and which carried things much as it wished. Acts of violence, including in several cases the burning of houses, had not been uncommon and the power of the "Bennington Mob," as it was called, was much increased by the publishing of a notice that anyone who should try to arrest any of them would meet with "immediate death." [2]

Poverty, the fear of ejectment from their homes, the frontier spirit of lawlessness and the dislike of New York on the part of many, all roused opposition to the courts erected by that colony within the limits of the Grants after a portion of that territory had been made into a new county. Finally, an armed clash occurred between the people, and the sheriff and judges in the court house at Westminster, in which two citizens were killed and several wounded.[3] There had long been trouble brewing but "at this time" we read in the Whig account "there were Tory parties forming, although they were under disguise; and had laid a plan to bring the lower sort of the people into a state of bondage and slavery. They saw that there was no cash stirring and they took that opportunity to collect debts, knowing that men had no other way to pay them than by having their estates taken by execution. . . . There were but very few

---

[1] Ira Allen, *The natural and political History of the State of Vermont*, (London, 1798), p. 24.

[2] J. H. Smith, *Our Struggle for the fourteenth Colony*, (New York, 1907), vol. I, pp. 114 *f.*

[3] Hall, *Eastern Vermont*, pp. 209 *ff.*; Force, *American Archives*, Ser. IV, vol. II, pp. 214 *f.*; *Records of the Council of Safety and Governor and Council of the State of Vermont*, (Montpelier, 1873), vol. I, pp. 330 *ff.*

among us that were able to buy; and they were so disposed that they would take all the world into their own hands, without paying anything for it, if they could, by law." [1] This situation has all the familiar ear-marks of an acute economic crisis on any frontier. The New York assembly, however, had refused to endorse the actions of the Continental Congress, and many if not most of the capitalists were Loyalists, so that the insurrection that occurred cloaked itself, as did the machinations of the Connecticut speculators, under the guise of resistance to England and "the enemies of American liberty." On the tombstone of William French, a lad of twenty-two who lost his life in the riot, we read that he was shot "by the hands of Cruel Ministerial tools of Georg the 3d," and below

> Here William French his Body lies.
> For Murder his Blood for Vengeance cries.
> King Georg the tird his Tory crew
> That with a bawl his head Shot threw [*sic*] [2]

It is by no means intended to try to prove that the major movement was wholly made up of such minor ones, but it is interesting to note how many such small rivulets rising from springs far remote from the central issue fed the main stream and immensely increased its volume and violence.

Meanwhile the Provincial Congress in Massachusetts by addresses and proclamations had been doing their best to arouse a spirit of resistance among the people. In October 1774 they had appointed a treasurer to receive taxes, but six months later he had accumulated only £5,000. [3] The day after his appointment it was also resolved that the people should arm themselves for "the security of their lives, liberty and property," and in February they were urged to make every military preparation, as otherwise they could expect nothing "but the vilest and most abject slavery." [4] The organization of the Minute Men was effected, and on April 8th it was decided to apply to

---

[1] *Records of Council of Safety*, vol. I, p. 333.
[2] Hall, *Eastern Vermont*, p. 215; F. Moore, *Diary of the American Revolution*, (New York, 1860), vol. I, p. 51 *n*.
[3] *The Journals of each Provincial Congress in Massachusetts in 1774 and 1775 and of the Committees of Safety*, ed. W. Lincoln, (Boston, 1838), pp. 45, 151.
[4] *Journals of Provincial Congresses*, pp. 48, 92.

Connecticut, Rhode Island and New Hampshire for raising an army for the general defence.[1] Although the Massachusetts Congress cautioned the people against being the aggressors in any action, they did their best by inflammatory language to bring about a conflict. They published statements in which they spoke of that "lust of power which of old oppressed, persecuted and exiled our pious ancestors from their fair possessions in Britain" and which "now pursues with ten-fold severity, us, their guiltless children." "So sanguinary are those our enemies, as we have reason to think, so thirsty for the blood of this innocent people" they said in another document, that the danger "is imminently great."[2] This is surely the language of men who are striving not to control but to arouse passion.

Meanwhile General Gage and his troops had remained for the most part cooped up in Boston save for a small and unsuccessful foray after stores at Salem, on which occasion peaceful opposition of the citizens resulted in an equally peaceful retreat of the British to Boston.[3] Owing to the cheapness of liquor in that godly and closed port the "Tommies," as they were already called, could get quite satisfyingly drunk at easily attainable figures, and there were occasional troubles between them and the townsfolk, although a restive young officer wrote home that "we are at present doing nothing with the Bostonians, but they are doing what they please with us."[4] Many citizens, particularly those identified with the patriot cause, had left town, and were staying at Lexington, among them Hancock and Sam Adams. In Parliament, against the votes of one-third of the members, the colonists had been declared in rebellion, and, indeed, impolitic as it may have been to use the word, they could be considered but little else.[5]

The seizure of government stores in Rhode Island and New Hampshire, the steady preparations for war by the Massachusetts Congress, and the accumulation of arms and ammunition

---

[1] *Journals of Provincial Congresses*, pp. 71, 103, 110, 120 *ff.*, 135.
[2] *Ibid.*, pp. 71, 120.
[3] R. Frothingham, *History of the Siege of Boston*, (Boston, 1849), pp. 47 *ff.*
[4] "A British Officer in Boston," *Atlantic Monthly*, vol. XXXIX, pp. 394 *ff.*; A. M. W. Stirling, *Annals of a Yorkshire House*, (London, 1911), p. 341.
[5] *Parlt. Hist.*, vol. XVIII, pp. 223, 265, 292.

In Congrefs, at Watertown, *April* 30, 1775.

Gentlemen,

THE barbarous Murders on our innocent Brethren on Wednefday the 19th Inftant, has made it abfolutely neceffary that we immediately raife an Army to defend our Wives and our Children from the butchering Hands of an inhuman Soldiery, who, incenfed at the Obftacles they met with in their bloody Progrefs, and enraged at being repulfed from the Field of Slaughter ; will without the leaft doubt take the firft Opportunity in their Power to ravage this devoted Country with Fire and Sword : We conjure you, therefore, by all that is dear, by all that is facred, that you give all Affiftance poffible in forming an Army : Our all is at Stake, Death and Devaftation are the certain Confequences of Delay, every Moment is infinitely precious, an Hour loft may deluge your Country in Blood, and entail perpetual Slavery upon the few of your Pofterity, who may furvive the Carnage. We beg and entreat, as you will anfwer it to your Country, to your own Confciences, and above all as you will anfwer to God himfelf, that you will haften and encourage by all poffible Means, the Inliftment of Men to form the Army, and fend them forward to Head-Quarters, at Cambridge, with that Expedition, which the vaft Importance and inftant Urgency of the Affair demands.

JOSEPH WARREN, Prefident, P. T.

PROCLAMATION BY THE PROVINCIAL CONGRESS, 1775

by the patriots, decided Gage, in the hope of preventing civil war, to strike a blow by seizing the stores gathered at Concord. The colonists had already seized those belonging to the king, and there was no particular reason why the general should not seize those of the colonists, palpably being accumulated to use against the royal authority. It was a rash step, however, for there were only about four thousand troops in Boston, and Gage through his intelligence service was well advised as to the situation. In a report made to him and which he considered reliable, he had been informed that there were fifteen thousand Minute Men well armed, and that "the first opposition would be irregular, impetuous, and incessant from the numerous bodys that would swarm to the place of action, and all actuated by an enthusiasm wild and ungovernable." [1] This advance information proved singularly correct. Nevertheless, he decided to send a detachment eighteen miles into the country on a hostile expedition, trusting to secrecy and despatch.[2] The Grenadiers and Light Infantry, under command of Lieutenant-Colonel Smith of the 10th Regiment and Major Pitcairn of the Marines, silently left Boston late in the evening of the 18th of April, but the news of the intended expedition and its object had already leaked out. Preparations had been made for conveying information of just such a contingency from the patriots within the town to those without, and William Dawes was at once despatched to Concord by way of Cambridge and Lexington, and Paul Revere to Lexington by way of Charlestown, to warn Hancock and Adams and to rouse the country.[3] Dawes accomplished his errand, and Revere succeeded in warning the patriot leaders at Lexington but was captured by the British on his way to Concord.

[1] Paper headed "Intelligence" enclosed in letter from Gage to Dartmouth, Mar. 4, 1775, *C.O. 5 No. 92.*

[2] Gage anticipated definite orders that were on their way from England to seize all rebel stores of war. Dartmouth to Gage, Apl. 15, 1775, Jared Sparks, *Writings of George Washington*, (Boston, 1834), vol. III, p. 509.

[3] The lights hung in the church belfry (there is some doubt as to which church), were to warn a third messenger at Charlestown in case the first two should not get away. *Cf.* H. W. Holland, *Wm. Dawes and his Ride with Paul Revere*, (Boston, 1878); E. H. Goss, *Life of Col. Paul Revere*, (Boston, 1897), vol. I, pp. 179 *ff.*; *Mass. Hist. Soc., Proceedings*, vol. XVI, pp. 371 *ff.* It is needless now to point out that the details in Longfellow's well-known poem are almost wholly incorrect.

The country was roused, however, and as this was evident to Smith he ordered Pitcairn to press ahead with six companies to secure the two bridges at Concord, and a request was sent back to Gage for reinforcements. When Pitcairn reached Lexington he found Captain Parker and a small body of Minute Men drawn up on the village green. When ordered to disperse they did not do so and the parley soon ended in an exchange of shots between the two bodies, killing eight and wounding ten of the colonials. It is impossible to say which side fired first and it is a question today of no historical importance. At the time it was a matter of political moment, and each side tried to fasten the responsibility upon the other. The Massachusetts leaders, though anxious to bring on a crisis, realized that the other colonies were not all prepared to force radical measures, and that Massachusetts might be left alone if it failed to appear that the contest was forced upon her. The patriot account, therefore, insisted that the regulars had fired the first shot. On the other hand, Pitcairn, who was an able officer and who, as even the rebels admitted, was a remarkably fine fellow, always insisted to the day of his death that the Americans had fired first. The important point at the moment was to impress the Americans throughout all the colonies with the belief that the British had been the aggressors, and this the patriots saw was thoroughly done by means of reports and affidavits.[1]

After the slight affray at Lexington, the British pressed on to Concord where they again came into collision with Minute Men, but destroyed such small quantities of stores as had not been removed. By the time, however, that they started back for Boston, the whole countryside was swarming with patriots who were now thoroughly aroused in just the manner that Gage had

[1] There is a large literature on the fights at Lexington and Concord. Bibliographies, very complete up to the time of their publication may be found in Winsor's *Narrative and Critical History of America*, (Boston, 1888), vol. VI, pp. 174 *ff*., and his *Memorial History of Boston*, (Boston, 1882), vol. III, pp. 101 *ff*. Many of the older accounts were based on that by Elias Phinney, *History of the Battle of Lexington*, (Boston, 1825), in which affidavits made by men over 70 years of age as to events of 50 years before were used entirely uncritically. Percy's report to Gage, Apl. 20, Smith's report to Gage, Apl. 22, and Gage's report to Dartmouth are in *C.O. 5 No. 92*. The general reader may find longer accounts in Frothingham's *Siege of Boston*, pp. 60 *ff*., and Albert Lee's *History of the 10th Foot*, (London, 1911), vol. I, pp. 225 *ff*. *Cf.* also *Literary Diary of Ezra Stiles*, ed. F. B. Dexter, (New York, 1901), vol. I, pp. 604 *ff*.

been warned they would be. From behind trees and houses and stone walls, they picked off the brightly-clad redcoats. Near Lexington the English were reinforced by Lord Percy and fifteen hundred fresh troops, and covered by these the whole expedition, exhausted and unsuccessful, made their way with difficulty back to the town. The pursuers settled down outside to begin the blockade of the British, and on the 23d the Massachusetts Congress resolved to raise immediately an army of thirty thousand men, of whom thirteen thousand were to be supplied by that colony.[1] The news of the conflict was despatched to all the colonies, and in just three weeks from that 19th of April it had reached Charlestown, South Carolina.[2] A carefully prepared version for English consumption was also at once sent to London, and although the ship carrying it sailed four days after that bearing Gage's official account, it arrived in London some days ahead of the government despatch.[3]

The effect on sentiment was great, although it probably merely intensified the feelings that Englishmen already had concerning the situation rather than changed any from one side to another. During the months from late December, when the papers had been received from the Continental Congress, vote after vote in Parliament had revealed the state of parties, an unshakable majority of about two-thirds of the members in favor of strong measures invariably defeating the one-third in favor of conciliation. Chatham, Shelburne, Camden, Rockingham, the Duke of Richmond, Fox, Burke and a hundred and more others with less well-known names, fought daily against the ministerial majority for measures that would be just to America and might save the empire, but without avail. On the opening of the new session in January, the papers with reference to the whole dispute were laid before Parliament, and on the 20th, Chatham moved to withdraw the troops from Boston. It was merely "an army of irritation" he said, and "the people of America, con-

[1] *Journals Provincial Congresses*, p. 148.

[2] The receipts and despatching orders are given by R. W. Gibbes, *Documentary History of the American Revolution*, (New York, 1855), vol. I, pp. 82 *ff.*, and show remarkable organization.

[3] R. S. Rantoul, "The Cruise of the Quero," *Essex Institute Historical Collections*, vol. XXXVI, pp. 1 *ff.*

CARTOON FROM THE "LONDON MAGAZINE," 1774

demned and not heard, have a right to resist."[1] Some days later
he introduced his plan for conciliation in the form of a provi-
sional Act for settling the troubles, to be succeeded throughout
the session by other plans of Burke, Hartley and others.[2] Even
North surprised his own party by moving such a plan which,
however, was wholly inadequate.[3] Both houses had already
agreed upon an address to the king proclaiming the colonies in
rebellion, and pledging their aid to subdue it. The line thus laid
down was far more popular, both within Parliament and among
the people, than any efforts at conciliation.

Early in March a restraining Act was passed cutting the
people of New England off from the northern fisheries and con-
fining their commerce wholly to the British empire. Some weeks
later this was extended to the other colonies as well.[4] On the
22d Burke made his famous speech on conciliation, extracts
from which are still spoken annually by hundreds of American
schoolboys. It was, however, only the most eloquent of scores
upon scores of speeches delivered by himself and others in favor
of the American cause in the progress of the year's debates.
Although the non-importation agreement by no means produced the distress among the English merchants that the first
resort to that method of coercion had done, nevertheless, petitions were presented in favor of America from many of the large
mercantile towns.[5] The extreme seriousness of the situation for
the West Indies had more effect. At a meeting of the merchants
and planters interested in the islands it was voted two hundred
to seven to petition Parliament to take measures to "quiet the
minds" of the Americans.[6] "Men do not break glass windows
with guineas" wrote one pamphleteer, and another feared that
if non-exportation was maintained by the continent, over one

[1] *Parlt. Hist.*, vol. XVIII, pp. 151, 158.

[2] *Ibid.*, pp. 198 ff., 478 ff., 552 ff.

[3] *Ibid.*, pp. 319 ff.

[4] 15 Geo. III, c. 10; *Parlt. Hist.*, vol. XVIII, pp. 298 ff.

[5] *Parlt. Hist.*, vol. XVIII, pp. 168 ff., 181 f., 184 ff., 194. Curwen, who was in England, wrote in August that "one of the warmest of the friends of America told me that
letters from Manchester expressed joy that no American orders had been sent, otherwise there must have been disappointment somewhere. What effects may follow in the
spring if orders from Russia and Spain are not received, I cannot foresee." G. A. Ward,
Journal and Letters of Samuel Curwen, (Boston, 1864), p. 37.

[6] Force, *American Archives*, Ser. IV, vol. I, pp. 1147 ff.

quarter of the four hundred thousand island slaves would die of starvation.[1] The assembly of the island of Jamaica "alarmed with the approaching horrors of an unnatural conflict between Great Britain and her colonies," in which the destruction of the sugar islands was imminent, petitioned the king to mediate and denied the sovereignty of Parliament.[2]

The English public was showered with pamphlets showing interest in the American question, but few revealed any real grasp of the fact that under new conditions a new nation was arising in the West, the relations of which to the mother country could not be decided by cheap wit or legal quibbling. In one, the long series of Parliamentary Acts serving as precedents were set forth as full answer to the contentions of the colonists.[3]

"If they are condemned unheard," wrote that solemn old dogmatist, Sam Johnson, in another, "it is because there is no need of a trial. The crime is open and manifest. All trial is the investigation of something doubtful." "We hear the loudest yelps for liberty" he added, "among the drivers of negroes,"[4] ignorant of the fact that at this time there was a stronger anti-slavery sentiment in America than would again appear for nearly a century, and that the Continental Congress and several of the colonies had passed a vote to discontinue the slave trade forever.[5] Dean Tucker adopted a similar tone and wrote of those "who protest against everything, and who would dissent even from themselves and their own opinions if no other means of dissen-

---

[1] [Sir John Dalrymple] *The Address of the People of Great Britain to the Inhabitants of America*, (Dublin, 1775), p. 15; R. Glover, *The Evidence delivered on the Petitions presented by the West India Planters and Merchants* . . . (London, 1775), p. 71.

[2] G. W. Bridges, *The Annals of Jamaica*, (London, 1828), vol. II, pp. 463 ff.

[3] *The Supremacy of the British Legislature over the Colonies candidly discussed*, (London, 1775), pp. 15 ff., 21 f., 30.

[4] *Taxation no Tyranny* . . . 3d. edit. (London, 1775), pp. 60, 89.

[5] *Congress Journals*, vol. I, p. 77. Rhode Island had passed an act setting forth that as the inhabitants were engaged in a struggle for liberty themselves, it should be extended to others, and therefore the slave trade was prohibited and any slave brought into the colony was to be freed, with certain exceptions. *R. I. Col. Records*, vol. VII, pp. 251 f. Connecticut forbade the importation of any more slaves. *Conn. Col. Records*, vol. XIV, p. 329. There had been many articles in the papers on the subject and a number of pamphlets appeared in New England. *Vide* e.g. *Connecticut Courant*, June 13, 1768; *Boston Gazette*, Mar. 2, 1767, Sept. 21, 1767, Nov. 16, 1772; *Massachusetts Gazette*, Jan. 4, 1773.

sion could be found."[1] Another wrote of that "fungous and luxurious growth, that Series of inflammatory Libels and nefarious Publications, which have wasted the Manufacture of Paper and troubled the Peace of the World."[2] Here and there a pamphleteer showed a truer comprehension of the real question at issue,[3] or an officer of the army would refuse to serve against his countrymen in America in an unjust cause.[4] On the whole, however, it must be admitted that among the people as in Parliament, the coercionists were in the majority.

That party in England, the long train of ministerial acts, the radicals in America, and the influence of a century and a half of the American environment, had created a situation in which the logic of events could have but one outcome at this stage. Nevertheless, although the extremer radicals in the colonies welcomed the bloodshed at Lexington as forcing the issue, there were still able patriots who did not wish to proceed to extremities. The assembly of Connecticut sent two of the colony's distinguished citizens with a letter from Governor Trumbull to Gage enquiring if there were no alternative but absolute submission or war, attempting to reopen negotiations.[5] This Gage was willing to do and he replied in a straightforward letter. News of this immensely alarmed the Massachusetts radicals, who at once took steps to block the negotiations. The Provincial Congress wrote to the Connecticut authorities that although not doubting the loyalty of that colony they were alarmed at their treating for a cessation of hostilities with a man who was engaged in "massacring" innocent people.[6] As part of that violent propaganda that war breeds, it now became advisable to blacken Gage's

---

[1] Josiah Tucker, *A Letter to Edmund Burke, Esq.*, (Gloucester, 1775), p. 18. The Americans believe the voice of the people is the voice of God, he wrote, and if anyone denies it they tar and feather him. *Ibid.*, p. 14.

[2] [Ambrose Serle] *Americans against Liberty, or an Essay on the Nature and Principles of true Freedom* . . . (London, 1775), p. 8.

[3] *E.g. An Answer to a Pamphlet entitled Taxation no Tyranny*, (London, 1775). The author contended that the matter could not be settled by "abstract notions of government at large" and that Parliament was contending "with your countrymen for nothing, at the hazard of everything." pp. 8, 48.

[4] *E.g.* the Earl of Effingham, *Rockingham Memoirs*, vol. II, p. 275.

[5] *Conn. Col. Records*, vol. XIV, pp. 416, 440 ff.; Force, *American Archives*, Ser. IV, vol. II, pp. 433 ff.

[6] *Journals of Provincial Congresses*, pp. 180 ff.

character as far as possible, and Philip Freneau, "the poet of the revolution," began to transform the green at Lexington with its eight dead into

> Vast plains all white with human bones
> That bleaching lie and ask sepulchral stones . . .

> And let your rocks, and let your hills proclaim,
> That Gage and Cortez' errand is the same.

In the argument it was stated that one of the themes of the poem was "the striking similarity of Gage's temper and conduct to that [sic] of Hernando Cortez." [1]

The Connecticut negotiation naturally led to nothing, though the failure was not due to any Cortez-like qualities in the not very able or wise but by no means bloodthirsty English general. The sweep of the movement was now too vast to be stayed by any such epistolary episode, and the radicals need not have been so nervous as to its possibilities. In the east, the siege of Boston continued, punctuated only by minor skirmishes between the beleaguered troops and the colonials over efforts to seize or secure the stock on islands in the harbor.[2] In the west, however, a daring exploit resulted in the colonial capture of Ticonderoga. Both Benedict Arnold and Ethan Allen had realized how easily the fort might be captured if surprised, and the former, after securing unofficial backing in both Connecticut and Massachusetts, marched westward for the attempt only to find that Allen with some of the "Green Mountain Boys" was already engaged in the project. Arnold joined Allen's forces as a volunteer, and on the night of May 10th the small garrison surrendered to the Vermont leader after a surprise attack.[3] A number of cannon and a very considerable and much needed supply of military stores rewarded the victors. A few days later, Crown Point was also taken by another Vermonter, Seth Warner. This invasion of New York, however, created serious inter-colonial friction, and the act of war against England also raised questions for the second Continental Congress which met the very day the for-

[1] [Philip Freneau] *A Voyage to Boston,* (New York, 1775), Argument and p. 9.
[2] Frothingham, *Siege of Boston,* pp. 105 *ff.*
[3] Smith, *Struggle for the 14th Colony,* vol. I, pp. 119 *ff.*

tress fell. A tradition connected with the capture is interesting as showing how far the spirit of the Vermont farmers was removed from that of the old-type Puritan. It is said that the Reverend Jedidiah Dewey in a long prayer gave the glory of the exploit to God and that the picturesque Allen, who happened to be present, called out "Parson Dewey, Parson Dewey, please mention to the Lord that I was there." [1]

On May 25th, Gage had received considerable reinforcements from England with three general officers, Burgoyne, Clinton and Howe, and on June 12th he issued a proclamation declaring martial law and that all who should refuse to lay down arms should be treated as rebels and traitors. Amnesty was offered to all who should do so, however, with the exceptions of Sam Adams and John Hancock, the latter now president of the Continental Congress.[2] Dartmouth had sent Gage instructions to issue such a proclamation, offering a reward for the capture of the "President, Secretary, and any other of the members of the Provincial Congress" whom Gage might consider to have been most active in promoting sedition, and the wording of the proclamation followed in part that of the instructions.[3]

Outside the town, behind slight works, poorly supplied with arms and ammunition, the American forces numbered about sixteen thousand men, drawn from the New England colonies, of whom Massachusetts claimed to have supplied three-quarters. The question had been discussed of extending the lines so as to include the hilly eminences on the Charlestown peninsula, but this was wisely considered as too dangerous a move on account of the lack of ammunition. On June 13th, it was learned that Gage intended to take possession of Dorchester Heights, the counter position to those on the peninsula. Of these Bunker Hill was the nearer to the narrow neck which connected the peninsula with the mainland, Breed's Hill lying beyond it seaward. As the British had complete command of the water and so could control the neck, valuable as the hills might be could forces be maintained upon them, the whole peninsula in reality

---

[1] Smith, *cit. supra*, p. 151.
[2] Force, *American Archives*, Ser. IV, vol. II, pp. 968 *ff*.
[3] I am greatly indebted to Albert Matthews, Esq., of the Colonial Society of Massachusetts, for having sent me copies of the documents.

formed a trap in which the forces placed there could readily be cut off from the mainland. In fact when, as a result of the decision of a council of war acting upon the recommendation of the Committee of Safety, troops were hastily moved to take possession of Bunker Hill on the night of the 16th some of them feared treachery on the part of the officers, suspecting from the obvious danger of the position that they had been trapped and "were brought there to be all slain." [1]

Although from its position, Bunker Hill was much the safer of the two to occupy, a hasty decision, after the ground was actually reached, was made to press forward and occupy Breed's Hill, where breast-works were begun at midnight. When day dawned and the Americans were discovered, one of the ships at once opened fire, soon joined by the rest of the fleet and by the battery on Copp's Hill in Boston. At a council of war held by the British, Gage over-ruled the advice of Howe to land troops at the neck and so cut off the Americans at once and attack in the rear. Instead, it was decided to attack by an assault upon the hill from the front. The ships, however, raked the narrow neck with their guns, and hampered the much needed reinforcements and supplies from reaching the colonials. It was the middle of the afternoon when the first assault was made. The Americans, under command of Colonel William Prescott, were expert marksmen, and protected by a six foot embankment they mowed down the British as they advanced, wavered and fled. [2] The smoke from Charlestown, which had been set on fire by the English, blew toward the mainland and did not hide the troops as they made their second assault. Although this was also repulsed, by the time that the intrepid regulars advanced for the third time, the ammunition of the Americans was almost exhausted, and after some hand to hand fighting over the breast-works they were forced to retreat to intrenchments at Bunker

---

[1] H. B. Dawson, "Bunker's Hill," *The Historical Magazine*, vol. III, p. 335. For accounts of the battle and criticisms, *vide* Frothingham, *Siege of Boston*, pp. 115 *ff.*; C. F. Adams, "The Battle of Bunker Hill from a strategic point of view," *American Antiquarian Society, Proceedings*, New Series, vol. X, pp. 387 *ff.* Burgoyne's account is in *New Eng. Hist. and Gen. Register*, vol. XI, pp. 125 *f.*

[2] For the disputed question as to who was in supreme command, *vide* Frothingham, *cit. supra*, pp. 159 *ff.* For a recent account favorable to the claims of Ward, *vide* C. Martyn, *Life of Artemas Ward*, (New York, 1921), pp. 154 *ff.*

Hill which Israel Putnam had been preparing during the day. The works were not finished, the British had gained momentum, and the colonials, resisting stubbornly, were pushed down the back of the hill and across the neck to the mainland under heavy fire. Prescott complained bitterly and not without reason of the failure to support him in his dangerous position. However, the soldiers had faced British regulars with marked courage, and reckless and ill-advised as the enterprise had been, it was a tremendous victory in its political and moral effect for the radical patriots, although one of the ablest of them, Dr. Joseph Warren, had died upon the field. The contest had been no affair of sniping from stone walls along a road or of half-concealed fighting Indian fashion among woods. The colonials had met British regulars face to face and the losses of the latter had been remarkably heavy.[1] The news of the battle following so closely upon Lexington, Concord, Ticonderoga and Crown Point fanned the war spirit into a fiercer blaze among the extremists throughout all the colonies. With each successive act of war there was less inclination on their part to temporize, and the necessity of definitely choosing sides for or against open rebellion became daily more insistent. The assertion by the English government that the colonies were in rebellion had made many of "the People desperate" wrote a conservative from Philadelphia, who added that "this is putting the Halter about our Necks, and we may as well die by the Sword as be hang'd like Rebels."[2] The way the untrained colonials had mowed down the British must have given many the thought that, after all, these might not be the only alternatives.

Meanwhile, the Continental Congress at Philadelphia, which had reassembled in May, had been taking steps that tended more and more toward definite separation from England, little as that was as yet desired by many of the members themselves. Although owing to the manner in which the delegates had been elected they could by no means be considered as representatives

---

[1] Channing accepts the figure of from 1,000 to 1,500 as against 411 killed and wounded on the American side, a greater proportionate loss for the British than they had suffered in any battle in Europe or America in the Seven Years' War. *History of U. S.*, vol. III, pp. 169 *f.*

[2] Burnett, *Letters of Members*, vol. I, p. 114.

of the people as a whole, they displayed remarkable courage, even to audacity. Their counsels, however, were by no means unanimous. "Every important step was opposed and carried by bare majorities" wrote John Adams.[1] The abilities of that patriot were now beginning to outshine those of his political relative Sam, but the efforts of both for revolution were constantly thwarted by the more conservative patriotism of such men as Dickinson. Feeling ran high. "Adams and Dickinson now look ascance at each other" wrote one observer, "and are not upon speaking terms, except in the language in which Cats talk together." [2] However, Congress moved steadily in a more radical direction. In answer to a request for advice from the Provincial Congress of Massachusetts as to the establishment there of some more definite form of civil government, there being "alarming symptoms of the abatement of the sense of private property," the congress advised the reëstablishment of the charter as nearly as might be, denying the validity of the recent Act of Parliament modifying it, and thus sanctioned the setting up of a revolutionary government in which Gage and the other royal appointees bore no part.[3] In October, New Hampshire was advised to form a government similar to that of Massachusetts.[4] The reorganization of the colonial forces was also begun and the troops around Boston were taken into the service of the continent. On June 15th, as a political stroke to bind the southern vote, George Washington was unanimously elected commander-in-chief and he immediately hastened to join the forces at Cambridge. Unwittingly, the greatest step toward the achievement of eventual independence had been taken, although on his way through New York he assured the assembly there that he would make every effort to restore harmony with the mother country. This was unquestionably still desired by a large proportion of the people throughout America. Even in Congress, John Adams wrote on the day of Bunker Hill that he

[1] *Works*, vol. II, p. 503.
[2] Extract of a letter not signed to Isaac Wilkins, Oct. 3, 1775, *C.O. 5 No. 134.*
[3] *Journals of Provincial Congresses*, pp. 319, 359; Cushing, *Transition from Provincial to Commonwealth Government in Massachusetts*, pp. 167 *ff.*
[4] Burnett, *cit. supra*, vol. I, pp. 232 *ff.*, 245 *f.*; *N. H. Prov. Papers*, vol. VII, pp. 641 *ff.*, 685 *ff.*

"found a strong jealousy of us from New England, and Massachusetts in particular; suspicions entertained of designs of independency; an American republic; Presbyterian principles, and twenty other things." "America is like a great, unwieldy body," he continued after noting a hopeful increase in radical sentiment. "Its progress must be slow. It is like a large fleet sailing under convoy. The fleetest sailors must wait for the dullest and slowest." [1]

On July 6th he wrote that there was in Congress "a strange oscillation between love and hatred, between War and Peace-Preparations for War and Negociations for Peace. . . . This Negociation I dread like Death: But it must be proposed." [2] A few days later an address to the people of Great Britain, popularly dubbed "the olive branch," was issued, and on the 18th the Declaration on taking up arms.[3] Jefferson's more violent draft of the latter was distinctly disavowed.

The wildest rumors were afloat among the common people of assistance that might be derived from an insurrection in England and these were eagerly believed by many. A mob in London under the strange leadership of John Wilkes, Burke and Lord Effingham was supposed to have destroyed the Parliament buildings, and North was reported to have fled to France and Bute to Scotland. Holland was said to have called for immediate payment of £50,000,000 and England to have become bankrupt.[4] Of more serious import than such eagerly swallowed fantasticalities was the fact that the French were active in intrigue. They even ran much needed powder into Philadelphia under their flag. "I have lived here these five years past," wrote a resident there, "and never saw so many Frenchmen in the time as are here now." [5] Evidently a new chapter was soon to be written in the long story of the struggle for empire, and revenge seemed to be within the grasp of France. The letters of the French minister to England are full of the colonial situation and

[1] Burnett, *Letters of Members*, vol. I, pp. 131 *f.*
[2] Burnett, *cit. supra*, p. 152.
[3] *Congress Journals*, vol. II, pp. 129 *ff.*, 163 *ff.*
[4] Letter, unsigned to — Stephens, Philadelphia, July 29, 1775; Letter from a captain in H. M. Navy to Stephens, Sept. 29, 1775, *C.O. 5 No. 122.*
[5] First letter *cit. supra*.

give one the impression of a hawk biding his time to strike. New secret agents were sent to America for information. By the end of the year Vergennes had made up his mind that the colonists did not desire simply "redress of grievances but that they had taken the resolution of cutting the throat of the mother-country."[1] Within a few months the French government was giving active but secret aid to the revolutionists.

The latter had decided to carry the war vigorously into the enemy's camp, and after long negotiations with the Canadians, and addresses to the inhabitants of that colony, an expedition had been set on foot to capture Quebec and Montreal. This change from "a defensive opposition" to "the extremity of an offensive war" by no means met with general approval and is said to have been voted down in Congress and subsequently acquiesced in by the change of one vote.[2] It was finally undertaken with the hope that the Canadians would join with the revolting colonies and would welcome the invasion as a means of freeing them from what the Americans considered the tyranny of the Quebec Act. From a military standpoint it met with Washington's approval, and in September he wrote to the Congress from Cambridge that he had detached Benedict Arnold and a thousand men for the attempt.[3]

The plan was a modification of the old standard one with which the reader of this and the preceding volume is already familiar. A western force, under command of Richard Montgomery of New York was to advance by way of Lake Champlain, take Montreal, and then unite with the expedition under Arnold for an attack upon Quebec. Arnold, however, was to

[1] H. Doniol, *Histoire de la participation de la France à l'établissement des États Unis d'Amerique*, (Paris, 1886), vol. I, pp. 67 ff., 138, 153 f., 243.

[2] "As the expedition into Canada is one of the most important Subjects of Conversation, it may not be amiss just to say, that the Measure was proposed by Md. towards the Close of the last sitting & met with a spirited & warm Opposition, & was upon a Division carried against the Proposition 6 Colonies to 5. Not content with this Determination, the subject was resumed the next Day, when N. Y., N. J., L. C. Md. & N. C. were still against the measure; N. H., M. C. V. & S. C. were for the measure; R. Id. lost their vote by a Division on the two Members. The Determination of this unhappy & ill-judged project rested on P. — a Majority of whose Members had the Day before voted against it, but that unstable Man No. 5, uniting with No. 4, determined the Vote in the affirmative." Letter from Thos. Wharton to Saml. Wharton, in Mr. Todd's of Nov. 17, 1775, *C.O. 5 No. 134.*

[3] Washington, *Writings*, ed. W. C. Ford, vol. III, p. 144.

march through the Maine wilderness by way of the Chaudière instead of proceeding by sea to the St. Lawrence.[1] The first part of the enterprise was even more successful than could have been hoped. Not only did Montreal surrender to Montgomery on November 13th, but a few days later the British fleet in the river also hauled down their colors to the Americans. Meanwhile, after a terrific march through the wilderness, Arnold and his men had reached Quebec on the 8th. It was impossible to take the city by assault and the little army retreated to Pointe aux Trembles. Montgomery, in spite of heavy depletion of his forces due to the refusal of men whose term of enlistment had expired to remain for a winter campaign, moved down from Montreal to join Arnold, and on December 31st an unsuccessful assault was made in which the gallant New Yorker lost his life. From that time forward, the action of the American force "seems nothing but a scene of confusion, cowardice, negligence and bad conduct."[2] A large proportion of the troops were "licentious, mercenary, and wholly without discipline," and although the French were not loyal to England, they were entirely alienated from any attachment to the American cause by the treatment they received from the soldiery.[3] Reinforcements sent by Congress introduced dissensions among the commanding officers, and finally in May 1776 the besiegers suffered a disgraceful rout.[4]

Meanwhile, however, in England the opinion as to the seriousness of the opposition of the colonists was changing. In November, in the House of Lords, Grafton stated that although England could coerce America if it were a question merely between her and her colonies, yet "we cannot exert our whole force against America, nor with prudence or safety one-half of it. . . . It is no longer a secret that France will not permit us."[5] "Is any minister weak enough to flatter himself with the conquest of all North America?" thundered Wilkes. "The Americans

[1] The most complete account of the campaign is by Smith, *Struggle for the 14th Colony*, vol. I, pp. 467 *ff.*, vol. II, pp. 1 *ff.* For Arnold's march *vide* the same author's *Arnold's March from Cambridge to Quebec*, (New York, 1903).

[2] Coffin, *Province of Quebec and the early American Revolution*, p. 525.

[3] *Ibid.*, pp. 514 *ff.* *Cf.* Smith, *Struggle for the 14th Colony*, vol. II, pp. 225 *ff.*

[4] Smith, *cit. supra*, pp. 320 *ff.*

[5] *Parlt. Hist.*, vol. XVIII, p. 961.

will dispute every inch of territory with you, every narrow pass, every strong defile, every Thermopylae, every Bunker's Hill." [1] A less important member of the Commons spoke of three of the military officers in command in America as among those who "were last session among the deceived at home, and have already this year been disgraced abroad." [2] Nevertheless, the ministerial majority though occasionally lessened was still overwhelming. In the Lords, it was voted fifty-two against twenty-one that the petition of the Continental Congress did not afford ground for conciliation. [3] In September, Dartmouth instructed the Admiralty that every harbor in the colonies should be visited and that the masts and rudders of every colonial ship should be removed or they should otherwise be so disabled that they could not be used for purposes of rebellion. [4] In November, North introduced his bill to prohibit all trade and intercourse of any sort with the colonies south of Canada, the bill finally passing the Commons by the extraordinary majority of a hundred and twelve to sixteen. [5] In February 1776, the treaties with the German princes for the hire of Hessian troops were laid before Parliament, and a motion by the Duke of Richmond in the Lords that the orders for the marching of the Germans be countermanded and that hostilities in America be suspended was lost by one hundred to thirty-two. [6] Step by step, events had marched as inexorably as the Hessians themselves, and the fact of open and avowed warfare had now to be acknowledged by all men. A doubly fratricidal war it was to be, a war between England and her colonies in the empire, and between Loyalist and Patriot in every hamlet in America; a war not only between the old world and the new across three thousand leagues of ocean, but between colonial friends and neighbors dwelling hitherto in peace across many a small town street and country lane.

[1] *Parlt. Hist.*, vol. XVIII, p. 1009.
[2] *Ibid.*, p. 1018.
[3] *Ibid.*, p. 910.
[4] Dartmouth to Lords of Admiralty, Sept. 12, 1775, *C.O. 5 No. 122.*
[5] *Parlt. Hist.*, vol. XVIII, pp. 992 *ff.*, 1028 *ff.*, 1056 *ff.*
[6] *Ibid.*, pp. 1156 *ff.*, 1228.

CHAPTER XVIII

CIVIL WAR

Patriots Secure Control of Colonial Governments — English Plunder the Coast — Character of Patriot Troops — Washington's Difficult Position — Evacuation of Boston by British — Thomas Paine and "Common Sense" — Radicals Shift Their Ground — The Radical Spirit — Declaration of Independence — The Loyalists — Civil War

EVEN though the colonists might disrelish the title of rebels there was no doubt that they were in open rebellion. The Congress had published to the world the reasons for taking up arms, and throughout America there was the stir and bustle of military operations. Everywhere the royal governors came into conflict with the popular party. In Connecticut and Rhode Island the governors were elected by the people, and in the former there was no trouble as Governor Trumbull was of the patriot side. In Rhode Island Governor Wanton, who had been successively elected for seven terms, had protested against raising an army and had refused to sign the commissions for the officers, and on that account he was formally suspended from office by the assembly in May 1775.[1] In Massachusetts Gage shut up in Boston had ceased to have any control over the rest of the colony, and having been recalled to England sailed on October 10th, being succeeded in military command by General Howe. In New Hampshire the formerly popular John Wentworth had been forced to take refuge in the castle in Portsmouth harbor in June, and although when he sailed for Boston in August he fully intended to return, he was not able to do so and never saw the colony again.[2] In all four provinces, therefore, the victory of the patriots in securing control of the organs of government, either

[1] *R. I. Col. Records*, vol. VII, pp. 325 f., 334 f., 355, 372, 392 f.
[2] Mayo, *John Wentworth*, pp. 156 ff.

established or revolutionary, had been complete by the middle of 1775.

Meanwhile Dartmouth had instructed the Lords of the Admiralty to send orders to the Admiral commanding on the Boston station to "carry on operations upon the sea coasts of the four New England colonies as "he shall judge most effectual for suppressing . . . the rebellion which is now openly avowed" and to seize all colonial ships not owned by Loyalists.[1] The orders were obeyed. On August 30th Stonington was bombarded, the British naval vessels firing on the houses of the undefended little port.[2] On October 7th sixteen ships appeared off Bristol and began a heavy cannonading, withdrawing only after the town had yielded a supply of provisions.[3] Eleven days later a smaller fleet of four vessels arrived at Falmouth, Maine, and the commanding officer at once sent a message ashore stating that the town was to be destroyed and giving the two thousand inhabitants two hours in which to leave. He also said that his orders from Admiral Graves were to burn and destroy all towns on the seaboard without warning, but that if the inhabitants would deliver up their arms the town might be saved. This they refused to do, and the following morning the vessels opened fire. The new church, the town house, one hundred and thirty dwellings, two hundred and thirty stores, and many other buildings were wholly destroyed. One hundred and sixty families lost all their property and were rendered homeless upon the approach of winter.[4] In December an expedition landed at Conanicut in Rhode Island, and burned the houses and plundered the inhabitants of their goods.[5] These wanton attacks and the fear and uncertainty that they caused along the seaboard aroused the people to furious anger against the British and greatly strengthened the patriot party. A policy of "frightfulness" must always fail against people of any courage, and the Americans, as Englishmen living in an environment in which self-reliance was of

---

[1] Dartmouth to Lords of Admiralty, July 1, 1775, *C.O. 5 No. 121.*
[2] Force, *American Archives*, Ser. IV, vol. III, pp. 461, 470 *f.*
[3] *Ibid.*, pp. 990, 1108.
[4] *Ibid.*, pp. 1169 *ff.*; W. D. Williamson, *History of Maine*, (Hallowell, 1832), vol. II, pp. 434 *ff.*
[5] Force, *American Archives*, Ser. IV, vol. IV, p. 230.

necessity a cardinal virtue, were by no means lacking in that quality however much they might be wanting in discipline.

The absence of the latter, as well as the almost negligible supplies of powder, were causing Washington serious anxiety as he maintained the siege of Boston. The English were making every effort to prevent the Americans from importing stores of war from any quarter. Even the ballast of ships leaving England was examined lest it should contain flints, and war-ships were sent to range the African coast for fear ammunition might be procured even in that remote quarter.[1] A plan was made in Rhode Island, which received the unofficial sanction of Washington, to raid the stores in Bermuda and seize the considerable amount of powder collected there, but a similar expedition had been successfully carried out by Pennsylvanians before the Rhode Islanders arrived.[2]

We have already had occasion to note several times certain faults in New England troops which made any sustained operations difficult if not impossible — such as the poor quality of the minor officers due to the system of their election by their men, the lack of discipline, due partly to this cause and partly to the character of the men themselves, and the dislike of long enlistments. "Our own Troops are raw, irregular, and undisciplined," wrote General Greene from Rhode Island in June 1775, "yet, bad as they are, they are under much better government than any Troops around Boston."[3] Washington at times was almost in despair. "I am sorry to be under a necessity of making such frequent examples among the Officers when a sense of honor, and the interest of their country might be expected to make punishment unnecessary," he wrote of some cases of cowardice and fraud. Again, in connection with other cases he wrote "I have made a pretty good slam among such officers as the Massachusetts Government abound in since I came to this camp." He thought too many of the officers were of "nearly the same

[1] Pownall to Stephens, Aug. 3, 1775, *C.O. 5 No. 121*; Dartmouth to Lords of Admiralty, Aug. 29, 1775, *C.O. 5 No. 122*; Same to same, Sept. 18, 1775, *ibid.*

[2] Washington, *Writings*, ed. Ford, vol. III, pp. 81 *f.*, 133; James Young to the Council at Antigua, Aug. 14, and Aug. 22, 1775; same to Commander-in-chief at Leeward Ids., Oct. 22, 1775, both in *C.O. 5 No. 122*; Force, *American Archives*, Ser. IV, vol. III, pp. 682 *f.*, 808, 1181 *f.*

[3] Force, *cit. supra*, p. 1126.

kidney as the privates" and that there was no such thing as "getting of officers of this stamp to exert themselves in carrying orders into execution — to curry favor with the men (by whom they were chosen, and on whose smiles possibly they may think they may again rely) seems to be one of the principal objects of their attention." [1]

If democracy in the army was thus working badly, so was that false sentiment of independence among the men which had so often before plagued the New England authorities. The men deserted wholesale. "The Connecticut regiments have deserted, and are about to desert, the noble cause we are engaged in," Washington wrote to the governor of Rhode Island, "nor have I any reason to believe, that the forces of New Hampshire, this government, or Rhode Island, will give any stronger proof of their attachment to it, when the period arrives that they may claim their dismission." Of the militia reinforcements, he wrote that they "are not to be depended on for more than a few days; as they soon get tired, grow impatient, ungovernable, and of course leave the service." [2] He wrote similarly to Governor Trumbull of Connecticut who replied that the troops had given the same trouble in the preceding war, and that it was difficult "to support liberty, to exercise government, to maintain subordination, and at the same time to prevent the operation of licentious and levelling principles." [3] Fraud and profiteering were rife both within the army and among the people. "Notwithstanding all the public virtue which is ascribed" to the New Englanders, Washington wrote on another occasion, "there is no nation under the sun, (that I ever came across) pay greater adoration to money than they do." Officers absented themselves from duty, took privates with them and worked them on their own farms while both drew pay from the government. "Such a dearth of public spirit, and want of virtue, such stock-jobbing and fertility in all the low arts to obtain advantages of one kind and another . . . I never saw before, and pray God I may never be witness to again" wrote the general in another letter. "Such a dirty, mercenary spirit pervades the whole, that

[1] Washington, *Writings*, vol. III, pp. 67, 97 *f.*
[2] *Ibid.*, pp. 264 *f.*, *Cf.* Force, *American Archives*, Ser. IV, vol. III, p. 327.
[3] Washington, *Writings*, vol. III, p. 255 *n.*

JONATHAN TRUMBULL
From a portrait by Colonel John Trumbull

I should not be at all surprised at any disaster that may happen." [1] General Greene in commenting on Washington's strictures admitted that the country people were extremely avaricious and were profiteering shamelessly at the expense of the army, but thought that the general had looked for too much virtue from having been led to believe that the New Englanders were "a superior race of mortals," and that reaction came when he discovered they were ordinary human beings. [2] From the time, nearly a century and a half before, when the Purtians smugly accepted and spread the dictum that "God sifted a whole nation that he might send choice grain over into this wilderness," they had been diligently insisting that they did constitute such a superior race, and one can sympathize with the father of his country when he found the full complement of human vices underlying this pharisaical self-satisfaction.

It was difficult to get any men to reënlist, and Washington feared that the entire force would melt away. Congress wrote to each of the New England governments pointing out the alarming situation. The hope of a volunteer army made up of patriots enlisting out of love to the cause was given up. Bounties were offered, and furloughs to as many as fifty men in a regiment were granted, to secure enlistments. Even so, by February 1776, Washington found that instead of twenty thousand troops he had less than half that number including the sick and those on leave. [3] The war was not to be an affair of sniping from the stone walls of Lexington and Concord, or even a detached engagement such as Bunker Hill, but was to be made up of years of gruelling campaigns against trained and disciplined European troops. Fortunately the people had leaders, and the New England governments did their best to bring about order and to instil a nobler spirit. Officers such as Schuyler, overcome with disgust at the sordid greed and selfish spirit so generally manifested, tried to resign their commissions. The soul of Washington, sorely tried as it was, endured. "The cause we are engaged in is so just and righteous," he wrote to Schuyler,

---

[1] Washington, *Writings*, vol. III, pp. 72, 246 *f.*, 413.
[2] *Ibid.*, p. 247 n.
[3] *Ibid.*, pp. 138, 251, 264, 408, 412; Force, *cit. supra*, pp. 217 *f.*

"that we must try to rise superior to every obstacle in its support."[1] In this first great crisis the country was saved by a
leader drawn from the most wealthy and the most aristocratic
section of society, himself a product of the old order. In the
next, that leader was to come from the common people themselves, and perhaps there is no other single fact in the history
of American democracy that goes so far to justify the new order
as the fact of Abraham Lincoln.

Although the conditions in the American camp were known to
Lord Howe, he was in no position to take advantage of them,
and throughout the early winter the two armies watched each
other across narrow lines. Washington had several times considered the possibility of an assault upon the town, and had
been anxious to attempt it.[2] Finally, it was decided to occupy
Dorchester Heights in hopes of bringing on an engagement and
possibly of attacking Boston. On the night of March 4th, after
diversions had been made for a couple of days to mislead the
British, the Heights were occupied and the first rude works
quickly erected. When they were discovered after day broke, it
was immediately decided by Howe to attempt to dislodge the
rebels as neither the fleet nor town was safe so long as they
remained. Preparations were made for an attack in which the
fleet was to share, but a fierce storm lasting two days prevented
the plan from being executed, and the Americans had time
greatly to strengthen their defences. By the 7th Howe's position had become critical under the bombardment from the rebel
works. No word had been received from the English government since October, and at a council of war the decision was
taken to save the army at all costs and to evacuate the town
immediately. The movement, carried out gradually, was complete by the 19th, and on the following day the main body of the
patriot army entered Boston.[3] Soon after, Washington ordered
all but five regiments to proceed to New York and on April 4th
he himself followed them. From that time to the end of the
war, the more important military events all took place outside
the boundaries of New England.

[1] Washington, *Writings*, vol. III, pp. 267 *f.*
[2] *Ibid.*, pp. 145, 425.
[3] The details may be found in Frothingham's *Siege of Boston*, pp. 295 *ff.*

The temporary abandonment of the colonies by the English forces was an event of the greatest importance in forming sentiment and increasing the ranks of the patriot party. Even more so had been one in the intellectual sphere. In January there appeared in Philadelphia a pamphlet by Thomas Paine entitled *Common Sense*, which was to sell by the hundred thousand and to do more than any other utterance to turn the tide definitely toward independence. Crude and coarse as it was, it was written in words of power, and brushing away all the sophistries of the long-drawn legal discussions, it spoke to the common man in words which appealed to him as wisdom. Both in this and in the amazing succession of pamphlets that were to follow, Paine seemed to become to his readers the very incarnation of that "common sense" that he used both as a title and *nom de plume*. "To know whether it be the interest of this continent to be Independent, we need only ask this easy, simple question: Is it the interest of a man to be a boy all his life?" To those weary of attempting to defend their position against British encroachment by constitutional argument in which they became more and more entangled, this seemed like opening the window of a stuffy and darkened room to the air and sunshine. Knowing that loyalty to the person of the king was holding back many from taking the final step, Paine attacked the very idea of kingship. A king in England, he said, can only make war and give away places. "A pretty business indeed for a man to be allowed eight hundred thousand sterling a year for, and worshipped into the bargain! Of more worth is one honest man to society, and in the sight of God, than all the crowned ruffians that ever lived." He denied that the colonies owed England anything for protection, and laid stress on that composite character of America which has always been too much overlooked. "Europe, and not England, is the parent country of America. This new world hath been the asylum for the persecuted lovers of civil and religious liberty from every part of Europe. Hither have they fled, not from the tender embraces of the mother, but from the cruelty of the monster." It is absurd to think of a continent being ruled by an island, he continued, and to be constantly running three thousand miles with a tale or a petition and waiting months or years for a decision. England and America belong to different systems, "England to Europe, America to itself." In florid rhetoric perfectly adapted to his audience he pictured the destiny of the new nation. "Freedom hath been hunted round the globe. Asia, Africa, have long expelled her. Europe regards her like a stranger, and England hath given her warning to depart. O! receive the fugitive, and prepare in time an asylum for mankind." "We have it in our power," he continued, "to begin the world over again. A situation, similar to the present, hath not happened since the days of Noah until now. The birth-day of a new world is at hand, and a race of men perhaps as numerous as all Europe contains, are to receive their portion of freedom from the event of a few months. The Reflection is awful — and in this point, How trifling, how ridiculous, do the little, paltry cavellings of a few weak or interested men appear, when weighed against the business of a world." [1] A formal declaration of independence was urged as the only step that would at once regularize the position of the colonies and bind them together.

Indeed, the radicals had reached the point at which they were prepared to abandon a sophistical debate in which they could but be worsted on purely legal ground.[2] Sir George Savile in England had clearly foreseen the situation as early as 1768. "I am almost ready to believe that George Grenville's Act only brought on the crisis twenty or, possibly, fifty years sooner than was necessary," he wrote to Rockingham, adding that "it is in the nature of things that, some time or other, colonies so situated, must assume to themselves the rights of nature, and resist the law, which is rebellion. By *rights* of nature, I mean advantage of situation, or their natural *powers*." [3] In their attempt to work our their destinies in their own way, the colonists had been driven from one logical and legal stand to another. The ground had been constantly shifted. Their only refuge finally was in pure dogmatism. The natural rights claimed might be the most unnatural things in the world of nature, unless the

[1] *Common Sense*, 2d. edit. (Philadelphia, 1776), pp. 31, 36, 45, 58, 89.
[2] *Cf.* A. M. Schlesinger, "The American Revolution reconsidered," *Pol. Science Quarterly*, (Mar. 1919), pp. 75 *ff*.
[3] *Rockingham Memoirs*, vol. II, p. 76.

term is stretched to denote merely all that is. The law of nature is rather that the stronger ever preys upon the weaker, and the natural right to life, liberty and the pursuit of happiness appears quite differently to the worm, the bird, the cat, the dog, as each successively pursues his happiness in the destruction of the next in a world admirably adapted for that pursuit. Men seem to require, however, a dazzling major premise as a stepping stone to their desired conclusions and an apparent sanction of their acts. In the earlier New England days it had been the word of God. The conclusions drawn from different interpretations might be wide apart but unanimity with that of the ruling group could be secured by imprisonment, banishment or the gallows. The roots of political philosophy lie deep in the history and psychology of human kind, but glittering *a priori* statements seem to the average man to afford a more sure foundation. He is obsessed by the two illusions of unity and permanence. The thought that everything he knows and holds dear is transient, that nothing abides, terrifies him. When at moments he vaguely senses the eternal flux, it is as though a flood threatened to sweep him from all to which he instinctively clings. It is the illusion of permanence that causes the poignancy of a child's grief. We smile, knowing that grief or joy comes and goes. But in our own more mature life, made up of customs, of property, of many institutions, we carry the same illusion and would fain believe that each is a permanent mould instead of a passing balance of social forces as transient as a child's trouble. We grasp at anything, the "word of God," the "rights of man," that seems to be true *semper et ubique*, as a shipwrecked sailor in the tumbling chaos of waves clutches at a spar.

Moreover, in criticising natural rights, we must recall that however absurd historically was the eighteenth-century doctrine of the original state of nature, the state depicted was that of "the ideal of man as a rational creature," and that natural rights and the idea of natural law transcending the law of the courts and codes, did serve to shape and guide the idea of legal rights so as more effectually to secure the interests of personality.[1] It was the passionate desire of the individual to

[1] *Cf.* Roscoe Pound, *An Introduction to the Philosophy of Law*, (Yale Press, 1922), pp. 42 *ff.*

secure those interests for himself that gave strength to the revolutionary doctrine.

In England it had long been the theory that those best qualified should rule, qualified by property, education, a "stake in the country," or a great position. In New England in the seventeenth century it had been that the "Saints" should do so. Both these theories had lingered on in America, but democracy and the frontier had been gradually undermining each of them. By 1776 the question had become less one of Parliamentary taxation than of the ultimate source of political power. The stupidity of the English government had hastened the crisis. The obstinacy of the king and his ministers had proved the fulcrum against which the colonial radicals pressed in heaving over not only Parliamentary supremacy but privilege as the basis of political rights. Throughout all the colonies there was a veritable onslaught upon even such meagre privileges as existed. Congress early advised an extension of the franchise, and in the provincial conventions new and more radical men came to the front. In the early years of the revolution this radical movement became increasingly apparent. Two colonies in their new constitutions declared that no men were entitled to special privileges except in consideration of public service. Four abolished the entailing of estates, and primogeniture followed. When in Virginia it was suggested, as an amelioration, that the eldest son might at least have a double share, as had been the New England custom, Jefferson replied "not until he can eat a double allowance of food and do a double allowance of work." [1] In the plan for the government of New Hampshire proposed by General Sullivan in 1775, he stated that such revolutions as had formerly occurred in other countries had always been due to too little and not to too much power being lodged in the hands of the people. Short terms and rotation in office were urged as essential to retain control in the electors.[2] In Vermont, this rotation in office was considered necessary in order to "keep up that equality of mankind in which by nature we are all formed." [3]

[1] C. H. VanTyne, *The American Revolution*, (New York, 1905), p. 148.
[2] *N. H. Prov. Papers*, vol. VII, pp. 685 ff.
[3] Hall, *Eastern Vermont*, p. 260.

Somewhat later, in Massachusetts, in the discussion over the broadening of the franchise, the town of Stoughton voted that this was not a civil but a natural right and could not be denied.[1]

Although we have no accurate population statistics for several decades beyond this period, it is evident that the interior agricultural and frontier sections outnumbered eastern Massachusetts many times. There were approximately forty thousand people in Maine, seventy-two thousand in New Hampshire, one hundred and ninety thousand in Connecticut, thirty thousand in what is now Vermont and a hundred thousand in western Massachusetts, out of perhaps a total for all New England of six hundred and fifty thousand.[2] The bulk of the people in the outlying districts were but little affected directly by the acts of England and it is interesting to note the effects of ten years' discussion of political questions and principles upon them by 1776. In October of that year the little town of Ashfield, in the extreme north-western section of Massachusetts, voted that "as the Old Laws that we have Ben Ruled by under the British Constitution have Proved Inefectual to Secuer us from the more then Savige Crualty of tiranical Oppressars and Sense the God of Nature hath Enabled us to Brake that yoke of Bondage we think our Selves Bound in Duty to God and our Country to Opose the Least Apearance of them Old Tiranical Laws taking Place again" and resolved that "we will take the Law of God for the foundation of the forme of our Government" and that "it is our opinion that we Do not want any Govinor but the Govinor of the univarse, and under him a States Ginaral to Consult with the wrest of the united States for the Good of the whole."[3]

It was this radical and democratic spirit and the natural feeling of pride and independence upon the part of a people that felt they had a continental destiny before them that made a break with the mother country inevitable, whenever and however the exact occasion might arise. There was then, and there is today,

---

[1] Cushing, *Transition from Provincial to Commonwealth Government in Massachusetts*, p. 269.

[2] Approximated from the figures in *A Century of Population Growth* and other sources.

[3] S. B. Harding, *The Contest over the Ratification of the Federal Constitution in the State of Massachusetts*, (Harvard University Press, 1896), p. 3.

no place in the strict interpretation of the English Constitution
for a mature colony of freemen. It does not, perhaps, become
an outsider to comment upon what appears to be the Constitutional anomaly, if not chaos, of the relations between the great
self-governing dominions and England, and those dominions and
foreign nations, at the present time. In the flood of conflicting pronouncements from English and colonial statesmen and
publicists it may at least be inferred that the British empire of
after the war is an emotional complex rather than a political
organism, though the bonds of union may be no less strong.
In 1776 there was the possibility of such a relationship between
England and the cultivated merchant and professional classes
of the colonial seaboard. But there was no common ground
between the majority of English statesmen in power and such
as the men of Ashfield. Moreover, England always laid the
whole stress upon a commercial empire. Statesmen and merchants there had always said frankly that the only value of the
colonies to England was their trade value. Scarcely anywhere is
there to be found a trace of pride in the growth of the colonies
or of interest in their problems and destiny. The mother country acted like a parent whose sole thought for her child is of the
earnings it brings home of a Saturday night. There was to some
extent a filial sentiment in the colonies, but this England killed
by word and act. The result of England's considering her colonial policy merely as a trade policy was Paine's *Common Sense*.
If there was no affection, no sympathy, was it unnatural that in
time the child should appraise the relationship in the same
terms and find it worthless? Moreover, crude and raw as it may
have been, there was an ideal for which the seamen and farmers
and loggers and Americans of many other types began the
struggle. There was a hope for a life larger than the economic.
The seed planted by the merchants in the economic field was
choked by other growth. That class abandoned the economic
contest and the revolutionary party carried on the social one.

From the beginning of 1776 the sentiment in favor of independence strengthened rapidly. In January only a third of the
members of the Congress at Philadelphia were willing to vote
for a definite break with England, but the destruction of Nor-

folk early in that month, the news of the Restraining Act, the appearance of Paine's pamphlet, and the steady radical propaganda, all had their effect. The Congress authorized privateers, suggested to the colonies that they establish new governments, opened the ports of America to the commerce of the world, and step by step independence was made actual though unacknowledged.[1] The anticipated arrival of commissioners from England to treat on the questions at issue delayed decision, but the unsatisfactory nature of their powers, when after delay they finally arrived, and the increasing demand from many quarters, brought the final moment nearer. In May the Rhode Island assembly passed an act absolving the citizens from all allegiance to Great Britain. In June many of the Massachusetts towns voted for independence, and on the 14th the New Hampshire assembly instructed the delegates to vote for the declaration. In the same month Connecticut omitted the king's name from public documents and also instructed her delegates to support the motion made in favor of independence by Richard Henry Lee of Virginia and seconded by John Adams.[2]

That resolution was placed before Congress on June 7th and recited that the colonies "are, and of right ought to be, free and independent states," and that a plan of confederation should be prepared. As it was introduced before Connecticut and New Hampshire had acted, and as the sentiment of the middle colonies was not yet ready for such a final step, the question was postponed for three weeks. New York, Pennsylvania, Maryland and South Carolina had still to be won over. On July 1st the motion was again brought before Congress, and although New York was excused from voting, the Delaware delegation was tied, and Pennsylvania and South Carolina opposed, nevertheless nine colonies voted in favor of it. The following day, the arrival of Caesar Rodney from Delaware changed the vote of that colony, John Dickinson and Robert Morris of Pennsylvania absented themselves so that the Pennsylvania vote could be cast in favor of the resolution, and the South Carolina dele-

[1] H. Friedenwald, *The Declaration of Independence*, (New York, 1904), p. 50; Burnett, *Letters of Members*, vol. I, pp. 410, 421, 434, 445, 447, 460, 468 *f.*, 483 *f.*, 508, 514, 516.
[2] *R. I. Col. Records*, vol. VII, pp. 522 *f.*, 545; Force, *American Archives*, Ser. IV, vol. VI, pp. 603, 649, 698 *ff.*, 902.

gates, without authority, also gave their assent. Two days later, on the 4th, the Declaration in its final form was adopted, although not signed until some weeks later.[1] It is interesting to note that of the signers one-third were of non-English stock and one-seventh had been born outside of the colonies. [2]

The document, which consisted of a preamble and a list of grievances was easily open to attack. The philosophy in the former had at once all the weakness and all the idealistic inspiration which we have already attributed to the doctrine of natural rights. In the list of specified grievances, some were overstated, some difficult to prove, and many related to acts of the British government which had occurred only after the colonists had taken up arms in actual rebellion. In England, ex-governor Hutchinson submitted them to a searching analysis in one of the many pamphlets which at once appeared.[3] The Declaration was of necessity a party document in which only one side of the case could be presented and in which the most had to be made of that in order to influence as far as possible all the colonies and all shades of opinion.

With its publication the die was cast. Parties both in England and America were now sharply aligned. All lingering hopes of compromise, of adjustment, were now past. In the mother country the party in favor of America was still large though too much in the minority to accomplish any alteration in policy. If in order to preserve the theoretical unity of the empire, wrote Price, "one half of it must be enslaved to the other half, let it, in the name of God, want Unity." [4] In Parliament, the ever faithful minority group continued its attacks upon the administration. Even the adoring Boswell told Sam Johnson that he

---

[1] Cf. Friedenwald, *Declaration of Independence*, pp. 99 ff.; Burnett, *Letters of Members*, vol.I, pp. 528 ff.; M Chamberlain, *John Adams*, (Boston, 1899), pp. 99 ff.; J.H. Hazelton, *The Declaration of Independence*, (New York, 1906), pp. 193 ff. The latest work is that by Carl Becker, *The Declaration of Independence*, (New York, 1922).

[2] A. M. Schlesinger, *New Viewpoints in American History*, (New York, 1922), p. 7.

[3] *Strictures upon the Declaration of the Congress at Philadelphia in a letter to a noble lord.* . . . (London, 1776). Cf. also [James Macpherson] *The Rights of Great Britain asserted against the Claims of America.* . . . (London, 1776); [John Roebuck] *An Enquiry whether the Guilt of the present Civil War in America ought to be imputed to Great Britain or America,* (Dublin, 1776); John Lind, *An Answer to the Declaration of the American Congress,* (London, 4th. edit. 1776).

[4] Richard Price, *Observations on the Nature of Civil Liberty,* (London, 1776), p. 22.

had never differed from him but on two political questions and that America was one.[1] In England, however, the war between parties was but a war of words, in America it was a war of deeds.

Throughout the entire controversy with England there had been two sides, either of which could be taken by honest and well-meaning men. As we have already noted, there were few, even of the more violent Tories, who approved the acts of the ministry. Many, like Hutchinson, had opposed the Stamp Act and all or nearly all that followed, but they wished to remain within the empire, securing redress by peaceful means, and it must be recalled that the later Acts of Parliament had been only in response to American violence. In fact, so rapidly had the radicals shifted their ground that in the Declaration of Independence, the main stress was not laid at all on the original issues, and that of taxation without representation was hidden away in a single phrase only in the thirteenth paragraph of the list of grievances. Whether redress might have been obtained, in time, had it not been for the mob actions and armed resistance of the minority during the early days, it is impossible to say. Very possibly not, but the Loyalists believed that it could, and as Professor Tyler has said, their side "was even in argument not a weak one, and in motive and sentiment not a base one, and in devotion and self-sacrifice not an unheroic one." [2]

Now that the issue was sharply defined as forcible secession from the empire, and the possible creation of an untried and radical democracy, the question was by no means simple for the more conservative and loyal. They must all have searched their hearts to guide their conduct. Nor were such men in an inconsiderable minority. Outside of New England, they were in the great majority in Georgia, outnumbered the Whigs in South Carolina, and at least equaled them in Pennsylvania and New York. John Adams said that if it had not been for New England on one side and Virginia on the other, the two latter colo-

[1] "Criticisms made by the Majority during the War with America," *United Service Magazine*, New Series, vol. LVI, p. 46.
[2] M. C. Tyler, "The Party of the Loyalists in the American Revolution," *Am. Hist. Review*, vol. I, p. 26.

nies would have joined the British.[1] He thought that in the colonies as a whole at least one-third of the people were openly opposed to independence, and later researches bear this out.[2] Perhaps the fairest estimate is that which places the Tories at one-third, the Whigs at one-third, and the indifferent, who were willing to stampede to either side, at the same figure. Even in New England there was a large Loyalist element. When Howe evacuated Boston, although many of them had left previously, eleven hundred took refuge on the British fleet, and Lieutenant-Governor Oliver had estimated the number under his charge in January at "upwards of two thousand." In New Hampshire, in March, although many Tories had fled, about one in every eleven adult men refused to sign the test provided by Congress. In Connecticut, Stephen Hoit of Norwalk claimed in affidavits that he alone raised over eight hundred men to serve in the British ranks.[3]

The coercive measures adopted throughout New England, as elsewhere, more especially from 1775 onward, undoubtedly forced many to give lip-service to the American cause who were either indifferent or Loyalist at heart. Banishment, the ruin of their business, complete ostracism, tarring and feathering and imprisonment were freely resorted to even before the bitterness engendered by the struggle had become acute in its latter years.[4] Washington was for humaner methods, and was in favor of a general amnesty.[5] The detailed story of the sufferings of the Loyalists and of their treatment during the struggle belong to a later volume, and we may merely note here the general character of the Loyalist element. It is a mistake to think of them

[1] *Works*, vol. X, p. 63.

[2] *Ibid.*, pp. 87, 110. Lorenzo Sabine thought that the "Whigs were a minority in some of the states, barely equalled their opponents in others, and in the whole country composed but an inconsiderable majority." *Biographical Sketches of Loyalists in the American Revolution*, (Boston, 1864), vol. I., p. 143.

[3] W. H. Siebert, "The Dispersion of the American Tories," *Mississippi Valley Historical Review*, vol. I, p. 192; *Mass. Hist. Soc., Proceedings*, vol. XVIII, pp. 266 ff.; W. H. Siebert, "The Loyalist Refugees of New Hampshire," *Ohio State University Bulletin*, (1916), p. 3; Same, "The Refugee Loyalists of Connecticut," *Transactions Royal Society of Canada*, Ser. III, vol. X, pp. 75 f.

[4] *Cf.* Force, *American Archives*, Ser. IV, vol. II, pp. 1711, 1749, vol. III, pp. 59, 84 f., 138, 289, 641, 851, 1024, 1028, 1444, vol. IV, p. 1340, vol. V, pp. 806, 822, 1275, 1301. *Cf.* C. H. Van Tyne, *The Loyalists of the American Revolution*, (New York, 1902), *passim*.

[5] *Writings*, vol. IV, p. 6.

as only office-holders or place-seekers under government. The large numbers in the party were drawn from the most conservative, able and cultivated classes in the community as well as from the humbler ranks in every village. The possessors of inherited wealth, the lawyers, physicians, merchants and a majority of those usually accounted as "sound and conservative" in any society, were largely to be found in the Loyalist ranks. Of the three hundred and ten more prominent ones in Massachusetts singled out for banishment by the act of 1778, it has been said that the list of their names reads "like the bead roll of the oldest and noblest families concerned in the founding and upbuilding of New England civilization." [1] In courage and devotion they equaled if, indeed, it should not be said that they excelled, those in the patriot party, for during the war more colonials fought in the ranks of the British army than joined the American one.[2] Before the struggle was over, more than a hundred thousand had died or been exiled, and the loss of so large a number of substantial citizens, comparable only to the expulsion of the Huguenots from France, was to be felt severely in the years following.[3] This great body of conservative opinion was ballast that the new ship of state could ill afford to lose. Found in almost every hamlet, even throughout New England, the intensely bitter war waged against them, and their sufferings and eventual losses, form part of the story of that civil war within the colonies which used formerly to be largely lost to sight, as contrasted with the imperial war against England.

In the preceding two volumes, we have tried to indicate the real nature of the revolutionary contest and to show how the seeds of separation were present from the outset. These were not merely political, not merely commercial, but were rooted deep in the fundamental factors of the relationship between mother country and colonies under the conditions of time, distance, differing environments and heritage. "We are not a free state," William Pynchon had written to John Winthrop in

[1] Tyler, *Loyalists, cit. supra,* p. 31.
[2] Channing, *History of U.S.,* vol. III, pp. 215 *f.,* and notes.
[3] Van Tyne, *Loyalists,* p. vii; W. S. Duncan, *The United Empire Loyalists,* (Toronto, 1914), pp. 3 *f.*

1646, "neither do I think it our wisdom to be a free state; though we had our liberty, we cannot as yet subsist without England." [1] The dream that a few of the early settlers appear to have dreamed in those days passed. Fewer of the leaders thought, even vaguely, of independence in 1750 than they had a century earlier. Subtly and unconsciously, however, a thousand influences had been at work to loosen the bonds, and to make the American something different from the Englishman. If there is much false history and no little absurdity in the old legend of a practically unanimous population of Americans suddenly rising in the few years from 1763 to 1776, to resist the slavery that a king and his tools were said to be consciously striving to force upon them, no less unhistorical is the view that the revolution was the work of a few scheming radicals. Like Niagara, the rush and tumult of those years seem deafening, and we are too apt to watch the stunning crash of waters without questioning whence they come. But there would be no such mighty cataract were it not for the innumerable lakes and rivers and tiny streams, fed by the springs and rains of years and of many a thousand square miles of upland and hills far remote from where we stand to watch their waters take their final plunge. Some outlet to the sea, they would, in time, have found in any case.

In telling the story of New England from the first scattered settlements founded in cold December upon the little strip of land between the stormy wintry sea and the illimitable forests, down to the time when four populous colonies, strong and proud in their strength, united with the rest of their younger and older sisters to form a new nation, we have been able to indicate but a few of the sources from whence, both for good and for ill, that new nation drew its own peculiar character and life. Much of the ground, indeed, remains wholly unmapped, and many an historical explorer must study the records of obscure villages and whole districts before we can understand all the causes that led to the double revolution of 1776. Much we can learn from English records, much from those of Boston and the larger towns, much from the contemporary literature of the day, but

[1] *Cf.* my *Founding of New England*, p. 155.

behind it all we must still learn more than we yet know of the daily life and problems, the discontents and ambitions, of the many thousands who never saw a town and who never expressed themselves in the printed page. Until then, we cannot be sure that we understand aright that great movement which spread through the throngs of common men who sailed the ships and tilled the fields and felled the forests of New England, and wrought a new hope in the heart of the world.

INDEX

INDEX

ABERCROMBY, GEN. JAMES, 239, 244, 245, 246.
Abnakis, 44, 64.
Acadia, boundaries of, 44, 104, 212, 222; in King William's War, 44; conditions in, 224; deportations, 224, 225.
Acton, John E. E. D., Lord, 289 n.
Adams, John, quoted, 159, 176, 222, 254, 276, 286, 304, 343, 373, 375, 393, 407, 408, 409, 429, 447, 448; delegate to Continental Congress, 406, 428; 118, 272 and n., 273 n., 331, 355, 377 and n., 379.
Adams, Samuel, Sr., 157.
Adams, Samuel, Jr., character, 302, 303; begins early to work for immediate rupture, 303; resolutions adopted by Mass. assembly, 332; independence always his aim, 332, 374; and Stamp Act, 337; quoted, 359, 374; *An Appeal to the World*, 370; and the tea question, 390; delegate to Continental Congress, 406 ff.; excepted from amnesty, 225; 289, 304, 305, 330 n., 353, 355, 357, 366, 371, 379, 382, 383, 392, 393, 394, 395, 402, 404, 405, 416, 418, 428.
Addison, Joseph, 139.
Admiralty, the, functions of, 22.
Aix-la-Chapelle, peace of, 186 and n., 187 ff., 212.
Alaska, 19 and n.
Albany, fort at, 50; inter-colonial conference at, 178, 214–217.
Alleghany Mts., boundary, 222.
Allen, C. D., *The Early Federation Movement in Australia*, quoted, 219 n.
Allen, Ethan, 414, 424, 425.
Allen, John, quoted, 385.
Allen, Samuel, 56, 57, 124.
Alvord, C. W., 397.
American colonies, political doctrines in, 8, 9, 10; expansion, 8, 9; struggle between sections, 10 ff.; frontier of English civilization, 13; liberty in, 14, 15; causes of friction, 17; loyalty in, 17; administration of, 19–23; subject to legislation of Parliament, 21; communication with, 26; control of the purse their chief weapon, 29; population in, 1650–1700, 30 and n.; law in, 40 and n.; in King William's War, 45; their selfishness and jealousy, 46, 47; plans for union, 48; particularism of, 65 ff.; and Canadian Expedition, 77;

relations of, with England, 109, 110; their value to England, 117; manufacture of wool in, prohibited, 118; variety and interest of life in, 138; and the act concerning debts, 154; no thought of separation in mid-18th century, 163; and the "War of Jenkins's Ear," 164 ff.; new attempt at coöperation with England, 168; bishops in, 201; economic motive of, in relations with England, 207 ff.; to be taxed for their own support, 210 and n., 211; expense of military establishment of, 211; failure to realize their common interest, 220; conditions in, at outbreak of Seven Years' War, 225 ff.; boundary disputes between, 231; question of providing money for defence, 231, 232; financial position of merchant class in, 264, 265; salaries of judges in, 275; effect of retention of Canada and the West, 281; Proclamation of 1763 distasteful to, 282, 283, 284; Bernard advises remodeling government of, 285, 286; fundamental action of revolutionary movement in, 288; relations between classes in, and in England, 290, 291; plan to tax them, 291; naval commanders to serve as customs officers in, 292, 293; and the supposed plans of home government as to taxation, 297, 298; issue of paper money by, prohibited, 298; business depression in, 298, 299, 350, 351; opposition to acts of England never unanimous, 301; opinion in, 301; taxation, 308 ff.; franchise of judges in, 315, 316; why England wanted them, 318; proportion of population in favor of extreme measures (1765), 331; friction with England after 1765, 345 ff.; efforts to form a constitutional theory, 346; approaching revolution, 367, 368; conservatives and radicals, 369; basis of quarrel of merchants of, with England, 372, 373; political speculative thought in, 380; tone of press in, 380; views of radical leaders, 381; and England, mutual lack of understanding, 397–399; general congress of, agreed upon, 402; prohibition of export of arms to, 412; violent action on local questions, 412, 413; proclaimed in rebellion, 420; war-spirit in, intensified by battles of Lexington, etc., 427; reconciliation desired by

Moore, John, Commodore, 268.
Morely, Bishop, 169.
Morley, John, Viscount, *Notes on Politics and History*, quoted, 138.
Morris, Gouverneur, quoted, 400.
Morris, Robert, 445.
Morris, Robert H., 205, 217 *n.*
Mount Desert Island, 260.
Murray, James, *Letters*, quoted, 253, 367, 368, 375.
Mutiny Act, 350.

"NATURAL RIGHTS," 114, 441, 442.
Navigation Acts, 50 *ff.*
Nevis, 336.
New England, tendency toward expansion in, 8; literary taste in, 33; people of, touched their lowest point, intellectually and socially, in early 18th century, 35, 38; trade of, 41, 42; divergence of interest between British W. Indies and, 42; frontier of, in French war, 43, 44, 45; conditions in, in 1700, 49 *ff.*; and the Navigation Acts, 51; smuggling in, 52; relations of, with England in War of Spanish Succession, 66, 67; policy of unified control in, 66; conditions in, after 1713, 86 *ff.*; emigration from, to southern colonies, 87; effect of speculation on land policy of, 88, 89; power of money in, 90; trade of, with French W. Indies, 90, 91, 148, 151 *ff.*, 264 *ff.*, 281; influence of liberal writers on thought in, 96, 97; relations between different authorities in, 99, 100, and between official and non-official classes, 101, 102, 117; accumulation of wealth in, 115, 116; capitalists of, closely bound to England, 117; tenure of land in, 125; change of taste in, from religious to secular, 139 *ff.*; commercial interests supersede religious, 142, 195, 196; growth of large estates, 143; growth of parties in, shown in currency disputes, 160; limited franchise in, 160, 161 and *n.*; representation of townships in General Court, 161, 162; alignment of classes in, 163; undermining of theology in, 169, 170, 173; the great awakening, 177, 178; practically bankrupt in 1748, 180; commercial morality in, 191; had no purpose to separate from England, 196, 197; increased vigor of radicals in, 197, 198; changes in, between 1740 and 1750, 199; economic interests of, always inimical to those of British W. Indies, 209; conditions in, in 1750's, 226-236; number of troops provided by, 248; strength of, lay in her farming class, 252; poverty of bulk of population, 252; increase and concentration of wealth, 253, 254; feeling between court and country parties in, 254, 255; growing power of wealthy merchant class, 255, 256; dearness of labor in, 256; economic mainstays of life in, 256-258; effect of cheapness of new lands on land values, 262, 263; political conditions in, in 1761, 274; still strongly Puritan in feeling, 286; mental characteristics of people of, 286, 287; financial crisis in, 299; conditions in, in 1765, ideal for agitators, 302; radicals and conservatives act together in opposition to first steps of new imperial policy, 302, 303; main subjects of discussion in, in 1765, 318, 319; springs of mob-action in, 320, 321; triumph of radicals in, 364, 366; estimated population of colonies of, in 1775, 443. And *see* American colonies.
New England Courant, 139
New England Weekly Journal, 139.
New Hampshire, population of, in 1700, 30; conditions in, in 1700, 56, 57; created a royal province, 56; controversy over land titles in, 124; extension of frontier, 124; boundary dispute with Mass., 148; Wentworth first governor of, as separate colony, 148 *n.*; issues paper money, 155; in expedition against Louisbourg, 182; war debt claimed by, 251; logging centers in, 256, 257; new towns in, 259, 260; political feeling in, 348; seizure of government stores in, 416; assembly of, instructs delegates in Congress to vote for independence, 445; 23, 39, 40 *h.*, 48, 65, 67, 79 *n.*, 87, 94, 120, 121, 145, 161, 181, 226, 284, 298, 361, 369, 412, 428.
New Hampshire Gazette, quoted, 380, 381.
New Hampshire Grants, 413, 414.
New Haven, 288, 298.
New Jersey, boundary dispute with New York, 231; question of independence of judiciary in, 274; rioting in, 367; 48, 77, 78.
New London Society United for Trade and Commerce, 155.
New Orleans, 279.
New York, Colony of, conditions in, in 1700, 49, 50; piracy in, 53; boundary disputes with Mass. and New Jersey, 231; troops furnished by, in French and Indian War, 251; towns settled under New Hampshire Grants claimed by, 260, 413, 414, 415; question of independence of judiciary in, 274, 275, 276; mobs in, 360; suggests a general congress, 402; refuses to support the Association, 411; inter-colonial Congress meets at, 330; 41, 43, 46, 48, 77, 79, 107, 125 *n.*, 178, 194, 206, 207, 215,

Printed by McGrath-Sherrill Press, Boston
Bound by Boston Bookbinding Co., Cambridge